UNDERSTANDING
CONSUMER BEHAVIOUR

UNDERSTANDING CONSUMER BEHAVIOUR

First Canadian Edition

J. PAUL PETER
University of Wisconsin, Madison

JERRY C. OLSON
Pennsylvania State University

JERRY A. ROSENBLATT
Concordia University

Represented in Canada by:

**Times Mirror
Professional Publishing Ltd.**

IRWIN

Toronto • Chicago • Bogotá • Boston • Buenos Aires
Caracas • London • Madrid • Mexico City • Sydney

Dedicated to the loving memory of my father, Abe Rosenblatt.

Irwin Book Team

Publisher: *Roderick T. Banister*
Sponsoring editor: *Evelyn Veitch*
Developmental editor: *Karen Conlin*
Marketing manager: *Murray Moman*
Project editor: *Jean Lou Hess*
Production supervisor: *Bob Lange*
Manager, Prepress Purchasing: *Kimberly Meriwether David*
Designer: *Crispin Prebys*
Coordinator, Graphics and Desktop Services: *Keri Johnson*
Photo researcher: Michael J. Hruby and Associates
Compositor: *Weimer Graphics, Inc.*
Typeface: *9/12 Helvetica*
Printer: *Von Hoffmann Press, Inc.*

**Times Mirror
Higher Education Group**

ISBN 0-256-17048-7

Library of Congress Catalog Number 95-82010

Printed in the United States of America
1 2 3 4 5 6 7 8 9 0 VH 3 2 1 0 9 8 7 6

Preface

Consumer behaviour is an exciting, dynamic field critically important to the success of business firms and nonprofit organisations. *Understanding Consumer Behaviour* (first Canadian edition) captures the many fascinating aspects of Canadian consumer behaviour while presenting an integrated, coherent approach to its study. The text reflects the authors' lifelong involvement with consumer behaviour research.

In recent years, managers have become aware that satisfying consumers is the best way to develop and maintain a successful organisation, a fact marketers have long recognised. Even managers in such areas as engineering and production are emphasising consumer satisfaction. Many successful firms encourage everyone in the organisation to put the consumer first when developing strategies.

Managers who want to satisfy consumers need an in-depth understanding of those consumers. *Understanding Consumer Behaviour* identifies the essential elements of consumer behaviour and provides the knowledge and skills to analyse the reasons for consumers' behaviour. The text also shows how consumer understanding can be used to develop effective marketing strategies.

Unlike other texts that present students with many complex models, *Understanding Consumer Behaviour* is based on a simple model for analysing consumers, called the Wheel of Consumer Analysis. This model provides a conceptual framework for thinking about consumer behaviour issues and is used throughout the text to focus students' attention on the key elements in consumer analysis. It also provides the organising framework for the text. Section One provides an overview of the field of consumer behaviour, introduces the Wheel of Consumer Analysis framework for analysing consumers, and discusses how Canadian marketers use consumer analysis in segmenting markets and designing marketing strategies. The three remaining sections of the text concern the three elements of the Wheel of Consumer Analysis. Section Two focuses on affect and cognition, the feelings and thoughts consumers have about such things as products, advertisements, and stores. Section Three discusses behaviour, the overt actions of consumers as they engage in marketing exchanges with organisations. Section Four examines the many factors in the physical and social environment that influence how consumers think, feel, and behave. Overall, the text produces a comprehensive, interesting, and highly readable treatment of the essential elements of consumer behaviour analysis and application.

**NEW AND
UNIQUE
CONCEPTS**

Compared to other texts, *Understanding Consumer Behaviour* includes more unique material useful in understanding consumers.

The book is organised around the simple Wheel of Consumer Analysis, which is a big advantage over other texts. After reading *Understanding Consumer Behaviour,* students will know a simple framework they can use in virtually any consumer analysis situation to develop more effective understanding of consumers and better marketing strategies.

Understanding Consumer Behaviour has a superior treatment of affect, showing clearly its relationship to cognition and the implications of how affect and cognition influence each other. Means-end chains are used throughout the text to analyse consumer/ product relationships. *Understanding Consumer Behaviour* has superior coverage of involvement, attention and comprehension, and attitudes, including the marketing implications of these concepts.

The text offers a realistic treatment of consumer decision making as a part of the larger problem-solving process. Students learn that consumers make other decisions during problem solving besides brand choice. The chapter on communications includes new concepts such as narrative or drama advertising and the MECCAS model, which uses means-end chains to design effective advertising strategies.

Understanding Consumer Behaviour is distinctive among texts in its detailed attention to the centrally important concept of behaviour (four chapters) and how to analyse and influence consumers' behaviours.

The chapter on the physical environment is exceptional and includes a detailed treatment of situations. The chapter on culture provides a unique and compelling framework for understanding the various cultures and subcultures in Canada and developing marketing implications. The chapter on subcultures presents original material concerning acculturation and covers ethnic, gender, and income subcultures.

**SPECIAL
PEDAGOGY**

Understanding Consumer Behaviour contains a variety of pedagogical aids to enhance student learning and enjoyment of the course.

> ▷ **Learning objectives.** Listed at the beginning of each chapter are several learning objectives that direct students to important knowledge and skills they should acquire in studying the chapter.

> ▷ **Summaries focusing on learning objectives.** To help students focus on the key material, each chapter closes with a summary that provides concise responses, based on the chapter concepts, for each of the learning objectives.

> ▷ **Chapter introductory examples.** Each chapter opens with an example of a real-world marketing situation that generates student interest in the concepts presented in the chapter.

> ▷ **Consumer Perspectives.** Each chapter contains several longer examples that describe how marketers use consumer analysis to develop marketing strategies. These Consumer Perspectives are set off in colour to distinguish them from the text material. Each CP is referenced in the text so students easily grasp its relevance.

> ▷ **Real-world examples and photographs.** *Understanding Consumer Behaviour* is replete with real-life examples illustrating the concepts discussed. Photos and ads provide visual examples and increase student interest.

> ▷ **Marketing implications.** Implications of consumer analysis for designing marketing strategies are incorporated into the text material. In addition, most chapters include separate sections titled "Marketing Implications" that provide in-depth discussion of the marketing applications of chapter concepts.

▷ **Key terms and concepts.** Important terms and concepts are listed at the end of each chapter and are highlighted in boldface type within the chapter text.

▷ **Review and discussion questions.** End-of-chapter review and discussion questions emphasise the understanding and application of chapter material to strategic marketing issues. The questions can be used for written assignments, in-class discussions, essay exam questions, or student self-study.

▷ **Cases.** The text concludes with a set of short discussion cases that focus on consumer analysis issues facing well-known companies. The cases include several questions to focus student thinking on key issues of consumer analysis. The case questions also can be used for written assignments or in-class discussion.

▷ **References.** References are provided for text material and frequently include additional references students can use for more detailed study of selected topics.

▷ **Glossary.** The text includes a glossary of key consumer behaviour terms and concepts as a reference source for students during the course and in their future careers. Many of the glossary definitions were originally prepared by the authors for the American Marketing Association's *Dictionary of Marketing Terms.*

▷ **Writing style and clarity.** *Understanding Consumer Behaviour* is written in an engaging, relaxed style, using simple sentence structure and minimal jargon. The presentation of concepts is straightforward and is accompanied by definitions and immediate examples to help students grasp both the concept and its application.

▷ **Design.** The large size, two-colour, inviting design, and easy-to-use layout enhance student interest and comprehension.

INSTRUCTIONAL AIDS

The comprehensive **Instructor's Manual,** prepared entirely by the authors, includes a wealth of useful information and suggestions for teaching each of the chapters. Reviewers have applauded both the quantity and the quality of the material in the Instructor's Manual and have called it the best in the discipline. For each chapter, the manual provides teaching objectives, teaching suggestions, additional topics not covered in the text, materials for mini-lectures, examples not found in the text, and suggested projects to be completed outside of class. The manual also includes notes and answers to the review and discussion questions, notes on the cases, and a guide to the transparency masters. An extensive selection of multiple-choice and essay test questions is also provided.

ACKNOWLEDGMENTS

I am indebted to the many people who contributed to the development of this book. First, to J. Paul Peter and Jerry Olson, for their tremendous effort in developing the first edition of this text for use in the United States. Second, I thank my students, past and present, for their contributions to my understanding of consumer behaviour and the educational process. A special thanks to the many undergraduate and graduate students at Concordia University in Montreal who helped research the many original Canadian Consumer Perspectives (in particular Gord Spicer, Janice Cousin, and Carolyn Vogelesang). Third, a special thanks to Evelyn Veitch, sponsoring editor, and Karen Conlin, developmental editor, as well as Jean Lou Hess, Irwin project editor, and Irwin production, art, and design staffs for their efforts, insights, and patience in the development of *Understanding Consumer Behaviour,* first Canadian edition. Fourth, I thank our reviewers for their excellent comments and suggestions: Kay Sequeira, Ph.D., Professor, Centennial College; Auleen Carson, Wilfrid Laurier University; Deborah Lawton, University College of the Caribou; Robert M. MacGregor, Bishop's University; Zoe Wharton, University of Manitoba; and Louise Heslop, School of Business, Carleton University.

I also thank the many researchers and teachers in marketing who have contributed to our thinking about consumer behaviour and how it can best be taught to future managers. In particular, even though we have not worked together for some time, a special debt of gratitude is owed to Michel Laroche, professor of marketing, Concordia University, who has always been my consumer research mentor. Finally, my deepest debt of gratitude is owed to my family, Rhona, Jeffrey and Sara, for their love, encouragement, and patience during this project.

Jerry Rosenblatt
Montreal

To the Student

"Why are textbook prices so high?"

This is, by far, the most frequently-asked question heard in the publishing industry. There are many factors that influence the price of your new textbook. Here are just a few:

▷ **The Cost of Instructor Support Materials:** Your instructor may be making use of teaching supplements, many of which are provided by the publisher. Teaching supplements include videos, colour transparencies, instructor's manuals, software, computerized testing materials and more. These supplements are designed as part of a learning package to enhance your educational experience.

▷ **Developmental Costs:** These are costs associated with the extensive development of your textbook. Expenses include permissions fees, manuscript review costs, artwork, typesetting, printing and binding costs, and more.

▷ **Author Royalties:** Authors are paid based on a percentage of new book sales and **do not** receive royalties on the sale of a used book. They are also deprived of their rightful royalties when their books are illegally photocopied.

▷ **Marketing Costs:** Instructors need to be made aware of new textbooks. Marketing costs include academic conventions, remuneration of the publisher's representatives, promotional advertising pieces, and the provision of instructor's examination copies.

▷ **Book Store Markups:** In order to stay in business, your local book store must cover its costs. A textbook is a commodity, just like any other item your bookstore may sell, and bookstores are the most effective way to get the textbook from the publisher to you.

▷ **Publisher Profits:** In order to continue to supply students with quality textbooks, publishers must make a profit to stay in business. Like the authors, publishers **do not** receive any compensation from the sale of a used book or the illegal photocopying of their textbooks.

We at Times Mirror Professional Publishing hope you will find this information useful and that it addresses some of your concerns. We also thank you for your purchase of this new textbook. If you have any questions that we can answer, please write to us at:

Times Mirror Professional Publishing
College Division
130 Flaska Drive
Markham, Ontario
L6G 1B8

Brief Contents

Section I

CONSUMER BEHAVIOUR OVERVIEW

Chapter 1   Introduction to Consumer Behaviour   2

Chapter 2   The Wheel of Consumer Analysis: A Framework for Understanding Consumers   14

Chapter 3   Using Consumer Analysis: Market Segmentation and the Marketing Mix   30

Section II

AFFECT AND COGNITION

Chapter 4   Introduction to Affect and Cognition   52

Chapter 5   Product Knowledge and Involvement   72

Chapter 6   Exposure, Attention, and Comprehension   98

Chapter 7   Attitudes and Intentions   120

Chapter 8   Decision Making   144

Chapter 9   Communication and Persuasion   168

Section III

BEHAVIOUR

Chapter 10   Introduction to Behaviour   194

Chapter 11   Classical and Operant Conditioning   210

Chapter 12   Vicarious Learning and the Diffusion of Innovation   228

Chapter 13   Analysing Consumer Behaviour   244

Section IV

ENVIRONMENT

Chapter 14   Introduction to the Environment   266

Chapter 15   Cultural and Cross-Cultural Influences   292

Chapter 16   Subculture and Social Class Influences   322

Chapter 17   Reference Groups and Family Influences   350

Chapter 18   Environmental Influences on Marketing Practices   374

Section V

CASES IN CONSUMER BEHAVIOUR

1. Toyota   390
2. Wal-Mart Canada   391
3. Ralph Lauren   393
4. Nike   395
5. Black & Decker   397
6. Coca-Cola   399
7. Buying a Lancer   401
8. A Business Trip   404
9. Intel Pentium: Word of Mouth and Group Influence   406
10. Price-Costco   408

11. Elegant Traditions   410
12. Bauer In-Line Skates   412
13. The Train Trip   414
14. Movie Theatres   417
15. Selling in Foreign Markets   419
16. Hyatt and Marriott Building
    Retirement Housing   421
17. Breast-Feeding in Canada in
    the 1990s   424
18. The Tylenol Crisis   429
19. Advice for a New Friend   431
20. Purchasing a Treadmill   434

Notes   437
Glossary of Consumer Behaviour Terms   461
Credits and Acknowledgments   471
Name, Company, and Brand Index   473
Subject Index   483

Table of Contents

Section I

CONSUMER BEHAVIOUR OVERVIEW

Chapter 1   **Introduction to Consumer Behaviour**   2

The Phenomenon of the Grateful Dead   3
Applying the Marketing Concept   4
Value-Laden Products   5
Improved Quality of Marketing Research   5
Development of Consumer Behaviour Research and Theory   6
What Is Consumer Behaviour?   7
Consumer Behaviour Is Dynamic   8
Consumer Behaviour Involves Interactions   8
Consumer Behaviour Involves Exchanges   9
Beginnings of Consumer Behaviour   9
Who Is Interested in Consumer Behaviour?   9
Marketing Implications   10
Summary   11
Key Terms and Concepts   13
Review and Discussion Questions   13

Chapter 2   **The Wheel of Consumer Analysis: A Framework for Understanding Consumers**   14

Sara Lauren Buys Some "Peace of Mind"   15
The Wheel of Consumer Analysis   16
Affect and Cognition   16
Behaviour   17
Environment   17
Identifying the Wheel Components   18

Applying the Wheel of Consumer Analysis   20
Levels of Consumer Analysis   22
Society   22
Industry   22
Market Segment   23
Individual Consumer   23
Summary   25
Key Terms and Concepts   28
Review and Discussion Questions   28

Chapter 3   **Using Consumer Analysis: Market Segmentation and the Marketing Mix**   30

Gillette and the Drugstore Dinosaurs   31
Market Segmentation   32
Analyse Consumer/Product Relationships   33
Determine Segmentation Bases   35
Select Segmentation Strategy   42
Marketing Mix Decisions   43
Product Decisions   44
Price Decisions   44
Promotion Decisions   46
Channels of Distribution Decisions   46
Marketing Implications   48
Summary   49
Key Terms and Concepts   50
Review and Discussion Questions   50

Section II

AFFECT AND COGNITION

Chapter 4   **Introduction to Affect and Cognition**   52

What Does "Dole" Mean?   53

Affect and Cognition as Psychological
  Responses   54

Types of Affective Responses   *54*

The Affective System   *55*

What Is Cognition?   *55*

*How Are Affect and Cognition
  Related?*   *56*

Marketing Implications   *58*

Cognitive Processes in Consumer
  Decision Making   61

*A Model of Consumer Decision
  Making*   *61*

*Other Characteristics of the Cognitive
  System*   *63*

Marketing Implications   *64*

Knowledge Stored in Memory   65

Types of Knowledge   *65*

Structures of Knowledge   *67*

Types of Knowledge Structures   *68*

Marketing Implications   *69*

Summary   69

Key Terms and Concepts   71

Review and Discussion Questions   71

Chapter 5   **Product Knowledge and
Involvement**   72

Chrysler in the Minivan Driver's Seat   73

Levels of Product Knowledge   74

Consumers' Product Knowledge   76

Products as Bundles of Attributes   *76*

Products as Bundles of Benefits   *77*

Products as Value Satisfiers   *79*

Means-End Chains of Product
  Knowledge   81

Examples of Means-End Chains   *83*

Measuring Means-End Chains   *84*

Consumers' Product Involvement   85

Focus of Involvement   *86*

Factors Influencing Involvement   *87*

Marketing Implications   89

*Understanding the Key Reasons for
  Purchase*   *89*

*Understanding the Consumer/Product
  Relationship*   *90*

*Influencing Personal Sources of
  Involvement*   *93*

*Influencing Situational Sources of
  Involvement*   *93*

Summary   93

Key Terms and Concepts   95

Review and Discussion Questions   95

Chapter 6   **Exposure, Attention, and
Comprehension**   98

TV Viewers Exposed   99

Exposure to Information   101

Selective Exposure   *101*

Marketing Implications   *102*

Attention to Information   104

Factors Influencing Attention   *104*

Marketing Implications   *106*

Comprehension of Information   108

Variations in Comprehension   *108*

Inferences during Comprehension   *110*

Factors Influencing Comprehension   *111*

Marketing Implications   *114*

The Interpretation Process   116

Summary   117

Key Terms and Concepts   118

Review and Discussion Questions   118

Chapter 7   **Attitudes and Intentions**   120

Canadian Wine Producers Want
  Consumers to Stop Whining   121

What Is Attitude?   122

Attitudes toward What?   *124*

Marketing Implications   *125*

Attitudes toward Objects   128

Salient Beliefs   *128*

The Multiattribute Attitude Model   *129*

Marketing Implications   *131*

Attitude-Change Strategies   132

Add a New Salient Belief   *132*

Change Strength of Salient Belief   *132*

Change Evaluation of Existing Belief   *133*

Make Existing Belief More Salient   *133*

Attitudes toward Behaviours   133

The Theory of Reasoned Action   *135*

Marketing Implications   *137*

Intention and Behaviour   138

Summary   139

Key Terms and Concepts   141

Review and Discussion Questions   141

Chapter 8   **Consumer Decision Making**   144

The Dinner Party   145

Consumer Decisions   146

The Problem-Solving Process   148

Problem Recognition   *149*

Search for Relevant Information   *150*

Marketing Implications   *152*

Evaluation of Alternatives   *153*

Determining Choice Criteria   *153*

Choice Decision   *154*

Purchase 156
Postpurchase Use and Re-evaluation 156
Levels of Problem Solving 159
Extensive Problem Solving 159
Limited Problem Solving 159
Routinized Choice Behavior 160
Changes in Problem Solving with
    Experience 160
Marketing Implications 160
Summary 163
Key Terms and Concepts 166
Review and Discussion Questions 166

Chapter 9   Communication and Persuasion 168

CFL Chief Is American Marketing
    Association's Marketer of the Year 169
Types of Promotion Communications 170
Advertising 170
Sales Promotions 170
Personal Selling 170
Publicity 171
The Promotion Mix 172
The Communication Process 173
Source 173
Message 174
Transmission via Media 176
Receiver 177
Consumer Action 179
Effects of Promotion Communications 180
Simulate Product Need 180
Create Brand Awareness 180
Create a Favourable Brand Attitude 181
Form an Intention to Purchase the
    Brand 181
Influence Other Behaviours 182
The Persuasion Process 182
The Elaboration Likelihood
    Model (ELM) 182
Marketing Implications 184
Understanding the Consumer/Product
    Relationship 184
Developing Advertising Strategy 188
Summary 190
Key Terms and Concepts 192
Review and Discussion Questions 192

Section III

BEHAVIOUR

Chapter 10   Introduction to Behaviour 194

Canadian Companies Partnering to
    Create Value Offers to Customers 195

Behaviour versus Cognitive Views 191
Influencing Overt Consumer
    Behaviour 200
Sales Promotion 200
Social Marketing 205
Misconceptions about Behaviour
    Approaches 206
Are Behaviour Approaches
    Manipulative and Unethical? 207
Do Behaviour Approaches Deny that
    People Can Think? 207
Summary 208
Key Terms and Concepts 209
Review and Discussion Questions 209

Chapter 11   Classical and Operant Conditioning 210

Lotto Mania 211
Classical Conditioning 212
Classical Conditioning as a
    Marketing Tool 213
Consumer Research on Classical
    Conditioning 214
Operant Conditioning 217
Discriminative Stimuli 217
Behaviours 218
Consequences 218
Reinforcement Schedules 219
Shaping 220
Consumer Research on Operant
    Conditioning 221
Marketing Implications 223
Brand Loyalty 223
Store Loyalty 224
Summary 225
Key Terms and Concepts 226
Review and Discussion Questions 226

Chapter 12   Vicarious Learning and the
    Diffusion of Innovation 228

Vidio Game Challenge 229
Uses of Overt Modeling 230
Developing New Responses 230
Inhibiting Undesired Responses 231
Facilitating Desired Responses 232
Covert and Verbal Modelling 233
Factors Influencing Modelling
    Effectiveness 233
Characteristics of the Model and the
    Modelled Behaviour 234
Characteristics of the Observers 234
Characteristics of the Modelled
    Consequences 235
Marketing Implications 236

Diffusion of Innovation   236
The Adoption Process   236
Characteristics of Products   238
Summary   242
Key Terms and Concepts   242
Review and Discussion Questions   242

Chapter 13   Analysing Consumer Behaviour   244

Ford Explores the Four-Wheel-Drive
   Market   245
Model of Consumer Behavior   246
Information Contact   247
Funds Access   250
Store Contact   252
Product Contact   253
Purchase Transaction   254
Consumption   255
Communication   256
Marketing Implications   257
Identify Problem Behaviour   259
Analyse Contingencies   260
*Develop and Apply Behaviour
   Change Strategy*   261
Measure Behaviour Change   261
Maintain Behaviour   261
Summary   263
Key Terms and Concepts   264
Review and Discussion Questions   264

Section IV

THE ENVIRONMENT

Chapter 14   Introduction to the Environment   265

High-Tech Bingo Palace Lures
   Gamblers   267
The Environment   268
Aspects of the Environment   269
The Social Environment   269
The Physical Environment   272
Marketing Implications   274
Situations   279
Analysing Situations   280
Common Consumer Situations   281
Summary   288
Key Terms and Concepts   289
Review and Discussion Questions   290

**Chapter 15   Cultural and Cross-Cultural
Influences   292**

Birth of the Consumer Society   293

What Is Culture?   294
The Content of Culture   296
The Core Values of Canadian Culture   299
Changing Values in North America   300
Culture as a Process   302
*Moving Cultural Meanings into
   Products*   302
Cultural Meanings in Products   305
*Moving Meanings from Products into
   Consumers*   306
Cultural Meanings in Consumers   308
*Moving Meanings to the Cultural
   Environment*   309
Marketing Implications   309
Cross-Cultural Influences   312
Cross-Cultural Differences   312
*Developing International Marketing
   Strategies*   314
Summary   319
Key Terms and Concepts   320
Review and Discussion Questions   320

**Chapter 16   Subculture and Social Class
Influences   322**

The Boomers Meet the Dockers   323
Subcultures   324
Age Subcultures   327
Ethnic Subcultures   332
Gender as a Subculture   338
Income as a Subculture   339
Geographic Subcultures   341
The Acculturation Process   341
Social Class   342
Social Class and Values   343
Social Class and Income   343
Summary   346
Key Terms and Concepts   347
Review and Discussion Questions   348

**Chapter 17   Reference Groups and Family
Influences   350**

Barneymania and the Baby Boomlet   351
Reference Groups   352
Type of Reference Group Influence   353
*Reference Group Influence on
   Product and Brand Purchase* 356
Marketing Implications   357
Family   358
Family Decision Making   359
Consumer Socialisation   361
Changes in Canadian Families   364
Family Life Cycle   366
Marketing Implications   368

Summary   371
Key Terms and Concepts   373
Review and Discussion Questions   373

**Chapter 18   Environmental Influences on
Marketing Practices**   374

Fast Food Stuffed with R&D   375
The Rights of Marketers and
  Consumers   376
Legal Influences   378
Political Influences   381
Competitive Influences   382
Ethical Influences   382
Conclusions about Consumer
  Behaviour and Marketing Practice   386
Summary   386
Key Terms and Concepts   387
Review and Discussion Questions   387

Section V

CASES IN CONSUMER BEHAVIOUR

1. Toyota   390
 2. Wal-Mart Canada   391
 3. Ralph Lauren   393
 4. Nike   395
 5. Black & Decker   397
 6. Coca-Cola   399
 7. Buying a Lancer   401
 8. A Business Trip   404
 9. Intel Pentium: Word of Mouth
    and Group Influence   406
10. Price-Costco   408
11. Elegant Traditions   410
12. Bauer In-Line Skates   412
13. The Train Trip   414
14. Movie Theatres   417
15. Selling in Foreign Markets   419
16. Hyatt and Marriott Building
    Retirement Housing   421
17. Breast-Feeding in Canada in
    the 1990s   424
18. The Tylenol Crisis   429
19. Advice for a New Friend   431
20. Purchasing a Treadmill   434

Notes   437
Glossary of Consumer Behaviour Terms   461
Credits and Acknowledgments   471
Name, Company, and Brand Index   473
Subject Index   483

CONSUMER BEHAVIOUR OVERVIEW

OUTLINE

► 1. Introduction to Consumer Behaviour

► 2. The Wheel of Consumer Analysis: A Framework for Understanding Consumers

► 3. Using Consumer Analysis: Market Segmentation and the Marketing Mix

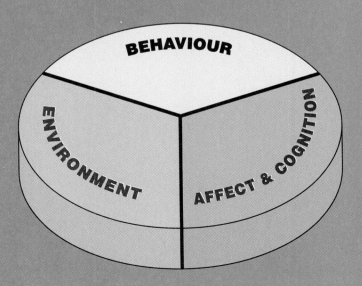

CHAPTER 1

Introduction to Consumer Behaviour

LEARNING OBJECTIVES

After completing this chapter, you should be able to:

► 1. Explain the marketing concept.

► 2. Cite three reasons companies today are changing to serve consumers better.

► 3. Define consumer behaviour.

► 4. Explain three points emphasised in the definition of consumer behaviour.

► 5. Explain why three major groups are interested in consumer behaviour.

► 6. List five elements of a marketing strategy for which knowledge of consumer behaviour can help companies make better decisions.

THE PHENOMENON OF THE GRATEFUL DEAD

One of the most successful operations in the history of rock music has been the rock 'n' roll group the Grateful Dead. The group always understood its customers and gave them what they wanted. The Dead pioneered such innovations as mail-order tickets, recorded phone messages about performances, and special locations at shows to allow fans (known as "tapeheads") to record the performance, something other rock groups actively discouraged.

The Grateful Dead would change its offerings every show to give variety to consumers going to more than one concert. The Dead also offered concerts that ran almost twice as long as those of its competitors but at no more cost. This market-sensitive approach allowed the Grateful Dead to be successful for nearly 30 years. In fact, on one of the band's last tours, more than $29 million worth of tickets were sold in 63 different cities. Few bands in the history of rock music could attract such crowds for so many years.

Hamilton, Ontario, was a favourite stop on the Dead's North American tour. The concerts in this city in 1990 and 1992 brought in an estimated $10 million to the community.

In recent years the band had branched out into new endeavours with its own merchandising division. Fans were able to order downhill skiis, neckties, dolls, backpacks, books, videos and equipment for perhaps the least likely of Deadhead sports: golf.

With the death of guitarist and inspirational leader, Gerry Garcia, in the Summer of 1995, many of the Grateful Dead's diehard fans were left shaken and distraught. It is truly safe to say that no band in the history of rock has been closer to its fans, knew what its customers wanted, and endeavoured to deliver more customer service than the Grateful Dead.

APPLYING THE MARKETING CONCEPT

In the 1990s more organisations have recognised that satisfying consumers with quality products and offering superior service are the foundation for success in highly competitive markets.

Marketers have long argued that the marketing concept is the appropriate philosophy for conducting business. Simply stated, the **marketing concept** suggests that to be more profitable an organisation must satisfy consumer needs and wants. To implement the marketing concept, organisations must understand and stay close to their customers to provide products and services consumers will purchase.

For many years, Canadian firms have not fully understood the marketing concept. All too often, even firms that accept it in principle do not recognise that its implementation requires an organisation to make dramatic changes in its approach to doing business. In general, these firms have viewed implementation of the marketing concept as a marketing task only, certainly not a comprehensive strategy the entire organisation has to buy into. While these companies may carry out marketing and consumer research, they seldom use this research as the basis for designing an entire organisational strategy.

Today, many of the world's most successful companies have designed their entire organisations to serve and stay close to consumers.[1] These companies are committed to developing quality products and services and selling them at prices that give consumers high value. In these successful companies, not only the marketing department but also design, engineering, production, human resources, finance, and other departments focus on doing their jobs in ways that enhance the value of their products to consumers. Some firms find they can improve product quality and reduce costs at the same time, and they

---

CONSUMER PERSPECTIVE

▶ 1.1

Top firms stay close to customers

Staying close to the customer can mean the difference between boffo success and abysmal failure. The techniques used by the top firms to find out what the customer wants include focus groups, field surveys, questionnaires, complaints, and—above all—quality products and services that both respond to clients and anticipate their needs.

"We're trying to limit the customer we potentially have," said Bob Hitchcock, marketing director of A&B Sound Ltd. of Vancouver, a music and consumer electronics retailer. Nor is the treatment of that customer limited to what a customer might expect from a firm like A&B: large inventory and in-store discount specials. For example, in A&B's new 40,000 square-foot stores in Calgary and Edmonton, there are listening posts where potential buyers can sample the music before they buy and cappuccino bars to create an ambience. One store has a children's play centre. "Quality of service depends on staff knowledge, something that A&B Sound looks for in new employees then tries to improve upon," Hitchcock said.

Customers need to feel special, even if they're buying an otherwise mundane service like house or institutional cleaning. "A hundred years ago only the ultrarich had servants," said Gary Franklin, president and CEO of ServiceMaster Canada Ltd. of Mississauga, Ontario. "Today, even the ordinary person can afford services like lawn care, housecleaning, and ordering in dinner."

Moyer Vico Corp. knows that knowing your firm's core strength is crucial to reaching the customer. Moyer Vico, a Toronto-based seller of educational products and school supplies, stays away from faddish items like Mutant Ninja Turtles or Biker Mice. "The emphasis isn't on getting sales," said Adam Okhai, president and CEO. "I want the customer's trust."

At Toronto's Rider Travel, no incoming phone call is allowed to ring more than three times before it's answered by a counsellor. A quality control card is sent with encourage employees throughout the company to seek ways to do this. Others first determine what consumers want and how much they are willing to pay for a product, and then they design, produce, and market the best-quality product they can for the price consumers are willing to pay. Consumer Perspective 1.1 discusses several companies that owe their success, if not their survival, to their focus on customers.

What accounts for the changes companies are making to serve consumers better? There are likely three major reasons: competition from value-laden products, improved marketing research, and the development of consumer behaviour theory.

First, the dramatic success of Japanese companies such as Toyota and Sony, which focus on providing value-laden products, has spurred other companies to focus on the consumer. During the 1960s and 70s, many Canadian companies could sell almost anything they could produce. Consumers accepted products and services as being as good as could be expected. As Canadian consumers discovered the superior quality and lower prices of Japanese products, they realised that many North American products offered inferior value, and they shifted to purchasing foreign-made goods. Faced with this flight of sales, North American companies had to redesign their organisations to serve consumers so they could survive.

Value-laden products

The second major reason for a shift to focusing on consumers is a dramatic increase in the quality of consumer and marketing research. In the past, firms often had no detailed information on people who bought and used their products. While they may have

Improved quality of marketing research

---

every ticket asking for the client's views on the service, As a result of this customer focus, the firm has reduced its error ratio (typically defined as a wrong quote or routing mistake) to 1 percent. Twice a year, Rider senior management meet with an advisory council consisting of 10 clients for a morning feedback session. Quarterly internal reports measure changes in service levels. Each client gets a formal annual satisfaction review survey.

One of the most successful ways to keep customers happy is to have high-quality employees who know their jobs. "Hire the best, then get the hell out of the way," advised Gary Santini of ParkLane Ventures Ltd., a Burnaby British Columbia housebuilder. "People can accomplish incredible heights if they're given the chance. My people don't work for me; they work for themselves."

Toronto-based Delta Hotels and Resorts is putting its money where its mouth is. The company has introduced the Great Meetings Guarantee to attract more convention business. Delta will pay $100 to any customer if the hotel does not provide same-day telephone response to meeting space requests. It will also pay $100 if meeting rooms are not set up to the client's specifications, if the final bill is not mailed within three business days of the conference, or if the room is not equipped with the requested office supplies. If audiovisual equipment is not set up on time, it's free for the day. If coffee breaks are late, they're free too. Simon Cooper, president and COO, said the company instituted this program because "Customers want to know that they're not going to have any hassles, and if they do, there's a penalty to us."

Source: Adapted from "Top Firms Stay Close to Customer," *Financial Post*, Dec. 18–20, 1993; "Delta Puts Its Money Where Its Mouth Is," *Financial Post*, Oct. 28, 1994.

Advertising firms such as this one can help marketers understand and stay close to consumers by knowing more about them.

commissioned research to investigate new product concepts and to try to understand consumers, often this research was not ongoing and did not identify the firm's actual customers. Today, computer technology and scanner and other data sources can tell firms who their customers are and how marketing strategy and strategy changes affect them. Both manufacturers and retailers now have ways to track consumer reactions to new products and services and to evaluate marketing strategies more effectively than ever before. Thus, companies are now in a better position to implement the marketing concept. Consumer Perspective 1.2 provides examples of segmented mailing lists that offer companies information about specific types of consumers.

Development of consumer behaviour research and theory

A third reason for today's increased emphasis on consumers is the development of consumer behaviour as a field of study. In the past, marketers had some useful views of consumer behaviour to work from, but both the number and the sophistication of theories, concepts, and models to describe and understand consumer behaviour have grown dramatically in recent years. Although there is no consensus on what approaches are best, marketers today have a greater variety of useful ideas for understanding consumers than they once did.

In sum, many successful companies recognise the importance of consumers, and they use sophisticated approaches and detailed data to develop organisational and marketing strategies. All of this indicates a consumer behaviour course is an important component of a business education. In the remainder of this chapter, we discuss the nature of consumer behaviour and the parties involved in studying and analysing it. We also investigate some relationships between consumer behaviour and marketing strategy and the

Companies today can buy or rent a variety of mailing lists to focus their marketing efforts on individual consumers. These mailing lists include the names and addresses of consumers who have demonstrated certain kinds of behaviour that indicate they might be interested in a given company's products. Examples of lists available for sale follow:

► 48,000 recent residential movers per month.

► 101,000 Canadian investors who have a $100,000+ investment portfolio.

► 360,000 parents with children under 6 years of age.

► 493,000 active direct-mail buyers of French cosmetics.

► 750,000 real estate investors.

► 828,000 retired active Canadian citizens, 50+ years of age.

► 1,785,000 respondents to socioeconomic and consumer behaviour surveys.

► 7,500,000 retail store buyers with assorted geographic, demographic, and consumer behaviour data.

Sources: Canadian Direct Mail Association and CICOMA, 1994.

value of this course for a successful career. While this text focuses on consumer behaviour and marketing strategy, employees in every business function in a successful company are involved in serving consumers. Consumer Perspective 1.3 lists some companies that have stayed close to their customers for many years.

WHAT IS CONSUMER BEHAVIOUR?

The American Marketing Association defines **consumer behaviour** as "the dynamic interaction of affect and cognition, behaviour, and environmental events by which human beings conduct the exchange aspects of their lives."[2] There are at least three important ideas in this definition: consumer behaviour is dynamic; it involves interaction among affect (WHAT PEOPLE FEEL), cognitions (WHAT PEOPLE THINK OR BELIEVE), behaviours (WHAT PEOPLE DO), and environmental events; and it also involves exchanges.

Consumer behaviour involves exchanges such as this one at a Blockbuster Video store.

CONSUMER PERSPECTIVE

▶ **1.3**

Staying close to customers— for a long time!

Some analysts argue that brand names are becoming less important to consumers. But clearly some companies have stayed close to their customers and kept their brands on top for many years. Some brands have been sales leaders for decades.

	Leading brand in	
Category	1923	1991
Cameras	Kodak	No. 1
Canned fruit	Del Monte	No. 1
Chewing gum	Wrigley's	No. 1
Crackers	Nabisco	No. 1
Razors	Gillette	No. 1
Soft drinks	Coca-Cola	No. 1
Soap	Ivory	No. 1
Soup	Campbell	No. 1
Toothpaste	Colgate	No. 2

Source: Mark Landler, Zachary Schiller, and Lois Therrien, "What's in a Name? Less and Less," *Business Week*, July 8, 1991, pp. 66–67.

Consumer behaviour is dynamic

First, the definition emphasises that consumer behaviour is *dynamic.* This means individual consumers, consumer groups, and society at large constantly change and evolve. Change has important implications for the study of consumer behaviour as well as for developing marketing strategies. One implication is that generalisations about consumer behaviour are usually limited to specific time periods, products, and individuals or groups. Thus, students of consumer behaviour must be careful not to overgeneralise theories and research findings.

The dynamic nature of consumer behaviour implies that one should not expect the same marketing strategy to work all of the time, or across all products, markets, and industries. While this may seem obvious, many companies do not recognise the need to adapt their strategies in different markets. For example, Philip Morris was unable to make 7UP a leading brand despite use of strategies that had been successful in other industries.

Further, a strategy that is successful at one time may fail miserably at another. For example, the automobile industry had no problem selling cars of relatively modest quality until consumers learned about the superior quality and value of Japanese cars. This resulted in North American manufacturers working hard to improve the quality of their offerings. As health-conscious consumers became aware of the cholesterol problems associated with palm and coconut oils, Kellogg's adapted its marketing strategy by removing these oils from its Cracklin' Oat Bran. In sum, the dynamic nature of consumer behaviour makes marketing strategy development an exciting, yet challenging, task.

Consumer behaviour involves interactions

A second important point that comes out of the definition of consumer behaviours is that it involves interactions among affect and cognitions, behaviours, and environmental events. To understand consumers and develop superior marketing strategies, we must understand what they think (cognition) and feel (affect), what they do (behaviour), and the things and places (environmental events) that influence and are influenced by *what consumers think, feel, and do.* We believe it is shortsighted to analyse only the effects of an environmental event on affect, cognitions, or behaviours, as is common in basic research. Instead, whether we are evaluating a single consumer, a target market, or an entire society, analysis of all three elements is useful for understanding and developing marketing strategies.

A final point in the definition of consumer behaviour is that it involves exchanges between human beings. Typically, consumers exchange their money for products and services. This definition of consumer behaviour is consistent with current definitions of marketing that also emphasise exchange. In fact, the role of marketing is to facilitate exchanges with consumers by formulating and implementing marketing strategies.

Consumer behaviour involves exchanges

It is generally agreed that the field of consumer behaviour grew principally out of economics but also has as its roots the disciplines of anthropology, cognitive psychology, communication theory, demography, personality theory, social psychology, and sociology. While marketers have always known that it is the consumer who is central to all business success, it wasn't until the 1960s that consumer behaviour emerged as a distinct field of study through the influence of researchers such as Katona, Ferber, and Howard. Today, consumer behaviour is a core discipline in the field of marketing, and every marketing major follows a course in this topic.

Beginnings of consumer behaviour

Two broad groups are interested in consumer behaviour: a basic research group and an action-oriented group. The basic research group is mainly academic researchers interested in studying consumer behaviour to develop a unique body of knowledge about this aspect of human behaviour. The majority of published work on consumer behaviour is basic research, which forms the foundation for our text. The major thrust of our book is applying this research to marketing problems.

WHO IS INTERESTED IN CONSUMER BEHAVIOUR?

The action-oriented group can be divided into three subgroups as shown in Exhibit 1.1: marketing organisations, government and political organisations, and consumers. Each of these is interested in consumer behaviour not just for the sake of knowledge, but for using this knowledge to influence the other subgroups.

Marketing organisations include not only conventional business firms but also other organisations such as charitable foundations, museums, law firms, and universities. Marketing organisations include all groups that have a market offering and seek exchanges with consumers. The primary focus of our text is on relationships between marketing strategy and consumers from the perspective of business firms, but the ideas we present can also be applied to other marketing organisations, from the World Wildlife Fund of Canada to your college or university.

The second group, government and political organisations, includes government agencies such as Health Canada and Industry Canada, which are concerned with monitoring and regulating exchanges between marketing organisations and consumers. They do this through the development of public policy, which affects marketing strategies and consumer activities. Political organisations in this subgroup include activists, such as the Consumers' Association of Canada or the Canadian Automobile Protection Association. While these relationships are not the major concern of our text, they are considered, particularly in Chapter 18.

The third group is consumers, which includes both individual consumers and organisational buyers who exchange resources for various goods and services. Their interest in consumer behaviour is primarily to make exchanges that help them achieve their goals.

EXHIBIT 1.1

Relationships among action-oriented groups interested in consumer behaviour

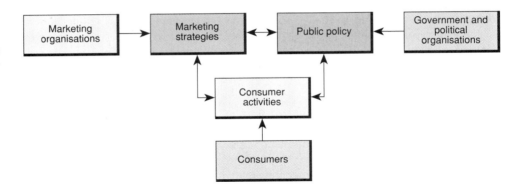

Although our major concern is with ultimate consumers, the logic presented here can be applied in organisational markets. Several examples of organisational buyer behaviour are discussed later in the text.

MARKETING IMPLICATIONS

From the viewpoint of marketing organisations, a **marketing strategy** is a plan designed to influence exchanges to achieve organisational objectives. Typically, a marketing strategy is intended to increase the probability or frequency of certain consumer behaviours, such as frequenting particular stores or purchasing particular products. This is accomplished by developing and presenting marketing mixes directed at selected target markets. A marketing mix consists of product, promotion, pricing, and distribution elements.

Exhibit 1.2 presents consumer behaviour issues involved in developing various aspects of marketing strategy. Such issues can be addressed through formal marketing research, informal discussions with consumers, or thinking about the relationships between consumer behaviour and marketing strategy.

Exhibit 1.2 shows that understanding consumers is a critical element in developing marketing strategies. Virtually every strategy decision involves a consideration of consumer behaviour. Analysis of the competition, for example, requires an understanding of

EXHIBIT 1.2

Examples of consumer issues for marketing

Marketing Elements	Consumer Issues
Segmentation	▷ Which consumers are the prime prospects for our product? ▷ What consumer characteristics should we use to segment the market for our product?
Product	▷ What products do consumers use now? ▷ What benefits do consumers want from this product?
Promotion	▷ What promotion appeal would influence consumers to purchase and use our product? ▷ What advertising claims would be most effective for our product?
Pricing	▷ How important is price to consumers in various target markets? ▷ what effects will a price change have on purchase behaviour?
Distribution	▷ Where do consumers buy this product? ▷ Would a different distribution system change consumers' purchasing behaviour?

Successful companies can stay close to their customers by making products their customers can trust.

what consumers think and feel about competitive brands, which consumers buy these brands and why, and in what situations they buy them. In sum, the more a firm learns about consumers (and approaches to analysing them), the better its chances for developing successful marketing strategies. Consumer Perspective 1.4 discusses the importance of understanding consumers for developing marketing strategies.

Finally, marketing strategies, particularly as developed and implemented by successful corporations, exert a powerful force on consumers and society at large. Marketing strategies not only adapt to consumers but also change what consumers think and feel about themselves, about various market offerings, and about the appropriate situations for product purchase and use. This does not mean marketing is unethical or devious. But the power of marketing and the ability of marketing research and consumer analysis to gain insight into consumer behaviour should not be underestimated or misused.

CONSUMER PERSPECTIVE

Consumer behaviour principles and marketing strategies

▶ **Know your customers**
Consumer-goods companies are using high-tech techniques to find out who their customers are—and aren't. By linking that knowledge with data about ads and coupons, they can fine tune their marketing.

▶ **Make what they want**
In an age of diversity, products must be tailored to individual tastes. So where once there were just Oreos, now there are fudge-covered Oreos, Oreo Double Stufs, and low-fat Oreos, too.

▶ **Use targeted and new media**
Companies aiming for micro markets are advertising on cable TV and in magazines to reach special audiences. And they're putting their messages on walls in high-school lunchrooms, on videocassettes, and even on blood-pressure monitors.

▶ **Use nonmedia**
Marketers are sponsoring sports, festivals, and other events to reach local markets. The Montreal Jazz Festival focuses on a young, hip audience and is very popular. So are sports ranging from golf to hydroplane racing.

▶ **Reach customers in the store**
Consumers make most buying decisions while they're shopping. So marketers are putting ads on supermarket loudspeakers, shopping carts, and in-store monitors.

▶ **Sharpen your promotions**
Couponing and price promotions are expensive and often harmful to a brand's image. Thanks to better data, some companies are using fewer, more effective promotions. One promising approach: Aiming coupons at a competitor's customers.

▶ **Work with retailers**
Consumer-goods manufacturers must learn to micro market to the retail trade, too. Some are linking their computers to the retailers' and some are tailoring their marketing and promotions to an individual retailer's needs.

Source: Adapted from Zachary Schiller, "Stalking the New Consumer," *Business Week*, Aug. 28, 1989, p. 54.

▶ SUMMARY

Learning objective 1: *Explain the marketing concept.*
The marketing concept suggests an organisation must satisfy consumer needs and wants to make profits. To implement the marketing concept, organisations must understand their customers and stay close to them to provide products and services that consumers will purchase and use appropriately.

Learning objective 2: *Cite three reasons companies today are changing to serve consumers better.*
First, the success of Japanese companies such as Toyota and Sony that focus on providing value-laden products has spurred other companies to do the same. Second, a dramatic increase in the quality of consumer and marketing research has made it easier for companies to implement consumer-oriented strategies. Third, consumer behaviour research has developed markedly in recent years, offering more sophisticated views to help companies understand customers.

Learning objective 3: *Define consumer behaviour*

Consumer behaviour is the dynamic interaction of affect and cognition, behaviour and environmental events by which human beings conduct the exchange aspects of their lives.

Learning objective 4: *Explain three points emphasised in the definition of consumer behaviour.*

First, the definition emphasises that consumer behaviour is dynamic. This means individual consumers, consumer groups, and society at large constantly change and evolve.

Second, the definition emphasises the interactions among affect and cognitions, behaviours, and environmental events. This means that to understand consumers and develop successful marketing strategies, a firm must understand what consumers feel (affect) and think (cognition), what they do (behaviour), and the things and places (environmental events) that influence and are influenced by what consumers feel, think, and do.

Third, the definition emphasises that consumer behaviour involves exchanges between human beings. Typically, consumers exchange their money for products and services, although other exchanges are also important.

Learning objective 5: *Explain why three major groups are interested in consumer behaviour*

The three major groups are marketing organisations, government and political organisations, and consumers. Marketing organisations, such as businesses, are interested in consumer behaviour primarily because they want to develop marketing strategies to influence consumers to purchase their products. Government and political organisations are interested mainly for purposes of monitoring and regulating exchanges between marketing organisations and consumers. Consumers are interested because they want to make exchanges that satisfy their goals.

Learning objective 6: *List five elements of a marketing strategy for which knowledge of consumer behaviour can help companies make better decisions.*

The five elements are market segmentation, product, promotion, pricing, and distribution. The last four elements are called the marketing mix.

---

marketing concept	consumer behaviour	marketing strategy	▶ **KEY TERMS AND CONCEPTS**

▶ **REVIEW AND DISCUSSION QUESTIONS**

1. Why is consumer behaviour an important course in business education?
2. Do you think marketing is a powerful force in society? Why or why not?
3. What is the role of consumer analysis in developing marketing strategies?
4. Describe three examples of situations where a marketing strategy influenced your purchase behaviour. Why did each succeed over competitive strategies?
5. Using Exhibit 1.2 as a take-off point, discuss other questions and decisions in marketing strategy that could be affected by a study of consumer behaviour.
6. Select a market segment of which you are not a member. With other students in the class, discuss the kinds of information you would need to develop a strategy aimed at that segment.
7. Using a campus organisation of interest (for example, student government, student association, or political interest group), discuss how a better understanding of the consumer behaviour of students could help the organisation improve its influence strategies.

2

The Wheel of Consumer Analysis: A Framework for Understanding Consumers

LEARNING OBJECTIVES

After completing this chapter, you should be able to:

► 1. List the three elements of the Wheel of Consumer Analysis.

► 2. Define affect and cognition and give an example of each.

► 3. Define behaviour and give an example.

► 4. Define environment and give an example.

► 5. Explain four points concerning use of the Wheel of Consumer Analysis.

► 6. Describe four levels of consumer analysis.

SARA LAUREN BUYS SOME PEACE OF MIND

Sara Lauren is a 35-year-old single mother to daughter Jessica. The increasingly uncertain times have meant that she's changed jobs twice in the last five years. Moreover, since the birth of her daughter, she's been more and more concerned about the future.

Sara's been contributing for years to the Canada Pension Plan but now wonders about the future viability of the government's retirement system. Frequent news reports warn that the system is doomed because the relatively small work force of the early 21st century will be unable to support its vast group of retired citizens.

Sara decides to stop by her local bank on the way to work to discuss ways of safeguarding her retirement savings with someone who knows the ropes.

After analysing her situation with the investment officer at the bank, she decides to purchase RRSPs. She also signs up for a retirement planning seminar the bank is offering next month. Learning about the Canadian Registered Retirement Savings Plan makes Sara feel much more secure about her financial future.

Although the description of this purchase is brief, it contains all of the major elements of consumer analysis. First, Sara Lauren had feelings of fear and worry for her security and that of her daughter. Feelings like this are called **affect.** Second, Sara did some planning, remembering, analysing, thinking, and decision making before she purchased the RRSP. Thinking like this is called **cognition.** Third, Sara paid attention to the media reports, stopped by the bank, met with an investment banker, registered herself in an investment seminar, and then purchased the RRSP. Doing things like this is called **behavior.** Finally, a number of factors influenced her behaviour, such as the future viability of the Canada Pension Plan (the national economic situation), the general media hype for RRSPs in the first 60 days of the new year, the convenience of her local bank, and her own financial situation. Such things taken together are called the **environment.** To understand even a simple purchase such as this one, marketers must analyse all of these elements: affect (what people are feeling), cognition (what people are thinking), behaviour (what people are doing), and the environment (what other factors contribute to what individuals think, feel, and do).

To help understand consumer behaviour, researchers have borrowed ideas from other fields, including economics, psychology, social psychology, sociology, and cultural anthropology. A number of ideas about consumers also come from marketing experience. Valuable insights have been obtained from all of these areas, but no one approach can completely explain a consumer purchase. In many cases, ideas borrowed from different areas overlap and even compete with each other as useful descriptions of consumers. To date, no one approach is fully accepted. A single, all-encompassing theory of consumer behaviour that everyone accepts is unlikely to be devised.

Even without a grand theory of consumer behaviour, marketers need a general framework for studying and understanding consumers. Such a framework should encompass all of the useful ideas and theories in the field. Marketers can use such a general model to guide their analyses of consumers, develop a deeper understanding of consumers, and create more effective marketing strategies.

THE WHEEL OF CONSUMER ANALYSIS

This chapter describes one useful framework for studying, analysing, and understanding consumers. We call this framework the **Wheel of Consumer Analysis.** Exhibit 2.1 presents the three parts of the wheel: affect and cognition, behaviour, and environment. You saw these components in the story about Sara Lauren's RRSP purchase. These three categories describe the major concepts and events that marketers must analyse to understand consumers. Each element is the focus of a major section of this book. We believe an analysis of consumers' affect and cognition, behaviour, and environment is the foundation for understanding consumers and for developing effective marketing strategies. In this section, we discuss the major elements of the Wheel of Consumer Analysis and how they are related, and we show how to identify these components.

Affect and cognition

In this text, affect and cognition refer to two types of internal psychological reactions that consumers may have in response to objects and events in the external environment or to their own behaviour. In simple language, *affect* concerns *feelings,* while *cognition* involves *thinking.*

Affect varies in evaluation (either positive or negative) and intensity. Some affective feelings are positive and favourable (love, joy, relaxed), while others are negative and unfavourable (boredom, anger, fear). Affect includes relatively intense emotions such as

EXHIBIT 2.1

The Wheel of Consumer Analysis

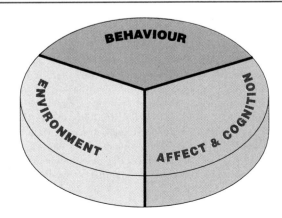

CONSUMER PERSPECTIVE

2.1

Some basic questions about consumer affect and cognition

Although many competing ideas about consumer affect and cognitions have been proposed, no single theory completely describes the workings of consumers' minds. Carefully studying and thinking about the information in Section II of this text should help you develop informed answers to questions about affect and cognition such as:

1. How do consumers interpret information from marketing stimuli such as products, stores, and advertising?
2. How do consumers choose from among alternative product classes, products, and brands?
3. How do consumers form evaluations of products and brands?
4. How does memory affect consumer decision making?
5. How do affect and cognition influence behaviour and environments?
6. How do behaviour and environments influence affect and cognition?
7. How do consumers interpret the benefits of marketing offerings?
8. Why are consumers more interested in some products or brands than others?
9. How do marketing strategies influence consumers' affective and cognitive responses?
10. How do affective and cognitive responses influence each other?

love or anger, less strong feelings such as satisfaction or frustration, diffuse moods such as relaxation or boredom, and rather mild evaluations such as "I like McDonald's french fries."

Cognition refers to the knowledge and thinking processes involved in people's responses to the environment. Cognition includes the knowledge, meanings, and beliefs people have acquired from their experiences and have stored in their memories. Cognition also includes the psychological processes associated with paying attention to and understanding aspects of the environment, remembering past events, forming attitudes, and making purchase decisions. Many cognitive processes are conscious; others are unconscious and essentially automatic.

Section II explores consumer affect and cognition. Consumer Perspective 2.1 offers a sample of the types of questions marketers ask about affect and cognition.

Behaviour

In this text, **behaviour** refers to the overt acts of consumers. Examples of behaviours include watching a TV commercial, visiting a store, or buying a product. Thus, while affect and cognition are concerned with what consumers feel and think, behaviour deals with what consumers actually *do*. Despite the importance of behaviour for developing marketing strategy, little consumer research has been conducted on the topic. Section III discusses ways to analyse consumers' overt behaviour. Consumer Perspective 2.2 illustrates the types of questions marketers might ask in analysing consumers' behaviours.

Environment

In this text, **environment** refers to all the physical and social characteristics of consumers' external world. The environment includes objects, places, and other people that influence consumers' affect, cognition, and behaviour. Section IV explores the physical and social aspects of the environment. Consumer Perspective 2.3 offers a sample of the types of questions marketers might ask about the environment.

CONSUMER
PERSPECTIVE

▶ 2.2

Some basic
questions about
consumer
behaviour

Little attention has been given to studying the overt behaviour of consumers, but many behaviour influence techniques seem to be commonly used by marketing practitioners. Carefully studying and thinking about the information in Section III of the text should help you develop informed answers to questions about behaviour such as:

1. How do behaviour approaches differ from affective and cognitive approaches to studying consumer behaviour?

2. What is classical conditioning, and how do marketers use it to influence consumer behaviour?

3. What is operant conditioning, and how do marketers use it to influence consumer behaviour?

4. What is vicarious learning, and how do marketers use it to influence consumer behaviour?

5. What consumer behaviours are of interest to marketing managers?

6. How much control does marketing exert on consumers' behaviour?

7. How do affect and cognition and environments affect behaviour?

8. How does behaviour influence affect and cognition and environments?

9. How can marketing managers use behaviour theory?

10. How does consumer behaviour vary by individuals, products, and situations?

The marketing strategies designed by managers create part of the physical and social environment consumers experience. For instance, products, packaging, advertisements, presentations by salespeople, price tags, signs, and stores are physical and social stimuli in the environment that marketers create to influence consumers. How marketers use consumer behaviour analysis to develop marketing strategy is introduced in Chapter 3 and is discussed throughout the text.

Identifying the wheel components

Marketers can analyse any consumer behaviour situation in terms of the three elements of the Wheel of Consumer Analysis: the environment, behaviour, and affect and cognition (see Exhibit 2.1). Because these factors influence each other, no one factor can be fully understood in isolation. Understanding consumers requires studying all three elements. To help you identify the components of the Wheel of Consumer Analysis, we examine an everyday grocery shopping situation.

Like millions of other consumers, Bruce Macklin makes a weekly trip to a local supermarket to buy groceries. On this sunny Saturday morning, Bruce has driven to Loblaw's supermarket with his three-year-old daughter, Angela. As he walks through the front doors, Bruce enters one of the most complex information environments a consumer can face. The average Canadian grocery store stocks some 5,000 items, but some very large stores may carry as many as 20,000. Most supermarkets offer many alternatives in each product category. For instance, one large store offers 18 brands of mustard in a variety of sizes. Moreover, most product packages show lots of information. The average package of breakfast cereal, for example, provides some 250 pieces of information! During the next 50 minutes (the average time consumers spend in the store on a major shopping trip), Bruce will see much of this information and make numerous purchase decisions. Most of his choices will be made easily and quickly, seemingly with little effort. Some choices, though, will involve noticeable thinking and may require a few seconds. And some may require several minutes and substantial effort.

Environmental psychology seeks to extend knowledge about the relationships between environmental stimuli and human behaviour. In consumer research, the major environmental factors examined have been concerned with the impact of various societal aspects. Careful study of the information in Section IV should help you develop informed answers to questions about the environment such as:

1. In what physical environments do consumer behaviours occur?
2. How do marketing environments influence consumers' affect, cognition, and behaviour?
3. How do consumer affect, cognition, and behaviour influence the environment?
4. What influence does culture have on consumers?
5. What influence does subculture have on consumers?
6. What influence does social class have on consumers?
7. What influence do reference groups have on consumers?
8. What influence do families have on consumers?
9. In what ways do people influence each other in consumer environments?
10. How powerful are interpersonal influences on consumer behaviour?

CONSUMER PERSPECTIVE

2.3

Some basic questions about consumer environments

Environment

What is the physical and social environment of the supermarket like? On a Saturday morning, it is likely to be *busy,* with many people *crowding* the aisles. The store is likely to be somewhat *noisy.* Because Bruce is shopping with Angela, her *chatter* adds to the commotion. These social aspects of the environment will influence Bruce's affect, cognition, and overt behaviour. The store *layout,* the *width* of the aisles, the special sale *signs* on the shelves, the product *displays* at the ends of the aisles and elsewhere in the store, the *lighting,* and other physical aspects of the supermarket environment may also have an effect. Other environmental factors such as the *temperature,* background *music,* and the *wobbly wheel* on his shopping cart may also influence Bruce's affect, cognition, and behaviour.

Much of the in-store environment Bruce experiences is the result of marketing strategy decisions made by the retailer and the manufacturers of the products. A grocery store is a good place to observe marketing strategies in action. The huge number of products sold in such stores requires an equally large number of marketing strategies. A firm's distribution strategy (for instance, place products only in discount stores) determines whether that product is even present in a store. A variety of pricing strategies (reduced price on Oreo cookies) and promotion strategies (free samples of cheese) are evident in a supermarket environment. Package designs (easy-opening milk containers) and specific product characteristics (low-calorie frozen entrée) are also market strategies. Finally, specific environmental details such as point-of-purchase displays (a stack of Pepsi six-packs near the store entrance) are important aspects of marketing strategy. All these marketing strategies create changes in the physical and social environment that are intended to influence consumers' affect and cognitions and their behaviours.

Behaviour

What behaviours occur on a shopping trip? Bruce is engaged in many behaviours, including *walking* down the aisles, *looking* at products on the shelves, *picking* up and *examining* packages, *talking* to Angela and a friend he meets in the store, *steering* the wobbly cart, and so on. While many of these behaviours are not of much interest to a marketing manager, some have important effects on Bruce's affect and cognitions and his eventual purchases. For example, unless Bruce *walks* down the aisle containing breakfast cereals, he cannot *notice* and *buy* a package of Kellogg's Raisin Squares. Typically, marketers are most concerned about purchase behaviour. In the supermarket environment, purchase requires several behaviours such as *picking up* a package, *placing* it in the cart, and *paying* for it at the checkout counter.

Affect and cognition

Bruce's affective and cognitive systems are active in the supermarket environment, but only some of this internal activity is conscious. Many affective and cognitive responses occur without much awareness. For instance, Bruce may feel *irritated* about getting a cart with a wobbly wheel. He also *pays attention* to certain aspects of the store environment and *ignores* other parts. Some products capture his attention; others do not. He *interprets* a large amount of information in the store environment, from aisle signs to brand names to price tags to nutrition labels. In addition, he *evaluates* some of the products in terms of meeting his needs and those of his family. He *remembers* what products he has at home and what he has run out of and needs to replace. He *chooses* from among the thousands of items available in the store. In addition, he *makes decisions* about other specific behaviours. Should he go down aisle 3 or skip it this week? Should he stock up on canned peaches or buy just one can? Should he give Angela a cookie for being good? Should he take the wobbly cart back and get another one? Should he pay with cash or check?

Summary

About 45 minutes after entering Loblaw's, Bruce emerges with five bags of groceries containing 48 different products. His grocery shopping activities on this Saturday morning are influenced by the social and physical environment of the store (including the marketing strategies found there), his own behaviours, and his affective and cognitive processes. Moreover, each factor influences the others.

APPLYING THE WHEEL OF CONSUMER ANALYSIS

The Wheel of Consumer Analysis gives marketing managers a powerful tool for analysing and understanding consumers and for developing marketing strategies. Four points need to be emphasised about how marketers should apply this framework.

First, any comprehensive analysis of consumer behaviour must consider all three elements of the wheel. Descriptions of consumer behaviour expressed in terms of only one or two of the elements are incomplete. For example, to assume that affect and cognition cause behaviour and to ignore the influence of environment underestimates the dynamic nature of consumer behaviour and may lead to a less effective marketing strategy.

Second, it is important to understand the relationships among the elements of the wheel.[1] At any given time, any one of the elements can influence either or both of the other elements. For example, suppose today a consumer is interested in Cooper hockey equipment and decides to buy some. He purchases the equipment, uses it for a week, and then decides he doesn't like it. Expressed in terms of the Wheel of Consumer Analysis, his initial liking of the equipment and his decision to buy are affect and cognition; purchasing and using the equipment are behaviours. Initially, his affect and cognitions influenced his behaviours. The behaviours, or purchase and use, however, then influenced his affect and cognition (his feelings toward and understanding of the product) and he came to dislike the product. The direction of influence between any of the model elements depends on the particular time and scope of the analysis.

Third, any of the three elements may be the starting point for consumer analysis. In the Cooper hockey equipment example, the starting point was the consumer's affect and cognition (feeling and thinking). But an analysis could begin before this point by determining which environmental events, such as ads for hockey equipment, influenced his feelings and beliefs about Cooper and his decision to purchase. Or the analysis could begin by examining an earlier behaviour such as trying a friend's equipment. Fundamentally, marketers are interested in influencing specific behaviours. Therefore, consumer analysis usually begins with a focus on the desired behaviour (buying a particular brand, going

CONSUMER PERSPECTIVE

2.4

LePage's glued to Child's Play

When LePage's, based in Brampton, Ontario, launched a new consumer glue, it was hoping for strong sales. But no one expected the product to finish the year as one of LePage's top-selling products.

Laird Robertson, brand manager on LePage's Child's Play School Glue, attributed the success of Child's Play to its positioning as an environmentally friendly product. He noted that because the glue market is already saturated with quality products, it has to be the positioning that accounts for Child's Play's strong sales performance. Key to its environmental positioning are its packaging and overall design presentation: Child's Play is a clear substance packaged in a clear polyethylene container. And it is labelled nontoxic.

Consumers have responded positively to Child's Play because it is less harmful to the environment than most glue products.

Source: "Green Product Is Big Seller: LePage's Glued to Child's Play," *Strategy*, Jan. 27, 1992. p. 15.

into a store, entering a sweepstakes contest) and attempts to determine the factors that influence that behaviour.

Fourth, the Wheel of Consumer Analysis views consumer behaviour as a dynamic process of continuous change. A marketer might develop a sound marketing strategy based on careful analysis of the components of the wheel at a particular time and a good description of consumers. But when any or all of the wheel elements change, the original marketing strategy becomes less effective. So, even if consumer analysis leads to an excellent marketing strategy, changes in consumers' affect and cognition, behaviour, or environment may necessitate a change in strategy. For example, because many consumers have developed strong values about protecting the environment and begun to use environmentally safe products, businesses have tried to improve their products to meet this market need. Consumer Perspective 2.4 discusses one company that has successfully responded to such changes.

LEVELS OF CONSUMER ANALYSIS	The Wheel of Consumer Analysis is a flexible tool for analysing and understanding consumers and for developing marketing strategies. It can be used fruitfully by both marketing managers and officials concerned with public policy to understand the dynamics of consumer behaviour. The wheel can be applied at four levels to analyse an entire society, an industry, a market segment, or an individual consumer.

Society

Changes in what a society believes and how its members behave can be analysed using the Wheel of Consumer Analysis. For example, a long-term trend in our society is increasing concern with health and fitness. How did this change occur? Surely, consumers have always wanted to live long, happy lives. For one thing, the media have widely publicized a growing body of medical research indicating people can be healthier and live longer if they eat properly and exercise regularly. This research may have changed some consumer's attitudes about eating and exercise. As these consumers began living more healthful lifestyles, other consumers copied their behaviour and developed their own positive values and attitudes toward health. Another factor that may have accelerated the health and fitness movement is that healthy, well-shaped people are considered more attractive in our society and are more prominent in ads, films, and public life. Also, a variety of health-related industries, such as health foods, exercise equipment, and sports apparel, promoted eating right and exercising regularly, which exposed many consumers to these ideas and contributed to adopting an active lifestyle.

Clearly, changes in the environment (medical research reports), cognition and affect (beliefs about how to live longer and healthier), behaviour (eating more healthful foods and exercising), and marketing strategies (development and promotion of health food, equipment, and exercise apparel) have interacted to influence this dynamic change in society. Of course, not everyone has been affected by these changes. But the wheel can help marketers think about changes in affect and cognition, behaviour, and environment in various societies around the world.

Industry

The Wheel of Consumer Analysis can be used to analyse and understand consumers who purchase products from companies in a specific industry. For example, changing health concerns have influenced beer consumers and companies in the beer industry. Changes in consumer beliefs and behaviour about calorie intake influenced Miller Brewing to develop a low-calorie beer, Miller Lite. This marketing strategy, in turn, helped reinforce and spread the changes in consumer beliefs and behaviours. Then, the success of Miller Lite prompted competitors, such as Molson and Labatt, to offer other brands of light beers, further stimulating demand for this product category.

Another change affecting the beer industry is consumers' increasing concern with responsible drinking, which decreases demand for alcohol products in general. This led to the marketing of low-alcohol beer (and nonalcoholic drink products such as mineral waters, juices, and soft drinks). Consumer groups such as Mothers Against Drunk Driving and Canadians Against Drunk Driving have also influenced many members of society to reduce their alcohol consumption or abstain. In fact, while drunken and boisterous behaviour was once considered acceptable, many people no longer find it funny. Similarly, smoking was once considered a sign of maturity and sophistication, but today it is not tolerated in most public places.

In sum, changes in consumer cognition, affect, and behaviour can weaken the appeal of certain products at the industry level. But such changes can also create opportunities for new products more consistent with emerging values and behaviours. Successful marketing strategies depend on analysing consumers' relationships with your own company's products and those of your competitors, and then creating an advantage over competitive offerings.

Market segment

The Wheel of Consumer Analysis can be used to identify segments of consumers with similar affect and cognitions, behaviours, or environments. Most successful firms divide the total market into segments and try to appeal most strongly to one or more segments. The emphasis on health, for example, has encouraged many consumers to take up sports. In the past, specific shoes were not designed for each particular sport. Today, there are many varieties and styles of shoes for running, bicycling, aerobics, soccer, basketball, and other sports. These shoes vary in design, features, and price ranges to appeal to groups of consumers who are similar in some way.

Reebok, for example, developed its Blacktop shoes for young basketball fans who play on urban outdoor courts. The shoe is a few ounces heavier than its competitors, moderately priced, and designed for use on asphalt and concrete. The shoe looks good, so it appeals to the 80 percent of consumers who buy athletic shoes solely for fashion, but it is also tough enough to stand up to rugged outdoor play. The shoe sold out in many stores in its first two months and was expected to sell over 2.2 million pairs in its first year, a smashing marketing success.[2] Thus, Reebok developed a successful marketing strategy by understanding the wants and preferences (cognitions and affect) of urban youths (target market) for a good-looking, moderately priced, long-wearing shoe, for regular guys who play basketball (behaviour) on outdoor courts (environment).

Marketers can use the Wheel of Consumer Analysis to monitor consumers in various segments. Successful marketers continuously monitor consumers' affect and cognition, behaviour, and the environment and are ready to modify their marketing strategies in response to significant changes in these factors. Such changes occur rapidly in some industries (pop music, computer software), and marketers must respond quickly. In other industries, changes occur more slowly (men's suits, home furnishings), and marketers have the luxury of time to develop effective strategies. Consumer Perspective 2.5 and Consumer Perspective 2.6 describe how Madonna (an international entertainment celebrity) and Harry Rosen (a Canadian menswear company executive) have changed their images and marketing strategies over the years to keep their loyal customers and attract new ones.

Individual consumer

Finally, the Wheel of Consumer Analysis can be used to analyse a single consumer in a variety of ways. For example, it could be used to understand the consumption history of an individual by analysing all the major purchases made in the past five years. The wheel could also be used to understand a series of purchases an individual makes in a particular product class, such as automobiles. Analyses such as these could reveal the

CONSUMER
PERSPECTIVE

▶ 2.5

Madonna's
changing
marketing
strategies

Staying in business over the long run is a matter of creating and keeping customers in the face of continuous change. Managers must be able to adapt their marketing strategies to dynamic changes in the three components of the Wheel of Consumer Analysis: consumers' environment, affect and cognition, and behaviour. Few marketers have done so as successfully as Madonna Ciccone, the pop music star.

Madonna is a rarity in show business—a star who runs her own business affairs. People who know her (and will talk about her) speak of her business skill in deal making, financing, and marketing. Throughout the late 1980s and early 1990s, Madonna was one of the top-earning female entertainers in North America, earning an estimated $39 million in 1990 alone. Since her career began in the early 1980s, Madonna has changed her image and her position in the marketplace several times. How does she do it?

1983: Madonna's original image was punk and trampy. She dressed in skimpy black clothes showing an exposed navel. She produced upbeat "dance music" with sexy lyrics sung in a girlish voice. Her premier album, "Madonna," sold 9 million copies.

1984: Madonna's second album hit the stores showing her dressed in a white wedding dress with a belt buckle reading "boy toy." She began wearing underwear as outerwear. Her album "Like a Virgin" sold 11 million copies.

1986–1988: Madonna dropped the sex kitten look for a more traditionally feminine appearance. Her singing voice became deeper and more serious. She appeared in a video with honey-blond hair and a demure flowered dress. In 1987, she was on the cover of *Cosmopolitan* as a glamorous blond; she appeared on the cover of *Harper's* in 1988 as a brunette. Her "True Blue" album sold 17 million copies.

1989: Madonna once again changed her image to a combination of gypsy and hippie. In the video accompanying "Like a Prayer," she flirted with religious symbols. That album sold 11 million copies.

1990: Madonna went futuristic with her blond hair tied back, a microphone strapped to her head, and a bustier that looked more like armor than underwear.

1992: Madonna became more sexually explicit in her songs and her behaviour. She released the CD "Erotica" along with a $50 book titled *Sex* showing nude pictures of herself.

Madonna continually redesigned and updated her product (both her music and herself as a personality) to stimulate new interest from her fans and to appeal to new market segments. Part of her strategy has been to stimulate controversy among some

consumption dynamics of an individual consumer. Comparing such profiles across consumers in the same and in different cultures could provide insights into the meaning of consumption at different times in history and in different parts of the world.

For marketing purposes, the Wheel of Consumer Analysis can be used to analyse and describe an individual shopping trip, an individual purchase, or some aspect of them. For segments of the population, usually with a sexual theme, to the delight of her fans. She also tried to expand her appeal by appearing in movies such as *Dick Tracy* and *Body of Evidence.*

One thing Madonna does shy away from is product endorsements. The only North American endorsement she has done was for Pepsi, in 1989. For a $5 million fee, Madonna contracted to do three ads and allow Pepsi to sponsor her tour. The expensive ads were to be aired just after the release of her album "Like a Payer." But the video for the title song showing her kissing a black saint and dancing provocatively in front of burning crosses caused so much controversy that Pepsi cancelled the contract. Madonna still collected her fee, along with millions in free publicity.

Although she hates to be described as an astute businesswoman (it isn't consistent with the image she is selling), Madonna is a very successful marketer who adapts her marketing strategies to changing market conditions as suggested by the Wheel of Consumer Analysis.

Source: Adopted from Matthew Schifrin and Peter Newcomb, "A Brain for Sin and a Bod for Business," *Forbes*, Oct. 1, 1990, pp. 162–66. Reprinted by permission of *Forbes* magazine, © Forbes Inc., 1990.

example, to understand Sara Lauren's purchase of an RRSP discussed at the beginning of the chapter, we needed to consider her cognitions, affect, behaviour, and environments. Bruce Macklin's grocery shopping trip is another example of consumer analysis at the individual level.

CONSUMER PERSPECTIVE

▶ 2.6

Harry Rosen's changing marketing strategies

Staying in business over the long run is a matter of creating and keeping customers in the face of continuous change. Managers must be able to adapt their marketing strategies to dynamic changes in the three components of the Wheel of Consumer Analysis: consumers' environment, affect and cognition, and behaviour. Few marketers have done so as successfully as Harry Rosen, the menswear retailer.

It would be difficult to find anyone in Canada who does not know the name and face of Harry Rosen. He has come to represent quality fashion clothing for men all over Canada and in parts of the United States. Harry Rosen, the man, is approachable, unpretentious, and very popular among his customers. Harry Rosen, the store, is upbeat and exciting and offers a unique shopping experience to its customers. The man and the store have created high standards in the fashion industry, which competitors have tried to emulate over the last three decades. How has he done this?

1954: Harry Rosen started a made-to-measure business in Toronto. At the time, upscale consumers were inclined to search out their tailor. Quality and longevity, along with personal service, were the prevailing values.

1957: Harry brought natural shoulder clothing to Canada, along with button-down shirts and repp silk ties. Young university graduates in search of their own identity found the clothing different but within conforming guidelines.

1961: Harry Rosen moved downtown to be closer to his market. His new store had the feel of an exclusive men's club.

1968: Harry broadened his merchandise to appeal to customers who sought out upscale men's clothing with greater variety.

1976: Harry Rosen introduced Polo to Canada. His objective was to attract younger consumers and counter the perception that he was establishment and expensive.

1980: During the recession, Harry Rosen did not trade down. He determined that it was more important than ever for men to have the advantage of appropriate dress. His ads became more informational.

1982: Harry Rosen opened his first store outside Toronto at a time when many retailers were experiencing difficulties. The stores got considerable support from many customers who had moved out West or knew of the name from business travels to Toronto.

1987: Harry Rosen had stores in five major markets in Canada. He emphasized training. As many menswear merchants went out of business, Harry opened his flagship store at Bloor and Belair in Toronto. It benefitted all his stores and generated a profitable volume of business.

1990: The recession and the introduction of the GST saw sales drop. Two stores were closed and four downsized.

1992: Strategies were developed to strengthen service and provide value-added benefits. Advertising focused on the sales associates' outstanding service. Harry Rosen himself appeared in his ads because market research showed that it was important for customers that Harry was a real person, with a real ideology, watching over the business.

1993:   Harry Rosen continued to position his company as a retailer with a broad fashion focus. He formed strategic alliances with well-known international brands such as Hugo Boss. "Tell Harry" cards were developed; their feedback revealed ways merchandise assortment and services could be enhanced.

1994:   Business was buoyant. Harry Rosen targeted a larger share of the menswear business by broadening his merchandise assortment, adding higher price points, expanding stores, and intensifying training. So far this strategy has been successful. Harry Rosen customers have little tolerance for unfulfilled promises and are quick to complain when something goes wrong. Harry still takes all customer phone calls and letters—both good and bad.

Harry Rosen continually redesigned and updated his product to stimulate demand and appeal to new market segments. A critical success factor has been Harry Rosen's involvement in the business. He tries to spend at least four days a year in each of his stores, which helps him to keep abreast of changes in consumer needs. Moreover, his appearance in numerous ads has made his face synonymous with the store. Harry has created a relationship with his customers through his ads. The company's advertising is continually changing to respond to new customers and consumer trends and lifestyles. Harry Rosen's marketing strategies have always been adaptive to changing market conditions as suggested by the Wheel of Consumer Analysis.

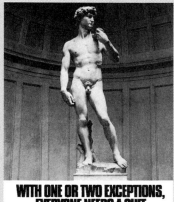

▶ SUMMARY

Learning objective 1: *List the three elements of the Wheel of Consumer Analysis.*
The three elements of the wheel are affect and cognition, behaviour, and environment.

Learning objective 2: *Define affect and cognition and give an example of each.*
Affect refers to feelings the consumer may have. Affect varies in evaluation: positive or negative, favourable or unfavourable. Affect also varies in intensity or level of arousal. Affect includes emotions (joy), feeling states (guilt), moods (bored), and evaluations (liking).

Cognition refers to the knowledge and mental processes involved in thinking responses to the environment. For instance, cognition includes knowledge that people have acquired from their experiences and have stored in their memories. Cognition also includes psychological processes associated with paying attention to and understanding aspects of the environment, remembering past events, forming attitudes, and making purchase decisions.

Learning objective 3: *Define behaviour and give an example.*
Behaviour refers to the overt acts or actions of consumers that can be directly observed. It deals with what people actually do rather than what they think or feel.

Learning objective 4: *Define environment and give an example.*
Environment refers to all the physical and social features of consumers' external world. The environment includes objects (products, store displays), places (factory outlet malls, the checkout area), and other people (friends, relatives, salespeople) that can influence the consumer's affect, cognition, and behaviour. An important part of the environment for consumer analysis includes the stimuli that marketers create to influence consumers (products, stores, ads, signs).

Learning objective 5: *Explain four points concerning use of the Wheel of Consumer Analysis.*
To use the wheel appropriately, analysts should recognise that (1) all elements of the wheel must be included for a comprehensive analysis: (2) at any given time, any one of the elements can influence the other two elements; (3) any of the elements could be the starting point for a consumer analysis, but behaviour is often the best one to start with; and (4) the wheel views consumer behaviour as a dynamic process of continuous influences.

Learning objective 6: *Describe four levels of consumer analysis.*
Four levels of consumer analysis include society, industry, market segment, and individual consumer. Societal analysis focuses on the affect and cognition, behaviour, and environment of very large groups of consumers in a society. Industry analysis is applied to all consumers who are customers for the products of a particular industry (blue jeans, athletic shoes, stereo systems). Segment-level analysis focuses on the affect and cognition, behaviour, and environment of consumers in a particular market segment. Individual-level analysis is intended to understand the affect and cognition, behaviour, and environment of a single consumer.

▶ KEY TERMS AND CONCEPTS

Wheel of Consumer Analysis	affect	behaviour
	cognition	environment

▶ REVIEW AND DISCUSSION QUESTIONS

1. Explain the relationship between the environment and marketing strategy.
2. Relate each of the four points the text makes about the Wheel of Consumer Analysis to the impact these issues would have on marketing strategy.

3. The text says analysis can begin with affect and cognition, behaviour, or environment. Why not begin with marketing strategy?

4. Offer three examples of changes in a marketing strategy that led to changes in your affect/cognition and behaviour.

5. Bring three magazine advertisements to class. Be prepared to explain what effect the ads are intended to have on your affect/cognition and behaviour.

6. List the four levels of consumer analysis and give a specific example of a recent change at each level.

3

Using Consumer Analysis: Market Segmentation and the Marketing Mix

LEARNING OBJECTIVES

After completing this chapter, you should be able to:

► 1. Define market segmentation and explain why marketers segment markets.

► 2. List five major types of segmentation and give examples of each.

► 3. Explain psychographic, benefit, and usage situation segmentation.

► 4. List the elements of the marketing mix.

► 5. Offer examples of marketing mix issues for which consumer analysis is important.

► 6. Explain product positioning.

GILLETTE AND THE DRUGSTORE DINOSAURS

Gillette is one of the best marketers of personal care products for men. The company invented the disposable razor blade and has a history of success with new styles of razors and blades. In 1990, it hit the jackpot again with the Sensor blade and a razor whose spring mechanism makes for what the company claims is the closest shave ever. With margins of 30 percent or more, Gillette can make profits of over $500 million per year on blades and razors alone. It benefits from loyal customers and dominates the market with a 63 percent share.

For all its success in the male market, however, Gillette has had problems marketing personal care products to women. Gillette's women's products include Silkience hair conditioner, White Rain shampoo, Dippity-Do hair treatment, Toni home permanent, Aapri facial cleanser, and Deep Magic skin cream. All were hot brands in their day, but young trendsetting women today view them as drugstore dinosaurs. Revitalizing these products has been difficult. For example, a $20 million campaign to relaunch Silkience conditioner did not succeed.

Gillette apparently has done excellent consumer analysis of men's shaving products and understands this market. What Gillette doesn't seem to understand is that women's hair care products require different marketing strategies. For one thing, fresh, new products tend to do better in the hair care market. While shaving products for men have reached the stage where they satisfy the bulk of the market, many women are still searching for a shampoo that meets their specific needs. Another factor is that in our culture the appearance of their hair is important to many people. Given the many variables of colour, texture, thickness, and style of hair, it is not likely that one shampoo will meet everyone's needs as one type of razor may. In other words, careful consumer analysis is needed to develop products and strategies that can succeed in varying target markets.[1]

As we noted in Chapter 1, marketing organisations, government and political organisations, and consumers are all interested in understanding consumer behaviour. Marketing organisations need to analyse consumers to develop successful marketing plans and strategies. To stay close to its customers, a company needs to carry out consumer analysis to understand consumer affect and cognitions, behaviours, and environments for its products and those of its competitors. This chapter focuses on some ways marketing organisations can use consumer analysis to make marketing decisions.

Marketing managers have two major tasks: selecting target markets and developing marketing mixes. This chapter discusses consumer analysis in terms of these two tasks. First, we examine the concept of **market segmentation,** that is, dividing consumers into groups that are similar in one or more ways to market to them more effectively. The group or groups a firm seeks to serve is called a **target market.** Second, the chapter discusses some important marketing mix questions that consumer analysis can help answer to develop more effective marketing strategies.

MARKET SEGMENTATION

Market segmentation is one of the most important concepts in the consumer behaviour and marketing literature. A primary reason for studying consumer behaviour is to identify bases for effective segmentation, and a large portion of consumer research is concerned with segmentation. Selecting the appropriate target market is paramount in developing successful marketing strategy.

The logic of market segmentation has a simple basis: a single product usually will not appeal to *all* consumers. People's purchase goals, product knowledge, and purchase behavior vary, and successful marketers often adapt their marketing strategies to appeal to specific consumer groups. Even a simple product such as chewing gum comes in multiple flavours and package sizes and varies in sugar content, calories, consistency, and colours to appeal to different consumers. While a single product seldom appeals to all consumers, it can almost always be attractive to more than one consumer. Thus, there are usually *groups of consumers* to whom a single item will appeal. If a particular group can be reached profitably by a firm, it constitutes a viable market segment or target market. A marketer should then develop a marketing mix to serve that group.

In the past, many marketers focused on target markets in a general, nonpersonal way. As we note in Chapter 1, marketers may have operated with some notion of the general characteristics of their target market, but they could not identify particular consumers who actually purchase and use their products. Today's technology, including scanner and other personal data sources, improved methods of marketing research, and efficient computers to handle large databases, now gives marketers detailed personal information on many members of its target market.

For example, one tobacco company is reported to know the names, addresses, and purchasing patterns of over 30 million smokers. Holt Renfrew + Co. Ltd spent $250,000 to implement a new point-of-sale technology to improve customer profiles and its frequent-flyer club. HR has a database where its credit-card holders earn points and receive gifts when they accumulate enough points. As Consumer Perspective 3.1 shows, one insurance company can now target niche customer groups as well as promotional material they are most likely to respond to.

We define *market segmentation* as the process of dividing a market into groups and individuals for the firm to target. We can break the process of market segmentation into three tasks, as shown in Exhibit 3.1. We discuss each of the market segmentation tasks shown. While these tasks are related, and firms may approach them in a different order (depending on the firm and the situation), market segmentation analysis can seldom (if ever) be ignored. Even if the final decision is to mass market and not to segment, this

The starting point for building database marketing programs is usually the information in existing files, but North America Life Insurance Co. of Toronto took a different tack. It set up a wholly owned subsidiary to develop niche markets.

The first target groups were women professionals, business owners, executives, and managers, all in Toronto. The results were so impressive that the company decided to take this approach across Canada.

The company began by using dozens of outside sources such as census information from Statistics Canada, tax filer data from Revenue Canada, lists of medical professionals, and people making large donations to charities and city directories. This was supplemented by an extensive telemarketing program.

In the case of professional women, the company developed a profile of their best prospects: aged 30 to 44, established career, financially secure, living in a two-income family, beginning to think about long-term investments, and interested in education funds and other investments for their children. Focus groups determined the most effective sales and marketing approaches for this group. Armed with this profile and the knowledge from tax filer information which neighbourhoods were likely to have a high ratio of prospects, the company began distributing promotional material by Canada Post. After the targeted direct-mail campaign, a telemarketing department followed up with evening calls.

Response was good. More than 12 percent agreed to see a company representative. The industry norm is 8 percent and drops to 4 percent in oversolicited neighbourhoods. "What's also impressive is the cost of getting these appointments," said company director Mclean. "We conducted tests with a telemarketing company and came up with a cost of $104 for every appointment. Our costs worked out at $86 for every appointment, and leads were better, resulting in better sales. We proved the value of database marketing and the benefits of understanding your customer. And we also proved that you can take each niche market in turn, as long as you listen, understand, and deliver exactly what they want."

Source: Adapted from "How One Insurance Firm Found a Niche," *Globe and Mail*, Feb. 15, 1994, p. B27.

CONSUMER PERSPECTIVE

3.1 ◀

"How One Insurance Company Found a Niche"

---

decision should be reached only *after* market segmentation analysis has been conducted. Thus, market segmentation analysis is critical for sound marketing strategy development.

The first task involved in segmenting markets is analysing consumer/product relationships. This entails analysis of the affect and cognitions, behaviours, and environments involved in the purchase/consumption process for a particular product. Managers take

Analyse consumer/product relationships

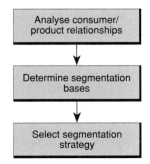

EXHIBIT 3.1

Tasks involved in market segmentation

Marketing attempts to
communicate the consumer/
product relationship for a
target segment of
consumers.

three general approaches to this task. First, marketing managers may brainstorm a product concept and consider what types of consumers are likely to purchase and use the product and how they might differ from those less likely to buy. Second, focus groups and other types of primary research can be useful for identifying differences in attributes, benefits, and values of various potential markets. Third, secondary research may be used to investigate specific differences in potential target markets, determine the relative sizes of these markets, and develop a better understanding of consumers of this or similar products.

For many established product categories, considerable information is available for analysing various markets. For product categories such as automobiles, toothpaste, and many food products, various target markets are well established. For example, the car buyer category includes luxury, sports, midsize, compact, and subcompact markets. Within each of these markets, further analysis may offer insights into market opportunities. One market of great concern to General Motors, for example, is the group that purchases foreign autos. Only one in five of these buyers even considers a General Motors car. GM executives believe that if they produce a car comparable to cars that Honda and Toyota make, they can recapture up to 80 percent of this market. In fact, GM has spent $3.5 billion to produce the Saturn to appeal to this market. Given the fact that many owners of Japanese vehicles are reported to be highly satisfied with their cars, GM's decision would be a risky strategy unless GM has thoroughly analysed the affect and cognitions, behaviours, and environments of foreign car buyers and can build a car these consumers will purchase instead of foreign brands.

For many products, the initial breakdown in markets is between the prestige and mass market. The prestige market seeks the highest-quality (and often the highest-priced) product available. Often, particular products in this market have very important meanings for their purchasers, such as expressions of good taste, expertise, and status. Rolex watches, Mercedes-Benz automobiles, Hartmann luggage, and Gucci handbags are targeted to these consumers. The marketing strategies for these products generally involve selling them in exclusive stores at high prices and promoting them in prestige media. For consumers in this market, affect and cognitions (feelings about and meaning of the product), behaviours (shopping activities), and environments (information and store contact) differ from those of consumers in the mass market. Thus, the initial analysis of consumer/ product relationship has important implications for all the subsequent tasks involved in market segmentation and strategy development.

Analysis focusing on specific differences in consumers is also important when companies seek new target markets. In the 1980s, when recessionary pressures caused many Canadian companies to tighten their travel expenditures, hotel developers capitalised by constructing economy hotels. Holiday Inn responded by opening Hampton Inns. Other chains that specialised in limited-service economy accommodations in Canada included Journey's End, Relax Hotels, Choice Hotels, and Embassy Suites.

Here, a difference in consumers' cognitions about lodging prices led to a change in marketing strategy (resegmenting the midpriced market) and the lodging environment (creation of limited-service hotels), which led to a change in consumer behaviour (staying at limited-service hotels). This example demonstrates how analysis of consumer/product relationships led to a successful marketing strategy for Canadian hotel developers. A number of other tasks occur after an initial analysis of consumer/product relationships and before marketing strategies are finalised. A logical next step is to investigate various bases on which markets could be segmented. Consumer Perspective 3.2 explores a marketing strategy to reach the college market.

There is no simple way to determine the relevant bases for segmenting markets. In most cases, however, at least some initial dimensions will be obvious from previous research, purchase trends, managerial judgment, and analysis of consumer/product relationships. For example, suppose we wish to segment the market for all-terrain vehicles. Several dimensions come to mind for initial consideration: gender (male); age (18 to 35); lifestyle (outdoors); and income level (perhaps $25,000 to $40,000). At a minimum, these variables should be included in subsequent segmentation research.

Determine segmentation bases

Exhibit 3.2 presents five ways a consumer market could be segmented, with a number of segmentation categories for each. The five types are geographic, demographic, sociocultural, affective/cognitive, and behavioural segmentation. While there are other bases for segmenting markets, they usually represent combinations of the types and bases discussed here.

Geographic segmentation

Geographic segmentation calls for dividing markets on the basis of location. Common bases for segmenting a market geographically include region, size of cities, population density, and climate. City (and trading area) size is a popular segmentation basis for retailers. For example, Canadian Tire has intentionally located many of its stores in smaller towns capable of supporting few stores, thereby hoping to corner markets. This way it did not have to compete directly with larger chains and could monopolise the trading area. Success with this strategy led the retailer eventually to larger trading areas, and, as a result, Canadian Tire became one of the largest chain stores in Canada.

Like small towns across Canada, the university and college market, once attractive only to beer marketers, continues to mature. This group represents "an incredible market segmentation opportunity of relatively homogeneous demographics at a particularly attractive stage of life," says Cameron Killoran, president of The Campus Network, the advertising sales arm of 50 college and university publications.

The importance of the campus market potential continues to be recognised by a growing number of marketers who want to build brand loyalty at this formative stage. Computer, music, car, banking, telecommunications, and personal care companies are marketing their products to this group. They believe that graduates ultimately turn into higher-earning, higher-spending, more acquisitive consumers. According to Statistics Canada, Canada's 69 universities and 203 community colleges were populated by more than 921,000 students in 1993, with women outnumbering men by more than 100,000. The majority fall into the 18–24 age group, with 12.5 percent in the 25–29 age group and a further 11 percent over 30.

The beer-guzzling, sex-crazed, party-hungry students characterized by movies like *Animal House* and *Porky's* are a rare sight on Canadian campuses in the 1990s. They have been replaced by more responsible young adults who are serious about their education. Students respond to on-campus marketers that offer them real value for their money. Ford Motor Co. claims that its $750 cash-back rebate offered to college graduates has been a huge success in part because Ford recognizes the needs of students. Rick Wilson, direct marketing manager, says, "I don't think they're horribly different from the public at large in their demand for new products and value. They're obviously at the beginning stage of their career development, and, hence, the program was created to give them some added benefit. We have consistently grown in the number of vehicles sold [since 1985]".

A 1993 Campus Plus "Canadian Campus Survey" found that students are not merely subsisting. This group's income is far greater than perceived. In 1989, 26 percent owned Visa cards and 13 percent held MasterCards. In 1993, those numbers rose to 40 percent and 20 percent respectively, with 66 percent owning a credit card of some type. Their incomes ranged from $3,000 to $15,000. Since 43 percent still live at home, this significantly increases their potential disposable income. Nearly half (44 percent) owned a computer, 20 percent took at least one round trip in Canada, 37 percent owned a car, and 14 percent planned to buy one in the next year. Other major purchases include clothing and CDs and tapes.

Zeroing in on the campus newspaper is one of the most effective ways to reach students. "Many advertisers feel like they have to be earth-shattering, but bells and whistles won't get these people," says Bill Cotric from Campus Plus. "It's a matter of approaching them in a direct way, and you can impress them with a simple, honest ad in the campus newspaper."

Source: Adapted from "Special Report: Campus Marketing," *Strategy*, May 16, 1994, p. 29.

Demographic segmentation

Demographic segmentation divides the market on the basis of a population's characteristics. The most common ones are age, gender, household size, income, occupation, and education. Even if a market is segmented on other bases, it is common for companies also to obtain a demographic profile of customers to know their market better.

A good example of demographic segmentation can be found in the increased attention many companies are giving to marketing products to women. Labatt, for example, traditionally marketed beer exclusively to men. However, recognising the need to expand its market, the company now promotes its new beers equally to men and women. Jockey International bucked the prevailing silk-and-lace mindset of the competition and devel-

EXHIBIT 3.2

Examples of segmentation bases for consumer markets

Segmentation Types/Bases	Illustrative Categories
Geographic Segmentation	
Region	West, Prairies, Ontario, Quebec, Atlantic Canada
City size	Up to 100,000; 100,001+
Population density	Urban, suburban, rural
Climate	Temperate, cold
Demographic Segmentation	
Age	Up to 12; 13–19; 20–39; 40–59; 60+
Gender	Female, male
Household size	1, 2, 3, 4 or more persons
Income	Up to $25,000; $25,000–$50,000; over $50,000
Occupation	Professional, blue-collar, retired, unemployed
Education	High school or less, some college or university, college/university graduate
Sociocultural Segmentation	
Culture	French–Canadian, American, European
Subculture	
Religion	Protestant, Catholic, Jewish, Muslim
National origin	British, Italian, French, Greek, German
Race	East Indian, Asian, African-American
Social class	Upper, middle, working, lower class
Marital status	Single, married, divorced, widowed
Psychographics	Aggressive achievers, joiner activists, day-to-day watchers, old-fashioned puritans
Affective and Cognitive Segmentation	
Degree of knowledge	Expert, novice
Benefits sought	Convenience, economy, prestige
Attitude	Positive, neutral, negative
Behavioural Segmentation	
Brand loyalty	None, divided, undivided loyalty
Store loyalty	None, divided, undivided loyalty
Usage rate	Light, medium, heavy
User status	Nonuser, ex-user, current user, potential user
Payment method	Cash, credit card, time payments
Media usage	Newspapers, magazines, TV, radio
Usage situation	Work, home, vacation

oped Jockey for Her. In five years it captured 40 percent of the women's underwear market. The Gap clothing store offers four different cuts of jeans for women and three for men, recognising differences in body shapes both between and within the sexes.

Sociocultural segmentation

Sociocultural segmentation divides markets on the basis of similarities and differences in social and cultural factors, such as religion or marital status. One of the most popular of these is **psychographic segmentation,** which groups consumers on the basis of similarities and differences in their lifestyles.

Marketers usually measure lifestyles by asking consumers about their *activities* (work, hobbies, vacations), *interests* (family, job, community) and *opinions* (about social issues, politics, business). The activity, interest, and opinion **(AIO)** questions in some studies are of a very general nature. In others, at least some of the questions are related to specific products. Psychographic information can be obtained from sources other than company-sponsored research projects, as illustrated in Consumer Perspective 3.3.

Psychographic segmentation studies often include hundreds of questions and provide a tremendous amount of information about consumers. Such segmentation is based on the idea that the more you know and understand about consumers, the more effectively you can communicate and market to them.

However, different psychographic studies reach different conclusions about the number and nature of lifestyle categories, and the validity of psychographic segmentation is sometimes questioned.

One well-known psychographic segmentation applicable to the populations of Canada and the United States was developed at SRI International in California. The original segmentation divided consumers into nine groups and was called **VALS**™, which stands for "values and lifestyles." Although commercially successful, this segmentation tended to place the majority of consumers into only one or two groups, and SRI updated VALS to reflect changes in society. The new typology is called VALS 2™.[2]

CONSUMER PERSPECTIVE

▶ **3.3**

An interesting source of lifestyle information

Here's how marketers get lifestyle information about consumers who use 800 and 900 telephone numbers. Do you have an opinion about their access to this information?

1. **Make a phone call:** You call an 800 or 900 number to buy a product, get information, or express an opinion.

2. **Connect to computer:** Calls are treated by one of two service control points (SCPs) in Toronto or Calgary. The technology is produced by Northern Telecom and is the property of Stentor, an alliance of Canada's full-service telecommunications companies (nine in total across Canada). The SCPs treat roughly 700 calls per second.

3. **Computer identifies you:** Using your phone number, the computer connects with a marketing service to get your name and address and display it on a salesperson's computer screen. Millions of names can be searched in a second or two.

4. **Do your business:** The salesperson greets you by name and then takes your order, answers questions, or asks for more information.

5. **Instant check on your credit:** If you order something by credit card, the computer checks an electronic credit authorization bureau to make sure your credit is good.

6. **Your call is recorded:** Your name, address, phone number, and the subject of your call are provided electronically to the sponsoring company or organisation, which then can use it for targeted mailing lists or marketing campaigns.

7. **Marketers analyse your lifestyle:** The sponsoring company can match this data with information in other databases (voter lists, magazine subscriptions) to find out even more about your lifestyle.

Source: Adapted from Robert S. Boyd, "How Big Brother Sees Consumers," © 1990 by Knight-Ridder Newspapers, by permission of Knight-Ridder/Tribune News Service.

VALS 2 is based on two surveys of 2,500 consumers who responded to 43 lifestyle questions. The first survey developed the segmentation, and the second validated it and linked it to buying and media behaviour. The questionnaire asked consumers to agree or disagree with statements such as "My idea of fun at a national park would be to stay at an expensive lodge and dress up for dinner" and "I could stand to skin a dead animal." Consumers were then clustered into the eight groups described in Exhibit 3.3.

The VALS 2 groups are arranged in a rectangle according to vertical and horizontal dimensions. The vertical dimension represents resources, which include income, education, self-confidence, health, eagerness to buy, intelligence, and energy level. The horizontal dimension represents self-orientation and includes three different types. *Principle-oriented consumers* are guided by their views of how the world is or should be; *status-oriented consumers* by the actions and opinions of others; and *action-oriented consumers* by a desire for social or physical activity, variety, and risk taking.

Each of the VALS 2 groups represents from 9 to 17 percent of the adult population. Marketers can buy VALS 2 information for a variety of products and can have it tied to a number of other consumer databases. Depending on the validity of the psychographic approach, VALS 2 could provide a useful basis for segmenting markets.

Toronto-based Goldfarb Consultants developed the Goldfarb Psychographic Profiles to describe the lifestyles of Canadians. Marketers may access the database, which describes six segments.

The more traditional segments

▷ *Day-to-day watchers* are a realistic group, satisfied with what life has to offer. They keep a close watch on the world around them and probably are early followers, not leaders. This group stands for some of the more traditional, upstanding attitudes and values in Canada. They have strong moral convictions, although they also demonstrate a certain tolerance for opposing viewpoints.

▷ *Old-fashioned puritans* are conservative to the point of being defensive, traditional to the point of inflexibility, and indifferent to the world to the point of apathy. They try to avoid issues that might require a commitment, and they tend to resist change. They are terrified of technology. These people rely heavily on others for guidance; in a sense, they live vicariously through others, particularly their families. They are least likely to use credit cards or cable TV or to try new brands.

▷ *Responsible survivors* are people who are not particularly confident about themselves or their own abilities. They are cautious and tend to respect the status quo. They accept direction well and do a set task efficiently but are not particularly ambitious. These people are likable, very ethical, good neighbours.

The less traditional segments

▷ *Disinterested self-indulgents* are an insular, self-centred group. They are not interested in the world's problems. These people tend to refuse to accept solutions to social problems or issues, because they do not admit the problem exists. They put themselves and their own wants and desires first. Moreover, they tend to indulge their desires, although not necessarily because they want to make a statement about themselves. They are simply interested in making their own lives easy and convenient.

▷ *Joiner-activists* are leading-edge thinkers, nonconformists who help to shape current opinion. Their thinking tends to be global rather than short term or personal, so they are involved in issues with broad social or political impact. They tend to be strong-willed, liberal in their attitudes, and big spenders. They are

EXHIBIT 3.3   VALS 2™ eight lifestyle segments

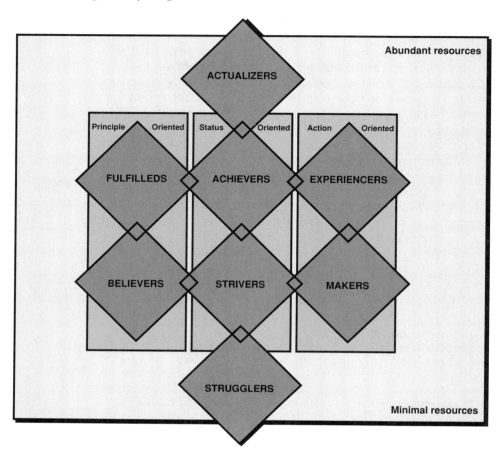

Actualizers. These consumers have the highest incomes and such high self-esteem and abundant resources that they can indulge in any or all self-orientations. They are located above the rectangle. Image is important to them as an expression of their taste, independence, and character. Their consumer choices are directed toward the finer things in life.

Fulfilleds. These consumers are the high resource group of those who are principle-oriented. They are mature, responsible, well-educated professionals. Their leisure activities centre on their homes, but they are well-informed about what goes on in the world and they are open to new ideas and social change. They have high incomes but are practical consumers.

Believers. These consumers are the low resource group of those who are principle-oriented. They are conservative and predictable consumers who favor domestic products and established brands. Their lives centre on family, church, community, and the nation. They have modest incomes.

Achievers. These consumers are the high-resource group of those who are status-oriented. They are successful, work-oriented people who get their satisfaction from their jobs and families. They are politically conservative and respect authority and the status quo. They favor established products and services that show off their success to their peers.

Strivers. These consumers are the low-resource group of those who are status-oriented. They have values very similar to achievers but have fewer economic, social, and psychological resources. Style is extremely important to them as they strive to emulate people they admire and wish to be like.

Experiencers. These consumers are the high-resource group of those who are action-oriented. They are the youngest of all the segments with a median age of 25. They have a lot of energy, which they pour into physical exercise and social activities. They are avid consumers, spending heavily on clothing, fast foods, music, and other youthful favourites—with particular emphasis on new products and services.

Makers. These consumers are the low-resource group of those who are action-oriented. They are practical people who value self-sufficiency. They are focused on the familiar—family, work, and physical recreation—and have little interest in the broader world. As consumers, they appreciate practical and functional products.

Strugglers. These consumers have the lowest incomes. They have too few resources to be included in any consumer self-orientation and are thus located below the rectangle. They are the oldest of all the segments with a median age of 61. Within their limited means, they tend to be brand-loyal consumers.

Source: Martha Farnsworth Riche, ''Psychographics for the 1990s,'' *American Demographics,* July 1989, pp. 24–25ff. Reprinted with permission © *American Demographics,* July 1988. For subscription information, please call (800) 828-1133.

interested in quality and intrigued by technology. This is probably the most dynamic segment.

▷ *Aggressive achievers* as a group are confident, success-oriented people who hunger for power and position. They need to demonstrate to others that they are successful and they do this by both their consumer behaviour and the way they deal with other people. In reality, they are continually looking over their shoulder to see who is coming up behind. They can lose sight of their ethical standards if they feel their own position is being threatened.

Exhibit 3.4 shows the size of each Goldfarb segment, as well as the regional distribution. Marketers will find it useful to know that Atlantic Canada has the highest proportion of day-to-day watchers, British Columbia has the highest percentage of old-fashioned Puritans, Quebec has the lowest percentage of disinterested self-indulgents, and Ontario and the Prairies have the highest percentage of responsible survivors.

Affective and cognitive segmentation

Dividing markets on the basis of similarities and differences in consumers' knowledge, beliefs, or other internal psychological states is called **affective and cognitive segmentation.** For example, different hardware and software can be marketed to consumers who have a lot of knowledge about computers as opposed to those who are just beginning to learn what a keyboard is.

A traditional type of such segmentation is **benefit segmentation.** The assumption underlying this approach is that the *benefits* consumers seek in using a particular product are the basic reasons for differences in true market segments. This approach measures consumer perceptions of various brands in order to understand the benefits they look for in a product class.

Exhibit 3.5 shows three possible benefit segments for blue jeans. Hardy workers want durable jeans that can be purchased at a price that gives them good value for their money. Casual wearers want jeans that are comfortable and fit well for shopping and weekend activities. This segment is less price conscious than the hardy workers. The third segment is the trendies, who want expensive brands of jeans that make a statement about them. This segment is the least price conscious and prefers expensive jeans with brand marks identifying them as costly.

These segments differ on a number of criteria, so different marketing approaches are likely to be successful for each. For example, because hardy workers shop in stores such as Mark's Work Warehouse, Levi's made a good move in selling its jeans in these outlets several years ago. Different types and sizing of jeans, different packaging and labelling, different advertising appeals and media, and different retail outlets are generally needed to appeal to different benefit segments.

Segment	Total	BC	Prairies	Ontario	Quebec	Atlantic
Day-to-day watchers	23%	19%	21%	23%	23%	32%
Old-fashioned puritans	15	19	15	14	15	16
Responsible survivors	12	7	14	14	10	11
Joiner activists	23	25	25	22	26	15
Disinterested self-indulgents	15	19	15	16	12	14
Aggressive achievers	12	11	10	11	14	12

Source: Goldfarb Consultants

EXHIBIT 3.4

Goldfarb psychographic segments by region, 1995

EXHIBIT 3.5

Three benefit segments for blue jeans

	Hardy Workers	Casual Wearers	Trendies
Principal benefits sought	Durability, value	Comfort, fit	Social identity
Common demographics	Blue-collar males	Young professionals over 30 years of age	Middle- and upper-income teenagers, young adults
Brands favoured	Levi's, Wranglers, Plain Pockets	Lees, Gap, Zena	Guess?, Polo, President Stone, Jeans Gasoline
Usage situations	Daily work and home wear	Shopping, weekend activities	Social events, including school
Lifestyle characteristics	Conservative	Active	Pleasure seeking

Behavioural segmentation

Dividing markets on the basis of similarities and differences in the overt actions of consumers is called **behavioural segmentation.** An example is a credit-card promotion. Toronto-Dominion Bank (TD) and General Motors of Canada Ltd. (GM) launched the TD–GM Visa card in June 1993. Cardholders build credits toward buying or leasing a GM vehicle with each TD–GM Visa purchase. By early 1994, about 510,000 had registered, most of whom were not former TD–Visa cardholders. Over 3.5 million TD–GM transactions worth about $250 million have been made since the program started, and 65 GM vehicles have been bought or leased using TD–GM Visa credits. In the saturated credit-card market, focusing on a particular behaviour turned out to be a successful strategy.[3]

An extension of behavioural segmentation involves segmenting on situations in which the behaviours occur. This is called **usage situation segmentation.** For example, clothing and footwear markets are divided not only on the basis of gender and size, but also on the usage situation—weather conditions (boots), physical activities (basketball shoes), and social events (pumps). As another example, Doulton china is designed for special occasions; Corelle dinnerware is designed for everyday family use. One advocate for this type of segmentation claims, "In practice, the product whose unique selling proposition (quality, features, image, packaging, or merchandising) is not targeted for particular people in particular usage situations is probably the exception rather than the rule."[4]

Usage situation is a more complete approach to segmentation than some others. To use this segmentation technique successfully, marketers have to understand what consumers think and feel about using a product, what actions they take, and what environmental events occur in the condition of use. In other words, marketers must understand differences in consumer affect and cognitions, behaviours, and environments to target the best markets for their products.

Select segmentation strategy

Once the analysis of consumer/product relationships and the bases for segmentation is completed, the appropriate segmentation strategy can be considered. There are four basic alternatives. First, the firm may decide not to enter the market. Analysis so far may reveal there is no viable market niche for the product, brand, or model. Second, the firm may decide not to segment but to be a mass marketer. This may be the appropriate strategy in at least three situations:

1. When the market is so small that marketing to a portion of it is not profitable.
2. When heavy users make up such a large proportion of the sales volume that they are the only relevant target.

Usage situations can be effective means for segmenting markets.

3. When the brand is dominant in the market, and targeting to a few segments would not benefit sales and profits.[5]

Third, the firm may decide to market to only one segment. Fourth, the firm may decide to market to more than one segment and design a separate marketing mix for each.

In any case, marketers must have some criteria on which to base segmentation strategy decisions. Three important criteria are that a viable segment must be measurable, meaningful, and marketable:

1. **Measurable.** For a segment to be selected, marketers must be able to measure its size and characteristics. One of the difficulties with segmenting on the basis of social class is that the concept and its divisions are not clearly measurable. Alternatively, income is much easier to measure.

2. **Meaningful.** A meaningful segment is one that is large enough to have sufficient sales and growth potential to offer long-run profits.

3. **Marketable.** A marketable segment is one that can be reached and served profitably.

Segments that meet these criteria are viable markets for the product. The marketer must now give further attention to the marketing mix.

MARKETING MIX DECISIONS

The **marketing mix** consists of product, price, promotion, and channels of distribution. These are the primary elements marketing managers can control to serve consumers. The aim is to develop a consistent mix where all elements work together to serve the target market or markets the company has selected. Selecting target markets and developing marketing mixes are related tasks.

Companies increasingly recognise that the starting point for making marketing mix decisions is a thorough understanding of consumers in their target markets. Each of the marketing mix elements involves many decisions, and analysis of consumers can make the decisions more effective for achieving company goals.

Product decisions

A product is any offering made for the purpose of exchange. Marketing questions in this area include such issues as:

▷ What function does this product or service serve for consumers in a target market, and what does it mean to them?

▷ What attributes or features of the product are most important to the target market?

▷ What types of packaging and labelling information would best serve consumers and attract them to purchase the product?

▷ What brand name and trademark for the product would create the appropriate image in the target market?

▷ What kinds of pre- or post-sale service would satisfy consumers in the target market?

▷ How many models, variations, or sizes of the product are needed to satisfy various target markets?

While this list is not exhaustive, it demonstrates that many product decisions depend on understanding consumers in various target markets. Think about tennis racquets, for example. Analysis of this market reveals that most tennis players do not spend the time to practice often and to get into good playing condition. Standard racquets let them enjoy the game but do not give them the power good players have. For many of these players, however, tennis performance is important, and they are willing to pay more for a racquet that can improve their game. Weekend players can purchase high-tech, wide-body design graphite racquets that offer exceptional power, yet are lighter, so players can swing them harder than conventional racquets. The names of these expensive racquets—Wilson's Hammer, Prince's Vortex, and Head's Discovery—communicate the idea of superior performance.

In the case of tennis racquets, redesign of a conventional product to serve a particular target market using new technology resulted in a dramatic change in demand. In fact, the 10 top-selling rackets today are all wide-body models. Wide-bodies account for about 90 percent of tennis racquet sales. Understanding what the target market wanted and how they play the game allowed racquet manufacturers to score a huge marketing success.[6]

Price decisions

Price is what consumers must give up to purchase a product. Marketing questions in this area include such issues as:

▷ How much are consumers in a target market willing to pay for a particular product?

▷ At what price would consumers in this market consider this product a good value?

▷ What do specific prices communicate to consumers about the quality of a particular product?

▷ If the price of a product were lowered in the short run, would consumers continue to buy the product when it goes back to full price?

▷ Would consumers stop purchasing the product if the price were increased permanently?

▷ How important is price to consumers in a particular target market?

Whether a company is introducing a new product or planning a short-term or long-term price change, it needs to analyse how consumers will respond to the price variable. For example, consumers view nationally branded motor oil as essentially a commodity, where price is the most important determinant of purchase. In this market, price wars are common among brands such as Pennzoil, Quaker State, and Motomaster.

Quaker State motor oil, at one time the market leader, tried to avoid competing on the basis of price. The company promoted its long warranty and its new synthetic oil line in an attempt to convince consumers that its products were of superior quality and should command a higher price than other brands. Consumers cannot detect differences in major brands of motor oil, though, and were not willing to pay a higher price for Quaker State. The company's market share dropped from 22 percent to 14 percent, and Pennzoil gained the market lead. Overall, Quaker State's volume dropped from almost 125 million gallons in the mid-1980s to about 85 million in the early 1990s. Analysis of consumers' beliefs and the way they buy and use motor oil could have saved Quaker State from making this mistake in its pricing strategy. Even so, some companies do find ways of charging higher prices that do not decrease consumer demand, as Consumer Perspective 3.4 shows.

Manufacturers can raise the price consumers pay for products in a number of ways. Prices can be increased outright for the same quantity and quality, or maintained for less quantity, less quality, or fewer auxiliary services. Price deals could be reduced or eliminated, or interest rates and charges could be increased. Examples of maintaining the same price but offering less quantity include:

CONSUMER PERSPECTIVE

3.4 ◀

Increasing consumer prices

Brand	Product	It Looks Like . . .	You Pay . . .	But You Get . . .
Knorr	Leek soup and recipe mix	**More:** Box is ½" deeper	**The same**	**Less:** Makes three 8-oz. servings, reduced from four
StarKist	Canned tuna	**A bit less:** Can is ¹⁄₁₆" less tall	**The same**	**Less:** Weight of tuna reduced by ⅜ oz., or 5.8%
Lipton	Instant lemon-flavoured tea	**The same**	**The same**	**Less:** Weight reduced by 7.5%; company claims it contains same number of servings as before
Brim	Decaffeinated coffee	**The same**	**The same**	**Less:** Weight reduced by 4.2%; company claims it contains same number of servings as before

Source: David E. Kalish, "Prices Stable, but Products Are Less Filling," *Wisconsin State Journal,* Jan. 6, 1991, p. 1D. Reprinted by permission of the Associated Press.

Promotion decisions

Promotion refers to the variety of ways marketers communicate with consumers about products to influence their affect, cognitions, and behaviours. Marketing questions in this area include such issues as:

▷ What are the best media for reaching a target market for a particular product?

▷ What message should be communicated to consumers about a product?

▷ What image should advertising try to create about a product?

▷ What types of sales promotions would be most effective for getting consumers to buy a product?

▷ What approach should salespeople use to match consumers' needs and wants with particular products?

▷ What role should publicity play in communicating with consumers about a product?

Decisions about these questions clearly depend on knowing a lot about consumers. For example, Buick, like many North American car brands, suffered losses in sales and market share through much of the 1980s. Part of the problem was that it came to ignore its traditional target market in favour of a younger market. The "traditional" Buick buyer has a median income of $42,700, a median age of 61 years, and a high-school education.

To re-establish Buick in its traditional market, GM promoted it as a premium motorcar— a substantial, distinctive, powerful, and mature automobile. Buick ads changed to feature more mature people and emphasised automotive features that consumer analysis indicates this market prefers, such as powerful engines, comfortable ride, and easy control.

While sales of other General Motors brands continued to decline in the early 1990s, Buick division sales increased sharply. In fact, Buick moved ahead of Pontiac and Oldsmobile to rank second only to Chevrolet in General Motors sales. One of the reasons for Buick's success was that it learned to promote the appropriate image and features for its target market.[7]

Channels of distribution decisions

Channels of distribution are the system by which products are directed from producers to consumers. Channels for consumer goods often include wholesalers and retailers. Consumers typically purchase from retail stores but may also buy from mail-order houses, TV home shopping networks, and other sources. Marketing questions in this area include such issues as:

▷ Would consumers prefer to purchase a product in stores or from different channels, such as mail-order catalogues or in-home salespeople?

▷ What image do various stores and chains have that might influence consumer preference and purchase behaviour for various products?

▷ Do various stores have particular atmospheres that might influence consumer purchase of a product?

▷ How do such things as in-store layout, signs, and displays influence consumer affect, cognition, and behaviour toward various products?

▷ Where should service facilities be located to make them readily available for consumers?

▷ What role do in-store salespeople play in educating consumers about various products?

Decisions like these influence not only the specific retail channels that a manufacturer selects, but also what other intermediaries are involved. For example, a major trend for many manufacturers in recent years is to sell directly to major discount chains and bypass wholesalers.

CONSUMER
PERSPECTIVE

3.5

**Coffee shops
keep perking**

Samuel Pepys would have been shocked. Painted in vivid colours and populated by people rushing in and out clutching foam cups, modern specialty coffee shops bear no resemblance to the famous diarist's 17th-century haunts.

They also seem to be remarkably healthy in an economy that has devastated retailing like a plague. In 1983 gourmet coffee accounted for 10 percent of the coffee market. By 1989 it had reached 19 percent. It's now growing 13 percent per year. This in the face of an overall drop in coffee consumption of almost 50 percent since the 1960s.

The main reasons are the store environment and the twin mantra of quality and service. The big players in Canada are The Second Cup (224 stores), A. L. Van Houte (95 stores), Timothy's (50 stores), Gourmet Cup (50 stores), and Starbucks (25 stores). These outlets all provide similar advantages for consumers. They can walk into one of these specialty shops and within one or two minutes be on their way with a fresh cup of mocha, java, or Colombian coffee. If they wish to sit, they can, for much less than the cost of sitting in a bar having an alcoholic beverage, sip on a cappuccino or linger over an espresso—in a store environment that is not smoke-filled.

One owner of a small shop in east-end Toronto says that she "wants people to feel better when they leave the store." She has developed a rather unusual in-store environment for her clientele, made up of mostly mothers with young children. She purchased high chairs and unbreakable cups and saucers.

What seems to be most important in this business is having the right mix of store environment and product. What sells depends on the location. Stores in office buildings do a better trade in coffee by the cup, while shopping centre stores may sell more coffee beans, teas, and gift items.

Source: Adapted from "Gourmet Coffee Sales Defy Trends for Luxury Goods," *Globe and Mail*, March 6, 1993, p. B1-4: "Coffee College Is a Tough Grind," *Globe and Mail*, March 6, 1993, p. B1-4; "Coffee Shops Perk Despite Economy," *Globe and Mail*, Aug. 20, 1992.

Distribution decisions can also play an important role in determining what consumers think about various products. For example, OshKosh B'Gosh has had an image as a manufacturer of high-quality, trendy clothes for kids under seven, earned in part by selling only in exclusive department and specialty stores. In the early 1990s, however, the company decided to sell its products in chains like Sears. Such a move might damage its image, but if the quality of the product remains high, the company could increase sales dramatically by reaching a larger target market of parents and grandparents. The important point is that the specific stores that sell a product can influence what consumers think about the product.

As another example, consider the coffee market. For the last 30 years, demand for this product has decreased. Coffee consumption dropped from 3.1 cups per day in the early 1960s to 1.75 cups in the early 1990s. In spite of this drop, sellers of gourmet coffee have managed to thrive in this declining market. Specialty retail chains sell gourmet coffee beans, brewed gourmet coffee, and related products. The Second Cup, A. L. Van Houte, and Timothy's have taken advantage of social trends away from alcoholic beverages to offer an affordable luxury for many consumers. Offering a specialty product through a unique channel formed the basis for a successful marketing strategy. Consumer Perspective 3.5 describes several coffee stores that use a unique in-store environment to develop a successful marketing strategy and attract a specific target market.

Shimano positioned its
Calcutta reel as a prestige
product with ads like
this one.

**Marketing
implications**

Marketing mix decisions clearly depend heavily on understanding consumers and selecting appropriate target markets. One way to summarise this process is to consider product
positioning. **Product positioning** involves conveying an image in order to influence consumer behaviour. To position a product effectively, all four of the marketing mix elements
should be designed to work toward creating a consistent image. For example, consider
the situation facing Shimano, a fishing-tackle company with a reputation for producing
quality rods and reels. In the early 1990s, other companies such as Daiwa introduced
several more expensive reel models and threatened to take over the market for high-
priced, high-quality reels.

Shimano developed an excellent positioning strategy to combat this threat. First, it developed the Calcutta 200, a distinctive bait-casting reel machined very precisely from a
single piece of aluminium, with a brushed aluminium finish that makes it stand out from
its competition. And the reel sold for $139.95, a good deal more than most other reels.

In this case, each marketing mix element fits with and reinforces the other elements to encourage purchase. The Calcutta 200 reel is clearly positioned as a top-quality product for serious purchasers, promoted only in selected media, and sold primarily by independent retailers. The fact that the product is unlikely to be discounted reinforces the image of quality. The high price implies quality. In essence, this company developed a successful positioning strategy that involved all four elements of the marketing mix and was appropriately targeted at a group of consumers. Consumers' affect, cognition, and behaviours changed as a result of this strategy.

► SUMMARY

Learning objective 1: *Define market segmentation and explain why marketers segment markets.*
Market segmentation is the process of dividing markets into groups of similar consumers and selecting the most appropriate groups and individuals for the firm to serve. Marketers segment markets because seldom does a single product appeal to all consumers. Consumers vary in terms of product knowledge, involvement, and purchasing behaviour. Thus, marketers group consumers who are similar on some dimensions so a particular product will appeal to and satisfy them better.

Learning objective 2: *List five major types of segmentation and give examples of each.*
Five major types of segmentation include geographic segmentation with bases such as city size and population density; demographic segmentation with bases such as age and income; sociocultural segmentation with bases such as race and social class; affective and cognitive segmentation with bases such as benefits sought and attitudes; and behavioural segmentation with bases such as brand loyalty and usage rate.

Learning objective 3: *Explain psychographic, benefit, and usage situation segmentation.*
Psychographic segmentation involves segmenting consumers on the basis of similarities and differences in their lifestyles. Benefit segmentation involves segmenting consumers on the basis of the benefits they are looking for in purchasing a product. Usage situation segmentation involves segmenting consumers on the basis of the circumstances surrounding their use of a product.

Learning objective 4: *List the elements of the marketing mix.*
The marketing mix includes product, price, promotion, and channels of distribution.

Learning objective 5: *Offer examples of marketing mix issues for which consumer analysis is important.*
Product decisions about product features, packaging, and branding, and the number of models and sizes to be offered can benefit from consumer analysis. Decisions on pricing a new product or making a short-term or long-term price change can benefit from an understanding of what price means to consumers of a particular product. Promotion decisions concerning appropriate images, messages, and media for advertising and appropriate types of sales promotion can benefit from analysis of consumers. Finally, consumer analysis is useful in channel of distribution decisions such as the effects of store location and in-store stimuli on consumer purchasing behaviour.

Learning objective 6: *Explain product positioning.*
Product positioning involves conveying an image of a product to influence consumer behaviour. Successful product positioning depends on combining all four of the marketing mix elements to create a consistent image in the minds of consumers.

▶ **KEY TERMS AND CONCEPTS**

market segmentation

target market

geographic segmentation

demographic segmentation

sociocultural segmentation

psychographic segmentation

AIO

VALS™

Goldfarb Psychographic Profiles

affective and cognitive segmentation

benefit segmentation

behavioural segmentation

usage situation segmentation

marketing mix

product positioning

▶ **REVIEW AND DISCUSSION QUESTIONS**

1. Define market segmentation and describe the management tasks involved in applying the concept.

2. Select a product (not blue jeans) that you know something about, and draw up possible benefit segments following the structure used in Exhibit 3.5.

3. Identify potential advantages and problems associated with marketing to benefit segments.

4. Use the VALS 2 or Goldfarb Psychographic Profiles categories to suggest marketing strategies for psychographic segments of buyers for hotel/motel services.

5. Consider usage situation segmentation as a way to view the snack-food market. State the needs and objectives of people in situations for at least three segments that you identify.

6. How does the concept of segmentation relate to positioning strategies?

7. What options might an organisation choose after identifying segments in the market? When would each of these options represent a reasonable choice?

8. Are segmentation and positioning decisions different for a small business entrepreneur compared to a large corporation? If so, in what way?

AFFECT AND COGNITION

OUTLINE

▶ 4. Introduction to Affect and Cognition
▶ 5. Product Knowledge and Involvement
▶ 6. Exposure, Attention, and Comprehension
▶ 7. Attitudes and Intentions
▶ 8. Consumer Decision Making
▶ 9. Communication and Persuasion

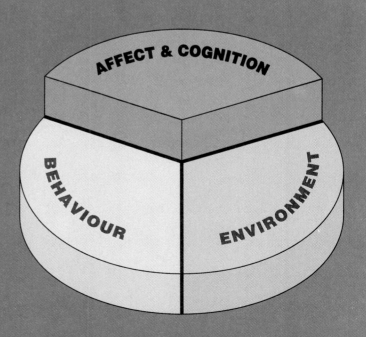

4

Introduction to Affect and Cognition

LEARNING OBJECTIVES

After completing this chapter, you should be able to:

► 1. Describe the affective system and identify the types of affective responses it produces.

► 2. Describe the cognitive system and the types of meanings it creates.

► 3. Explain how the affective and cognitive systems influence each other.

► 4. Describe the components of the model of consumer decision making.

► 5. Explain how knowledge in memory can be activated for use in cognitive processing.

► 6. Describe the differences between general and procedural knowledge.

► 7. Give examples of associative networks of knowledge in the form of schemas and scripts.

WHAT DOES "DOLE" MEAN?

Dole, the packaged-foods company, is attempting to cash in on its well-known brand name in some surprising ways. It has introduced three new juice cocktails in western Canada. Dole must be careful that its new products convey the same image as the brand name. According to focus groups, Dole conveys feelings of "warmth, sunshine, exotic places, and vacations."

In extending their valuable brand names to other products, companies must ensure that the meanings and feelings associated with the brand name are appropriate for the new product. For example, Campbell licensed its name and the familiar red-and-white packaging to a line of cooking utensils. This worked because the Campbell's name and logo conjures up emotional images of hearth and home.

There are advertising firms that specialise in finding the hidden meanings and feelings in familiar brands. Landor Associates, for example, found that Dole also suggests "sunshine foods," which led the company to introduce fruit sorbets, carrots, and nut snacks. Companies must be careful because brand names with clear and distinctive meanings cannot be applied to everything. Playboy stands for swanky self-indulgence as well as sex, and the Playboy name was used successfully for a line of men's shoes. But a Playboy line of suits didn't work—a college graduate may not want to walk into his first job interview with a new haircut and a Playboy suit.[1]

These examples show that marketers need to understand the feelings (affect) and meanings (cognition) that consumers associate with products and brands. In this chapter we begin our examination of affect and cognition. First, we define affect and cognition. Then we explain how consumers' affective and cognitive systems produce affective and cognitive responses. Next, we present a model of consumer decision making that describes the key cognitive processes involved in decision making. Finally, we discuss several types of knowledge stored in memory that consumers can use to make decisions. Our goal is to understand how consumers' affective and cognitive responses to the environment influence their decision making.

AFFECT AND COGNITION AS PSYCHOLOGICAL RESPONSES

Affect and cognition are different types of psychological responses. **Affect** refers to feeling responses; **cognition** is a mental response (thinking, evaluating, planning). Consumers can have both affective and cognitive responses to any element in the Wheel of Consumer Analysis—the environment, behaviours or other affective and cognitive responses. Affect and cognition are produced by the affective and cognitive systems, respectively. Although the two systems are distinct, they are richly interconnected, and each system can influence and be influenced by the other.[2]

In distinguishing affect from cognition, you can think of affect as something people *are* or something people *feel* (I *am* angry; Linda *is* in a good mood; Joe *feels* bored).[3] Because people experience affect in their bodies, affect seems to be a part of the person at the time he or she experiences it. In contrast, people *have* cognitions (your father *believes* Diet Pepsi is not fattening; Susan *knows* where the grocery store is; you *think* your interview suit is stylish). Cognitions are mental states; they usually are not felt in the body.

Types of affective responses

People can experience *four broad types of affective responses*: emotions, specific feelings, moods, and evaluations. Exhibit 4.1 identifies these affective responses and gives examples of each type. Each type of affect can involve positive or negative responses. Feelings, for example, can be favourable (Joan was satisfied with her T-shirt) or unfavourable (John was disgusted with the service he received). Moods can be positive (relaxed) or negative (sad).

The four types of affect differ in the level of bodily arousal or the intensity with which they are experienced.[4] The stronger affective responses, such as *emotions,* may involve physiological responses like increased heart rate or blood pressure, perspiration, dry mouth, tears, rushes of adrenaline, or butterflies in the stomach. *Specific feelings* involve somewhat less intense physiological reactions (Robert was sad when he was forced to throw out his old Edmonton Oilers sweatshirt). *Moods,* which involve lower levels of felt intensity, are rather diffuse affective states (Jennifer was bored by the long shopping

EXHIBIT 4.1

Four types of affective responses

Type of Affective Response	Level of Physical Arousal	Intensity of Feeling	Examples of Positive and Negative Affect
Emotions	Higher arousal	Stronger feelings	▷ Joy, love ▷ Fear, guilt, anger
Specific feelings			▷ Warmth, appreciation, satisfaction ▷ Disgust, sadness
Modes			▷ Alert, relaxed, calm ▷ Blue, listless, bored
Evaluations	Lower arousal	Weaker feelings	▷ Like, good, favourable ▷ Dislike, bad, unfavourable

trip).[5] Finally, *evaluations* of products or other concepts (I like Colgate toothpaste) often are rather weak affective responses accompanied by low levels of arousal (one hardly "feels" anything).

Affective responses are produced by the affective system. Although researchers are still studying how the affective system operates, they generally agree on *five basic characteristics*.[6] One important property is that the affective system is *largely reactive:* it cannot plan or purposefully direct its responses toward a goal. Rather, a person's affective system usually responds immediately and automatically to significant aspects of the environment. An obvious example is colour. Most people have an immediate positive affective response when they see a favourite colour on a car or item of clothing. Consumer Perspective 4.1 discusses how the affective system responds to colour.

The affective system

People have *little direct control* over their affective responses. For instance, if you are insulted by a rude salesclerk, your affective system may immediately, automatically produce feelings of frustration or anger. However, people can indirectly control their affective feelings by changing the behaviour that is triggering the affect or moving to another environment. For instance, you might complain about the rude clerk to the manager, which could reduce the negative affect you felt and create a new feeling of satisfaction. Consumers who have negative affective reactions to a crowded clothing shop (feelings of discomfort, frustration, or even anger) might leave the store to shop in a less crowded environment that stimulates more positive affective feelings.[7]

A third feature of the affective system is that affective responses are *felt physically in the body*. Consider the "butterflies" in the stomach associated with the excitement of making an important purchase, such as a car or a house. These physical reactions can be powerful feelings for the people experiencing them. Body movements often reflect their affective states (smile when happy, frown when disturbed, clench fists in anger, sit up straight in anticipation, slouch in boredom) and communicate emotional states. Successful salespeople read the body language of their prospects and adapt their sales presentations accordingly.

Fourth, the affective system can *respond to virtually any type of stimulus*. For instance, consumers can have an affective response to a physical object (I *love* my Pioneer stereo system) or a social situation (I *disliked* talking to the salesperson in the electronics store). People's affective systems can also respond to their own behaviours (I *enjoy* playing my stereo system). Finally, consumers' affective systems can respond to thoughts produced by their cognitive systems (I *like* to think about stereo systems).

Fifth, most *affective responses are learned*. Only a few basic affective responses, such as preferences for sweet tastes or negative reactions to loud, sudden noises seem to be innate. Consumers learn some of their affective responses (evaluations or feelings) through classical conditioning processes (discussed later in the text). Consumers also acquire many affective responses through early socialisation experiences as young children. Because affective responses are learned, they may vary widely across different cultures, subcultures, or other social groups. Thus, people's affective systems are likely to respond in different ways to the same stimulus.

Human beings have evolved highly sophisticated cognitive systems that support the higher mental processes of thinking, understanding, evaluating, planning, and deciding (see Consumer Perspective 4.2). We use the term *cognition* broadly to refer to these mental processes as well as the thoughts and meanings produced by the cognitive system.

What is cognition?

A major function of cognitive systems is to interpret, make sense of, and understand significant aspects of personal experience. To do so, the cognitive system creates

CONSUMER
PERSPECTIVE

▶ 4.1

Automatic
affective
responses
to colour

All living creatures have certain innate responses to the environment, and the response to colour is one of the most important. The first thing people react to in evaluating an object (a product or building) is its colour, and their automatic affective response can account for as much as 60 percent of their acceptance of the object. Your affective response to colour influences your emotions and feelings, as well as your cognitions and behaviours. Colours can attract or distract you, make you feel good or bad, attract you to other people or repel you, make you want to eat more or less.

A person's affective response to colour involves automatic reactions of the eye, optic neurons, parts of the brain, and various glands. Consider the response to red. When the eye sees primary red, the pituitary gland (embedded in the brain) is stimulated to send out a chemical signal to the adrenal medulla (located above the kidneys), which secrete adrenaline that activates and arouses the body. Emotions such as anger and fear are enhanced by this automatic reaction to red—danger signs are usually red. Affective feelings of excitement are generated by red. Thus, cosmetics such as lipstick are based on red. In the presence of red, people tend to eat more, which is why red is a popular colour for restaurants.

People have similar automatic reactions to other colours. For instance, a particular shade of vivid pink causes the brain to secrete norepinephrine, a chemical that inhibits the production of epinephrine. Thus, pink is a useful colour for places where angry people must be confronted (a principal's office, certain areas of a prison, or the complaint centre in a department store).

Yellow is the fastest colour for the eye to see because the electrochemical reactions that produce vision work fastest in response to yellow stimulation. Thus, yellow is an excellent colour to use to command attention (traffic signs and Post-it notes are examples). Placing a yellow car in the auto showroom will attract more attention from passing motorists. Although many people think of yellow as cheerful and sunny, the yellow kitchen they often request may increase anxiety and loss of temper.

People's reactions to favourite colours tend to vary by socioeconomic status (income and education level). Lower-income people tend to like primary colours that are pure, simple, and intense. Primary colours can be described in two words, such as sky blue

symbolic, subjective meanings that represent our personal interpretations of the stimuli we encounter, such as our interpretations of the Dole products. Our cognitive systems can interpret virtually any aspect of the environment. We also can interpret our behaviours (Why did I buy that CD?) and our own affective states (Do I really like this sweater? Why did I get so angry at the salesclerk?). Cognitive interpretations can include the deeper, symbolic meanings of products and behaviours (see Consumer Perspective 4.3). Finally, people can interpret the meaning of their own cognitions or beliefs (What does it mean when Zellers says "the lowest price is the law"?). Exhibit 4.2 lists some of the interpretations of cognitive systems.

A second function of our cognitive systems is to "process" (think about) these interpretations or meanings in carrying out cognitive tasks such as identifying goals and objectives, developing and evaluating alternative actions to meet those goals, choosing an action, and carrying out the behaviours. The amount and intensity of cognitive processing vary widely across situations, products, and consumers. Consumers do not always engage in extensive cognitive activity. In fact, many behaviours and purchase decisions involve minimal cognitive processing.

How are affect and cognition related?

The relationship between affect and cognition remains an issue in psychology.[8] Several researchers consider the affective and cognitive systems to be (at least somewhat) independent. Others argue that affect is largely influenced by the cognitive system.[9] Still oth-

and forest green. Upper-income people tend to prefer more complex colours that require three or more words to describe (say, a sort of grayed green with a little blue in it). To lower-income people, such colours seem "muddy" or washed out.

According to the experts, there are sex-based preferences for certain colours, too. The eye sees all colours as having either a yellow base or a blue base. Thus, red can be yellow based (tomato red) or blue based (raspberry). Men inherit a preference for yellow-based reds, while most women like blue-based reds. Thus, when women buy cosmetics that look good to themselves or their female friends, they usually gravitate toward the blue-based reds. However, most men tend to react more favourably to a woman wearing yellow-based red make-up.

Finally, blue is the stated favourite colour of 80 percent of North Americans. Blue is considered a calming colour, but a very strong sky blue is much more calming than other shades. In its presence, the brain sends out some 11 tranquilising chemicals to calm the body. Some hospitals use this colour in the cardiac unit to calm fearful patients. In contrast, a very pale sky encourages fantasy, so it might be a good colour for the creative department in an ad agency.

The affective system reacts strongly to certain colours. Red is arousing and exciting.

Source: Adapted from Carlton Wagner, "Color Cues," *Marketing Insights*, Spring 1990, pp. 42–46.

ers argue that affect is the dominant system.[10] We believe that some degree of independence is plausible because the affective and cognitive systems appear to involve different parts of the brain. However, the affective and cognitive areas are richly connected by neural pathways, so we also recognise that each system can influence the other.

For understanding consumers, it is more useful to emphasise the interactions between the affective and cognitive systems than to argue about which system is more important. Exhibit 4.3 presents a simple model to illustrate how the two systems are related. Note that each system can respond independently to aspects of the environment, and each system can respond to the output of the other system. For instance, the affective responses (emotions, feelings, or moods) the affective system produces in reaction to stimuli in the environment can be interpreted by the cognitive system (I wonder why I am so happy. I don't like the insurance agent because she is too serious). These cognitive interpretations, in turn, may be used to make decisions (I won't buy insurance from this person).

We also know that consumers' affective reactions to the environment can influence their cognitions during decision making. For instance, if you go grocery shopping when you are in a good mood, you may spend more money than if you had been in a bad mood. The affect associated with being in a good mood influences cognitive processes during shopping, so you are more likely to think about the favourable qualities of things to buy.

CONSUMER
PERSPECTIVE

▶ 4.2

"Higher"
mental
processes

What do we mean by higher mental processes?

▶ **Understanding**—Interpreting specific aspects of environment, especially determining the meaning of environmental features in terms of their personal relevance.

▶ **Evaluating**—Judging whether an aspect of the environment, or one's own behaviour, is good or bad, positive or negative, or favourable or unfavourable.

▶ **Planning**—Determining how to achieve a solution to a problem.

▶ **Deciding**—Comparing alternative solutions to a problem and selecting the best (or a satisfactory) alternative.

▶ **Thinking**—The cognitive activity that occurs during all these processes.

Source: Adapted from John R. Anderson, *Cognitive Psychology and Its Implications* (San Francisco: W. H. Freeman, 1985).

As another example, your cognitive interpretation of a TV commercial can be influenced by your affective reactions to the preceding programme.[11]

In contrast, consumers' cognitive interpretations of information in the environment can trigger affective reactions. (Oh, is that a Honda Civic? I like it.) We know that people's affective systems can be influenced by their cognitive interpretations of their experiences in a situation.[12] For instance, if you interpret a salesperson's behaviour as pushy, you probably will have a negative evaluation of the salesperson. If, on the other hand, you interpret the salesperson's behaviour as helpful, you probably will have a favourable affective response.

**Marketing
implications**

Both affect and cognition are important for understanding consumer behaviour. Consider, for instance, the cognitive and affective components of brand image.[13] A brand image includes consumer knowledge and beliefs (cognitions) about brand attributes and the consequences of brand use, as well as the evaluations, feelings, and emotions (affect) associated with brand use. Also, marketers need to understand both affective and cognitive responses to marketing strategies such as product design, advertisements, and store

---

EXHIBIT 4.2

**Types of
Interpretations
created by the
cognitive system**

Interpretations of physical stimuli
This sweater is made of lambswool.
This car gets 12 kilometers per liter.

Interpretations of social stimuli
The salesperson was helpful.
My friends think Pizza Hut is the best.

Interpretations of affective responses
I love Sealtest ice cream.
I feel guilty about not sending Dad a birthday card.
I feel mildly excited and interested in a new store.

Interpretations of behaviours
I drink a lot of Diet Pepsi.
I am a clever shopper.

Interpretations of symbolic meanings
This car is sexy.
This style of dress is appropriate for older women.
Wearing a Rolex watch means you are successful.

Interpretations of sensations
Colours on a box of breakfast cereal.
Sound of a soft-drink can being opened and poured.
Sweet taste of chocolate-chip cookies.
Smell of a favourite cologne.
Feel of a favourite pair of jeans.

Most marketers recognise that consumers choose products because of their symbolic meanings as well as their functional utility. In fact, symbolic qualities can be key determinants of product evaluation and purchase. Take food, for example.

Some foods symbolise age and gender differences. Milk and soft mushy foods are appropriate for babies or the elderly. Boys are supposed to prefer chunky peanut butter, while girls like smooth. Hamburgers are for kids; steak and lamb chops are appropriate for adults.

Certain foods are symbols of social status. Everyday foods such as hamburgers and French fries symbolise traditional values. More exotic and expensive foods, such as lobster or caviar, symbolise high status and sophisticated palates. Drinking wine with meals connotes higher status in parts of Canada, but probably not in Quebec, where as in France or Italy wine is expected at many meals.

Eating elsewhere than kitchen or dining room also has symbolic meaning. Eating outdoors, for instance, whether in the backyard, on the deck, or at the beach, symbolises freedom from convention and a return to more basic ways of cooking (on an open fire) and eating (with fingers). The symbolic meanings of going to a restaurant depend on the type of restaurant. Truck stops, outdoor cafés, bars, and cafeterias have very different symbolic meanings. Fast-food restaurants symbolise youth and unpretentious values. Going to better restaurants involves dressing up and using company manners, which helps create a ceremonious atmosphere and contributes to the symbolic meanings of the experience.

The method of food preparation also has symbolic meaning. Elaborate cooking procedures (haute cuisine) signify rarefied and sophisticated tastes. Raw foods tend to symbolise meeting more basic needs, although a few foods that are served uncooked have higher status meanings—caviar, sushi (raw fish and rice), steak tartare (raw ground beef)—perhaps because they symbolise mature or refined tastes.

Sources: Sidney J. Levy, "Interpreting Consumer Mythology: A Structural Approach to Consumer Behavior," *Journal of Marketing*, Summer 1981, pp. 49–61; Michael R. Solomon, "The Role of Products as Social Stimuli: A Symbolic Interactionism Perspective," *Journal of Consumer Research*, December 1983, pp. 319–329.

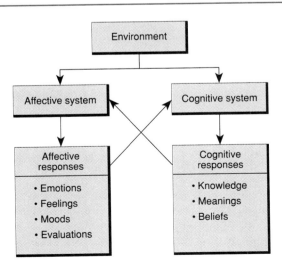

EXHIBIT 4.3

The relationship between the affective and cognitive systems

layouts. For some marketing purposes, consumers' affective responses are more important; in other cases, cognitions are key.

Affective responses are especially important for so-called feeling products.[14] These include certain foods (doughnuts, snacks, pizza), beverages (soft drinks, beer, wine), greeting cards, fragrances, skin care products, and sports cars. For instance, consider consumers' affective responses to ice cream. For most people, eating ice cream is a highly sensory experience, and they associate the product with affective feelings of happiness, fun, and contentment, even sensual pleasure. When Haagen-Dazs, the maker of superpremium ice cream noted for its high butterfat content and intense flavours, expanded into Europe, the company promoted people's affective, sensual reactions to ice cream.[15] One British ad portrayed a semiclothed couple feeding ice cream to each other. Haagen-Dazs was extremely successful in England, France, and Germany; sales grew from $2 million to $30 million in just two years.

As another example, consumers' initial affective responses to the smell of a cologne may be critical to its purchase. To promote its new scent Spellbound, Estée Lauder inserted 11 million scent strips in magazines such as *Vanity Fair* and *Vogue*.[16] Once a scent is bought and used, however, consumers' affective responses become influenced by their cognitive interpretations of other people's reactions to the scent. Fragrance advertising may try to convey both affective and cognitive responses. For example, Estée Lauder's ads for Spellbound picture attractive models looking intently into each other's eyes. Apparently, Lauder hopes to communicate both affective and cognitive meanings associated with romance, sensuality, and physical attraction. (Consumer Perspective 4.4 discusses the affective and cognitive aspects of romance.)

CONSUMER PERSPECTIVE

▶ **4.4**

The return of romance

Romance as a concept gained ascendancy in North America during the late 1980s and early 1990s, as people sought some refuge from the pressures of work and economic stress. Wedding advertising in *Bride* magazine portrayed increasingly romantic settings. Sales of romance novels were strong. The growing interest in Victorian furniture and flowery decoration was seen as a nostalgic return to a more romantic time. Advertising showed much more romantic settings and situations for restaurants, vacation locales, and male/female situations in general.

Romance is difficult to define, but it surely involves affective states, including emotions, feelings, and moods. Romance is about relationships, fantasy, imagery, nostalgia, and tradition. The affective responses associated with romantic love are quite different from those associated with more explicit sexual feelings. Look at Calvin Klein cologne ads, for example. To promote Obsession cologne, ads pictured nude, interlocked bodies to create an image of intense sexuality. Different advertising imagery was used to promote Eternity cologne. Here the goal was to elicit different types of affective responses—romantic emotions and moods, and feelings of commitment and close relationships.

Romance also involves cognitive responses. Romantic love is a whole psychological package that combines cognitive beliefs (equality of men and women), ideals (marriage is forever), and expectations (sharing as the most important aspect of marriage) with various affective responses (feelings of "true love" and of closeness, warmth, comfort, and mutual respect).

Interestingly, the trend toward romance may not be limited to our society. The engagement ring, a romantic concept indeed, is catching on in Japan.

Source: Adapted from Lea Bayers Rapp, "The Return of Romance," *Marketing Insights*, June 1989, pp. 31–39.

The most important aspect of consumer behaviour for marketers to understand is how consumers make decisions. Consumers make decisions about a variety of behaviours.

> What product or brand should I buy?

> Where should I shop?

> What TV shows should I watch tonight?

> Should I pay for this purchase with cash or credit card?

> How much money should I borrow?

> Should I read this ad carefully?

> Which friend should I consult?

> Which salesperson should I buy from?

COGNITIVE PROCESSES IN CONSUMER DECISION MAKING

Consumers use information to make such decisions. From the consumer's perspective, most aspects of the environment are potential information. In a supermarket, for instance, marketing strategies such as a price tag, a coupon, sale signs in a store window, or a tasting demonstration of a new product provide information. In addition, people's internal affective responses and their own behaviours constitute information that can be interpreted by their cognitive systems. If this information is to influence consumers' decisions, it must be *processed* (taken in, interpreted, and used) by their cognitive systems. To explain how the cognitive system processes information, researchers have developed information processing models.[17] These models identify a sequence of cognitive processes where each process transforms or modifies information and passes it on to the next process, where additional operations occur. The decisions that underlie many human actions can be understood in terms of these cognitive processes.

Reduced to its essence, consumer decision making involves three important cognitive processes. First, consumers must *interpret* relevant information in the environment to create personal meanings or knowledge. Second, consumers must combine or *integrate* this knowledge to evaluate products or possible actions and to choose among alternative behaviours. Third, consumers must *retrieve product knowledge in memory* to use in integration and interpretation processes. All three cognitive processes are involved in any decision-making situation.

Exhibit 4.4 presents a model of consumer decision making that highlights these three cognitive processes of interpretation, integration, and product knowledge in memory. We provide an overview of this decision-making model here (in Chapters 5–7 we discuss each element of the model in more detail).

A model of consumer decision making

Consumers must interpret or make sense of information in the environment around them. In the process, they create new knowledge, meanings, and beliefs about the environment and their place in it. **Interpretation** involves *exposure* to information and two related cognitive processes: attention and comprehension. *Attention* governs how we select which information to interpret and which to ignore. *Comprehension* refers to how we determine the subjective meanings of information and thus create personal knowledge and beliefs. We discuss exposure, attention, and comprehension processes in Chapter 6.

In this book, we use the terms **knowledge, meanings, and beliefs** interchangeably to refer to the various types of personal or subjective interpretations of information produced by interpretation processes. Exhibit 4.4 shows that knowledge, meanings, and beliefs may be stored in memory as well as used in integration processes.

Integration describes how we combine different types of knowledge (1) to form overall evaluations of products, other objects, and behaviours and (2) to make choices among alternative behaviours, including purchase. In the first instance, consumers combine knowledge and affective feelings about a product or a brand to form an overall evaluation or a *brand attitude* (I like Baskin-Robbins chocolate-chip cookie dough ice cream. Or

EXHIBIT 4.4

Cognitive processes in the model of consumer decision making

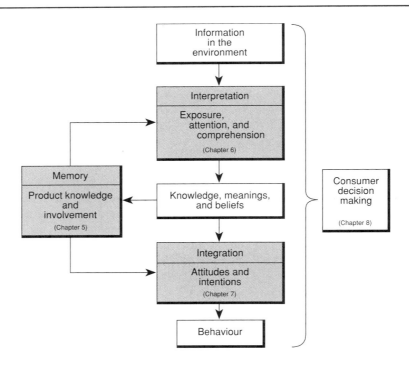

Wrangler jeans are not as good as Gap jeans). We discuss attitudes and intentions in Chapter 7. In the second case, consumers combine knowledge and affective responses to choose a behaviour (Should I go to Eaton's or The Bay?). When consumers choose between different purchase behaviours, they form an *intention or plan* to buy (I intend to buy a new Bic pen this afternoon). Integration processes also are used to choose among other types of behaviours. For instance, a consumer might combine knowledge in deciding when to go on a shopping trip, whether to pay with a check or a credit card, or whether to recommend a movie to a friend.

Product knowledge and involvement describes the various types of knowledge, meanings, and beliefs that are stored in memory. For example, consumers may have product knowledge about the characteristics or attributes of a brand of athletic shoe (gel inserts in the heel), the outcome of using the brand (I can run faster), or the brand's ability to satisfy important objectives (I will be fit). Product knowledge retrieved from memory can influence interpretation and integration processes. Canadian consumers, for example, need a certain amount of knowledge about nutrition to interpret and understand the many health claims made by food companies. Product involvement refers to consumers' knowledge about the personal relevance of the product in one's life (Nutrition information is important to my health goals). People's level of involvement with health issues influences how much effort they exert in interpreting a nutritional message. We discuss product knowledge and involvement in Chapter 5.

In summary, Exhibit 4.4 shows that consumer decision making involves the cognitive processes of interpretation and integration, as influenced by product knowledge, meanings, and beliefs in memory. In Chapter 8, we discuss how all these factors work together in consumer decision making.

The cognitive system interprets this ad to create knowledge, meanings, and beliefs about how the product works.

Other characteristics of the cognitive system

Several aspects of the cognitive system influence consumer decision making. *Activation*, for instance, refers to the process by which product knowledge is retrieved from memory for use in interpreting and integrating information. Activation of knowledge in memory is often automatic in that little or no conscious effort is involved.[18] Consumers typically experience activated knowledge as thoughts that "just come to mind." Daydreaming is a good example of activation: various bits of knowledge or meanings surface as a person's mind drifts from one thought to another. Activation also operates when consumers intentionally try to remember certain bits of knowledge. Examples include trying to recall the location of a particular shop in the mall, the salesperson's name, or the price of that black sweater. Remembering such knowledge involves giving ourselves "cues" that may activate the desired knowledge (Let's see, I think her name begins with a B).

The product knowledge in consumers' memories can be activated in various ways. The most common way is by exposure to objects or events in the environment. Seeing something, such as the distinctive BMW grille, can activate various meanings (you might think about sportiness or that this is a rich person's car). People's internal, affective states also can activate knowledge. For instance, positive knowledge and beliefs tend to be activated when a person is in a good mood, while more negative meanings are activated when the same person is in an unpleasant mood. Finally, product knowledge in memory can be activated because it is linked to other activated meanings. Because meanings are associated in memory, activation of one meaning concept may trigger related concepts and activate those meanings as well. Consumers have little control over this process of

CONSUMER PERSPECTIVE

▶ **4.5**

Increasing automatic cognitive processing: learning to drive a car

People who are skilled at doing something can do what seems impossible to both the novice and the theorist. Think about your experience in learning to drive a car. When you first learned to drive, you probably couldn't drive and talk at the same time. The task of driving seemed to require all your concentration. Today, if you are used to driving, you can probably drive in traffic, listen to music on the radio, and carry on a conversation. Could you have done this when you first started driving? Probably then you kept the radio off. If anyone tried to talk to you, you could not pay attention. (Of course, even experienced drivers stop talking if something unfamiliar occurs such as an emergency on the road ahead.)

Learning to drive illustrates how cognitive processes (and associated behaviours) become increasingly automatic as they are learned through practice. However, even highly automatic skills such as eating seem to require some "capacity." Perhaps you like to munch on something while you study. You might snack on pretzels or eat an apple while you read this chapter. But if you come on a passage that requires more thought, you'll probably stop eating while you interpret the meaning of what you are reading.

spreading activation, which occurs unconsciously and automatically.[19] For instance, seeing a magazine ad for Jell-O might activate first the Jell-O name and then related knowledge and meanings such as jiggly, tastes sweet, good for a quick dessert, and Bill Cosby likes it. Through spreading activation, various aspects of one's knowledge in memory can spring to mind during decision making.

Another important characteristic of the human cognitive system is its *limited capacity*. Only a small amount of knowledge can be considered consciously at one time. This suggests that the interpretation and integration processes during consumer decision making are fairly simple. For instance, it is unlikely that consumers can consider more than a few characteristics of a brand in forming an attitude or intention to buy the brand. At the same time, we know people are able to handle rather complex tasks such as going to a restaurant because cognitive processes tend to become more *automatic* with experience. That is, over time, cognitive processes gradually require less capacity and conscious control (thinking).[20] Grocery shopping, for instance, is routine and cognitively easy for most consumers because many of the interpretation and integration processes involved in choosing food products have become automatic. Consumer Perspective 4.5 describes a common example of how automatic processes develop.

Marketing implications

The simple model of consumer decision making that we have described has many implications. Because the next several chapters cover the elements of the model in detail, we mention only a few examples here.

Obviously, it is important for marketers to understand how consumers interpret their marketing strategies. For instance, a store might put a brand on sale because it is overstocked; the consumer, however, might interpret the sale price to indicate lower product quality. Marketers need to know the knowledge, meanings, and beliefs that consumers have for their products or brands or stores.

The integration processes involved in forming brand attitudes (Do I like this brand?) and purchase intentions (Should I buy this brand?) are critically important for understanding consumer behaviour. Marketers need to know what types of product knowledge are used in integration processes and what knowledge is irrelevant. Because the cognitive system has a limited capacity, marketers should recognise that consumers can integrate only small amounts of knowledge when choosing brands to buy or stores to patronise.

CONSUMER PERSPECTIVE

4.6

Automatic activation of meanings from memory

Most activation tends to be automatic and very rapid. Normally, we are not conscious of the activation process that retrieves stored knowledge from memory. The (usually appropriate) meanings just "come to mind."

("The Family Circus" by Bil Keane. Reprinted with special permission of Cowles Syndicate, Inc.)

Source: © 1992 King Features Syndicate, Inc. All Rights Reserved. Reprinted with special permission of King Features Syndicate.

Activation of product knowledge has many implications for marketing. The choice of a brand name, for example, can be highly important for the success of the product because a name can activate particular meanings in the consumer's memory. Jaguar is a good name for a sports car because it activates meanings like speedy, agile, exotic, rare, beautiful, powerful, and graceful.[21] Another implication is that marketers need to pay attention to differences between consumers because the same stimulus may activate different meanings for different consumers. The cartoon in Consumer Perspective 4.6 illustrates this point.

KNOWLEDGE STORED IN MEMORY

The model in Exhibit 4.4 shows that knowledge in memory influences the cognitive processes involved when consumers make decisions. We discuss product knowledge and involvement in the next chapter, but here we describe two broad types of knowledge and how this knowledge is organised in memory.

Types of knowledge

The human cognitive system can interpret virtually any type of information and thereby create knowledge, meanings, and beliefs.[22] People can create two types of knowledge: (1) general knowledge about their environments and behaviours and (2) procedural knowledge about how to do things.[23]

General knowledge concerns people's interpretations of relevant information in their environments. For instance, consumers develop general knowledge about product categories (compact discs, fast-food hamburger restaurants, mutual funds), stores (Sears, Wal-Mart, and Kmart), particular behaviours (shopping in malls, ordering at restaurants, talking to salespeople), other people (one's best friend, the cashier at the Tim Horton's on the corner, teachers), and even themselves (I am shy, intelligent, and honest).

General knowledge is stored in memory as *propositions* that connect two concepts:

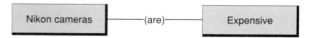

Essentially, every meaning concept in memory is linked to at least one other concept via such propositions. Most propositions are based on a meaningful relationship between the two concepts. For instance, your knowledge that a favourite clothing store is having a sale creates a simple proposition:

Consumers can have episodic or semantic knowledge.[24] *Episodic knowledge* concerns the specific events that have happened in a person's life. "Yesterday I bought a Snickers candy bar from the vending machine" and "My last bank statement had a mistake" are examples of episodic knowledge. Consumers also have *semantic knowledge* about objects and events in the environment. For instance, the personal meanings and beliefs you have about Snickers candy bars—the peanuts, caramel, and calories it contains; the wrapper design; the aroma or taste—are part of your semantic knowledge. When activated from memory, episodic and semantic knowledge can have important influences on consumers' decision making and behaviour.

Consumers also have **procedural knowledge** about how to do things.[25] Procedural knowledge is stored in memory as a *production,* which is a special type of "if . . . , then . . ." proposition that links a concept or an event with the resulting appropriate behaviour.

Examples of productions include, "If the phone rings when you are busy, don't answer it," or "If a salesperson presses you for a quick decision, say no and leave."

Over a lifetime of experience, consumers learn a great deal of procedural knowledge, much of which is highly specific to particular situations. When activated from memory, these productions directly and automatically influence a person's overt behaviour. For instance, Susan has a production: "If the price on a piece of clothing is reduced by 50 percent or more, I will consider buying it." If this procedural knowledge is activated when Susan sees a half-price sign in the jeans section, she will stop and decide whether now is the time to buy a new pair of jeans.

Like general knowledge, people's procedural knowledge is relevant in many everyday situations. Consider the procedural knowledge consumers need to operate equipment such as computers, videocameras, VCRs, stereo receivers, and televisions. Some people feel such products have become too complex and difficult to operate.[26] One survey found that only 3 percent of total TV viewing time is spent watching shows that were recorded in advance because many people have not taken the time to acquire the procedural knowledge necessary to programme their VCRs.[27] Understanding that relatively few consumers use all the features on their high-tech equipment, some manufacturers are simplifying their products, which reduces the procedural knowledge necessary to use them. For example, Philips, the giant Dutch electronics firm, has developed a group of easy-to-use clock radios, VCRs, and tape players called Easy Line.

Both general knowledge and procedural knowledge can have important influences on consumers' behaviours. Consider the grocery shopping trip described in Chapter 1. Various aspects of Bruce Macklin's general and procedural knowledge were activated as he moved through the grocery store environment. This knowledge affected his interpretation and integration of information as he made his purchase decisions.

Consumers' general and procedural knowledge is organised to form structures of knowledge in memory. Our cognitive systems create networks that organise and link many types of knowledge.[28] Exhibit 4.5 presents an **associative network of knowledge** for Nike running shoes. In this knowledge structure, the Nike product is connected to various types of general knowledge, including episodic knowledge about past events (shopping at Sports Experts) and semantic knowledge about the features of Nike shoes (their appearance, weight, and cushioning). Also included in knowledge of affective responses (memory of one's feelings after a hard run) and the interpretations of those affective feelings (relaxed and proud). This structure of Nike knowledge also contains productions (how to run lightly, when to wear cushioned socks) and related semantic knowledge about the consequences of these behaviours (avoid sore knees).

Parts of this knowledge structure might be activated in certain circumstances. For example, seeing an athlete on TV wearing Nike shoes or noticing the Nike swoosh symbol on a billboard could activate some knowledge. Experiencing the pleasant affective feelings of satisfaction and relaxation after a hard workout could activate other knowledge associated with Nike. Finally, spreading activation could activate some meanings associated with Nike as "activation energy" spreads from one meaning concept in the network to related meanings. Whatever element of Nike knowledge is activated during decision

Structures of knowledge

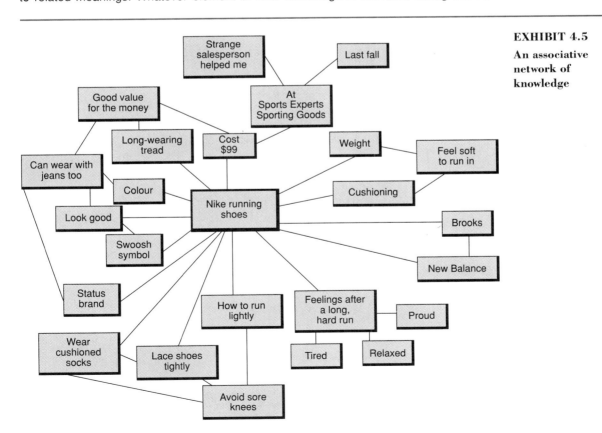

EXHIBIT 4.5

An associative network of knowledge

making has the potential to influence consumers' interpretation and integration processes at that time.

Types of knowledge structure

People's cognitive systems create and use two types of knowledge structures—schemas and scripts. Each structure is an associative network of linked meanings, but **schemas** include mostly episodic and semantic general knowledge, while scripts contain procedural knowledge. Both schemas and scripts can be activated during decision making, and both can influence cognitive processes. The knowledge structure in Exhibit 4.5 is a schema that represents one consumer's general knowledge about Nike running shoes.[29] Marketers have a vital interest in understanding consumers' schemas about brands, stores, and product categories.

Scripts are organised networks of production knowledge. When consumers experience common situations, they learn what behaviours are appropriate in that situation. This knowledge may be organised as a sequence of if . . . , then . . . productions called a script.[30] Here is a simple script relating to eating in a fast-food restaurant.

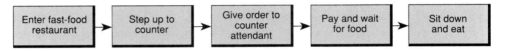

As another example, consumers who go to auctions develop a generalised script containing production knowledge about how to register with the auctioneer before the sale starts, how to bid, and how to pay for their purchases. When activated at the auction, the script automatically guides and directs many (but not necessarily all) of the consumer's overt behaviours. Thus, consumers who have a well-delivered script do not have to make conscious decisions about many auction-related behaviours because those behaviours are controlled by the script. Exhibit 4.6 presents a simplified script for eating in a "fancy" restaurant. Exhibit 4.7 shows the major processes in the cognitive system.

EXHIBIT 4.6

A hypothetical script of appropriate procedures for dining at a "fancy" restaurant

▷ Enter restaurant.

▷ Give reservation name to maitre d'.

▷ Wait to be shown to table.

▷ Walk to table and sit down.

▷ Order drinks when server asks.

▷ Select dinner items from menu.

▷ Order meal when server returns.

▷ Drink drinks and talk until first course arrives.

▷ Eat soup or salad when it arrives.

▷ Eat main course when it arrives.

▷ Order dessert when finished with dinner.

▷ Eat dessert when it arrives.

▷ Talk until bill arrives.

▷ Examine bill for accuracy.

▷ Give server credit card to pay for bill.

▷ Add tip to credit card form and sign.

▷ Leave restaurant.

Source: Reprinted with permission from Gordon H. Bower, John B. Black, and Terrence J. Turner, "Scripts in Memory for Text," in *Cognitive Psychology*, April 1979, pp. 177–220.

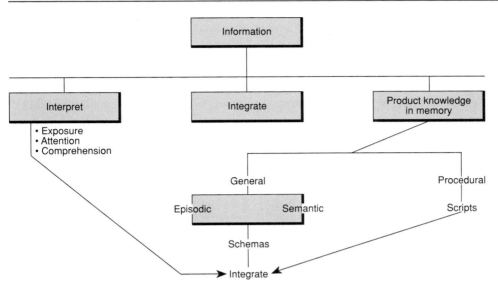

EXHIBIT 4.7

Cognitive processes

To understand consumers, marketers need to know what product knowledge they have acquired and stored in memory. For instance, a coffee company may want to determine how consumers organise the coffee category into product forms (Do consumers see ground, freeze-dried, and instant coffee as different forms of coffee?). Marketers might want to know the contents of consumers' product schemas (associative networks of general knowledge about whole-bean coffee) or shopping scripts (associative networks of procedural knowledge about where to shop for whole-bean coffee). They also might need to know what types of knowledge are activated by particular marketing strategies. This could require a detailed analysis of the meanings activated when consumers are exposed to a celebrity spokesperson or a certain typeface for a magazine ad. Finally, marketers need to know how consumers' affective systems react to the knowledge, meaning, and beliefs created by their cognitive systems and to the cognitive processes used in decision making. Understanding consumers requires attention to both affect and cognition.

Marketing implications

▶ **SUMMARY**

Learning objective 1: *Describe the affective system and identify the types of affective responses it produces.*
The affective system produces affective responses to objects and events in the environment. The affective system also responds to specific behaviours (I'm pleased with the way I negotiated the price on my new car) and to cognitions (Thinking about that meal makes me mad). The affective system is reactive in that it can only respond to things and events; it cannot think or plan. The four types of affective responses vary in intensity and level of physical arousal. Emotions (love, joy, anger) are the most intense and arousing affective responses. Feelings (frustration, interest) are somewhat less intense and arousing. Moods (bored, calm, blue) are rather diffuse (nonintense) affective states that involve relatively low levels of arousal. Evaluations (judgments of how much you like a product) typically involve relatively low levels of intensity and arousal.

Learning objective 2: *Describe the cognitive system and the types of meanings it creates.*
A primary function of the cognitive system is to interpret and make sense of the environment, one's behaviours, and one's affective responses. The cognitive system creates

knowledge and beliefs that represent the personal, subjective meanings of these factors. This knowledge could be about physical objects (a car), social events (a party), affective responses (the reasons for sadness). The cognitive system is capable of creating symbolic meanings (These sunglasses are for kids. This product is for women, not men). The cognitive system also interprets physical sensations (This cookie has too much sugar). Finally, the cognitive system can interpret one's own overt behaviours (I bought that CD because my girlfriend likes it). Another function of the cognitive system is to integrate or combine knowledge to form attitudes (I like this textbook) and intentions (I will go shopping for new shoes).

Learning objective 3: *Explain how the affective and cognitive systems influence each other.*

Because the affective and cognitive systems are highly related, they can influence each other. For instance, people's thoughts can influence their affective responses. Marketers may use nostalgic music from the past to prompt recall of pleasant events and create positive affective feelings and moods. Many affective responses require cognitive interpretation, as when people try to determine the reasons they like a certain sweater. Marketers often want to create a certain mix of affective and cognitive responses in consumers. Consider the combined affective and cognitive responses that might be created by ads for cars, cologne, or beer that portray fantasy, romance, and sexual attraction.

Learning objective 4: *Describe the components of the model of consumer decision making.*

The model of consumer decision making (Exhibit 4.4) identifies two major cognitive processes: interpretation and integration. Interpretation involves making sense of information in the environment, as well as one's own behaviours and affective responses. Interpretation processes give rise to knowledge and beliefs that represent the personally relevant meanings of these factors. Interpretation involves exposure to information, attention to selected aspects of the information, and comprehension of the information's meaning. Integration describes how we combine knowledge (1) to form attitudes toward products, brands, and stores, and (2) to make choices by forming intentions to act (I want to buy a Big Mac). The third major component of the model is knowledge and involvement. Involvement refers to consumers' interest in the information. Relevant knowledge that is activated in memory can influence interpretation processes and can be used in integration processes. All of these components are involved in consumer decision making. The outcome of decision making is behaviour, such as the purchase of a product.

Learning objective 5: *Explain how knowledge in memory can be activated for use in cognitive processing.*

The knowledge that consumers have acquired and stored in memory must be activated, or retrieved from memory, to influence interpretation and integration processes. Only activated knowledge is available for use in various cognitive processes. Knowledge that is not activated remains stored in memory and cannot influence decision making. Thus, marketers need to understand the factors that can activate desirable knowledge in memory. These factors include exposure to some object or event in the environment. Seeing a picture of the movie star Leslie Nielsen can activate knowledge about him; noticing a can of Green Giant peas may activate knowledge and feelings about the Jolly Green Giant; hearing a song might activate episodic knowledge about special events in your life. Finally, because activation is a kind of "energy" that can spread through a knowledge structure, activation of one knowledge concept can activate related concepts. For example, thinking about the cushioning qualities of Nike or Reebok basketball shoes might activate recollection of related attributes.

Learning objective 6: *Describe the differences between general and procedural knowledge.*

General knowledge concerns various aspects of the world: the environment, one's own behaviours, and even one's affective responses. There are two types of general world knowledge. Episodic knowledge concerns memory for past events in one's life. Semantic knowledge concerns general knowledge and beliefs about the world. Procedural knowledge is knowledge about how to do things—how to behave and the circumstances in which certain behaviours are appropriate. Both general and procedural knowledge can have important influences on consumer decision making.

Learning objective 7: *Give examples of associative networks of knowledge in the form of schemas and scripts.*

An associative network of knowledge links various meaning concepts to form a network-like structure. The basis for the network organisation is the meaningful connections or associations between or among concepts. Associative network structures that contain general knowledge related to some concept or some product are schemas. Marketers are interested in understanding the knowledge contained in consumers' schemas for brands, stores, ads, and the like. Exhibit 4.5 gives an example. Associative network structures that include procedural knowledge about how and when to perform certain behaviours are called scripts. A script knowledge structure provides a sequence of behaviours that are appropriate to perform in certain circumstances. See Exhibit 4.6 for an example.

▶ **KEY TERMS AND CONCEPTS**

affect

cognition

interpretation

knowledge, meanings, and beliefs

integration

product knowledge and involvement

general knowledge

procedural knowledge

associative network of knowledge

schema

script

▶ **REVIEW AND DISCUSSION QUESTIONS**

1. Describe the four broad types of affective responses that are produced by the affective system.

2. How do you distinguish between the cognitive and affective systems? How are they interrelated?

3. Consider a product such as an automobile or a perfume. Describe at least three types of subjective meanings that consumers might construct to represent various aspects of the product and explain ways marketers might try to influence the meaning.

4. Find an advertisement or some other type of marketing information, and assume you are trying to make a decision about this product. Using the model of consumer decision making, describe how a consumer might make a purchase decision. Be sure to describe the cognitive processes of interpretation and integration and discuss how knowledge in memory might influence these cognitive processes.

5. Give a specific example of how exposure to a marketing strategy could activate certain knowledge and lead to spreading activation within a consumer's associative network of product knowledge.

6. Compare and contrast general and procedural knowledge. Are they related?

7. Discuss the type of knowledge assumed in a script and describe a simple script that you follow (e.g., going to a bank, buying textbooks, getting up in the morning).

CHAPTER 5

Product Knowledge and Involvement

LEARNING OBJECTIVES

After completing this chapter, you should be able to:

▶ 1. List the four categories of product knowledge and give examples.

▶ 2. Give examples of concrete and abstract attributes, functional and psychosocial consequences, and instrumental and terminal values.

▶ 3. Define benefits and risks.

▶ 4. Describe a means-end chain and give an example.

▶ 5. Discuss two marketing implications of means-end chains.

▶ 6. Define involvement and describe how personal and situational sources influence involvement.

▶ 7. Give examples of marketing strategies that can influence personal and situational sources of involvement.

CHRYSLER IN THE MINIVAN DRIVER'S SEAT

Less than two years after the first minivan rolled off the production line at Chrysler's refurbished Windsor plant, where all the highly successful Mini Ram, Caravan, and Voyageur cars are made, more than 200,000 per year are shipped to dealers. The company is back-ordered—a problem Chrysler's Big Three competitors would love to have.

While Chrysler was cranking out 1,018 minivans a day, the competition could hardly get their entries into dealer showrooms. As a result, Chrysler continued to enjoy virtually a free rein in the minivan segment, which grew from less than 1 percent of the total Canadian truck market to 13 percent by 1985 and was 35 percent in 1995. Because of Chrysler's jump on the competition in terms of understanding and predicting consumers' needs in the huge family car market, the company enjoyed a market share in Canada of over 85 percent for at least the first five years in the market. Between 1990 and 1995, Chrysler maintained between 40 and 50 percent of the minivan market. The company's objective is for its share to be 50 percent, in the face of ever-increasing competition from Ford (28 percent share in 1995) and GM (24 percent share in 1995).

Chrysler's strategy was very clear all along. Instead of attempting to manufacture more me-too products at a competitive disadvantage to Ford Canada and General Motors of Canada, it committed to developing products with superior attributes that deliver important benefits to consumers. There is no doubt that Chrysler revolutionised the North American car market with its introduction of the minivan. As a result, the company scored big in the family passenger car market.[1]

Chrysler's experiences illustrate the importance of understanding consumers' reactions to product attributes and benefits. In this chapter, we examine consumers' product knowledge and involvement, two important aspects of the affect and cognition portion of the Wheel of Consumer Analysis. We begin by identifying four types or levels of product knowledge. Then we discuss consumers' knowledge about product attributes as well as the benefits and values the product provides. Then we show how these attributes, benefits, and values fit into a simple associative network of knowledge called a means-end chain. In the second half of the chapter, we consider consumers' product involvement or feelings of interest and personal relevance. We describe how consumer involvement is influenced by intrinsic (internal) and situational (external) factors. We conclude by discussing how means-end chains can be used to understand the consumer/product relationship and how marketing strategies can influence consumers' product involvement.

LEVELS OF PRODUCT KNOWLEDGE

Consumers have different levels of product knowledge that can be used to interpret new information and make purchase choices. Levels of meaning are formed when people combine separate meaning concepts into larger categories of knowledge.[2] For instance, you might combine knowledge about the braking, acceleration, and cornering ability of an automobile to form a more inclusive concept that you call handling. In a sense, your knowledge of handling "contains" these separate meanings.[3] Another example is the various types of bicycles that make up the overall bike category—racing, mountain, BMX, city bikes. Each of these meaning categories can be separated into more specific knowledge (different types of racing bikes or mountain bikes). Thus, a person's knowledge about bikes, mountain bikes, and types of mountain bikes may form a hierarchical structure of bicycle knowledge at different levels.

This idea of related meanings at different levels can help us understand consumers' product knowledge. Consumers can have product knowledge at four levels: the product class, product forms, brands, and models. Exhibit 5.1 gives examples of each level of product knowledge.

Marketers are very interested in consumers' knowledge about *brands*. Most marketing strategies are brand oriented in that they are intended to make consumers aware of a brand, teach them about a brand, and influence them to buy that brand. Most marketing research focuses on consumers' knowledge and beliefs about brands. Likewise, much of our discussion in this text concerns customers' brand knowledge.

For some products, consumers can have knowledge about models, a more detailed level of product knowledge than brands. A *model* is a specific example of a brand that has one or more unique product features or attributes (Exhibit 5.1 gives several examples). For instance, Nikon 35mm cameras are available in several different models; Coca-Cola comes in diet, caffeine-free, cherry-flavoured, and other versions; and Baskin-Robbins ice cream is sold in different flavours. The 325, 525, and 850 models of BMW automobiles vary in size, price, and exterior design and have distinctive features and options such as air conditioning, fancy wheels, automatic braking systems, and leather seats.

Going in the other direction from the brand and model levels of knowledge, a *product form* is a broader category that includes several brands similar in some important way. Often the basis for a product-form category is a physical characteristic the brands share. For instance, freeze-dried, instant, ground, and whole-bean coffee are defined by their physical form. In some cases, certain product forms become so well established in consumers' minds that marketers can treat them as separate markets. Diet soft drinks, sports sedans, fast-food hamburger restaurants, and laptop computers are examples.

Product Class	Product Form	Brand	Model/Feature
Coffee	Ground	Folgers	1-pound can
	Instant	Maxwell House	8-ounce jar
Automobiles	Sedan	Ford	Taurus with air and power steering
	Sports car	Nissan	300EX with air and 5-speed
	Sports sedan	BMW	Model 325e with air and automatic transmission
Pens	Ballpoint	Bic	$.79 model, regular tip
	Felt tip	Pilot	$.99 model, extra-fine tip
Beer	Imported	Foster's	12-ounce can
	Light	Miller Lite	Keg
	Low alcohol	Labatt .5	12-ounce can
	Dry	Molson Dry	Tall Bottle

EXHIBIT 5.1

Levels of product knowledge

The *product class* is the broadest and most inclusive level of product knowledge and may include several product forms. Coffee, cars, and soft drinks are examples. Marketing strategies to promote the entire product class can be effective for brands with a high market share. For example, Hostess might promote consumption of the product class salty chip snacks (various types of potato and flavoured chips). Because the company enjoys a substantial market share, any increase in overall consumption of the product class is likely to benefit Hostess more than its competitors.

Marketers need to understand how consumers organise their product knowledge in terms of these different levels, because consumers may make separate purchase decisions at each level of knowledge.[4] For instance, a consumer might choose between alternative product classes (Should I buy a television or a stereo system?), different product forms (Should I purchase a large-screen TV or a portable?), various brands (Should I buy an RCA or a Sony TV?), and alternative models (Should I choose a 27-inch RCA TV with stereo speakers or a 25-inch RCA set without stereo?). In sum, all levels of product knowledge are relevant to the marketing manager, and the brand level is of particular importance.

This ad focuses on a key functional consequence of the product.

**CONSUMERS'
PRODUCT
KNOWLEDGE**

Consumers can have three types of product knowledge: knowledge about product attributes or characteristics, benefits or positive consequences of using the product, and values the product helps to satisfy or achieve. Exhibit 5.2 presents examples of these types of knowledge about Nike running shoes.

**Products as
bundles of
attributes**

As the Chrysler example illustrates, decisions about product characteristics or attributes are important elements of marketing strategy. Within the limits imposed by production capabilities and financial resources, marketing managers can add new attributes to a product ("Now, Diet 7UP contains 100% NutraSweet"), remove old attributes ("Caffeine-free Diet Pepsi"), or modify existing attributes (in 1985, Coca-Cola managers modified the century-old secret recipe for Coke). Marketers change brand attributes to make their products more appealing to consumers. For instance, to give Liquid Tide its cleaning power, chemists at Procter & Gamble created a new molecule and included twice as many active ingredients as competitive brands. The 400,000 hours of research and development time seemed to pay off, as Liquid Tide's initial sales skyrocketed.[5] Consumer Perspective 5.1 describes another successful change in a product attribute.

Even the simplest products have multiple attributes. Pencils, for examples, have different shapes, sizes, and colours as well as varying densities of lead and eraser softness.

EXHIBIT 5.2

**Types of product
knowledge**

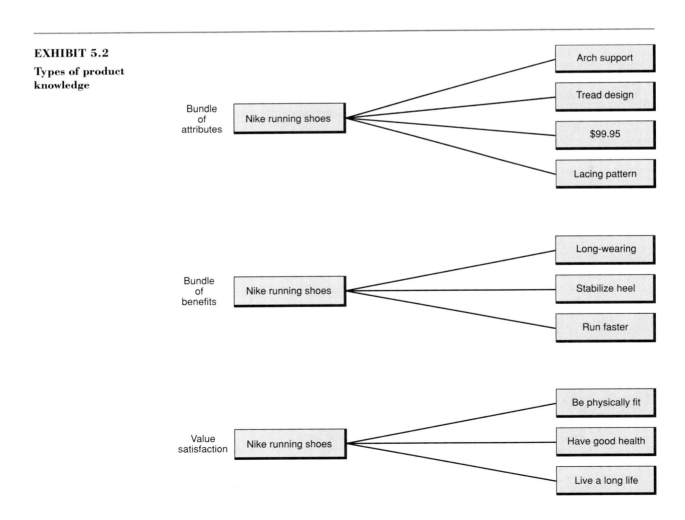

The old Pyrex measuring cup made by Corning Glass Works was a kitchen classic. The glass cup with its familiar attributes—a simple volume gauge printed in red on one side, the pouring lip, and the nice big handle—was found in as many as 80 percent of households. Even though the bulky handle made the three sizes (1-, 2-, and 4-cup) difficult to stack, no one complained. In fact, the cups had not changed much since they had been introduced some 50 years before. Why should marketers change the attributes of a product this successful?

The idea for changing the attributes of the Pyrex measuring cup came about by accident when the handle on a test product sagged during heating. This gave designers the idea of an "open" handle that was attached to the cup at only one end. Besides being cheaper to produce, this handle would make the cups stackable and therefore more convenient to store in a cupboard. Corning also added a second new attribute, making the cup a bit deeper so that foods could be heated in microwave ovens without boiling over. However, the designers kept the familiar red measuring gauge on the side. What was the result of making these simple changes in the attributes of this product? Sales increased 150 percent.

Source: Toni Mack, "What's in a Handle?" *Forbes*, Jan. 25, 1988, p. 87. Reprinted by permission of *Forbes* magazine. © Forbes Inc. 1988.

CONSUMER PERSPECTIVE

5.1

What's in a handle?

Many marketers treat products and brands as *bundles of attributes* (see Exhibit 5.2). From a cognitive processing perspective, however, it is not certain that consumers have extensive knowledge about product attributes or use their attribute knowledge to make purchase decisions. Marketers need to know which product attributes are important to customers, what those attributes mean to consumers, and how consumers use this knowledge to make purchase decisions about products and brands.

Consumers can have knowledge about the concrete and abstract attributes of products.[6] **Concrete attributes** refer to physical product characteristics such as the type of fibre or thickness of a blanket. The colour of a car and its front-seat legroom are also concrete attributes. Concrete attributes have a tangible, physical reality that consumers can experience directly. (A high butterfat content in ice cream is experienced as a rich taste.) In contrast, **abstract attributes** are nonmaterial product characteristics such as the warmth and quality of a blanket or the stylishness and comfort of a car. Abstract attributes are intangible in that consumers cannot experience them directly, but must judge them subjectively. (You cannot see quality directly; it must be inferred.) In addition to abstract and concrete attributes, consumers' product knowledge may include affective evaluations of each attribute. ("I don't like itchy wool blankets." "I love chocolate ice cream.")

Products as bundles of benefits

Marketers also recognise that consumers often think about products and brands in terms of their consequences, not their attributes.[7] *Consequences* are outcomes that happen when the product is purchased and used or consumed. Positive consequences are known as *benefits*. For instance, an electric shaver might give a close shave, require repairs, or make the user feel more attractive; a facial cream might cause an allergic reaction or cost too much. Consumers can have knowledge about two types of outcomes: functional and psychosocial consequences.

Functional consequences are the tangible outcomes of product use that consumers usually experience directly and immediately. For instance, functional consequences include the immediate physiological outcomes of product use (eating a Harvey's hamburger satisfies your hunger, drinking orange juice quenches your thirst, the tennis racquet grip fits your hand). Functional consequences also refer to the tangible performance outcomes of using a product (a hair blower dries your hair quickly, a car gets 12 kilometres per liter, a toaster browns bread evenly, an ink pen writes without skipping).

Psychosocial consequences refer to knowledge about the psychosocial and social outcomes of product use. *Psychological consequences* are internal, personal outcomes about how the product makes you feel. For example, using Nexxus shampoo might make you feel attractive, wearing Gap sportswear might make you feel stylish, eating an ice-cream cone from Baskin-Robbins might make you feel satisfied. Consumers also think about the *social consequences* of product use, the reactions of other people. ("My friends will be impressed if I buy this Sony stereo system." "My mother will think I'm a smart shopper if I buy this jacket on sale.")

When people experience functional and psychosocial consequences, their affective and cognitive systems produce responses that may be stored as knowledge in memory. For instance, most consumers would feel negative affect (dissatisfaction) if a product needed repairs soon after it was bought. Or a consumer might have positive feelings of pride and self-esteem if other people comment favourably on a new sweater. Beliefs about these functional and psychosocial consequences and related affective reactions are part of consumers' product knowledge in memory. This knowledge may later be activated from memory and used in interpretation or integration processes.

Consumers can think about the positive and negative consequences of product use as possible benefits or potential risks. **Benefits** are the desirable consequences consumers seek when buying and using products and brands. ("I want a car with fast acceleration." "I want a car with good mileage.") Benefit knowledge can be described in terms of cognition and affect. Cognitive aspects of benefits include consumers' knowledge of desired functional and psychosocial consequences. ("I want my stereo system to have excellent sound reproduction." "People will notice me.") Affective aspects of benefits include positive affective responses associated with the desired consequence. ("I feel good when people notice me.")

Consumers often think about products and brands as *bundles of benefits* rather than bundles of attributes (see Exhibit 5.2). Thus, marketers can divide consumers into subgroups or segments according to their desire for particular product consequences, a process called *benefit segmentation*.[8] For example, some toothpaste consumers are looking for appearance benefits (whiter teeth), while others are more interested in health benefits (preventing tooth decay).

Perceived risk concerns the undesirable product consequences that consumers try to avoid when buying and using products. Several types of negative consequences might occur. Some consumers worry about the *physical risks* of product consumption (side effects of a cold remedy, injury on a bicycle, electric shock from a hair dryer). Other types of unpleasant consequences include *financial risk* (finding out the warranty doesn't cover fixing your microwave oven; buying new athletic shoes and finding them on sale the next day), *functional risk* (an aspirin product doesn't get rid of headaches very well; a motor oil additive doesn't really reduce engine wear), and *psychosocial risk* (my friends might think these sunglasses look weird on me; I won't feel confident in this suit). As with benefits, perceived risk includes consumers' cognitive knowledge about unfavourable consequences and the negative affective responses associated with them (unfavourable evaluations, bad feelings, and negative emotions).

The amount of perceived risk a consumer experiences is influenced by two things: (1) the degree of unpleasantness of the negative consequences and (2) the probability that these negative consequences will occur. In cases where consumers do not know about potential negative consequences (a side effect of a health remedy, a safety defect in a car), perceived risk will be low. In other cases, consumers have unrealistic perceptions of product risks because they overestimate the likelihood of negative physical consequences. Consumer Perspective 5.2 describes marketplace problems created by consumers' misperceptions of risk.

Because consumers are unlikely to purchase products with high perceived risk, marketers should manage consumers' perceptions of the negative consequences of product purchase and use. For example, a highly successful mail-order company tries to reduce consumers' perceptions of financial and performance risk by offering an unconditional money-back guarantee. A different marketing strategy is to intentionally activate knowledge about product risk to show how using a particular brand avoids the negative consequences. For instance, Federal Express continually employs an advertising theme intended to generate doubt and anxiety among businesspeople by pointing out the negative consequences of not using its services.

Consumers also have knowledge about the personal, symbolic values that products and brands help them to satisfy or achieve (see Exhibit 5.2). **Values** are people's broad life goals. ("I want to be successful." "I need security.") Values also involve the affect associated with such goals and needs (the feelings and emotions that accompany success). Recognising when a value has been satisfied or a basic life goal has been achieved is rather intangible and subjective. ("I feel secure." "I am respected by others." "Am I successful?") Functional and psychosocial consequences are more tangible, and it is more obvious when they occur. ("Other people noticed me when I wore that silk shirt.")

> **Products as value satisfiers**

There are many ways to classify values.[9] One useful scheme identifies two types or levels of values—instrumental and terminal. **Instrumental values** are preferred modes of conduct or *ways of behaving* (having a good time, acting independent, showing self-reliance). **Terminal values**, on the other hand, are preferred ultimate *states of being* or broad psychological states (happy, at peace, successful). For example, one might employ the instrumental value of being self-reliant to achieve the terminal value of peace of mind

---

CONSUMER PERSPECTIVE

5.2 ◄

Risk: perception versus reality

In 1990, analyses of Perrier water revealed minute amounts of benzene, a known carcinogen. Benzene is a natural ingredient in the carbon dioxide gas that bubbles up in the springs in France. The benzene usually was removed by filters, but they had not been changed frequently enough. The amount of benzene detected in Perrier was 19 parts per billion, a level that could not have been detected 15 years earlier. This example illuminates a problem in risk assessment. Our technologies for measuring tiny quantities of "harmful" compounds in products have outstripped our ability to make reasonable judgments about the degree of possible harm.

Was Perrier dangerous? That depends on your perceptions of and tolerance for very small risks. The actual risk of developing cancer from drinking Perrier was extremely small. One expert estimated the additional cancer risk from drinking one litre of the "contaminated" Perrier every day for 70 years as somewhere between 1 in 100,000 and 1 in 10 million. This means that if all Canadians drank one litre of Perrier every day of their lives, the additional number of cancer deaths might be 250 or so per year. Of course, virtually no one consumes that much mineral water. Yet in the emotional climate of 1990, Perrier thought it had to recall $40 million of essentially harmless product.

Source: Adapted from Warren T. Brookes, "The Wasteful Pursuit of Zero Risk," *Forbes*, April 30, 1990, pp. 161–72. Reprinted with permission of *Forbes* magazine. © Forbes Inc. 1990.

EXHIBIT 5.3

Instrumental and terminal values

Instrumental Values (Preferred Modes of Conduct)	Terminal Values (Preferred End States of Being)

Competence
  Ambitious (hardworking)
  Independent (self-reliant)
  Imaginative (creative)
  Capable (competent)
  Logical (rational)
  Courageous
	Social harmony
	  World at peace
	  Equality (brotherhood)
	  Freedom (independence)
	  National security
	  Salvation (eternal life)

Compassion
  Forgiving (pardon others)
  Helpful (work for others)
  Cheerful (joyful)
  Loving (affectionate)
	Personal gratification
	  Social recognition
	  Comfortable life
	  Pleasure (enjoyable life)
	  Sense of accomplishment

Sociality
  Polite (courteous)
  Obedient (dutiful)
  Clean (neat, tidy)
	Self-actualization
	  Beauty (nature and arts)
	  Wisdom (understanding)
	  Inner harmony (no conflict)
	  Self-respect (self-esteem)
	  Sense of accomplishment

Integrity
  Responsible (reliable)
  Honest (sincere)
  Self-controlled
	Security
	  Taking care of family
	  Salvation (eternal life)

	Love and affection
	  Mature love (sexual and spiritual intimacy)
	  True friendship (close companionship)

	Personal contentedness Happiness (contentment)

Source: The values are from Milton J. Rokeach, *The Nature of Human Values* (New York: Free Press, 1973). The underlined category labels for groupings of Rokeach's values are identified by Donald E. Vinson, J. Michael Munson, and Masao Nakanishi, "An Investigation of the Rokeach Value Survey for Consumer Research Applications," in *Advances in Consumer Research*, vol. 4, ed. W. D. Perreault (Atlanta, Ga.: Association for Consumer Research, 1977), pp. 247–52.

or independence. Instrumental and terminal values (goals or needs) represent the broadest and most personal consequences that people are trying to achieve in their lives. Exhibit 5.3 lists some of the instrumental and terminal values consumers hold.

Another perspective is that values that are a central aspect of people's self-concept—their knowledge about themselves—are called *core values*.[10] Because they have a major influence on cognitive processes and behaviours, these core values are of particular interest to marketers. Consumer Perspective 5.3 describes how the core value of protecting the environment has created new marketing opportunities.

Because they represent important, personally relevant consequences, values often are associated with strong affective responses. Satisfying a value usually elicits positive affect (happiness, joy, satisfaction), while blocking a value produces negative affect (frustration, anger, disappointment). For many people, buying their first car satisfies the values of independence and freedom and generates positive affective feelings of pride and satisfaction. On the other hand, your security value is blocked if your new bicycle lock is broken by a thief, which could create substantial negative affect (anger, frustration, fear).

In summary, consumers can have product knowledge about product attributes, consequences of product use, and personal values. Most marketing research focuses on the attribute level of product knowledge, but consequences are studied occasionally (usually benefits rather than risks). Values are examined less frequently. The problem is that studying only one type of knowledge gives marketers an incomplete understanding of consumers' product knowledge.

CONSUMER PERSPECTIVE

5.3

The greening of corporate Canada

Many Canadian companies are finding green pastures by responding to consumer demand for environmentally friendly products and production methods. It's paying off in increased sales and public relations as concern about global dangers to the environment grows steadily.

While most consumers are willing to pay a little extra to help clean up waste and pollution, they are also looking to our big companies for leadership in adopting a new philosophy, not only in business, but in our way of life. As Patrick Carson, vice president of environmental affairs for Loblaw International Inc. of Toronto says, "Businesses have to realise they can no longer divorce their balance sheets from nature's bottom line."

Many companies have already recognised this. They have invested billions of dollars in pollution abatement, new manufacturing techniques, recycling, and the reduction of hazardous waste.

The following is a sample of companies that have won the *Financial Post* Green Star awards for genuine corporate concern for the environment.

Loblaw Co., Toronto, Ontario: One year after the launch of its green program of environmentally and body-friendly consumer products, from phosphate-free fertilisers and detergents to beef that hasn't been treated with antibiotics or hormones, it sold more than $60 million worth of these products.

Mohawk Oil, Burnaby, British Columbia: The firm has developed the technology to reprocess used motor oil into high-quality base oil. Its plant can produce 30,000 metric tons a year of this refined oil. Mohawk is also researching cleaner-burning fuels such as ethanol made from grain, a renewable resource.

The Body Shop Canada, Toronto, Ontario: The company, which sells natural source skin and hair-care products, joined with the World Wildlife Fund to raise money to save tropical rainforests in Central and South America. To date the company has raised millions of dollars.

Dofasco Inc., Hamilton, Ontario: The company spent close to $20 million to develop and install chemical-based technology that cleans up the cleaning liquid used to remove sulphur from its coke oven gases. The company adapted the technology from the pulp and paper industry and is now marketing it to other steel companies around the world.

Shell Canada Ltd., Calgary, Alberta: The company has adopted sustainable development as the principle for running its business, integrating environmental concerns into economic decision-making. It was first to install ultrahigh-efficiency sulphur recovery technology. The technology can recover up to 99.8 percent of sulphur from petroleum and natural gas.

Source: Adapted from "The Greening of Corporate Canada," *Financial Post*, June 4, 1990, pp. 33–44. Johanna Powell, "Companies get their due for public service," *Financial Post*, Nov. 12/14, 1994, p. S15.

The three levels of product knowledge can be combined to form a simple associative network called a means-end chain. A **means-end chain** is a knowledge structure that connects consumers' meanings about product attributes, consequences, and values.[11]

MEANS-END CHAINS OF PRODUCT KNOWLEDGE

Attributes	→	Consequences	→	Values

The means-end perspective suggests that consumers define product attributes in personal, subjective terms: "What is this attribute good for?" or "What does this attribute do for me?" In other words, consumers see a product attribute as a means to some end, which could be a consequence or a value.[12]

Dividing each of the attribute, consequence, and value levels into two categories creates a more detailed means-end chain:[13]

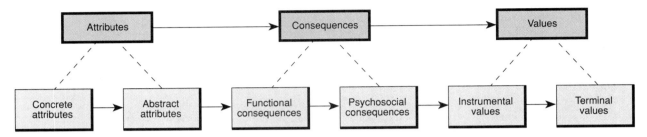

Exhibit 5.4 defines the six levels in the means-end chain and gives examples of each level. Some of the distinctions between levels can be a bit fuzzy. For instance, you might be uncertain whether "being with friends" is a psychosocial consequence or an instrumental value. For the most part, however, marketers don't have to worry about such issues when using the means-end chain model to develop marketing strategies. The main point of the model is that consumers create knowledge structures of linked meanings that connect tangible product attributes to more abstract attributes and consequences, which in turn are associated with more subjective, self-relevant values and goals.

The means-end chain model is based on the idea that the meaning of a product attribute is given by its consequences.[14] Consider the attributes Gillette designed into its popular Sensor razor—a spring suspension and a lubricating strip. These product attributes probably don't mean much to most consumers until they use the product or learn about its consequences from advertising or other consumers. Some consumers might form the means-end chains on page 83.

EXHIBIT 5.4

A means-end chain model of consumers' product knowledge

Level of meaning	Explanation	Example
Terminal values	Preferred end states of being, very abstract consequences of product use.	Self-esteem
Instrumental values	Preferred modes of conduct, abstract consequences of product use.	Being centre of attention
Psychosocial consequences	Psychological (How do I feel?) and social (How do others feel about me?) consequences of product use.	Others see me as special
Functional consequences	Immediate, tangible consequences of product use. What does the product do? What functions does it perform?	Handles easily
Abstract attributes	Product characteristic standing for several more concrete attributes. Subjective, not directly measurable or perceived.	Good quality
Concrete attributes	Knowledge about physical characteristic of product. Directly perceived.	Price

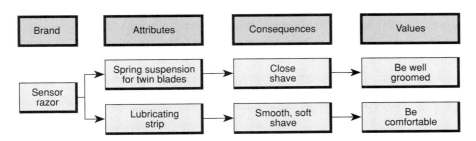

Exhibit 5.5 shows several means-end chains that represent one consumer's product knowledge for a product class (hair spray), a product form (flavoured potato chips), and a brand (Scope mouthwash). This exhibit illustrates *four important points* about means-end chains. *First*, actual means-end chains vary considerably in the number and types of meanings they contain. *Second*, not every means-end chain leads to an instrumental or terminal value. In fact, the end of a means-end chain can be any type of consequence, from a functional consequence (This toothpaste will give me fresh breath), to a psychosocial consequence (My friends will like being close to me), to an instrumental value (I will be clean), to a terminal value (I will be happy).

Third, some of the means-end chains in Exhibit 5.5 are incomplete, with missing levels of meaning. Actual means-end chains do not necessarily include all six levels of product knowledge. Two other points are not shown in Exhibit 5.5. Some product attributes can

Examples of means-end chains

EXHIBIT 5.5   Examples of means-end chains

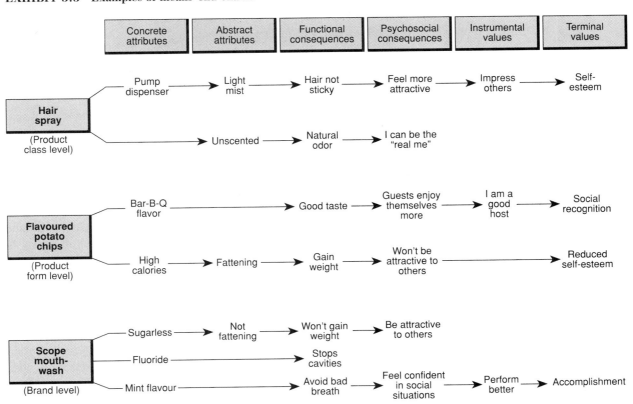

have more than one means-end chain. These multiple means-end chains may conflict if they lead to both positive and negative ends (benefits and perceived risks). For example, consider the positive and negative consequences sometimes associated with price for relatively expensive products such as a watch or television:

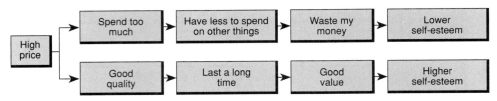

Fourth, because consumers create their own personally relevant knowledge structures, their means-end chains are unique. However, consumers in the same market segment often share enough meanings about a product that a marketer can identify a set of common meanings.

Measuring means-end chains

Measuring means-end chains is best accomplished with one-on-one, personal interviews where the researcher tries to understand a consumer's meanings for product attributes and consequences. The process involves two basic steps. First, the researcher must identify the product attributes that are most important to each consumer. One approach is to ask consumers what attributes are most relevant to them when they make decisions about a product. Another approach is for management to specify the attributes of greatest interest. Second, the researcher conducts a *laddering* interview by asking consumers a progression of questions in the format of "why is that important to you?"[15] Exhibit 5.6 shows a sample laddering interview. By describing why each prior response is important, consumers reveal the connections they make between product attributes, consequences, and values, which is their personal means-end chain.

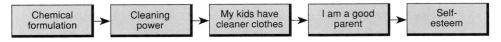

To summarise, the means-end chain provides a more complete understanding of consumers' product knowledge than methods that focus only on attributes or benefits.[16] For instance, consider the following means-end chain for Ultra Tide laundry detergent:

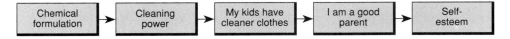

This hypothetical consumer interprets the chemical attributes of Ultra Tide in terms of the more abstract attribute, "cleaning power." Cleaning power, in turn, is seen as providing the functional benefit of "cleaner clothes for the kids," which is seen as helping to achieve the instrumental value of "being a good parent," which finally leads to the terminal value of "feeling good about myself" or "self-esteem."

By identifying the sequence of connections between product-related meanings, marketers can see more clearly what consumers are really communicating when they mention an attribute or a consequence such as "cleaning power." Means-end chain analyses also identify and help us understand the basic ends (values and goals) consumers are seeking when they buy and use certain products and brands. This gives insights into consumers' purchase motivations. Finally, means-end chains reflect the product/self relationship—that is, they show how consumers relate product attributes to important aspects of their

Researcher: "You said that a shoe's lacing pattern is important to you in deciding what brand to buy. Why is that?" **Consumer:** "A staggered lacing pattern makes the shoe fit more snugly on my foot." [physical attribute and functional consequence] **Researcher:** "Why is it important that the shoe fit more snugly on your foot?" **Consumer:** "Because it gives me better support." [functional consequence] **Researcher:** "Why is better support important to you?" **Consumer:** "So I can run without worrying about injury." [psychosocial consequence] **Researcher:** "Why is it important for you not to worry while running?" **Consumer:** "So I can relax and enjoy the run." [psychosocial consequence] **Researcher:** "Why is it important that you can relax and enjoy the run?" **Consumer:** "Because it gets rid of tension I have built up at work." [psychosocial consequence] **Researcher:** "Why is it important for you to get rid of tension from work?" **Consumer:** "So when I go back to work in the afternoon, I can perform better." [instrumental value: high performance] **Researcher:** "Why is it important that you perform better?" **Consumer:** "I feel better about myself." [terminal value: self-esteem] **Researcher:** "Why is it important that you feel better about yourself?" **Consumer:** "It just is!" [the end!]	**EXHIBIT 5.6** **An example of a laddering interview**

self-concepts. In sum, by providing a more complete understanding of consumers' product knowledge, means-end analysis helps marketers devise more effective advertising, pricing, distribution, and product strategies.

CONSUMERS' PRODUCT INVOLVEMENT

Why do consumers seem to care about some products and brands and not others? Why are some consumers highly motivated to seek information about products, or to buy and use products in certain situations, while other consumers seem to have no interest? Why did some Coke drinkers make such a big fuss when Coca-Cola managers made a minor change in an inexpensive, simple, and seemingly unimportant soft drink (see Consumer Perspective 5.4)? These questions concern consumers' involvement, an important concept for understanding consumer behaviour.[17]

Involvement is the perceived importance or personal relevance of an object or event.[18] Involvement with a product or brand has both cognitive and affective aspects.[19] Cognitively, consumers feel involved when knowledge about the relevance of a product is activated from memory. This knowledge includes means-end beliefs about important consequences or values produced by the product (This CD would be fun to play at parties). Involvement also includes affective states such as product and brand evaluations (I like "CBC Newsworld"). If product involvement is high, people may experience stronger affective responses, including emotions and strong feelings (I really love my Mazda).

Marketers often treat consumers' product involvement as either high or low, but involvement can vary from very low (little or no perceived relevance) to moderate (some perceived relevance) to high levels (great perceived relevance). The level of product involvement a consumer experiences during decision making is determined by the type of means-end knowledge activated in that situation.[20] Consumers who believe product attributes are strongly linked to important end goals or values will experience higher levels of involvement with the product. In contrast, consumers who believe the product attributes lead only to functional consequences or are only weakly linked to important values will experience lower levels of product involvement. Finally, consumers who believe the

In the spring of 1985, the Coca-Cola Company shocked consumers and other soft-drink manufacturers by announcing it was changing the 99-year-old formula for Coke. The "new" Coke was a bit sweeter, and marketing research showed it was preferred to Pepsi-Cola. The original Coke formula was to be retired to a bank vault and never again produced.

What happened then was the beginning of Coke's lesson in consumer involvement. Outraged consumers complained bitterly to the company about the loss of "a great American tradition." A group of strident loyalists calling themselves "Old Coke Drinkers of America" laid plans to file a class-action suit against Coca-Cola. They searched out shop owners, vending-machine owners, and others willing to claim that the company's formula change had cost them business. Then, when June sales didn't pick up as expected, the bottlers also joined in the demand for old Coke's return—and fast.

Although Coca-Cola had spent some $4 million testing the new formula, it had missed one important factor. Millions of consumers had a strong *emotional involvement* with the original Coke. They drank it as kids and still did as adults. Many consumers had a personal attachment to Coke. Says a Coke spokesperson, "We had taken away a little part of them and their past. They [consumers] said, 'You have no right to do that. Bring it back.'"

Coca-Cola had learned a costly lesson. Although consumers preferred the new taste in blind taste tests, Coca-Cola did not measure consumers' emotional reactions to removing the original Coke from the marketplace. Coca-Cola learned that a product is more than a production formula; extra meanings such as emotions and strong connections to self-image may also be present.

Source: Reprinted with permission from "Coke's Brand-Loyalty Lesson," by Anne B. Fisher, *Fortune*, © 1985 Time Inc. All rights reserved.

product attributes are not associated with any relevant consequences will experience little or no involvement with the product.

Involvement is a motivational state that energises and directs consumers' cognitive processes and behaviours as they make decisions. For instance, consumers who are involved with cameras are motivated to work harder at choosing which brand to buy. They may spend more time and effort shopping for cameras (visiting more stores, talking to more salespeople). They may interpret more product information in the environment (read more ads and brochures). And they may spend more time and effort in integrating this product information to evaluate brands and make a purchase choice. We suspect that in the typical purchase decision, most consumers experience low to moderate levels of involvement for most products and brands.[21]

Consumers do not continually experience feelings of involvement, even for important products such as a car, a home, or special hobby equipment. Rather, people feel involved with such products only on certain occasions, when knowledge about the personal relevance of products is activated. As circumstances change, that knowledge is no longer activated, and people's feelings of involvement fade (until another time).

Focus of involvement

Marketers are interested in understanding consumers' involvement with products and brands. But people also may be involved with other *physical objects* such as advertisements. During the 1990s, some people became involved with a series of ads for Taster's Choice coffee that portrayed flirtatious situations between a man and a woman. Consumers may also be involved with other *people* (friends, relatives, lovers, perhaps even

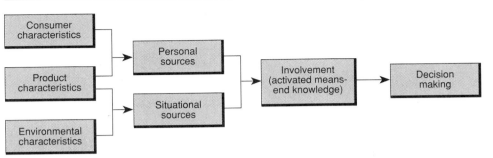

EXHIBIT 5.7

A model of consumer product involvement

Sources: Adapted from Richard L. Celsi and Jerry C. Olson, "The Role of Involvement in Attention and Comprehension Processes," *Journal of Consumer Research,* September 1988, pp. 210–24; Peter H. Bloch and Marsha L. Richins, "A Theoretical Model for the Study of Product Importance Perceptions," *Journal of Marketing,* Summer 1988, pp. 69–81.

salespeople). People can also become involved with certain *environments* (their home or backyard, amusement parks, a lake or the seashore). Some of these may be marketing environments—a clothing store the consumer especially likes, a shopping mall, or a favourite restaurant. People may be involved with specific *activities* or behaviours such as playing tennis, working, skating, or reading. Finally, some consumers become involved with marketing-related activities such as collecting coupons, shopping for new clothes, finding the cheapest price in town, or bargaining with vendors at flea markets.

Marketers need to understand the focus of consumers' involvement by identifying exactly what consumers consider personally relevant: a product or brand, an object, a behaviour, an event, a situation, an environment, or several of these together. In principle, marketers can analyse consumers' involvement with virtually anything, although our main focus here is on products and brands.

Factors influencing involvement

Exhibit 5.7 shows that a person's level of involvement is influenced by two sources, personal and situational.[22] Each source can activate or generate means-end chains that link product attributes to personally relevant consequences and values.

Personal sources of involvement refer to means-end knowledge stored in consumers' memories.[23] Consumers acquire this means-end knowledge through their past experiences with a product. As they use a product (or observe others using it), consumers learn that certain product attributes have relevant consequences that lead to important goals and values. For example, a consumer may learn that various attributes of a stereo system have favourable and unfavourable consequences ("digital readout—This will impress my friends," "remote control—I can be comfortable and relaxed," "programmability—This feature is too much trouble"). This means-end knowledge in memory is a potential source of involvement. To the extent that this knowledge is activated in a decision situation, the consumer will experience feelings of personal relevance or involvement.

Exhibit 5.7 shows the means-end knowledge stored in memory or personal sources of involvement are influenced by characteristics of both the consumer and the product. Consumer characteristics include people's values and life goals. Relevant product characteristics are the concrete and abstract product attributes that lead to important benefits and perceived risks (consumers tend to feel involved in decisions that might have negative consequences). Other product factors that may influence personal sources of involvement include social visibility (Do people know you own the product?) and time commitment (Buying a refrigerator is involving because you are committed to your choice for a long time).

Some people became involved with the long-running ad campaign for Taster's Choice.

SHARON: Hi
TONY: Hi.
SHARON: Was it something I said?
TONY: I came over last night
    . . . you had company.
SHARON: You mean my brother.
    He just loves my coffee.

TONY: Your brother.
ANNCR: Savor the sophisticated
    taste of Taster's Choice.
TONY: No just business.
SHARON: How long?
TONY: A month.
SHARON: That's long.

TONY: Hi.
SHARON: Don't tell me—you forgot
    to pack your Taster's Choice.
TONY: Listen, I though you should
    know I'm going to be in Paris.
SHARON: Paris. How romantic.
TONY: Well, it can be.

Situational sources of involvement are aspects of the immediate physical and social environment that activate important consequences and values and link them to product attributes, thus making products and brands seem self-relevant. For instance, a "50% Off" sign on fishing rods might activate self-relevant thoughts in a person interested in fishing (I can get a good deal on a new rod). Because many environmental factors change over time, situational sources often create temporary means-end links between a product and important consequences or values. These connections between the product and personal consequences may disappear when the situation changes. For example, the person's involvement with buying a fishing rod might last only as long as the sale continues.

Aspects of the social environment can be situational sources of involvement. For instance, shopping with others could make some consumers more self-conscious than when shopping alone (I want to impress my friends with my sense of style). A chance observation in the physical environment can be a situational source of involvement. For example, noticing a window display in a clothing store might activate knowledge about consequences and values that become associated with the clothing in the display (That sweater would be good for the party next week). More general aspects of the physical environment can also be situational sources of involvement. High temperatures on a summer day could activate desirable consequences (I need to take a break, cool off, or relax) that make buying an ice cream cone or going to an air-conditioned movie theatre relevant and involving.

Exhibit 5.7 shows that consumers' overall level of involvement is always determined by a combination of personal and situational sources. Although personal sources have the most influence on involvement in some cases, situational sources have a major influence in many circumstances. Consider the common situation when a consumer's personal source of involvement concerning a product is low (the product is not very important). For instance, many people do not consider water heaters very self-relevant. But if yours develops a leak, it becomes important to replace it quickly. The negative consequences of showering and washing in cold water are highly self-relevant. This means-end knowledge (which is activated only because your old heater broke) is a situational source of involvement with choosing and buying a new water heater. You are likely to feel this involvement and motivation only for the short time it takes to evaluate a few alternatives and make a purchase choice.

Marketers need to understand the *focus* of consumers' involvement and the *sources* that create it. Although most consumers are not personally involved with products such as water heaters, they can become temporarily involved with the process of buying the product. Having to replace a broken water heater (a situational source of involvement) makes people think about particular consequences of *purchase* (paying money, taking time and effort to shop, creating stress and hassle) that are important to them. The purchase situation also might activate product knowledge that is important during decision making (purchase price, speed of delivery, ease of installation) but is not relevant later when the product is being used. Involvement declines after the purchase, because most of the involvement consumers experienced concerned the decision process, not the product itself.

This is not an isolated example. Situational sources always combine with consumers' intrinsic or personal sources to create the level of involvement consumers actually experience during decision making. So consumers usually experience some level of involvement when making purchase choices, even for relatively unimportant products. Even though personal sources of involvement are low for many everyday consumer products (soap, bread, socks), situational sources are likely to influence the level of involvement consumers feel. This suggests marketers can influence consumers' product involvement by manipulating aspects of the environment that might function as situational sources of involvement.

MARKETING IMPLICATIONS

A means-end approach to product knowledge and involvement is useful for understanding the critical consumer/product relationship and developing effective marketing strategies. Marketers need a deep understanding of the cognitive and affective factors underlying purchase decisions. They need to develop marketing strategies that will connect their products and services to consumers' goals and values and influence consumers' product involvement.

Understanding the key reasons for purchase

Marketers can use means-end chain analyses to identify the key attributes and consequences underlying a consumer's product purchase decision. Restaurant choices are a good example. Unlike the people in cultures like France, many Canadians do not feel highly involved with food. Fast-food industry research suggests the three major factors in a decision on where to eat are: (1) time of day, (2) how long the customer wants to spend eating, and (3) price.[24] According to one expert, "We used to eat when the food was ready. Now we eat when we are ready." Speed and convenience are critical consequences, not the food itself.

Toronto-based Harvey's is a chain of 263 restaurants that has developed marketing strategies to provide these desired consequences. The typical Harvey's is small enough to be placed anywhere. A Harvey's can be built for significantly less than the $1 million the average McDonald's costs. Harvey's offers limited seating; food is ordered at walk-up or drive-through windows. The drive-in line at Harvey's restaurant moves relatively fast. The company has carved out its niche in the marketplace with the slogans "You can have it your way" and "Harvey's makes a hamburger a beautiful thing." You will typically pay about $5.00 for a cheeseburger, french fries, and a large Coke, which is less than the nearby McDonald's charges. Nutrition is not a big issue. As one Harvey's customer claims,

"The food isn't the most nutritious here, but it's cheap, really quick and easy—and it tastes OK too!" Harvey's understanding of what attributes and consequences its loyal customers really want led to muscling its way into the No. 2 spot in sales in 1992, ahead of A&W Food Services of Canada, Burger King, and Wendy's.

Understanding the consumer/product relationship

One of the most important concepts in marketing concerns consumers' relationships with products and brands.[25] A good example is the relationships many Canadians have with hockey, described in Consumer Perspective 5.5. Marketers need to understand the cognitive and affective aspects of these consumer/product relationships. For instance, teenagers may link the general attributes of cars to important self-relevant consequences (self-respect, admiration of peers, freedom). A key task of marketing management is to manage this important customer/product relationship.[26] Marketing strategies should be designed to create and maintain meaningful consumer/product relationships and to modify relationships that are not optimal.

There are innumerable examples of the importance of the consumer/product relationship. Consider the huge market for athletic shoes. Canadians spent $600 million in 1990 on brand-name athletic shoes. In 1991, Nike was the worldwide leader in the athletic

CONSUMER PERSPECTIVE

▶ **5.5**

Consumers' relationships with hockey

Hockey is part sport and recreation, part entertainment, part business, but in Canada hockey is also part community builder, social connector, and fantasy maker. It is played in every part of every province and territory in the country.

Many Canadians feel highly involved with the game of hockey. In fact, a careful look at this relationship reveals a lot about life in Canada. Today, hockey is square in the mainstream of Canadian life. It has taken on life's purposes and ambitions; it suffers life's conflicts and temptations, its weaknesses and abuses. Hockey *is* Canada's game. It may also be Canada's national theatre. On its frozen stage, each night the stuff of life is played out: ambition, hope, pride and fear, love and friendship, the fight for honour for the city, team, each other, oneself. It is a place where the monumental themes of Canadian life are played out: English and French, East and West, Canada and the United States, Canada and the world, the timeless tensions of commerce and culture, our struggle to survive and civilise winter.

But why does this game matter so much to Canadians? Because communities matter. Kids matter. Kids and parents and common experiences, common memories; myths and legends; common imaginations; stories that tell us about how we were, how we are, how we might be. Links, bonds, connections, things in common, things to share. And that is why hockey matters to Canadians.

To highlight the incredible relationship Canadians have with hockey, during the 1994–95 hockey strike/lockout, many sports fans called radio sports talk programs to say they didn't know how they would get through the season without their team. Radio programmes in Vancouver (Canucks), Calgary (Flames), Edmonton (Oilers), Toronto (Maple Leafs), Montreal (Canadiens) and Quebec (Nordiques) all reported great caller interest in talking about the strike, much more than the interest level that is normally associated with the (generally uninteresting) first half of the hockey season.

Hockey is simply a part of life in Canada. Thousands play it, millions follow it, and millions more surely try their best to ignore it altogether. But if they do, their disregard must be purposeful, for hockey's evidences are everywhere—on television and radio, in newspapers, in playgrounds and offices, on the streets, in sights and sounds, in the feeling of the season.

Source: Adapted from Ken Dryden and Roy MacGregor, *Home Game: Hockey and Life in Canada*, Toronto: McClelland and Stewart, 1989.

shoe market with sales of $2.2 billion. It was the leading brand in both the United States and Canada.[27] Nike's revenues soared during the past decade, partly because of the re-lationships marketing strategies created between fashion-conscious youth and the Nike brand. Muggings and even murders have been blamed on kids' desire for a trendy pair of athletic shoes or a jacket—a tragic manifestation of the consumer/product relationship.

If marketers can understand the consumer/product relationship, they may be able to segment consumers in terms of their personal sources of involvement. For instance, some consumers may have positive means-end knowledge about a product category, while oth-ers may have favourable beliefs and feelings for a brand. Still other consumers may have favourable means-end knowledge about both the product category and a brand. Con-sumer Perspective 5.6 shows the varying levels of brand loyalty in different product categories.

We can identify four segments with different personal sources of involvement for the product category and brand.[28] Those with the strongest feelings are brand loyalists and routine brand buyers.

▷ *Brand loyalists* have strong affective ties to one favourite brand they regularly buy. They also perceive the product category in general to provide personally relevant consequences. Their positive means-end knowledge about both the brand and the product category leads them to experience high levels of involve-ment during decision making. They strive to buy "the best brand" for their needs. For instance, consumers often have strong brand loyalty for sports equipment such as tennis racquets or athletic shoes.

▷ *Routine brand buyers* have low personal sources of involvement for the product category, but they do have a favourite brand they buy regularly (little brand switching). For the most part, their personal sources of involvement with a brand are not based on knowledge about the means-end consequences of product attributes. Instead, these consumers are interested in other types of conse-quences associated with regular brand purchase (It's easier to buy Colgate each time I need toothpaste). These beliefs can lead to consistent purchase, but these consumers are not so interested in getting the "best" brand; a satisfactory one will do.

Consumers who are highly involved with a brand tend to be brand loyal.

CONSUMER PERSPECTIVE

▶ **5.6**

Consumers' relationships with brands

Of the various types of relationships consumers can have with products and brands, brand loyalty is a highly desirable goal for most marketers. Although brand loyalty seems to have eroded considerably over the past 30 years because of increased brand competition and extensive sales promotions (coupons and price reductions), it is not dead. A survey of some 2,000 customers found wide variations in brand loyalty across product classes.

Faithful or Fickle?
Percentage of users of these products who are loyal to one brand

Product	Percentage
Cigarettes	71%
Mayonnaise	65%
Toothpaste	61%
Coffee	58%
Headache remedy	56%
Film	56%
Bath soap	53%
Ketchup	51%
Laundry detergent	48%
Beer	48%
Automobile	47%
Perfume/aftershave	46%
Pet food	45%
Shampoo	44%
Soft drink	44%
Tuna fish	44%
Gasoline	39%
Underwear	36%
Television	35%
Tires	33%
Blue jeans	33%
Batteries	29%
Athletic shoes	27%
Canned vegetables	25%
Garbage bags	23%

Source: Reprinted by permission of *The Wall Street Journal*, © 1989 Dow Jones & Company, Inc. All Rights Reserved Worldwide.

The other two segments have weaker personal sources of brand involvement. Information seekers and brand switchers do not have especially positive means-end knowledge about a single favourite brand.

▷ *Information seekers* have positive means-end knowledge about the product category, but no particular brand stands out as superior (You may be "into" skis, but know that many ski brands are good choices). These consumers use a lot of information to help them find a "good" brand. Over time, they tend to buy a variety of brands in the product category.

▷ *Brand switchers* have low personal sources of involvement for both the brand and the product category. They do not see that either the brand or the product category provides important consequences and have no interest in buying "the best." Such consumers tend to respond to environmental factors such as price deals or other short-term promotions that act as situational sources of involvement.

In sum, different marketing strategies are necessary to address the unique types of product knowledge and involvement of these four segments.

If marketers understand the means-end knowledge that makes up consumers' personal sources of involvement, they can design product attributes that consumers will connect to important consequences and values.[29] A good example is Chrysler's design of the mini-van (mentioned at the beginning of the chapter). Marketers can also try to strengthen consumers' personal sources of involvement with a given brand. Mazda once asked owners of Mazda cars to send in pictures of themselves with their cars, and some of these pictures were included in national magazine ads. This promotion may have enhanced the personal relevance of Mazda cars for their owners.

Influencing personal sources of involvement

In the short run, it is difficult to modify consumers' personal sources of involvement for a product or brand. Over longer periods, though, consumers' means-end knowledge can be influenced by various marketing strategies, including advertising.[30] The outcome of this process is not completely predictable, because many factors besides marketing strategy can modify consumers' means-end knowledge. For instance, the direct experience of using a product or brand can have a strong impact on means-end knowledge. If the actual product experience doesn't measure up to the image created by advertising, consumers are not likely to form the desired means-end meanings.

Marketers use many strategies to create, modify, or maintain consumers' situational sources of involvement, usually with the goal of encouraging purchase. Semi-annual clearance sales on summer or winter clothing are situational factors that may temporarily raise consumers' involvement with buying such products. Likewise, premiums such as stickers or small toys in cereal boxes or candy packages may temporarily increase children's involvement with a brand. Special pricing strategies, including rebates on new car models ("Get $1,000 back if you buy in the next two weeks"), may function as situational influences that create a temporary increase in involvement with buying the product.

Influencing situational sources of involvement

Another situational source of involvement is to link a product to a social cause.[31] For instance, in Quebec, IGA, Metro, and Provigo (the three largest grocery stores) collaborated with Centraide to offer coupons whose proceeds benefit all charities in Canada. These stores reaped lots of publicity and some new customers. Johnson & Johnson has promoted Shelter Aid, a program that makes donations to shelters for battered women. Finally, Esso has promoted the development of hockey programs for years and sponsors the Esso Medals of Achievement in almost every city in Canada where there is organised amateur hockey.

Learning objective 1: *List the four categories of product knowledge and give examples.*

▶ **SUMMARY**

Consumers can have knowledge about a product class or product category (cameras, TV, cars); various forms of a product (35mm SLR cameras, automatic 35mm cameras, disposable cameras); brands (Nikon, Canon, Olympus, Konika); and models (Olympus Infinity with a zoom lens, Olympus Infinity with a fixed lens).

Learning objective 2: *Give examples of concrete and abstract attributes, functional and psychosocial consequences, and instrumental and terminal values.*
Consumers can have knowledge about the attributes of products, the consequences of product use, and the values that products can satisfy. Concrete attributes are physical characteristics of products that are tangible and can be perceived directly (the type of fabric covering a chair; the amount of padding in the chair). Abstract attributes refer to more intangible product characteristics that cannot be perceived directly (the comfort of a chair; the quality of a pizza). Consequences are the specific outcomes that occur when a product is purchased and used. Functional consequences refer to the relatively immediate and tangible outcomes concerning product performance (the support a chair gives your back; the rich taste of ice cream; the sharpness of a photograph). Psychosocial consequences refer to less tangible and more personal outcomes (feeling relaxed in a chair; feeling proud when driving your car; fearing other people think your new shoes look ridiculous). Values are very intangible and subjective consequences, goals, or ends that consumers are trying to achieve in their lives. Instrumental values are preferred modes of behaviour (being comfortable; being the centre of attention; acting knowledgeable). Terminal values are desirable end states of being (happiness, achievement, security).

Learning objective 3: *Define benefits and risks.*
Benefits are the desirable functional and psychosocial consequences that people seek when buying and using products and brands. (I want a bike that can handle city potholes; I want a suit that makes me feel confident in myself.) Perceived risks are the undesirable functional and psychosocial consequences that consumers want to avoid when buying and using products and brands. (I don't want to spend too much money for this belt; I don't want people to laugh at me behind my back.) When making purchase decisions, consumers may have to make trade-offs between the benefit and risk consequences of a purchase.

Learning objective 4: *Describe a means-end chain and give an example.*
Means-end chains are simple knowledge structures that link product attributes to their consequences for the consumer. These consequences, in turn, may be linked to values (which actually are very abstract consequences). For example, the special tread design on an automobile tire (a concrete product attribute) might be seen as providing "good traction in the snow" (a functional consequence), which in turn helps to satisfy the terminal value, "keep my family safe." The links among attributes, consequences, and values are based on meaningful relationships as perceived by the consumer (not the marketer). Essentially, a means-end chain answers the consumer's basic question, "What does this product or brand do for me (mean to me; give me)?" The means-end chain perspective recognises that consumers tend to see a product attribute as a means to a desirable end.

Learning objective 5: *Discuss two marketing implications of means-end chains.*
Means-end chains can provide marketers with a detailed understanding of consumers' product knowledge (and also their knowledge about services, stores, and behaviours). By showing how concepts are related to each other, means-end chains reveal the meanings of an attribute or a consequence (from the consumer's perspective). Means-end chains reveal what end values, if any, consumers associate with a product. Means-end chains also reflect the important product/self relationship. To develop effective marketing strategies, marketers need to understand how consumers perceive the product and service offered. Understanding consumers' means-end knowledge is a help in designing marketing strategies such as what attributes to add to a product, what product benefits to emphasise in advertising, or how to reduce the product's perceived risks.

Learning objective 6: *Define involvement and describe how personal and situational sources influence involvement.*

Involvement refers to consumers' perceptions of personal relevance or feelings of interest and importance for an object, activity, or situation. Product involvement is experienced by consumers as cognitions about product consequences and related affective feelings. Involvement influences consumers' motivation to interpret information and integrate knowledge in decision making, as well as their overt behaviour, such as searching for product information in stores. Involvement is influenced by personal and situational sources. Personal sources concern consumers' means-end knowledge about how a product (or some other concept) is related to important end values in their lives. For instance, a sophisticated 35mm camera might be highly involving because it helps satisfy important values of accomplishment. Situational sources are aspects of the environment that create temporary associations between some behaviour or product attribute and consumers' valued ends. For instance, a half-off sale on camera equipment might be a situational source that increases consumers' involvement with buying a new camera.

Learning objective 7: *Give examples of marketing strategies that can influence personal and situational sources of involvement.*

Typically, consumers form personal sources of involvement over long periods of experience with a product. Marketing strategies can reinforce these means-end associations and encourage the development of new links. During the 1980s, Nike used extensive advertising to generate high levels of involvement for its basketball shoes among young males. Many marketing strategies are attempts to create situational sources of involvement. Price deals (two for the price of one), contests and sweepstakes (enter for a chance to win $1,000), and "cause marketing" (buy one and we will donate 25 cents to a charity) may be situational sources that create a level of involvement with buying or trying a product or brand.

▶ **KEY TERMS AND CONCEPTS**

concrete attributes

abstract attributes

functional consequences

psychosocial
  consequences

benefits

perceived risk

values

instrumental values

terminal values

means-end chain

involvement

personal sources of
  involvement

situational sources of
  involvement

▶ **REVIEW AND DISCUSSION QUESTIONS**

1. Select a product category and identify examples of product forms, brands, and models. Give examples of the attributes, consequences, and values associated with each of these categories.

2. Analyse the possible meanings of mouthwash or deodorant in terms of positive (perceived benefits) and negative (perceived risks) consequences of use. Why are both types of meanings important?

3. Describe the fundamental assumptions underlying means-end chains. Give examples of how marketing managers can use means-end chains.

4. Define the concept of involvement and illustrate it by discussing products that, for you, would be very low, moderate, and high in involvement.

5. Using the purchase of a personal cassette player as an example, describe how personal and situational sources combine to influence a consumer's involvement with the purchase.

6. Do you agree that the personal sources of involvement for most products are low to moderate for most consumers? Why or why not?

7. Using the concept of means-end chains, discuss why different people might shop for athletic shoes at department stores, specialty athletic footwear shops, and discount stores. Why might the same consumer shop at all these stores on different occasions?

8. Discuss how a marketer of casual clothing for men and women can use consumers' product knowledge (means-end chains) and involvement to understand the consumer/product relationship. What can this marketer do to influence consumers' personal sources of involvement with the product?

9. Identify three ways marketers can influence consumers' situational self-relevance and discuss how this will affect consumers' overall level of involvement. For what types of products are these strategies most suitable?

CHAPTER 6

Exposure, Attention, and Comprehension

LEARNING OBJECTIVES

After completing this chapter, you should be able to:

► 1. Describe the differences between accidental and intentional exposure.

► 2. Define selective exposure and give an example of how marketers can influence consumers' selective exposure to marketing information.

► 3. Define attention and identify three factors that influence customers' attention to marketing information.

► 4. Define comprehension and describe four ways comprehension can vary.

► 5. Define inferences and give an example.

► 6. Describe how consumers' knowledge (expertise) influences their comprehension of marketing information.

► 7. Describe how comprehension processes can influence consumers' ability to recall marketing information.

TV VIEWERS EXPOSED

Researchers have been trying to measure viewer exposure and attention to TV commercials since the inception of television in the 1950s. A. C. Nielsen Co. began measuring local Canadian viewer exposure in 1950. It still uses paper diaries to produce the Nielsen Broadcast Index (NBI), a viewership report that divides Canada into 42 separate designated market areas (DMAs). Diaries are sent out to the panel and returned by mail. The data are then cleaned up and interpreted. This is a slow process with a four- to six-week time delay.

This procedure has other obvious problems. Filling out diaries describing the TV viewing behaviour of an entire family is very difficult. Most Canadian households receive multiple TV channels via cable and have more than one TV set. If the diaries are not completed immediately, it is almost impossible to remember which family member was watching which programme and when.

To respond to this problem, Nielsen, in conjunction with Arbitron, developed the Network People Meter Service (NTI), which provides daily information 36 hours later. Launched in 1989, its panel consists of 1,500 Canadian households representative of the country by region, cable status, the presence of children under 18, age of head of household, and language. Personal interviews are also conducted to gather information on the type of cars driven, family pets, household income, the primary grocery shopper and ownership of goods such as microwaves and CD players. A remote control device has eight buttons that signal a small monitor box wired to the set. Each family member is assigned a number to push each time he or she starts and stops watching television. The viewing records are stored in a microcomputer and transmitted over telephone lines to Nielsen's main computers. While this technology is excellent for determining who is turning on and off sets and when, it still cannot measure the extent to which someone is actually watching or, more importantly, paying attention.

Nielsen has entered into a joint venture with Compusearch Market and Social Research to develop the Television Spending Index, which links television ratings and viewership with Compusearch's lifestyle data and with Statistics Canada information. The index allows users to look at consumer lifestyles by neighbourhood and to match up television viewing.

In 1993, the Bureau of Broadcast Measurement (BBM) concluded that viewing should be measured using portable TV meters, since individuals do not watch all of their programmes on their own sets at home (for example, sports bars, such as La Cage Aux Sports, have steadily increased in popularity). In conjunction with Arbitron, the company will launch a special personal portable meter that will record TV and radio tuning by picking up inaudible codes broadcasters will embed in programming soundtracks.

All of these technologies are not without problems. Nevertheless, TV advertisers will continue to search for the ultimate measure of who's watching what, given the $1 million a minute it will cost to purchase a 30-second commercial on next year's Super Bowl.[1]

Consumers' everyday environments contain a great deal of information, much of it created by marketing strategies such as TV commercials. Marketers need to understand how consumers are exposed to marketing information, whether they pay attention to the information, and how they comprehend it. The opening example illustrates the effort and difficulty in measuring exposure and attention to and comprehension of TV programmes and commercials, given multiple-TV households, the proliferation of channels, and remote controls that make changing channels easy.

In this chapter, we consider the interpretation process shown in Exhibit 6.1. Interpretation is a key cognitive process in the general model of consumer decision making. We begin by examining how consumers become exposed to marketing information. Then we discuss attention processes by which consumers focus the cognitive system on certain types of information. Finally, we examine the comprehension processes by which consumers understand the meanings of this information and store that knowledge in memory. We emphasise the effects of existing knowledge, meanings, and beliefs in memory on attention and comprehension. Understanding these aspects of interpretation has implications for developing more effective marketing strategies.

EXHIBIT 6.1

The interpretation process

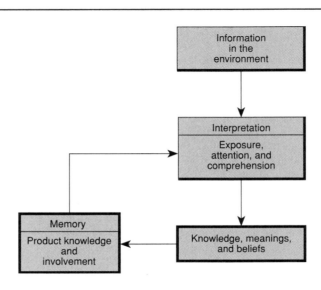

Exposure, defined as contact with information, is the first stage of interpretation. Consumers are continually exposed to information in their environments, including marketing information. Their exposure to marketing information can be accidental or intentional.

Intentional exposure to marketing information occurs when consumers purposefully search for information relevant to a goal or problem they have. Before buying a camera, for instance, a consumer might read product evaluations of 35mm cameras in *Consumer Reports* or photography magazines. Or a consumer might ask a friend or salesperson for their opinion on which brand of earphones to buy for a Walkman radio. Most investigations of consumer search behaviour indicate relatively little intentional exposure to marketing information.[2] For many purchases, buyers visit few stores (often only one) and consult few salespeople or other sources of information. Most consumers already have substantial product-related knowledge stored in memory. If they feel confident in their existing knowledge, or if they feel little involvement with a purchase, consumers have little need or motivation to search for more information. We discuss search behaviour more fully in Chapter 8, in the context of consumer decision making.

Most exposures to marketing information are not the result of consumers' intentional search behaviour, but happen by chance. **Accidental exposure** occurs when consumers unexpectedly encounter marketing information in their environments. The consumer-oriented environments of most industrialised countries offer many opportunities for accidental exposure to marketing information. We see advertisements in magazines and newspapers, on radio and TV, in direct-mail brochures, and on bus placards and bus-stop shelters. The sheer amount of promotion in Canada is increasing. Signs promoting products, services, and retail stores are found everywhere, and nearly all exposures are accidental. Stores provide a great deal of marketing information, including signs, point-of-purchase displays, product demonstrations, and brochures, in addition to the information on packages. While the total amount of promotion is increasing, there is no doubt that the mix of promotional expenditures is shifting from major media advertising (22 percent of Canadian marketing budgets in 1993) to consumer promotions (17 percent) and trade promotion (61 percent).[3]

Although some exposures to this information are due to intentional search, many exposures occur accidentally as consumers browse in the retail environments.[4] Some retailers design store environments to maximise the amount of time consumers spend browsing, which increases the likelihood they will be exposed to products and make a purchase. Finally, many exposures to product information in the social environment occur by chance in casual conversations with friends and relatives, salespeople, or even strangers.

Television viewing is a prime example of accidental exposure. Few consumers watch TV to seek information about products and services, yet they are exposed to plenty of commercials during an evening. Such accidental exposure to product information can have powerful effects on behaviour. During the Gulf War in early 1991, news viewership skyrocketed to twice previous levels (up to 20 times higher in some time periods).[5] Companies that advertised on networks such as CBC Newsworld and CNN enjoyed higher levels of accidental exposure to their commercials and big increases in sales.

As the amount of marketing information in the environment increases, consumers become more adept at avoiding exposure. Some consumers avoid reading product brochures or talking to salespeople. Others throw all junk mail away unopened. Consider the problems with exposure to TV commercials. People can leave the room as soon as the ads come on or quickly switch to another channel. One simple observation study of family members watching network TV indicated only 47 percent of viewers watched all or almost

EXPOSURE TO INFORMATION

Selective exposure

all of the ads, while about 10 percent left the room. Thanks to remote controls, viewers can easily turn off the sound or switch to another channel during a commercial break. Consumers with VCRs can fast-forward past commercials in programs they have taped. These practices are known as channel-surfing, *zapping*, and *zipping*.[6] In homes with remote controls, conservative estimates suggest 10 percent of viewers zap the average commercial. About one fifth of households include heavy zappers, who switch channels every two minutes. Advertisers paying media rates based on a full audience of viewers ($100,000 to more than $300,000 for 30 seconds of prime time) worry about getting their money's worth. One strategy to combat zapping is to develop commercials that are so interesting people want to watch them. Pepsi created extravagant ads featuring Michael Jackson that were zapped by only 1 to 2 percent of the audience.[7]

Marketing implications

Because exposure to marketing information is crucial to interpretation and to the success of marketing strategies, marketers need to develop strategies to increase the probability consumers will be exposed to product information. There are three ways to do this: facilitate intentional exposure, maximise accidental exposure, and maintain exposure once begun.

Marketers can *facilitate intentional exposure* by making appropriate marketing information available when and where consumers are searching for information. This requires that marketers anticipate consumers' needs for product information. IBM trains its retail salespeople to answer technical questions on the spot so consumers don't have to wait while the salesperson looks up the answer. Elaborate product brochures describing the various brands and models are available in most car showrooms and audio-equipment stores. Home Depot and Reno-Depot provide numerous in-store seminars on such home building projects as how to build a masonry wall or install a screen door.

Marketing information should be placed in locations that will *maximise accidental exposure*. For instance, when people park their cars, they see the parking meter for about 14 seconds as they find and deposit the right change.[8] This is plenty of time to be exposed to an ad. Media planners must carefully select a mix of media (magazines, billboards, radio, and TV) that increases the chances the target segment of consumers will be exposed to the ads.

Companies also attempt to increase accidental exposure by placing ads in taxicabs, in sports stadiums, and on boats, buses, and blimps. Another strategy is to put four-colour ads on grocery-store shopping carts.[9] A big advantage of shopping-cart ads is their low cost—only 50 cents per 1,000 exposures, compared to $10 to $20 per 1,000 exposures for network television. Advocates also claim this "reminder advertising" reaches consumers at the critical point when they make their purchase choices (an estimated 65 to 80 percent of brand buying decisions occur in the supermarket). Consumer Perspective 6.1 describes another way to expose consumers to marketing information in the grocery store.

Certain types of retail outlets such as convenience stores, ice-cream shops, and fast-food restaurants should be placed in locations such as malls and busy intersections where the target group of consumers receives high levels of accidental exposure.[10] Consider A. L. Van Houte, Timothy's, or the Second Cup. All are gourmet coffee shops selling freshly ground coffee and fresh-baked French bread, muffins, and croissants. Using a saturation distribution strategy, Van Houte packed more than 50 stores into the Montreal area, with more than half of the stores located in the downtown area (there are a dozen cafés on St. Catherine and De Maisonneuve streets alone). Besides being highly convenient for regular customers, this saturation strategy maximises the chances of accidental exposure. The thousands of busy Montrealers can hardly avoid walking by an A. L. Van Houte café. Consumer awareness levels in the city are high, although the company has

After a long day at work, Lisa stops at the supermarket to pick up dinner. As she wheels the grocery cart down the coffee aisle, an ad for Nescafé coffee flashes on the screen attached to her cart's handle. Seeing the ad reminds Lisa that she needs coffee, and she drops a can of Nescafé into her cart. Next, she notices on the screen that a coupon for 50 cents off Lipton's Noodles & Sauce is available at the touch of a button. Provided Lisa buys the product, the 50 cents will be automatically deducted when she arrives at the checkout where all purchases are scanned. In the next aisle, VideOcart's "Aisle Features" alerts Lisa that Sealtest ice cream is available at a reduced price.

It's a marketer's dream to promote items right at the point where consumers make that purchase decision. In April 1988, VideOcart, Inc., unveiled a prototype of the VideOcart, a standard grocery cart outfitted with a flat 6- by 8-inch liquid crystal display mounted on the cart handle. The animated graphics displayed on the screen are created and stored on a personal computer. Once the weekly "show" is finalised, it is sent to each VideOcart store via high-speed network communications and then transferred to the carts via a low-power FM transmitter. VideOcart can customise and change informative messages by market, chain, or individual store at a moment's notice.

Infrared sensor devices mounted in the ceiling cause these messages to be displayed at the precise moment shoppers pass the products being referenced. The system also can convey other useful information such as an item locator, store map, recipes, and CBC or CTV news, entertainment, and sports features as customers arrive at the checkout.

The average supermarket has roughly 100 shopping carts, and in stores using VideOcart, approximately 60 percent of the carts are equipped with the VideOcart unit. While few stores in Canada have opted for this technology, its use will probably increase with the growth in super retailers.

Test results suggest that VideOcart is a very powerful marketing tool. On average, shoppers pushing VideOcarts spend about $1 more per visit than shoppers using regular carts.

Source: VideOcart, Inc., 1993.

never advertised. According to a local marketing professor, "The stores themselves are a substitute for ads." So are the customers carrying the plastic coffee mugs and paper bags emblazoned with the A. L. Van Houte name and logo.

Another strategy to increase accidental exposure is to get a brand into movies or TV programmes.[11] Sometimes actors will use familiar brands—Coke or Pepsi cans are often seen in movies, as are certain brands of PC's (Compaq, Mac) and cars (Cadillac, Mercedes). Companies usually do not pay for such exposure, which is considered part of the new realism in television and film. In fact, it is illegal for marketers to pay to place a product on TV unless the payment is disclosed. However, products can be provided free to be used as props: a box of Quaker Oat Squares was seen on "Roseanne" and the announcers on NHL Hockey Night in Canada often wear Starter sports clothes. In other cases, marketers can hire companies that specialise in placing products in movies and on TV in hopes of "accidentally" exposing their brands to millions of viewers.

The process of maintaining exposure has probably been best exemplified by McDonald's. It is almost impossible for one day to go by where a consumer does not either hear, read or see some type of promotional exposure from this company.

ATTENTION TO INFORMATION

Attention involves focusing the cognitive system on information that is relevant to important goals and values.[12] Once consumers are exposed to marketing information, whether accidentally or through their own intentional behaviour, the interpretation processes of attention, and then comprehension, begin (see Exhibit 6.1). Marketers use many creative strategies to attract consumers' attention to their products and communications.

Attention implies *selection*. Because our cognitive systems have limited capacity, only a portion of information in the environment can be chosen for interpretation; in fact, most information is ignored. In a busy department store, people attend to information selectively—they tend to see and hear what helps them achieve their purchase goals and values. Thus, consumers in a Wal-Mart or Zellers store might notice signs directing them to a relevant product, grocery shoppers might read ingredients on the food label, and someone buying a car might consider a deal from a salesperson. At the same time, these consumers can disregard what other shoppers are doing or saying or even ignore product information that doesn't seem relevant at the moment. From a means-end perspective, consumers will selectively attend to information about product attributes and consequences that is perceived as relevant to their goals and values.

Attention varies in *awareness* and *intensity*—from automatic, essentially unconscious levels to controlled, intense levels.[13] In some cases, attention is uncontrolled and unconscious. For instance, you immediately turn your head when someone calls your name, or the word *free* might automatically attract your attention. Even though your attention may be at such a low level of intensity that you are not consciously aware of attending to information, it can still influence your behaviour (the bright lights in a jewellery store draw your attention to the products). At higher levels of intensity, people consciously focus their attention on marketing information that is relevant to their currently active goals and values. People who are thinking about buying a new bicycle are likely to selectively attend to bike ads, the dieter in a restaurant pays careful attention as the waiter recites the daily specials, a fan of a heavy metal band listens intently to a radio announcement about a concert.

Consumer reactions to the shopping-cart ads described in Consumer Perspective 6.1 provide some insight into these varying levels of attention. ActMedia, a dominant company in the cart ad business, claims cart ads increase sales of advertised brands by an average of 8 percent, but some research has found rather low levels of attention to the ads.[14] Interviews of shoppers in stores with the ad carts indicated only 60 percent of these consumers were aware of *ever* having seen any cart ads. The remaining 40 percent of shoppers who were exposed to the ads did not consciously attend to them. Only 13 percent of the shoppers interviewed were aware of seeing any ads on that particular shopping trip, and only 7 percent of the interviewed shoppers could name any brands advertised on the cart they were pushing. Apparently, only a few consumers paid enough attention to the ads to create a memory for the brand. Such results question the effectiveness of shopping-cart ads. Perhaps in the crowded information environment of the supermarket, most consumers do not pay attention to ads, even those on their grocery cart.

Factors influencing attention

Many factors can influence attention to marketing information, including the consumer's general affective state, the consumer's involvement with the information, and the prominence of the information in the environment. Marketers try to influence consumers' attention by developing strategies to address these factors.

Affective states

People's affective states influence their attention.[15] For instance, people in a good mood selectively attend to positive information in the environment, while people in a bad mood tend to notice negative information. Shopping when in a good mood stimulates the cognitive system to attend to favourable product attributes and benefits and positive reasons to buy, while shopping in a bad mood tends to focus attention on negative attributes and risky consequences and activate reasons not to purchase. A related issue is whether the affective responses created by a TV programme (happy, depressed, amused, sad) can influence consumers' attention to (and comprehension of) the commercials placed within that programme.[16]

Involvement

Involvement with marketing information is a motivational state that can influence selective attention and the intensity of attention.[17] Consumers who experience high levels of involvement because of an intense need (you desperately need new tires for your spring break trip) tend to focus their attention on marketing information (ads for tires) that seems relevant to their goals. A consumer's level of involvement with product information is determined by the activated means-end beliefs about the relationships between product attributes and relevant goals and values. This means-end knowledge is a function of personal and situational sources (refer back to Exhibit 5.7). Thus, hobby photographers for whom cameras are personally relevant are more likely to notice and attend to ads for photo products. Likewise, the involvement felt by consumers who need to replace a refrigerator influences them to notice and attend to ads and sales announcements.

Personal sources of involvement

In the short run, marketers have little ability to influence consumers' personal sources of involvement for a product. Therefore, the usual approach is to analyse and understand consumers' existing means-end knowledge about the relationships between product attributes and important goals and values. Basically, marketers must identify the goals and values consumers consider most self-relevant. A successful marketing strategy should activate these meanings and link them to product attributes. The involvement thus produced should motivate consumers to attend to this information, comprehend it, and possibly use it in making a purchase decision.

For instance, many marketers of antiperspirants emphasise qualities such as "stops odour" and "stops wetness"—ordinary functional consequences of using the product. The marketers of Sure deodorant, however, identified two more self-relevant and emotionally motivating consequences of using their product—social confidence and avoiding embarrassment. They communicated these psychological consequences in a long-running ad campaign, "Raise your hand if you're Sure," which showed coatless consumers in social situations raising their arms free of embarrassment due to damp spots on their clothing. The marketers of Vaseline Intensive Care lotion identified a similar consequence to invoke the key meaning of many consumers' perceived self-relevance with hand lotion. While brands such as Touch of Sweden discussed their greaseless formula, Vaseline marketers promoted skin restoration. They communicated the implied psychosocial consequence of "looking younger" in ads showing dried-up leaves before and after rejuvenation with Intensive Care lotion.[18]

Situational sources of involvement

All marketing strategies involve creating or modifying aspects of consumers' environments. Some of these environmental stimuli may act as situational sources of involvement by creating a temporary association between a product and important self-relevant consequences. Situational sources of relevance generate higher levels of involvement and motivation to attend to marketing information. Consider consumers who receive a brochure in the mail describing a $1 million sweepstakes contest sponsored by a magazine publisher. This marketing information might generate affective feelings of excitement and personal relevance with the details of the contest. The resulting involvement could motivate consumers to maintain exposure and focus their attention on the marketing offer for magazine subscriptions that accompanies the sweepstakes announcement.

Environmental prominence

The physical form of marketing information can influence consumers' attention. Because the most prominent information in the environment attracts the most attention, marketers often try to make their information noticeable. For instance, some radio and TV commercials are louder than the surrounding programme material to capture consumers' attention.[19] Many bakeries exhaust the fragrances of baking products onto sidewalks or into malls. Consumer Perspective 6.2 describes how large amounts of advertising can influence consumers' attention and brand awareness.

Marketing implications

Many marketing strategies attempt to increase consumers' involvement with marketing information by addressing personal or situational sources of involvement. Other strategies are designed to attract or maintain consumers' attention to marketing information by making the information more prominent in the environment.

Factors affecting environmental prominence

Marketers attempt to influence the prominence of their marketing information by designing bright, colourful, or unusual packages; by developing novel advertising executions; or by setting unique prices (a sale on small items, all priced at 88 cents). Because they must attract the attention of consumers hurrying by the newsstand, magazine covers often feature objects known to have high attention value—celebrities, babies, or dogs, or attractive, seductively clothed models (that old standby, sex).

Vivid images attract consumers' attention and help focus it on the product.[20] Nike, for instance, places powerful graphic portrayals of athletes (wearing Nike shoes, of course) on large billboards. Window displays in retail stores attract the attention (and subsequent interest) of consumers who happen to pass by. Ogilvy's (a famous Montreal department store) produces an extravagant window display every Christmas that always draws a huge crowd. The display has nothing to do with Ogilvy products; it is intended to attract the attention of shoppers during the busy Christmas season. Many stores use creative lighting to emphasise selected merchandise and thus attract and focus consumers' attention on their products. Mirrors are used in clothing shops and hair salons to focus consumers' attention on their appearance.

Novel or unusual stimuli that don't fit with the consumers' expectations can capture additional attention time to figure out what is happening. For instance, a British ad agency created a dramatic ad to attract attention to the staying qualities of an adhesive called Araldite. The agency attached a car to a billboard along a major road into London. The caption read, ''It also sticks handles to teapots.''

Even a novel placement of an ad on a page can influence consumers' attention. Sisley, a manufacturer and retailer of trendy clothing owned by Benetton, has run its print ads upside down on the back pages of magazines like *Elle* and *Outdoors*. Other marketers have experimented with ads placed sideways, in the centre of a page surrounded by editorial content, or spanning the top half of two adjacent pages.

Marketers must be careful in using novel and unusual stimuli over long periods, though, because prominence due to novelty tends to wear off. Also, novelty is a relative concept. Placing a black-and-white ad in a magazine where all the other ads are in colour will capture consumers' attention only as long as few other black-and-white ads are used.

What is Avia International, Ltd.?

    a. A small Italian commuter airline.

    b. An up-and-coming courier service.

    c. A map exporter specialising in exotic spots.

If you answered "none of the above," you may be among the 4 percent of people who know that Avia makes sneakers and sports apparel. According to a company vice president, Avia has a big problem: "There's a whole segment of people who are not buying our shoes because they don't know who we are." In contrast, Nike and Reebok are known by more than 70 percent of consumers.

The power of a well-known brand name, supported by strong advertising, is so great (and long lasting) that 20 of the top 25 leading brands in 1990 were also among the top 25 70 years ago. But with the clutter of new products, brands, and advertising in the environment, companies find it increasingly difficult to attract the customer's attention and create brand awareness. Today, approximately 90 percent of new products are pulled from the market within two or three years of their introduction. Most of them fail for lack of name recognition—consumers were just not aware of them.

The risks in creating a new brand are so great that many companies instead develop so-called line extensions. Rather than developing a new brand name, marketers apply their existing, well-known brand name to new products. Bud Light, Diet Coke, and Liquid Tide are but a few well-known examples.

Building name recognition can be difficult and expensive, especially for small companies. Market leaders often command budgets up to 10 times greater than smaller companies. For instance, Nike spends about $100 million and Reebok $70 million on annual advertising, compared to Avia's $10 million. Coca-Cola and Pepsi-Cola can afford to spend hundreds of millions on extensive advertising campaigns and still commit a small percentage of income. Coke typically spends only 4 to 5 percent of its total sales on advertising while smaller competitors may allocate upward of 40 percent of total revenues to advertising and promotion.

Small companies that cannot afford large advertising budgets have used creative marketing strategies to gain exposure for their brands and attract consumer attention. When Nevica, a British manufacturer of high-quality ski clothing, lacked advertising funds, it offered freelance photographers complimentary ski gear and a fee for every picture of a Nevica-clad skier published in a magazine. A lot of Nevica clothes were pictured, which increased brand awareness.

Sources: William M. Bulkeley, "It Needn't Always Cost a Bundle to Get Consumers to Notice Unknown Brands," *The Wall Street Journal*, Feb. 14, 1991, pp. B1, B4; and Joseph Pereira, "Name of the Game: Brand Awareness," *The Wall Street Journal*, Feb. 14, 1991, pp. B1, B4.

The strategy of trying to attract consumer attention by making stimuli more prominent sometimes backfires. When many marketers are trying very hard to gain attention at one time and place, consumers may tune most of the stimuli out. Consider the "miracle-mile strips" of fast-food restaurants, gas stations, and discount stores—each with a large sign—that line highways in many cities. Individually, each sign is large, bright, colourful, and vivid. Together, the signs produce clutter, and none is very prominent in the environment. Consumers find it easy to ignore individual signs, and their attention levels are likely to be low. Unfortunately, the typical marketing response is to put up even larger, more garish signs in hope of gaining slightly more environmental prominence. The clutter gets worse, consumer attention decreases further, and communities become outraged and pass ordinances limiting signs.

Vivid pictures and unusual images enhance environmental prominence and attract consumers' attention.

Just don't expect it to roar.

In an effort to become swifter and more ferocious, many organizations may be tempted to make superficial changes. But this approach will rarely improve performance. Especially when information technology is part of the plan. Which is why Andersen Consulting

works with companies to link technology to the heart of their business. Their strategies, operations and human resources. Because these days, becoming a more aggressive competitor often means transforming the organization. And not just hopping on a technological bandwagon.

ANDERSEN
CONSULTING
ARTHUR ANDERSEN & CO. SC

Where we go from here.

Clutter is also relevant for print and television advertising (too many commercials during programme breaks). To avoid the ad clutter found in most magazines, some publishers limit the number of ads.[21] One company has developed more than 40 magazines targeted at rather narrow audiences, including *GO* (Girls Only) for girls aged 11 to 14 and *in View* for college-aged women. Some of these magazines have only one advertiser, thus maximising possibilities of exposure and attention to that company's marketing messages.

COMPREHENSION OF INFORMATION

Comprehension refers to the cognitive processes by which consumers understand or make sense of their own behaviours and relevant aspects of their environment. As a key aspect of the interpretation stage in consumer decision making (see Exhibit 6.1), comprehension produces knowledge, meanings, and beliefs about concepts, objects, behaviours, and events. When attention is focused on particular information, comprehension of that information is guided by relevant knowledge activated from memory. This means information is interpreted in terms of existing knowledge. The resulting knowledge, meanings, and beliefs from comprehension can be stored in memory and can be activated for use in another interpretation process. The process of creating new meanings and using them to interpret new information is ongoing.

Variations in comprehension

Exhibit 6.2 shows that comprehension processes can vary in four ways: comprehension may be automatic or controlled, produce concrete or abstract meanings, generate few or many meanings, and create weaker or stronger memories.

Automatic processing
Like attention, simple comprehension processes tend to be *automatic*. For instance, most consumers around the world who see a can of Coca-Cola or a McDonald's restaurant immediately comprehend "Coke" or "McDonald's." Direct recognition of familiar products

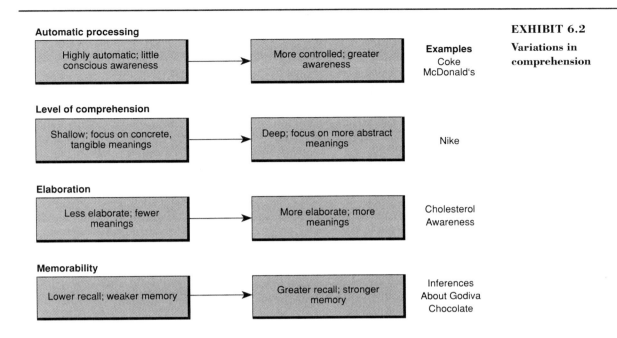

EXHIBIT 6.2

Variations in comprehension

is a simple comprehension process in that exposure to the familiar brand automatically activates its relevant meanings, perhaps its name and other associated knowledge, from memory.

In contrast, comprehending less familiar information usually requires more conscious thought and control. Because consumers do not have well-developed knowledge structures for new products or brands, they may have to construct the meanings of such things consciously (or else intentionally ignore them).

Level of comprehension

The specific meanings that consumers construct to represent products and other marketing information in their environment depend on the **level of comprehension** that occurs during interpretation.[22] Comprehension can vary in level from shallow to deep. *Shallow comprehension* produces concrete meanings about tangible things. For example, a consumer could interpret a product in terms of its physical product attributes (these Nike running shoes are black, size 10, and made of leather and nylon).

Deep comprehension produces more abstract meanings that represent broader, more subjective, and more symbolic concepts. For instance, deep comprehension of product information might create meanings about the functional consequences of product use (I can run faster in these Nike shoes) or the psychosocial and value consequences (I feel confident when I wear these shoes). From a means-end perspective, deeper comprehension generates product-related meanings that are more relevant to the consumer; shallow comprehension tends to produce meanings about product attributes. In general, more personal meanings have greater influence in a purchase decision than shallow product meanings.

Elaboration

Comprehension also varies in extensiveness or level of **elaboration**.[23] The degree of elaboration during comprehension determines the amount of knowledge or the number of meanings produced as well as the complexity of the interconnections between those meanings. Less elaborate (simpler) comprehension produces few meanings connected by simple relationships; more elaborate comprehension produces a greater number of meanings organised into more complex knowledge structures (schemas and scripts).

Memorability

Both the level and elaboration of comprehension influence consumers' ability to remember the meanings that are created during comprehension.[24] First, deeper comprehension processes create more abstract, more self-relevant meanings that tend to be remembered better (better recall and recognition) than the more concrete meanings created by shallow comprehension processes. Second, more elaborate comprehension processes create greater numbers of interconnected meanings. This enhances memory because when activated, one meaning can spread and activate other connected meanings.[25] In sum, marketing strategies that stimulate consumers to engage in deeper, more elaborate comprehension processes tend to produce meanings and knowledge that consumers remember better.

Inferences during comprehension

Deeper, more elaborate comprehension often produces **inferences,** which are beliefs or knowledge that are not based on information directly present in the environment.[26] Inferences are interpretations that go beyond the information given. For instance, some consumers might infer (form a belief) that a product is of good quality because it is heavily advertised on T.V.[27] The quality of the product is not visible in the environment; it is an inference based on other information (the amount of advertising).

Inferences are heavily influenced by consumers' knowledge that is activated during comprehension.[28] For instance, consumers who believe that more expensive brands of chocolates are higher in quality than cheaper brands are likely to infer that Godiva or Laura Secord chocolates are high quality when they learn that they cost up to $20 per pound.[29] As another example, incomplete or missing product information sometimes prompts consumers to "fill in the blanks" by forming inferences based on prior knowledge.[30] For instance, consumers highly knowledgeable about clothing styles may be able to infer the country of origin and even the designer of a suit or dress merely by noticing a few details.

Inferences play a large role in the construction of means-end chains.[31] By making inferences during comprehension, consumers form beliefs about relationships between tangible attributes of a product and its functional consequences and perhaps even the psychosocial and value consequences of product use. In highly familiar products, these inferences may be made automatically without much conscious awareness. For instance, some consumers draw inferences from the colour of detergent granules: blue and white seem to be *cues* connoting cleanliness. Packaging cues are another example. Hershey sells a premium-priced candy bar, Golden Almond, wrapped in gold foil, a characteristic that implies quality to many consumers. Finally, as Consumer Perspective 6.3 illustrates, even the brand name of a product can prompt consumer inferences during comprehension.

To stimulate consumers to form inferences, Kellogg's once promoted All-Bran with the headline, "At last, some news about cancer you can live with." The ads repeated the National Cancer Institute's recommendation for increasing levels of fibre in the diet and then stated that "no cereal has more fibre" than All-Bran. Apparently, Kellogg's hoped consumers would make the inference that the product attribute of high fibre leads to the desirable consequence of reduced cancer risk. Probably, most consumers then made additional inferences that a reduced risk of cancer helps one achieve the universal values of

CONSUMER
PERSPECTIVE

6.3

What's in a
name?

A key aspect of the marketing strategy for a new product is the brand name. Consumers can form inferences about important meanings just from the brand name—and those meanings, of course, should be consistent with the intended brand image. For instance, Ford selected a nonword, *Merkur*, for its imported car. Although the word really doesn't mean anything, it is German-sounding and connotes a high-tech image, just the meanings Ford wanted consumers to infer.

A primary function of a brand name is to differentiate the item from the competition. That is, the name should be different from other names and should help create a distinctive image (a unique network of meanings). The dominant image for most fragrances has been romance, so many of the brand names are quite similar—Cie, Ciara, Cerissa, Chimere, Cachet, and Chanel. Marketers of some fragrances have tried to create more distinctive images by using different types of names like Votre, Charlie, Scoundrel, and Babe.

The brand name should describe or connote the key meaning of the product, if possible. Consider how clearly names such as Pudding Pops frozen snacks, Liquid-Plumr drain cleaner, Head & Shoulders shampoo, Easy-Off oven cleaner, and Seduction cologne convey the product's basic function or key benefit.

Finally, a brand name should be memorable and easy to pronounce. Many believe that short names have an advantage here. For instance, the name *Acura* was selected for Honda's luxury car because it was thought to connote precision (as in accuracy). *Acura* also meets other important criteria for a coined word. Because it ends with an "a," it is read as a noun and is obviously the name of something. Also, the word begins and ends with the same letter, making it more memorable. Finally, *Acura* contains three clearly voiced syllables in only five letters, making it easy to pronounce.

In sum, the key consideration in selecting a brand name, whether short or long, is that it conveys a set of distinctive meanings that are consistent with the image intended by the marketing strategy.

Source: Daniel Doeden, "How to Select a Brand Name," *Marketing Communications*, November 1981, pp. 56–61; and Jeffrey A. Trachtenberg, "Name That Brand," *Forbes*, April 8, 1985, pp. 128, 130.

long life, health, and happiness. Consumer Perspective 6.4 describes some other health-related inferences that have come under government and public scrutiny.

Many factors affect the depth and elaboration of comprehension that occur when consumers interpret marketing information.[32] Three important influences are consumers' existing *knowledge in memory*, their *involvement* at the time of exposure, and the nature of their *exposure environment*. These factors influence consumers' ability, motivation, and opportunity to comprehend.

Factors influencing comprehension

Knowledge in memory
Consumers' *ability to comprehend* marketing information is determined largely by their knowledge in memory. The particular knowledge, meanings, and beliefs that are activated determine what level of comprehension will occur and what meanings will be produced.

Marketing researchers often discuss consumers' knowledge in terms of expertise or familiarity.[33] *Expert consumers* are quite familiar with a product category, product forms, and specific brands. They tend to have substantial amounts of knowledge about the product. When parts of this knowledge are activated, these expert consumers can comprehend marketing information at relatively deep, elaborate levels.

CONSUMER
PERSPECTIVE

▶ 6.4

Cholesterol
inferences

Just because a package of cookies or potato chips is stamped "cholesterol free," it does not necessarily mean the product is healthy to eat. In fact, many so-called cholesterol-free products contain certain types of fats that also can contribute to heart disease, said Bruce Holub, a leading nutritional scientist at the University of Guelph. "That also makes them no better, or perhaps worse, than some products containing cholesterol," Holub told reporters.

Holub argued that major food manufacturers are acting irresponsibly in their marketing practices and called on the federal government to tighten labelling regulations.

Health and Welfare Canada is aware of the problem but is concerned that more nutritional labelling on packages may only add to the confusion. "We have to take it one step at a time," said S. W. Gunner, director general of the food directorate of the department's Health Protection Branch.

Bretta Maloff, a public health dietician in Calgary and president of the 5,000-member Canadian Dietetic Association, advised, "When you see the term *cholesterol-free* on a label in the supermarket, ignore it. One of our major concerns in the Canadian diet is fat intake. The statement about fat on the label is far more informative and important for consumers than the phrase *cholesterol-free*."

Due to misleading claims about cholesterol, the federal government in 1993 further reviewed the rules for labels. "Consumers and health professionals are not in a position to judge the merits of these claims," argued Margaret Cheney, Canada's chief nutritionist. "Cholesterol-free has come to mean heart-healthy to consumers, and some manufacturers are doing nothing to clear up this misconception." That is why further government legislation and monitoring are required.

Trusting consumers are purchasing products they believe are healthier choices, such as cholesterol-free potato chips—a product that never had cholesterol to begin with.

Sources: Adapted from "Ottawa to Review Food Labels," *Strategy,* Nov. 1, 1993; "Labels Confuse, Officials Argue," *Winnipeg Free Press,* July 7, 1993; "Cholesterol-Free Label Challenged," *Globe and Mail,* Jan. 9, 1991.

Novice consumers have little prior experience or familiarity with the product or brand. They tend to have poorly organised knowledge structures, with relatively few, typically shallow meanings and beliefs. When parts of these knowledge structures are activated during exposure to marketing information, novices comprehend the information at shallow and nonelaborate levels that produce a few concrete meanings. They would need more knowledge to comprehend at a deeper, more elaborate level.

Marketers need to understand the knowledge structures of their target audience to develop effective marketing strategies that consumers can comprehend. For instance, the S. C. Johnson Co., manufacturer of Raid and other bug killers, knows that most consumers have limited technical knowledge about how insecticides work.[34] Because customers want to see action, the formulation for Raid bug spray lets them comprehend quickly that the product works. Raid attacks bugs' central nervous systems and drives them to race around in circles before they die—a highly satisfying result for the buyer.

Involvement

Consumers' involvement with a product influences their *motivation to comprehend* information about the product.[35] Consumers with high personal sources of involvement associate the product with values and goals that are central to their self-concept. The

CONSUMER PERSPECTIVE

6.5

In defence of an underrated advertising medium

The average Canadian listens to at least 22 hours of radio per week. Most homes have at least three radios (and 2.1 kids, but who can explain that statistic). And 90 percent of all vehicles have radios. So radio seems an obvious choice for advertising, unless you're exclusively targeting Zamboni drivers.

Radio finds itself competing for consumers' attention as they curse their way through a traffic jam, sit down to a plate of rigatoni, or gasp through a three-mile run. But overcome those hurdles, and a provocative radio spot involves the listener in a way few newspaper or television commercials could.

Capture your listeners' imagination and they become the best art directors you could hope for. Tell them you're speaking from the bottom of the Atlantic and their minds bring all the kelp, plankton, and squid for you.

Great radio often involves a very visual situation. In one quite successful commercial for Bell Mobility Cellular, Thom Sharpe calls his buddy Mel from the ledge outside the 17th floor of a building to demonstrate the virtues of his portable phone. Remember the great radio spots for Eastern Airlines about a chess champion who had simultaneous games in Pittsburgh and Toronto? Thanks to Eastern's frequent flights between those two cities, he not only kept the games going by flying back and forth—he won them.

In radio, the impossible becomes ridiculously possible. For example, one spot for a beverage company had George Bush and Brian Mulroney enjoying a casual barbecue while Dan Quayle trimmed the hedges and lawns of 24 Sussex Drive.

So the next time your favourite account person or media guru asks what medium you were thinking of using, remember—you're a creative person. Don't go around committing blasphemy by saying stuff like, "Gee, how about radio because of reach and frequency?" Just peer at them over the edge of your layout pad, and say "I dunno, radio might be kinda cool. . . ."

Source: Adapted from "In Defence of an Under-Rated Advertising Medium" by Karen Howe, *Marketing,* March 8, 1993, p. 19.

involvement experienced when such self-relevant knowledge is activated motivates these consumers to comprehend the information in a deeper and more elaborate way. For instance, a person highly involved in music is likely to construct complex meanings for a new CD from a favourite artist. Consumers who experience low levels of involvement when exposed to marketing information will not engage in extensive comprehension and will interpret the information at a relatively shallow, concrete level (This is a pair of socks).

Exposure environment

Various aspects of the exposure environment can affect consumers' *opportunity to comprehend* marketing information. These include time pressure, a person's affective state (a good or a bad mood), and distractions (noise, crowds). Consumers who are in a hurry and under a lot of time pressure don't have much opportunity to interpret marketing information, even though they may be motivated to do so (high involvement).[36] In this environment, they are likely to engage in relatively shallow and nonelaborate comprehension. Consumer Perspective 6.5 describes attention and comprehension in the exposure environment for radio advertising.

Savvy marketers consider these environmental factors in designing marketing strategies. Some retailers, for instance, aim for a relaxed, slow-paced environment that encourages people to slow down and comprehend all the information marketers make available. For instance, most Ralph Lauren's Polo shops are full of glowing wood, antique furniture,

Oriental carpets, and warm lighting fixtures—all to simulate an elegant English manor house. This environment helps create the desired images for the casually elegant clothing Lauren designs and sells.

Marketing implications

Marketers need to understand consumer comprehension in order to design marketing information that will be interpreted appropriately. They must consider the characteristics of the target consumers and the environment where consumers are exposed to the information.[37]

Knowledge and involvement

To encourage appropriate comprehension, marketers should design their messages to fit consumers' knowledge structures and involvement (ability and motivation to comprehend). For instance, marketers of high-involvement products such as luxury cars usually want consumers to form abstract, self-relevant meanings about their products. Many print ads for Saab, BMW, or Mercedes-Benz describe in great detail technical attributes and functional aspects of the cars. To comprehend this information at a deep, elaborate level, consumers must have fairly sophisticated knowledge about automobiles and sufficient involvement to motivate extensive interpretation processes.

For other types of products, however, marketers may not want consumers to engage in extensive comprehension processes. Sometimes they want to create simple, non-elaborate meanings about their product. For example, simple products (cologne or beer) are promoted largely through *image advertising*, which is not meant to be comprehended deeply or elaborately.[38] Consider the typical advertising for beer or soft drinks. Often these ads contain virtually no written information beyond a brief slogan such as "Bud, the King of Beer" or "Coke is it." Most consumers probably comprehend such information in a nonelaborate way that produces an overall image and perhaps a general affective reaction, but not detailed means-end chains. Other ads, such as billboards, are reminders intended mainly to activate the brand name and keep it at "top-of-mind" awareness. In such cases, comprehension might be limited to simple brand recognition.

Remembering

Consumers' ability to recall meanings from memory is important to marketers. Because many purchase decisions are made well after exposure to marketing information, marketers usually want consumers to remember certain key meanings associated with their marketing strategy, particularly the brand name and main attributes and benefits. Retailers want consumers to remember their name and location, the types of merchandise they carry, and the dates of the big sale. Keeping accessible knowledge in memory requires that consumers attend to the information and comprehend it at an appropriate level.

Despite the millions spent each year on advertising and other marketing strategies, much marketing information is not remembered well. Few advertising slogans are accurately recalled. Although some people can remember a slogan, many of them cannot associate it with the right brand name.[39] For instance, 60 percent of consumers recognised the slogan "Never let them see you sweat," but only 4 percent correctly associated it with Dry Idea deodorant. Although 32 percent recognised "Cars that make sense," only 4 percent associated it with Hyundai. Apparently, slogans have to be very heavily advertised to be remembered—two higher scorers are General Electric's "We bring good things to life" and Avis's "We try harder."

Miscomprehension of marketing information

Research shows that a substantial amount of marketing information is miscomprehended, in that many consumers form inaccurate, confused, or inappropriate interpretations. In

**CONSUMER
PERSPECTIVE**

**Confusing
brand names**

Molson Breweries of Canada Ltd. and Miller Brewing Co. filed a joint lawsuit in federal court asking for both a temporary and permanent injunction to stop John Labatt
Ltd. from marketing and selling its Labatt Genuine Draft. Molson and Miller claimed
that the beer violates Canada's trademark laws by copying much of the label of Miller
Genuine Draft, sold in the United States. Molson and Miller are backing up their
claim with research studies showing that consumers recognise Miller Genuine Draft
and that many identify the Labatt product with Miller's. Molson, which has exclusive
rights to Miller Genuine Draft in Canada, was planning to launch the brand in Canada, but is concerned that it will be seen as a second-best to Labatt Genuine Draft.

Source: "Molson, Labatt Face Legal Battle over Draft," *Financial Post*, March 31, 1992.

fact, all marketing information can be miscomprehended by at least some consumers.[40]
Miscomprehension can range from confusion over similar brand names (see Consumer
Perspective 6.6) to misinterpreting a product claim by forming an inaccurate means-end
chain. People may miscomprehend an average of 20 to 25 percent of the many different
types of information they encounter, whether advertising or news reports.[41] Although
unethical marketers may intentionally create deceptive or misleading information, most
professional marketers work hard to create marketing information that is understood correctly. For those who don't, Industry Canada's *Misleading Advertising Bulletin* monitors
deceptive marketing information and can fine a company for deceptive practices as well
as force a company to correct the false beliefs it creates.[42]

Exposure environment

Many aspects of the environment in which exposure to marketing information occurs can
influence consumers' comprehension processes. The type of store, for instance, can affect how consumers comprehend the product and brand sold there. Thus, for some customers, a brand of jeans purchased in a "high-image store" like Holt Renfrew may have a
more positive set of meanings than the same brand bought at Zellers or Kmart. Store
characteristics such as size, exterior design, or interior decoration can activate networks

EXHIBIT 6.3

**Relationships among
exposure, attention,
and comprehension**

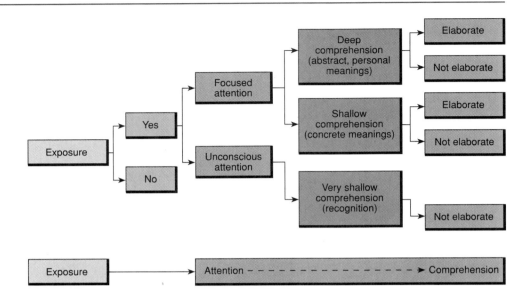

of meanings that influence consumers' comprehension of the products and brands displayed there.

Another aspect of the exposure environment concerns the actual content and format of the marketing information.[43] Some information may be confusing, unclear, and hard to comprehend. For instance, the volume of nutritional information on food product labels and in advertising claims can be difficult for many consumers to comprehend in a meaningful way.[44]

THE INTERPRETATION PROCESS

Interpretation is an ongoing process of sense-making or meaning creation. Interpretation involves three separate processes of exposure, attention, and comprehension. Exhibit 6.3 shows the relationships among exposure, attention, and comprehension. These interpretation processes are related in a sequence, so what happens later depends on earlier stages. An obvious example is that if exposure does not occur, attention and comprehension are not possible. Exhibit 6.3 also shows the various types and levels of interpretation that might occur under different conditions. For instance, deep and elaborate comprehension of marketing information requires focused attention on that information.

To design and implement successful marketing strategies—whether price, product, promotion, or distribution—marketers must consider the flow of effects that occur during interpretation. There are three basic issues concerning exposure, attention, and omprehension.

1. How can I *maximise and/or maintain exposure* of the target segment of consumers to my marketing information?
2. How can I *capture and maintain the attention* of the target consumers?
3. How can I influence the target consumers to *comprehend* my marketing information at the *appropriate level of depth and elaboration?*

Learning objective 1: *Describe the differences between accidental and intentional exposure.*

In accidental exposure, a person unintentionally comes into contact with information, essentially at random. A key marketing strategy is to place marketing information in the environment where the chances of accidental exposure are maximised: ads on buses, most TV commercials, most ads in magazines, and billboards on highways. Intentional exposure occurs when consumers purposefully seek out marketing information, often to decide on a purchase. An important marketing strategy is to make sure relevant information is available when and where consumers look for it. Examples include placing product brochures in the store to give to interested shoppers or training salespeople to be knowledgeable about the products they are selling.

Learning objective 2: *Define selective exposure and give an example of how marketers can influence consumers' selective exposure to marketing information.*

Selective exposure occurs when consumers intentionally seek certain types of marketing information. For instance, consumers tend to look for information they think is relevant to a decision. So they seek out information that is linked, through means-end chains, to the important goals and values in that situation. Selective exposure also implies that consumers can intentionally avoid exposure to certain types of marketing information. For instance, some consumers immediately discard unsolicited catalogues or hang up on telemarketers before hearing the sales pitch. Many marketing strategies can be developed to influence selective exposure, including sending junk mail in an envelope like a telegram so it looks important and won't be thrown away unopened. Advertisers try to capture people's interest in the first few seconds of a TV commercial so they won't look away or leave the room. Another strategy is to place marketing information in places where consumers cannot avoid being exposed and maintaining the exposure. The VideOcart screens on grocery carts (described in the text) are one example. Another example is to show ads on TV monitors placed above the checkout aisles in some grocery stores.

Learning objective 3: *Define attention and identify three factors that influence consumers' attention to marketing information.*

Attention involves focusing the cognitive system on information that is relevant to one's goals and values. Attention involves selecting certain information for interpretation from the vast array of potential information in the environment. Attention varies in terms of awareness (from unconscious to highly conscious) and intensity (from casual levels to highly focused levels of attention). Attention can be influenced by many factors: consumers' affective states, consumers' involvement with the information, and the information's prominence in the environment.

Learning objective 4: *Define comprehension and describe four ways comprehension can vary.*

Comprehension refers to the interpretation processes by which consumers make sense of relevant aspects of the environment as well as their own affective responses and behaviours. Comprehension processes can vary in four important ways. First, comprehension varies in the degree of processing from automatic (knowing to stop when a traffic light turns red) to more controlled comprehension (intentionally trying to figure out what something means). Second, the level of comprehension can vary from shallow to deep, from producing simple, relatively concrete meanings to producing more abstract, self-relevant meanings. Third, comprehension can vary in elaboration: few meanings versus many interrelated meanings. Fourth, comprehension varies in memorability, with lower levels of recall for some meanings and greater recall for others.

Learning objective 5: *Define inferences and give an example.*

Inferences are beliefs that are based on more than direct information in the environment. Inferences go beyond the information given because they are partially based on consumers' knowledge in memory. For example, consumers might infer the cleaning ability of laundry detergent based on stored (perhaps unconscious) meanings about the product's scent or colour. Inferences play a major role in the formation of means-end chains of product knowledge. During comprehension, consumers may make inferences about product attributes, consequences of product use, or abstract value outcomes. For instance, some consumers infer the quality of a product from its price or country of origin. Thirty years ago, a made-in-Japan label was interpreted as poor quality, but now most Canadians infer that Japanese products are high quality. Consumers' inferences can have important marketing implications. For example, Canadian Airlines tries to keep the interior of all its aircraft spotless because consumers might infer that engine maintenance is poor if the company can't even keep the plane clean.

Learning objective 6: *Describe how consumers' knowledge (expertise) influences their comprehension of marketing information.*

Consumers vary considerably in their knowledge or expertise concerning products. For example, expert consumers know a great deal about cars, while novice consumers know little. The amount of knowledge affects comprehension processes. More knowledgeable consumers are able to comprehend complex product information at a deeper and more personal level because they understand the means-end connections between product attributes and relevant consequences. In contrast, novice consumers are likely to have difficulty comprehending complex product information. They may be able to form meanings and beliefs only about rather concrete product attributes or simple functional consequences. These variations in consumer expertise suggest that marketers need to understand the type and amount of knowledge their target consumers have about the product category so they can create marketing information that "fits" these knowledge structures and is comprehended appropriately.

Learning objective 7: *Describe how comprehension processes can influence consumers' ability to recall marketing information.*

Typically, marketers want consumers to recall marketing information and use it in making a purchase decision. Consumers' ability to remember marketing information depends on the comprehension processes used to interpret the information. Deeper, more elaborate comprehension tends to create more memorable knowledge, meanings, and beliefs in memory. That is, knowledge that is more related to personal goals and values and is more richly interrelated with other knowledge tends to be easier to call up from memory. Thus, marketers who wish their marketing information to be well remembered should design information that consumers will process at deeper, more elaborate levels.

▶ **KEY TERMS AND CONCEPTS**

exposure	selective exposure	level of comprehension
intentional exposure	attention	elaboration
accidental exposure	comprehension	inferences

▶ **REVIEW AND DISCUSSION QUESTIONS**

1. Describe accidental and intentional exposure to marketing information in the context of a retail clothing store. Identify a clothing product such as socks or suits and discuss effective marketing strategies for both types of exposure.

2. Choose a product (such as breakfast cereal or CDs) and describe two factors that influence consumers' selective exposure to product information. How can marketers influence consumers' selective exposure to marketing information?

3. Describe two marketing strategies that could influence consumers' attention to marketing information for a product.

4. Consumers may engage in automatic processing during comprehension of marketing information. What are two marketing implications of such automatic processing?

5. Describe the differences in the knowledge, meanings, and beliefs produced by varying levels of comprehension. By example, explain when marketers should encourage shallow comprehension of their marketing information. Deep comprehension?

6. Describe the differences in the knowledge, meanings, and beliefs produced by more elaborate and less elaborate comprehension processes. By example, explain when marketers should encourage and when they should discourage elaborate comprehension of their marketing information.

7. Discuss how consumers' existing knowledge structures and their level of involvement can influence their (a) attention to and (b) comprehension of marketing information about the prices (or some other attribute) of brands in a product category.

8. Identify three factors that can affect the inferences formed during comprehension of ads for a packaged food product. Give two examples of marketing strategies that could influence the inferences consumers form.

9. Describe a marketing strategy that you think might result in consumer miscomprehension. Discuss how miscomprehension might occur in this case and describe how a marketer might reduce the chances of miscomprehension.

10. Discuss how interpretation processes of attention and comprehension can influence consumers' ability to recall marketing information. Give an example of a marketing strategy designed to influence this recall.

7

Attitudes and Intentions

LEARNING OBJECTIVES

After completing this chapter, you should be able to:

▶ 1. Define attitude and give two examples of its relevance for marketers.

▶ 2. Describe salient beliefs and give an example of how marketers can influence belief salience.

▶ 3. Using the multiattribute attitude model as a guide, describe the information integration process by which consumers form an A_o.

▶ 4. Describe four attitude-change strategies based on the multiattribute attitude model.

▶ 5. Explain how A_o differs from A_{act}.

▶ 6. Describe how the components of the theory of reasoned action are combined to create a behavioural intention.

▶ 7. Identify three factors that can reduce the accuracy of a measure of behavioural intention in predicting the actual behaviour.

CANADIAN WINE PRODUCERS WANT CANADIANS TO STOP WHINING

Canadian wines have won a number of international prizes over the years, but Canadian consumers retain a tenacious image of domestic wines as low quality. In 1990, for example, consumption of Ontario-produced wines had fallen by 9 percent despite the industry's attempt to develop high-quality, internationally acclaimed vintages. David Ringer of Andres Wines of Winona, Ontario stated that, "consumers are stuck with the impression that Ontario wines are sub-standard."

In order to combat continual declines in domestic wine consumption, Ontario launched a $4 million television and print campaign to change consumers' negative perception of domestic wines. Ontario wineries have since made a commitment to enter international competitions. They are winning more medals each year, taking 17 medals for reds and whites at Vinexpo 1995, the world's most prestigious competition. In 1991, British Columbia's Okanagan Valley wineries also spent over $1 million in an aggressive campaign to promote their high-end products.

The results of these campaigns were positive. Canadian consumers' attitudes toward Canadian-made wines has improved. Current public opinion polls indicate that 87 percent of all wine drinkers now believe that Ontario wines are good quality. British Columbia's campaign was quite successful—it resulted in a 60 percent increase in the sales of the province's best wines.

Attitudes toward products like wine can be quite strong and enduring. What Canadian wine producers have learned is that it is critical to understand how attitudes for certain types of products are developed, that a variety of strategies are required to change attitudes, and that this change in attitude will take time.[1]

Consumer attitudes are important for understanding consumer behaviour. Marketing managers spend millions of dollars each year researching consumer attitudes toward products and brands. They spend many more millions on advertising, sales promotion, and other sorts of communication to influence those attitudes. By modifying consumer attitudes, marketers hope to influence purchase behaviour.

In this chapter, we examine two types of attitude: attitudes toward objects and attitudes toward behaviours. We begin by defining attitude. Then we describe the integration process by which people combine beliefs to form attitudes toward objects in their environment. Next, we distinguish between attitudes toward objects and behaviours. We then discuss how knowledge is integrated to form attitudes toward behaviours and intentions to perform specific behaviours. Finally, we discuss the relationship between behavioural intentions and actual behaviours. All these attitude issues have implications for marketing strategy.

WHAT IS ATTITUDE?

Attitude has been a key concept in psychology for more than a century, and more than 100 definitions and 500 measures of attitudes have been proposed.[2] Nearly all these conceptions of attitude have one thing in common: they refer to people's evaluations. We define **attitude** as a person's *overall evaluation of a concept*.[3] The concept can be an object (including products, services, or ideas) or a behaviour, and the evaluation can be created by both the affective and cognitive systems.

Evaluations created by the affective system are immediate, automatic, positive or negative reactions to simple objects or behaviours. These affective responses are at relatively low levels of intensity and arousal (refer back to Exhibit 4.2) and are produced without conscious, cognitive processing of information. Examples are people's immediate affective responses to the taste of spicy chili or chocolate ice cream, the colour of a new car, or another person's appearance. An attitude may be formed when these affective evaluatives become associated with a product or brand through the classical conditioning process, which is discussed in Chapter 11.[4]

In this chapter, we will most often treat *attitudes as evaluations produced by the cognitive* (not the affective) *system*. These **evaluations** take the form of pro/con, favourable/unfavourable, like/dislike judgments of an object or behaviour. The model of consumer decision making in Exhibit 7.1 shows that people form an overall evaluation or attitude toward a concept by integrating or combining relevant knowledge, meanings, or beliefs about the concept. The purpose of this **integration process** is to evaluate the concept in terms of its *personal relevance* for the individual consumer. In means-end terms, consumers judge whether the concept has good or bad attributes and favourable or unfavourable consequences: "What does this concept have to do with me? Does this object have positive attributes? Is this a good or bad thing for me? Do I like or dislike this object?"

Exhibit 7.1 shows that the evaluations produced in the integration process may be stored in memory. Once an attitude has been formed and stored in memory, the consumer does not have to repeat the integration process to reconstruct the attitude. Instead, the preformed attitude can be activated from memory and used to interpret new information or be integrated with other knowledge in making a decision.[5] These existing attitudes can have a strong influence on consumers' cognitive processes. This is the reason researchers conduct "blind" taste tests where consumers do not know what brands they are tasting. This approach avoids activating brand attitudes that could bias the taste judgments.

We measure attitudes simply and directly by asking consumers to evaluate the concept of interest. For instance, marketing researchers might ask consumers to indicate their attitudes toward McDonald's french fries on three evaluative scales:

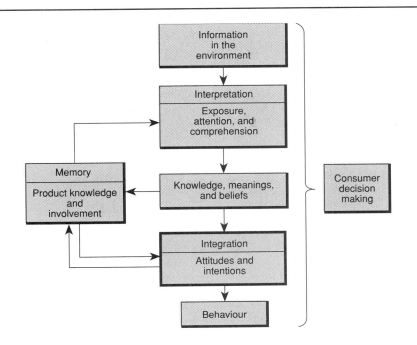

EXHIBIT 7.1

A model of consumer decision making

McDonald's French Fries

Extremely Unfavourable	−3	−2	−1	0	+1	+2	+3	Extremely Favourable
Dislike Very Much	−3	−2	−1	0	+1	+2	+3	Like Very Much
Very Bad	−3	−2	−1	0	+1	+2	+3	Very Good

The overall attitude toward McDonald's french fries is measured by the average rating across the evaluative scales. Note that attitudes in this case can vary from *negative* (ratings of −3, −2, −1) through *neutral* (a rating of 0) to *positive* (ratings of +1, +2, or +3). Also note that attitudes are not necessarily intense or extreme. On the contrary,

Many consumers have positive attitudes toward the Body Shop in part because of the well publicized committment by Anita Roddick, Managing Director, to recycling and Amnesty International.

<table>
<tr><td>

**CONSUMER
PERSPECTIVE**

▶ **7.1**

**Marketing middle
brands**

</td><td>

As a result of the recession of the early 1990s, the impact of the North American Free
Trade Agreement (NAFTA) and the continual increase in cross-border shopping at
favourite U.S.-Canadian borders, Canadian retailers have to work harder than ever
before to earn Canadian consumers' loyalty and dollars. These factors have all con-
tributed to the creation of a much more demanding consumer. As a result, middle-
brand products and retailers are suffering the most.

At one time, it was a blessing to be "in the middle" of a market. Brands that were
midpriced and had middle-of-the-road attributes appealed to the mass market and
often enjoyed great success. But by the late 1980s and early 1990s, many consumers
no longer held strong, positive attitudes toward brands that were "just OK." Thus,
many "middle brands," such as Eaton's, The Bay, Sears, Holiday Inn, Ford and
Labatt found it difficult to retain existing customers and acquire new ones.

Traditional department stores are being squeezed from both above and below their
traditional market segments. Eaton and The Bay, for example, are being squeezed by
discount stores such as Zellers and specialty stores such as Fairweather and Reit-
man's. Grocery stores and office supply stores face significant competition from ware-
house-style competitors such as Price Costco, Business Depot, and Club Biz, which
offer the lowest prices on brand-name merchandise. Stores like Buck or Two Stores
and Dollar Bill are taking away more consumers by offering very low-priced products.

Middle-brand retailers are using a number of methods to win back consumers.
Kmart reorganised its departments, widened its aisles, brightened its floor space, and
began to target single mothers and families. Ford Motor Company of Canada's mar-
keting strategy includes value-pricing and full-line roadside assistance to combat the
onslaught of the more prestigious European and Japanese car manufacturers such as
BMW, Mercedes, Lexus and Infinity. To fight back against warehouse-style competi-
tors, Grand and Toy has opened supercentres and guarantees next-day-or-it's-free
delivery on brand merchandise, from fluorescent highlighters to fax paper. Labatt's
redesigned its Blue and Blue Light packaging to modernise its look and further dif-
ferentiate itself from the competition. Eaton's advertises that its everyday prices are
as good or better than its competitors' including their sale prices. To regain consumer
loyalty, Eaton's uses the slogan, "Why Wait for Sales?" to focus on its competitive
prices.

Source: Daniel Girard, "The New Retail Giants," *Toronto Star*, Feb. 9, 1992, p. H1; Giles Gherson, "Now
the Good News," *Financial Times*, Aug. 3, 1992, p. 1; Mark Evans, "Dollar Stores Buck Retail Downtrend,"
Financial Post, July 30, 1992, p. 11; "Labatt Adopts New Design for Blue Line," *Marketing*, June 1993.

</td></tr>
</table>

consumers can have essentially neutral evaluations (neither favourable nor unfavourable)
toward relatively unimportant, noninvolving concepts. A neutral evaluation is still an attitude, however, although probably a weakly held one. Consumer Perspective 7.1 describes the problems marketers face in dealing with brands toward which consumers hold
weak attitudes.

**Attitudes toward
what?**

Attitudes are always *toward* some concept. We can distinguish between two broad types
of concepts—objects and behaviours. Consumers can have *attitudes toward objects in
the physical and social environment* (A_o) such as products, brands, models, stores, or
people (a salesperson at the camera store), as well as aspects of marketing strategy (a
coupon offer from Hostess potato chips, an ad for the Players' Challenge tennis tournament). Consumers also can have attitudes toward imaginary objects and concepts (an
ideal desk chair, a fair price for gasoline, capitalism). Second, consumers can have
attitudes toward their own behaviours or actions (A_{act}), including their past behaviours

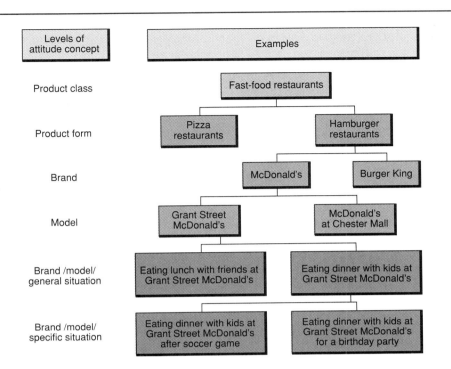

EXHIBIT 7.2

Variations in level of attitude concept

(buying that sweater was stupid), current actions (I like talking to this salesperson), and future behaviours (I'm looking forward to going to the mall tomorrow afternoon).

Consumers can have distinct and quite different attitudes toward many variations or levels of essentially the same product or brand. Exhibit 7.2 shows several attitude concepts for fast-food restaurants that vary in level of specificity. We can say that an individual has a moderately positive attitude toward fast-food restaurants (the product class), but he has a highly favourable attitude toward hamburger restaurants (one product form). His attitude toward McDonald's, a specific brand of hamburger restaurant, however, is only slightly favourable (he prefers Wendy's). Finally, his attitude toward a particular "model"—the McDonald's on the corner of Grant Street—is somewhat negative (he had an unpleasant meal there).

Some attitude concepts can be defined in terms of a particular behaviour and situation (eating dinner with the kids at the Grant Street McDonald's after a soccer game). Consumers can have different attitudes toward these concepts that are not necessarily consistent. Our sample consumer has an unfavourable attitude toward eating lunch with his friends at the Grant Street McDonald's (he'd rather go to a full-service restaurant), but he has a somewhat favourable attitude toward eating dinner there with his kids (it's easy and fast).

Note that although the same McDonald's "object" is present in each of these concepts, the attitudes are toward the *combination* of the object and situation, which is quite a different concept from the object alone.[6] Because consumers can have very different attitudes toward only slightly different attitude concepts, *marketers must precisely identify the attitude concept that is most relevant to the marketing problem of interest.*

Consumer brand attitudes are the subject of much marketing research. Two application areas are brand equity and attitude tracking studies.

Marketing implications

Brand equity

Brand equity refers to the *value* of the brand.[7] John Forsyth Co. Ltd., maker of ties and shirts for the Canadian market, formed alliances with well-known foreign companies (Gitano, Van Heusen) because it believed exclusive rights to market these popular brands in Canada would significantly increase sales. Hitachi, a Japanese electronics company, and GE once co-owned a factory in England that made identical televisions for both companies.[8] The only differences were the brand name on the set and a $75 higher price for the Hitachi, reflecting its greater brand equity value. From the marketer's perspective, brand equity implies higher profits, more cash flow, and greater market share.

The consumer/brand relationship is the basis for brand equity, and brand attitude is an important aspect of that relationship. Brand equity involves a *positive brand attitude* (a favourable evaluation of the brand) based on favourable meanings and beliefs about the brand. Strong, consistently positive brand attitudes are an important asset for a company. Consumer Perspective 7.2 illustrates the importance of attitudes in brand equity.

Basically, marketers have three ways to get brand equity: they can build it, borrow it, or buy it. Companies can *build brand equity* by ensuring the brand actually delivers relevant consequences and by communicating these important consequences through consistent advertising. Consider the considerable brand equity developed over time by Campbell's soup, President's Choice foods, Mercedes-Benz automobiles, and NutraSweet artificial sweetener. Classy Formal Wear and Harry Rosen consistently invest heavily in advertising and promotion to create positive consumer attitudes and brand equity.

Companies can *borrow brand equity* by associating a positive brand name with other products. For example, Tide no longer refers to only one type of detergent. When the brand name is extended to other products (Liquid Tide, Ultra Tide), the notion is that some of Tide's original equity is passed along to these new products. Brand extension is an increasingly popular marketing strategy. Coca-Cola once produced a single product, but now the product line includes Classic Coke, Diet Coke, caffeine-free Coke, and cherry Coke. How brand equity is transferred by brand name extensions is still an issue for

---

CONSUMER PERSPECTIVE

▶ **7.2**

Brand equity and brand attitudes

From a means-end perspective, equity is based on the degree to which consumers value the consequences the brand delivers. A key aspect of equity is substitutability. For instance, Suzy and Julie are next-door neighbours who routinely buy Monarch margarine. Each receives an advertisement and coupon for Country Crock margarine. On their next shopping trips, Julie buys a pound of Country Crock, but Suzy buys her usual pound of Monarch. These different behaviours are determined by their beliefs and attitudes, or their perceptions of brand equity. Julie believes Country Crock is essentially the same as Monarch, so she switches brands when offered the small inducement of the coupon. Suzy, however, believes Monarch is the superior product, and she will buy it "no matter what."

People like Suzy are a marketer's dream because they create brand equity. If a brand has high equity, it is less vulnerable to competition. Consumers are less willing to accept substitutes for a brand with high equity, because they want the consequences they believe the brand uniquely provides. Thus, marketers can spend less money promoting brands with strong equity. This, in turn, makes high-equity brands more profitable.

Source: Adapted from Gretchen Morgenson, "The Trend Is Not Their Friend," *Forbes*, Sept. 16, 1991, pp. 114–19; William Moran and Kenneth Longman, "Boosting Profit Potential," *Marketing Insights*, Summer 1991, pp. 24–32.

The following brands have built up considerable brand equity as reflected by their leadership positions.

research. The success of a brand extension may depend on the key meanings consumers associate with a brand name and whether those meanings are appropriate for the new product.[9]

Finally, a company can *buy brand equity* by purchasing brands that enjoy strong consumer attitudes. The rash of mergers and leveraged buyouts of the 1980s was motivated partially by a desire to buy brands with equity clout. For instance, when Canada Post acquired control of Purolator Courier Ltd., it hoped to capitalise on Purolator's brand equity.

Attitude tracking studies

Large-scale attitude surveys, called *tracking studies*, are conducted to monitor brand attitudes over time. The results of such surveys can indicate the success of marketing strategies intended to influence attitudes toward a brand. As these studies identify trends in consumer attitudes, marketers can adjust their marketing strategies, as Canadian wine producers did in the opening example.

An example of a company that almost failed to keep in touch with changing consumer attitudes is Timex. In the 1970s it clung to mechanical watches in the digital revolution. In the 1980s it turned down the chance to handle the world-wide business for Swatch watches, not realising that these brightly coloured watches would dramatically open up the watch-as-fashion accessory market. However, in the 1990s Timex Canada had to completely rethink its strategies and product lines. It implemented a multibrand strategy promoting fashion and sports/activity styles. The corporation and product lines have been completely restructured. The new products will account for as much as 40 percent of the Canadian market by taking market share from Seiko, Swatch, and Citizen. Part of the corporate strategy was to acquire distribution rights for the funky Guess and upscale Monet watch lines world-wide. Timex has come a long way since it began making Mickey Mouse watches for Disney in the 1930s.

EXHIBIT 7.3

Relationship between salient beliefs about an object and attitude toward the object

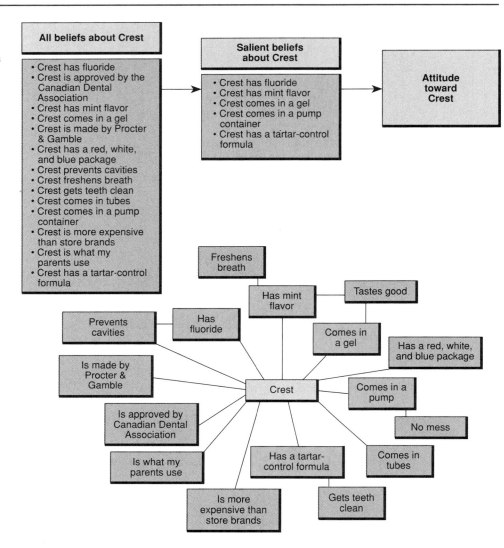

ATTITUDES TOWARD OBJECTS

Consumers form **attitudes toward objects (A_O)** such as products, brands, and stores by integrating or combining selected product knowledge, meanings, and beliefs to form an overall evaluation of the object (see Exhibit 7.1). The relevant knowledge, meanings, and beliefs that are integrated may be produced by interpretation processes or activated from memory.

Salient beliefs

Consumers acquire many beliefs about products, brands, and other objects in their environments (stores, catalogues, a salesperson) through their past experiences. Exhibit 7.3 presents some of the beliefs a consumer might have about Crest toothpaste. These beliefs are organised in an associative network of linked meanings that is stored in memory. Because the cognitive system has a limited capacity, only a few of all the beliefs in a consumer's memory can be activated and integrated consciously when a person evaluates an object. These few activated beliefs (highlighted in Exhibit 7.3) are called **salient**

beliefs, and it is only these beliefs that influence a person's attitude toward a concept.[10] To understand consumer attitudes, marketers must understand salient consumer beliefs.

Consumers can have salient beliefs about any level of meaning in a means-end chain, including the attributes of a product (Roots sweatshirts are made of thick material), its functional and psychosocial consequences (Roots sweatshirts keep me warm and my friends think they're really cool), and/or the values it might help achieve (I can relax in a Roots sweatshirt). Other beliefs such as the product's country of origin (made in Japan, Taiwan, or Canada) may be salient in certain circumstances.[11] Consumers also can have salient beliefs about various tactile, olfactory, and visual images (this blouse feels good, these tacos smell spicy, that car looks like a boat). Once activated from memory, any type of belief can be salient and influence a consumer's attitude toward a product.

The **multiattribute attitude model** attempts to explain how consumers' salient beliefs about the multiple attributes of an object influence their attitudes toward the object. Several versions of the multiattribute attitude model have been proposed, but all take the same basic approach.[12] The key idea is that consumers' overall attitudes toward an object (A_o) are based on two things: the *strength* of their salient beliefs about the object's attributes and their *evaluation* of those beliefs.[13] Simply put, the multiattribute attitude model proposes that people like objects they believe are associated with "good" characteristics and dislike objects they believe to have "bad" attributes.

The multiattribute attitude model

The most popular multiattribute attitude model has the following form:

$$A_o = \sum_{i=1}^{n} b_i e_i$$

where
A_o = Attitude toward the object

b_i = The strength of the belief that the object has attribute i

e_i = The evaluation of attribute i

n = The number of salient beliefs about the object

This multiattribute attitude model describes an integration process by which product knowledge (the evaluation and strength of salient beliefs) can be combined to form an overall evaluation or attitude. It is not meant to indicate, however, that consumers mentally multiply belief strength and evaluation when forming attitudes toward objects. Rather, it is designed to predict the attitude produced by the actual integration process. We see the multiattribute model as a useful tool for investigating attitude formation and predicting attitudes.

The typical number of salient beliefs about an attitude object is unlikely to exceed seven to nine.[14] Given the limited capacity of the cognitive system, we might expect even fewer salient beliefs for many objects. In fact, brand attitudes for low-involvement products might be based on very few salient beliefs, perhaps only one or two.

Exhibit 7.4 illustrates how the *strength* and *evaluation* of salient beliefs are combined in the multiattribute model to predict attitudes toward two brands of soft drinks. Note that this hypothetical consumer has salient beliefs about three attributes for each brand. These beliefs differ in content, strength, and evaluation. The multiattribute model predicts this consumer will have a more favourable attitude toward 7UP than toward Diet Pepsi.

Belief strength (b_i) is the perceived probability of association between an object and some relevant attribute. Asking consumers to rate this probability of association for each of their salient beliefs can measure belief strength:

EXHIBIT 7.4

An example of the multiattribute attitude model

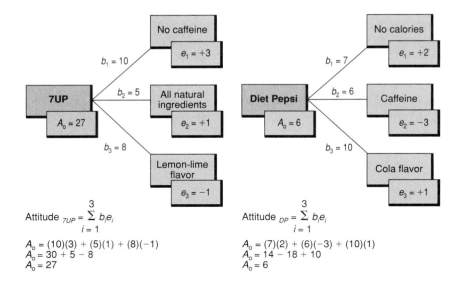

$$\text{Attitude}_{7UP} = \sum_{i=1}^{3} b_i e_i$$

$$A_o = (10)(3) + (5)(1) + (8)(-1)$$
$$A_o = 30 + 5 - 8$$
$$A_o = 27$$

$$\text{Attitude}_{DP} = \sum_{i=1}^{3} b_i e_i$$

$$A_o = (7)(2) + (6)(-3) + (10)(1)$$
$$A_o = 14 - 18 + 10$$
$$A_o = 6$$

"How likely is it that 7UP has no caffeine?"

Extremely unlikely   1 2 3 4 5 6 7 8 9 10   Extremely likely

"How likely is it that 7UP is made from all natural ingredients?"

Extremely unlikely   1 2 3 4 5 6 7 8 9 10   Extremely likely

Consumers who are quite certain that 7UP has no caffeine would indicate a very strong belief strength, perhaps 9 or 10. Consumers who have only a moderately strong belief that 7UP is made entirely from natural ingredients might rate their belief strength as 5 or 6.

The strength of consumers' product or brand beliefs is affected by their past experiences with the object. Beliefs about product attributes or consequences tend to be stronger when they are based on actual use of the product. Beliefs formed indirectly from mass advertising or conversation with a salesperson tend to be weaker. For instance, consumers are more likely to form a strong belief that "7UP tastes good" if they actually drink some and taste it themselves than if they read a product claim in an ad.[15] These stronger beliefs based on direct experience tend to have a greater impact on A_o, so marketers try to give their potential customers actual use experience with their product. They may distribute free samples; sell small, less-expensive trial sizes; offer cents-off coupons; or have a no-obligation trial policy.

The **evaluation (e_i)** associated with each salient belief reflects how favourably the consumer perceives that attribute. Marketers measure the e_i component by having consumers indicate their evaluation of (favourability toward) each salient belief, as shown below.

"Sodas that have no caffeine"

Very bad   -3 -2 -1 0 +1 +2 +3   Very good

"Sodas with all natural ingredients"

Very bad   -3 -2 -1 0 +1 +2 +3   Very good

Exhibit 7.4 shows how the evaluation of each salient belief influences the overall A_o in proportion to the strength of that belief (b_i). Thus, strong beliefs about positive attributes have greater effects on A_o than do weak beliefs about equally positive attributes.

Likewise, negative evaluations reduce the favourability of A_o in proportion to their belief strength "weights."

Marketers have been using multiattribute models since the late 1960s to understand consumer behaviour. The models are popular because managers find them appealing and relatively easy to use.[16] Three of the many applications of these models are understanding customers, diagnosing marketing strategies, and understanding environmental influences.

Marketing implications

Understanding customers

The multiattribute attitude model is useful for understanding which attributes are the most salient or important to consumers. For instance, airline passengers are loud in complaining about the food served on planes.[17] Yet in one large-scale survey, only 40 percent of passengers rated good food and beverage service as important. Other attributes were seen as much more important, including convenient schedules (over 90 percent), fast check-in (about 80 percent), comfortable seats (about 80 percent), and good on-time performance (about 85 percent). Perhaps airlines use such data to justify not improving the quality of the food they serve (airlines spend only about $4.25 per passenger on food). Of course, the relative importance of different product attributes varies across market segments. For instance, three segments of the airline market—light travellers (1 or 2 trips per year), moderate travellers (3 to 9 trips per year), and frequent travellers (10 or more trips per year)—evaluate some attributes differently. Light travellers have greater concerns about safety and efficient baggage handling, while heavier travellers are more concerned with convenient schedules and the frequent-flyer program.

Diagnosing marketing strategies

Although multiattribute models were developed to predict overall attitudes, marketers often use them to diagnose marketing strategies. By examining the salient beliefs that underlie attitudes toward various brands, marketers can learn whether their strategies are influencing those beliefs and make adjustments to improve their effectiveness. For instance, in the "value conscious" 1990s, marketers found that many consumers were more concerned with price and with the quality and value of products relative to price.[18] It became fashionable to seek a bargain, spend one's money wisely, and not overpay for quality. Many companies adjusted their strategies in light of these beliefs and values. Consider the motto of the world's largest retailer, Wal-Mart, "The low price on the brands you trust." Price Club, Price-Costco, and Club Biz combined low prices with friendly but bare-bones service to enhance consumers' value beliefs and overall attitudes. In the United States, Taco Bell reduced its operating costs enough to price several items on the menu under $1 and create stronger beliefs about the value provided. Tim Horton's now offers tidbits (a dozen) for under $2.00. Consumer Perspective 7.3 presents another example of marketing strategies directed at consumers' beliefs about value.

Understanding environmental influences

Finally, marketers can also use the multiattribute attitude model to examine the influence of the product use environment on the relative salience of beliefs about product attributes. The usage environment can vary in many ways, including time of day, presence of others, physical setting, weather, or hundreds of other variables. These environmental factors influence which beliefs are activated from memory, which in turn influences attitudes toward the brand that might be purchased for use in that situation. A study of snack products, for example, found that beliefs about economy and taste were most important in three common snacking situations: for everyday desserts at home, for watching TV in the evening, and for kids' school lunches.[19] However, beliefs about nutrition and convenience were most important in the environmental situation of providing snacks for a children's party. Different salient beliefs in various usage environments can lead to different brand attitudes in those situations.

ATTITUDE-CHANGE STRATEGIES

The multiattribute model is a useful guide for devising **attitude-change strategies**.[20] Basically, a marketer has four ways of changing consumers' attitudes: (1) add a new salient belief about the attitude object—ideally, one with a positive e_i; (2) change the strength of an existing belief; (3) increase the evaluation of a strongly held belief; or (4) make an existing favourable belief more salient.

Add a new salient belief

Adding a new salient belief to the beliefs that consumers already have about a product or brand is probably the most common attitude-change strategy. This strategy may require an actual change in the product. Hasbro Inc. is the biggest and perhaps the most successful toy marketer in North America.[21] One of Hasbro's marketing strengths is its ability to manage "old" products effectively, which involves adding new attributes and creating new salient beliefs for these products. In fact, its goal is to achieve 70 percent of revenues from existing products. In 1989, for example, as its G.I. Joe sales dropped, Hasbro discovered that many kids were becoming bored with the action figures (attitudes were becoming less favourable). In response, Hasbro redesigned 80 percent of the line by discarding old attributes such as combat fatigues and adding new attributes such as spacesuits, jetpacks, and combat helicopters. Kids loved the new look, and sales jumped back quickly. As another example, when Hasbro acquired the languishing Tonka brand of toy trucks and other vehicles, the company considered adding a salient attribute to the Tonka brand—a lifetime guarantee—to strengthen positive consumer attitudes.

Change strength of salient belief

Marketers can also try to change attitudes by *changing the strength of already salient beliefs*. They can attempt to increase the strength of beliefs about positive attributes and consequences, or they can decrease the strength of beliefs about negative attributes and consequences. Consider the millions of dollars spent by the Beef Industry Council and the milk producers of Canada to develop more favourable attitudes toward beef and milk. Beef consumption had fallen steadily in the 1970s and 1980s at a time when the consumption of chicken rose dramatically. Consumers' attitudes also changed dramatically. The percentage of people who described themselves as meat lovers dropped from 22 percent in 1983 to only 10 percent in 1985. Many consumers in Canada also switched from whole milk to 2 percent and skim milk. To weaken consumers' negative beliefs that beef and milk are fattening and have high levels of cholesterol, TV and print ads claimed, for example, that three ounces of trimmed sirloin has about the same calories and cholesterol as three ounces of chicken breast. Milk producers made claims about the importance of calcium in our diets. To strengthen consumer beliefs that both products are healthful, charts displayed at many supermarket counters showed the calorie and cholesterol levels for a cut of beef comparing favourably with the dietary standards recommended by the Canadian Heart Association, as well as the amount of calcium milk provides.

Marketers can try to change consumers' attitudes by *changing evaluations of an existing, strongly held belief* about a salient attribute. They can do this by linking a more positive consequence to that attribute, with the aim of changing the consumer's means-end knowledge. Cereal manufacturers such as Kellogg's, for instance, have tried to enhance consumer attitudes toward cereal brands by linking the food attribute fibre to cancer prevention. Along the same line, consider how evaluations of food attributes have changed as their means-end meanings have changed.[22] Attributes such as butterfat or egg yolks once were seen as favourable because they gave foods a rich, satisfying taste. But by the late 1980s, they had become negative attributes, while attributes once seen as rather undesirable, such as low fat or low salt, had become more highly valued. For instance, Sealtest linked non-fat characteristics of Sealtest 1 percent ice cream to important values such as health and fitness. Likewise, Kraft linked the key attributes of its fat-free line of salad dressings and mayonnaise (egg whites, skim milk, cellulose gel, and various gums) to important health consequences and values (lower risk of heart disease and longer life).

Change evaluation of existing belief

The final strategy for changing consumer attitudes is to *make an existing favourable belief more salient*, usually by convincing consumers that an attribute is more self-relevant than it once seemed. This strategy is similar to the previous one, in that it attempts to link an attribute to valued consequences and values. Creating such means-end chains increases both the salience of consumers' beliefs about the attribute and the evaluations (e_i) of those beliefs. For example, the marketing strategies of sun-lotion manufacturers such as Bain de Soleil and Hawaiian Tropic emphasize the perceived risks of not using products with a sunscreen attribute. By linking the sunscreen attribute to important ends such as lessening the risk of skin cancer and avoiding premature wrinkling, marketers sought to make the sunscreen attribute more salient (more self-relevant) for consumers. Such means-end chains are intended to make sunscreen beliefs more salient and more influential during decision making.

Make existing belief more salient

ATTITUDES TOWARD BEHAVIOURS

Consumer attitudes toward products and brands have been the subject of extensive research, but it is consumers' actual behaviours in which marketers are most interested, especially their purchasing behaviours. Many managers expect a strong relationship between a consumer's attitude toward an object (A_o) and his or her purchase of that same object. Thus, a marketer might measure consumers' attitudes toward Pizza Hut and use those attitudes to predict whether each person will purchase a pizza at Pizza Hut in the

EXHIBIT 7.5

Relationships among beliefs, attitude, and behaviours regarding a specific object

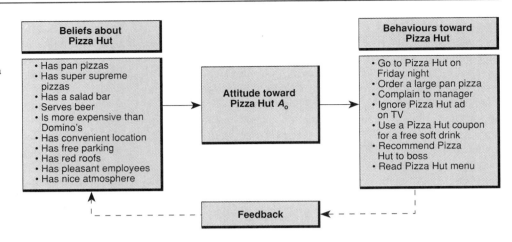

next two weeks. Although this approach might seem reasonable, overall A_o seldom is a good predictor of a specific behaviour.[23]

Exhibit 7.5 shows why it is not so simple to relate an overall brand attitude to a single behaviour. This exhibit presents the relationships among the beliefs, attitude, and behaviours of one consumer (we'll call her Judy) concerning a particular object—Pizza Hut. Judy has a single attitude, A_o, toward Pizza Hut, which is based on several salient beliefs she holds about Pizza Hut. In her case, this is a favourable overall evaluation. Note that Judy can engage in many different behaviours that involve Pizza Hut, some positive and some negative. For instance, she might go to Pizza Hut on Friday night and order a pizza, she might ignore a Pizza Hut ad on television, she might use a Pizza Hut coupon for a free soft drink, or she might complain to the store manager about an improperly cooked pizza.

None of Judy's specific behaviours, however, is necessarily strongly related to or even consistent with her overall A_o, although some might be. This is because a specific behaviour is influenced by many factors besides A_o, including various aspects of the physical environment and social pressures from other people. Does this mean attitudes are irrelevant to behaviours? Of course not. Exhibit 7.5 shows that, although Judy's overall attitude is not necessarily related to any specific behaviour, her A_o is related to *the entire pattern of her behaviours* involving Pizza Hut (all her behaviours taken together). If someone likes a product, most of her behaviours regarding that product are likely to be positive.

There are many examples of consumers with favourable attitudes toward products that are not purchased. Many consumers have positive attitudes toward fancy cars, diamond jewellery, 45-inch TVs, and vacation homes, but most do not own these products. Favourable attitudes toward products can be expressed in many different behaviours (besides purchase), so it is difficult to predict which behaviour will be performed. Consider three consumers who have highly favourable attitudes toward Porsches, although none owns a Porsche. One consumer may read ads and reports about Porsches, while another consumer may go to showrooms to look at Porsches. A third consumer may just daydream about owning a Porsche. Having a generally favourable (or unfavourable) attitude toward a product or brand does not mean the consumer will engage in every possible favourable behaviour regarding the product, including purchase. Marketers need a model that identifies the specific attitudinal factors leading to specific behaviours, such as the theory of reasoned action.

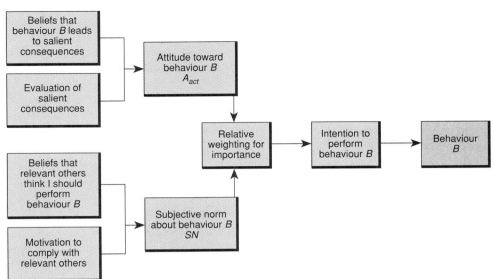

EXHIBIT 7.6

The theory of reasoned action

Source: Adapted from Martin Fishbein, "An Overview of the Attitude Construct," in *A Look Back, A Look Ahead*, ed. G. B. Hafer (Chicago: American Marketing Association, 1980), p. 8.

A particular behaviour is determined by the consumer's *intention* to perform the behaviour, not his or her attitude toward the object of the behaviour.[24] Whether you buy a university sweatshirt depends on your intention to take that action, not on your attitude toward the university or the sweatshirt brand. To explain how intentions are formed, researchers extended the basic multiattribute attitude model to create the model shown in Exhibit 7.6.[25] This model is called the **theory of reasoned action** because it assumes that consumers (1) consciously evaluate the consequences of the alternative behaviours they are considering and (2) choose the behaviour that is perceived to lead to the most desirable consequences.[26] The theory of reasoned action is not relevant in the case of simple, involuntary behaviours such as sneezing, turning your head at the sound of a telephone, or jumping at a loud sound. Such behaviours are performed automatically, without conscious analysis of their consequences.

Exhibit 7.6 shows the four main components of the theory of reasoned action: behaviour (*B*), intention to behave (*BI*), attitude toward the behaviour (A_{act}), and subjective norm (*SN*).[27] If you start with a behaviour, such as buying a pair of socks, and work backward through the theory of reasoned action, you see that the behaviour is determined by a person's intention to perform it. The behavioural intention, in turn, is a function of two factors: the person's *attitude toward the behaviour* and the *subjective norm* (or perceived social pressure) to engage in that behaviour. A_{act} is based on beliefs about the functional and psychosocial consequences of the behaviour, while *SN* is based on beliefs about what other people expect you to do. Simply stated, the theory of reasoned action proposes that people perform behaviours that are perceived to have desirable consequences and that are favoured by other people who are important to them. People are assumed to refrain from behaviours that have unfavourable consequences and are unpopular with others.

All the components of the theory of reasoned action are defined in terms of a specific behaviour. **Behaviour (*B*)** is an action directed toward an object for the purpose of

The theory of reasoned action

achieving one or more goals. Examples of behaviours include driving to the store, buying a swimsuit, drinking a soda, and looking for your lost pen. Behaviour always occurs *in an environment* or context, at a particular time (reading at home last night, shopping in the grocery store this afternoon).[28] Marketers have not always been careful in their measures of behaviour. To make more accurate measurements of behaviour, marketers should specify as precisely as possible its environmental context.

The theory of reasoned action proposes that every *voluntary* behaviour is determined by a behavioural intention. A **behavioural intention** is a plan to engage in a specific behaviour to reach a goal.[29] Behavioural intentions vary in strength, which can be measured with a simple rating scale:

"All things considered, how likely are you to use newspaper coupons when buying groceries this week or next?"

Extremely unlikely   1 2 3 4 5 6 7   Extremely likely

Exhibit 7.6 shows that a behavioural intention is created when consumers integrate or combine two types of information about the behaviour: their own attitude toward the behaviour or action (A_{act}) and the perceived social pressures from other people to perform that behaviour (*SN*). The relative influence or weight of these two factors depends on the particular behaviour that is involved. For example, private behaviours such as what toothpaste you use are determined largely by A_{act}, whereas more social behaviours such as what clothing you wear tend to be influenced by what others think (*SN*).

Consumers develop an overall evaluation of a behaviour or **attitude toward the behaviour or action (A_{act})** by integrating their *beliefs* about the salient consequences of the behaviour with their *evaluations* of those consequences. For example, if buying a Ford pickup is seen as producing more favourable consequences than buying a Chevy pickup, buying a Ford will have a more favourable A_{act}. Marketers can measure the strengths and evaluations of the salient beliefs about the consequences of a behaviour in the same way they measure beliefs about product attributes.

A_{act} can be quite different from A_o because the consequences of a behaviour regarding a product often are different from the product attributes. For instance, consider the salient beliefs about the attributes of "Chevrolet" versus the consequences of "buying a Chevrolet next week."

Chevrolet (A_o)	Buying a Chevrolet next week (A_{act})
Moderately priced (+)	Gives me a mode of transportation (+)
Ordinary (−)	Will put me in financial difficulty (−)
Well built (+)	Will lead to high upkeep costs (−)
Dependable (+)	Will cost more now than later (−)
Easily serviced (+)	Will lead to high insurance rates (−)

To the extent that the salient beliefs about the product and about the behaviour are evaluated differently, A_o and A_{act} will be different. Also, marketing strategies can have varying effects on A_o and A_{act}.[30] For instance, advertising the advantages of visiting Hallmark stores might influence consumers' attitudes toward shopping in a Hallmark store (A_{act}), but would not necessarily affect their attitudes toward Hallmark greeting cards (A_o).

The **subjective norm (*SN*)** component reflects the social pressures consumers may feel to perform (or avoid performing) certain behaviours. Exhibit 7.6 shows that the *SN* component results when a consumer considers his or her beliefs about whether important people want him or her to perform the behaviour along with his or her motivation to comply with these people's wishes.[31]

To summarise, the theory of reasoned action proposes an integration process where A_{act} and *SN* combine to form an intention to behave, which in turn determines the actual

CONSUMER
PERSPECTIVE

7.4

Increasing A_{act}
and behavioural
intentions

Marketers of credit cards have a difficult marketing task to influence specific consumer behaviours. First they have to get consumers to *accept* the cards; then they have to get consumers to *carry* and *use* the cards. According to the *Nilson Report*, a credit-card newsletter, the average cardholder carries about 7.5 pieces of plastic. Issuers can't make money on credit cards that aren't used, so they need strategies to make A_{act} and *BI* more positive.

Over the years, marketers have tried such inducements as free flight insurance when air travel is charged to the credit card and discounts on merchandise that most consumers probably wouldn't buy anyway. Neither of these promotions was evaluated very highly, and card usage was not affected very much.

Then, in the mid-1980s, some credit-card marketers finally got serious and began giving away cold, hard cash as an incentive. In the late 1980s, Royal Trust MasterCard of Canada offered a 1 percent discount on all outstanding balances that were paid in full by the due date. The use of this card rose significantly. Visa became very aggressive in the 1990s by combining forces with four of Canada's largest corporations. The Toronto Dominion Bank and General Motors of Canada teamed up to offer the TD/GM Visa card; members would accumulate potential rebates on the purchase of a GM car or truck. The Canadian Imperial Bank of Commerce and Air Canada teamed up to offer the CIBC/Aerogold Visa card, which offered Air Canada Aeroplan members one frequent-flyer point for every dollar spent on the card.

Will these marketing strategies work? Well, they add a belief about a new consequence (getting money back or free air travel) to the behaviour they want consumers to perform more often—using the credit cards. Of course, nearly everyone has a positive evaluation for receiving "free" money. Therefore, we would expect most consumers' attitudes toward using the cards to become more favourable. This, in turn, should increase their intentions to use the card.

Source: Adapted from Mary Kuntz, "Credit Cards as Good as Gold," *Forbes*, Nov. 4, 1985, pp. 234–36; "GM Rolls Out New Credit Card," *Toronto Star*, March 9, 1993, p. D1.

behaviour. When combined, A_{act} and *SN* may have different amounts of influence on *BI*.[32] Some behaviours may be influenced primarily by the *SN* factor. For instance, a person's intention to wear a certain style of clothing to a party is more likely to be determined by beliefs about what others expect than by the functional consequences of wearing those clothes. For other behaviours, normative influences are minimal, and consumers' intentions are largely determined by A_{act}. For example, a consumer's intention to purchase Contac cold remedy is probably due more to A_{act} based on beliefs about the functional consequences of using Contac than on *SN* and beliefs about what other people expect. Marketers need to understand how A_{act} and *SN* are integrated to create *BI* so they can focus their strategies on the dominant influence. Consumer Perspective 7.4 describes a strategy to increase A_{act} and *BI*.

Marketing implications

The environmental context can have powerful influences on consumers' behavioural intentions and their eventual behaviours. Consider Brian, an assistant brand manager for General Foods of Canada. Last week, Brian had to decide whether to buy imported or domestic beer in two different contexts. In the first, Brian wanted to have beer on hand at home over the weekend while he watched sports on TV. In the other context, he had a beer after work in a plush bar with a group of his co-workers. The different sets of product-related and social beliefs activated in the two situations created different A_{act} and *SN* components. In the at-home situation, Brian's product beliefs and A_{act} had the dominant effect on his intentions (he bought an inexpensive domestic beer). In the bar, his normative beliefs and *SN* had the stronger influence on his intentions (he bought an expensive imported beer).

To develop effective marketing strategies, marketers need to determine whether the A_{act} or the *SN* component has the major influence on behavioural intentions (and thus on behaviour). If the primary reason for a behaviour (shopping, searching for information, buying a particular brand) is normative (you think others want you to), marketers need to emphasise that the relevant normative influences (friends, family, co-workers) are in favour of the behaviour. Often this is done by portraying social influence situations in advertising. Conversely, if intentions are largely influenced by A_{act} factors, the marketing strategy should attempt to create a set of salient beliefs about the positive consequences of the behaviour, perhaps by demonstrating those outcomes in an ad.

INTENTION AND BEHAVIOUR

Predicting consumers' future behaviour, especially their purchase behaviour (sales, to marketers), is a critically important aspect of forecasting and marketing planning. According to the theory of reasoned action, predicting purchase behaviours is a matter of measuring consumers' intentions to buy just before they make a purchase. In almost all cases, however, this is impractical. Marketing strategies require prediction of consumers' purchase and use behaviours weeks, months, or sometimes years in advance.

Unfortunately, predictions of specific behaviours based on intentions measured well before the behaviour occurs may not be very accurate. One survey indicated that only about 60 percent of people who intended to buy a car actually did so within a year.[33] And of those who claimed they did not intend to buy a car, 17 percent ended up buying one. Similar examples could be cited for other product categories (where predictions may be even farther off). This does not mean the theory of reasoned action is wrong in identifying intention as an immediate influence on behaviour. Rather, failure to predict the behaviour of interest is often due to *when* and *how* intentions are measured.

To accurately predict behaviour, marketers should take careful measures of *BI*, being certain to identify precisely the behaviour of interest and specify clearly the environmental context. Exhibit 7.7 lists several factors that can weaken the relationship between measured behavioural intention and the observed behaviour. In situations where few of these factors operate, measured intentions should predict behaviour quite well.

In a broad sense, *time* is the major factor that reduces the predictive accuracy of measured intentions. Intentions, like other cognitive factors, change over time. The longer the intervening time period, the more likely it is that unanticipated circumstances (such as exposure to competing market strategies) will occur and change consumers' original purchase intentions. Of course, unanticipated events can also occur during very short time periods. An appliance manufacturer once asked consumers entering an appliance store what brand they intended to buy. Of those who specified a brand, only 20 percent came back out with it.[34] Apparently, events occurred in the store to change these consumers beliefs, attitudes, intentions, and purchase behaviours.

Despite their less-than-perfect accuracy, measures of purchase intentions are often the best way to predict future purchase behaviour. For instance, Air Canada, Canadian Airlines, and KLM Canada often conduct passenger surveys measuring intentions to travel by air during the next one to three months. Although many events in the ensuing time period can change consumers' beliefs, A_{act}, and *SN* about taking a personal or business trip by airplane, aggregated intentions can provide useful predictions of future airline travel.

Certain behaviours cannot be accurately predicted from beliefs, attitudes, and intentions.[35] Obvious examples include nonvoluntary behaviours such as sneezing or getting

Factor	Examples
Intervening time	As the time between measurement of intention and observation of behaviour increases, more factors can occur that act to modify or change the original intention, so that it no longer corresponds to the observed behaviour.
Different levels of specificity	The measured intention should be specified at the same level as the observed behaviour. Suppose we measure Judy's intentions to wear jeans to class (in general). But we observe her behaviour (not wearing jeans) on a day when she made a class presentation and didn't think jeans were appropriate.
Unforeseen event	Sam fully intended to buy Pringle's potato chips this afternoon, but the store was sold out. Sam could not carry out his purchase intention. He had to form a new intention on the spot to buy Hostess chips.
Unforeseen environmental context	Sometimes the environmental context the consumer had in mind when the intentions were measured is different from the situation at the time of behaviour. In general, Peter has a negative intention to buy André champagne. When he decides to prepare a holiday punch calling for eight bottles of champagne, however, Peter formed a positive intention to buy the inexpensive André brand.
Degree of voluntary control	Some behaviours are not under complete volitional control. Thus, intentions may not predict the observed behaviour very accurately. For instance, Becky intended to go shopping on Saturday when she hoped to be recovered from a bout with the flu, but she was still sick and couldn't go.
Instability of intentions	Some intentions are not stable, if they are founded on only a few weakly held beliefs that may be easily changed. Such intentions cannot predict actual behaviour accurately.
New information	Consumers may receive new information about the salient consequences of their behaviour, which leads to changes in their beliefs and attitudes toward the act and/or in the subjective norm. These changes, in turn, change the intention. The original intention is no longer revelant to the behaviour and does not predict the eventual behaviour accurately.

EXHIBIT 7.7

Factors that reduce or weaken the relationship between intention and behaviour

sick. It is also difficult to predict purchase behaviours when alternative brands are very similar and the person has positive attitudes toward several of them. Finally, behaviours about which consumers have little knowledge and low levels of involvement are virtually impossible to predict, because consumers have very few beliefs in memory on which to base attitudes and intentions. In such cases, a consumer's expressed intention may have been created to answer the marketing researcher's question. Such intentions are likely to be unstable and poor predictors of the eventual behaviour. In sum, before relying on measures of attitude and intentions to predict future behaviour, marketers need to determine whether consumers can reasonably be expected to have well-formed beliefs, attitudes, and intentions toward those behaviours.

▶ **SUMMARY**

Learning objective 1: *Define attitude and give two examples of its relevance for marketers.*

An attitude is a person's overall evaluation of a concept, whether an object or a behaviour. This overall evaluation (pro/con, favourable/unfavourable, positive/negative) develops when people combine or integrate relevant knowledge, meanings, and beliefs about the concept in judging its personal relevance to them. Many marketing strategies (advertising, pricing, product design) are intended to influence consumer attitudes. Marketers often use consumer attitudes toward a brand as criteria for marketing success. Marketers may measure consumers' product or brand attitudes over time to track the performance of a brand or the effectiveness of a marketing strategy.

Learning objective 2: *Describe salient beliefs and give an example of how marketers can influence belief salience.*

Salient beliefs are the most important or relevant beliefs out of all those in memory that are likely to be activated in a particular situation and used in integration processes. Because the cognitive system has a limited capacity, only a few beliefs can be salient at one time. Marketers hope favourable beliefs about their brand will be salient and activated to influence a purchase decision. Means-end chains are relevant for understanding belief salience. Beliefs about attributes or consequences that are linked to the important goals and values in a situation are most likely to be salient, so marketers can try to influence belief salience by linking product attributes to those important goals or values.

Learning objective 3: *Using the multiattribute attitude model as a guide, describe the information integration process by which consumers form an A_o.*

The multiattribute attitude model describes how consumers form an overall evaluation of a concept by combining salient beliefs about the concept. The model states that a consumer's attitude toward an object (A_o) is a combination of the strengths of the consumer's salient beliefs about product attributes and his or her evaluations of each attribute. The multiattribute attitude model proposes that consumers like objects that have good attributes and dislike objects that have bad attributes. The model represents this integration process by the formula:

$$A_o = \sum_{i=1}^{n} b_i e_i$$

The multiattribute attitude model does not claim that consumers actually calculate their attitude by multiplying and adding numbers according to this formula. Rather, the formula is an organised way for marketers to predict consumers' attitudes toward products and brands and to identify the salient beliefs that underlie those attitudes.

Learning objective 4: *Describe four attitude-change strategies based on the multiattribute attitude model.*

The multiattribute attitude model suggests four ways to change consumers' attitudes toward a concept (a brand, store, or product category). One strategy is to alter the strength of a salient belief. Marketing strategies that increase the strength of positive beliefs should produce a more positive A_o, while strategies directed at weakening negative beliefs should also increase A_o. Another strategy is to modify the evaluative component of a salient belief. Convincing consumers that a certain belief is more positive or less negative should produce a more positive A_o. The means-end perspective suggests that a marketer can create a more favourable belief by linking a product attribute to desirable end goals or values. A third strategy is to add a new belief about positive attributes to the set of salient beliefs. Commonly, this occurs when a new product attribute is added to a product (Kellogg's now has more fibre). Finally, marketers could try to increase the salience of an existing positive belief. From a means-end chain perspective, this would require making a product attribute more important or personally relevant by linking it to important goals or values.

Learning objective 5: *Explain how A_o differs from A_{act}.*

Attitudes toward an object (A_o) can be quite different from attitudes toward an action involving the same object (A_{act}) because each type of attitude is based on a different set of salient beliefs. A_o is based on beliefs about product *attributes*, while A_{act} is based on beliefs about the *consequences* of buying and using a product. Although the two are related, they can be rather different. For certain objects and behaviours, there may be little overlap between the salient beliefs. If so, A_o and A_{act} will be quite different. For instance, Joe might like a particular restaurant very much (it has good food, service, and mosphere), yet have a negative attitude toward eating there on Friday night (it is too far away, too crowded, and short on parking spaces).

Learning objective 6: *Describe how the components of the theory of reasoned action are combined to create a behavioural intention.*

The theory of reasoned action claims that behavioural intentions are based on two factors—consumers' attitudes toward the behaviour or action (A_{act}) and the subjective norm (SN)—each of which is based on a set of salient beliefs that consumers find relevant. A_{act} is based on consumers' beliefs about the consequences of a behaviour (buying a soft drink from the vending machine is quick and easy, shopping for clothes at the Gap is fun and exciting). The SN component reflects consumers' beliefs about the social pressures to perform a behaviour. These beliefs reflect consumers' perceptions about what significant other people want them to do (my mother thinks I should buy the green shorts, my friend wants me to buy the Blue Rodeo CD). In a particular situation, A_{act} and SN are integrated, perhaps with different weights, to form a behavioural intention, BI. In some situations, A_{act} may be the dominant influence on BI, while in other cases, SN has the greater effect on intentions.

Learning objective 7: *Identify three factors that can reduce the accuracy of a measure of behavioural intention in predicting the actual behaviour.*

In general, measures of behavioural intentions become less accurate as the time increases between BI measurement and the actual behaviour. This is because many other things can intervene between the intention and the actual behaviour. When the original intention is no longer the relevant determinant of the behaviour, the measure is not accurate. Other factors that affect the accuracy of behavioural intentions include consumers' uncertainty about the intention. Sometimes consumers don't really have a clear intention, yet they are asked to indicate what they are likely to do. Sometimes the measure of intention asks consumers about the likelihood they will perform a general behaviour, but their actual behaviour is constrained by the specific environmental context in which it occurs. To the extent that unanticipated environmental factors influence behaviour, the intention measure will be less accurate. When behaviours are not completely voluntary, behavioural intentions may not be entirely relevant. Finally, consumers can get new information that leads to changes in their beliefs and eventually creates a new behavioural intention, making the original BI irrelevant.

			▶ **KEY TERMS**
attitude	salient beliefs	theory of reasoned action	**AND**
evaluations	multiattribute attitude	behaviour (B)	**CONCEPTS**
integration process	model	behavioural intention	
brand equity	belief strength (b_i)	attitude toward the behav-	
attitudes toward	evaluation (e_i)	iour or action (A_{act})	
objects (A_o)	attitude-change strategies	subjective norm (SN)	

---

1. Define *attitude* and identify the two main ways consumers can acquire attitudes.
2. How are salient beliefs different from other beliefs? How can marketers attempt to influence belief salience?
3. According to the multiattribute attitude model, how does a consumer integrate beliefs to form an attitude?
4. Consider a product category in which you make regular purchases (such as toothpaste or shampoo). How have your beliefs and evaluations changed over time? Is your attitude accessible in memory?

▶ **REVIEW AND DISCUSSION QUESTIONS**

5. Use an example to describe the key differences between A_o and A_{act}. Under what circumstances would marketers be most interested in each type of attitude?

6. Describe the theory of reasoned action and discuss the two main factors that are integrated to form a behavioural intention. Describe one marketing strategy implication for each factor.

7. Develop an example to distinguish between the multiattribute attitude model and the theory of reasoned action. How could each model contribute to the development of a more effective marketing strategy for the products in question?

8. Discuss the problems in measuring behavioural intentions to (a) buy a new car; (b) buy a soft drink from a vending machine; and (c) save $250 a month toward the eventual purchase of a house. What factors could occur in each situation to make the measured intentions a poor predictor of actual behaviour?

9. How could marketers improve their predictions of behaviours in the situations described in Question 8? Consider both measurement improvements and alternate research or forecasting techniques.

10. Negative attitudes present a special challenge for marketing strategy. Consider how what you have learned about attitudes and intentions could help you to address a consumer who has a brand relationship described as "Doesn't like our brand and buys a competitor's brand."

8

Consumer Decision Making

LEARNING OBJECTIVES

After completing this chapter, you should be able to:

► 1. Define a decision and describe why consumer decision making is part of the problem-solving process.

► 2. Describe the six stages of the problem-solving process.

► 3. Define end goals and discuss their role in problem solving.

► 4. Define a consideration set, discuss how it can be formed, and describe an implication of consideration sets for marketers.

► 5. Define choice criteria and give examples of how positive and negative choice criteria might be used in problem solving.

► 6. Describe the difference between compensatory and noncompensatory integration processes and give an example of each.

► 7. Describe three types of heuristics and give an example of each.

► 8. Describe the three levels of problem-solving effort and give a marketing implication for each.

THE DINNER PARTY

In mid-September, Barbara decided to have a dinner party for 10 people on October 17. She immediately called and invited all the guests. But now she had a problem: she didn't have enough dishes to serve 10 people. Actually Barbara had two sets of dishes—Wedgwood stoneware and Lenox china—but several pieces of the stoneware had broken over the years, and she had only seven place settings of the china. Barbara decided she had to buy some new dishes. Given her budget restrictions, Barbara decided to replace the missing pieces of stoneware, which she thought would be less expensive than the china.

That Friday, Barbara called several department stores, only to discover that none of them had her pattern in stock. In fact, they said it would take from two to six months to get the dishes and that Wedgwood would probably discontinue the pattern soon. Barbara decided to order the stoneware and borrow dishes for the party. First, though, she would check with her husband.

Barbara's husband was not very enthusiastic. He thought replacing the stoneware might be more expensive than buying a complete set of new dishes, especially with sales at the department stores, and he noted that a six-month wait was also a high cost. Besides, the stoneware they would be matching was chipped and scratched. Barbara might instead add three place settings to the china. Barbara developed a complex plan to take all of these factors into consideration. She decided that if finishing her set of china cost under $200 more than the stoneware replacements, she would buy three place settings of china. If a new set of stoneware cost under $100 more than replacing the missing china, she would buy the new set of stoneware dishes. But if these two alternative actions were more expensive, she would order the replacement pieces for her Wedgwood stoneware.

When she called stores to check sale prices, Barbara learned the sales offered 25 percent off all dishes in stock. She also learned that one store was selling a service for eight of Chinese porcelain for $100. At that price, she could buy two sets (a service for 16) for less than any of her other options would cost. She decided to buy the Chinese porcelain, if she liked it.

Later that Saturday, Barbara's mother-in-law happened to call, and Barbara told her what she was thinking about. Barbara's mother-in-law said to forget the Chinese porcelain because it is too fragile—either bone china or stoneware is much stronger. She also told Barbara about a warehouse "club" store that had a large inventory and very low prices. Barbara decided to go back to her previous plan, but to check out the warehouse, too.

Barbara visited The Bay, Eaton's and Sears. She learned from one salesperson that porcelain and bone china are equally strong and both are stronger than stoneware. She also discovered that ordering the replacement Wedgwood would cost several hundred dollars and could take up to 12 months. Barbara saw an Imari stoneware pattern she liked that was on sale and within her budget. She decided to check with the warehouse store to see whether it had the Imari pattern, because she might be able to save a lot of money buying at the outlet. If the price was low enough, it might be worth the 90-minute round-trip drive.

Barbara found the number of the warehouse and called it. The Imari pattern was out of stock and an order would take two months, but the outlet had many other patterns. Now, Barbara was in a quandary. She could probably save considerable money by going to the warehouse, but it was a long drive and she couldn't go until the weekend. But by then the department store might be sold out of the Imari pattern she liked. And there was a chance that she wouldn't find anything she liked at the warehouse. Barbara decided to check out the Chinese porcelain and buy it if she liked it. Otherwise, she would drive to the warehouse on the weekend and buy something.

On Wednesday, Barbara went to the department store to look at the Chinese porcelain. Although it was pretty, it came only in a delicate flower pattern she did not care for. She decided to drive to the warehouse right away. If it didn't have anything she liked, she could go back to the department store and buy the Imari pattern.

Barbara drove 45 minutes to the warehouse. It had a huge inventory at much lower prices than the department store, but no stoneware with the Oriental pattern she wanted. So she telephoned the department store to see whether it still had the Imari pattern. It did, but there were no longer 10 place settings left. Perhaps this disappointment led Barbara to ask once again if the warehouse had the Imari pattern. She was surprised to find that it did have the pattern in stock, and even better, it was on sale for 25 percent off the already low price. Unfortunately, the dishes were at central distribution and couldn't be picked up for 7 to 10 days. Barbara was pleased to find a complete set of the dishes she liked best at a great price. Her only worry was that her dinner party was exactly 10 days away. She decided to order the Imari dishes and take the chance that they would be there on time. They were, and Barbara was pleased with her choice.[1]

CONSUMER DECISIONS

Barbara made several decisions during the complex process of buying her new tableware. Each **decision** involved a choice between two or more alternative actions [or behaviours].[2] For instance, Barbara had to decide between travelling to the warehouse store or buying the tableware at the department store. *Every decision requires a choice between possible behaviours.* For instance, when Joe bought a Snickers candy bar from a vending machine, his actual choice was not among different brands of candy but between the alternative *behaviours* of buying Snickers versus buying one of the other brands. When Jill is trying to decide whether to see a particular movie, her choice is really between the behaviours involved in attending the movie versus the behaviours involved in staying home (or going bowling, or whatever other activities she is considering). Marketers are particularly interested in consumer's purchase behaviours, especially their choices of which brands to buy (Should I get Levi's or Guess? jeans?). But consumers also make many decisions about behaviours other than brand choice (Should I go shopping now or wait until after lunch? Should I pay with cash or Visa?). Some of these other behaviours are targets of marketing strategies: "Come down to our store this afternoon for free coffee and doughnuts."

Even though marketers often refer to consumers making decisions about objects (products, brands, or stores), consumers actually choose among alternative behaviours involving those objects. This means the components of the theory of reasoned action—attitude toward the behaviour or action (A_{act}), subjective norms (SN), and behavioural intentions (BI)—are relevant for understanding consumer decision making (refer back to Exhibit 7.6).

Exhibit 8.1 shows that each decision a consumer makes involves the cognitive processes of interpretation and integration as influenced by the knowledge, meanings, and beliefs activated from memory. **Integration** is a key process in decision making. During integration, consumers combine salient beliefs about the possible consequences of the behaviours being considered in order to evaluate the alternative behaviours (form A_{act} and SN). By integrating these factors, consumers make a **choice** of which behaviour to perform and form a behavioural intention (BI). A behavioural intention (I am going to buy Wilson tennis balls) can be thought of as a *plan* to engage in the chosen behaviour.

We assume that every voluntary behaviour is determined by a behavioural intention created by a decision-making process. However, this does not mean people engage in conscious decision making before every behaviour.[3] Some voluntary behaviours have become habitual and occur with little or no decision-making effort (Sara always buys Canada Dry when she wants a soft drink). These routine behaviours still are based on intentions that once were produced by a decision-making process, but the intentions or plans are stored in memory. When activated, these behavioural intentions automatically produce the habitual behaviour. Conscious decision making is not necessary on each occasion. Also, decision making does not occur for simple involuntary behaviours (sneezing is an example) or for behaviours controlled largely by the environment (the layout of aisles and product displays partly determines consumers' movements through a store).

This chapter treats consumer decision making as part of a problem-solving process. This means consumers evaluate and choose behaviours (Should I go to Zellers or Wal-Mart?) *in the context of a perceived problem.* During a problem-solving episode like

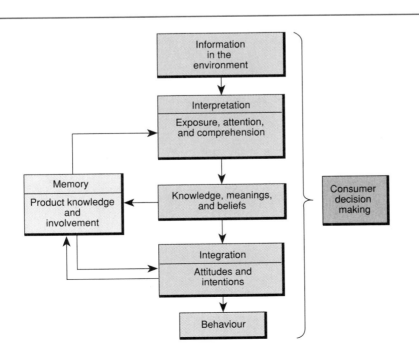

EXHIBIT 8.1

A model of consumer decision making

Barbara's, consumers make many types of decisions. "Where and when should I shop? What products or brands might solve my problem? What product attributes are most relevant to my goals? Who should I consult about this purchase? What brand should I buy? How should I pay for my purchase?" We begin by presenting a general model that identifies several stages of problem solving, each of which may involve decisions. We discuss each stage of problem solving, along with the decision-making processes of interpretation, integration, and activation of knowledge that may occur. Then, we describe three levels of problem-solving effort and discuss the implications of these levels for marketing strategies.

THE PROBLEM-SOLVING PROCESS

As Barbara's tableware buying experience illustrates, **problem solving** involves a goal-directed sequence of interactions among cognitive and affective responses, behaviours, and environmental factors—the three components of the Wheel of Consumer Analysis.[4] To help understand these complexities, researchers have developed models of problem solving.

Exhibit 8.2 presents a model of six basic stages in problem solving. The first stage is *problem recognition,* where the consumer recognises that the current situation is not ideal and thus identifies one or more goals. (The upcoming dinner party made Barbara aware of a problem and her goal: she needed a set of nice dishes for 10 people.) In the next stage, consumers *search for relevant information.* (Because Barbara had little relevant knowledge about dishes in memory, she had to search for information by calling and visiting stores, talking to salespeople, and discussing the problem with her husband and mother-in-law.) In the *evaluation of alternatives* stage, the consumer compares alternative behaviours in terms of their potential to achieve the activated goals. (Barbara evaluated the act of buying the different tableware she found during her search in terms of her desired price, delivery, and design criteria.) At the *choice decision* stage, the consumer

EXHIBIT 8.2

A model of consumer problem solving

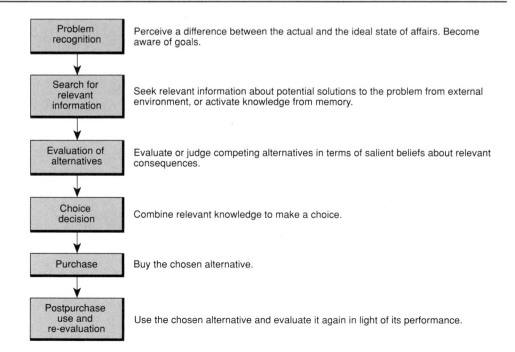

Problem recognition	Perceive a difference between the actual and the ideal state of affairs. Become aware of goals.
Search for relevant information	Seek relevant information about potential solutions to the problem from external environment, or activate knowledge from memory.
Evaluation of alternatives	Evaluate or judge competing alternatives in terms of salient beliefs about relevant consequences.
Choice decision	Combine relevant knowledge to make a choice.
Purchase	Buy the chosen alternative.
Postpurchase use and re-evaluation	Use the chosen alternative and evaluate it again in light of its performance.

forms an intention to buy. (Barbara finally decided to buy the Imari pattern at the warehouse store.) At the *purchase* stage, the purchase intention or plan is carried out. (Barbara ordered the dishes, and a few days later she returned to pay for the dishes and pick them up.) The final stage of problem solving is *postpurchase use and re-evaluation,* where consumers use the purchased product and reconsider their choice decision. (Barbara had her dinner party and was glad to have the new stoneware.)

Understanding consumer problem solving requires a careful analysis of the goals that are activated during problem recognition. A *goal* is a desired consequence or value in a means-end chain. (Dana wants a car that gives her reliable transportation. Steve wants a shampoo that gives his hair extra body. Rhona wants to go to a restaurant where her kids won't have to wait.) **Problem recognition** occurs when a consumer notices that the current state of affairs is not the ideal or desired state. At this point, a goal is activated. For instance, a man who notices dandruff on his shoulder and recognises a problem and wants to get rid of the dandruff (a goal). Depending on the perceived importance of the problem, he experiences a certain level of involvement with solving the problem and achieving the goal. This involvement motivates his problem-solving activities and focuses his decision making on reaching the goal.

Problem recognition

The most basic consequences or values that consumers want to achieve or satisfy are called **end goals.** They provide a frame that gives a direction and focus to the entire problem-solving process.[5] Some end goals represent concrete, tangible consequences; others are more abstract. For instance, a purchase decision to replace a flashlight bulb involves a concrete end goal of buying a bulb that lights—a simple functional consequence. Other product choices involve more abstract end goals such as desired psycho-social consequences of a product—some people want to serve a fine French wine that indicates their sophisticated taste to their guests. Finally, end goals such as instrumental

This ad shows how the product is relevant for solving five different problems.

EXHIBIT 8.3

Types of purchase end goals and related problem-solving motivations

Dominant End Goal	Basic Purchase Motivation	Examples
Optimise satisfaction	Seek maximum positive consequences	Buy dinner at the best restaurant in town
Prevent problem	Avoid potential unpleasant consequences	Buy rust-proofing for a new car
Resolve conflict	Seek satisfactory balance of positive and negative consequences	Buy a moderately expensive car of very good quality
Escape from problem	Reduce or escape from unwanted circumstances	Buy a shampoo to get rid of dandruff
Maintain satisfaction	Maintain satisfaction of basic need with minimal effort	Buy bread at the nearest convenience store

Source: Adapted from Geraldine Fennell, "Motivation Research Revisited," *Journal of Advertising Research*, June 1975, pp. 23–28; J. Paul Peter and Lawrence X. Tarpey, Sr., "A Comparative Analysis of Three Consumer Decision Strategies," *Journal of Consumer Research*, June 1975, pp. 29–37.

and terminal values are even more abstract and general—consumers might choose a car that makes them feel sporty or enhances their self-esteem. End goals also vary in evaluation. Some consumer decisions focus on achieving positive, desirable end goals, while others focus on negative end goals—distasteful consequences the consumer wishes to avoid.

The particular end goals consumers are striving to achieve have a powerful effect on the problem-solving process and the many decisions they make. Exhibit 8.3 presents very broad types of end goals that motivate quite different problem-solving processes. For instance, consumers who have an *optimising* end goal are likely to expend substantial effort searching for the best possible alternative. At the other extreme, consumers with a *satisfying/maintenance* end goal are likely to engage in minimal search behaviour. In yet other decisions, consumers may have conflicting end goals that must be resolved during problem solving.

Marketers have relatively little direct influence over consumers' abstract end goals, including values. However, marketers do use promotional strategies to influence more tangible goals, such as desired functional or psychosocial consequences. For instance, a London Life insurance salesperson might try to influence consumers' end goals by convincing them that buying life insurance is a way to guarantee their children's college educations or to maximise the payout from a company pension. The usual strategy is to identify the major goals activated by problem recognition and design product and promotion strategies consistent with those goals.

Search for relevant information

To decide which behaviour is likely to satisfy their goals, consumers need knowledge that is relevant to the choice problem. Consumers who have past experience in choosing products to satisfy their goals may have considerable relevant knowledge stored in memory that can be activated for use in interpretation and integration processes. The end goal is a major influence on what product knowledge is activated during decision making.[6] Product attributes and functional consequences that have strong means-end links to the end goal are more likely to be used in making a purchase decision.

Those without suitable knowledge in memory must **search for relevant information** in the environment.[7] Because Barbara had no experience with buying tableware and little relevant knowledge in memory about dishes, prices, and shops, she had to exert considerable effort searching for useful information. In problem-solving situations with less important goals, consumers may engage in casual search behaviour. For instance, people

Sometimes consumers browse as part of a vague search plan. Frequently, however, browsing consumers have no specific decision plan in mind. They are shopping for other reasons: recreation, stimulation from store environments, social contact, escape from home or work, or even exercise. In other words, some consumers get satisfaction from shopping/browsing, apart from solving a purchase problem. Browsing can be both a problem-solving strategy and a form of leisure activity.

One motivation for browsing without a specific decision plan in mind is that the consumer is involved in some way with a particular product class or form and likes to be around it. Consumers who are interested in music may enjoy browsing in record shops. Some consumers are involved with a particular store or set of stores in a mall or shopping area, perhaps because they like the atmosphere.

Trillium Terminal 3 at the Pearson International Airport in Toronto, which has been called an Eaton Centre with 24 gates, is one example of how architecture and imagery can stimulate the consumer to browse. A significant amount of space goes to revenue-generating retail—a precedent-setting 100,000 square feet, a tenth of the whole. The spending opportunities seem endless. To make the browsing experience more enjoyable, Trillium's panels are painted a soothing aqua, and street furniture and drinking fountains are spread throughout the terminal. The overwhelming message consumers receive at the Pearson International Airport is to savour the delays—and start browsing.

Retail stores need to pay attention to browsers because they can have a major impact on the success of the store (although the retailer may have a problem if browsers crowd the store and keep serious customers away). Discouraging browsers is easy: follow them around the store being "helpful." But driving browsers away can be risky. Many browsers become buyers. If a particular store creates a negative environment, browsers may take their business to a different store.

Since browsers play a significant role in relaying information to other consumers, they are doubly important. Not only may they buy something themselves, but they are likely to spread word-of-mouth information to less well-informed consumers.

Sources: "Terminal 3: A Shopping Mall with 24 Gates" Adele Freedman, *Globe and Mail*, Feb. 23, 1991; Peter H. Bloch and Marsha L. Richins, "Shopping without Purchase: An Investigation of Consumer Browsing Behavior," in *Advances in Consumer Research* 10, ed. R. P. Bagozzi and A. M. Tybout (Ann Arbor, Mich.: Association for Consumer Research, 1983), pp. 389–93.

CONSUMER PERSPECTIVE

8.1

Browsing as search and entertainment

can pick up relevant information while browsing in Eaton's or through the Sears catalogue. Consumer Perspective 8.1 describes how consumers use browsing for casual search and entertainment at Toronto's Pearson International Airport. Finally, consumers can acquire relevant knowledge through purely accidental exposure to marketing information (learning about a new store through a radio ad).

To make a choice decision, consumers need relevant knowledge about possible solutions to their problem that may help them to achieve their goals. The alternative behaviours consumers consider during decision making are called **choice alternatives.** For purchase decisions, the choice alternatives are different product categories, product forms, brands, or models the consumer is considering buying. For other types of decisions, the choice alternatives might be different stores to visit, times of the day or week to go shopping, or methods of paying (cash, cheque, credit or debit card). Given their limited time, energy, and cognitive capacity, consumers seldom consider every possible choice alternative; instead, they evaluate a limited subset of all possible alternatives, called the **consideration set.**[8]

Exhibit 8.4 illustrates how a manageable consideration set of brands can be identified during problem solving. Some brands in the consideration set may be activated directly

EXHIBIT 8.4

Forming a consideration set of brand choice

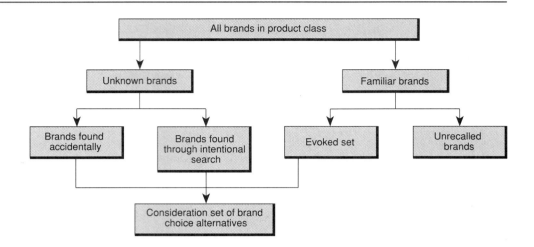

from memory—this group is the *evoked set*.[9] For highly familiar decisions, consumers may not consider any brands beyond those in the evoked set; they are confident they already know the best choice alternatives.

In other decisions, they may find choice alternatives through intentional search activities such as reading the results of product tests, talking to knowledgeable friends, or examining brands in a store.[10] Finally, consumers may learn of still other choice alternatives through accidental exposures to information in the environment, such as overhearing others talking about new Sun Chips snacks, a new store like the Future Shop, or a sale at Mark's Work Warehouse. Barbara learned about the warehouse store from her mother-in-law, essentially by accident. However the choice alternatives are generated, they form a *consideration set* of possible purchase options to be evaluated in decision making.

To be chosen, a brand must be included in the consideration sets of at least some consumers. Marketers therefore develop strategies to increase the likelihood that a brand will be activated from consumers' memories and included in their evoked sets of choice alternatives. The activation potential of a brand, sometimes called its *top-of-mind awareness,* is the result of many factors. One is the amount of past experience consumers have had with the brand. Consumers are much more likely to think of (activate) brands they have used before. For this reason, popular brands with higher market share, such as Molson Export, have a distinct advantage.[11] The more a brand is used, the more likely it is activated, and the greater the probability of its purchase, which in turn increases its activation potential, and so on. Unfamiliar and low-market-share brands, such as Lakeport beer, are at a disadvantage, since they are much less likely to be included in consumers' evoked sets and to be considered choice alternatives.

Marketing implications

One marketing strategy to increase the activation potential of a brand is to adopt repetitive (and costly) advertising campaigns such as those promoting Du Maurier cigarettes, Labatt Blue beer, Pepsi and Coke, and Colgate and Crest.[12] Such heavy expenditures may pay off, because brands with high top-of-mind awareness are more likely to be included in the evoked set of choice alternatives that "come to mind" during problem solving.

Finally, distribution strategies, such as those used by the Canadian Milk and Poultry Marketing Boards can have a critical influence on whether a brand or product is in the consideration set. Consider food products, where an estimated 65 percent of decisions are made in the store. A key marketing strategy in this case is making sure the product is on the shelf. Availability in the store enhances the likelihood that consumers will encounter the brand at the time of the decision, which increases its chances of entering consumers' consideration sets.

To make purchase decisions, consumers need knowledge about the consequences of the choice alternatives. **Evaluation of alternatives** in the consideration set (forming A_{act}) is based on consumers' beliefs about the consequences of buying and using those products or brands. The specific consequence beliefs a consumer uses to evaluate choice alternatives are called **choice criteria**.[13] Virtually any type of product-related consequence can be a choice criterion in a brand choice decision, including beliefs about functional consequences (product performance), psychosocial consequences (approval of friends), or value consequences (a sense of achievement or self-esteem).

Evaluation of alternatives

For many common problems, consumers may have some beliefs in memory about the consequences of the choice alternatives in the consideration set. If more knowledge about choice criteria is desired, consumers must search for information by visiting stores, reading *Consumer Reports,* or talking to salespeople. For unfamiliar problems, consumers may not know which product attributes and consequences are appropriate as choice criteria, and they may have to search for relevant information.[14] Barbara spent considerable effort searching for information about what attributes and consequences were appropriate as choice criteria.

Consumers do not necessarily consider a large number of choice criteria in the evaluation integration process. In fact, given their limited cognitive capacity, the number of choice criteria considered at one time may be only one or two.[15] The probability that product beliefs will be used as choice criteria (activated and integrated in evaluating choice alternatives) depends on how relevant they are to the end goal. If the end goal is self-esteem, for instance, then beliefs about product consequences that are linked to self-esteem are likely to be used as choice criteria. The end goal generated by problem recognition is an important influence. Different end goals may be activated in different problem contexts, such as buying a sweater for yourself versus buying one as a gift ("I want to be seen as stylish" versus "I want to be seen as generous"). Different choice criteria (unique design versus expensive looks) may be relevant to these end goals.

Determining choice criteria

Marketers can try to activate certain choice criteria by placing marketing information in prominent places in the decision environment. For instance, special sale signs can activate beliefs about financial consequences (saving money). Prominent labels on food packages, such as "fat free" or "low cholesterol," enhance the likelihood that the consumer will use these consequences as choice criteria. Finally, salespeople tend to emphasise certain product benefits in their sales pitches, which increases the probability that beliefs about those consequences will be used as choice criteria.

An important influence on choice criteria is the set of product attributes of the choice alternatives in the consideration set.[16] Only *discriminant consequences*—consequences that are perceived to differ across choice alternatives—can be used as choice criteria.[17] If several choice alternatives have a similar consequence, that consequence cannot discriminate between the alternatives and cannot be used as a choice criterion. For example, if all the soft drinks in a vending machine are caffeine-free, the consequences of non-stimulation (I will get to sleep) is the same for all alternatives and cannot be used as a choice criterion.

Consumers' choice criteria can have varying evaluations. Some choice criteria are desirable consequences that elicit positive affective responses, produce positive A_{act}, and lead to a favourable *BI*. Other choice criteria, such as price, may have unpleasant consequences and elicit negative affective responses.[18] Over the past decade, for example,

CONSUMER
PERSPECTIVE

▶ 8.2

Marketing
strategies
aimed at price

Many consumers see shopping for certain luxury items as a risky venture, because they are uncertain about their abilities to negotiate the best price. A common retailer strategy is to offer consumers both a money-back guarantee with no questions asked and a price protection guarantee. Thus no financial loss can be incurred if the product does not meet expectations or if it is found at a lower price elsewhere.

The Audio Centre of Montreal, a retailer of high-quality audio and video equipment, has a somewhat unusual price strategy to give consumers confidence that they are getting the best deal, a powerful desired consequence for most purchasers. Note that such a pricing strategy has the added advantage of building shopping loyalty toward the company.

Price Performance Guarantee
"Most of you know us as a place to buy better than average audio and video components in an environment that's friendly and helpful. We pride ourselves on that perception. Our surveys tell us though, that the perception in the marketplace is that while we have great equipment and nice people, we are felt to be more expensive. We know this is not true and many of you know that too. To combat this perception, we have come up with a revolutionary new policy that is unique in Canada, it's called Audio Cheque and it goes like this . . .

If you buy something at the Audio Centre and it's advertised for less in a major local newspaper within 30 days, we'll automatically mail you a cheque for the difference . . . it's that easy!

HOW IT WORKS: We scour the major newspapers for advertisements of electronic equipment we sell, then enter all the advertised prices into our computer. The computer scans all our invoices written in the last 30 days and compares the prices. If

many Canadians have acquired the negative choice criterion of caffeine content for soft drinks as a result of the increasing value of good health. 7UP used this negative choice criterion as the basis for its no-caffeine marketing strategy: "Never had it, never will." Most other soft-drink manufacturers also responded to consumers' increasing negative beliefs about this choice criterion by introducing caffeine-free soft drinks.

Consumers usually see negative choice criteria as perceived risks to be avoided. One strategy to reduce perceived risk is to offer warranties and guarantees of product quality, as Consumer Perspective 8.2 illustrates. Usually, a consumer will reject a choice alternative with negative consequences, unless it also has a number of positive consequences. Consumers who believe a choice alternative has both positive and negative consequences experience a conflict between its perceived benefits and risks, which may motivate them to search for information to resolve the conflict.[19]

Choice decision

Making a **choice decision** requires that consumers integrate their product knowledge about choice criteria to evaluate the choice alternatives in the consideration set and choose one.[20] Researchers have identified two types of integration processes: *formal integration processes* and simpler procedures called *heuristics*. A key distinction in formal models of the integration process is between compensatory and noncompensatory integration processes.[21]

Compensatory integration processes combine the salient beliefs about choice criteria (perhaps only two or three beliefs) to form an overall attitude (A_{act}) toward each behavioural alternative in the consideration set. The multiattribute attitude model (discussed in Chapter 7) is a compensatory process in that a negative consequence there is a variance, where our invoiced price is higher, it will automatically print and mail you a cheque for the difference . . . it's that easy!

All other "Price Protection Policies" put the onus on the customer to find the same product at a lower price, and return to the store and claim their refund; a time consuming practice rarely done by anyone!

WE WANT YOU . . . to know that you never have to waste time shopping around. We have the best products at the best prices; and if we don't, we'll send you a cheque for the difference.

(expensive) can be balanced or compensated by a positive consequence (status). Combining a favourable and an unfavourable belief leads to a neutral overall attitude. The multiattribute attitude model does not specify how a consumer chooses between the choice alternatives once they have been evaluated, but most researchers assume consumers will select the behaviour with the most positive A_{act}.

Noncompensatory integration processes do not combine or consider all the salient beliefs about choice criteria at once. Thus, the positive and negative consequences may not balance or compensate for each other. For instance, Edie might reject a particular model of Bauer in-line skates if it has one negative consequence (too expensive), even though it also has several positive consequences (firm support, comfortable, trendy). In another example of a noncompensatory integration process, Tina might evaluate a pair of dress shoes favourably and buy them because they were superior to all the alternatives on the most important consequence (the colour matched her dress). She did not even consider the other product consequences, which were unfavourable (less durable, expensive, and not very comfortable).

Research suggests consumers do not follow any single integration process in evaluating and selecting choice alternatives.[22] Because people do not have enough cognitive capacity to integrate several beliefs about several choice alternatives at once, they probably use a combination of simple integration processes in most problem-solving situations.[23] For instance, a consumer might use a noncompensatory process to reduce the choice alternatives to a manageable number by rejecting all those that fail to meet one or two critical choice criteria. Bill might reject all restaurants that do not have a salad bar. Then he could evaluate the remaining choice alternatives in the consideration set (perhaps only two or three) on price and atmosphere using a more demanding compensatory integration process. Consumers probably construct most integration processes at the time they are needed, to fit the problem-solving situation. This suggests that most integration processes are rather simple, quite flexible, and easily adaptable to changing problem situations.[24] Such simple integration "rules" are called *heuristics.*

Heuristics are simple "if . . . , then . . . " integration rules that link an event to an appropriate behaviour. Because they are applied to only a few bits and pieces of knowledge at a time, heuristics are highly adaptive to the specific problem-solving situation and are not likely to exceed the person's cognitive capacity. Some heuristics may be stored in memory like miniature scripts that are activated and applied automatically in certain situations. Other heuristics may be constructed on the spot in response to information encountered in the environment.

Exhibit 8.5 presents examples of three types of heuristics that consumers use in problem solving. *Search heuristics* are simple rules for seeking information relevant to a goal. A consumer might have a search heuristic for buying any small appliance—first read the product tests in *Consumer Reports. Evaluation heuristics* are integration procedures for evaluating choice alternatives in light of the end goal. Dieters might have a heuristic that identifies the most important choice criteria for food—low calorie or low fat content—which is strongly linked to the problem-solving goal of losing weight. *Choice heuristics* are simple integration rules for comparing evaluations of alternative behaviours in order to make a choice. A choice heuristic is to select the alternative you bought last time, if you were satisfied.

Purchase

Purchase is determined by a behavioural intention (*BI*) to buy. The integration processes of evaluating choice alternatives and then choosing one produces a **decision plan,** made up of one or more behavioural intentions. Decision plans vary in specificity and complexity.[25] Specific decision plans contain intentions to perform particular behaviours in highly defined situations: This afternoon Jim intends to go to the Gap and buy a blue cotton shirt to go with his new jeans. Other decision plans involve rather general intentions; Paula intends to shop for a new car sometime soon. Some decision plans contain a simple intention to perform a single behaviour: Andy intends to buy a large tube of Colgate toothpaste. More complex decision plans involve a set of intentions to perform a series of behaviours: Val intends to go to Eaton's and The Bay to browse through their sportswear departments and look for a lightweight jacket.

Although forming a decision plan greatly increases the likelihood that the consumer will perform the intended behaviour, not all behavioural intentions are carried out. A purchase intention may be blocked or modified if environmental factors make it difficult to carry out. The problem-solving process may recycle to problem recognition, new goals may be formed, and a new decision may be made: if Andy finds the store is sold out of large tubes of Colgate, he may decide to buy two medium-sized tubes. Sometimes unanticipated events bring other choice alternatives to light, or change consumers' beliefs about appropriate choice criteria, which could lead to a revised decision plan. While reading the paper, Val learned Wal-Mart was having a 30 percent off sale on lightweight jackets, so she decided to shop there first instead of Eaton's.

Postpurchase use and re-evaluation

In the **postpurchase use and re-evaluation** stage of the problem-solving process, consumers use the purchased product, and they may re-evaluate their decision choice: "Am I happy with the purchase choice or not?"[26] The level of **satisfaction/dissatisfaction** with the purchase choice is a useful concept for understanding consumer behaviour.[27] For instance, consumer satisfaction can be used to measure the success of a company's marketing strategies. Satisfied consumers are more likely to repurchase a product and

Search heuristics	Examples
Purchase	If you are buying stereo equipment, always go to the Audio Centre.
Sources of information	If you want to know which alternatives are worth searching for, read the test reports in *Consumer Reports*.
Source credibility	If a magazine accepts ads from the tested products, don't believe its product tests.

Evaluation heuristics	Examples
Key criteria	If you are comparing processed foods, examine sodium content.
Negative criteria	If a salient consequence is negative (high fat content), give this choice criterion extra weight in the integration process.
Insignificant differences	If alternatives are similar on a salient consequence (all low cholesterol), ignore that choice criterion.

Choice heuristics	Examples
For familiar, frequently purchased products:	If choosing among familiar products, then . . .
Works best	Choose the product that you think works best—provides the best level of performance on the most relevant functional consequences.
Affect referral	Choose the alternative you like best overall (the alternative with the most favorable attitude).
Bought last	Select the alternative you used last, if it was satisfactory.
Important person	Choose the alternative that some "important" person (spouse, child, friend) likes.
Price-based rule	Buy the least expensive alternative (or buy the most expensive, depending on your beliefs about the relationship of price to product quality).
Promotion rule	Choose an alternative you have a coupon for or can get at a price reduction (seasonal sale, promotional rebate, special price reduction).
For new, unfamiliar products:	If choosing among unfamiliar products, then . . .
Wait and see	Don't buy any software until someone you know has used it for at least a month and recommends it. Don't buy a new car (computer, etc.) until the second model year.
Expert consultant	Find an expert or more knowledgeable person who will evaluate the alternatives in terms of your goals, then buy the alternative the expert selects.

EXHIBIT 8.5

Examples of consumer heuristics

become brand loyal. They are more likely to tell other people about the product and spread positive word of mouth. Dissatisfaction, on the other hand, can lead to complaints and negative word of mouth, behaviours with unfavourable consequences for a company.[28] Consumer Perspective 8.3 describes Molson Breweries' system for handling consumer complaints.

Marketers often study satisfaction and dissatisfaction in terms of the *disconfirmation of consumers' expectations.*[29] *Satisfaction* occurs when the product positively disconfirms consumers' expectations by performing better than expected (This magazine is more interesting than I thought it would be). Satisfaction can also occur when the product

CONSUMER
PERSPECTIVE

► 8.3

Handling
consumer
complaints

Marketers can use consumer complaints to understand their customers and keep them satisfied. Unfortunately, consumers complain to family, friends, and co-workers, but rarely to the company itself. When companies make it easy for dissatisfied customers to complain, the problem can be addressed and unhappy customers can be avoided.

Molson Breweries had been facing a decrease in sales due to the migration of dissatisfied customers, who were being lured away by upstart microbreweries. When Molson surveyed beer drinkers, it discovered that many consumers viewed the company as big and inaccessible. So Molson embarked on a new campaign—to get close to its customers.

Molson introduced a toll-free hotline customers could call with complaints or comments. Disturbingly, many customers questioned the quality and distinctiveness of Molson's beer. So the company stopped using preservatives and introduced a new "signature series." Under this new line, Molson will experiment with seasonal beers and may vary recipes by region. The series comes with a money-back guarantee, which helps reposition Molson as "the brewery that cares," not the manufacturer distinguished by its averageness.

Thanks to Molson's renewed interest in catering to customers' needs and handling customer complaints, its market share finally stopped sliding in the last quarter of 1993.

Source: Mark Stevenson, "My Dear, Beer Friend," *Canadian Business*, March 1994, pp. 52–58. Ellen Lee, "Problem with a Retailer? How to Complain Effectively," *Montreal Gazette*, June 20, 1994, p. F13.

confirms a consumer's favourable prepurchase expectations (I thought this would be a great CD, and it is). *Dissatisfaction* occurs when expectations are negatively disconfirmed, when performance of the product is worse than the consumer anticipated (This frozen lasagna doesn't taste very good). The amount of dissatisfaction depends on the extent of disconfirmation and the consumer's level of involvement with the product and the problem-solving process. To avoid disconfirmation and resulting dissatisfaction, marketers should try to manage consumer expectations by not under- or overpromising product performance. When marketing promotions promise more quality or performance than a product can deliver, consumers are more likely to become dissatisfied with the product.

A disconfirmation experience that leads to dissatisfaction also creates a state of cognitive dissonance (I bought brand X, but X is not very good).[30] *Cognitive dissonance* refers to an inconsistency between two cognitions (beliefs) or attitudes (I like the $350 one best, but I bought the $200 model). Consumers who are not sure they made a good decision may experience cognitive dissonance (I wonder if I could have bought that camera more cheaply somewhere else).

The unpleasant affective feelings associated with cognitive dissonance can motivate the consumer to do something to reduce the dissonance. A consumer might reduce postpurchase dissonance by switching to another band, returning the product for a refund or exchange, telling friends how bad it is, or throwing it away. Or a consumer might rationalize a choice by changing an inconsistent belief or attitude (This shirt isn't so bad after all; I sort of like it). Some consumers have reduced their cognitive dissonance by persuading friends to buy the same product or brand, which validates their product evaluations and supports their choice decision. Other consumers pay selective attention to ads and other positive information about the chosen product or brand in an attempt to convince themselves they made a good decision. A marketing strategy is to send direct-mail information to people who might experience cognitive dissonance, reassuring them

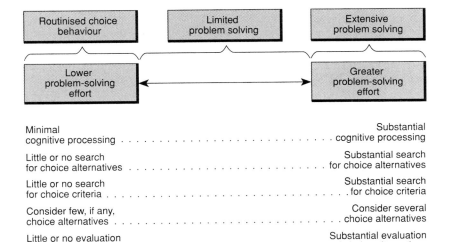

EXHIBIT 8.6

Levels of problem-solving effort

about their good choice (Congratulations! Buying your Nikon camera was an excellent decision).

LEVELS OF PROBLEM SOLVING

Consumers put varying amounts of cognitive and behavioural effort into different problem-solving situations. Problem-solving effort ranges from considerable (Barbara's extensive activities in buying new tableware) to very little (buying a soft drink from a vending machine). For convenience, marketers divide problem-solving activity into three levels: extensive, limited, and routine or habitual.[31] Exhibit 8.6 summarizes the major ways these three levels differ.

Extensive problem solving

During **extensive problem solving,** consumers usually put substantial effort into search activities to identify potential choice alternatives and to learn the choice criteria with which to evaluate them. When engaged in extensive problem solving, consumers often make multiple decisions involving significant cognitive effort. For instance, in making a purchase decision, consumers are likely to consider several choice alternatives and carefully evaluate them using choice criteria linked to their personal goals. Extensive problem solving occurs because the important goals activated by problem recognition create high levels of involvement and motivation to engage in problem solving. Extensive problem solving also may occur because consumers do not have enough relevant knowledge in memory to solve the problem. Because consumers care about the consequences of their actions, they may have strong affective responses during problem solving. Extensive problem solving can take a long time, ranging from hours to months. Relatively few consumer purchases require extensive problem solving (buying a house, a car, furniture, a major investment, special items of clothing).

Limited problem solving

In **limited problem solving,** consumers exert low to moderate levels of cognitive and behavioural effort. Many common purchase problems tend to activate moderately important end goals, producing low to moderate levels of involvement and motivation. Based on their past experiences with these problems, many consumers have some relevant knowledge in memory they can activate in evaluating alternatives and making a choice decision. Compared to extensive problem solving, consumers in limited problem-solving situations conduct fewer search activities, make fewer decisions, consider fewer choice alternatives, and have less complex integration processes. Limited problem solving is usually carried out quickly, requiring only minutes or hours. Limited problem solving is common for many consumer purchases.

Routinised choice behaviour

Routinised choice behaviour occurs relatively automatically, with minimal effort and little or no decision making. For many simple, everyday purchases, consumers' buying behaviour has become habitual or routine—buying another lunchtime Nestea from the vending machine or always purchasing gum at the grocery checkout counter. Because such purchase problems activate relatively unimportant goals, consumers tend to have low involvement and motivation in the purchase process. Also, because such purchases tend to be made frequently (people buy milk or bread every week), consumers have considerable knowledge in memory to use in making decisions. Given the low involvement and adequate knowledge of routinised choice behaviour, consumers perform little or no search for information. In fact, consumers may do little or no conscious decision making (they don't compare alternative behaviours' ability to satisfy the problem goals). In most cases, a previously formed decision plan is activated from memory (*BI* to buy a Pepsi) and is carried out automatically to produce the purchase behaviour. Consumer Perspective 8.4 describes an example of routinised choice behaviour.

Changes in problem solving with experience

The amount of effort consumers exert in problem solving tends to decrease with experience.[32] As they make repeated decisions to solve a problem, consumers form means-end chains of product and brand knowledge that is linked to their goals and values. Consumers also learn simple scripts and heuristics regarding the problem that are stored in memory. When activated, these heuristics can automatically direct search and evaluation processes (decisions about what to do are not needed). Consumers also learn which products and brands can successfully solve the problem. This knowledge may be stored in memory as decision plans (*BI*), which can automatically direct purchase behaviour when activated. Running down to the convenience store for a loaf of bread or stopping to fill up at a favourite gas station are simple decision plans that require little or no problem solving or decision making to carry out.

The degree to which a problem-solving process becomes routinised depends on the amount of knowledge a consumer has about the problem and the consumer's level of involvement with the problem. Consumers are more likely to develop habitual choice behaviour for frequently purchased, less involving products such as food and personal care items. In contrast, problem-solving processes for higher involvement, infrequently purchased products (low knowledge in memory) are likely to remain limited (or extensive). Because these products tend to be purchased infrequently, consumers' knowledge in memory may be seen as obsolete, and some search for relevant information is necessary.

Marketing implications

To develop effective marketing strategies, marketers need to know at which level the consumer is making purchase decisions. The level of problem solving has different implications for marketing strategies.

Extensive problem solving
Although relatively few consumer decisions involve extensive problem solving, marketers must recognise and satisfy consumers' special needs for information when they do engage in extensive decision making. In many extensive decision-making situations,

CONSUMER
PERSPECTIVE

8.4 ◄

Routinised
choice
behaviour

In one study, 120 consumers were observed buying laundry detergent in three chain grocery stores. An observer coded shoppers' activities as they moved down the aisle and picked out the detergent they wanted. The results showed that, for most consumers, laundry detergent choice behaviour was quite routinised. They examined few if any packages when deciding which laundry detergent to purchase.

Grocery chains in Canada, such as Loblaw's, Metro, and Safeway are challenging this routine behaviour by offering their own private-label products. These merchants hope consumers will be drawn away from merely purchasing their "old favourites" to trying the more visible store brands. Purchases of private-label products now account for 21.4 percent of retail grocery spending. They rose 18 percent in volume and 13 percent in dollar value in 1993 alone, according to Nielsen Marketing Research of Markham, Ontario. These private labels are particularly well-entrenched in Ontario and the West, where the large chains dominate.

With the increasing availability of private-label products, consumers' routinised behaviour, such as buying detergent, is now being challenged. The question is: will private labels continue to lure customers away from name brands in the future?

Sources: Vivian Smith, "Behind the Battle of the Brands," *Globe and Mail*, June 6, 1994, p. A11; Wayne D. Hoyer, "An Examination of Consumer Decision Making for a Common Repeat Purchase Product," in *Journal of Consumer Research*, Dec. 1984, pp. 822–29. Used by permission of the University of Chicago Press. © 1984 by the University of Chicago.

consumers need information about everything—which end goals are important, which choice alternatives are relevant, which choice criteria are appropriate, and so on. Marketers should strive to make the necessary information available, in a format and at a level of presentation that consumers can understand and use in the problem-solving process.[33]

Because consumers intentionally seek product information during extensive decision making, interrupting their problem-solving processes is relatively easy. Informational displays at the point of purchase—say, displays of mattresses that are cut apart to show construction details—or presentations by salespeople can be effective sources of information. Complex sales materials such as brochures and product specifications may be effective, along with high-information advertisements. Consumers operating at extensive decision-making levels will attend to relevant information and are motivated enough to comprehend it. Marketers may take advantage of their information receptivity by offering free samples, coupons, or easy trial (take it home and try it for a couple of days) to help consumers gain information about a brand.

Limited problem solving

Most consumer decisions involve limited effort. Because most consumers already have a lot of information about a product from previous experience, the basic marketing strategy here is to make additional pieces of information available when and where consumers need them. Ads to increase top-of-mind awareness may help to move a brand into the evoked set of choice alternatives at the beginning of the decision process. Such a position is important, because most consumers are not likely to search extensively for other alternatives. Moreover, it is critical that the brand is perceived to possess the few key choice criteria used in the evaluation process. Ads that capture consumers' attention and communicate favourable beliefs about salient attributes and consequences of the brand may be able to create that knowledge. Marketers may also try to design a store environment that stimulates impulse purchases, a type of limited decision making.[34]

Ads that capture consumers' attention can create knowledge about important product consequences.

Routinised choice behaviour

Much consumer choice behaviour is routinised. Consumers may feel they know all they need to about a product category, and they are not motivated to search for new information. Their choice behaviour is based on a learned decision plan. In such cases, the appropriate marketing strategy depends on the strength of the brand's position in the market.

In general, the more automatic the choice behaviour becomes, the more difficult it is for marketers to interrupt and influence the choice. Marketers of established brands, such as Molson or Labatt, with substantial market share want to maintain their brand in the evoked sets (the choice alternatives activated at the beginning of the problem-solving process) of a significant segment of consumers. When consumers engage in little or no search, marketers have minimal opportunities to propel their brand into consumer consideration sets during problem solving.

Marketers of new brands or brands with a smaller market share, such as Lakeport beer, must somehow interrupt the automatic problem-solving processes. They could develop strategies of producing prominent environmental stimuli such as large or unusual store displays (Reebok with Shaquille O'Neal's life-size poster to compete with Nike), creating strong package graphics that stand out on the shelf (Pringle's potato chips), giving away free samples (new shampoos), or running sales promotions (buy one, get one free).[35] Such strategies are intended to catch consumers' attention and interrupt their routine choice behaviour. The goal of "interrupts" is to prompt a more conscious level of decision making that might persuade the consumer to include the new brand in the consideration set.

Of course, marketers of leading brands such as Hostess snack chips, Snickers candy bars, Labatt beer, and IBM computers may *want* consumers to follow a routine choice process. Because these brands already have a high market share, they are in the evoked sets of most buyers. Marketers of such products want to avoid marketing-related environmental interrupts such as stockouts, which could push consumers into a limited decision-making process and lead them to try a competitor's brand. One critical aspect of the overall marketing strategy for high-market-share brands is an efficient distribution system

CONSUMER
PERSPECTIVE

8.5

Routinising
consumers'
choice
behaviour

The basic purpose of marketing is to create and keep customers. The secret to keeping customers is to keep them satisfied. One way the giant warehouse Price Club (Price-Costco) keeps its customers satisfied is by routinising consumer decision-making processes.

Price Club relies on the revolutionary world of electronic data interchange (EDI), which enables warehouses like Price Club to be linked with suppliers like Black & Decker so merchandise can be reordered quickly without the need for paper shuffling.

The result is that suppliers and customers lock together in unusual intimacy. A common tactic is for a supplier to provide such an excellent computer order-entry or value-added service that customers switch to that supplier. In some industries, computerised sellers have driven noncomputerised competition out of business.

D. H. Howden & Co. Ltd. of London, Ontario, has been providing its Pro Hardware dealers with electronic ordering since 1973. About 1,200 client stores have hand-held ordering devices that download over phone lines and about 350 large Pro Hardware stores are even better served through PCs or display phones. These stores can get fast order-entry confirmations and approvals for returns, as well as extra services that are attractive to retail customers, such as a special order tag stating the name of the customer who placed the order.

There are some problems with integrating EDI into established computer applications and with understanding the technology, but most industry analysts agree that "You will not be in business tomorrow if you don't gear up for EDI today."

Source: John Heinzl, "Supply and Command," *Globe and Mail*, Dec. 15, 1992, p. B20; Jim Steinhart, "Electronic Ties That Bind Firms," *Globe and Mail*, Sept. 28, 1993, p. B23.

to keep the brands fully stocked and available whenever consumers can make choices. In order to do business with most major department or warehouse stores, Canadian manufacturers and distributors have had to develop electronic data interchange (EDI) technology. Consumer Perspective 8.5 shows how Black and Decker Canada makes the Price-Costco decision-making process more routine.

▶ SUMMARY

Learning objective 1: *Define a decision and describe why consumer decision making is part of the problem-solving process.*

A decision is a choice between two or more possible behaviours or actions. Decisions are always choices between behaviours—what to *do* with an object. In decision making, consumers integrate or combine knowledge about the consequences of alternative actions to evaluate the possible behaviours and choose one. The outcome of this integration process produces attitudes toward a behaviour (A_{act}) and the social influences concerning the behaviour (*SN*), which in turn are combined to form a behavioural intention—a plan to perform the chosen behaviour (I will buy Colgate toothpaste tomorrow). Consumer decision making is part of the problem-solving process. Recognizing a problem—"I am thirsty"—activates a goal—"I would like a soft drink." Because the goal is not yet attained, the consumer has a problem to be solved. Solving the problem may involve making multiple decisions. Every decision during problem solving is influenced by the overall goal associated with the problem.

Learning objective 2: *Describe the six stages of the problem-solving process.*

The problem-solving process includes six stages: problem recognition, search for relevant information, evaluation of alternatives, the choice decision, purchase, and postpurchase use and re-evaluation. Problem recognition occurs when people become aware of an unsatisfied goal or problem and are motivated to do something to achieve the goal and solve the problem. The search for relevant information involves looking for information that is relevant to the perceived problem, including information about potential choice alternatives (different products or brands) and information about choice criteria. Evaluation of alternatives (forming A_{act}) involves combining salient beliefs about the consequences of each considered behaviour. The choice decision involves integrating information to form a decision plan (a behavioural intention to buy one of the alternatives). Purchase involves carrying out the decision plan. The postpurchase stage involves using the chosen alternative and re-evaluating it by comparing its performance with one's expectations. Satisfaction with the choice usually results if expectations are confirmed or surpassed, while a negative disconfirmation of expectations creates dissatisfaction.

Learning objective 3: *Define end goals and discuss their role in problem solving.*
End goals are the important consequences or values that consumers want to achieve or satisfy (Seth wants to be more popular with his classmates). End goals are a key influence in the problem-solving process. The activated end goals are the basis for involvement, provide the motivation for decision making, and focus consumers' attention on information that is relevant to the perceived problem. End goals can be simple and concrete (Bill wants to buy gas for his car) or more complex and abstract (Mary Lou wants to buy a new dress that makes her feel attractive). We can identify five broad categories of end goals. Consumers who have an end goal of optimising satisfaction are motivated to find the best possible choice alternative (buy the best tennis racquet under $200). Other consumers with a goal of maintaining satisfaction try to find an acceptable (just OK) alternative, while expending little effort (going to the convenience store to buy milk—any brand is OK). Other types of end goals include preventing problems (buying snow tires to avoid the unfavourable consequences of getting stuck in the snow), resolving conflict (buying a moderately expensive brand such as Sony to balance the positive and negative consequences of purchase), and escaping a problem (buying mouthwash to reduce unpleasant consequences of bad breath).

Learning objective 4: *Define a consideration set, discuss how it can be formed, and describe an implication of consideration sets for marketers.*
The consideration set is the various choice alternatives (different behaviours) a consumer evaluates and seriously considers performing during decision making. A purchase consideration set may contain different product categories, product forms, brands, or models. The choice alternatives in a consideration set (different brands, for instance) could be activated from memory, found through intentional search, or "discovered" by accident. If a brand is not in a person's consideration set, it cannot be evaluated or purchased. Brands that are included in many consumers' consideration sets have the potential for a high market share. Thus, marketers may engage in costly marketing strategies (lots of TV advertising and sales promotions, as with Coke and Pepsi) to help their brand get into the consideration set.

Learning objective 5: *Define choice criteria and give examples of how positive and negative choice criteria might be used in problem solving.*
Choice criteria are the specific consequences used to evaluate different behaviours (buy Sony, buy Panasonic, buy Technics) and to choose among them. Virtually any consequence can be a choice criterion, including salient beliefs about functional and psychosocial consequences as well as values. Some choice criteria are beliefs stored in memory that may be activated during the problem-solving process. In other cases, consumers search for information about choice criteria, which they must interpret and convert into

personal beliefs and knowledge. Many choice criteria are benefits or positive consequences consumers wish to avoid or escape from.

Learning objective 6: *Describe the difference between compensatory and noncompensatory integration processes and give an example of each.*

Compensatory and noncompensatory processes describe two ways consumers combine information about choice alternatives to make a purchase decision. In a compensatory integration process, a consumer considers all the salient beliefs about the consequences of the choice alternatives (considered behaviours). That is, a consumer considers all the positive and negative consequences at once so they can balance or compensate for each other. Thus, a choice alternative with mostly positive consequences and a few negative consequences will be evaluated less favourably than an alternative with all positive consequences. In a noncompensatory integration process, consumers do not consider all their salient beliefs about choice criteria at once. Thus, beliefs about consequences are combined in ways that do not balance or compensate for each other. For instance, a consumer might reject a choice alternative with one negative consequence (such as high price) without considering its several positive consequences (high quality, excellent style, good warranty).

Learning objective 7: *Describe three types of heuristics and give an example of each.*

Heuristics are simple "if . . . , then . . ." rules that connect an event with an appropriate action: "If you get junk mail, throw it away unopened." Heuristics can be activated to direct cognitive processes and overt behaviours automatically. Heuristics do not require consumers to use much information at a time, so they do not exceed the limited capacity of the cognitive system. Heuristics are adaptive in that they are activated and used in specific situations where appropriate. There are three broad categories of heuristics: search, evaluation, and choice heuristics. Search heuristics refer to simple rules about how and where to search for relevant information. For example, some consumers may have a heuristic of seeking advice from a friend with expertise in the problem topic. Evaluation heuristics are procedures for evaluating choice criteria in terms of the current end goal. For instance, some consumers might infer that a product is good quality if it advertises on television. Choice heuristics are rules of thumb for choosing an alternative. For instance, an affect referral heuristic says to buy the product you like the best overall. A wait-and-see heuristic for a new product says to wait several months before buying to make sure it is good.

Learning objective 8: *Describe the three levels of problem-solving effort and give a marketing implication for each.*

The amount of cognitive and behavioural effort that consumers put into their problem-solving processes is highly variable. Three levels of problem-solving effort have been identified. In extensive problem solving, consumers exert a substantial amount of effort in searching for relevant information and evaluating choice alternatives. Extensive problem solving may require a substantial mental and behavioural effort over long periods. For most consumers, buying a car or a new suit for job interviews involves extensive problem solving and considerable decision making. In contrast, routinised choice behaviour involves low levels of problem-solving effort and little or no decision making. There may be little or no search for choice alternatives or choice criteria and no consideration of alternative behaviours. Rather, a behavioural intention or decision plan stored in memory is activated and carried out automatically. Between these two extremes is the moderate amount of decision-making effort expended during limited problem solving. Limited problem solving involves a modest amount of searching for relevant information, consideration of a few choice alternatives, and modest amounts of decision making.

▶ **KEY TERMS AND CONCEPTS**

decision

integration

choice

problem solving

problem recognition

end goals

search for relevant information

choice alternatives

consideration set

evaluation of alternatives

choice criteria

choice decision

compensatory integration processes

noncompensatory integration processes

heuristics

purchase

decision plan

postpurchase use and re-evaluation

satisfaction/dissatisfaction

extensive problem solving

limited problem solving

routinised choice behaviour

▶ **REVIEW AND DISCUSSION QUESTIONS**

1. Discuss what it means to say that decisions are always between alternative behaviours. Illustrate your answer.

2. Why do products or brands not in the consideration set have a low probability of being purchased?

3. Identify three ways that choice alternatives can enter the consideration set. Describe a marketing strategy that could get your brand into consumers' consideration sets for each situation.

4. Discuss why decision making can be treated as a problem-solving process.

5. Think of a purchase decision from your own experience in which you had a well-developed end goal. Describe how it affected your problem-solving process. Then select a decision in which you did not have a well-developed end goal and describe how it affected your problem-solving process.

6. Assume the role of a product manager for a product about which you (and your management team) have a fairly high level of product knowledge. Consider how each of the formal integration processes would result in different responses to your product and how you could adjust marketing strategy to deal with these differences.

7. Give at least two examples of how a marketing manager could use routinised choice behaviour to increase the likelihood of purchase of his or her new product.

8. Discuss how consumers' involvement and their activated product knowledge might affect the problem-solving processes during purchase decisions for products or services such as new cars, an oil change, or cold remedies.

9. Relate the examples of decision heuristics shown in Exhibit 8.5 to the concept of involvement. When are these heuristics likely to be useful to the consumer? Under what conditions might they be dysfunctional?

10. Describe the differences between extensive and limited decision making. How should marketing strategies differ for these two types of problem-solving processes?

CHAPTER 9

Communication and Persuasion

LEARNING OBJECTIVES

After completing this chapter, you should be able to:

► 1. Describe the four types of promotion communications.

► 2. Describe the components of the basic communication model.

► 3. Describe the various effects that promotion communications can have on consumers.

► 4. Discuss the two routes to persuasion specified by the Elaboration Likelihood Model and describe the role of attitude toward the ad in persuasion.

► 5. Describe how the FCB Grid and vulnerability analysis can be used to understand the consumer/product relationship and help marketers create effective communication strategies.

► 6. Describe the MECCAS model of advertising strategy.

► 7. Distinguish between lecture and drama advertising.

CFL CHIEF IS AMERICAN MARKETING ASSOCIATION'S MARKETER OF THE YEAR

Canadian Football League commissioner Larry Smith was named marketer of the year by the Toronto chapter of the American Marketing Association. Smith, an ex-CFL player himself, has faced the daunting task of end-running the erstwhile Canadian franchise deep into the United States.

In winning, Smith beat runners-up Richard Gallop of Ontario's Heart and Stroke Foundation and Don Woodley, managing director of computer firm Compaq Canada Ltd. Smith was the winner "for his success in reviving the Canadian Football League despite the many obstacles facing him." Smith was cited for making sure that his customers are pampered. He pushes for comfort in the stadium, day care, food service in the stands, nonsmoking and nondrinking sections, handicapped access and many types of consumer promotions, including family-oriented pricing and promotions. Key to success in markets south of the border in places such as Sacramento and Las Vegas are finely tuned regional promotions that have lured customers to the stands. For all this, Smith was credited with reviving the league and named marketer of the year.

Along with the American Marketing Association Awards, every year *Marketing* magazine honours companies for their sales promotion efforts. In 1993, a record 1,832 entries were among the competition, including more than 140 advertising agencies that sent in their best work.

Most previous winners are justly proud of their work. Are awards self-serving to the industry? Yes. Do they set a standard for creative people to aspire to? Yes. And is the work that wins at award shows the same work that wins customers' hearts? Yes.[1]

Successful sales promotions illustrate the importance of communication and persuasion in influencing consumer behaviour. Marketers develop promotions to *communicate* information about their products and to *persuade* consumers to like and buy them. This chapter discusses the four types of marketing promotion communications. Then we present a general model of the communication process that helps us understand how marketing promotions communicate information to consumers. Next, we discuss the persuasion processes by which promotions influence consumers to change their beliefs, attitudes, and behavioural intentions. We conclude by discussing implications for developing and managing promotion strategies.

TYPES OF PROMOTION COMMUNICATIONS

The four types of **promotion communications**—advertising, sales promotions, personal selling, and publicity—constitute a promotion "mix" that marketers try to manage. The most obvious form of promotion communication is advertising, but the other forms can have important influences on consumers.

Advertising

Advertising is any paid, nonpersonal communication about a product, brand, company, or store. Ads may be conveyed via a variety of media including TV, radio, print (magazines and newspapers), billboards, signs, and unusual media such as hot-air balloons and T-shirts. Marketers use advertising to influence consumers' affect and cognitions (feelings, beliefs, attitudes, and intentions). But the vast majority of the hundreds of ads consumers are exposed to each day receive low levels of attention and comprehension.

The broad goal of advertising communication is image management: creating, and maintaining images and meanings in consumers' minds.[2] For instance, Nike once made a big splash with a series of billboards featuring strong visual images of athletes—Carl Lewis long jumping or Michael Jordan leaping for the basket. Besides the picture, the ads showed only the Nike "swoosh" logo in the corner. At first, viewers probably had to look twice to comprehend what product was being advertised, but the pictures conveyed strong symbolic meanings about Nike products. In markets where the billboards appeared, Nike sales increased 30 percent.[3]

Sales promotions

Sales promotions are communications offering inducements to the consumer to make a purchase. There are many types of sales promotions, including temporary price reductions through coupons and rebates, contests and sweepstakes, trading stamps, free samples, in-store displays, and premiums and gifts. TV advertising may be more glamourous, but more money is spent on sales promotions in Canada. In fact, almost 78 percent of the promotion budget is spent on sales promotions versus 22 percent on advertising.[4]

The main objective of sales promotions is to move the product today, not tomorrow. A sales promotion is designed to influence consumers to buy a product immediately by offering them something, such as premium or price reduction. Dow once designed a back-to-school promotion for its Ziploc sandwich bags that included a 15-cent coupon plus a mail-in offer for free bread with two proofs of purchase. A premium was also included in the package—stickers of the beasties from the movie *Gremlins*. This promotion was intended to get people to stock up on Ziploc products, thereby blocking purchases of competitive brands. Sales volume increased 42 percent, and Ziploc became the No. 1 brand in the category for the first time.[5]

Personal selling

Personal selling involves direct personal communications between a salesperson and a consumer. Personal communications may increase consumers' involvement with the product or the decision, making them more likely to pay attention and comprehend the information presented by the salesperson. Also, the interactive communication situation in personal selling allows the salesperson to adapt the presentation to each potential buyer. Certain products are traditionally promoted through personal selling, such as life insurance, cars, and houses. Personal selling in retailing has decreased over the past 20 years as self-service has become more popular. However, retailers like Harry Rosen and Ogilvy's have reversed this trend by emphasising personal selling and customer service. Besides lots of personal attention from a courteous sales staff, customers are often wooed by soft music.

For other businesses, a form of personal selling by telephone, or *telemarketing,* has become increasingly popular as the costs of a direct sales call increased to between $100 and $200 in 1985 and have remained at about that level.[6] Telemarketing selling differs considerably from face-to-face selling. The telemarketer usually follows a prepared script, never travels, makes 20 to 50 calls per day, which last from one to two minutes, works about four to six hours per day, and is closely supervised. In contrast, a conventional salesperson often travels, usually must improvise the sales presentation to fit the buyer's needs, makes only 2 to 10 sales calls per day that last about an hour each, works about 8 to 12 hours per day, and is loosely supervised.[7]

Both Avon and Mary Kay Cosmetics, among the largest marketers of skin care products, were built on personal selling. Neither company spends much on advertising or customer sales promotions. Mary Kay, for instance, spends less than 1% of sales on advertising. Instead, most of its promotion budget is spent on incentives for salespeople: symbolic prizes such as medals, ribbons, and commemorative certificates, and jewelry, calculators, briefcases, and furs. Top sellers receive the use of pink Cadillacs or Buick Regals. Mary Kay also spends heavily on motivational and training programs for sales personnel.

Publicity

Publicity is any unpaid communication about a company, product, or brand. An article in *PC World* comparing various brands of word-processing software is not paid advertising but provides useful product information to consumers at no cost to the marketers of the software. Descriptions of new products or brands; brand comparisons in trade journals, newspapers, or news magazines; or discussions on radio and TV talk shows provide similar product information to consumers.

Nabisco sales representatives are creating an in-store display of Ritz crackers.

Publicity can be positive or negative. A small Canadian company called Paas Products received a bonanza of free publicity in the form of favourable news stories when the Canadian government suggested that parents use make-up rather than masks for young children at Halloween. This story effectively linked Paas and child safety. Tylenol, on the other hand, received unfavourable publicity when people were poisoned by Tylenol capsules that had been tampered with.

Sometimes publicity can be more effective than advertising, because consumers do not screen out the messages so readily. In addition, publicity communications may be considered more credible because they are not being presented by the marketing organisation. Publicity is difficult to manage, however. Marketers sometimes stage media events in hopes of garnering free publicity. Procter & Gamble, for example, once held a glitzy news conference at a disco to introduce new Liquid Tide—complete with a 20-foot-high inflatable model of the product. It hoped the media would report the event and perhaps show a picture of the product. P&G had little control over what type of publicity (if any) would result, however.

The promotion mix   Ideally, marketing managers should combine the four types of promotion communications into a coherent overall strategy. In the past two decades, Canada has seen major changes in the balance of marketing effort devoted to the four types of promotion. Expenditures for sales promotions have increased much more rapidly than those for advertising. From 1976 to 1991, spending on sales promotions in North America increased more than four-fold (from $30 billion to $134 billion), while ad spending increased about 160 percent (from

---

CONSUMER PERSPECTIVE

▶ **9.1**

Hockey Hall of Fame corporate sponsors

By integrating marketing opportunities into their game plan from the onset, the creators of the Hockey Hall of Fame ensured longevity in corporate sponsorship.

The Hockey Hall of Fame opened June 18, 1993. The ideas behind it were put together by a group of dedicated people with one main goal: to create an international home for hockey greatness. The Hall honours all levels of hockey—men's and women's, amateur and professional, international and Olympic. Hockey's greatest treasure, the Stanley Cup, makes its home here.

Marketing was a key aspect in the hall's construction. The interactive games, evolving exhibits, on-site promotions, and special events encourage repeat visits and ensure financial stability. The project realised the importance of corporate sponsorship. Sponsors can achieve their sales and marketing objectives through traffic and loyalty-building promotions, hospitality opportunities within the facility itself, and on-site exposure.

Sponsorship programs were developed on three levels, each offering different opportunities in marketing. Founding sponsorship involved a 10-year partnership that integrates founding sponsors into the hall through exhibit entitlement, on-site programs, and promotions. Contributing sponsorship is typically a five-year partnership that is driven by promotion and lets sponsors work with the hall to develop programs that meet their individual marketing and sales plans. Supplier sponsorships are for three to five years. They were developed to ensure the participation of the hockey industry and the recognition of these companies' contributions to the sport.

Built primarily from private funding, the Hockey Hall of Fame sets a new standard in the creation of a customer-oriented sports attraction, one that integrates the corporate community as marketing partners in both the development of the facility and its ongoing operation.

Source: Peter Allemang, *Marketing*, Nov 29, 1993.

$22 billion to $58 billion).[8] During the recession of the early 1990s, sales promotions gained even more ground, while advertising expenditures, especially on network TV, decreased (down about 7 percent in 1991 over 1990). Moreover, new forms of promotion communications continue to be developed, such as direct marketing and magazines dedicated to a single advertiser, which allow highly accurate targeting of the desired consumer audience. Despite the attention on advertising and sales promotions, publicity and personal selling remain important promotion communications for certain products such as movies (publicity) and automobiles (personal selling).

Marketers have debated the relative importance of advertising versus personal-selling communications.[9] As you might expect, most advertising agencies argue that advertising is the best way to create a strong relationship between consumers and the brand. Other marketers believe sales promotions can also enhance the consumer/brand relationship while having the advantage of influencing immediate purchase behaviour. Some analysts see a long-range trend toward a broader promotion mix where advertising is no longer dominant. The promotion mix of the future may offer many more options, including event sponsoring (Alcan and Labatt sponsor the Montreal Jazz Festival), sports marketing (Matinee and Player's sponsor tennis matches), direct marketing (coupons are sent to purchasers of your competitor's brand), and public relations. Consumer Perspective 9.1 describes a major Canadian sports sponsorship promotion. These "new" promotion communications are valuable developments partly because of the high costs of advertising and partly because marketers need to target customers more precisely than mass advertising can.

THE COMMUNICATION PROCESS

The broad goal of marketing promotions is to communicate a certain set of meanings to consumers.[10] These meanings are intended to create positive beliefs about the product and positive attitudes toward buying (A_{act}) and a positive intention to buy the product (BI). Thus, developing successful marketing promotions is a communications issue.

Exhibit 9.1 identifies the key factors in the **communication process.** The process begins when the *source* of the promotion communication determines the communication strategy (decides what information to communicate) and creates the *message* (constructs the communication using appropriate symbols, words, pictures, actions). Then the message is *transmitted* over some medium such as a television show, direct mail, billboard, or magazine. The *receiver* or consumer, if exposed to the promotion, must interpret it by attending to it and comprehending its meaning Then the consumer might take *action,* which could include going to a store or making a purchase. Two stages are especially critical to the success of promotion strategies: (1) when the marketer creates the promotion message to convey the intended meaning and (2) when consumers are exposed to the promotion and interpret its meaning.[11] Exhibit 9.1 also shows the relevant agents or actors in each stage of the communication process and the key activities at each stage. Next, we discuss some factors that influence each of these stages in the communication process.

Source

The *source* of a promotion message influences its effectiveness.[12] For instance, salespeople whom customers perceive as credible, trustworthy, and similar to themselves tend to be more effective. These can include celebrity spokespeople, who are often hired to appear in ads to serve as the source for promotional messages. After extensive research, Zellers selected actor Alan Thicke from among many Canadian celebrities to help the company retain its dominance in the mid-level retail chain department store business against Kmart, Sears, Wal-Mart, and other competitors. Thicke was viewed as a solid, dependable person in tune with the image Zellers wanted to present. Zellers focused on

EXHIBIT 9.1   A general model of the communication process

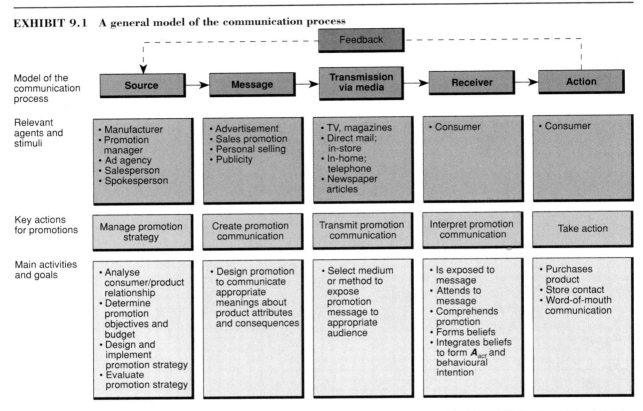

Source: Adapted from Figure 8.1 in Henry Assael, *Consumer Behavior and Marketing Action,* 3rd ed. (Boston: PSW-KENT Publishing Co., 1987), p. 210. © by Wadsworth, Inc. Used by permission of PSW-KENT Publishing Co., a division of Wadsworth, Inc.

Thicke's trustworthiness to launch its national campaign. Most Canadians responded favourably and Zellers management considered Thicke quite effective. Unfortunately, many other celebrity spokespeople don't seem to have this effectiveness.[13]

Message

The effectiveness of a promotion is influenced by the actual information contained in the promotion *message:* the product claim made in a print ad, the value of the coupon or sweepstakes prize, the promises made by the salesperson, or the attractiveness of the premium offer. Marketers work hard to devise effective promotions. For instance, they must trade off making a sales promotion (like those in the opening example) attractive enough to stimulate consumer response yet small enough that the costs don't outweigh the benefits.

Most research concerning message effects focuses on advertising. The effects of many message-related factors have been examined—including the use of fear appeals, sexual content, content that produces emotional responses, humour, gender roles, one-versus two-sided messages, evaluative visual material, and explicit versus implicit product claims.[14] Some studies have even examined subliminal messages (see Consumer Perspective 9.2).

The results of all this research are mixed, in that a given message characteristic does not always have the same effect on every consumer. This is partly because the effects of any ad message are influenced both by the activated knowledge and involvement of the consumers who receive the ad and by specific features of the environment in which

Drama ads like this tell a story in which the product has an important part.

exposure occurs. Thus, the effects of a fear appeal or humour may vary considerably from one situation to another. Because few generalisations can be drawn, marketers usually must research the effects of a new promotion strategy on consumers or rely on their intuition.

The type of information included in an advertising message influences how the ad communicates to consumers. For example, *informational ads* present verbal facts about the product; *image ads* show pictures and visual symbols.[15] Consumers' responses to informational ads are dominated by the cognitive system, which interprets the ad and creates knowledge and beliefs about product attributes and consequences (benefits and risks). Responses to image ads are dominated by the affective system, which produces a range of emotional, feeling, and mood responses.

An ad message can be delivered as a lecture or presented as a drama.[16] A *lecture ad* is like a classroom lecture in that a source offers information about the attributes and functional consequences of a brand. Consider an ad for toothpaste in which a person in a white doctor's coat describes two attributes—tartar-control formula and a special fluoride ingredient. The source claims these attributes reduce cavities and make it less necessary to visit the dentist for teeth cleaning and also presents scientific evidence to support these claims.

Lecture ads communicate product information with the intention of persuading consumers to form positive beliefs about product consequences, a favourable attitude toward purchasing the product, and an intention to buy. One possible problem with lecture ads is that consumers may react negatively to the obvious attempt to influence.

In contrast, a message delivered in dramatic form makes few or no explicit product claims. Instead, a *drama ad* tells a story in which the brand has a prominent role. Consider

Although most advertisers pay little or no attention to the topic, *subliminal persuasion* in advertising just won't go away. Writers like Wilson Key keep turning out widely read books that claim subliminal advertising is all around us. Key claims marketers intentionally embed stimuli such as sexual objects, symbols, or words, in advertisements. Moreover, he claims these hidden, subliminal stimuli affect us in powerful ways of which we are unaware.

What do we know about the effects of subliminal stimulation? First, it is clear that stimulation below the level of a person's conscious awareness *can* have measurable effects on some aspects of that person's behaviour. That is, people can respond to stimuli without realising the stimuli exist. But these stimuli are not necessarily subliminal—that is, they are not necessarily presented at intensities below our perceptual threshold. They just tend not to be noticed consciously as consumers go about their business; a great deal of cognitive activity occurs automatically. Thus, consumers often cannot report the existence of a stimulus or an awareness that some cognitive process has occurred.

With regard to Key's claims about sexual symbol embedding, two issues are in question. First, are subliminal embeddings made in advertisements as a matter of course, as Key claims? Virtually no evidence exists for this. Certainly, sexual stimuli are found in a great many ads, but not in subliminal embeds. Second, could subliminal stimuli affect goal-directed behaviours such as purchase choices?

A key finding in cognitive psychology that is basic to marketing strategy is that the meaning of a stimulus is not inherent in the stimulus itself. Rather, meanings are constructed by consumers in active and sometimes complex ways as they come into contact with the stimulus. Most stimuli have little or no influence on our cognitions or behaviours when presented at a recognisable level. Why, then, should they suddenly have a strong impact when presented subliminally? Key claims that humans have two processing systems, one of which operates on a completely unconscious level and immediately picks up on subliminal embeds. No psychological theories or data support such a system of cognition.

None of this is to say that ads may not have effects on consumers' meanings at a subconscious level—but the stimuli don't have to be subliminal for that to occur.

Sources: Jack Haberstroh, "Can't Ignore Subliminal Ad Charges," *Advertising Age*, Sept. 17, 1984, pp. 3, 42; and Timothy E. Moore, "Subliminal Advertising: What You See Is What You Get," *Journal of Marketing*, Spring 1982, pp. 38–47.

---

an ad showing an executive who has been working late on a cold winter night. As she leaves her office and walks to her car parked on a deserted city street, she wonders whether her car will start. She gets into the car and turns the key, and the engine immediately starts—to her obvious relief. She congratulates herself for buying a DieHard battery.

Such ads are miniature dramas, similar to a very short play or movie. In contrast to the hard sell of lecture ads, drama ads communicate product information more gently and indirectly. Effective drama ads draw viewers into the story and encourage them to identify with one or more characters in the story. Consumers who empathise with a character may experience affective feelings and emotions similar to those portrayed by that character.[17]

**Transmission
via media**

Marketing managers must decide what media to use to transmit the promotion message to consumers. For any given promotion, many media choices are available. Advertisements, for example, can be placed in magazines or newspapers, displayed on billboards, aired on television or radio programs, or sent through the mail. Consumer Perspective 9.3

Given the difficulty of keeping viewers' attention on 30- or even 15-second commercials, the promotion strategy Toyota used to sell its new minivan, Previa, might be considered a bit risky.

Toyota's ad agency, Saatchi and Saatchi, created an eight-minute videotape commercial for the Previa and mailed it to some 200,000 potential customers. (Toyota assumed these people owned VCRs.) The video had a fragile story line about a woman ad writer assigned to push the new Previa. It portrayed her family (husband and fresh-faced kids) driving around in the car, while she explained its special features. In the background, an orchestra played the Toyota theme song, "I love what you do for me."

The costs of this promotion were estimated at about $1.5 million, including buying the mailing list, producing the video, and mailing the $4 plastic cassettes. Future promotions may use cardboard cassettes, which work for about five plays and cost only about $2. The effectiveness of the Previa tape was hard to determine, but about 2 percent of those who received it visited a Toyota showroom within three months.

The big communications medium question is, would people actually watch such videos? If so, the video surely communicated the Previa name and its special attributes better than any TV commercial or print ad.

Source: Reprinted by permission of *Forbes* magazine. © Forbes Inc. 1990.

CONSUMER PERSPECTIVE

9.3 ◄

A new medium for transmitting promotion communications

describes a new advertising medium for transmitting product information. Coupons may be placed in magazines or newspapers, delivered by mail, or printed on the product package. Personal-selling messages can be delivered in face-to-face interactions in a store or in the consumer's home, or via telephone in telemarketing.

Because each medium has advantages and disadvantages for communicating with consumers, marketers must give careful attention to media choices for their promotion messages.[18] Clutter is a problem for most media because of the increases in the number of promotion messages over the past decade. In 1989, for instance, over 320,000 commercials were shown on American television network stations.[19] Consumer Perspective 9.4 discusses some implications of clutter in TV advertising. Sales promotions also suffer from clutter. In 1993, the number of coupons distributed to Canadians was 4 billion (only 174 million were redeemed). In the United States in 1992, 350 billion coupons were distributed. Obviously, getting the consumer's attention with another coupon promotion is difficult in this cluttered environment.[20]

Receiver

The effectiveness of a promotion message is influenced by the characteristics of the consumers who receive it. Two key factors are consumers' product knowledge and involvement, which affect their attention and comprehension of the promotion message. Another receiver characteristic is deal proneness—people's general inclination to use sales promotion deals such as coupons or rebates or to buy at reduced sale prices.[21] Some consumers have high personal sources of involvement with using coupons and may even belong to clubs where coupons are traded. They are much more likely to respond favourably to sales promotions than are consumers who consider coupons a nuisance.

Promotion messages have their initial impact on consumers' affect and cognitions. For a promotion communication to be effective, receivers must be exposed to the message, pay attention to it, and comprehend its meaning. Marketers hope the receiver will form positive beliefs about the consequences of buying and using the product and integrate these beliefs to form a favourable A_{act} and purchase intention (BI). Much research has

CONSUMER
PERSPECTIVE

▶ 9.4

Clutter and the
15-second
commercial

The 60-second commercial was once the most common ad on TV, bearing out research data that established benchmarks of effectiveness for ads of this length. Then, in the late 1960s, along came the 30-second commercial. At the time, it was thought that the shorter ads, and the extra "clutter" they would create, would raise havoc with advertising effectiveness and measurement. It didn't happen, and the 30-second ad became the standard.

Enter 15-second ads. What is their effect?

Preliminary evidence provided by a large-scale comparison of 15-second and 30-second ads suggests the new ads won't wreak havoc, either. When the average 30-second commercial scored 100 for communication performance, the average 15-second ad scored 78. The 15-second ads also scored well on a measure of the number of ideas in the ad recalled later by the viewer—2.6 versus 2.9 for the 30-second ads. Finally, both ad lengths scored about the same in terms of the sense of importance of the main idea created by the commercial. Yet the 15-second ad costs only slightly more than half as much money to run.

So, are the 15-second ads a problem? Probably not. It is not the length per se that makes an ad effective or ineffective. If an ad establishes a reason—a reward—for viewing it in the first few seconds, consumers are likely to pay attention and comprehend its meaning, no matter how short it is.

Certain communication goals are more difficult to achieve with 15-second ads: a feeling of newness, a multistep process, a sense of variety, creation of a mood or emotion, and humour. But the very same problems were once issues for the 30-second ads, and we know how that turned out.

Source: Adapted from Robert Parcher, "15-Second TV Commercials Appear to Work 'Quite Well,' " *Marketing News* 20 (Jan. 3, 1986), pp. 1 and 60. Published by the American Marketing Association.

focused on measuring these affective and cognitive effects of promotion communications, especially advertising.[22] Three indicators of advertising effectiveness have been used: recall, persuasion, and sales.

Consumers' ability to *recall* the promotion message is a simple measure of communication effectiveness. In day-after recall studies, researchers telephone consumers the day after a TV commercial is run and ask them if they remember seeing any ads on TV the day before, and if so, what they can recall about the ads they remember. Viewers who can remember a visual element or a product claim are counted as having recalled the ad. Recall indicates whether consumers were exposed to the ad and attended to it enough that they can remember seeing it, but recall does not measure whether the ad created appropriate product meanings or elicited the desired affective responses.[23] Exposure and attention to individual ads have decreased due to consumers' use of remote controls to zap ads and sagging loyalty to favourite brands (lower involvement). In 1968, nearly two-thirds (64 percent) of consumers could remember an ad campaign seen in the previous month; by 1990, this figure had plunged to 48 percent. Recall of single ads gradually declined from an average of 24 percent in the late 1970s to 21 percent in 1988 (of course, some ads scored higher or lower than this).[24]

A promotion message may have a persuasive effect on the receiver.[25] *Persuasion* occurs when consumers' interpretation of the ad message produces positive beliefs about the product's attributes and consequences, leading to favourable brand attitudes toward buying the brand (A_{act}) and intentions to purchase (BI). Persuasion also involves creation of means-end chains of product knowledge, linking the brand to important end goals such as terminal and instrumental values.[26]

CONSUMER PERSPECTIVE

9.5

Single-source advertising research

Information Resources Inc. (IRI), knows what Paxton Blackwell of Williamsport, Pennsylvania, eats for breakfast, what television shows he watches, the coupons he uses, where he shops, the products and brands he buys, and which newspapers he reads. He says he doesn't mind the meters on his TV or the frequent surveys he fills out. Blackwell is monitored in an evolving methodology called *single-source research*. This methodology could revolutionize the advertising research business and may be able to show how—or perhaps whether—advertising works to affect brand purchase choices.

IRI is poised to expand its data-gathering service to include Canada. However, it is facing strict competition from A.C. Nielsen Co. of Canada, which IRI believes is engaging in anti-competitive practices. A federal competition tribunal is currently considering whether Nielsen has an unfair monopoly on the scanner data market, which comprises prized sales data gathered from retailers. Nielsen's practice of sealing ironclad contracts with grocery chains prevents a rival (like IRI) from entering a business that could be worth up to $70 million annually in Canada.

Of course, there are problems with the single-source system, not the least of which is figuring out how to analyse and summarize the mountains of data the system generates. In addition, single-source research can't tell who, if anyone, in the household actually saw each commercial. Moreover, there are so many other possible influences on purchase besides the advertisement, that concluding an ad is solely responsible for a sale is usually not possible. Finally, and most important of all, single-source research does not answer the all-important question of *why* consumers purchase a particular brand.

Despite the drawbacks, most marketers agree that this form of collecting data is very useful. Scanner data is very focused and fine-tuned. You might say it's the voice of the people. Consumers tell manufacturers what brands they want to purchase—an invaluable source of information for marketers.

Source: Marina Strauss, "War at the Check-out Counter," *Globe and Mail*, Nov. 1, 1994, p. B1; Marina Strauss, "Competition Bureau Targets Nielsen: Contractual Lock on Grocery Chain Scanner Data Assailed," *Globe and Mail*, April 6, 1994, p. B2; Marina Strauss, "Nielsen's Market Share Challenged: U.S. Rival Wants to Expand In Canada," *Globe and Mail*, Dec. 14, 1993, p. B3; Felix Kessler, "High-Tech Shocks in Ad Research," *Fortune*, July 7, 1986, pp. 58–62; Joanne Lipman, "Learning about Grape-Nuts in Denver," *The Wall Street Journal*, Feb. 16, 1988, p. 36; Joanne Lipman, "Single-Source Ad Research Heralds Detailed Look at Household Habits," *The Wall Street Journal*, Feb. 16, 1988, p. 36.

The basic objective of most promotion communications is to influence *sales* of the brand. But linking sales to a particular promotion message such as a coupon or an ad is difficult because many other factors influence purchase behaviour besides the promotion. However, technological advances associated with the scanner devices described in Consumer Perspective 9.5 are moving marketers closer to understanding the relationship between promotions and sales.

Consumer action

Although the key consumer action of interest to marketers is purchase of the promoted product or brand, other behaviours may also be the targets of marketing strategies. For instance, some promotions are intended to generate visits to the store. Some grocery stores offer a double-coupon strategy (each coupon is worth twice its face value) in an effort to build store traffic.

Other promotions may attempt to stimulate product conversations between customers. Word-of-mouth communications help to spread awareness beyond people who come into direct contact with the promotion. For example, you may call a friend who is looking for tires to say Sears is having a sale. Consumers sometimes recommend that their friends see a particular salesperson who is especially pleasant or well informed or who offers good deals on merchandise. Consumers often pass on impressions of a new restaurant or retail store to their friends. Because mention of a product by someone we know is such a powerful form of promotion, marketers design some promotions to encourage word-of-mouth communication (sign up a friend to join the health club, and you get two months' membership free).

EFFECTS OF PROMOTION COMMUNICATIONS

A promotion communication can have five types of effects on consumers, but certain promotion strategies are best suited to produce each effect.[27]

▷ Stimulate a need for the product category or product form.

▷ Create awareness of the brand.

▷ Create a favourable brand attitude.

▷ Form an intention to purchase the brand.

▷ Influence various behaviours that are necessary for brand purchase (travelling to store, finding the brand in the store, talking to salespeople).

Stimulate product need

Before consumers can make a brand purchase, they must recognise a need for the product category or the product form. Problem recognition motivates consumers to consider which product category or product form is most likely to solve their problem and satisfy their end goal. Consumers are said to be "in the market" for the product if they believe the product is relevant to their problem and they have formed a general intention to purchase it. At any given time, relatively few consumers are in the market for a particular product category. (At any moment, perhaps 15 to 20 percent of consumers intend to buy laundry detergent, compared to only 1 or 2 percent who intend to buy a new car.) This means many consumers are potentially susceptible to communication strategies designed to stimulate a product need.

To stimulate a need for a product, marketers must convince a consumer that using the product category or product form will have desirable consequences that are linked to the consumer's end goal. For instance, having dinner in a nice restaurant could be promoted as enjoyable and relaxing and a deserved reward for working hard. Essentially, marketers must create a positive means-end chain for the product category or form. Marketers often use advertising communications to stimulate a category need, but publicity and personal selling also have an influence.

Create brand awareness

Because consumers cannot buy a brand unless they know about it, brand awareness is a general communication goal for all promotion strategies. By creating brand awareness, marketers hope the brand will be activated from memory whenever consumers recognise a category need and will be included in the consideration set of choice alternatives.

Advertising probably has the greatest influence on brand awareness, and much of the advertising for frequently purchased products such as beer, soda, and cigarettes is designed to create and maintain high levels of brand awareness.[28] But the other types of marketing promotion also can influence brand awareness. Sales personnel generate brand awareness in the store by calling attention to certain brands. Various sales promotion strategies such as colourful price discount signs and in-store displays (a large stack of Ritz cracker packages at the end of the supermarket aisle) draw consumers' attention to brands. The position of brands on the shelf can influence brand awareness (for most products, eye-level placements tend to be noticed more). Finally, prominent displays of brand name signs on stores, buses, and billboards remind consumers of the brand name and help maintain brand awareness.

The level of brand awareness necessary for purchase depends on how and where consumers make their purchase decisions. Many brand choice decisions are made in the store (grocery and personal care products, clothing items, appliances, and electronic products), so consumers do not need to recall a brand name from memory. They need only to recognise the brand when they see it, which then activates their relevant brand knowledge in memory. Thus, a common communication strategy is to show the brand package in the advertising so consumers can more easily recognise the brand in the store.[29] In other decision contexts, brand awareness must be higher to influence consumers' brand choice. If the purchase decision is made at home where there are few brand-name cues, consumers must recall the brand from memory before it can be included in the consideration set. Restaurant choices are an example. In such cases, knowledge in memory can be more influential than environmental factors.

The appropriate promotion strategy to influence brand awareness depends on how well known the brand name already is. In some cases, the marketing goal is to maintain high levels of brand awareness and make it more likely that the brand is activated during decision making.[30] Much of the advertising for well-known brands such as Coca-Cola, McDonald's, and Tim Horton's serves as a reminder of the brand name. To create brand awareness for less familiar brands, managers may have to spend heavily on advertising.

Create a favourable brand attitude

Every promotion communication has the potential to influence brand attitudes by creating favourable beliefs about the consequences of salient brand attributes.[31] For instance, mint flavour for toothpaste might be associated with the functional consequence "makes my mouth feel fresh," which in turn could connect to a means-end chain of positive consequences, including "eliminate bad breath, avoid offending others, feel confident." These beliefs may be integrated to form an attitude toward buying the brand, which, in turn, could influence an intention to buy the brand. Consumers form positive attitudes toward purchasing a brand if the promotion message creates means-end links between the brand and important consequences and values.

Form an intention to purchase the brand

Most promotion communications are intended to influence the probability that consumers will buy the brand (BI). A purchase intention can be formed through integration processes in decision making (This T-shirt is such a good deal, I am going to buy it) or activated from memory as a preformed decision plan (When Tammy runs low on mouthwash, she buys Scope).

To design effective promotion communications, marketers need to know *when* most consumers form a brand purchase intention. For instance, only consumers who are actively in the market for the product category are likely to form an intention to buy a brand at the time of exposure to an ad.[32] More typically, consumers form a brand BI well after exposure to advertising, perhaps when they are making a decision in a store. (It's estimated that intentions to buy are formed in the store for about 85 percent of candy purchases, 83 percent of snack purchases, and 45 percent of soft drinks.)[33] This delay in forming BI means the consumer must remember advertising information about brand attributes and consequences to activate and use in integration processes during decision making.

Most sales promotions and personal-selling strategies are designed to influence consumers' purchase intentions (and behaviours) *at the time of exposure*.[34] The goal of these promotion communications is to persuade consumers to buy right away. This can happen if the consumer forms beliefs that the brand is connected to important consequences and values and immediately integrates these beliefs to form an A_{act} and a BI to purchase. If a consumer interprets a 25-percent-off sales promotion as leading to "saving money" and "having more money to use for other things," which in turn is linked to the value of "being a careful consumer," that consumer might immediately form a favourable A_{act} and BI and make a purchase on the spot.

Influence other behaviours

Finally, some promotion communication strategies are designed to influence behaviours other than purchase. Consumers often must perform certain behaviours to make a brand purchase. To buy a brand such as Ralph Lauren's Polo, consumers must enter the high-quality clothing shops that carry it, making store choice a critical factor in sales of Polo. All types of promotion communications, including sales promotions, publicity, and personal selling, can influence the probability that consumers will perform these "other" behaviours. For instance, consumers might be invited to an auto dealership for free doughnuts and coffee and a test drive in a new car. Publicity and word-of-mouth communications can influence movie sales or visits to a restaurant. Real estate salespeople might help consumers get a mortgage loan, which greatly increases the probability of their buying a house.

THE PERSUASION PROCESS

Persuasion refers to changes in beliefs, attitudes, and behavioural intentions caused by a promotion communication. For the most part, marketing researchers have studied the persuasive effects of advertising communications, but sales promotions, personal selling, and publicity also can persuade consumers.

The Elaboration Likelihood Model (ELM)

The **Elaboration Likelihood Model (ELM)** identifies two cognitive processes by which promotion communications such as advertising can persuade consumers: the central and peripheral routes to persuasion.[35] Exhibit 9.2 shows how these two processes work. Which persuasion process occurs is determined by consumers' level of involvement with the product message. The central route to persuasion is more likely when consumers' involvement is higher; the peripheral route to persuasion is more likely when involvement is lower. The ELM also distinguishes between two types of information in the promotion communication. Specific claims about product attributes or demonstrations of functional and psychosocial consequences, along with the supporting evidence, are "central" information; information about anything other than the product is "peripheral."

In the *central route to persuasion,* consumers who experience higher levels of involvement with the product or promotion message are motivated to pay attention to the central, product-related information and comprehend it at deeper and more elaborate levels.[36] Consumers' comprehension of the product-related information is indicated by their cognitive responses to the promotion message.[37] *Support arguments* are positive thoughts about product attributes and the self-relevant consequences of product use (Head and Shoulders does seem like an effective dandruff shampoo). Support arguments enhance persuasion by leading to favourable product beliefs, positive brand attitudes, and stronger intentions to buy the product. During comprehension, consumers may produce unfavourable thoughts about the product called *counterarguments* (I don't think taking this vitamin every day will make a difference in my health). Counterarguing reduces persuasion by leading to unfavourable product beliefs, negative brand attitudes, and weaker intentions or no intention to buy the product.

The *peripheral route to persuasion* is quite different. Consumers who have low involvement with the product message (they are not in the market for the product) have little motivation to attend to and comprehend the central product information in the ad. Therefore, direct persuasion is low because these consumers form few brand beliefs and are unlikely to form brand attitudes or purchase intentions. However, these consumers may pay attention to the peripheral (nonproduct) aspects of the promotion communication,

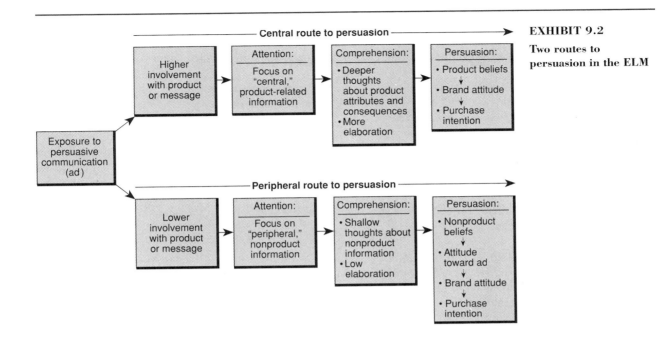

EXHIBIT 9.2

Two routes to persuasion in the ELM

such as the pictures in a print ad or the scenery or actors in a TV commercial, perhaps for their entertainment value. For instance, ads for Reebok featuring basketball star Shaquille O'Neil might attract such attention. Consumers' affective and cognitive responses to these peripheral features may be integrated to form an attitude toward the ad (A_{ad})—"This is a good ad." Later, if a brand evaluation is called for during decision making, these ad-related meanings can be activated and used to form a brand attitude, since there are no relevant brand beliefs or attitudes in memory. Substantial evidence indicates consumers' affective feelings about an ad (A_{ad}) can influence their brand attitudes and purchase intentions.[38] Thus, the peripheral route to persuasion can persuade consumers to buy, but in an indirect way.

At any given time, relatively few consumers are in the market for a particular product, so much of the advertising consumers are exposed to daily is not particularly relevant to their end goals and values. This suggests that most mass media advertising receives peripheral processing. The low levels of recall for most ads (about 20 percent on average) suggest this is the case. In some cases, marketers might want consumers to engage in peripheral route processes. If a brand is similar to competing brands (soft drinks, beer, and cigarettes are examples), marketers may not be able to make credible claims about unique product attributes or consequences. Promotion strategies, therefore, tend to focus on image advertising for which peripheral processing is appropriate.

In situations where a brand has a distinctive advantage, marketers may want to encourage consumers to engage in central route processing by increasing their involvement with the ad message and the product or brand.[39] Making explicit comparisons with other brands in comparative advertisements tends to make the ad message more interesting and involving.[40] Sending promotion messages directly to consumers who are in the market for the product category or product form ensures some level of motivation in the brand information and should stimulate central processing.

**MARKETING
IMPLICATIONS**

Developing and implementing effective promotion communication strategies can be difficult. Although no single approach or magic formula can guarantee success, the process begins with an understanding of the consumer/product relationship.

**Understanding the
consumer/product
relationship**

To analyse the relationships between consumers and products or brands, marketers begin by identifying the appropriate target market of consumers. Then they identify the end goals and values of these consumers, their knowledge and beliefs about product attributes and consequences, their involvement with the product and brand, and their current brand attitudes, behaviour intentions, and actual behaviour. Marketers of established brands may already know a great deal about consumer/product relationships. For new products or brands, marketers may have to conduct considerable marketing research. This could include laddering interviews to identify the dominant means-end chains that reveal how consumers perceive the relationship between the product and their own self-concepts.[41]

The FCB Grid

The **Foote, Cone & Belding (FCB) Grid** shown in Exhibit 9.3 offers a way to analyse consumer/product relationships.[42] Developed by a major advertising agency to help its clients understand consumers' relationships with products, the FCB Grid is based on two concepts discussed in earlier chapters: consumers' involvement with the product and their dominant mode of psychological response to the product—either cognitive or affective.

Consumers' level of product involvement depends on how closely product attributes are linked, via means-end chains, to self-relevant goals and values. For most products, it is possible to identify the typical level of involvement experienced by most consumers. The FCB Grid divides products into two levels, *higher involvement* and *lower involvement.*

Most consumers have a typical mode of psychological response to a product—cognitive or affective. Consumers respond to some products primarily in rational, cognitive

---

EXHIBIT 9.3

**The Foote, Cone &
Belding Grid for
analysing consumer/
product relationships**

	Think products	**Feel products**
Higher involvement	• RRSP account • 35mm camera • ———▶ • Car battery	• Car • Wallpaper • Refrigerator • Perfume
Lower involvement	• Insecticide • Clothespins	• Greeting card • Rum • Ice cream bar

Source: David Berger, "Theory into Practice: The FCB Grid," *European Research,* Jan. 1986, p. 35.

A "think" ad for a "feel" product.

meanings, creating beliefs about product attributes and the functional consequences of using the product.[43] These are *think products* in the grid model. Examples of this category are financial investments, cameras, and car batteries. Cognitive responses produced by the cognitive system dominate consumer reactions to such products.

The affective system is the dominant mode of psychological response for *feel products*. Consumers react to these products with emotion and feeling, and they may form visual or other sensory images of the product.[44] These affective responses may be associated with the psychosocial consequences and value outcomes of product use. Feel products in the FCB Grid are purchased primarily for their sensory qualities (ice cream, beverages, cologne) or for their emotional consequences (greeting cards, jewelry, some types of clothing).

Exhibit 9.3 shows the placement of several products within the FCB Grid, based on extensive consumer research. Because consumers have different types of relationships with products in the four quadrants, the appropriate communication strategy depends on a product's position. For instance, drama or visual advertising that emphasises emotional, feeling responses and visual images might be appropriate for feel products but probably not for think products. Lecture ads containing verbal claims about product attributes and consequences would be more appropriate for think products.

Sometimes a product can be moved within the grid by a promotion strategy. This is illustrated in Exhibit 9.3 by the shift of the refrigerator from a think to a feel product. A South American client of FCB presented a problem: 5,000 ugly green refrigerators were

EXHIBIT 9.4

An analysis of consumer vulnerability

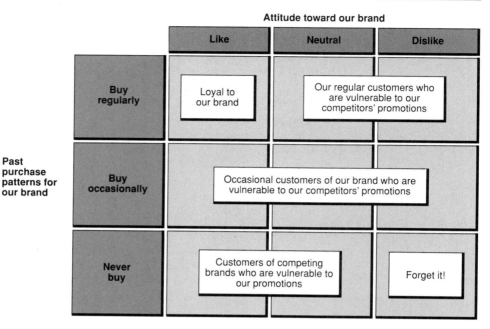

Source: Adapted from Yoram Wind, "Brand Loyalty and Vulnerability," in *Consumer and Industrial Buying Behavior*, ed. A. G. Woodside, J. N. Sheth, and P.D. Bennett (New York: North Holland Publishing, 1977), pp. 313–20. Reprinted by permission of A. G. Woodside.

not selling. High-involvement products like refrigerators tend to be marketed as think products and sold in terms of functional consequences, but in this case there was no unique benefit to promote. So FCB designed a promotion strategy to move refrigerators from the think to the feel quadrants. The agency created ads featuring Venezuelan beauty queens and called the refrigerators "another Venezuelan beauty." The 5,000 refrigerators sold out in 90 days, showing that even traditional think products sometimes can be promoted using affective, feel communication strategies. In sum, the FCB Grid can help marketers understand consumer/product relationships to develop more effective promotions.

Vulnerability analysis

Vulnerability analysis is another tool for understanding the consumer/product relationship and developing promotion strategies. By analysing consumers' attitudes toward its brand and people's past purchases of the brand, a company can identify segments of consumers who vary in their vulnerability to its promotion communications and those of competitors. Exhibit 9.4 provides an example of vulnerability analysis. For instance, people who dislike a brand and never buy it (lower right quadrant) are not likely to be persuaded to buy and can be ignored. Consumers who never buy the brand but have a favourable (or at least neutral) attitude toward it are vulnerable to the company's promotions. Free samples, premiums, contests, or coupons might create an intention to try the brand and move consumers to an occasional-user segment.

Occasional purchasers of the brand are vulnerable to the promotion strategies for competing brands, so the marketer might have a promotion objective to encourage repeat purchases. Offering a free doughnut after the consumer has bought 12 or a premium for saving proofs of purchase may be effective. Or a firm might try to demonstrate the

The business of buying consumer loyalty is booming. For consumers, it means savings that can amount to 14 percent off airline tickets, more than 10 percent off phone bills, and thousands of dollars toward the cost of a new car or home.

Frequent-flyer programs remain the best deals on the market, at least for foreign or full-fare passengers. Although Air Canada and Canadian Airlines have tightened their requirements for domestic frequent-flyer programs, they remain generous in point allocations for foreign air travel.

Infrequent flyers have another alternative. They can earn free air trips without going on a plane. The plan is called Air Miles and it is operated by a Toronto-based company, Loyalty Management Group. A consumer can collect air travel points by making purchases at participating retailers, which include such giants as Bell Canada and Sears. Consumers can also generate Air Miles through the use of credit cards. With the Bank of Montreal MasterCard, for $35 a year, a consumer can earn one air mile for every $20 spent.

Source: Michael Prentice, "Buying Consumer Loyalty: Sharp Careful Shoppers Score Points in Reward Programs," *Montreal Gazette*, July 14, 1994, p. D3.

CONSUMER PERSPECTIVE

9.6

Promoting customer purchase loyalty

superiority of its brand over competing brands. For example, Burger King and Pepsi-Cola have used comparative advertising to "prove" their respective brands are better than McDonald's and Coca-Cola.[45]

Finally, brand-loyal consumers who like a company's brand and purchase it consistently can be influenced by promotions designed to keep them happy customers. Frequent-flyer programs have been a phenomenally successful promotion to reinforce the attitudes and purchase behaviour of airline customers. Consumers rack up mileage on flights taken with the airline and receive free trips when they accumulate sufficient mileage. The programs are supposed to be limited to frequent flyers, usually defined as those taking 12 or more plane trips per year. But today more than a third of air travelers are enrolled in four such programs—not exactly what the airlines had in mind when the promotion began. In any case, these incentive programs seem so successful that they are copied by hotels, car-rental firms, restaurants, and other types of companies (see Consumer Perspective 9.6).

Calls by salespeople to "check on how things are going" may reinforce past customers' attitudes and intentions to rebuy when the need arises. Joe Girard, the top car salesperson in the United States for 11 years in a row, sent out over 13,000 cards to his customers each month, wishing them Happy New Year from Joe Girard, Happy St. Patrick's Day, and so on.[46] Finally, promotions can inform current consumers of new uses for existing products. Advertising campaigns promoted Saran Wrap for use in microwave cooking and Static Guard to eliminate static electricity from carpets around computers.

These examples illustrate three important points. First, effective promotion communications depend on the type of relationship consumers have with the product or brand.[47] Second, promotion communications vary in their effectiveness for achieving certain objectives. Personal selling, for example, is usually more effective for closing sales, while advertising is more effective for increasing brand awareness among large groups of consumers. Third, promotion objectives will change over a product's life cycle as consumers' relationships with the product change.[48] The promotion strategy that worked well when the product was introduced is not likely to be effective at the growth, maturity, or decline stage.

EXHIBIT 9.5

The MECCAS model

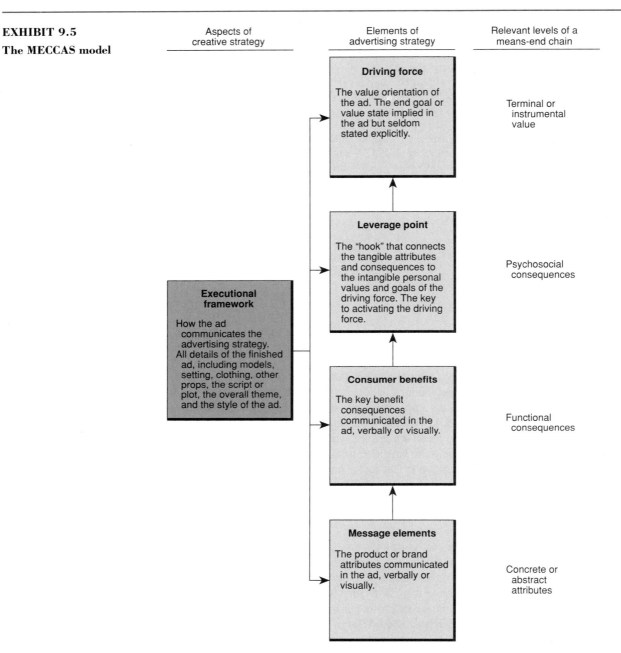

Aspects of creative strategy	Elements of advertising strategy	Relevant levels of a means-end chain

Driving force

The value orientation of the ad. The end goal or value state implied in the ad but seldom stated explicitly.

Terminal or instrumental value

Leverage point

The "hook" that connects the tangible attributes and consequences to the intangible personal values and goals of the driving force. The key to activating the driving force.

Psychosocial consequences

Executional framework

How the ad communicates the advertising strategy. All details of the finished ad, including models, setting, clothing, other props, the script or plot, the overall theme, and the style of the ad.

Consumer benefits

The key benefit consequences communicated in the ad, verbally or visually.

Functional consequences

Message elements

The product or brand attributes communicated in the ad, verbally or visually.

Concrete or abstract attributes

Source: Adapted with the permission of Lexington Books, an imprint of Macmillan, Inc., from Jerry C. Olson and Thomas R. Reynolds, "Understanding Consumers' Cognitive Structures Implications for Advertising Strategies" (pp. 77–90) in *Advertising and Consumer Psychology* by Larry Percy and Arch G. Woodside, editors.

Developing advertising strategy

Marketers should specify advertising strategy in terms of how the product will be related to the consumer. Then ads should be created to communicate the appropriate means-end connections between the product attributes and the consumer's goals and values.[49] The MECCAS model in Exhibit 9.5 can help marketers understand the key aspects of ad strategy and make better strategic decisions.[50]

The **MECCAS model** defines four elements of advertising strategy—the driving force, the leverage point, consumer benefits, and message elements—based on analysis of consumers' means-end chains. (MECCAS stands for means-end chain conceptualization of advertising strategy.) The fifth component of the MECCAS model, the executional framework, is part of the creative strategy that must develop the details of the actual advertisement to communicate the ad strategy.

The first step in creating an advertising strategy is to *understand the consumer/product relationship* by measuring consumers' means-end chains for the product category or product form. Then the marketer must select a means-end chain to convert into an advertising strategy. The most important means-end chain in the decision-making process is a likely candidate. Knowing which product attributes are most important for consumers helps marketers decide which information to include as *message elements* in the ad strategy. (Should the ads for Ruffles potato chips emphasise their flavour, their crunchiness, or their ridges?) Knowing what functional consequences are linked to these salient attributes helps marketers identify the key *consumer benefits* to emphasise. (If Ruffles chips are for dipping, focus on the ridges. If Ruffles are to accompany sandwiches, emphasise flavour and crunchiness.)

The *driving force* is the basic value or end goal to be communicated by the ad. The driving force is usually communicated indirectly and in a subtle fashion; values are seldom mentioned explicitly in ads. That would be perceived as heavy-handed by most consumers, who might react negatively to being told what value they should be thinking of. Values and end goals are part of the consumer, not the product, and must be aroused or activated in the consumer. Merely stating a value in an ad does not ensure that it is activated and felt by consumers. Once activated, the emotional and motivational power of the end goals or values provides the driving force for action, including purchase of the brand.

The final component of an ad strategy is the important *leverage point* by which the relatively concrete, tangible message elements and benefits (attributes and functional consequences of the product) are linked to the abstract driving force (values of the consumer). The leverage point can be thought of as a hook that reaches into the consumer and attaches the product to the activated value that is the driving force of the ad strategy. In advertising, the leverage point is often portrayed as a psychosocial consequence of using the brand. Because consumers automatically perceive the values associated with most psychosocial consequences, the leverage point should activate the driving force and form a connection to it. Thus, the ad does not have to explicitly mention the value to communicate the ad strategy.

In sum, an advertising strategy should specify how a brand will be connected to the important ends the consumer wants. The advertising team must then create an ad that will persuasively communicate these meanings and the links between them. The *executional framework* refers to the various details of the creative strategy (the type of models, how they are dressed, the setting, what people are saying) that are designed to communicate the ad strategy. In general, an effective advertisement should communicate each of the four means-end levels of meaning in the ad strategy (from message elements to driving force) and the links or connections between the levels.

The MECCAS model is not a foolproof tool for creating successful ads; it is a guide to developing advertising strategies and creating effective ads.[51] Marketers still must conduct careful analyses of consumers and use their imaginations. Marketers can use the MECCAS model to translate several means-end chains into possible ad strategies, which can then be evaluated for their competitive advantages. Although any means-end chain can be translated into an advertising strategy using the MECCAS model, not every means-end chain is a viable strategy. Some strategies, for instance, may already be taken by one's competitors. Marketers also can use the MECCAS model as a framework for analysing the meanings their current advertising communicates and for considering how to make these ads more persuasive.[52]

▶ **SUMMARY**

Learning objective 1: *Describe the four types of promotion communications.*
Marketers use four types of promotions to communicate with consumers and influence them to buy. Advertising is any paid, nonpersonal communication about a product, brand, company, or store. Advertising can be transmitted via many different media, including TV and radio, print ads in magazines and newspapers, billboards and signs, and direct mail. Sales promotions are communications offering inducements to buy a product or brand; they include price reductions, coupons, rebates, premiums and gifts, trading stamps, and sweepstakes contests. Personal selling involves direct personal communications between a salesperson and a potential buyer. Among the forms of personal selling are in-store sales, telemarketing, professional sales to business customers, and door-to-door sales. Publicity is any unpaid communication about a product, brand, company, or store; it includes feature stories and news items in popular media, photos on TV or in newspapers, and discussions on talk shows. Advertising is probably the most noticeable promotion communication, although more marketing dollars are spent on sales promotions than on advertising.

Learning objective 2: *Describe the components of the basic communication model.*
The basic communication model identifies the key elements in the communication process. The source (a company, an advertising agency, or a corporate spokesperson) creates a message designed to convey certain meanings. The message could be in the form of an ad, a sales promotion offer, a script for a sales presentation, or a publicity story. The message is transmitted through a medium such as broadcast (TV or radio), print (magazines, newspapers, or mail) signs (billboards), or personal appearance (direct selling). The message is apprehended by a receiver (consumers in the target audience) and comprehended (interpreted). Finally, the receiver initiates some action, perhaps purchase of the product, although other behaviours are possible, such as word-of-mouth discussions with friends, visits to stores, or reading reports of product tests.

Learning objective 3: *Describe the various effects that promotion communications can have on consumers.*
Promotion communications can have at least five types of effects on consumers. Some promotion communications are intended to stimulate a need for the product category or product form by inducing consumers to recognise a problem that the product can solve. Other promotion communications are intended to create or maintain brand awareness. Many promotion communications are designed to persuade consumers by creating positive beliefs about the brand, favourable attitudes toward the brand, and a strong intention to purchase the brand. Finally, some promotion communications are intended to influence other behaviours, such as visiting a store or showroom or telling a friend about the brand. Promotion communications can have multiple effects.

Learning objective 4: *Discuss the two routes to persuasion specified by the Elaboration Likelihood Model and describe the role of attitude toward the ad in persuasion.*
A promotion communication such as an ad transmits two sorts of information: central information about the product or brand being promoted, and peripheral information about all other factors. The Elaboration Likelihood Model describes two cognitive processes or "routes" to persuasion that focus on these types of information. The route taken depends on consumers' involvement. Consumers who are interested in the brand (perhaps

because they are in the market for the product) have higher levels of involvement with the product. This motivation focuses their attention on the central product and/or brand information in the message, and these consumers are likely to form brand beliefs and attitudes toward buying the brand. This process is the central route to persuasion.

When involvement with the brand and/or product message is low, consumers are not interested in the central product information in the message and are unlikely to form brand attitudes or purchase intentions. Any attention that occurs is likely to be focused on peripheral aspects of the message, such as the setting or the models used in an ad. Consumers engaged in peripheral processing might form an attitude toward the ad (A_{ad}) instead of toward the product. This peripheral route to persuasion is indirect and based on processing of nonproduct information. In several marketing research studies, A_{ad} has been shown to have an influence on brand attitudes and purchase intentions.

Learning objective 5: *Describe how the FCB Grid and vulnerability analysis can be used to help marketers understand the consumer/product relationship and create effective communication strategies.*

Before they can design effective promotion communication strategies, marketers need to understand the nature of the consumer/product relationship. The text described two models that are useful for developing such an understanding. The FCB Grid combines two dimensions to categorise products in terms of the types of relationships consumers may have with them: consumer involvement with the product (higher and lower levels of involvement) and think/feel, which refers to the dominant way consumers react to the product—either cognitive or affective. Think products like laundry detergent, insecticides, and lawnmowers are evaluated in terms of rational, cognitive factors such as product attributes and functional consequences. Feel products like cologne, ice cream, and beer are evaluated in terms of their affective qualities. The combinations of higher/lower involvement and think/feel describe four broad types of consumer/product relationships.

The vulnerability matrix also describes the relationships consumers may have with a company's brand. The matrix identifies segments of consumers who vary in terms of their attitudes toward the brand (like, are neutral to, or dislike the brand) and their past purchasing behaviour (buy the brand regularly, occasionally, or never). These groups differ in terms of their vulnerability to the promotion communication strategies of competing companies. The vulnerability matrix also suggests that different types of promotion communications strategies are necessary for each segment. Consumers who like a brand and buy it regularly are loyal and should be rewarded occasionally to keep them satisfied. Consumers who dislike a brand and never buy it are poor targets and probably should be ignored.

Learning objective 6: *Describe the MECCAS model of advertising strategy.*

The MECCAS (means-end chain conceptualization of advertising strategy) model identifies the basic components of advertising strategy. The model is based on the means-end chain approach that identifies the associations consumers make among product attributes, consequences, and value outcomes. According to MECCAS, a fully specified advertising strategy has four elements: message elements, product benefits, the leverage point, and the driving force. The message elements refer to the basic product attributes to be communicated in the ad. The product benefits refer to the functional consequences mentioned or shown in the ad. Typically, the leverage point is a psychosocial consequence that is portrayed or implied in the ad. The leverage point helps consumers link the relatively tangible product benefits or functional consequences the ad shows with the abstract, intangible personal values it implies. The driving force is the end consequence (perhaps a value) that is implied in the ad (most ads do not explicitly mention the value the ad attempts to link the brand with). A good ad strategy should specify the meanings to be communicated at all four levels. The last part of the MECCAS model is the executional framework, which refers to all the details of the ad's creative execution (including the scenes, dialogue, models and their clothing, actions portrayed, lighting, and camera angles).

Learning objective 7: *Distinguish between lecture and drama advertising.*
Lecture and drama advertising elicit different reactions from consumers and persuade consumers in different ways. Lecture ads resemble a classroom lecture in that the source makes claims about the product and may present evidence to support them. Essentially, lecture ads present rational arguments why consumers should buy and use the product. Lecture ads persuade by creating favourable beliefs about product attributes and consequences. Drama ads (sometimes called narrative ads) tell a story in which the product is somehow relevant. A drama ad may not feature any explicit product claims. Drama ads persuade by drawing consumers into the story and encouraging them to identify with the characters. They let receivers vicariously experience some of the product experiences the characters in the drama are portraying and thereby learn about the product. These beliefs in turn may lead to positive attitudes and intentions to buy.

▶ **KEY TERMS AND CONCEPTS**

promotion communications	publicity	Foote, Cone & Belding (FCB) Grid
advertising	communication process	MECCAS model
sales promotions	persuasion	
personal selling	Elaboration Likelihood Model (ELM)	

▶ **REVIEW AND DISCUSSION QUESTIONS**

1. As a consumer of fast-food products, evaluate the effects of promotion communications on your decision processes.

2. Using the soft-drink industry as an example, define and illustrate each major type of promotion strategy.

3. Suggest reasons for the growing emphasis on sales promotion in the promotion mix of many marketing organisations.

4. Select an ad or sales promotion strategy and discuss it in terms of the elements in the communication model.

5. Describe the two routes to persuasion in the ELM and suggest how to develop effective advertising strategies.

6. Use the FCB Grid to describe your consumer/product relationship for two products you recently purchased.

7. Describe how the MECCAS model can be used to develop an effective advertising strategy for a brand of athletic shoe.

8. Discuss the circumstances under which lecture and drama ads might be effective formats.

9. Identify a specific promotion communication and suggest how marketers could measure its effects.

III SECTION

BEHAVIOUR

OUTLINE

▶ 10. Introduction to Behaviour
▶ 11. Classical and Operant Conditioning
▶ 12. Vicarious Learning and the Diffusion of Innovation
▶ 13. Analysing Consumer Behaviour

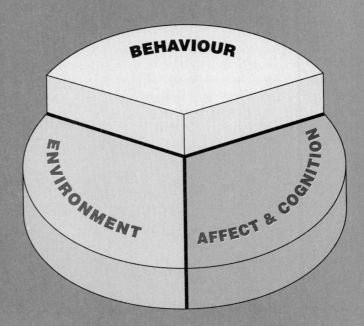

10

Introduction to Behaviour

LEARNING OBJECTIVES

After completing this chapter, you should be able to:

► 1. Explain some basic differences between behaviour and cognitive approaches.

► 2. List a number of different types of consumer promotions.

► 3. Explain four ways promotions are used to influence consumer behaviour.

► 4. Explain the uses of behaviour approaches in social marketing.

► 5. Discuss ethical questions concerning the use of behaviour approaches in marketing.

Think No Fee.

Think 5% Towards a New Car.

What else is there to think about?

Thinking about a Visa* card? You'd be smart to think about the GM Visa. No fee.
Never has been. And you'll earn 5% of every dollar you spend towards
a new GM car, truck or van.

Call 1 800 461-3279. Now You're Thinking.

Up to $500 per Cardholder Year or maximum of $3,500 over 7 years.
Subject to GM Card Program Rules. *TD and GM are licensed users of Marks.

CANADIAN COMPANIES PARTNERING TO CREATE VALUE OFFERS TO CUSTOMERS

In June of 1993, two prominent companies, General Motors of Canada and the Toronto-Dominion Bank, partnered to create a new value-added Visa credit card. Consumers using the GM Visa Card pay no annual fee and earn five percent of everything they spend toward a new GM car, truck or van (you can earn up to $500 per cardholder year, for a maximum of $3,500 over seven years). The advertising campaign ("Now You're Thinking") encouraged viewers thinking about getting a Visa card to obtain the GM Card™, where they would not have to think about any annual fee, and would only have to think about five percent toward a new car.

Canadian ethnic cultures were targeted by Telecom Canada and Teleglobe Canada with a contest that asked contestants to guess the cost of long-distance calls "back home." Prizes awarded twice daily included 10-minute phone calls. There were 10 grand prizes of 10-minute calls monthly for a year.

A bilingual promotion by Toronto's Consumer Health Care Division for Sinutab's non-drowsy hot drink for cold sufferers featured a point-of-purchase entry-form sweepstakes. The grand prize was a trip to the city that never sleeps—for those who don't want to sleep. It included airfare for four, selected day and evening activities, and $500 U.S. spending money.

Ten-second spots that ran throughout the National Football League season and the playoffs invited viewers to their local Ford dealerships. Those who completed a test drive became eligible to win a Ford Escort.

The CBC network ran a contest on its youth-oriented music show "Video Hits." Teens had to watch the show for contest information. From the entries they mailed in, 10 winners from across Canada were chosen to 'party in L.A.' with the musical group Kris Kross.

These promotions, run by different companies for different purposes, all have something in common: the companies were trying to change not consumers' attitudes or beliefs but their behaviour. Both Telecom Canada and the Ford dealerships wanted to get consumers more involved with their services, while Warner-Lambert tried to get more consumers buying Sinutab. Toronto Dominion wanted consumers to spend more on their credit cards, while CBC wanted more teens to watch its programs more regularly. Such strategies are consistent with the behaviour approaches introduced in this chapter.

The previous section of this book presented an in-depth analysis of consumer cognitive and affective processes. Its major focus was on understanding the psychological or mental aspects of consumer behaviour. In this section, the focus changes to another element of the Wheel of Consumer Analysis. Our concern here is with attempting to understand overt consumer behaviour: behaviour that can be directly observed and measured. We focus on what consumers *do* rather than on what they *think* and *feel,* and we delineate some processes by which this behaviour can be changed to achieve marketing objectives.

In this chapter, we first compare the *cognitive* and the *behaviour* approaches in terms of their basic differences so far as marketing is concerned. We do this so that you can appreciate why there are so few attempts to integrate them. Both cognitive and behaviour approaches have value for the study of consumer behaviour and for achieving marketing management objectives. We then discuss two areas of consumer research that have recognised the value of behaviour approaches: sales promotion and social marketing. The chapter concludes with a discussion of some common misconceptions about behaviour approaches.

In Chapter 11, classical and operant conditioning are explained and illustrated with a variety of marketing examples. We then turn to vicarious learning and its value for marketing (Chapter 12). These two chapters provide an overview of the major technology employed in applied behaviour analysis. In Chapter 13, the last chapter of this section, we develop a model of overt consumer behaviour and a management model for systematically influencing these behaviours.

BEHAVIOUR VERSUS COGNITIVE VIEWS	Cognitive approaches, including some aspects of affect, dominate the field of consumer behaviour and much of the thinking in marketing. Behaviour approaches, which have been an important part of psychology for many years, are relatively new to consumer research and often are not well understood. For this reason, we think it is important to give a brief account of some differences between the two approaches.

There are, of course, many types of cognitive theories and assumptions, as there are a variety of behaviour positions. Some cognitive approaches, for example, attempt to apply cognitive theories in explaining overt behaviour. Others are concerned only with explaining the mind and mental processes. Some behaviourists view cognitive events as covert behaviour to be analysed in the same way as overt behaviour. Other behaviourists see cognitive events as little more than words that may be useful for communication purposes but are of no value as scientific explanations. It is unlikely that any discussion of differences between cognitive and behaviour perspectives would be accepted by all advocates of either position, but we will attempt to offer representative accounts of them.

The **behaviour approach** is based on a view called "applied behaviour analysis." The **cognitive approach** is based on current research on topics such as information processing and cognitive science. These two perspectives tend to conflict: they often involve quite different views of the world, with conflicting positions, assumptions, and beliefs about what is scientifically important. Most important for our purposes, the behaviour and

Issues	Behaviour Approaches	Cognitive Approaches
Role of the environment	Environment controls consumer behaviour	Environment is one of many influences on consumer behaviour
Role of cognition	Cognitions may mediate behaviour environment interactions	Cognitions cause and control behaviour
Role of behaviour	Behaviour is the central focus of research and strategy development	Behaviour is the result of cognition and is secondary in importance
View of affect	Affect refers to observable behaviours	Affect refers to internal feelings
View of freedom	Consumer behaviour is controlled by the environment	Consumers have free will and buy what they need and want

EXHIBIT 10.1

A comparison of behaviour and cognitive approaches

the cognitive approaches often have different implications for designing marketing strategies.

Some differences between the two approaches are shown in Exhibit 10.1. Behaviour approaches tend to view the environment as the cause of behaviour, so they focus on the effects of different environmental situations and stimuli on what consumers actually do. For example, setting up a store display for Duracell batteries and observing the effects on consumer purchase behaviour would be consistent with the behaviour approach. Cognitive approaches, which tend to view mental processes and states as more important, focus instead on what consumers report they think and feel about various aspects of the environment. Giving consumers a questionnaire asking them about their attitudes toward Duracell batteries would be consistent with the cognitive approach.

The question of freedom deserves more discussion. Not many people like to think they are controlled or even strongly influenced by the environment. We like to think of ourselves as making free choices and determining our own destiny in a variety of circumstances. Behaviourists look at circumstances from a different perspective. An example will illustrate what behaviourists mean when they argue that the environment controls consumer behaviour.

Most adults in our society use products such as deodorant and toothbrushes. In fact, it is socially unacceptable not to use these products, and consumers who do not can be looked down on. Serious health problems can also result from not brushing one's teeth. In other words, some consequences are connected with use or nonuse of these products. In behaviour terms, the environment conditions the use of these products by in some way rewarding consumers who use them and punishing consumers who do not.

Given these consequences, how free are we to choose whether to use deodorant or brush our teeth? In fact, our "choice" is influenced to a great extent by the consequences of not engaging in the behaviours. Because behaviour is strongly influenced by its consequences, behaviourists argue that consumers are not free to do whatever they want. In this sense, consumer behaviour is seen as controlled by the environment.

It is also worth noting that the behaviour and the cognitive approach take a different view of affect. So far in the text, we have treated affect as a psychological phenomenon dealing with the way consumers feel. Affect includes such things as consumer attitudes and emotions. To behaviourists, however, affect refers to observable behaviours, not internal states.

Rebates are often effective at changing purchase probabilities, even for big-ticket items.

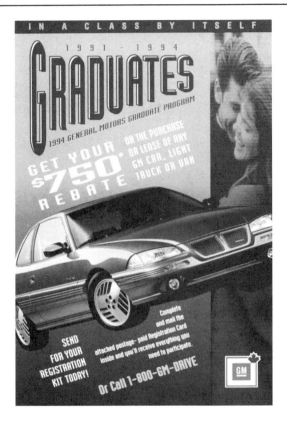

The concept of attitude is one example. In cognitive approaches, attitudes deal with what consumers mentally like and dislike. So to a cognitivist, a favourable attitude toward a product means the consumer likes the product a lot. In behaviour approaches, the term *attitude* refers instead to the probability of a behavioural response. To a behaviourist, a favourable attitude toward a product means the consumer has a higher probability of purchasing it.

Another example of the difference in cognitive and behaviour approaches concerns emotions, such as anger. Cognitivists view anger as an internal feeling. To a behaviourist, anger is a summary statement to describe a set of behaviours. For example, if they see a consumer yelling and throwing ice cream at a store clerk, behaviourists would have no problem saying the person seems angry. Yet by "angry" they do not mean what the person feels inside; they refer specifically to the behaviours they are observing. Thus, whether affect is an internal feeling or an observable behaviour depends on your view. In this section of the text, we treat affect as observable behaviours.

Exhibit 10.2 offers further comparison of these approaches in the ways they tend to view marketing issues. Cognitive approaches assume that the role of marketing action is to satisfy needs at a profit, a theory that requires two further cognitive assumptions. First, it assumes that consumers have something called "needs," which they attempt to satisfy through purchase and consumption. Second, consumers are somewhat autonomous and rational and largely control their preferences and purchases. Marketing strategies may attempt to change consumer affect and cognitions, such as beliefs and attitudes, the cognitive approach would say, but marketing cannot *create* consumer needs and wants or even modify them very much. Similarly, cognitivists seldom address the question of whether marketing is very effective at changing consumer behaviour.

Marketing Issues	Behaviour Approaches	Cognitive Approaches
Role of marketing	Modify and control consumer behaviour to achieve organisational objectives	Satisfy needs of consumers at a profit
Role of marketing/ consumer research	Investigate strategies for predicting and controlling consumer behaviour	Investigate strategies for influencing consumer affect and cognitions
View of marketing effectiveness	Recognize the effectiveness of marketing in changing behaviour	Often overlook the effectiveness of marketing

EXHIBIT 10.2

A comparison of views of marketing

Behaviourists tend to offer a different account of marketing activity. They see marketing as an attempt to achieve organisational objectives by modifying consumer behaviour. A main objective typically is to increase profits and/or market share, usually by increasing sales. Two primary methods of increasing sales are: (1) influencing current buyers to buy more of the product, and (2) maintaining current buyers while influencing nonbuyers to become buyers. Both of these involve changing consumer purchase behaviour. Many behaviourists would argue that marketing strategies are often effective at changing consumer behaviour—and that a variety of current marketing tactics are quite consistent with behavioural principles. Some behaviourists might even suggest that marketers are far more concerned with making profitable sales than with satisfying consumer needs.

Clearly, the two approaches have considerable differences in marketing and consumer behaviour applications. Which approach is "true" or "right" is not at issue. What is important is which approach or combination of approaches is most *useful* in various stages of solving marketing problems and developing marketing strategies.

We believe that a combination of both approaches is superior to either one applied separately. That is, if consideration of consumer needs (cognitive approach) is helpful in the development of successful new products, and if operant conditioning (behaviour approach) is helpful in increasing market share for the product, it would be unwise to ignore either approach. Consumer Perspective 10.1 illustrates a successful marketing strategy using both approaches.

Behavioural principles form the foundation for marketing strategies in several areas. The first of these is sales promotion, an area of increasing interest to consumer researchers and marketing practitioners. A second area deals with social marketing issues. Here the behaviour approach is commonly used to develop strategies to influence socially desirable consumer behaviours.

One area of consumer research that assumes the value of a behaviour approach is sales promotion. In fact, leading experts define **sales promotion** as "an action-focused marketing event whose purpose is to have a direct impact on the behaviour of a firm's customers."[1] Two points are noteworthy in this definition.

First, the firm's customers may be industry members such as retailers, in which case the promotion is called a **trade promotion.** Companies use trade promotions like advertising or display allowances to push products through retailers to consumers. The alternative is that the firm's customers are the final consumers, in which case the promotions are called **consumer promotions.** Retailers (and manufacturers) use consumer promotions such as coupons and free samples to encourage consumers to purchase products and pull the product through the distribution channel. The Association of Canadian

INFLUENCING OVERT CONSUMER BEHAVIOUR

Sales promotion

CONSUMER PERSPECTIVE

▶ **10.1**

Ford's no longer missing company boat

Many marketing practitioners use a combination of cognitive and behavioural approaches effectively. For example, the Ford Motor Co. of Canada Ltd. conducted cognitive research on why its full-size cars were not on the list of choices available to senior corporate management. It found that half of the full-size car market was made up of "perk cars"—company vehicles turned over to executives. These cars were going to the movers, shakers, and opinion makers, a sector that Ford realised it no longer represented. Demographics showed its full-size models were selling to the 50-plus age group, where many customers were dying off.

Ford followed a behavioural marketing strategy and set two objectives: (1) to retain its present customers and (2) to make some new conquest sales by appealing to the slightly younger generation.

The strategy used to accomplish these objectives included a careful design process. For the first time the Grand Marquis and the Crown Victoria were slightly different from one another, with the former appealing to the older customers and the latter to the younger customers. To avoid disturbing its older customers, Ford talked directly to many of them during the design stage to tell them of the changes that were planned. As the introduction date neared, Ford mailed out more than 100,000 invitations, including many to owners of Ford's mid-size models who might be interested in moving up to the bigger car. At the same time, the company wooed corporate customers with VIP nights and test drives for the executive types across the country.

Ford's share of the full-size market jumped 38.6 percent after the new models were introduced. "It was a good fit," said John Radford, vice president of marketing for Ford. Old customers were happy with the new vehicles and new customers were coming into the fold. By analysing cognitions to identify the problem and devising a behavioural intervention to solve it, Ford developed a successful marketing strategy.

Source: Ken Romain, "Ford No Longer Missing the Company Boat," *Globe and Mail*, July 16, 1991, B1.

Advertisers 1993 survey of members found that 61 percent of marketing dollars were spent on trade promotions, 22 percent on advertising, and 17 percent on consumer promotions. Consumer Perspective 10.2 shows how much sales promotions have grown in recent years.

Second, the definition emphasises "direct impact on the behaviour of . . . customers," clearly a behavioural approach. In fact, few consumer promotions provide material designed to change consumer cognitions about a product. Rather, they are designed to influence the probability of purchase or other desired behaviours without necessarily changing any consumer attitudes about a brand. If the promotion is for a new brand, purchase and use may lead to favourable postpurchase attitudes and future purchases. If the promotion is for an existing brand, consumers with a neutral or slightly positive attitude may take advantage of the promotion to reduce their purchase risk and try a brand they do not normally use. For consumers who already purchase a brand, a promotion may be an added incentive to remain loyal to it. The list in Exhibit 10.3 covers most types of consumer promotions.[2] These basic types are often combined to increase the probability of desired behaviours. For example, Procter & Gamble offered a $1-off coupon plus a premium coupon for a free Duncan Hines cake mix for purchasing any size Folgers coffee. Some consumer promotions feature coupons plus a promise to make donations to specific charities for every coupon or refund certificate redeemed. For example, Kentucky Fried Chicken offered Toronto residents coupons for its restaurants. For each coupon that was redeemed, KFC donated 25 cents to Block Parents, an organisation that helps children in distress.

Although advertising remains an important promotional tool, sales promotion expenditures have grown rapidly in recent years. The Association of Canadian Advertisers' 1993 survey on the marketing practices of its members confirms the ongoing trend toward sales promotions. The study found that:

▶ 61 percent of marketing dollars went to trade or retail promotion.

▶ 22 percent of marketing dollars was spent on advertising.

▶ 17 percent of marketing dollars was directed at consumer promotions.

These numbers are quite dramatic, given that in 1990, the split was 35 percent for major media, 15 percent for consumer promotions, and 50 percent for trade promotion. If you go back to 1985, the split was 40 percent for major media, 10 percent for consumer promotion and 50 percent for trade promotion.

While these figures may be surprising, they are in sync with studies that have tracked the increasing dollar expenditures moving away from advertising to the other forms of promotions.

Many reasons are often given for the increasing use of consumer promotions, including the notion that advertising is becoming less effective, consumers are more price sensitive, and the sales effects of promotions are easier to measure than those of advertising. Another reason may be that promotions focus directly on changing consumer behaviour, a major goal of marketing.

Source: Adapted from "Advertising vs Promotion—Game Over?," *Marketing*, Feb. 7, 1994. p. 23.

CONSUMER PERSPECTIVE

10.2 ◀

The new order of promotions

Consumer promotions can be used to influence behaviour in a variety of ways. Four aspects of behaviour that promotions are designed to affect are purchase probability, purchase quantity, purchase timing, and purchase location.

Purchase probability

Most consumer promotions are designed to increase the probability that consumers will purchase a particular brand or combination of products, although a firm may have a number of subgoals it hopes to achieve in running a promotion. For a new product, the primary goal may be to get consumers to try it. For example, Hershey offered a free package of Reese's Crunchy peanut butter cups with the purchase of any other Reese's candy product to encourage trial of the new product. Kellogg's offered a coupon for an 18-ounce box of its popular corn flakes with the purchase of its new Kellogg's Mini Buns. General Motors of Canada offers special discounts to graduating university students.

A second subgoal of consumer promotions may be to position a particular brand or company to encourage consumers to purchase and continue to purchase the company's brand. In this case, the promotion is designed to maintain or change both consumer cognition and behaviour. One way to do this is to use frequent promotions to offer a competitive price on a brand that is positioned as a high-priced, high-quality product. A lower price in these circumstances has less chance of leading consumers to believe the product is of lower quality than competitive brands. For example, Kellogg's frequently offers coupons and premiums on its market-leading cereals.

Other uses of promotions for positioning include offering to contribute to charity for each coupon redeemed or to design in-house products specifically for fund-raising purposes (contributing donations equivalent to the receipts from the sale of those products). These tactics may increase consumer perceptions of the societal commitment of firms.

EXHIBIT 10.3

Types of consumer promotions

▷ **Sampling.** Consumers are offered regular or trial sizes of the product either free or at a nominal price. Hershey Foods has handed out 750,000 candy bars on 170 college campuses.

▷ **Price deals.** Consumers are given discounts from the product's regular price. For example, Coke and Pepsi are frequently available at discounted prices.

▷ **Bonus packs.** Bonus packs consist of additional amounts of the product provided in the package or container. For example, Gillette Atra occasionally adds a few extra blades to its blade packs without increasing the price.

▷ **Rebates and refunds.** Consumers are given cash reimbursements, either at purchase or by mail, for purchasing products. For example, consumers are often offered rebates on certain car makes or models.

▷ **Sweepstakes and contests.** Consumers are offered chances to win cash and/or prizes through either chance selection or games of skill. For example, Marriott Hotels teamed with Hertz Rent-A-Car in a scratch-card sweepstakes that offered over $90 million in prizes.

▷ **Premiums.** A premium is a reward or gift that comes from purchasing a product. For example, Procter & Gamble offered a free package of Diaperene baby washcloths with the purchase of any size Pampers.

▷ **Coupons.** Consumers are offered cents-off or added-value incentives for purchasing specific products. For example, Lenscrafters offered newspaper coupons for $20 off on the purchase of contact lenses from its stores.

Consumers who are socially and ecologically concerned may then switch to purchasing products from companies involved. For example, Quebec's four major grocery chains, normally fierce competitors, joined forces to support Centraide, the province's version of the United Way. For every "Save and Snip with Centraide" coupon redeemed at any of these four stores, the grocers donated 5.4 cents and the manufacturers remitted another 15 cents. The Toronto-based Grocery Industry Foundation Together (GIFT) distributes in-store coupons in 1,000 Ontario supermarkets. The participating grocery retailers and wholesalers donate their per-coupon handling allowance to the foundation. For the Lillehammer Olympics, McDonald's Canada produced its very popular Olympic Cap; 50 cents from the sale of each cap went to support the Canadian Olympic Team. Finally, Carleton Cards Ltd., Canada's largest greeting-card maker, produced a line of specially designed cards to raise funds for the Canadian Wildlife Federation.

A third subgoal of consumer promotions is to effect a brand switch. Consumer promotions result in brand switches by making the purchase of a brand on a deal more attractive than purchasing the usual brand at full price.

A final goal of consumer promotions is to develop brand loyalty. Some consumers are deal-prone and tend to purchase products on the basis of coupons and other deals, so frequent deals on the brands they use may keep them relatively loyal. Companies such as Kellogg's, Procter & Gamble, Gillette Canada, and Canstar (makers of Bauer and other sporting goods equipment) have broad product lines and a number of top-selling products. They frequently offer a variety of consumer promotions for their products. Even deal-prone customers who have preferred brands may remain loyal through a long succession of coupons and other deals.

Purchase quantity

A number of consumer promotions are designed to influence not only purchase of a brand but also the number or size of units purchased. For example, Quaker Oats offered a 70-cent coupon for purchasing two bottles of Gatorade. Best Foods offered a $1 coupon for purchasing two 18-ounce or larger jars of Skippy peanut butter. Procter & Gamble offered $2, $5, and $8, refunds for purchasing one, two, or three gallons of Tide or Cheer liquid laundry detergent. A free Mennen Speed Stick deodorant was offered with the purchase of two at the regular price.

Such promotions may increase the amount of a company's product sold and may increase brand loyalty, but consumers who are already loyal to particular brands may simply stock up on them during a promotion and wait until the next promotion to purchase again. Some consumers will purchase products only when they can get a deal on them. In fact, many Canadian furniture retailers may have unintentionally conditioned consumers to expect free credit deals ("no money down," "no payment until January"), making them reluctant to buy furniture otherwise.

Purchase timing

Consumer promotions can also influence when consumers purchase. For example, marketers may offer special discounts to encourage consumers to go to movie theatres on nights when business is slow. Many Canadian movie theatres offer discounts and special prices on Tuesday or Wednesday nights. Other retail stores have special sales on specific dates to encourage purchases at that time. Services such as airlines and telephone companies offer special rates to encourage consumers to use them at specific times and dates to even out demand. One trend in the case of coupons is to shorten the redemption period to encourage consumers to purchase sooner. Finally, most sweepstakes and contests are relatively short to encourage consumers to enter the contest by purchasing the product promptly.

Purchase location

Consumer promotions can also be used to influence the location or vendor of particular products. Retail stores and retail chains offer their own coupons, contests, and other deals to encourage consumers to shop at their outlets. Canadian Tire for years has offered 5 percent coupons with all cash purchases, redeemable at any store in Canada. National retail chains, such as Wal-Mart, and local retailers such as the Linen Chest in Montreal, have a standing offer to meet any other store's price on a product. The discount electronics store the Future Shop in Vancouver will give away its merchandise if it cannot beat the price of similar goods sold by stores in United States border towns. Such promotions and tactics can build store traffic and encourage store loyalty, as discussed in Consumer Perspective 10.3.

Effectiveness of sales promotions

There is little question that promotions are effective in influencing consumer behaviour, and this is shown by the growth of sales promotion expenditures, as shown in Consumer Perspective 10.2. Which promotion tools are generally most effective for achieving particular behavioural changes is not fully understood, however. One study compared four consumer promotion tools—coupons, rebates, sweepstakes, and premiums—for their impact on various consumer purchase behaviours.[3] These behaviours included purchasing a product consumers said they didn't need, purchasing a product they had never tried before, purchasing a different brand from their usual, purchasing more than usual, purchasing sooner than usual, and purchasing later than usual.

Exhibit 10.4 presents the results of that study. In general, consumers reported coupons were the most effective promotions at changing these various behaviours. Over 70 percent of the consumers said they purchased a product they had never tried before because of a coupon; over 75 percent said they purchased a different brand from their usual because of a coupon. Of course, of the four promotion tools, coupons are the most commonly available and easiest to use. Rebates and premiums were both effective in changing consumer behaviour in this study but to a lesser extent than coupons. The study found that the bigger the rebate, the more effort consumers would expend to obtain it. Finally, while some consumers also reported that sweepstakes influenced them, such promotions were the least effective overall.

CONSUMER PERSPECTIVE

▶ 10.3

Club Z is leaving its mark

Zellers Inc., with over 305 stores across the country is undoubtedly a force to be reckoned with. As the retail sector struggles through its worst slump in 30 years, Zellers' sales and profits continue to grow. It is marching along in a bid to become the biggest retailer in Canada. The chain has had phenomenal success with its innovative Club Z incentive program, which encourages customers to come back by allotting points redeemable for gifts on every dollar spent at Zellers. The more Club Z points, the greater the value of the free gift. For example, Zellers customers can obtain a free 12-cup coffee maker after accumulating 429,000 points, or they can get it with 199,000 points and $67.97 cash. The products offered generally are higher in quality than those sold in Zellers stores. Since its inception in 1986, Club Z has become one of the most successful customer loyalty programs in Canada and perhaps even North America. More than 9 million people (a participation rate of 75 percent) collect the points and 95 percent of Canadian households recognise the name Club Z.

Clearly, Club Z is an integral part of Zellers' marketing plan, says company president Paul Walters, because it adds value to the shopping experience and creates customer loyalty. "Some of our Club Z members have even included their Club Z points in their wills" Walters said.

Sources: John Heinzl, "Club Z Leaving Its Mark," *Globe and Mail*, Dec. 6, 1991, p. B1; Paul Brent, "Zellers Opens Up The Clubhouse," *Financial Post*, April 29, 1993, p. 12; Rick Haliechuk, "Imperial Oil To Join Zellers in Club Z Frequent Buyer Plan," *Toronto Star*, Sep. 15, 1993, p. B3, Danielle Bochove, "Zellers Primed For Any Wal-Mart Invasion," *Globe and Mail*, June 9, 1993, p. B16; Adele Weder, "Coming Out On Top," *Financial Times*, Dec. 31, 1991 p.4; Carolyn Green, "The Law of Retail," *Marketing*, Oct. 28, 1991, p. 1.

The study also found that changes in behaviour varied by the type of product and by the consumers' characteristics. For example, for products such as shampoo, coffee, batteries, toothpaste, and personal appliances, promotions could persuade the majority of consumers to try a different brand. But for products such as alcoholic beverages, automobiles, motor oil, pet food, and floor coverings, consumers said promotions would not persuade them to switch brands. In terms of consumer characteristics, consumers who are more affluent, educated, and older are more likely to participate in consumer promotions, according to this study.

In sum, promotions can change consumer behaviour, although many contingencies can influence their effectiveness. Consistent with behavioural principles, it seems that the

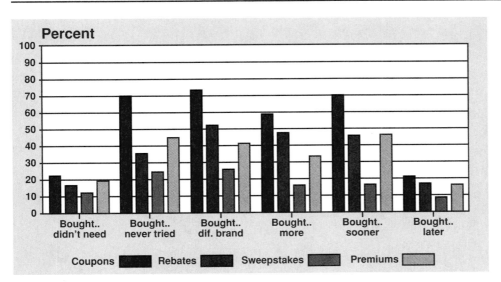

EXHIBIT 10.4

Promotion effects on consumer behaviour

Source: "Study: Some Promotions Change Consumer Behavior," *Marketing News,* Oct. 15, 1990, p. 12.

greater the reward, the less effort required to obtain it, and the sooner it comes after the behaviour, the more likely the promotion will be influential.

Social marketing refers to programs and strategies designed to change behaviour in ways deemed good for consumers and society. Much of the research on such programs is in the applied behaviour analysis literature rather than the traditional consumer behaviour literature. It focuses on methods of encouraging desired behaviours and discouraging undesired consumer behaviours.

Encouraging desired behaviours

Many forms of behaviour can be increased through the use of behaviour approaches. Research shows, for example, that various incentives increase the probability parents will

Social marketing

Free samples can increase the probability of trial and purchase.

This ad encourages walking—a desired behaviour.

see that their children get dental and health care. Providing information and counselling to Canadian high school and university students will encourage safe sex practices, which can save thousands of lives from the virus associated with AIDS. Companies like the Body Shop pay their employees for volunteer work, helping to increase awareness of community service and providing help to needy people. Small incentives can also increase the use of car pools, which can help save natural resources and reduce air pollution. Providing information in the grocery store about the amount of fat and fibre in products, and offering alternatives, can influence the purchase of particular foods.

Discouraging undesired behaviours

Many types of undesired consumer behaviours can also be decreased through applied behaviour analysis. Various types of interventions can reduce smoking, driving while impaired, dropping out of school, illegal drug use, and teenage pregnancies. While no program has been totally effective, even small advances against such major problems are valuable for both individuals and society in general.[4] Consumer research has contributions to offer to society in exploring better solutions to these problems outside traditional product marketing.

If applied behaviour analysis is a useful approach in sales promotion and social marketing, it may have extensions to other areas of consumer research. In the chapters that follow, we examine behaviour technology more fully and suggest how it can be used to help formulate successful marketing strategies.

MISCONCEPTIONS ABOUT BEHAVIOUR APPROACHES

Sales promotion and social marketing techniques normally do not engender any suspicion about the use of behaviour approaches to influence consumers. The application of sales promotion tools is well accepted in our society, and advancing societal goals through social marketing may not seem ethically problematic. We have not referred to these approaches as *behaviour modification,* for this term frequently generates strong negative feelings. Negative reactions may have to do with misconceptions about the nature of behaviour modification or applied behaviour analysis. Misconceptions centre on two major questions concerning the nature of the behavioural approach in general and its application in marketing in particular: (1) Are behaviour approaches manipulative and unethical? (2) Do behaviour approaches deny that people can think?

There is no question that behaviour approaches involve changing behaviour. They have been criticised as manipulative and unethical because they attempt to change behaviour in a systematic way. In fact, most human interactions concern people attempting to change the behaviour of other people. For example, professors attempt to get students to study, and students attempt to get professors to give them good grades; employers attempt to get employees to work hard, and employees attempt to get employers to pay them more money; parents attempt to get their children to behave well, and children attempt to get parents to give them treats; the government attempts to get people to pay taxes and obey laws, while people attempt to get the government to provide municipal services. Behaviour approaches should not be singled out as manipulative and unethical solely because they involve systematic methods for doing what most of us are attempting to do anyway.

Are behaviour approaches manipulative and unethical?

The ethical question involved in attempts by marketing managers to get consumers to change behaviour goes beyond questioning the use of behaviour technology. In fact, consumer choice is essential in a competitive, capitalistic system. Firms that survive and prosper in this system are those that are most effective at modifying consumer behaviour and encouraging purchase and repurchase of their products and brands.

Even the cognitive approach to marketing and consumer behaviour can raise questions of manipulation. The reason we study cognitive variables in marketing and consumer behaviour is because they are believed to influence overt behaviour. In some cases, marketers try to influence cognitive variables in order to change behaviour. In other cases, marketers look at cognitive variables to develop more efficient marketing strategies to change behaviour *without* changing the cognitive variable. That is, needs and benefits sought by consumers are often an issue for the purpose of segmenting markets; the knowledge gained is used to develop products and marketing strategies that reach a particular market segment seeking certain benefits or need satisfactions. In neither case is the cognitive approach of much value unless the firm develops a marketing strategy that effectively changes consumers' behaviours so that they actually purchase a product.

In summary, a major concern of human activity in general and of marketing in particular is to change or maintain overt behaviour. Our personal interactions cause this to occur, and society in many cases encourages it. And strategy development in marketing is clearly concerned with influencing overt consumer behaviour, whether behaviour or cognitive approaches are used. A claim that behaviour approaches are unethical and manipulative—but that societal, marketing, and cognitive approaches to marketing are not—does not seem to be logical.

The conventional wisdom is that behaviourists see people as at the mercy of their surroundings. In fact, while many behaviourists believe behaviour is controlled by the environment, few would argue that there is nothing going on in people's brains. Where behaviourists and cognitivists differ is on our ability analyse cognitive variables "scientifically," what causes cognitive processes, and the importance of thinking versus doing.

Do behaviour approaches deny that people can think?

Cognitive variables cannot be observed and measured easily and must instead be inferred. Historically, behaviourists have therefore been skeptical of the scientific value of cognitive events; they are not directly observable. To a behaviourist, cognitive events are usually not considered to be explanations of behaviour, because they cannot be analysed scientifically.

Many behaviourists accept self-report measures of cognitive events as supplemental, supporting information, but cognitive information is not a substitute for studying overt behaviour. Some marketing professionals believe it is useful to investigate *what* behaviours consumers perform before accepting cognitive theories designed to explain *why* the behaviours are performed.

Even if cognitive processes do mediate behaviour, behaviourists see these processes as developed through interactions with the environment. Such interaction teaches the individual which behaviours are rewarded and which are punished, and this becomes part of the individual's conditioning history. Cognitivists interpret the process as resulting in interactions that are stored in memory, while behaviourists say the person is changed through the interaction.

Most behaviourists believe that what people *do* is much more important than what they *think*. They believe that what goes on inside people's heads is of less consequence, because results occur only when people actually do something. In this sense, it is unimportant whether consumers need a product, want a product, like a product, plan to purchase a product, or think they would be satisfied with a product, until they engage in some overt behaviour, such as telling someone else about the product or actually buying it. For example, we may like a particular member of parliament, but only by working for and voting for the candidate do we have any impact. Simply liking the candidate makes no difference in the outcome of the election.

In summary, behaviourists view thoughts and feelings as not observable, as caused by the environment, and as less useful for scientific study than behaviour. For our purposes, the major limitation of behaviour approaches has been their exclusion of cognitive variables from study. At the same time, we acknowledge that a major limitation of marketing and consumer research has been to ignore overt behaviour.

▶ **SUMMARY**

Learning objective 1: *Explain some basic differences between behaviour and cognitive approaches.*

Behaviour and cognitive approaches differ most strongly on what factors control behaviour. Behaviour approaches see the environment as controlling, while cognitive approaches view mental processes and states as the controllers. Behaviour approaches view marketing as a means to modify and control behaviour to achieve organisational objectives; cognitive approaches view marketing as a means of satisfying consumer needs and wants to obtain profits. Behaviour approaches investigate strategies to influence behaviour; cognitive approaches investigate strategies to influence consumer affect and cognitions. Behaviour approaches tend to see marketing as more effective at influencing consumers than do cognitive approaches.

Learning objective 2: *List a number of different types of consumer promotions.*

Consumer promotions include practices such as sampling, price deals, bonus packs, rebates and refunds, sweepstakes and contests, premiums, and coupons.

Learning objective 3: *Explain four ways promotions are used to influence consumer behaviour.*

First, promotions are used to influence the probability that consumers will purchase a particular brand or combination of products. Ways of doing this include offering a premium or coupon on a normally high-priced product or offering to make a charitable contribution based on purchase. Second, promotions can be used to influence the number of units or the size of the package purchased. Ways of doing this include offering a coupon or premium only for purchasing multiple units or for purchasing the largest package of the product. Third, promotions are used to influence purchase timing. Ways of doing this include offering discounts on particular days and dates or limiting the redemption period on coupons. Fourth, promotions can be used to influence purchase location. Ways of doing this include offering store coupons or offering to meet competitive prices of other stores.

Learning objective 4: *Explain the uses of behaviour approaches in social marketing.*

Behaviour approaches are used for both encouraging desired behaviours and discouraging undesired behaviours. Behaviours that society values, such as providing medical and dental care for children, using seat belts, carpooling, practicing safe sex, and purchasing healthier products, can be encouraged via behavioural methods. Behaviours that society does not value, such as smoking, driving drunk, dropping out of school, and using illegal drugs, can be discouraged via behavioural methods.

Learning objective 5: *Discuss ethical questions concerning the use of behaviour approaches in marketing.*

Behaviour approaches are concerned with changing consumer behaviour. So are most of the day-to-day activities we all engage in, whether as teachers or students, parents or children, employers or employees. Marketers also use cognitive approaches to find strategies to change consumer affect and cognitions, with the objective of eventually changing behaviour. Thus, the ethical question of whether influencing and controlling consumer behaviour is manipulative requires analysis of more than behaviour approaches. Many types of marketing strategies, based on both cognitive and behaviour approaches, are acceptable to society.

---

behaviour approach	sales promotion	consumer promotions	▶ **KEY TERMS AND CONCEPTS**
cognitive approach	trade promotion	social marketing	

▶ **REVIEW AND DISCUSSION QUESTIONS**

1. Why have behaviour and cognitive approaches not been fully integrated in psychology or consumer research?

2. Explain how behaviour and cognitive approaches differ in their views of consumer research.

3. Give examples of purchase decisions where you believe the marketer need take only a behavioural view.

4. In what kinds of purchase decisions would understanding of consumer cognitive processes be superior to a marketing manager's behavioural view?

5. Describe three instances where you have attempted to modify someone else's behaviour, or where someone else has attempted to modify your behaviour.

6. Do you think behaviour modification is ethical or unethical as a marketing tool? Why or why not?

7. Consider a specific occasion, such as dinner at a restaurant. Offer both cognitive and behavioural views of the script you might observe.

8. Assume you want to change the response of restaurant patrons. Suggest strategies (*a*) based on a cognitive view and (*b*) based on a behavioural view.

9. Find at least two offers for products in magazines or newspapers designed to influence (*a*) purchase probability, (*b*) purchase quantity, (*c*) purchase timing, and (*d*) purchase location.

11

Classical and Operant Conditioning

LEARNING OBJECTIVES

After completing this chapter, you should be able to:

► 1. Define classical conditioning.

► 2. Offer examples of how classical conditioning is used to influence consumer behaviour.

► 3. Define operant conditioning.

► 4. Offer examples of discriminative stimuli used to influence consumer behaviour.

► 5. Explain four types of consequences that can occur after a consumer behaviour.

► 6. Describe three types of reinforcement schedules that can be used to influence consumer behaviour.

► 7. Explain shaping and offer a marketing example of it.

► 8. Offer examples of ways operant conditioning is used to influence consumer behaviour.

► 9. Explain brand loyalty and store loyalty.

LOTTO MANIA

Lotto fever has hit again! On the evening of Saturday, March 26, 1994, Lotto-Quebec drew its sixth ever jackpot of over $15 million just days after awarding a Granby, Quebec, couple the $12-million jackpot prize from Wednesday, March 23. The largest jackpot ever awarded was $19 million in October 1993. On the afternoon of the second big draw sales were brisk at nearly $225,000 an hour, almost double the normal sales for a regular draw. The odds of winning, at 13,983,816 to 1, do not deter people from waiting in long lines for hours. It is obvious from this example that lotteries have a powerful effect on consumer behaviour. Some of the reasons are discussed in this chapter.[1]

This chapter has two major sections. The first explains and illustrates the process of classical conditioning. The second section covers operant conditioning, describing some successful applications along with examples from marketing practice. We treat the two conditioning processes as conceptually distinct, although they overlap in a number of areas.[2] Each of these types of conditioning involves changing the environment to change overt behaviour. While the environmental changes may also influence cognition, the focus here is on the behaviour element of the Wheel of Consumer Analysis.

CLASSICAL CONDITIONING

You are likely familiar with Pavlov's experiments that conditioned a dog to salivate at the sound of a bell. Pavlov did this by first pairing the sound of a bell with sprays of meat powder for a number of trials. Eventually, he could eliminate the meat powder, and the dog would salivate at the sound of the bell alone. Pavlov's research provides the basis for classical conditioning.

In general, **classical conditioning** can be defined as a process by which a previously neutral stimulus (the bell in Pavlov's experiment), by being paired with an unconditioned stimulus (the meat powder), comes to elicit a conditioned response (salivation) very similar to the response originally elicited by the unconditioned stimulus. In other words, when they are repeatedly paired together, a new stimulus begins to elicit the same behaviour as a familiar stimulus. This process is depicted in Exhibit 11.1.

Four points are relevant in our discussion. First, classical conditioning can be accomplished not only with unconditioned stimuli but also with previously conditioned stimuli. For example, most of us are previously conditioned to the sound of a doorbell ringing and look in the direction of the sound almost automatically. This previously conditioned stimulus has been used at the beginning of Avon TV commercials to attract consumers' attention.

Second, classically conditioned behaviours are controlled by stimuli that occur *before* the behaviour. For example, in Pavlov's experiment the meat powder and the bell were presented before salivation occurred. Consumer Perspective 11.1 discusses the Coca-Cola Co.'s use of classical conditioning.

Third, the behaviours influenced by classical conditioning are assumed to be under the control of the autonomic nervous system. This system controls the smooth muscles that produce involuntary behaviour not under one's conscious control.

Last, and perhaps most important for the purposes of consumer behaviour analysis, the behaviours called *emotions* appear to follow the principles of classical conditioning. For example, when a new product for which people have neutral feelings is advertised repeatedly during momentous sports events (such as the Grey Cup or Stanley Cup finals), it is possible for the product eventually to generate excitement on its own solely through

EXHIBIT 11.1

The process of classical conditioning

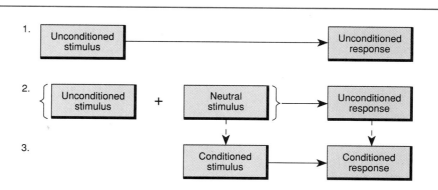

Do television commercials make people behave like Pavlov's dogs? The Coca-Cola Co. says the answer is yes. In the early 80s, the soft-drink company refined an ad-testing procedure based on the behavioural principles developed by the Russian physiologist. It found the new testing system worked remarkably well.

In his classic experiment, Ivan Pavlov discovered he could get dogs to salivate at the ring of a bell by gradually substituting the sound for a spray of meat powder. Coca-Cola says that just as Pavlov's dogs began to associate a new meaning with the bell, advertising is supposed to provide some new image or meaning for a product.

Although the specific's of Coke's test were kept secret, the company said it attempted to evaluate how well a commercial conditions a viewer to accept a positive image that can be transferred to the product. From 1981 to 1984, according to Coca-Cola, ads that scored well in its tests almost always resulted in higher sales of a soft drink.

"We nominate Pavlov as the father of modern advertising," said Joel S. Dubow, communications research manager at Coca-Cola. "Pavlov took a neutral object and, by associating it with a meaningful object, made it a symbol of something else; he imbued it with imagery, he gave it added value. That," said Dubow, "is what we try to do in modern advertising."

the repeated pairings with the significant event. Television commercials for Publisher's Clearinghouse sweepstakes frequently include exuberant past winners to generate excitement. Similarly, a political candidate may come to elicit patriotic feelings in voters simply through the effect of the Canadian flag constantly shown in the background of his or her commercials. Many companies, including Hallmark, Bell Canada, and Procter & Gamble, use stimuli in commercials and ads that are designed to generate emotions.

Classical conditioning has important implications for marketing and consumer behaviour. It can account for many of the responses that environmental stimuli elicit from individuals. Through classical conditioning, a particular stimulus can come to evoke positive, negative, or neutral feelings. Consequently, classical conditioning can influence an individual to work to obtain or avoid (or be indifferent to) a wide variety of products and services.

Classical conditioning as a marketing tool

Consider product-related stimuli. External stimuli that elicit positive emotions can be paired with a product so that the product itself elicits a positive effect. A response may then be triggered that changes the potential consumer's feelings about the product. That is, if a product elicits positive affect, an individual exposed to it is more apt to behave positively toward it than if negative emotions are elicited. Attending behaviour is also apt to be a function of classically conditioned affect. Stimuli that elicit stronger emotional responses (either positive or negative) are apt to receive more attention from a consumer than stimuli that are affectively neutral. To the degree that attending behaviour is necessary for product purchase, classical conditioning is influential.

Similarly, stimuli may produce certain learned responses, such as excitement, nostalgia, or some other emotion likely to increase the probability of a desired behaviour (such as product purchase). Radio and TV ads often use broadcasters whose voices have been associated for years with big-time sports events. Such repeated association of these voices with an advertised product can result in positive feelings of acceptance of the product. Stimuli that are irrelevant to the specific content of an ad or the function of a product

Wrangler attempts to classically condition positive emotional responses to its product by pairing its jeans with a cute dog.

Berke Clark and two of his greatest pleasures in life.

~ Avid duck hunter and trusted friend, Kelly. And comfortable jeans.

Wrangler
RUGGED WEAR
Since 1904

can likewise increase attention paid to the ad itself, as when Patrick Roy was featured in a series of ads for the Upper Deck trading card company.

Marketers use stimuli at or near the point of purchase to take advantage of their ability to elicit behaviours. Christmas music in a department store is a good example. Although no data are available to support the point, we suspect that carols are useful in eliciting the feeling labelled the "Christmas spirit." Once these feelings have been elicited, we suspect (and retailers seem to share our suspicions) that people are more apt to purchase a gift for a loved one. In other words, Christmas carols are useful in generating emotions that are compatible with purchasing gifts. Exhibit 11.2 highlights some marketing strategies that use the principle of classical conditioning.

Several points should be noted about classical conditioning as a marketing tool. First, classical conditioning assumes that the presentation of stimuli can elicit certain feelings in the consumer. These stimuli are meant to trigger emotions to increase the probability of certain desired behaviours (as with Christmas music). Second, in many cases, marketers can actually condition responses to stimuli. When the Liberal Party of Canada was promoting Jean Chretien for prime minister in 1993, repeatedly pairing him with the Canadian flag conditioned the feelings elicited by the flag to the candidate. After a while, the appearance of the candidate alone may stimulate the same feelings in voters as the flag does. Finally, repetition increases the strength of the association between stimuli.

Consumer research on classical conditioning

Several studies in the marketing/consumer behaviour literature demonstrate classical conditioning effects. The first demonstration of these effects in a marketing context is in a study by University of British Columbia professor Gerald Gorn.[3] This research investigates the effects of the music used in advertising on consumer choices. Consumers iden-

EXHIBIT 11.2

Some marketing tactics consistent with classical conditioning principles

Conditioning Responses to New Stimuli		
Unconditioned or Previously Conditioned Stimulus	**Conditioned Stimulus**	**Examples**
Exciting event	A product or theme song	New product advertised during the Stanley Cup finals
Patriotic events or music	A product or person	Patriotic music as background in political commercial

Use of Familiar Stimuli to Elicit Responses		
Conditioned Stimulus	**Conditioned Response(s)**	**Examples**
Popular music	Relaxation, excitement, "goodwill"	Christmas music in retail stores
Familiar voices	Excitement, attention	Famous sportscaster or movie star narrating a commercial
Sexy voices, bodies	Excitement, attention, arousal	Most soft-drink and beer commercials
Familiar cues	Anticipation, attention	Sirens sounding, telephones or doorbells ringing in commercials
Familiar social cues	Feelings of friendship and love	Television ads depicting calls from family or close friend

tified one musical selection that they liked and one that they disliked. They also identified two colours of pens toward which they had neutral evaluations (light blue and beige). Together there were four combinations: (1) liked music, light blue pen; (2) liked music, beige pen; (3) disliked music, light blue pen; (4) disliked music, beige pen. Subjects looked at an ad for one of the pens while hearing a tape of one of the types of music and then selected one of the pens to keep.

If classical conditioning were taking place, subjects would select the advertised pen when it was paired with the liked music. Similarly, they would select the other pen when the advertised pen was paired with the music they didn't like. Exhibit 11.3 shows the results of this experiment. Clearly, the vast majority of subjects appear to have been influenced by the pairing of the unconditioned stimulus (liked and disliked music) with the

EXHIBIT 11.3

Liked versus disliked music and pen choices

Pen Choice		
Advertised Pen	**Nonadvertised Pen**	
79%	21%	Liked music
30	70	Disliked music

EXHIBIT 11.4

Information versus music and pen choices

Decision-Making Situation	Nondecision-Making Situation	
71%	29%	With information
37	63	With music

Source: Adapted from Gerald J. Gorn, "The Effects of Music in Advertising on Choice Behavior: A Classical Conditioning Approach," *Journal of Marketing*, Winter 1982, pp. 94–101. Published by the American Marketing Association.

The brand manager of Moosehead Light beer in Nova Scotia believes that beer purchases can be classically conditioned. The beer was introduced in 1989 and since then sales have increased slowly. An ad campaign launched in the summer of 1991 was tied to summer themes and good times. Sales have always been good in the summer, but Moosehead felt this campaign would put it in the forefront.

Moosehead used two 30-second TV commercials with the support of five radio spots. These ads showed young men and women having a good time and featured an upbeat, catchy song. The ad employed a name game of sorts. In it a singer mentioned the names of people who enjoy Moosehead Light beer. As Stuart Baker, a senior account executive with the advertising agency, Harrod & Mirlin, said, "We used all the different names to get the feel of the popularity that we wanted."

Making young men and women associate Moosehead Light beer with good times and summer as well as popularity can increase awareness of the beer and induce feelings of belonging. The ad was clearly designed to act as the condition stimulus; it made the target audience want to go out and buy Moosehead Light beer to experience the good times promised in the ad. Even more importantly, the ad has the opportunity to change the behaviour patterns of the target audience.

Source: "Summer Campaign for Moosehead Has a Light Touch," *Marketing*, July 1, 1991.

neutral stimulus (light blue and beige pens), resulting in predicted choice behaviours (pen selection).

A second experiment compared the same pen selections after exposure to advertisements that contained either product information or music. Subjects were in either a decision-making or a nondecision-making situation. It was hypothesised that product information would influence pen choice in the decision-making situation, but music would influence pen choice in the nondecision-making situation. Exhibit 11.4 presents the results of this experiment. Clearly, the majority of subjects appear to be classically conditioned in the nondecision-making situation but less so in the decision-making situation. These differences might be explained in terms of involvement—the nondecision-making task may be less involving for subjects. In fact, some researchers have suggested classical conditioning may be most useful in low-involvement situations:

Consumer involvement is low when the products have only minor quality differences from one another . . . This is especially the case in saturated markets with mature products. It is exactly in these markets that product differentiation by means of emotional conditioning is the preferred strategy of influencing consumers.[4]

Because a variety of circumstances meet these conditions, classical conditioning should be a useful strategy for low-involvement purchases (see Consumer Perspective 11.2).

Another study of classical conditioning investigates the effects of a credit card on the amount of money consumers report they are willing to spend on specific items, including dresses, tents, sweaters, lamps, electric typewriters, and chess sets.[5] In a simulated buying task, consumers consistently reported they would spend more in the "credit-card present" condition. This research suggests credit cards and ads for them may become associated with spending, partly through classical conditioning.

In sum, classical conditioning may account for a wide variety of consumer responses. Advertising and in-store promotions commonly take it for granted, although marketing practitioners perhaps use classical conditioning techniques only intuitively. Further research in this area may clarify conditioning effects on information processing, attitude formation and change and, most importantly, overt consumer behaviour.

OPERANT CONDITIONING

Operant conditioning can be defined as the process of altering the probabilities of behaviours by affecting their consequences. Operant conditioning differs from classical conditioning in two ways. First, the behaviours influenced by operant conditioning are assumed to be voluntary behaviours controlled by the skeletal nervous system. Second, the focus of operant conditioning is on understanding how the consequences that occur after a behaviour influence the probability of the behaviour occurring again. Exhibit 11.5 identifies the major components in the operant view.

Discriminative stimuli

Discriminative stimuli occur before a behaviour and can influence whether the behaviour occurs. The mere presence or absence of a discriminative stimulus can affect the chance that a behaviour will follow. For example, if Pizza Hut runs an ad with a coupon for a free quart of Pepsi with every large pizza, this offer may increase the probability of consumers purchasing a large pizza. Since the offer occurs before the behaviour and influences the probability of purchase, the offer is considered a discriminative stimulus.

Many marketing stimuli are discriminative. Store signs ("50 percent off sale") and store logos (Wal-Mart's sign, Zellers' flashy Z) and distinctive brand marks (the Nike swoosh, the Petro-Canada maple leaf, the Polo insignia) are examples of discriminative stimuli. Previous experience may have taught consumers that purchase behaviour will be rewarded when the distinctive symbol is present and will not be rewarded when the symbol is absent. For example, many consumers purchase Ralph Lauren shirts, jackets, and shorts with the stitched polo player symbol and avoid other Ralph Lauren apparel without the symbol. A number of competitors have tried to copy the polo player symbol because of its power as a discriminative stimulus. Clearly, much of marketing involves developing effective discriminative stimuli that promote certain behaviours.

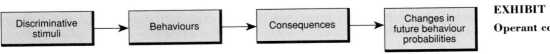

EXHIBIT 11.5

Operant conditioning

Credit-card stimuli can influence consumer behaviour

Behaviours

Marketers try to influence many types of consumer behaviour. They want consumers to read ads, watch TV commercials, obtain money to buy products, go to particular malls and stores, purchase products, and tell other consumers good things about their products. These behaviours are discussed in detail in Chapter 13, but at this point it is enough to say that marketers must influence overt consumer behaviours to sell products.

Consequences

Marketers can use four basic types of consequences to influence consumer behaviour: positive reinforcement, negative reinforcement, extinction, and punishment.

Some events or consequences increase the frequency with which a given behaviour is likely to be repeated. For example, if a reward, such as a cash rebate, is given at the time of purchase, it may increase the probability that a shopper will buy something in the same store in the future. In this case, because the reward increases the probability of the behaviour being repeated, it is called **positive reinforcement.** Positive reinforcement is the most common type of consequence used by marketers to influence consumer behaviour. In general, the greater the amount of the reward and the sooner it is received after the behaviour, the more likely it is that the behaviour will be reinforced and similar behaviour will occur in the future. For example, a $1 coupon for Tropicana orange juice would likely increase the probability of purchase more than a 50-cent coupon would and lead to future purchases of this product. Similarly, a coupon redeemable at the time of purchase is likely to be more effective than a mail-in coupon, when the consumer has to wait for the reward.

Marketers can also increase the frequency of consumer behaviour by removing aversive stimuli that operate to deter a consumer's purchase. This is called **negative reinforcement.** For example, if purchase of a product gets a salesperson to relax high-pressure techniques, the consumer may be negatively reinforced. That is, performing the behaviour of purchasing removes the aversive stimuli (the actions of the pushy salesperson). In the future, operant conditioning predicts that a consumer faced with pushy salespeople will be more likely to purchase again.

Sometimes operant techniques are used to decrease the probability of a response. If the environment is arranged so that a particular response results in neutral consequences, over a period of time that response will diminish in frequency. This process is referred to as **extinction.** The A&P grocery chain, at one time the largest retailer in the world, provides an unwitting example. One mistake it made was to overstock its own brands (which had higher profit margins) and understock nationally branded merchandise. Consumers who were loyal to a number of nationally branded products often could not find them at an A&P store. Eventually, many consumers quit shopping at A&P, partly

EXHIBIT 11.6

Operant conditioning methods

Operation Performed after Behaviour	Name	Effect
Present positive consequences	Positive reinforcement	Increases the probability of behaviour
Remove aversive consequences	Negative reinforcement	Increases the probability of behaviour
Neutral consequences occur	Extinction	Decreases the probability of behaviour
Present aversive consequences	Punishment	Decreases the probability of behaviour

because they could not obtain their favourite brands. Thus, A&P inadvertently used extinction on its own customers.

If a response is followed by a noxious or unpleasant result, the frequency of that response is likely to decrease. The term **punishment** is usually used to describe this process. For example, car insurance rates may increase if a consumer causes an accident. Punishment is often confused with negative reinforcement, although they are distinctly different concepts. Exhibit 11.6 summarises these four methods of operant conditioning.

Two other important characteristics of operant conditioning have major implications for designing market strategies to influence consumers' behaviour: reinforcement schedules and shaping.

Reinforcement schedules refer to how consistently a reward occurs after desired behaviours occur. Three reinforcement schedules used in marketing include continuous, fixed ratio, and variable ratio schedules.

Reinforcement schedules

The offer of a reward after every desired behaviour is called a **continuous schedule.** Marketers aim to keep the quality of their products constant so that a purchase is continuously reinforced every time it occurs, but this doesn't always happen. Frequent product recalls for automobiles, for example, indicate a failure to maintain product quality. Services like airlines may not be able to control contingencies such as bad weather, overbooked, cancelled, and late flights, and unfriendly employees, which can make flights not reinforcing at all. Sporting events, because they may turn out to be boring or the home team may take a beating, may not be continuously reinforcing for some consumers.

For other products or services, every second, third, tenth, or so time a behaviour is performed, a reward is given. This is called a **fixed ratio schedule.** Consumer Perspective 11.3 illustrates how a muffin chain uses this schedule to increase purchases.

Similarly, it is possible to have a reinforcer follow a desired behaviour on an *average* of one-half, one-third, one-tenth, or so of the time the behaviour occurs, but not necessarily every second time or third time. This is a **variable rate schedule.** A provincial lottery is an example of rewards occurring on variable ratio schedules. Tim Horton's "Roll up the r-r-r-rim to win" contest, where prizes are printed under the rim of a certain number of paper coffee cups, is another example.

Variable ratio schedules are of particular interest because they produce high rates of behaviour that are reasonably resistant to extinction. Gambling devices are good examples. Slot machines are very effective in producing high rates of response, even under conditions that often result in substantial financial losses. This property of the ratio schedule is particularly important for marketers, because it suggests a great deal of desired behaviour can be developed and maintained with relatively small, infrequent rewards. One

study found that giving a free token for riding a bus on a variable ratio schedule resulted in the same amount of bus riding as giving rewards on a continuous schedule.[6] Thus, for approximately one-third the cost of the continuous schedule, the same amount of behaviour could be sustained.

Other examples of variable ratio schedules include sweepstakes, contests, and door prizes, where individuals must behave in a certain way to be eligible for a prize. Consumer Perspective 11.4 discusses the use of variable ratio schedules for selling Pepsi, 7UP and Mountain Dew products.

Shaping

Another operant conditioning concept with important implications for marketing and consumer behaviour is shaping. **Shaping** involves arranging conditions that change the probabilities of certain behaviours not as ends in themselves, but *to increase the probabilities of other behaviours occurring*. Usually, shaping involves the positive reinforcement of successive approximations of a desired behaviour or of behaviours that must be performed before the desired response occurs.

Marketing activities that can be described as shaping include loss leaders and other special deals used to reward individuals for coming to a store. Once customers are in the store, the probability that they will make other desired responses (such as purchasing full-priced items) is much greater than when they are not in the store. Shopping centres or car dealers that hold carnivals in the parking lot are attempting to shape behaviour, because consumers are more likely to come in and purchase when they are already in the parking lot drinking the free coffee than when they are at home. Similarly, free trial periods make it more likely for a consumer to have contact with the product and then experience the product's reinforcing properties. Real estate developers that offer free trips to look over resort property are employing a shaping tactic, as are casinos that offer free trips to gamblers. In both cases, moving people to the place of purchase or place of gambling increases the probability that they will perform these behaviours.

CONSUMER
PERSPECTIVE

11.4

Using variable
ratio schedules
to increase Pepsi
purchases

Pepsi-Cola Canada Ltd. ran its "Taste the Wild Side" promotion in 1991. The grand prizes in the contest were 20 Jeep YJ Renegades. Other prizes included T-shirts, Pizza Hut discount coupons, and free bottles of Pepsi, 7UP, or Mountain Dew.

Consumers could receive a chance to win by purchasing a 500-ml bottle of one of the three soft drinks. Through a variable ratio schedule, consumers could receive either an instant-win prize or a letter from the word *Pepsi*. The person who collected all the letters that spell *Pepsi* would win the grand prize. The letter or the instant-win prize was indicated by an under-the-cap liner.

Variable rate schedules were used to allocate the chances to win prizes as well as the prizes themselves. By offering the chance to win instantly and after multiple purchases, Pepsi-Cola Canada Ltd. increased the probability of consumers making more than one purchase (However, it should also be noted that consumers were given a "no purchase necessary" alternative to participate in the contest by mailing a stamped, self-addressed envelope to a specified Ontario address, and in return received a randomly selected cap liner.) Costs to the company are another consideration. A variable ratio schedule is probably the only way expensive products can be used profitably as reinforcers for purchase of inexpensive products.

Source: Ken Riddell, "Pepsi Drives Jeep into Teens' Hearts," *Marketing*, July 8, 1991, p. 8.

Shaping is not necessarily a one-step process; it may affect several stages in a purchase sequence. Suppose a car dealer wants to shape an automobile purchase. She offers free coffee and doughnuts to anyone who comes to the dealership. She offers $5 cash to any licensed driver who will test drive a car. She offers a $500 rebate to anyone who purchases a car. In this case, operant principles are used in a multistep process to encourage high involvement. Exhibit 11.7 describes a number of marketing tactics applying operant conditioning principles.

Most of the research on operant conditioning procedures in consumer-related contexts is not reported in the traditional marketing literature. An exception investigated the effects of positive reinforcement on jewellery store customers.[7] The study divided charge-account customers into three groups. One group received a telephone call thanking them

**Consumer research
on operant
conditioning**

EXHIBIT 11.7

Some marketing tactics consistent with operant conditioning principles

A. Discriminative Stimuli Desired Behaviour	Reward Signal	Examples
Entry into store	Store signs	Half-off sale
	Store logos	Zellers' flashy Z, McDonald's golden arches
Brand purchase	Distinctive brandmarks	Levi's tag, Ralph Lauren polo player, Petro-Canada maple leaf

B. Continuous Reinforcement Schedules Desired Behaviour	Reward Given following Behaviour
Product purchase	Trading stamps, cash bonus or rebate, prizes, coupons

C. Fixed and Variable Ratio Reinforcement Schedules Desired Behaviour	Reward Given following Behaviour
Product purchase	Prize for every second, third, etc., purchase
	Prize to some fraction of people who purchase

D. Shaping Approximation of Response	Consequence following Approximation	Final Response Desired
Opening a charge account	Prizes, etc., for opening account	Expenditure of funds
Trip to point of purchase	Loss leaders, entertainment, or event at the shopping centre	Purchase of products
Entry into store	Door prize	Purchase of products
Product trial	Free product and/or bonus for using	Purchase of products

for their patronage; a second group received a telephone call thanking them and informing them of a special sale; the third group was a control group and received no telephone calls. The study reported a 27 percent increase in sales during the test month over the same month of the previous year, an impressive result because year-to-date sales were down 25 percent. Seventy percent of the increase came from the "thank-you only" group; the remaining 30 percent of the increase came from the "thank-you and sale-notification" group. Purchases made by customers in the control group were unchanged. Positive reinforcement resulted in sustained increases in purchases for every month but one the rest of the year.

Some operant conditioning research deals with behaviours such as encouraging energy conservation or charitable contributions, or discouraging smoking or littering. One application of operant conditioning concerns punishment in the form of charging telephone customers for local directory assistance, an expensive, labour-intensive service.[8] A study reported the effect of charging 20 cents per local directory-assistance call for more than three calls in a given period. Long-distance directory-assistance calls were not charged. Results show that local directory-assistance calls dropped dramatically. The fact that long-distance directory assistance did not change supports the conclusion that the charge, not some other factor, led to the change in consumer behaviour.

Classical conditioning is particularly relevant to marketers selecting stimuli for advertisements. Choice of the appropriate stimuli in ads can influence purchase behaviour. Classical conditioning is also useful in designing malls and retail stores. Operant conditioning is particularly useful to marketers deciding what types of products, packaging, and sales promotions would be most successful in the marketplace.

Of course, marketers are not merely concerned with influencing consumers to buy a brand once or shop at a store once. Rather, they want consumers to buy a brand repeatedly or shop at a retail store faithfully. These behaviours are called brand loyalty and store loyalty. Both classical and operant conditioning can be useful for developing such loyalties. If through classical conditioning consumers develop strong affect for a particular product or store, they may continue to buy the brand or shop at the store. If through operant conditioning consumer behaviour in buying a particular brand or visiting a particular store is reinforced, the probability that this behaviour will continue is increased.

Brand loyalty is defined as repeat purchase intentions and behaviour. While we focus mainly on brand loyalty as a behaviour, cognitive processes strongly influence the development and maintenance of this behaviour. Retaining brand-loyal customers is critical for survival, particularly in today's low-growth, highly competitive marketplace. Retaining customers is often a more efficient strategy than attracting new customers. Indeed, the average company spends an estimated six times more to attract a new customer than to hold a current one.

Brand loyalty can be viewed on a continuum, from undivided brand loyalty to brand indifference (shown schematically in Exhibit 11.8). Marketers can analyse the market for a particular brand in terms of the number of consumers in each category, as a first step in developing strategies to enhance the brand loyalty of particular groups. Loyalty categories are somewhat arbitrary, although there are clear degrees of brand loyalty.

Undivided brand loyalty is, of course, the ideal. In some cases, consumers will purchase only a single brand and forgo purchase if that brand is not available. *Brand loyalty with an occasional switch* is more common, though. Consumers may switch occasionally for a variety of reasons: their usual brand is out of stock, a new brand comes on the market and they try it once, a competitive brand is offered at a special low price, or they purchase a different brand for a special occasion.

Brand-loyalty switches are a marketing goal in low-growth or declining markets. Competitors in the blue-jean market or the distilled-spirits industry, for example, must encourage brand switches for long-run growth. Switching brand loyalty even within the same firm can be advantageous for the company. Procter & Gamble, for example, sells both

MARKETING IMPLICATIONS

Brand loyalty

Purchase Pattern Category	Brand Purchase Sequence									
Undivided brand loyalty	A	A	A	A	A	A	A	A	A	A
Brand loyalty/occasional switch	A	A	A	B	A	A	C	A	A	D
Brand loyalty/switch	A	A	A	A	A	B	B	B	B	B
Divided brand loyalty	A	A	B	A	B	B	A	A	B	B
Brand indifference	A	B	C	D	E	F	G	H	I	J

EXHIBIT 11.8

Examples of purchase pattern categories and brand purchase sequences

Marketing strategies aimed at reinforcing brand loyalty

Pampers and Luvs disposable diapers. A switch from Pampers to Luvs might be advantageous to P&G in that Luvs are more expensive and may have a higher profit margin.

Divided brand loyalty describes consistent purchase of two or more brands, as might happen in the shampoo market, which has a low level of brand loyalty. One reason is that households may purchase different shampoos for different family members or for different purposes. Johnson's Baby Shampoo may be the choice for youngsters and frequent shampoo users. Other household members may use Head & Shoulders. This household would divide its loyalty between two brands.

Brand indifference refers to purchases showing no apparent repurchase pattern. It is the opposite extreme from undivided brand loyalty. While total brand indifference across the board is not common, some consumers of some products exhibit this pattern. For example, a consumer may make weekly purchases of whatever bread is on sale, regardless of the brand.

Marketers of a particular brand would prefer that consumers have undivided brand loyalty for it. If appropriate reinforcers are used on appropriate schedules, this goal is achievable. More consumers in a target market, however, inevitably enjoy something less than undivided brand loyalty, because competitive brands may have marketing strategies that better reinforce consumer behaviour. Consider that a $750 rebate for a Ford may influence a college graduate to purchase a Ford at least one time, for one purchase. A major challenge for marketers is to come up with better reinforcers than the competition.

Store loyalty

Most retailers do not look for consumers to come to their stores once and never return: they want repeat patronage. Marketers can influence **store loyalty** (repeat patronage intentions and behaviour) by the arrangement of the environment, particularly the reinforcing properties of the retail store. These include such things as friendly salesclerks, good prices, quality merchandise, attractive decor, convenient location, and expeditious service.

Consider one tactic that may be used to develop store loyalty: in-store unadvertised specials. These specials are often marked with an attention-getting sign. Typically, consumers go to a store shopping for a particular product or just to "go shopping." While on their route, they find a favourite brand or a long-sought-after product as an unadvertised special. Such an experience could be quite reinforcing and strongly influence the probability of the consumer returning to the same store, perhaps seeking similar unadvertised specials. Quite likely the consumer would not have to find a suitable unadvertised special on every trip; a variable ratio schedule might be powerful enough to generate a considerable degree of store loyalty. These additional trips to the store allow the consumer to experience other reinforcing properties, such as fast checkout, a pleasant store atmosphere, or good-quality merchandise at competitive prices. In sum, reinforcing tactics and positive attributes of the store are used to develop store loyalty.

Store loyalty is a major objective of retail strategy that has an important financial impact. The loss of a single customer to a supermarket is estimated to cost the store about $3,100 per year in sales. Thus, analysis of the store environment and its impact on store loyalty is critical for successful marketing.

▶ **SUMMARY**

Learning objective 1: *Define classical conditioning.*
Classical conditioning is a process by which a previously neutral stimulus (such as a new product), by being paired with an unconditioned stimulus (such as a sexy male or female model), comes to elicit a response (excitement) similar to the response (excitement) originally elicited by the unconditioned stimulus. In other words, when they are repeatedly paired together, a new stimulus begins to elicit the same behaviours as a familiar stimulus.

Learning objective 2: *Offer examples of how classical conditioning is used to influence consumer behaviour.*
Ads and commercials for products often feature stimuli such as famous people and emotion-generating scenes. Repeated pairing of these stimuli with products could condition affect for the advertised products to be similar to that generated for the conditioned stimuli. Music that generates emotions is also used in ads and in stores. These too could classically condition consumers.

Learning objective 3: *Define operant conditioning.*
Operant conditioning is the process of altering the probabilities of behaviours by affecting their consequences.

Learning objective 4: *Offer examples of discriminative stimuli used to influence consumer behaviour.*
Discriminative stimuli are those that occur before a behaviour and can influence whether the behaviour occurs. Common examples of discriminative stimuli used to influence consumer behaviour are store signs, store logos, and distinctive brand marks.

Learning objective 5: *Explain four types of consequences that can occur after a consumer behaviour.*
Four types of consequences include: (1) positive reinforcement, where a reward follows a behaviour, to increase the probability of the behaviour being repeated; (2) negative reinforcement, where an aversive stimulus is stopped when the consumer engages in a behaviour, also to increase the probability of the behaviour being repeated; (3) extinction, where neutral consequences occur after a behaviour, again to decrease the probability of the behaviour being repeated; and (4) punishment, where aversive consequences occur after a behaviour, to decrease the probability of its being repeated.

Learning objective 6: *Describe three types of reinforcement schedules that can be used to influence consumer behaviour.*

In a continuous schedule, a reward is offered every time a desired behaviour occurs. In a fixed ratio schedule, every second, third, or tenth (for example) time the behaviour is performed, a reward is given. In a variable ratio schedule, a reward is offered on an average of half, one-third, one-fourth (and so on) of the time the behaviour occurs, but not necessarily every second or third or fourth time.

Learning objective 7: *Explain shaping and offer a marketing example of it.*

Shaping involves arranging conditions that change the probabilities of certain behaviours not as ends in themselves, but to increase the probabilities of other desirable behaviours occurring. A grocery store might offer one product below cost, not just to get consumers to buy it, but to increase the chances of consumers coming to the store and purchasing other full-priced items.

Learning objective 8: *Offer examples of ways operant conditioning is used to influence consumer behaviour.*

Marketers use many types of discriminative stimuli, such as store signs, store logos, and brand marks, to influence consumers. Various types of reinforcement schedules, including continuous, fixed ratio, and variable ratio, can be established to try to develop brand and store loyalty. Marketers also use various types of rewards, such as trading stamps, bonuses, and premiums, to reinforce purchase behaviour.

Learning objective 9: *Explain brand loyalty and store loyalty.*

Brand loyalty is defined as repeat purchase intentions and behaviour. The degree of brand loyalty varies among consumers from undivided brand loyalty, where consumers always purchase the same brand, to brand indifference, where consumers always purchase different brands. The challenge to marketers is to increase the degree of brand loyalty by offering appropriate reinforcers. Store loyalty is defined as repeat patronage intentions and behaviour. Reinforcing properties of a store itself, including store location and in-store stimuli like fast service and unadvertised specials, can help develop store loyalty.

▶ **KEY TERMS AND CONCEPTS**

classical conditioning	extinction	variable ratio schedule
operant conditioning	punishment	shaping
discriminative stimuli	reinforcement schedules	brand loyalty
positive reinforcement	continuous schedule	store loyalty
negative reinforcement	fixed ratio schedule	

▶ **REVIEW AND DISCUSSION QUESTIONS**

1. Describe classical conditioning and identify three responses in your own behaviour that are the result of classical conditioning.

2. Under what conditions would the use of classical conditioning be likely to produce positive results as part of a marketing strategy?

3. What are two differences between classical and operant conditioning?

4. Describe operant conditioning and identify three responses in your own behaviour that are the result of operant conditioning.

5. Give two marketing examples of positive reinforcement, negative reinforcement, extinction, and punishment.

6. Why are variable ratio reinforcement schedules of greater interest to marketing managers than other types of reinforcement schedules?

7. Define shaping and explain why it is an essential part of many marketing conditioning strategies.

8. Examine the marketing strategies used in selling fast-food hamburgers and automobiles. Identify specific examples of classical conditioning, operant conditioning, shaping, and discriminative stimuli for each product type.

12

Vicarious Learning and the Diffusion of Innovation

LEARNING OBJECTIVES

After completing this chapter, you should be able to:

► 1. Explain three uses of vicarious learning (modelling).

► 2. Describe three types of modelling.

► 3. Explain three factors that influence the effectiveness of modelling.

► 4. Describe five adopter categories.

► 5. Identify the characteristics that influence the success of new products.

VIDEO GAME CHALLENGE

In 1993, Sega spent millions of dollars to participate in the consumer electronics show in Chicago, where it introduced a new flight simulation game. Sega uses these trade shows to demonstrate its products to the public. Sega now leads Nintendo of Canada Ltd. in sales of video games. During the Christmas season of 1991, Sega sold 50,000 Genesis units in Canada, compared to the 25,000 Nintendo sold.

Video games such as Sega's Genesis and the Nintendo Entertainment System are good examples of companies in an industry that relies on its consumers to learn how to play the games by watching other people play. This is why companies spend millions of dollars on consumer shows. One topic of this chapter is watching how other people behave.

Vicarious learning is a deceptively simple idea. Basically, it refers to people changing their behaviour because they observe the behaviour of others and its consequences. In general, people tend to imitate others' behaviour when they see it leads to positive consequences and avoid performing others' behaviour when they see it leads to negative consequences.

Vicarious learning surprisingly has been almost ignored in published consumer and marketing research, although it has a variety of applications in marketing. In fact, vicarious learning offers a useful approach to developing marketing strategy and consumer education programs. We use the terms *vicarious learning, modelling, observational learning*, and *imitative learning* interchangeably in this chapter, although other writers sometimes draw distinctions among these terms.

We focus first on the most common form of vicarious learning, called *overt modelling*, where people actually watch a model perform some activity. Covert modelling involves no demonstration of activity, but rather asks the consumer to imagine one, while verbal modelling merely informs consumers of what other people have done. This chapter discusses how and why these various techniques work in marketing strategies.

USES OF OVERT MODELLING

Overt modelling requires that consumers actually observe the model in person, whether a salesperson demonstrating a product (*live modelling*) or TV commercials or in-store videos (*symbolic modelling*). Exhibit 12.1 depicts the modelling process. A common example is commercials for cosmetics and grooming aids, which show the model using the product and then becoming sought after by a member of the opposite sex. Clairol commercials frequently show a woman with dull, drab hair (and an equivalent social life) going out with a handsome, well-dressed man after she uses the Clairol product. The modelled behaviour (use of the product) is shown to have reinforcing consequences (attention from men).

There are three major uses of overt modelling in marketing. First, it can be used to help observers *develop new response patterns*. Second, modelling can be used to *inhibit undesired responses*. Third, modelling can *facilitate desired responses* whereby observing the behaviour of others facilitates the occurrence of previously learned responses.

Developing new responses

Modelling can be used to develop new behavioural responses that were not previously in the consumer's repertoire. It is a common technique for those selling technically complex organisational and consumer products. Consider, for example, the video that many stores provide to demonstrate use of a product. Sears has long used this method to demonstrate the safe use of its chainsaws. Exercise videos showing the consumer how to get those buns of steel and golf videos demonstrating how to develop the perfect swing are good

EXHIBIT 12.1

The modelling process

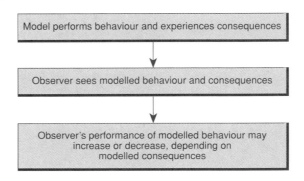

examples of direct marketing behavioural modelling techniques. New behaviours are often modelled in TV commercials. Sears used a modelling strategy when it began in-store sales of Allstate insurance, a departure from the traditional office or home sales method. A TV commercial shows a family coming to the Sears store and dropping off their old insurance policy for comparisons with Allstate rates. After their shopping trip, the family returns and learns Allstate can give them a better deal, thus modelling the positive consequences of the new behaviour. Similarly, Arm & Hammer baking soda ads showed new uses of the product as a carpet and refrigerator freshener and portrayed models being complimented on the freshness of their homes. WD-40 lubricant ads also model new uses of the product.

From these examples we can draw several generalisations about the use of modelling to develop new consumer behaviours. First, overt modelling can be used to develop behaviours that enable potential consumers to use products appropriately. Demonstrating ways to use a product may make purchase more profitable, particularly if the models appear to experience positive consequences. Moreover, repurchase, or influencing one's friends, may become more probable if the consumer has learned to use the product appropriately by watching someone else. Modelling can also be beneficial for consumers because it can help them to develop effective behaviours in the marketplace and to avoid costly errors resulting from poor product purchases or inappropriate uses of a product.

Second, models may be very helpful in developing particular desired purchasing behaviours. Suppose, for example, a firm has a product that is technically superior to its competitors'. It may be important to teach potential consumers to ask questions about such technical advantages at the point of purchase. Advertisements could show individuals doing this or behaving in other ways that appear to give the product a differential advantage.

Third, it is often necessary (particularly at early stages in the purchase process) to find ways to increase the degree to which potential customers attend to information in ads and other messages about a product. Marketers need to pay attention themselves to overt modelling factors such as incentive conditions, the characteristics of the observers, the characteristics of the model, and the characteristics of the modelling cues themselves. In fact, advertising practitioners seem to be sensitive to these issues. Many ads reflect their creators' awareness of salient characteristics of the target audience, of the models in the ads, and of the behaviours the models exhibit.

Inhibiting undesired responses

Modelling can also be used to decrease the probability of undesired behaviours. Because of the ethical (not to mention practical) problems involved in using punishment to affect consumer behaviour, there are not many direct ways to reduce the frequency of undesired responses. Overt modelling, however, lets bad things happen to models rather than to actual consumers.

Modelling research indicates that, under appropriate conditions, observers who see a model experience unpleasant results following a particular action will reduce their tendency to exhibit that behaviour. Thus, vicarious learning may be one of the few approaches that can reduce the frequency of unwanted elements in a potential or present consumer's behaviour.

Hefty bags, for example, are frequently advertised on TV using a modelling approach. Various family members are shown taking out the trash in "bargain bags." Of course, the bargain bag breaks and garbage is strewn all over, a visibly annoying experience! The frustrated family member is then told about Hefty bags, uses them successfully, and is socially reinforced for doing so. Head & Shoulders shampoo commercials show people initially found attractive by members of the opposite sex but then rejected when the models scratch their heads, indicating they may have dandruff. Following the use of the advertised product, the model is once again warmly greeted by an attractive member of the opposite sex.

A common use of this type of modelling is in public service advertising. Many behaviours considered socially undesirable can be modelled and shown to have unpleasant consequences. These behaviours include littering, smoking, driving drunk, using drugs, overeating, wasting energy, and polluting. One commercial, for example, showed a drunken driver being caught, taken to court, and given a considerable fine and jail sentence for his behaviour.

Facilitating desired responses

Besides developing new behaviours and inhibiting undesired ones, modelling can facilitate the occurrence of desired behaviours that the consumer already knows how to do. That is, the modelling not only illustrates uses of a product but also shows what types of people use it and in what settings. Because many of these uses involve behaviours already familiar to the observer, the model's function is merely to *facilitate these responses* by depicting positive consequences for using the product appropriately. For example, Nyquil ads show adult cold sufferers using the product before going to bed and then sleeping comfortably. This is a common technique in advertising for high-status products, where ads do not demonstrate any new behaviours, but show the positive consequences of using the product. An ad campaign by the Dairy Council of Canada showing a couple serving cheese at a party is a good example.

To the degree that marketers want to encourage positive emotions toward a product, vicarious emotional conditioning may also be useful for the design of effective advertisements. Many emotional behaviours can be acquired through observation of others, as well as through direct respondent conditioning.

> Vicarious emotional conditioning results from observing others experience positive or negative emotional effects in conjunction with particular stimulus events. Both direct and vicarious conditioning processes are governed by the same basic principles of associative learning, but they differ in the force of the emotional arousal. In the direct prototype, the learner himself is the recipient of pain- or pleasure-producing stimulation, whereas in vicarious forms somebody else experiences the reinforcing stimulation and his affective expressions, in turn, serve as the arousal stimuli for the observer.[1]

Exhibit 12.2 summarises some applications of overt modelling principles in marketing.

EXHIBIT 12.2

Some applications of overt modelling principles in marketing

Modelling Used	Desired Response
Instructor, expert, salesperson using product (in ads or at point of purchase)	Use product in correct, technically competent way
Models in ads asking questions at point of purchase	Ask questions at point of purchase that highlight product advantages
Models in ads receiving positive reinforcement for product purchase or use	Try product; increase product purchase and use
Models in ads receiving no reinforcement or receiving punishment for performing undesired behaviours	Discourage undesired behaviours
Individual or group (similar to target) using product in novel, enjoyable way	Use product in new ways

Source: Reprinted from Walter R. Nord and J. Paul Peter, ''A Behavior Modification Perspective on Marketing,'' *Journal of Marketing* 44 (Spring 1980), p. 43. Published by the American Marketing Association.

Two other forms of vicarious learning have marketing applications: covert modelling and verbal modelling.

Covert modelling techniques do not show any actual behaviours or consequences. Rather, people are asked to imagine someone behaving in a situation and subject to particular consequences.[2] A radio commercial might conjure up Doug, a construction worker who has just finished work. It's July, it's hot and humid, and Doug has worked for 12 hours pouring concrete. He's driving home; he's tired and thirsty. His mouth is parched and his throat is dry. Imagine how good that first cold, frosty mug of Molson Dry is going to taste!

Covert modelling has received less research attention than overt modelling, but a review of the literature suggests that:

1. Covert modelling can be as effective as overt modelling in modifying behaviour.
2. The factors that affect overt modelling should have similar effects on covert modelling.
3. Covert modelling can be tested and shown to be effective.
4. Covert modelling can be more effective if alternative consequences of the model's behaviour are described.[3]

While there appears to be no consumer or marketing research on covert modelling, we believe it could be a useful marketing tool.

The **verbal modelling** technique neither demonstrates behaviours nor asks people to imagine a model performing a behaviour. Instead, people are *told* how others similar to themselves behaved in a particular situation. Verbal modelling therefore suggests a social norm that may influence behaviour. One study, for example, investigated the effects of verbal modelling on contributions to charity.[4] In door-to-door solicitation for donations to the United Way, the solicitor manipulated the percentage of households that had already contributed to the drive: "More than (three-fourths/one-fourth) of the households that I've contacted in this area have contributed so far." People who were told three-fourths of their neighbours had contributed usually donated more. Verbal modelling also outperformed several other strategies, such as social responsibility arguments, arguments for helping less fortunate people, and the dollar amount people were told others had given. The study concludes that verbal modelling is an effective means of eliciting desired behaviour.

Verbal modelling is a natural technique in personal-selling situations. For example, salespeople sometimes tell potential buyers that people like them have purchased a particular product, brand, or model. This may be an effective tactic, but it may not necessarily be true, and thus not ethical. As with covert modelling, little is known about verbal modelling in consumer behaviour contexts.

Exhibit 12.3 compares overt, covert, and verbal modelling and suggests appropriate media for each. Investigations of the effectiveness of these procedures using different media and approaches could provide considerable insight into effective modelling processes and development of marketing strategies.

COVERT AND
VERBAL
MODELLING

Watching a model perform a behaviour often increases the likelihood that the observer will perform the behaviour. It is a well-established psychological principle that modelling is effective in changing behaviour, as Consumer Perspective 12.1 illustrates. Certain factors increase the likelihood that vicarious learning will occur: (1) characteristics of the model and modelled behaviour, (2) characteristics of observers, and (3) characteristics of modelled consequences.

FACTORS
INFLUENCING
MODELLING
EFFECTIVENESS

Type	Description	Example	Useful Media
Overt modelling (live and symbolic)	Consumer observes modelled behaviour and consequences	Allstate Insurance commercials demonstrating new method of purchasing insurance	TV, personal selling, in-store video machines, trade shows, auto shows
Covert modelling	Consumer is asked to imagine a model (or self) performing behaviour and consequences	Airline or travel agency commercial during winter inviting consumers to "imagine you're on the warm sunny beaches of Florida"	Radio, personal selling, possibly print advertising
Verbal modelling	Consumer is given a description of how similar people behave in purchase/ use situation	United Way solicitor reporting on gift-giving behaviour of neighbors	Personal selling, radio, direct mail, possibly other print advertising

Characteristics of the model and modelled behaviour

Several characteristics of the models observed influence the probability that an observer will imitate the modelled behaviour.[5] Models found to be attractive may be listened to, while less attractive models may be ignored. Models perceived to be credible and successful exert greater influence than those who are not. High-status and competent models are also more influential in determining model success.

The manner in which the modelled behaviour is performed is another influence. If the sequence of the modelled behaviour is detailed carefully and vividly, modelling effects tend to increase. Interestingly, models who display a bit of apprehension and difficulty and yet complete the task are more effective than models who display no struggle or difficulty. A reason for this has been suggested by Manz and Sims:

> It appears that an observer can identify more with a model who struggles and overcomes the difficulties of a threatening task than a model who apparently has no problem. A model who is seen as possessing substantially greater abilities may not be considered a reasonable reference point for the observer. However, experts who display little difficulty in completing a task (e.g., professional athletes) may serve as ideals to be emulated in nonthreatening situations.[6]

Another factor that influences modelling effectiveness is the model's perceived similarity to the observer. This finding supports the common practice of featuring models similar to members of the target market in commercials, as well as attempts to take advantage of similarities between customers and salespeople in hiring and assigning sales personnel.

Characteristics of the observers

Any number of individual difference variables in observers could be expected to affect successful modelling. For example, individual differences in cognitive processing as well as in physical ability to perform the modelled behaviour may affect the process. In covert modelling in particular, people differ in their ability to imagine modelled behaviour. Bandura suggests that observers who are dependent, who lack confidence and self-esteem, and who have frequently been rewarded for imitative behaviour are especially prone to adopt the behaviour of successful models.[7] Perceptive and confident people readily emulate idealised models who demonstrate highly useful behaviours.

CONSUMER
PERSPECTIVE

12.1

Modelling effects
in apes and
humans

One mistake zoos used to make was to remove new-born primates from their mothers and family groups. When these primates grew up, they turned out to be poor parents, sometimes beating their own babies and inflicting fatal injuries. Researchers determined that the early social isolation was the leading cause of the abuse and they had to alter the primate's environment for the animals to thrive. They made sure biological mothers reared infants in spacious group settings, exposed them to play with infants and peers, and introduced older mothers to help with the new mothers' caretaking. They found that inexperienced and even abusive mothers, once given examples of good mothering (modelling) and a chance to play with infants, became competent parents. Today, as few as 2 percent of primate mothers abuse or neglect their babies, compared to about 75 percent in the 1970s.

University researchers tested a similar program for human mothers, where nurses developed relationships with new mothers by regularly visiting them at home. The nurses showed the new mothers how to play with and talk to an infant, much as the older primates had modelled mothering skills. Attempts were made to get new mothers jobs and to obtain benefits to reduce tension at home. In the end, 4 percent of the low-income teen mothers who received the nurse visits neglected or abused their children, compared with 19 percent of those mothers who did not receive the visits. The nurses also succeeded in teaching parents who had been abused as children how to trust in their abilities as nurturing parents.

One important difference was found between the effects of modelling on humans and animals: the animals apparently learned much more quickly. Just two days of contact with new-born infants made primate females more likely to hug and feed their own infants, while the only programs effective for humans required intensive, long-lasting intervention. In this case, humans could have become more human by modelling the behaviour of primates.

Source: Adapted from Art Levine, "The Biological Roots of Good Mothering," *U.S. News & World Report*, Feb. 25, 1991, p. 61. © Feb. 25, 1991, *U.S. News & World Report*.

Perhaps most important is the value the observer places on the consequences of the modelled behaviour. For example, if consumers value the social approval enjoyed by Maurice Richard in a Grecian Formula (hair colouring) commercial, they are more likely to purchase and use the product.

Characteristics of the modelled consequences

Just as operant conditioning emphasises the consequences of behaviour, so does vicarious learning. Of course, in vicarious learning, the observer does not experience the consequences directly. Thus, a major advantage of vicarious learning for consumers is that they can learn effective purchase and use behaviour while avoiding negative consequences.

Research has demonstrated that positively reinforcing a model's behaviour is a key factor in facilitating vicarious learning, although little is known about what types of positive consequences would be most effective to model, in terms of consumer behaviour. This is also true for modelling applications that seek to decrease undesired behaviours; the most effective types of negative consequences to model in commercials are unknown. While it has been demonstrated that modelling is useful in deterring smoking, reducing drinking, reducing uncooperative behaviour of children, and reducing energy consumption, many other areas of consumer behaviour are unexplored. Consumer Perspective 12.2 presents an example of an emergent marketing tool based on modelling.

<table>
<tr><td>

**CONSUMER
PERSPECTIVE**

▶ **12.2**

**Marketing by
modelling through
infomercials**

</td><td>

Infomercials provide retailers and manufacturers with various ways to model products to consumers. In Canada, ads are not allowed to exceed 12 minutes per hour during the broadcast day, defined as the hours between 6:00 and 12:00 A.M.

    Companies must be creative to get their infomercials seen by their Canadian target market. Loblaw International Merchants Inc. overcame this scheduling dilemma. In order for its 30-minute infomercials to be seen in the Toronto area, Loblaw's purchased air time on WUTV in Buffalo. These infomercials highlight its line of President's Choice products and combine folksy humour with information and demonstrations of how to use the products in certain recipes.

    Since Loblaw's started modelling the use of its products on infomercials, sales of President's Choice products have risen by 50 percent and have generated sales of $27 million at the 135 Loblaw stores. It appears that modelling proper product usage through infomercials is a very effective marketing strategy.

Source: "Loblaw's Infomercials Boost Sales by 50%," *Marketing*, Jan. 20, 1992, pp. 1–4; "Loblaw's Tries Infomercials," *Marketing*, Nov. 18, 1991, p. 4.

</td></tr>
</table>

MARKETING IMPLICATIONS

Modelling clearly plays a role in marketing products, particularly in advertising and personal-selling approaches to influencing consumers. Modelling also plays a special role in the diffusion of innovation and the degree to which consumers adopt products.

Diffusion of innovation

Diffusion refers to the way innovations (new products, services, or ideas) are spread throughout society. Successful diffusion of innovations follows a common pattern. First, the innovation is introduced by prominent models. Wayne Gretsky, for example, the all-time leading goal scorer in the National Hockey League, introduced Easton's new aluminium hockey stick in 1991. Next, the innovation is adopted by others at an accelerating rate. After Gretsky endorsed the stick and was successful using it, Easton's market share grew from 1 percent to 25 percent within the first year. Finally, adoption then either stabilises or declines, depending on the functional role of the product. Easton was still one of the leading brands of aluminium hockey sticks in 1995.

    Modelling affects the diffusion of innovation in several ways. It instructs people about new products and new styles of behaviour through social, pictorial, or verbal displays. Some consumers may be reluctant to buy new products until they see the advantages gained by earlier adopters. After breaking countless records in the NHL, including Gordie Howe's old record of 801 career goals, Gretsky has doubtless influenced thousands of young Canadian hockey players to try Easton hockey sticks.

    Modelled benefits accelerate diffusion by weakening the resistance of the more cautious consumers. As acceptance spreads, the new users are evidence of further support for the product. Models not only exemplify and legitimise innovations but also serve as advocates for products by encouraging others to adopt them. Even weekend or pickup hockey players can influence their friends to purchase Easton hockey sticks, either by being observed playing better with them or by offering verbal support for their advantages.

The adoption process

Different types of consumers adopt new products at different stages. A well-known classification of these different types is shown in Exhibit 12.4. This **adoption curve** represents the cumulative percentage of purchasers of a product across time. It includes five groups. Traditionally, the five adopter groups are characterised as follows. **Innovators** are venturesome and willing to take risks. **Early adopters** are respectable and often influence

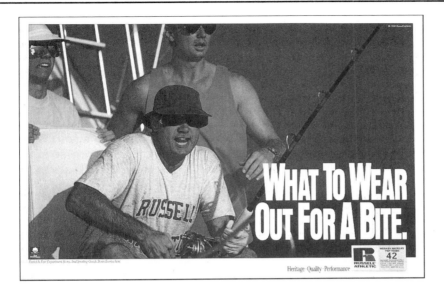

This ad models an appropriate occasion for using (wearing) a product.

the early majority. The **early majority** are risk avoiders and are deliberate in their purchases. The **late majority** are sceptical and cautious about new ideas. **Laggards** are quite traditional and set in their ways.

Marketing managers find innovators particularly important because they influence early adopters, who in turn may influence the early majority to purchase. A new product's chances of success increase greatly once innovators adopt the product and tell others about it. Modelling is important in this instance because early adopters may be influenced by seeing innovators using a product and being reinforced for doing so.

A major focus of consumer research has been to identify the characteristics of innovators and their differences from other consumers. Innovators tend to be more highly educated and younger, and to have greater social mobility, more favourable attitudes toward risk (more venturesome), greater social participation, and higher opinion leadership than other consumers.

Innovators also tend to be heavy users of other products within a product class. One study finds that adopters of home computers had greater experience with other technical

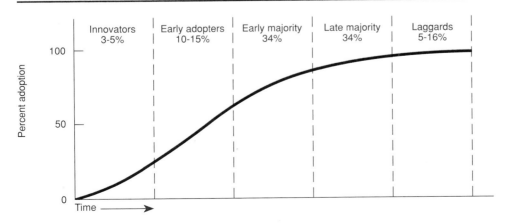

EXHIBIT 12.4

The adoption curve

products—such as programmable pocket calculators and video games—than did non-adopters.[8] Innovators may have better-developed knowledge structures for particular product categories, which may enable them to understand and evaluate new products more rapidly and thus adopt earlier than other consumers.

The idea that different types of consumers purchase products in different stages of the products' life cycles has important implications for marketing. Marketing strategies must change across time to appeal to different types of consumers.

Characteristics of products

Exhibit 12.5 lists a number of characteristics of new products and brands that influence whether consumers will purchase them. Modelling can play an important role in new-product success by demonstrating these characteristics of a product in advertising or in the product's actual use by innovators. Other influences are word-of-mouth communication, including verbal modelling, by innovators, salespeople, and other consumers about these characteristics. Observers are more likely to adopt a new product or brand if these characteristics are easily modelled for them.

Compatibility

Compatibility refers to the degree to which a product is consistent with consumers' current affect, cognitions, and behaviours. Other things being equal, consumers are more likely to try a product that does not require a major change in their values and beliefs or their purchase and use behaviours. For example, Freedent chewing gum—the gum that doesn't stick to your teeth—required little change by consumers to try the product.

Trialability

Trialability refers to the degree to which a product can be tried on a limited basis or divided into small quantities for an inexpensive trial. A product that facilitates a nonpurchase trial or a limited-purchase trial is more likely to influence the consumer to try it. Test driving a car, trying on a sweater, tasting bite-size pieces of a new frozen pizza, accepting a free trial of a new encyclopaedia, or buying a sample-size bottle of a new shampoo are ways consumers can try products on a limited basis and reduce risk.

Observability

Observability refers to the degree to which products or their effects can be perceived by other consumers. New products that are public and frequently discussed are more likely to be adopted rapidly. Many clothing styles, for example, become popular after consumers see movie and music stars wearing them. Satellite disks are highly observable, a feature that likely influences their purchase.

EXHIBIT 12.5

Characteristics that influence the success of new products

▷ **Compatibility:** How well does this product fit consumers' current affect, cognitions, and behaviours?

▷ **Trialability:** Can consumers try the product on a limited basis with little risk?

▷ **Observability:** Do consumers frequently see or otherwise sense this product?

▷ **Speed:** How soon do consumers experience the benefits of the product?

▷ **Simplicity:** How easy is it for consumers to understand and use the product?

▷ **Relative advantage:** What makes this product better than competitive offerings?

▷ **Product symbolism:** What does this product mean to consumers?

A marketing strategy to increase trialability.

Speed

Speed refers to how quickly the benefits of the product are experienced by the consumer. Because many consumers are oriented toward immediate rather than delayed gratification, products that can deliver benefits sooner rather than later have a higher probability of at least being tried. For example, weight-loss programs that promise results within the first week are more likely to attract consumers than those that promise results in six months.

Simplicity

Simplicity refers to the degree to which a product is easy for a consumer to understand and use. A product that does not require complicated assembly and extensive training to use has a higher chance of trial. For example, many computer products, such as those made by Apple, are promoted as user friendly to encourage purchase.

Relative advantage

Relative advantage refers to the degree to which an item has a *sustainable, competitive differential advantage* over other product classes, product forms, and brands. There is no question that relative advantage is a most important product characteristic not only for obtaining trial but also for continued purchase and the development of brand loyalty.

In some cases, a relative advantage may be obtained through technological developments. At the product-class level, for example, RCA introduced the videodisk player,

In 1984, General Motors reduced the length of its Cadillac by two feet, and sales dropped dramatically, forcing the company to rethink the way it designs cars. Traditionally, GM had interviewed car buyers only at the start of product development, but to deal with this new problem, the company decided to meet with five consumer groups over a three-year period. Each group consisted of 500 owners of Cadillacs and other models. GM planners sat these people behind the wheel of prototype cars, letting them fiddle with buttons and knobs on the instrument panel, with door handles and seat belts, while engineers sat in back and took notes.

What was the result? The new Cadillac De Villes and Fleetwoods that cruised into showrooms for 1988 were nine inches longer and sported subtle tail fins and fender skirts—reminiscent of the opulent automobiles of the 1950s. In the fourth quarter of 1988, Cadillac sold 36 percent more De Villes and Fleetwoods than it had a year earlier, and overall Cadillac volume grew for the first time in five years.

Why weren't the smaller Cadillacs successful? It seems clear that Cadillac buyers want a distinctive-looking car, and the smaller versions probably looked too much like other GM cars. Also, the larger versions, with features similar to those from the 1950s, may have special meanings to some consumers. For example, the 1950s were a relatively worry-free, secure period in history. For some Cadillac owners, the larger car may represent physical, social, and financial security, something they did not feel with the smaller models. In other words, the larger Cadillacs may be symbolic of important consumer values.

Source: Reprinted with permission from Patricia Sellers, "Getting Customers to Love You," *Fortune,* © 1989 Time Inc. All rights reserved.

which showed programs on any TV set. The disk player cost half as much as a VCR, and the disks were cheaper than videocassettes. But VCRs had a relative advantage over disk players: they could record programs. RCA assumed that recording ability was not an important factor to consumers—and lost more than $500 million finding out otherwise.

At the brand level, however, it is often difficult to maintain a technological relative advantage, because new or improved technology can be quickly copied by competitors. In addition, many brands within product groups are relatively homogeneous in terms of their functional benefits for consumers. For these reasons, one of the most important sources of a sustainable relative advantage is product symbolism rather than technological change or functional difference in products.

Product symbolism

Product symbolism refers to what the product or brand means to the consumer and what the consumer experiences in purchasing and using it. That is, consumption of some products may depend more on their social and psychological meaning than on their functional utility. For example, the blue-jean market is dominated by major brands such as Levi's and Guess, which show few clear differences except in pocket design and brand labelling. If these brand names meant nothing to consumers, and blue jeans were purchased only on the basis of product attributes such as materials and styles, it would be difficult to explain differences in market share, given the brand similarity. Obviously jeans brands have different symbolic meanings for consumers. Consumer Perspective 12.3 offers an example of the importance of product symbolism in the car market.

Learning objective 1: *Explain three uses of vicarious learning (modelling).*

First, modelling can be used to help observers acquire new behavioural responses that did not previously exist in their repertoires. In other words, it can help consumers develop new behaviours. Second, modelling can be used to inhibit undesired behaviours. That is, modelling can help decrease incidence of behaviours that are not good for consumers, marketers, or society. Third, modelling can be used to facilitate the occurrence of desired behaviours that are currently in the consumer's repertoire. In other words, it can help consumers engage in behaviours that they already know by showing appropriate occasions and reinforcement for performing them.

Learning objective 2: *Describe three types of modelling.*

The three types of modelling are overt, covert, and verbal. In overt modelling, observers actually observe a model either in person (live modelling) or on TV or video (symbolic modelling). Covert modelling asks consumers to imagine observing a model behaving in various situations and receiving particular consequences. In verbal modelling, people are told how people like them behaved in a particular situation.

Learning objective 3: *Explain three factors that influence the effectiveness of modelling.*

First, the characteristics of the model and the modelled behaviour influence the effectiveness of modelling. In general, attractive, credible, high-status, competent models are more effective. Modelled behaviour that is detailed vividly is also more effective. Second, the characteristics of the observers influence the effectiveness of modelling. Differences in consumers' cognitive processing and physical abilities, as well as factors such as self-confidence, dependence, and self-esteem, can influence the success of modelling. Third, the characteristics of the modelled consequences can influence the success of modelling. In general, showing a model receiving positive reinforcement after performing a behaviour is a key factor in successful modelling.

Learning objective 4: *Describe five adopter categories.*

Innovators (3 to 5 percent of purchasers) are venturesome and willing to take risks. They are the first group to adopt new products. Early adopters (10 to 15 percent of purchasers) are respectable and often influence the early majority. They follow innovators in purchasing. Members of the early majority (34 percent of purchasers) avoid risks and are deliberate in their purchases. The late majority (34 percent of purchasers) are sceptical and cautious about new ideas. Laggards (5 to 16 percent of purchasers) are traditional and set in their ways. They are the last group to adopt a product.

Learning objective 5: *Identify the characteristics that influence the success of new products.*

Seven major characteristics influence the success of new products. Compatibility refers to the degree to which a product is consistent with consumers' current affect, cognitions, and behaviours. Trialability refers to the degree to which a product can be tried on a limited basis or divided into small quantities for an inexpensive trial. Observability refers to the degree to which products or their effects can be perceived by consumers. Speed refers to how quickly the product's benefits are experienced by consumers. Simplicity refers to the degree to which a product is easy for a consumer to understand and use. Relative advantage refers to the degree to which an item has a sustainable, competitive differential advantage over other product classes, product forms, or brands. Product symbolism refers to what the product or brand means to the consumer beyond its strictly functional utility.

▶ **KEY TERMS AND CONCEPTS**

overt modelling	early adopters	observability
covert modelling	early majority	speed
verbal modelling	late majority	simplicity
diffusion	laggards	relative advantage
adoption curve	compatibility	product symbolism
innovators	trialability	

▶ **REVIEW AND DISCUSSION QUESTIONS**

1. Describe the steps necessary for behaviour change in the modelling process.
2. What are the three major uses of modelling in marketing strategy?
3. Why might a marketing organisation use symbolic rather than live overt modelling? Give examples to illustrate your points.
4. How are covert and verbal modelling different from overt modelling? How are they similar?
5. Give examples (not already discussed in the text) of marketing strategies you have observed that use each of the types of modelling.
6. In what situations would you recommend that a marketing manager use vicarious learning in advertisements?
7. How could modelling be used to facilitate the introduction of the newest models of lightweight portable personal computers?
8. To which adopter category do you belong in general? Explain.
9. Identify characteristics of new products (in different product/service categories) that would be useful for predicting success and for prescribing effective marketing strategies.
10. Discuss the problems and advantages of appealing to innovators when marketing a new consumer packaged good.

CHAPTER 13

Analysing Consumer Behaviour

LEARNING OBJECTIVES

After completing this chapter, you should be able to:

▶ 1. Describe a sequence of overt consumer behaviours involved in a retail consumer-goods purchase and explain the behaviours.

▶ 2. Suggest several tactics marketers could use to influence each of these behaviours.

▶ 3. Explain a model marketers could use to influence a sequence of consumer behaviours.

FORD EXPLORES THE 4-WHEEL-DRIVE MARKET

Throughout the 1980s, the Jeep Cherokee was the car of choice for many upscale buyers seeking a second car. In fact, common garage-mates for Cherokees were Mercedes-Benzes and BMWs. These consumers wanted a second car with four doors and enough room for the family to pile in for a trip to the beach or the mall. Chrysler, which acquired Jeep in 1987, made from $4,000 to $4,500 profit on each Cherokee it sold during this period.

In 1990, Ford Canada introduced the Explorer, a four-door, four-wheel-drive vehicle that competes directly with the Cherokee. Ford recognised that many more women were buying off-road vehicles or influencing purchase decisions, so it made changes for them as well as for men. As a result, the Explorer has safety features such as front-seat head restraints, rear shoulder belts, and a shift into four-wheel drive that requires simply pushing a button. In 1993 and 1994, Ford added standard four-wheel antilock brakes and dual air bags. In just six months, the Explorer outsold the Jeep Cherokee by almost two to one, and Ford Canada's share of the off-road-vehicle market went from 18 to 23 percent while Jeep's dropped from 33 to 22 percent.[1]

Many consumer behaviours are involved in purchasing a new vehicle, as the Cherokee/ Explorer example illustrates. There are also many behaviours involved in purchases of simpler, less-expensive products. This chapter investigates the types of consumer behaviours marketers try to influence.

By now you have a general understanding of the major aspects of the behaviour approach used in the Wheel of Consumer Analysis. Here we tie this approach more directly to consumer behaviour and marketing strategy development by explaining a model of the behaviours involved in a common purchase situation and how marketers use alternative strategies to change these behaviours.

MODEL OF CONSUMER BEHAVIOUR

Traditional models of the purchase or adoption process in marketing treat it as a series of cognitive events followed by a single behaviour usually called *adoption* or *purchase*. These models are consistent with the view that *cognitive variables* (awareness, comprehension, interest, evaluation, conviction) are the main concern of marketing and the primary controllers of behaviour. According to this view, the marketing task is to influence these cognitive variables and move consumers through each stage until a purchase is made.

An alternative approach is to analyse adoption or purchase as a *sequence of behaviours*. From this perspective marketing managers want to increase the frequency of a certain behaviour, and they design strategies and tactics for doing so. The assumption is that strategies and tactics to change affective and cognitive processes such as attention or attitude may be useful intermediate steps, but they must ultimately change behaviour to be profitable for marketers.

Exhibit 13.1 describes a model of a behaviour sequence that occurs in the purchase of many consumer goods. While this is a logical sequence, many other combinations of behaviour can occur. For example, an unplanned (impulse) purchase of a Mars chocolate bar could start at the store contact stage. Not every purchase follows the sequence shown in Exhibit 13.1, and not every purchase requires that all of these behaviours be performed. The model is generally useful all the same for categorising a variety of marketing strategies in terms of the behaviours they are designed to influence.

The model in Exhibit 13.1 is also intended to illustrate only one type of behaviour sequence for retail purchase; similar models could be developed for other types of purchases, such as mail-order, telephone, or catalogue-showroom exchanges. Further, the sequences involved with other behaviours of interest to consumer analysts, such as voting, physician care, banking, or consumer education, could also be modelled in much the same way. In fact, any attempt to influence behaviour should include an analysis of the behaviour sequence that is necessary or desired. Unfortunately, many marketing managers do not consider exactly what behaviours are involved in the actions they are attempting to get consumers to perform.

The time it takes for a consumer to perform behaviours in the model depends on a variety of factors. Different products, consumers, and situations may affect not only the total time to complete the process but also the length of time between stages. For example, an avid water-skier purchasing a Mastercraft powerboat likely will spend more time per stage, and more time between stages, than a consumer purchasing a Timex watch.

A seller's emphasis on any particular element of the sequence will vary according to the place in the distribution chain for the product or service. Retailers, for example, may be more concerned with increasing store contact than with purchase of a particular brand; manufacturers are less concerned with the particular store patronised, but want to increase brand purchase; credit-card companies may be less concerned with particular

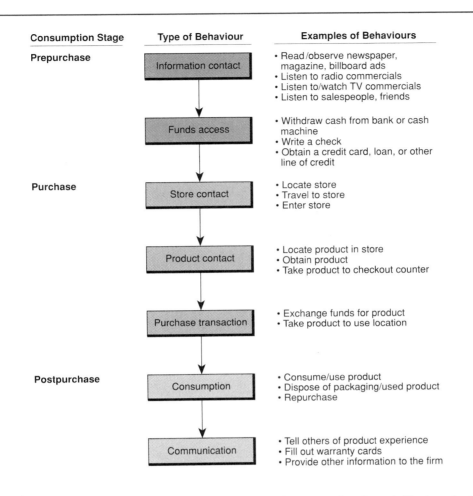

EXHIBIT 13.1

A common behaviour sequence for a retail consumer-goods purchase

Consumption Stage	Type of Behaviour	Examples of Behaviours
Prepurchase	Information contact	• Read/observe newspaper, magazine, billboard ads • Listen to radio commercials • Listen to/watch TV commercials • Listen to salespeople, friends
	Funds access	• Withdraw cash from bank or cash machine • Write a check • Obtain a credit card, loan, or other line of credit
Purchase	Store contact	• Locate store • Travel to store • Enter store
	Product contact	• Locate product in store • Obtain product • Take product to checkout counter
	Purchase transaction	• Exchange funds for product • Take product to use location
Postpurchase	Consumption	• Consume/use product • Dispose of packaging/used product • Repurchase
	Communication	• Tell others of product experience • Fill out warranty cards • Provide other information to the firm

store or product contacts so long as their credit card is accepted and used. Store contact, product contact, and transaction method are all common for a retail exchange, however, and all three sellers can benefit from the others' efforts. Consumer Perspective 13.1 discusses a creative strategy for influencing consumers' purchasing behaviour that involves offering air miles for buying products or services from many different corporate sponsors.

A common early stage in the purchase sequence, called **information contact,** occurs when consumers come into contact with information about products, stores, or brands. This stage includes behaviours such as reading product information, observing newspaper, magazine, and billboard ads, listening to radio commercials, watching TV commercials, and talking to salespeople and friends. At this point, the practical problem for marketers is to increase the probability that consumers will observe and attend to the information; they assume this will increase the probability of other behaviours.

Marketing managers for brands with low market share usually want to increase overall search behaviour, because it may increase the probability of brand switching. High-market-share brands may try to discourage extensive search behaviour, because it may result in a shift to another brand. For example, Heinz currently has a major share of the market for ketchup and does not want most consumers to search for information concerning other brands. Ads showing Heinz as the thicker, richer ketchup while depicting other

Information contact

CONSUMER PERSPECTIVE

▶ **13.1**

Creative strategies to influence purchase behaviour

The Loyalty Management Group Canada, Inc., of Toronto introduced a unique frequent-buyer scheme in early 1992 called Air Miles. The program involves blue-chip consumer-oriented sponsors such as gasoline retailers, credit-card firms, financial institutions, and major retail outlets. More than 100 Canadian companies, including Air Canada, American Airlines, Provigo, Shell, Ford, Bank of Montreal, MasterCard, Andre LaLonde Sports, and Ro-Na Hardware, are participating in the program.

Consumers join the program for free and accumulate Air Miles by buying products or services from the different sponsors. The number of miles for each dollar spent varies among the participating companies. After building up enough miles, consumers can book an airline ticket through the Air Miles reservation centre or redeem the miles for hotels and car rentals.

By 1994 more than 3.8 million households in Canada had signed up for the Air Miles program. Research shows that the most cherished promotions companies can offer Canadian consumers are vacation and travel-related offers.

Companies like Shell and MasterCard, which process thousands of transactions for Air Miles, put up with the administrative and labour costs associated with the program because they are convinced it has increased business. Louise Bourdeau, director of client services for the Bank of Montreal, said the volume of transactions of the Air Miles/MasterCard has significantly exceeded expectations.

This innovative program works because it offers consumers highly desired promotions at virtually no cost and offers retailers a competitive advantage that can increase customer loyalty.

Source: Adapted from "Frequent Buyers Get to Fly," *Financial Post*, July 25, p. 10, 1991; Gilles des Roberts, "Air Miles Deux Ans Plus Tard," *Les Affaires*, April 30, 1994, p. 7.

brands as thin and unsavoury may discourage loyal consumers from searching for an alternative. They may also help attract non-Heinz purchasers by demonstrating the negative consequences of using another brand. The extent of a consumer's search depends on many factors, some of which are listed in Exhibit 13.2.

In general, empirical research has shown:

1. Consumers tend to engage more in search when purchasing higher-priced, more visible, and more complex products—i. e., products that intrinsically create greater perceived risk.

2. Search is influenced by individual factors, such as the perceived benefits of search (e.g., enjoyment, self-confidence, role), demographic aspects, and product knowledge already possessed.

3. Search efforts tend to be influenced further by factors in the marketplace (such as store distribution) and by circumstances impinging on the shopper (such as time pressure).[2]

From a public policy standpoint, information search should develop more knowledgeable consumers, although there are differences in the effort consumers must exert to obtain information from different sources as well as in the believability of the information.[3] For example, Exhibit 13.3 rates five common sources of information on effort required and believability. Internal sources (stored experiences) and personal sources (friends and relatives) are easiest to access and the most believable. Marketing sources (advertising) are also readily available but not as believable, because advertisers have something to gain from the transaction. Finally, public sources (*Consumer Reports* and other impartial stud-

Influencing Factor	Increasing the Influencing Factor Causes Search to:
Market characteristics	
Number of alternatives	Increase
Price range	Increase
Store concentration	Increase
Information availability	Increase
Advertising	
Point of purchase	
Sales personnel	
Packaging	
Experienced consumers	
Independent sources	
Product characteristics	
Price	Increase
Differentiation	Increase
Positive products	Increase
Consumer characteristics	
Learning and experience	Decrease
Shopping orientation	Mixed
Social status	Increase
Age, gender, and household life cycle	Mixed
Perceived risk	Increase
Situational characteristics	
Time availability	Increase
Purchase for self	Decrease
Pleasant surroundings	Increase
Social surroundings	Mixed
Physical/mental energy	Increase

EXHIBIT 13.2

Factors affecting information search by consumers

Source: Del I. Hawkins, Roger Best, Jr., and Kenneth A. Coney, *Consumer Behaviour: Implications for Marketing Strategy*, 5th ed. (Homewood, Ill.: Richard D. Irwin, 1992), p. 478.

ies) and experiential sources (personally examining or testing the product) are less likely to be used, at least in this early stage, because they require more effort.

The main marketing task is to increase the probability that the target market comes into contact with product, brand, or store information and pays attention to it. Numerous

Source	Effort Required	Believability
Internal (stored experiences in memory)	Low	High
Personal (friends, relatives)	Low	High
Marketing (advertising)	Low	Low
Public (*Consumer Reports*, other studies)	High	High
Experiential (examining or testing product)	High	High

EXHIBIT 13.3

A comparison of information sources

Funds access can occur in
a number of ways.

marketing strategies are directed at encouraging attentive behaviour. For example, media scheduling, message content and layout, the use of colour and humour in advertising, and repetition all involve presenting stimuli to increase the probability that potential consumers will attend to relevant cues. *Fear appeals* can also be used to bring about attentive behaviours and to stimulate emotions vicariously by exposing the observers to possible distasteful consequences of certain conditions (inadequate insurance, faulty tires and batteries, the absence of smoke alarms, not using dental floss). Strategies such as contests and prizes encourage attentive behaviour and promise rewards for engaging in certain behaviour that brings the consumer into closer contact with the product or point of purchase. Finally, ads that show models receiving positive reinforcement in the form of social approval and satisfaction for purchasing a product provide stimuli that can move the consumer closer to purchase by stimulating the "buying mood." Consumer Perspective 13.2 discusses a strategy that encourages information contact for magazine subscriptions.

Funds access

Exchange is frequently seen as the key concept for understanding marketing, although relatively little attention has been given to *what consumers exchange* in the marketing process. Beyond time and effort costs, money is the primary medium of consumer exchanges. Before an exchange can occur, the consumer must access this medium in one form or another, engaging in what is known as **funds access.** The primary marketing issues at this stage are (1) the methods consumers use to pay for particular purchases and (2) the marketing strategies to increase the probability that the consumers can access funds for purchase.

CONSUMER PERSPECTIVE

13.2

Encouraging information contact for magazine subscriptions

Including subscription cards in magazines is a useful marketing tactic, because the cards are available at the time the magazine is being read and enjoyed. These cards make it convenient for readers of the magazine (the likely target market for future issues) to renew a subscription or start a new one.

Traditionally, magazine marketers have bound subscription cards to the magazines. One drawback to such "bind-in" cards is that readers often simply ignore them. They leaf past them without giving the card (or the idea of starting or renewing a subscription) any consideration.

An alternative method of including subscription cards in magazines is to place them between the pages, unbound. When magazines are open or read, these "blow-in" cards fall out and consumers need to handle them for at least a moment. In other words, blow-in cards increase the probability of information contact. It is not surprising, then, that blow-in cards are more effective than bind-in cards at generating subscription renewals.

There are, of course, a variety of ways consumers can pay for a product. These include cash in pocket; bank withdrawal of cash; writing a cheque; using credit cards such as Visa, MasterCard, and American Express; using a store charge account; using debit cards such as the Interac system; and drawing on other lines of credit, such as bank loans or car financing. Access may involve different degrees of effort exerted to obtain the money that is spent or that is used to repay loans. It seems likely that funds obtained from tax refunds, stock sales and dividends, gambling winnings, awards, or regular paycheques are valued differently by the consumer and spent in different ways. A manifestation of this effect is that some retailers (for example, Leon's and The Brick) encourage the purchase of big-ticket items, especially during the December shopping spree, by offering interest-free loans for a few months while people are waiting for their tax refunds ("Buy now, pay nothing down, no interest, no payment until June of next year").

A variety of other strategies may increase the probability that consumers can access funds for purchases. For example, The Bay often offers a small gift to anyone who fills out a credit-card application. The probability of purchasing at The Bay is increased when

Marketing strategies that increase the probability of access to funds.

a consumer has a credit card, because cash may not always be available. Other strategies include locating cash machines in malls, instituting liberal credit terms and check-cashing policies, and accepting a variety of credit cards. Deferred payment plans and layaway plans that allow the consumer additional time to raise the required funds help stores avoid lost sales. Gift certificates are also used to presell merchandise and to provide some consumers with another source of funds that is restricted for particular purchases. All these strategies have a common goal—to increase the probability of an exchange by increasing the probability of accessing funds.

Other strategies can be employed to increase certain types of purchases. For example, a store could offer a small discount for using cash to avoid the costs of paying credit-card fees. Canadian Tire has used this strategy, in the form of Canadian Tire money, for years. An analysis of the conditions surrounding particular purchases may recommend other successful tactics. Many major home appliances, for example, are purchased only when both husband and wife are present, and a necessary condition is that they can obtain funds. One tactic for an appliance store might be to offer a small gift to any couple who come to the store with their chequebook or approved credit card. This assures the appropriate contingencies for an appliance sale. Any number of other methods (such as offering rebates) could be used in conjunction with this tactic to increase the probability of purchase. Consumer Perspective 13.3 discusses strategies credit-card issuers use to encourage consumers to obtain and use their credit cards for funds access.

Store contact

Although catalogue and telephone-order purchases are important, most consumer-goods purchases are still made in retail stores. Thus, a major task of retailers is to get consumers into the store, where purchase can occur. **Store contact** includes (1) locating the store, (2) travelling to it, and (3) entering it.

One factor that affects the probability of store contact involves how consumers see their roles as shoppers. Some people enjoy shopping and spend many hours looking in stores. To others, shopping is drudgery. Some shoppers are primarily price oriented and favour particular low-price outlets. Others look for a high level of service, or unique products and stores that express their individuality. These differences are important dimensions in design of market segmentation strategies for stores.

Many strategies are designed to increase the probability of store contact. For example, consider the methods used to increase the probability that shoppers will be able to locate a particular outlet. Selecting convenient locations in high-traffic areas with ample parking, has been successful for retailers such as Mac's convenience stores and Harvey's restaurants. Major advantages for retailers locating in shopping malls are the increase in consumers' ability to find the outlet as well as the additional shopping traffic created by the presence of the other stores. Yellow Pages, newspaper, and other ads frequently include maps and information numbers to aid shoppers in locating an outlet. Outdoor signs and logos (such as the distinctive Domino's Pizza sign) are well-known discriminative stimuli. One consumer electronics store in Montreal used an interesting modelling approach to aid potential customers in locating its downtown store. Its TV ads showed the quickest way to get to the store from various points in the city using familiar access roads and public transportation.

Other tactics to encourage store contact include carnivals in mall parking lots, free style shows or other mall entertainments, and visits by Santa Claus, the Easter Bunny, Sesame Street characters, and soap-opera actors. Mall directories and information booths help shoppers find particular stores.

Finally, some tactics are used to get the potential customer physically into the store. Frequently advertised sales, sale signs in store windows, door prizes, loss leaders,

The road to redemption is getting easier. In the race to keep consumers charging with just one credit card, many card marketers are broadening rewards programs by making merchandise available at lower point levels.

Almost every dollar charged on a Canadian Gold Card and many spent on basic cards are now converted into points—that ubiquitous new currency—and redeemable for everything from sunny travel packages to merchandise from glossy catalogues.

American Express launched its membership awards program in early 1992 and recently reported that 40 percent of personal cardholders have paid the $30 to enroll.

Rewards members are spending an average of four times more on their card than nonmembers, apparently consolidating their spending. According to American Express, the number of redeemers in the first half of 1994 doubled over the same period a year ago. About 62 percent of the cardholders used their points for plane tickets; the balance chose such rewards as hotel packages, concerts, theatre, and restaurants.

The TD/GM Visa and the CIBC/Aeroplan Visa have also been huge successes. "This is more than just a credit card for the bank, it's a relationship-building product," said Lisa Driscoll, the bank's TD/GM card marketing director. "It's a share-of-wallet issue," said Tim Wallace, manager of cardholder services for Royal Bank of Canada.

Any effort to get core customers to use a product pays higher dividends than spending lots of money chasing new customers, who can be fickle. Plus the commitment to a credit card often translates into a customer's return to the same institution for his or her next banking product.

The people who benefit most from rewards programs are those who carry a Gold Card for its other benefits, such as travel insurance. These are usually business-people who charge thousands of dollars on their card and pay the balance every month. It is not uncommon for a Canadian business executive to earn 200,000 to 300,000 points per year using the CIBC Visa/Aeroplan Aerogold card. Every trip earns one point for every mile travelled as well as points for the cost of the ticket—a double bonus.

Source: Lisa Kassenar, "Card Holders Scramble for Points Payoff," *Financial Post*, Sept. 10, 1994, p. S23.

CONSUMER PERSPECTIVE

13.3

Cardholders scramble for points payoff

---

sounds (such as popular music), and tempting aromas (such as fresh popcorn) are commonly employed for these purposes.

Product contact

Manufacturers are concerned primarily with *selective demand* of consumers in stores— purchase of their particular brands and models. Many of the methods employed to accomplish **product contact** involve push strategies such as trade discounts and incentives to enhance the selling effort of retailers. For example, a free case of Tide liquid detergent for every 10 cases the retailer purchases can be a powerful incentive for retailers to feature liquid Tide in newspaper ads, put it in prominent displays, and even sell it at a lower price while maintaining or increasing profit margins. Other approaches involve pull strategies, such as cents-off coupons to encourage the consumer to purchase the manufacturer's brand. In any event, once potential buyers are in the store, three behaviours are usually necessary for a purchase to take place: (1) locating the product or brand in the store, (2) physically obtaining the product or brand, and (3) taking the product or brand to the point of exchange (e.g., the checkout counter).

Once consumers are in the store, it is important that they be able to locate products. Store directories, end-of-aisle and other displays, in-store signs, information booths, and store personnel all help consumers move into visual contact with products. While consumers are in the store, their visual contact with the many other available products increases the probability of purchase.

One tactic a major chain uses involves a variation of "blue-light specials." Blue-light specials, pioneered by Kmart, offer shoppers in the store the opportunity to purchase products at special prices when a blue light is flashing at a particular location. Usually, the sale item is low priced and sold at its normal location. A variation involves moving the sale merchandise and the blue light to an area where high-priced or high-margin items are located. This brings the blue-light shoppers into visual contact with such products—which, of course, increases the probability of making these more profitable sales. The tactic is reported to be quite successful.

Physically coming into contact with a product influences whether a purchase will occur. Attractive, eye-catching packaging and other aspects of product appearance influence the degree to which the consumer pays attention to the product. Trying the product in the store can also affect purchase probabilities, as can the behaviour of sales personnel. Salespeople can positively reinforce certain behaviours, extinguish or punish others, influence the stimuli attended to, and model appropriate consumer usage. Even negative reinforcement can be employed. For example, consider salespeople who are overly aggressive and use high-pressure tactics. One way for consumers to eliminate the pushy treatment is to purchase the product—and some people do this rather than walk away. Thus, the consumer is negatively reinforced to purchase; the probability of this response is likely to be increased in similar situations in the future. Note also that the salesperson is positively reinforced by making the sale using a high-pressure approach, so the salesperson's aggressive selling approach is also likely to persist.

Salespeople can also change the circumstances for purchasing versus not purchasing. Consider this approach to selling furniture to ambivalent customers who state their intention to "go home and think it over." Once the potential buyer leaves the store, of course, the probability of a sale is reduced, so the salesperson can change the contingencies for leaving. Potential buyers who want to think it over are told, "If you buy now, the price is $150. If you go home and come back later, the price will be the original $175." In this way a salesperson can modify the behaviour of potential buyers.

There are also a number of tactics for getting potential buyers to the checkout or payment location. Checkout counters are commonly located near the exit, and parking vouchers are usually validated there. Also, salespeople frequently escort the buyer to the checkout, where they may help arrange financing.

Purchase transaction

In a macro sense, *facilitating exchange* is viewed as the primary objective of marketing. In a micro sense, this involves **purchase transactions** where consumers exchange funds for products and services. Many marketing strategies involve removing obstacles to transactions. Credit cards are one example. So are express checkout lanes and electronic scanners that minimise the time consumers must wait in line. Some consumers will leave stores without making a purchase if checkout lines are too long. The Toronto-Dominion Bank offered customers $5 if they had to wait more than five minutes. Credit-card companies offer prompt purchase approvals to decrease the chances that a sale will be missed because of a long wait. American Express, for example, spends $300 million to $400 million annually to ensure prompt service for its 15 million customers. From its computer centre, the company approves 250,000 credit-card transactions a day from all over the world in an average of five seconds or less.[4] American Express also uses a separate phone number for its front-of-the-line service, which builds additional service for members.

Because the behaviour of checkout personnel is an important influence on purchase, checkout people are trained to be friendly and efficient. McDonald's personnel frequently offer *prompts* in an attempt to increase the total amount of purchase: "Would you like some fresh, hot french fries with that?" or "How about some McDonald's cookies today?" Because these are very low-cost tactics, few incremental sales are required to make them quite profitable.

The positive reinforcers are critical elements in encouraging purchase transactions. Tactics like rebates, friendly treatment and compliments by store personnel, and contest tickets may increase the probability of purchase and repurchase. The reinforcing properties of the product or service itself are also important. These may involve both functional and psychosocial benefits.

Consumption

While **consumption** would seem to be a simple behaviour to delineate, it is not, because of the vast differences in the nature of various products and services. For example, compare typical behaviours involved in the purchase of nondurables such as a fast-food burger and fries versus a durable such as a car. The burger and fries are likely to be consumed rather quickly and the packaging disposed of as directed. Certain strategies can increase the probability that consumption will be fast, such as seats in a restaurant that are comfortable for only short periods of time so customers do not take up space for too long. Prompts (like "Thank You" signs on refuse containers) are often used to encourage proper disposal of packaging.

On the other hand, an automobile purchase usually involves several years of consumption or use. In addition, periodic service is required, and additional complementary products such as gas must be purchased. Finally, a car may be disposed of in several ways (sold outright, junked, or traded in on another model). At present, little is known about the process by which consumers dispose of durable goods.

Regardless of the type of product, however, a primary marketing concern is to increase the probability of repurchase. For nondurable packaged goods, common tactics include the use of in- or on-package coupons to encourage the consumer to repurchase the same brand. Many consumers are frequent coupon users who take considerable satisfaction in the money they save. Proof-of-purchase seals are often used to encourage the consumer to purchase the same brand repeatedly to obtain enough seals to receive "free" gifts. Pampers diapers ran a promotion in which a coupon for diapers was sent to buyers who mailed in three proof-of-purchase seals. For durable goods, proper instructions on the care and use of the product may be useful, for they help the consumer receive full

Cents-off coupons encourage product contact.

product benefits. High-quality service and maintenance provided by the seller can similarly help to develop long-term client relationships.

Communication

A final set of behaviours that marketers attempt to encourage involves **communication.** There are two basic audiences with which marketers want consumers to communicate. They want consumers to (1) provide the company with marketing information and (2) tell other potential consumers about the product and encourage them to purchase it. Of course, consumers can communicate with the company or other consumers about products, brands, or stores any time, not just at the end of the purchase sequence. We describe this behaviour as a final step because consumers who have purchased and used a product are likely to be more knowledgeable about it and more influential in telling other consumers about it.

From consumer to marketer

Marketers typically want at least three types of information from consumers. First they want information *about the consumer* to help them investigate the quality of their marketing strategy and the success of market segmentation. Warranty cards are traditionally used for this purpose. They commonly ask about consumer demographics, what magazines consumers read, where they obtained information about the product, where they purchased it, and what competing brands they own or have tried. Free gifts are sometimes offered to encourage consumers to return warranty cards—as well as subtle threats that the warranty is not in force unless the card is filled out and returned promptly. Of course, legally, companies cannot void warranties for failure to return the cards promptly.

A second type of information sought from consumers is names of *other potential buyers* of the product. Some firms and organisations offer rewards or premiums if the names of several potential buyers are given and a larger reward if any of these prospects actually makes a purchase. Brokerage houses and real estate companies usually ask

Positive consumption experiences may increase the probability of repurchase, such as buying another pair of Avias.

their clients to give them names of new contacts. Scot Foto includes a mailer in its processing package: "Give this mailer to a friend and you will both receive a free film and free Scot coupon book worth up to $60 in savings."

Finally, marketers also seek consumer information about *defective products*. Money-back or other guarantees that require the consumer to contact the store or company provide this information and also reduce the consumer's risk of loss. Eaton's department stores pioneered money-back guarantees, a strategy that helped the company become one of the largest retail stores in Canada.

From consumer to consumer

Marketers also want consumers to tell others about the product. A product that is effective and performs well may encourage this behaviour, but other tactics can encourage it as well. Tupperware parties have long been used to take advantage of the fact that consumers respond favourably to information from their friends and to create an environment that encourages purchase. This approach has been so successful that in the first 25 years of existence Tupperware doubled its sales and earnings every five years.

Newly opened bars and lounges frequently offer customers free drinks to encourage them not only to return but also to tell others about the place and to bring their friends. Word-of-mouth communication is the primary way such establishments become popular. Health clubs, such as Nautilus Plus and Gold's Gym, often run promotions where members who bring in new customers get special rates for themselves as well as for their friends. One cable TV company offered $10 to any subscriber who got a friend to subscribe. Such tactics increase incidence of other behaviours in the purchase sequence as well.

MARKETING IMPLICATIONS

Managers can analyse consumer behaviour and develop marketing programs to increase the probability of behaviour that is advantageous to them. (This general approach could also be used to develop strategies for discouraging undesired behaviours, although we do not explore such strategies.)

Two tasks must be performed to use this analysis model. First, given appropriate marketing objectives, the manager must develop a sequential model of the behaviours that are needed or desired from the consumer. To develop this sequence, we use the seven-stage model (in Exhibit 13.1), but other models can be developed for various types of purchase/consumption situations.

Second, after the behaviours are identified, their frequency must be measured to determine baseline data, or a starting place for comparison. This step is necessary to provide a benchmark for evaluating the effectiveness of the strategy implemented. There are many ways to measure various consumer behaviours; some examples are provided in Exhibit 13.4. These measurement methods are commonly used in current marketing research, although they are not always used sequentially at every behaviour stage.

One approach that does allow monitoring of a number of stages in a purchase sequence is the **scanner cable method,** available from research companies such as Information Resources Inc. (IRI) and A. C. Nielsen Company of Canada. Because this method is consistent with the requirements of a consumer behaviour management model, we briefly describe how one such system works.

IRI's research systems are designed to predict which products will be successful and what ads work best to sell them. It has been expanded from grocery stores to include drugstores and mass merchandisers as well. IRI assembles consumer panels in a number of cities and monitors over 60,000 U.S. households. It plans to monitor purchases of 6,000 Canadian households. For example, it monitors purchases in 2,700 grocery stores in 66

EXHIBIT 13.4

Examples of methods used to measure consumption behaviours

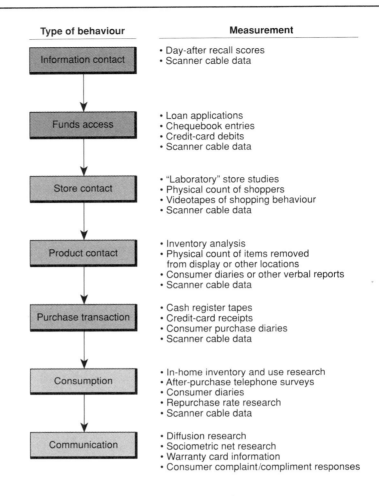

Type of behaviour	Measurement
Information contact	• Day-after recall scores • Scanner cable data
Funds access	• Loan applications • Chequebook entries • Credit-card debits • Scanner cable data
Store contact	• "Laboratory" store studies • Physical count of shoppers • Videotapes of shopping behaviour • Scanner cable data
Product contact	• Inventory analysis • Physical count of items removed from display or other locations • Consumer diaries or other verbal reports • Scanner cable data
Purchase transaction	• Cash register tapes • Credit-card receipts • Consumer purchase diaries • Scanner cable data
Consumption	• In-home inventory and use research • After-purchase telephone surveys • Consumer diaries • Repurchase rate research • Scanner cable data
Communication	• Diffusion research • Sociometric net research • Warranty card information • Consumer complaint/compliment responses

markets ranging from big cities to small towns. Many leading companies use IRI, including General Foods, Procter & Gamble, General Mills, and Frito-Lay.

Consumer panel members provide demographic information, how many TVs they own, the types of newspapers and magazines they read, and who does most of the shopping. IRI issues a special bar-coded identification card that shoppers present to the cashier when they pay for products in participating supermarkets or drugstores. By passing the card over the scanner or entering the digits manually into the register, the cashier records everything each shopper has purchased. One executive for Frito-Lay, which used IRI's services for the introduction of Sun Chips snacks, concluded, "The beauty of scanner data is that we get a complete description of a household from the panel and can match it with purchasing patterns. We know exactly who's out there buying our product and that helps us design marketing and advertising plans accordingly."[5]

A number of behaviours in the purchase sequence can be monitored and influenced using scanner methods. First, information contact can be influenced because media habits of households are monitored, and commercials can be changed until contact occurs. Funds access can be monitored on the cash register tape by recording prices and the method of payment. Because every purchase in the store is recorded, store contact, product contact, and purchase transaction information is available, along with dates and times of these behaviours. The relative effectiveness of various sales promotions and other

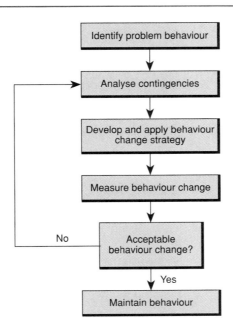

EXHIBIT 13.5

A model for managing consumer behaviour

marketing strategies on specific consumer behaviours can thereby be determined and successful promotions offered again to encourage store and brand loyalty. The time between purchases can be determined, so information is also available on consumption and usage rates.

Technology allows quite efficient measurement of consumer behaviours, although there presumably are limits to the benefits of extended research on such behaviour. While scanner data provide substantial benefits, many firms cannot afford the costs. Simpler, less expensive methods—such as analysis of advertising expenditures and shipping orders in various markets—may provide useful information about consumer behaviour.

Exhibit 13.5 offers a model for managing a sequence of behaviours that is based on ideas in applied behaviour analysis. In its emphasis on the development and maintenance of consumer behaviour, the model is fully consistent with the objectives of marketing management and common marketing strategies. It offers a more systematic, efficient approach than many models used in current marketing practice.

Each behaviour in the purchase/consumption sequence depends on many factors. In some cases—such as the promotion of a clearly superior product—information contact may be sufficient to drive the entire behaviour chain and result in performance of all the required behaviours. Even a simple comment about a product by a trusted friend may result in the performance of all behaviours in the sequence. In many cases, however, initial consumer behaviours are performed with sufficient frequency that they could lead to the other behaviours—yet the other behaviours do not occur. For example, consumers may go to retail stores where the product is carried and may even look at the product, but not purchase it. In other cases, information contact may not occur, so no additional behaviours follow.

Identify problem behaviour

The problem or **target behaviour** is the earliest behaviour in the sequence that is not being performed, or is not being performed appropriately or frequently enough to lead to the next behaviour. Such a problem could occur with any behaviour in the sequence. The marketer identifies the problem behaviour by examining the differences in behaviour frequencies from one stage to the next. Consumer research can provide information on results at each stage:

1. **Information contact:** 90 percent of the target market has been exposed to two commercials per week in the home for the past month. Unaided recall scores are 40 percent; 30 percent of respondents indicate they like the features of our product.

2. **Funds access:** 87 percent of the target market purchases a competitive brand at the same price as ours; 67 percent pays with credit cards.

3. **Store contact:** 96 percent of the target market shops at least once per week in stores where our brand is carried; 40 percent comes into the physical vicinity of our product once per week.

4. **Product contact:** 30 percent of the target market looks at our product; 14 percent picks up the product and inspects it; 2 percent takes our product.

5. **Purchase transactions:** slightly less than 2 percent pays for our product; a few replace it on the shelf.

6. **Consumption:** most purchasers use the product within two weeks of purchase.

7. **Communication:** no indication of significant communication with other consumers; 60 percent of warranty cards are returned in three weeks.

What is the problem behaviour in this example? Consumers' information contact, funds access, and store contact are all exceptionally good. Even some phases of product contact are good, but notice how few consumers actually take the product with them. There are several ways to deal with any problem behaviour in the sequence.

Analyse contingencies

Once the problem behaviour is identified, the contingencies or relationships among the behaviour and the environment can be analysed. Among the major contingencies are the effects of competition on maintaining or changing consumer behaviour. Many successful firms attempt to interfere with new-product test marketing (or other marketing efforts) of their competitors to avoid losing market share and to confound competitors' research results. Other contingencies that require analysis are the nature of the target market and the marketing mix elements, particularly those elements most closely related to the problem behaviour. Exhibit 13.6 suggests one way to link the major marketing mix elements with the stages of behaviours.

Analysing contingencies is an important step because it represents a search for the reasons particular behaviours do not occur. Assessment of affective and cognitive variables as well as behaviour environment interactions may also contribute valuable

---

EXHIBIT 13.6

Primary relationships between consumer behaviours and marketing mix elements

Consumer Behaviours	Elements			
	Product	Price	Promotion	Place
Information contact			X	
Funds access		X		
Store contact				X
Product contact	X			X
Purchase transaction	X	X	X	X
Consumption	X			
Communication	X	X	X	X

information. Many new products fail because consumers do not perceive a difference in them, so research on consumer perceptions and attitudes can be useful for investigating the problem and analysing contingencies.

Where product contact is the problem behaviour, analysis of the contingencies might begin with a comparison of our product and package with those of successful competitors. We could interview consumers to investigate their perceptions of and attitudes toward our product. We might directly investigate other contingencies, such as competitive differences in packaging, labelling, instructions for use, colours, and price.

Develop and apply behaviour change strategy

Once the problem behaviour is identified and the contingencies surrounding it analysed, a **behaviour change strategy** can be developed and applied. Such strategies might include any number of the processes we discussed earlier, such as positive reinforcement, negative reinforcement, shaping, classical conditioning, or modelling, among others. Positive reinforcement is generally recommended for encouraging behaviour because it is both effective and flexible. Of course, as with any marketing strategy, the costs and benefits of various procedures must be carefully assessed.

Returning to the example, suppose the analysis of contingencies reveals an important difference between our product and those of successful competitors. Their packaging gives detailed assembly and use instructions, while our package instructions are more sketchy. We might decide to improve the instructions and add pictures of models assembling and using the product. We could also include a toll-free number consumers can call for additional information or help.

Measure behaviour change

After implementing the strategy, we remeasure the target behaviour to determine whether the problem has been solved. If the behaviour has not changed sufficiently, we must re-analyse the contingencies and develop a new intervention strategy.

How much behaviour has to change for the strategy to be successful depends on the marketing objectives, the particular behaviour, and the situation. For example, if implementation of the strategy results in 3 percent (instead of 2 percent) of those who inspect the product actually purchasing it, this probably would not be considered a successful strategy. In fact, even this 50 percent increase might not cover the cost of the toll-free number. If the majority of those who inspect the product now purchase it, however, we might conclude we have successfully solved the behaviour problem.

In some cases, a very small amount of behaviour change may suffice for a strategy to be successful. For example, Procter & Gamble increased market share for Crest toothpaste from 35 percent to 41 percent by updating its formula, adding a gel version, and sharply increasing advertising and promotion. While a change in toothpaste market share of 6 percentage points may not sound impressive, it translates into millions of dollars in additional sales.

Maintain behaviour

If a new strategy is successful in developing a sufficient amount of behaviour, marketers must consider ways to maintain that behaviour. Because much consumer behaviour is habitual, maintaining behaviour is usually much easier and less expensive than developing it. In fact, one of the major reasons product introductions are so expensive is the promotional cost of developing the behaviour. Once a behaviour is developed, promotional costs usually can be decreased and behaviour can be maintained much more cheaply. As an example, in the most successful cigarette introduction in history, Brown & Williamson gave away free cartons of cigarettes and spent an estimated $150 million to develop use of Barclay cigarettes. Once the company obtained roughly a 2 percent market share (each share point is worth about $125 million to the manufacturer) it

CONSUMER
PERSPECTIVE

▶ 13.4

Developing loyalty
to Zellers

Zellers is determined to become the largest retailer in Canada. Unlike many other companies that either lost money or closed during the recession of the early 1990s, Zellers was very profitable. The company claims that it owes much of its success to aggressive advertising, precise market identification, and the Club Z program, which it claims is one of the most successful customer loyalty programs in North America. With every dollar spent in any Zellers store in Canada, a Club Z member earns points that can be used to purchase products for free. The company spent more than $20 million in 1994 in television advertising, much of it centred on the Club Z program. In 1994, there were more than 6 million Club Z members.

Zellers is not standing still in the customer-loyalty program game. In 1993, Imperial Esso and Zellers announced that all Esso cardholders could join the Club Z frequent-buyer program and collect 20 Club Z points for every dollar charged to the Esso credit card.

Source: Ken Riddell, "Pumping Up Promos," *Marketing,* April 18, 1994, p. 12; John Heinzl, "Club Z Leaving Its Mark," *Globe and Mail,* Dec. 6, 1991, p. B1.

eliminated carton giveaways and reduced promotional spending—and maintained much of the market share.

If positive reinforcers are used to develop a behaviour, very often their frequency and amount can be decreased to maintain the behaviour. If continuous schedules of reinforcement were initially employed, it may be possible to switch to ratio schedules and still maintain behaviour. Discount coupons of lower value may also be effective; requiring multiunit purchases to receive the same discount may maintain certain behaviours. In fact, encouraging multiunit purchases may not only help develop brand loyalty but also increase use of the product, because additional quantities are then readily available at home.

Different organisations will be concerned with maintaining different behaviours in the purchase/consumption chain. Credit-card companies want to maintain card use or loyalty across a variety of purchase situations; retailers want to maintain store contact or store loyalty; manufacturers want to maintain product contact or brand loyalty. From a behaviour viewpoint, these actions are controlled by contingencies in the environment, and loyalty is the degree to which the behaviours are repeated. Consumer Perspective 13.4 offers an example of Zellers' strategy to influence loyalty.

If a problem behaviour is changed and then maintained, marketers also need to investigate whether the remaining behaviours are now being performed appropriately and frequently enough to achieve the objectives. If not, they identify the new target behaviour that is blocking the behaviour chain—the next one in the sequence that is not being performed appropriately—and then repeat the stages in the model. This process continues until all of the behaviours are being performed appropriately.

No matter how successful a particular marketing strategy is, there is always room for improvement. In general, marketing strategies must be monitored continually for more efficient methods of maintaining behaviour as well as encouraging it.

Any consumer behaviour may decrease in frequency because of changes in the environment (such as more powerful or more frequent reinforcement by a competitor). Thus, while the model in Exhibit 13.5 provides a systematic way to focus directly on consumer behaviour, it does not replace analyses such as monitoring carefully and responding to competitive strategies. This is part of analysing contingencies in an ongoing marketing program.

Learning objective 1: *Describe a sequence of overt consumer behaviours involved in a retail consumer-goods purchase and explain the behaviours.*

▶ SUMMARY

A sequence of overt consumer behaviours includes information contact, funds access, store contact, product contact, purchase transaction, consumption, and communication.

Information contact occurs when consumers come into contact with products, stores, or brands. This stage includes behaviours such as reading or observing newspaper, magazine, and billboard ads, listening to radio commercials, watching TV commercials, and talking to salespeople and friends. Marketers encourage information contact and, in many cases, consumers also search for information.

Funds access involves the consumer behaviours involved in obtaining money for a purchase. These include withdrawing cash from a bank or cash machine, writing a cheque, opening a store charge account, or using other types of credit.

Store contact concerns the behaviours involved in coming into physical contact with a store. It includes locating, travelling to, and entering the store.

Product contact concerns the behaviours involved in coming into physical contact with products and brands. It includes locating a product in a store, obtaining it, and taking it to the point of exchange.

Purchase transaction refers to the exchange of consumer funds for products and services. It involves behaviours such as handing over payment, receiving change, and taking the product to where it will be used.

Consumption refers to consuming or using a product. It includes disposing of packaging or the used product itself and repurchase.

Communication involves behaviours in which consumers tell others about the product and their experiences with it. It includes communicating both with other consumers and with marketers through such means as warranty cards.

Learning objective 2: *Suggest several tactics marketers could use to influence each of these behaviours.*

Marketers could influence information contact by selecting and scheduling media consistent with the media habits of the target market. Attention-getting advertising features, such as colour, humour, and fear appeals, could also be used. Repetition of messages influences the probability of information contact.

Marketers could influence funds access by offering gifts to consumers who fill out credit-card applications, locating cash machines in malls, instituting liberal credit terms and cheque-cashing policies, and accepting a variety of credit cards.

Marketers could influence store contact by selecting convenient locations in high-traffic areas, using ads with maps and information phone numbers to aid shoppers, using outdoor signs and logos, featuring carnivals and other entertainment close to the store or mall, offering sales, and using window signs, displays, and other stimuli to attract consumers to enter a store.

Marketers could influence product contact by providing store directories and information booths, using displays and signs, and hiring helpful store personnel. Attractive, eye-catching packaging and salesclerks who escort consumers to product and exchange locations could also influence product contact.

Marketers could influence purchase transactions by having express checkout lanes, fast electronic scanners, and quick credit-card approvals. Prompts and reinforcers such as rebates could also influence purchase transactions.

Marketers could influence consumption by tactics such as providing seats in fast-food restaurants that are comfortable for only short periods and using prompts to encourage disposal of packaging. Repurchase of the same product or brand could be influenced by in- or on-package coupons and offers for bonus merchandise that require multiple purchases.

Marketers could influence communication by offering gifts for returning warranty cards and giving money-back guarantees. Free merchandise or discounts could also be used to reinforce consumers who bring friends to new retail outlets or give their friends' names to sellers of new services.

Learning objective 3: *Explain a model marketers could use to influence a sequence of consumer behaviours.*

The first thing marketers need to do is to identify the problem or target behaviour. This is the earliest behaviour in a sequence that is not being performed appropriately or frequently enough to lead to the next behaviour. The next step is to analyse the contingencies or relationships between the behaviour and the environment. Here marketers are looking for things in the environment that encourage or discourage the behaviour. Next, marketers can develop and apply a behaviour change strategy to encourage the target behaviour directly or overcome any barrier found in the previous stage that was discouraging it. Then they measure the amount of behaviour change resulting. If the strategy results in sufficient behaviour change, additional strategies can be employed to maintain the behaviour. If the strategy fails, the contingencies have to be reanalysed to find the problem.

▶ **KEY TERMS AND CONCEPTS**

information contact	purchase transaction	target behaviour
funds access	consumption	behaviour change strategy
store contact	communication	
product contact	scanner cable method	

▶ **REVIEW AND DISCUSSION QUESTIONS**

1. Describe the differences between traditional cognitive models of the adoption process and the behaviour sequence presented in Exhibit 13.1.

2. What advantages do you see in the use of the behaviour sequence model for marketing researchers and for marketing managers?

3. Use the behaviour sequence model to describe your recent purchases of a product and of a service.

4. Consider the challenge presented by the information contact stage of the behaviour sequence for each of the following: (*a*) a leading brand, (*b*) a new brand, and (*c*) an existing low-share brand.

5. Give some examples of marketing strategies aimed at addressing the funds access problems of university students.

6. Visit several local supermarkets and identify strategies used to increase product contact for grocery items.

7. List at least three situations where marketing efforts have been instrumental in changing your consumption or disposal behaviour for products you have purchased.

8. Assume the role of a marketing manager for each of the purchases you described for Question 3. Which behaviours would you want to change? Using the model in Exhibit 13.5, suggest behaviour change strategies you might recommend.

9. Use the model for managing consumer behaviour to suggest strategies for decreasing the frequency of post-holiday merchandise returns to a department store.

10. How would the concept of shaping relate to use of the consumer behaviour management model?

IV

THE ENVIRONMENT

OUTLINE

▶ 14. Introduction to the Environment
▶ 15. Cultural and Cross-Cultural Influences
▶ 16. Subculture and Social Class Influences
▶ 17. Reference Groups and Family Influences
▶ 18. Environmental Influences on Marketing Practices

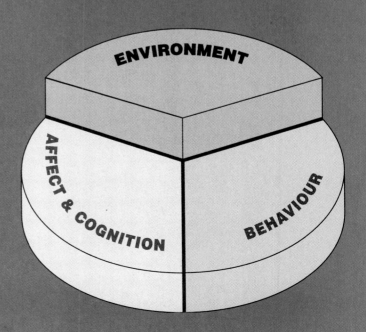

CHAPTER ▶ 14

Introduction to the Environment

LEARNING OBJECTIVES

After completing this chapter, you should be able to:

▶ 1. Define the environment and describe the difference between the macro- and micro-environment.

▶ 2. Define the social environment, identify the types of macro and micro social environments, and describe the flow of influence between the macro- and micro-environments.

▶ 3. Define the physical environment and give an example of how it can influence consumer behaviour.

▶ 4. Give two examples of how a marketing strategy can modify the environment and influence consumer behaviour.

▶ 5. Define a situation and describe the factors to be examined in a situation analysis.

▶ 6. Describe the five common consumer situations and identify behaviours that are important in each situation.

HIGH-TECH BINGO PALACE LURES GAMBLERS

Jean McCorry stood in line outside Club Regent for an hour to be the first to get her quarters into one of the slot machines. McCorry was one of hundreds of gamblers who stood in line in June 1993 to get into the first of two gambling palaces opening in Winnipeg. They represent the Manitoba Lottery Foundation's bid to grab an estimated $100 million in gambling dollars that drain out of the province every year.

The $15 million high-tech playing house is filled with the newest in gambling technology. "If we are going to compete with those glitzy gaming houses south of our border, there is no such thing as overdoing it," said one owner. Club Regent sports a Caribbean village theme, complete with a live calypso band, a forest of palm trees, silk flowers, and fountains.

With its upscale combination of theme rooms, slot machines, electronic horse racing and video blackjack, Club Regent is more akin to the Crystal Casino than the traditional smoke-filled halls associated with bingo. Traditionalists in the crowd can still play bingo, but they get to do so in a room landscaped with flowers and designed by architects and interior design consultants for improved acoustics and viewing.

Like the major U.S. casinos, Club Regent was designed to create an environment that impresses people yet makes them feel comfortable. All aspects of time, noise, and visual effects were taken into consideration to develop an adult playland.[1]

THE ENVIRONMENT

The **environment** refers to all the physical and social characteristics of a consumer's external world, including physical objects (products and stores), spatial relationships (location of products and stores in space), and the social behaviour of other people (who is around and what are they doing?). As one part of the Wheel of Consumer Analysis (see Exhibit 14.1), the environment can influence a consumer's affective and cognitive responses and behaviour. A consumer's cognitive and affective systems will respond to the environment of a new supermarket by interpreting features of this environment and deciding what behaviours to perform to accomplish the shopping goals.

Marketers are especially interested in the *perceived* or *interpreted environment,* sometimes called the functional environment, because this is what influences consumers' behaviours.[2] Because each consumer draws on a unique set of knowledge, meanings, and beliefs in interpreting any environment, the perceived or functional environment is somewhat different for each consumer. However, consumers within a society or culture perceive many parts of the physical and social environment similarly. For example, large groups of Canadian consumers probably have similar perceptions of shopping malls (or credit cards or fast-food restaurants) and therefore use them in similar ways. Marketers need to understand the interpretations of the environment shared by groups of consumers; they are seldom interested in the idiosyncratic perceptions of individual consumers. Fortunately, marketers can usually identify enough consumers who share common interpretations to form a target market segment.

The environment can be analysed at two levels, macro and micro. Marketers need to determine which level of environment analysis is relevant for a marketing problem and design their research and marketing strategies appropriately. The *macro-environment* includes large-scale, general environmental factors such as the climate, economic conditions, political system, and general landscape (seashore, mountains, prairie). Macro-environmental factors have a general influence on behaviour, as when the state of the economy influences aggregate purchases of homes, cars, and stocks. Consumer Perspective 14.1 describes how changes in the macro-environment can create a marketing opportunity.

The *micro-environment* refers to the more tangible physical and social aspects of someone's immediate surroundings: the dirty floor in a store, a talkative salesperson, the hot weather today, or the people in your family or household. Such small-scale factors can have a direct influence on consumers' specific behaviours and affective and cognitive responses. For instance, people tend not to linger in dirty or crowded stores; most

EXHIBIT 14.1

The Wheel of Consumer Analysis

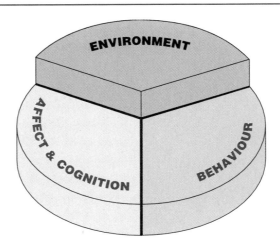

CONSUMER
PERSPECTIVE

14.1

Changes in macro-
environment
create market
opportunities

A red-faced young couple scope out the wares of the Condom Shack on Toronto's trendy Queen Street. As the woman reaches for a European brand of ultrathin condoms, a perky salesclerk approaches and asks her if she'd like to feel an inflated sample beside the display.

Stores like the Condom Shack, Epoch Condom, and Sexuality are trying to make buying condoms not only respectable but fun. And they aren't the only ones. Condom manufacturers are introducing new varieties, advertising on TV, and running contests and other promotions in drugstores, which are still their biggest retail distributors. As a result, condoms have finally moved out of the shadow of the prescription counter and into the mainstream.

According to Scot Matheson, product care manager for Carter Products, maker of Trojans, education programs linked to AIDS prevention are largely responsible for all this activity. The condom market took off in 1987 when the World Health Organization targeted AIDS as a major issue. Sales jumped by more than 25 percent in Canada that year, another 7 percent in 1988 and an estimated 5 percent in 1989. In 1993, the domestic market was worth more than $40 million annually.

Though the vast majority of condom sales still occur in the big drugstore chains, condom specialty shops are making an impact, partly because they've attracted a lot of positive publicity. "These stores have gotten away from the sleazy image of sex shops. They developed clean, modern-looking stores with friendly staff, and you can go in and touch the condom before you buy it," says a product manager for Ortho Pharmaceuticals, manufacturer of Shields. "They've done a great job at hyping awareness of the category."

Source: Hugh Filman "Making Safe Sex Respectable, Trendy and Fun," *Marketing*, March 29, 1993, pp. 14–15.

consumers wait until spring as opposed to February to go window-shopping outdoors; you get frustrated and angry in a slow-moving checkout line when you want to get home to prepare dinner. Consumer Perspective 14.2 gives an example of how the micro-environment can influence consumers' behaviour.

ASPECTS OF THE ENVIRONMENT

The environment has two aspects or dimensions—the social and physical environment. Marketing managers have direct control over some aspects of the social and physical environment, which they form into marketing strategies. But they have little or no control over large parts of the social and physical environment. Both the controllable and uncontrollable aspects of the social and physical environment can influence consumers' overt behaviours as well as their affective and cognitive responses.

The social environment

Broadly defined, the **social environment** includes all social interactions between and among people. Consumers can interact with other people either directly (you discuss sports equipment or clothes with a friend, you talk to a salesperson) or vicariously (you watch your father negotiate a car price, you observe the clothing other people are wearing). People can learn from both types of social interactions, direct and vicarious.

It is useful to distinguish between macro and micro levels of the social environment. The *macro social environment* refers to the indirect and vicarious social interactions among very large groups of people. Researchers have studied three macro social environments—culture, subculture, and social class—that have broad and powerful influences on the values, beliefs, attitudes, emotions, and behaviours of individual consumers in

CONSUMER PERSPECTIVE

▶ 14.2

The window-shopping environment

When Craig and Mary Ellen Budreau moved to Paisley, Ontario, they wanted a modern pharmacy with an old-fashioned feel. Window displays were part of the game plan even before the couple bought the store. They thought it would be a good way to attract customers. And they were right; the custom-made displays stop shoppers in their tracks.

Mary Ellen Budreau said the displays have more effect than an ad in the paper. "I think it's made a big difference and it's certainly improved business."

The creative displays are changed every month, and animated displays are produced at Christmas, Easter, Halloween, and a few other times to make the window snazzier than the typical pharmacy display.

There is no doubt in the Budreaus' minds that the window displays have increased window shopping, which has ultimately led to more customers coming into the store.

Source: Nancy Deutsch "Better than Advertising," *Drug Merchandising*, 75 (4), April 1993, pp. 36–37.

those groups. For instance, a marketer might find that consumers in different subcultures or social classes have quite different means-end chains concerning a product, which means they are likely to respond differently to marketing strategies. Such differences make macro social environments useful for market segmentation.

The *micro social environment* includes face-to-face social interactions among smaller groups of people such as families and reference groups. These direct social interactions can have strong influences on consumers' knowledge and feelings about products, stores, or ads and on their consumption behaviour. For instance, most people learn acceptable, appropriate behaviours and acquire many of their values, beliefs, and attitudes through direct social interaction with their families and reference groups. The influence of families can continue for years as some adult consumers purchase the same brands, patronise the same stores, and shop in the same way their parents once did.

Families and reference groups are influenced by the macro social environments of culture, subcultures, and social class. Exhibit 14.2 illustrates the flow of influence from the

This Japanese family constitutes a micro social environment for each person in the family.

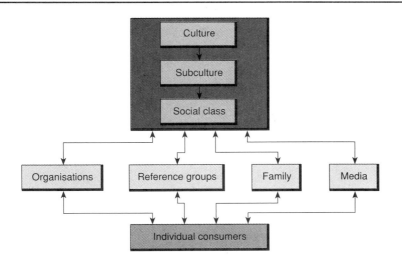

EXHIBIT 14.2

Flows of influence in social environment

macro social environments of culture, subculture, and social class to the micro social environments of reference groups and family and then on to the individual consumer (and the reverse influence too). We discuss these social influences at length in Chapters 15, 16, and 17.

The hierarchical relationships portrayed in Exhibit 14.2 can help us understand how various levels of the social environment influence consumers. For instance, consumers in different subcultures may have the same cultural value but reflect it in different ways, just

Visine reminds consumers of aspects of the physical environment that make the product self-relevant.

Certain products such as iced tea sell best in summertime when the weather is hot.

as consumers in different social classes may attempt to satisfy a subcultural value in different ways. Consider how people can satisfy the common Canadian value of sense of achievement. A person living in a rural subculture might fulfill this value by going to agriculture school, earning a degree, and becoming an excellent farmer. In an urban subculture, a person with the same achievement value might go to law school, earn a degree, and become a successful attorney. Similarly, the social class of an individual can influence the choice of higher education (a local community college, a large city university, or an internationally famous university). In turn, these macro social influences are filtered by a person's family situation (parents' expectations and financial support) and reference groups (where one's friends are going to school). In sum, while many individuals may share the same cultural values, their methods of achieving these values may differ considerably, depending on their macro and micro social environments. This means people in different social environments use different means to reach the same ends.

Exhibit 14.2 also identifies other social entities involved in transferring meanings, values, and behaviour norms from the macro social environment to individual consumers. These include media such as TV programs, newspapers, and magazines, movies, literature, and music, as well as religious and educational institutions, police and the courts, government—and business firms that develop marketing strategies to influence individual customers.

The physical environment

The **physical environment** includes all the nonhuman, physical aspects of the external world in which behaviour occurs. Virtually any aspect of the physical environment can affect consumer behaviour. The physical environment can be divided into spatial and nonspatial elements. Spatial elements include physical factors of all types (including products and brands) as well as landscapes, cities, stores, and design elements of the environment. Nonspatial elements include intangible factors such as climate (cold/hot, humid/dry), illumination, noise level, and time. Here we discuss four factors in the nonspatial environment: time, weather, lighting, and colour.

Time

Time has a great effect on consumer behaviour.[3] Behaviour can be influenced by the time of day (stores tend to be more crowded during lunch hour), the day of the week (Mondays are often slow days for restaurants), the day of the month (sales may drop off just before the end of the month and pick up again after the first), and the season of the year (in the pre-Christmas holiday season, people's shopping behaviours are quite different from other times of the year).

The recent battles in many markets across Canada over Sunday shopping laws show how sensitive marketers can be to the time factor. Different parties held many conflicting views. For instance, many retailers and grocers complained that pharmacies held an unfair advantage as they were legally open on Sundays though they sold more than pharmaceutical goods. Major chain retail stores complained that many customers were being lost to cross-border shopping on one of the few "family shopping" days. Indeed, once laws were changed, retail sales across the country rose significantly, in large part due to the decline in cross-border shopping. Smaller corner stores, however, suffered greatly due to the new liberal Sunday shopping regulations, which loosened their lock on Sunday consumers. Many have had to reorganise their marketing plans to adapt to the new environment. Thus, what seems to be a minor change in time effects often has a large impact on marketers and consumers.

Weather

Many firms recognise that weather influences consumer behaviour.[4] Obviously, tuques, gloves, and heavy coats are winter products, and most suntan lotion, air conditioners, and swimsuits are sold during the summer. Some firms pay even daily attention to the weather. For example, Campbell's Soup Co. bases some of its spot radio advertising on weather reports. When a storm is forecast, Campbell's ads urge listeners to stock up on soup before the weather worsens; after the storm hits, the ad copy changes to tell people to relax indoors and warm themselves with soup. While research on the relationships between weather and consumer behaviour is in its early stages, the extreme seasons in most parts of Canada are certainly an important influence on affect (such as moods), cognitions, and purchase behaviour. Consumer Perspective 14.3 presents some examples.

Lighting

There is considerable evidence that lighting affects behaviour. In general, people work better in brighter rooms, although they find direct overhead lighting unpleasant. In business meetings, people who intend to make themselves heard sit under or near lights, while those who intend to be quiet often sit in darker areas. Intimate candlelight may draw people together; bright floodlights can cause people to hurry past a location. Overall, lighting may affect the way people work and interact with others, their comfort, and even their mental and physical health.

While it seems likely that lighting affects consumers' moods, anxiety levels, willingness to shop, and purchase behaviour, little research directly addresses this topic. One discussion of lighting in retail stores and malls did suggest that specialised lighting systems can increase sales dramatically.[5] W. W. Electronics of Toronto offers a light projection system that allows companies to project their logo onto surfaces, such as in a mall, regardless of

CONSUMER PERSPECTIVE

▶ 14.3

Temperature and seasonal sales

Although many products sell uniformly throughout the year, it's essential for marketers to take into account seasonal factors. The seasons influence not only what consumers buy but how they think and feel during different times of the year. Canadian monthly trends include:

January: A depressing month with the highest death rate and guilt feelings about overindulging and overspending during the holiday season. A good time for the sale of fitness programs. A great sale can draw consumers out of the doldrums.

February: Kept indoors by wintery blasts, people develop cabin fever. Incentives are needed to get consumers to shop.

March: Consumers are eagerly awaiting spring weather, but the weather doesn't always cooperate. Caution is required regarding sales and promotions of spring-related items.

April: Spring weather inspires householders into action cleaning and fixing up. Product services to meet these demands and, with the growing concern for the environment, a green twist to promotion can boost sales.

May: Improvement in the weather draws people out to the stores. Getting in shape for the summer months ahead becomes a priority for many people. Sporting goods and sportswear retail sales usually begin. Mother's Day is a major drawing card.

June: The weather is usually delightful, and most of Canada is consumed with weddings (38 percent of Canadian adults attend or participate in a wedding each year, and June is the peak month).

the surrounding light diffusion. Trans-Optique of Montreal has point-of-purchase backlit signs that attach to existing light fixtures to attract consumers' attention without cluttering aisle space.

Colour

Colour has been shown to have a variety of physical and psychological effects on both humans and animals. A study of the effects of colour on consumer perceptions of retail store environment found that while consumers were drawn to warm colours (red and yellow), they felt that warm-colour environments were generally unpleasant; cool colors (blue and green) did not draw consumers, but were rated as pleasant.[6] The authors offer these implications of their work for store design:

> Warm-color environments are appropriate for store windows and entrances, as well as for buying situations associated with unplanned impulse purchases. Cool colors may be appropriate where customer deliberations over the purchase decision are necessary. Warm, tense colors in situations where deliberations are common may make shopping unpleasant for consumers and may result in premature termination of the shopping trip. On the other hand, warm colors may produce a quick decision to purchase in cases where lengthy deliberations are not necessary and impulse purchases are common.

Act Media Canada of Mississauga, Ontario, offers electronic coupon dispensers with blinking red lights that help attract shoppers' attention.

Marketing implications

Although much of the environment is uncontrollable, marketing managers can control certain aspects of it. In fact, every marketing strategy involves changing some aspect of the social and physical environment. In this sense, marketers can be seen as environmental managers.[7] A marketing strategy alters the social and physical environment in an attempt to influence consumers' affective and cognitive responses and their behaviours. For ex-

July: The hot summer weather allows Canadians to commit to having fun, with outdoor barbecues, picnics, summer camps—despite economic woes.

August: This is the peak month for travel and back-to-school planning.

September: This is the end of summer fun and the start of business as usual. A strong month for sales of books, jeans, shoes, and other school-related items. With kids back at school, older Canadians take advantage of less crowded and less costly travel opportunities (e.g., VIA Rail's Trans Canada Great Getaway Escape).

October: Thanksgiving and Halloween are the important marketing events. Other purchases often include home improvement and winter wear.

November: Santa Claus parades and holiday shopping, mostly for out-of-town relatives and friends, begin. While most people do not admit to being influenced by early season shopping displays, there is evidence to suggest that the earlier Christmas displays come out, the earlier people begin to shop.

December: Retail sales usually peak in December, particularly for toy and jewellery stores.

It is important for marketers to know when the consumer buying decision will be made and to advertise at that time. As Ecclesiastes said, "To everything there is a season."

Source: Jo Marney, "A Season for All Products," *Marketing*, Jan. 11, 1993, p. 10.

ample, aspects of the physical environment are changed by promotion strategies (a magazine ad, a billboard along the highway), product strategies (a new squeeze bottle for Crest toothpaste, a styling change in the Ford Escort), pricing strategies (a "sale" sign in a window, a price tag on a sweater), and distribution strategies (the location of a Harvey's, a product display in a store). Consumer Perspective 14.2 described how store displays, a simple aspect of the physical environment, can influence consumers. Marketing managers may also create marketing strategies that modify aspects of the social environment. For instance, Lexus trains its car salespeople to be less aggressive and less pushy than traditional car salespeople. A health club encourages its members to invite a friend for a free workout. Wal-Mart stations a greeter at the store entrance to smile and welcome customers.

Most environments contain an endless variety of stimuli that could influence consumer affect, cognition, and behaviour. For instance, retail stores include social factors such as salespeople and other shoppers, along with physical factors such as store layout, lighting, noise, scents, temperature, shelf space and displays, signs, and the merchandise. We discuss how four of these characteristics—store layout, signs and price information, shelf space and displays, and music—can influence consumers.

Store layout

Store layout can influence how long consumers stay in the store, how many products they come into visual contact with, and what routes they travel within the store. These behaviours in turn may affect the products bought and the number of purchases made. Two basic types of store layouts are grid and free-flow.

Exhibit 14.3a presents an example of a *grid layout* common in many groceries and drugstores.[8] Most counters and fixtures are at right angles to each other, which create structured channels, with merchandise counters acting as barriers to and guides for traffic flow.

EXHIBIT 14.3a

Basic store layouts

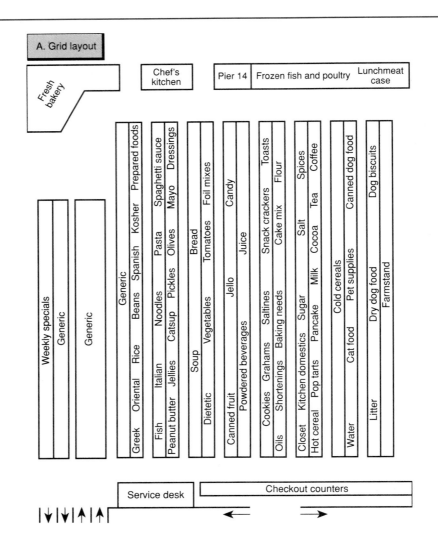

A supermarket grid layout is designed to increase the number of products a consumer comes into visual contact with, thus increasing the probability of purchase. Because produce, meat, and dairy products are typically high-margin items, the grid design is intended to channel consumers toward these more profitable products. In fact, 80 to 90 percent of all consumers shopping in supermarkets pass these three areas. Similarly, the location of frequently purchased items toward the back of the store requires consumers who may be shopping only for these items to pass by many other items. Because the probability of purchasing other items is increased once the consumer sees them, the grid layout can increase the number of items purchased.

The grid layout is used in department stores, mass merchandisers, and discount stores to direct customer traffic down the main aisles. Typically, these retailers put highly sought merchandise along the walls to pull customers past slower-moving merchandise. For example, sale merchandise may be placed along the walls not only to draw consumers to these areas, but also to reward consumers for spending more time in the store and shopping carefully. This may increase the probability of consumers returning to the store and following similar traffic patterns on repeat visits.

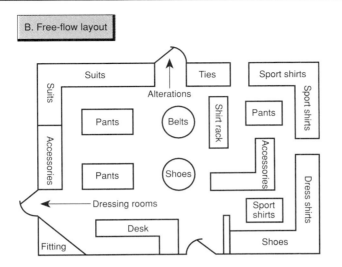

EXHIBIT 14.3b

Basic store layouts

Source: J. Barry Mason, Morris L. Mayer, and Hazel Ezell, *Retailing,* 4th ed. Burr Ridge, Ill.: Richard D. Irwin, Inc., 1991, pp. 461–62.

Exhibit 14.3b shows a *free-flow layout.* Here, the merchandise and fixtures are grouped into clusters that allow a free flow of customer traffic. Merchandise is identified by fixtures and signs, and customers can see other departments from any place in the store. The free-flow approach is often used in specialty stores, boutiques, and apparel stores to encourage relaxed shopping, browsing, and impulse purchases. Also, the free-flow layout helps salespeople show consumers different types of merchandise and sell multiple items, such as a shirt and a tie with a suit, or a purse along with a pair of shoes.

Signs

Retail stores often use *signs* to direct consumers to the merchandise and to communicate price information and product benefits. One study investigated how sales of several products were influenced by the type of product information on a sign (price or benefit) and

Signs are part of the in-store environment.

EXHIBIT 14.4

Effects of three types of signs on daily sales

Type of Sign	Units Sold at Regular Price	Units Sold at Sale Price
No sign	7.7	15.4
Price sign	6.1	19.1
Benefit sign	7.8	23.0

Source: Gary F. McKinnon, J. Patrick Kelly, and E. Doyle Robinson, "Sales Effects of Point-of-Purchase In-Store Signing," *Journal of Retailing*, Summer 1981, p. 57.

the price on the sign (regular or discounted price).[9] The results, presented in Exhibit 14.4, show that (a) the price level influenced sales more than the type of information on the sign, (b) a price sign did not increase sales at regular prices, but did when the item was on sale, and (c) a sign describing product benefits increased sales at both regular and sales prices, but had a greater effect when combined with a discounted price.

Shelf space and displays

Most marketers believe increased *shelf space* and more *in-store displays* capture consumer attention and generate sales.[10] A study compared sales generated by normal shelf space to sales obtained with expanded shelf space (twice the normal shelf space) and special displays (regular shelf space plus special end-of-aisle or within-aisle displays). Exhibit 14.5 shows that manipulating both aspects of the spatial environment increased sales in four product categories, but special displays consistently outperformed expanded shelf space.[11] Consumer Perspective 14.4 presents additional evidence of display effects on purchase behaviour.

Music

Considerable research supports the idea that background *music* played in retail stores or restaurants while other activities are being performed influences consumers' affect, cognitions, and behaviour.

One study found that the tempo of such music changes the behaviour of supermarket shoppers. No music, slow music, and fast music had different effects on the pace of in-store traffic.[12] Traffic flow was slowest when slow-tempo music was played and fastest under the fast-tempo treatment. The slow-tempo musical selections generated higher sales volumes because consumers spent more time in the store. On average, sales were 38.2 percent greater under the slow-tempo condition than under the fast-tempo condition. Interestingly, when questioned after shopping, consumers showed little awareness of the

EXHIBIT 14.5

Percentage increase in unit sales for expanded shelf space and special display

Product	Expanded Shelf Space	Special Display
Camay soap (bath)	39%	243%
Piggly Wiggly pie shells (2 per pkg.)	30	185
White House apple juice (32 oz.)	16	77
Mahatma rice (1 lb.)	27	103

Source: Reprinted from J. B. Wilkinson, J. Barry Mason, and Christine H. Paksoy, "Assessing the Impact of Short-Term Supermarket Strategy Variables," *Journal of Marketing Research* 19 (February 1982), p. 79. Published by the American Marketing Association.

CONSUMER PERSPECTIVE

14.4

The front end: Consolidating profits

Supermarket customers can be held captive at the checkout counter for up to two minutes, and today's experienced retailers know that a well-merchandised front end can earn increased profits.

It requires increased effort from retailers and manufacturers alike, but it has paid off; industry experts say from 1.5 to 3 percent of total sales are made at the front end. And it's generally agreed that the front end provides the greatest return on investment in terms of sales per square foot. Some say it's the most profitable area in the store.

Of customers entering the store, 99 percent buy something and leave through the checkout. Of those, 10 percent leave with a front-end product. Whether they leave with confectionary or candy items, cigarettes, disposable lighters or razors, batteries, camera film, or magazines, it's something that will be consumed in relatively short order. It's something they'll pick up again on their next trip.

Source: Kara Kuryllowicz, "The Front End: Consolidating Profit," *Canadian Grocer*, 102 (11), November 1988, pp. 40, 42–45.

music that had been playing in the supermarket. Thus, it seems likely that music affected behaviour without consumers being totally conscious of it. In terms of marketing strategy, the author suggests that:

. . . in some retailing situations, the objective may be to slow customer movement, keeping people in the store for as long as possible in an attempt to encourage them to purchase more. However, in other situations, the objective may be the opposite, that is, to move customers along as a way of increasing sales volume. A restaurant, for instance, will most likely want to speed people up, especially during lunch, when the objective is to maximize the "number of seats turned" in a very short period of time, normally about two hours or less. Playing slow-tempo music in a restaurant might result in fewer seats turned and lower profit, although it could encourage return visits if customers preferred a relaxed luncheon atmosphere. . . . the music chosen must match the objectives of the business and the specific market situation.[13]

SITUATIONS

Because a huge number of elements make up the social and physical environment, marketers may find it difficult to identify the most important environmental influences on consumers' affect, cognitions, and behaviours. It can be easier to analyse the influences of the environment in the context of a specific situation.[14] A situation is neither the tangible physical environment (a checkout counter, a storefront, your living room, the temperature today, a landscape) nor the objective features of the social environment (the number of people in a store, the time of day).[15] *A situation is determined or defined by a person who is acting in an environment for some purpose.* A situation occurs over a period of time that can be very short (buying a soda in a vending machine), somewhat longer (eating lunch), or protracted (buying a house). The person's goals define the situation's beginning (goal activation or problem recognition), middle (working to achieve the goal), and end (achieving the goal). Thus, a **situation** is described as a *sequence of goal-directed behaviours, along with affective and cognitive responses, and the various environments in which they occur.* For instance, going to the mall to look for a new tape or CD is a shopping situation. This view of situations as a series of goal-directed interactions among the environment, affect and cognitions, and behaviour is consistent with the Wheel of Consumer Analysis (see Exhibit 14.1).

Situations vary in *complexity*. Some situations involve simple goals, relatively few behaviours, and few affective and cognitive responses, all of which occur within a single physical and social environment. Examples of relatively simple consumption-related situations include buying a stamp at the post office, bargaining with a salesperson over the price of a stereo system, or discussing a winter break trip with your friends over dinner. Other consumer situations are more complex. Complex situations may take place in several physical and social environments, involve multiple (perhaps conflicting) goals, and require many different behaviours and cognitive and affective responses. Shopping for a new winter coat and browsing in antique shops on Sunday afternoon are examples of more complex situations.

Other consumer-related situations are common and *recurring*. For instance, Canadian consumers frequently buy gas for their cars, watch TV in the evening, shop for new clothes, rent videos, and go to grocery stores. As their experiences accumulate over time, consumers form clear goals, develop consistent cognitive interpretations of these recurring situations, and learn appropriate behaviours. Thereafter, when the consumer encounters a familiar situation, appropriate knowledge schemas and scripts may be activated from memory. They in turn influence consumers' behavioural, affective, and cognitive responses in that situation. To the extent that people tend to form approximately the same interpretations for common consumer-related situations, their behaviours will also tend to be similar. Consequently, marketers can develop marketing strategies that should affect consumers in a target segment in similar ways.

If consumers do not have clear goals or relevant knowledge when faced with a new or unfamiliar situation, they may have to engage in problem solving (interpretation and integration processes) to determine their goals, identify salient environmental factors, and evaluate alternative behaviours. Marketers should develop strategies to help consumers cope with unfamiliar situations. For instance, life insurance salespeople are trained to help consumers define their goals (college education for kids, retirement planning, pay off mortgage) and identify key environmental considerations (current income and savings, children's ages, time to retirement) before they demonstrate the personal relevance of life insurance.

Analysing situations

Marketers must identify and analyse important situations to understand the physical and social environment from the perspectives of the consumers who experience them.[16] To analyse a situation, marketers first determine the major goals of their target customers that define the situation. Then they identify the key aspects of the social and physical environments in those situations, including aspects of the marketing environment that might affect consumers. The next step is to understand consumers' affective and cognitive responses to these environmental characteristics. Finally, marketers need to identify the key product-related behaviours in this situation.

Marketers can learn a great deal about a consumption situation through detailed observation of consumers' behaviours in that situation. For instance, researchers could develop rich descriptions of ordinary consumer behaviours observed at discount malls, banks, garage sales, or auctions. Another approach is to ask consumers to describe the major occasions when they consume a product. For example, a university student described the following three situations when she ate candy. Each situation occurred in a different environment and involved different goals, affective and cognitive responses, and behaviours. Each consumption situation was defined by the consumer in highly personal terms of her own goals and her environments.

Situation 1. Hungry—in a rush.
Environment: hectic; many other people around; between classes.

Goal: satisfy hunger and get energy.
Affect/cognition: feeling hungry, stressed, anxious.
Behaviour: snack on candy between classes and during class.

Situation 2. Lazy—relaxed.
Environment: quiet; alone at home in evening.
Goal: relax so I can concentrate on work.
Affect/cognition: feeling relaxed and calm, but alert.
Behaviour: snack on candy while reading or studying.

Situation 3. Calm—at lunch.
Environment: no commotion; alone in kitchen at lunchtime.
Goal: reward myself.
Affect/cognition: feeling happy to be home after hectic class
schedule; starting to calm down.
Behaviour: eat candy for dessert.

Typically, marketers do not base their strategies on an analysis of a single consumer. Marketers are interested in identifying situations experienced similarly by large numbers of consumers. Then the marketer can develop marketing strategies (special products, prices, or advertising campaigns) for those consumption situations. For instance, consider a study of fast-food restaurants that identified four use situations: lunch on a weekday, a snack during a shopping trip, an evening meal when rushed for time, and an evening meal with family when not rushed for time.[17] The authors found different choice criteria were used in these situations (speed of service was more important at lunch, menu variety was more important in the evening when not rushed). Moreover, certain restaurants (different environments) were considered more appropriate for certain situations. Finally, even if the same fast-food restaurant is patronised in these different situations, consumers' behaviours and affective and cognitive reactions may be quite different (rushed/not rushed, relaxed/not relaxed).

In this section, we consider five common *consumer situations:* information acquisition, shopping, purchase, consumption, and disposition (see Exhibit 14.6). These situations are relevant for most products. Marketers analyse consumers' goals, relevant affect and

Common consumer situations

EXHIBIT 14.6

Five common situations for consumers

Situation	General Behaviour	Specific Behaviour and Environment
Information acquisition	Information contact Communication	Reading a billboard while driving Discussing running shoes with a friend at a track meet Watching a TV commercial at home
Shopping	Store contact Product contact	Window shopping in a mall Browsing through Consumers' Distributors catalogue Comparing brands of shirts in a store
Purchase	Funds access Transaction	Obtaining a Visa card at a bank Going to a checkout counter at The Bay Purchasing theatre or baseball tickets through Ticketron
Consumption	Use	Eating a doughnut at Tim Horton's Using a refrigerator for 15 years
Disposition	Disposal	Recycling aluminium cans Throwing away a hot-dog wrapper at a hockey game

cognitions, and the key environmental factors in these situations to develop strategies that will change, facilitate, or maintain the key behaviours.

Information acquisition

Relevant information may be acquired accidentally, as consumers randomly come across it in their environments, or intentionally, as they consciously seek information related to their current problem-solving goals, such as a brand or store choice. An **information acquisition situation** includes aspects of the social environment (discussions with friends, persuasion attempts by a salesperson), the physical environment (ads, prominent signs in a store, labels on the product package), the behaviours involved in exposure to this information, and the consumer's affective and cognitive responses.

Marketers have considerable control over many aspects of consumers' information environment through the advertising, sales promotion, and personal-selling elements of the promotion mix. Marketers can place signs in stores and on the front windows of shops, send direct-mail material about their products to consumers, and place ads on TV, in magazines, and on billboards.[18] They can add information to packages and labels or provide salespeople with special information to convey to customers.[19] Other aspects of consumers' information environment are not under marketers' direct control—for example, marketers can try to generate publicity and news articles about their product or encourage consumers to tell other people about a product, but they may not be successful in creating this environment information.

Two especially important behaviours in information acquisition situations are information contact and communication. Because approximately two-thirds of retail purchases come from decisions made in the store, *information contact* with relevant product information in a store can have a significant influence on choice. Various marketing strategies are designed to facilitate information contact, including product displays, point-of-purchase information, and signs. An example is the interactive computer display developed for Clarion Cosmetics. After answering a few simple questions, consumers receive information about which Clarion products are best for their skin color and tone.[20] Other strategies include placing ads on shopping carts and printing coloured ads on paper grocery bags.[21]

Modern technology enables marketers to make information contact with precisely defined target groups. In some supermarkets, coupon dispensers connected to the checkout scanners can issue different types of coupons, depending on which products and brands a consumer buys. Thus, people purchasing peanut butter might receive a coupon for bread, while customers who buy Folgers coffee might receive a coupon for Maxwell House. Electronic couponing could eliminate printing coupons in newspapers for clipping. Many Ontario-based retailers now offer special discount cards in exchange for basic demographic data. Shoppers present their cards at the checkout, where an electronic scanner notes all eligible discounts. Retailers prefer this system because it reduces coupon handling, cuts labour costs, and gives them consumer information.

Other marketing strategies focus on *communication*, such as how salespeople communicate with customers. For example, Toyota, manufacturer of the Lexus luxury car, trains its salespeople in all aspects of the car so they spend an average of 90 minutes presenting a car to a potential customer, much more than the industry average.[22] Communication is also relevant in service situations. Consumers' top complaint about auto service is having to bring the car back because the problem was not fixed properly the first time. Research indicated Lexus buyers saw this as a communication flaw in that their car problem was not adequately explained to the mechanic doing the work. The company modified the service situation so car owners could speak directly to the mechanic who would examine their car. Customers can even stay during the diagnosis to make sure the problem is clearly communicated to the mechanic.

Shopping

The **shopping situation** includes the physical, spatial, and social aspects of places where consumers shop for products and services, as well as shopping behaviours and related affective and cognitive responses. Shopping can occur in a variety of environments, such as boutiques, department and discount stores, factory outlets, malls, pedestrian-only retail areas, the home via catalogues and TV shopping programs, garage sales, auctions, and so on. The shopping situation also includes the merchandise (products and brands) available for sale in those environments. For instance, the shopping environment provided by an auto centre where several franchises are sold under one roof vastly increases the number of product alternatives. A customer can examine dozens of makes and models on a single shopping trip, much like shopping for a new dress or suit at a large department store.

The shopping environment also includes social factors such as how many salespeople and checkout personnel are in the store, how they act toward consumers, and the types of other customers in the store. Many people dislike going to an auto showroom where aggressive salespeople may pressure them, so at a Lexus dealership, no salespeople are in sight.[23] Instead, consumers are greeted by a receptionist behind a marble desk. They are encouraged to learn more about the Lexus by studying the "media wall" of videos and print materials, without interruption. Only on request will the receptionist call a sales representative to talk to the consumer.

Two general behaviours affected by the shopping environment are of particular importance: store contact and product contact. *Store contact* is critical for retailing success, and many marketing strategies are intended to get consumers to come to the store. Giving away a free cassette tape to the first 100 people to show up at an electronics store on a Saturday morning is an example of such a strategy.

Store location is another critical environmental influence on store contact for many types of stores; for example, fast-food restaurants and convenience stores need to be located in high-traffic locations. Consumer Perspective 14.5 describes an unusual strategy to increase store contact behaviour by changing the location of the store. As another example, consider how the location strategy of several small shopkeepers in an old Edmonton neighbourhood has evolved over the years. Once a run-down section of town avoided by most, a stretch of Whyte Avenue in Old Strathcona has taken on a new life. While the Edmonton area itself has been overrun by an explosion of shopping centre growth, including the massive West Edmonton Mall, marketers and shopkeepers in Old Strathcona have been smart enough to capitalise on a potentially difficult situation. The area has taken on a culture all its own. From the boutiques and bistros to the old-fashioned signage and secondhand stores, it has become one of the most popular and chic places to spend a day shopping. The popularity has even spread to the store owners themselves, most of whom can be found in the stores maintaining a close relationship with their consumers.

As another example of store contact strategies, the location in a mall of smaller boutiques selling candy, natural foods, or gifts can have a critical effect on store contact behaviour. One desirable location is close to the entrance of one of the anchor stores, usually large department stores found at the ends or the middle of the mall. Because these anchor stores draw so many consumers, smaller stores benefit from the traffic flowing past their doors. The importance of mall location within the general environment can also have a large effect on consumers and marketing success. In the early '90s, many

**CONSUMER
PERSPECTIVE**

▶ **14.5**

**Mobile shopping
environments**

Canada's smallest McDonald's is in a parking lot in Grand Bend, Ontario, for the summer. But the experimental mobile restaurant will move on to more populated areas after the holiday crowd leaves the Lake Huron resort town.

The "QuickBreak" trailer is an experiment for McDonald's in Canada, and it may be the first of many. "It's something we picked up from the U.S.," said Len Jillard, operations manager for southwestern Ontario. "It gives us flexibility to go to different venues."

The restaurant promises the same quality of food expected by McDonald's customers throughout the world—but not the same selection. The menu has been scaled down along with the size of the kitchen.

This concept is not new. Kentucky Fried Chicken, Pizza Hut, Taco Bell, and Dairy Queen all use mobile restaurants. McDonald's was very successful with the Grand Bend program. It serviced a customer group during the holiday season and employed 22 young people during the entire summer. McDonald's knows that its future success will depend on its quick reaction to changing consumer demographics and lifestyles. The mobile restaurant is one strategy for achieving this success.

Source: Heather Scoffield, "Mobile McDonald's Serves Holiday Crowd," *Winnipeg Free Press*, July 25, 1993, p. A3.

shopping centres across Canada experienced difficulty dealing with groups of unruly teenagers. In particular, the Dufferin Street Mall in Toronto began having trouble not only with teens but with drug pushers and their potential for violence. It was only through the extraordinary efforts of public and private agencies that the environment was able to re-establish itself as a prime shopping area. Changes, whether negative or positive, in a mall shopping environment can initiate a sequence of interactions among behaviours, affect and cognition, and the environment.

Product contact is another important behaviour affected by the environmental characteristics of the shopping situation. Consider how the probability of product contact is reduced in very large stores, or if shoppers are discouraged from lingering in a store by overcrowding or overly aggressive sales personnel. Some stores use restful music, warm colour schemes, and low-key salespeople to encourage shoppers to linger, thus enhancing the probability of product contact. In large self-service stores, signs are hung from the ceiling to identify product locations. To facilitate product contact, Hallmark recently redesigned its product displays, using coloured strips to identify different types of greeting cards and to help customers find the right card quickly.[24]

Certain stores are designed to make the shopping environment more fun and exciting so consumers will spend more time in the store and be more likely to make contact with the merchandise.[25] When a small chain of clothing stores for young women called Ups and Downs redesigned its store interiors, it added kinetically controlled display racks.[26] This innovation allows customers to spin an entire carousel of clothes with just a light touch. These kinetic displays facilitate product contact and make the shopping experience more fun. Consumer Perspective 14.6 describes another example of a store environment that makes shopping fun and increases product contact behaviour.

Although the retail store environment is certainly important, other types of shopping environments are becoming quite significant. These include shopping at home by phone or by mail. Consider the great popularity of TV shopping programs and the continued rise of catalogue or mail-order shopping. A new example of mail-order shopping is the increasing popularity of mail-order prescription medications, which offer customers savings

CONSUMER PERSPECTIVE

14.6

The store environment

Seduce them, then abandon them; speed them in, then slow them down. Such, in a nutshell, is the retailing recipe at Clinique's revamped Canadian flagship boutique at The Bay, Queen Street, Toronto. "This is the first open-service installation in North America," said the vice president and general manager of Clinique Canada. "The customer can penetrate it."

In place of the familiar, barrier-like rows of glass cases in front of mirrored columns, Clinique's new look boasts corner counters with welcoming sensuous curves. A central area opens into separate little zones: here a cosy, upholstered seating banquette, there a circular display table flanked by barstools.

The change is about making customers feel more welcome. "We want the customer to get information on product lines herself, without having to be told," said a Clinique executive. "The customer wants to read, browse, and perhaps identify needs we can't identify. There is always a consultant within arm's reach without invading the customer's space."

Source: David Lasker "Shop Until You Drop In," *The Globe and Mail*, Sept. 2, 1993, p. D2.

of up to 35 percent. Obviously, the environment at home is dramatically different from the in-store shopping environment. Other shopping environments are relevant for some products, including garage sales, flea markets and swap meets, auctions, sidewalk sales, and private sales of merchandise by individuals and street vendors. In some cities, you can even avoid shopping situations altogether, by hiring someone else to shop for you.[27]

Purchasing

The **purchase situation** includes the social and physical stimuli present in the environment where the consumer actually makes the purchase. Consider, for instance, the differences in the purchasing environment when you buy fresh vegetables at a supermarket versus at an outdoor farmers' market. In some cases, the purchasing environment is similar to the shopping environment, but they are seldom identical. In most self-service stores, for instance, consumers pay for the products they have selected at a checkout counter at the front of the store or at various cash register locations scattered around the store. Some purchasing environments are quite distinct from the shopping environment. For instance, the central checkout counter at one trendy music store is designed to look like a giant piano keyboard with black and white keys.

In other retail environments, such as a car dealership, the purchasing environment may be a separate room used exclusively for the purchase transaction. This is where the salesperson and the customers retire to negotiate the final details of the purchase. Sometimes the shopping environment intrudes into the purchasing environment. For instance, checkout lines at grocery stores usually include displays of products such as magazines, gum and candy items, and cigarettes to stimulate impulse purchases.

The information acquisition and purchase environments may overlap. For instance, A&P experimented with showing ads on TV monitors placed at the checkout aisle, but many consumers complained that this type of information contact was too intrusive. Besides, few customers wanted to leave the line to get an advertised product.

Marketers are particularly interested in influencing two behaviours in purchasing situations: *funds access* and the *final transaction.* For instance, Sotheby's, the world-famous auction house for fine art, found that the extreme escalation of art prices in the late 1980s had created a funds access problem for its customers. Buyers did not have the large sums of cash (millions, in some cases) necessary to buy fine works of art, so Sotheby's instituted a credit policy allowing a loan of up to half the cost of an artwork, using the purchased painting or other works of art owned by the borrower as collateral. Many grocery stores and other retail stores have streamlined the transaction procedures in the purchasing situation by installing scanner equipment to speed up the checkout process. Most retail outlets in Canada accept the Interac access card, which has simplified payment in stores that have traditionally not accepted credit cards (grocery chains, liquor stores).

Consumption

The **consumption situation** includes the social and physical assets of the environments where consumers actually use or consume the products and services they have bought. Obviously, consumption behaviours (and related cognitive and affective processes such as enjoyment, satisfaction, or frustration) are most relevant in such situations. Consider how clean, tidy, well-lighted, and attractively decorated consumption environments in full-service and fast-food restaurants, pubs and bars, nightclubs and discos, and ice-cream parlors can enhance consumers' enjoyment of the purchased products. For such businesses, the design of the consumption environment may be critically important to consumers' satisfaction with their purchase.

Consider the consumption environment of two cafés in Toronto. At the Help Wanted Café, started by two enterprising marketers, customers can order bacon and eggs with complete resumé and job-search services on the side. Included in the deal is the use of computers, fax machines, and photocopiers (even access to the Internet!). Taking advantage of the economic times has proven successful here through a positive manipulation of the consumption environment. The Second Cup, on the other hand, decided that manipulating the store environment to emphasise the social atmosphere and feel of a coffee house should improve sales. A successful artist was commissioned to create original artwork for the walls of several of the chain's outlets in an effort to garner interest and give the shops a unique and trendy atmosphere.

For other products such as appliances, clothing, cars, and furniture, marketers have almost no direct control over the consumption environment. When purchased, these products are removed from the retail environment and consumed elsewhere. Moreover, for many of these products, the consumption situation involves multiple consumption behaviours over long periods (most people own and use a car or a microwave oven for several years). In some cases, the consumption environment might change during the useful life of the product, which could affect consumption-related cognitive and affective responses (satisfaction) and behaviours (repairs and service). Perhaps the best marketers can do is to monitor consumer satisfaction levels and behaviours in these consumption situations over the lifetime of the product.

In other cases, however, marketers have a great deal of control over the consumption environment. For instance, many service businesses, such as hair stylists, dentists and doctors, and hotels and motels, have total control over the consumption environment, because consumption of these products and services occurs on the premises of the seller. Obvious examples are Disneyland and Canada's Wonderland in Toronto (or any other theme or amusement park) where the consumption environment is a major part of the product/service that consumers buy. These large theme parks go to great lengths to ensure the consumption environment meets rigorous standards. The Edmonton Mall is another example of a consumption environment that attracts consumers from all over the world (in this case to experience the world's largest mall).

Another instance where the design of the consumption environment can be critical is the restaurant industry. Japanese restaurants such as Benihana simulate traditional Japanese values: you take off your shoes and are served by waitresses wearing traditional

West Edmonton Mall, the world's largest mall, is a mixture of shopping and consumption environments, including a Galaxyland amusement park inside the mall.

Japanese kimonos. The chefs provide the floor show while preparing your dinner at your (oven) table. Sports restaurants, such as La Cage Aux Sports, are less popular for their food than for their noisy, beer-drinking sports environment. Moishe's is Canada's most famous steak restaurant. While the food is excellent, the hustle and bustle, the seeing and being seen, are as much a part of the ambiance as is the decor. Hooter's Restaurants are probably less known for their food than for their servers' attire (or lack of it). Le Festin du Gouverneur is a Montreal restaurant that replicates a New France feast. The decor is 18th-century Quebec City and the food is traditional French cuisine.

Disposition

For certain products, marketers may need to consider other types of environmental situations. For instance, **disposition situations** are highly relevant for businesses like used car lots and used clothing stores. Here the key behaviour of interest is *disposal* of products. Many people simply throw away unwanted products or give them to charity. Others sell their unwanted products at flea markets, garage sales, and swap meets. These situations offer interesting environments for study in and of themselves.[28] Disposition situations are relevant for public policy issues, too.

Consumers in many countries, including Canada, are developing stronger concerns about quality. Cost-consciousness and concern for the natural environment, in turn, are fueling interest in used products and the recycling of waste. The markets for recycled goods and used products (furniture and appliances, clothing, and housewares) are likely to increase in the future, and we can expect entrepreneurs to develop strategies to serve these markets.

Marketing implications

Marketers need to identify the key social and physical environmental features of the information, shopping, purchase, consumption, and disposition situations for their products. Perhaps some aspects of the particular environment are blocking behaviours crucial to the marketing success of the firm's product. If so, marketing strategies can be developed that modify the environment to stimulate, facilitate, and reinforce the desired behaviours. For instance, if funds access is a problem for consumers, the company might introduce debit cards, accept regular credit cards, or allow charge accounts. If consumers are becoming increasingly discouraged with the shopping environment in many cities (noisy streets, difficult parking, crowded stores), clever marketers are likely to introduce alternative shopping environments, such as home shopping opportunities through the mail or by telephone. Canadian businesses have witnessed strong growth for such businesses in the 1990s.

▶ **SUMMARY**

Learning objective 1: *Define the environment and describe the difference between the macro- and micro-environment.*

The environment refers to all the physical and social characteristics of consumers' external world. The environment includes *(a)* physical objects such as products and stores, *(b)* spatial aspects such as the position of a product in a store or the location of a store in a mall, and *(c)* social aspects associated with other people and their social behaviours. The micro-environment refers to a person's immediate physical and social surroundings (your bedroom, house, or workplace). The macro-environment refers to the large-scale, broad environmental factors such as the climate or type of landscape where you live, the economic conditions of your region, and whether you live in a large or small city or in a rural environment. Each consumer responds to aspects of the macro- and micro-environment in terms of his or her personal interpretations of those factors. Usually, marketers can identify groups of consumers (possible market segments) with enough common experience that they interpret major environmental factors similarly.

Learning objective 2: *Define the social environment, identify the types of macro and micro social environments, and describe the flow of influence between the macro- and micro-environments.*

The social environment includes all social interactions among people. The macro social environment includes the social interactions that occur among very large groups of people. Marketers are interested in three such groups: culture, subculture, and social class. The micro social environment includes the social interactions that occur between small groups of people such as families and reference groups. The macro- and micro-environments have a hierarchical relationship; the values, norms, and meanings of the overall culture flow to the subcultures within it and on to social class groups. The micro social environments of family and reference groups act as a filter in transmitting these influences of the macro social environments to the individual consumer. In turn, the flow of influence can go back up the hierarchy, as when the behaviour of many families influences the values of a social class or subculture.

Learning objective 3: *Define the physical environment and give an example of how it can influence consumer behaviour.*

The physical environment includes all the nonhuman, physical aspects of the external world of consumers. The physical environment can be divided into spatial and nonspatial elements. Spatial factors include physical objects such as products, brands, and the layout and design of stores, malls, and cities. Nonspatial aspects of the physical environment include the weather, time, colour, odours, and other factors. Any aspect of the physical environment can influence consumer behaviour. For example, the availability of parking (an aspect of the spatial environment) influences consumers' shopping behaviours. Time factors have major effects on behaviours—more sports activities or more shopping during daylight hours.

Learning objective 4: *Give two examples of how a marketing strategy can modify the environment and influence consumer behaviour.*

Each marketing strategy modifies some aspect of the social and physical environment. For instance, promotion strategies create physical objects in the environment (ads on TV, billboards, signs in the store) and may also influence the social environment (phone calls from telemarketers, product descriptions by salespeople). These aspects of the environment may attract consumers' attention or persuade them to buy the product. Product strategies may involve physical changes in the product (removing fat from a food product, increasing the horsepower of the Pontiac Grand Am), pricing strategies create small changes in the environment (a sale sign in the store window, a price tag on a blouse), and distribution strategies can change the spatial environment (building a Wal-Mart store, creating a product display in a drugstore). Any of these environmental stimuli may influence consumers' affect and cognition and behaviour.

Learning objective 5: *Define a situation and describe the factors to be examined in a situation analysis.*

A "raw" physical environment is not a situation—a shopping mall is not a situation. Rather, a situation is a sequence of goal-directed behaviours that occur in a physical and social environment, accompanied by related affective and cognitive responses. A situation is defined and created by the consumer who is behaving in an environment for some purpose. Thus, going to the mall to buy a sweater is a shopping situation. Situations are like a story in that they have a beginning, a middle, and an end.

To understand the product-related situations that are important to consumers, marketers should analyse the major components of those situations. These factors include the consumers' and goal(s), the major features of the environments in which the situation occurs, the key behaviours involved, and the dominant affective responses and cognitions related to those behaviours.

Learning objective 6: *Describe the five common consumer situations and identify behaviours that are important in each one.*

Consumers define particular situations in terms of their own perspectives and goals. However, each culture or society has common or generic situations that most people experience. Five consumer situations are relevant for many marketing problems and most products. To understand each situation, marketers would identify the key behaviours, related affect and cognitive responses, and major aspects of the physical and social environments in which these behaviours occurred. Marketers are particularly interested in the key behaviours for each situation because they focus their strategies on changing or maintaining these behaviours.

In information acquisition situations, consumers acquire or learn relevant information about products or brands; two important behaviours are information contact and communication. In shopping situations, people search for appropriate products to solve their problems; two important behaviours are store contact and product contact. In purchasing situations, consumers make the buying exchange, and funds access and the final transaction are important behaviours. In consumption situations, the product is used or consumed, and consumption behaviours are important. In disposition situations, consumers discard products, and disposition behaviours are important.

---

environment	situation	purchase situation	▶ **KEY TERMS**
social environment	information acquisition	consumption situation	**AND**
physical environment	situation	disposition situation	**CONCEPTS**
	shopping situation		

► **REVIEW AND DISCUSSION QUESTIONS**

1. Pick a fast-food restaurant and identify the social and physical aspects of the marketing environment. Which factors seem most important?

2. Discuss the distinction between the macro- and micro-environment in terms of grocery shopping. How is each level of the environment relevant for developing marketing strategies?

3. Describe how the various levels of the social environment are related and how they affect the individual consumer.

4. Research suggests that about 80 percent of grocery purchase decisions are made while consumers are in the store. What aspects of the physical environment in the store could influence those decisions? (You might choose a product category such as frozen entrées or snack chips to focus your answer.)

5. What is a situation? Using examples from your personal purchasing experience, differentiate situations from the "raw" environment.

6. Describe the key factors in a situation that marketers need to understand, and give an implication for marketing strategy.

7. Consider how you might go about buying a portable cassette player (or another product of your choice). Describe the information acquisition and shopping situations and identify critical behaviours. What implications for marketing strategies do you see in your analysis?

8. Consider how you might go about buying a portable cassette player (or another product of your choice). Describe the purchase and consumption situations and identify critical behaviours. What implications for marketing strategies do you see in your analysis?

9. Describe a disposition situation for a portable cassette player (or another product of your choice), and identify critical behaviours. What implications for marketing strategies do you see in your analysis?

15

Cultural and Cross-Cultural Influences

LEARNING OBJECTIVES

After completing this chapter, you should be able to:

► 1. Define culture and cultural meaning.

► 2. Discuss aspects of the content of culture, including core values.

► 3. Describe the cultural process by which cultural meaning is moved from the environment into products and then into consumers.

► 4. Give examples of how rituals move meaning from products into consumers and vice versa.

► 5. Give some examples of important cross-cultural differences.

► 6. Discuss three approaches to developing international marketing strategies.

BIRTH OF THE CONSUMER SOCIETY

Modern consumption cultures are a rather recent historical development. According to one analysis, the birth of the consumer society occurred in England during the late 18th century with several important events. For one, the mass production technologies developed during the Industrial Revolution allowed companies to produce larger amounts of standardised goods at relatively low prices. But a *cultural revolution* also occurred about the same time, without which the Industrial Revolution would not have been successful.

During the 18th century, England was gradually transformed from a largely agrarian society into a more urban society. As people moved into towns, their culture changed dramatically. They performed different types of work, established new ways of living, and developed new values. Many people developed an increased desire for material goods, stimulated partly by "new" marketing strategies such as advertising. Increasingly, ordinary citizens (not just the wealthy) became concerned with the symbolic meanings of goods and felt it necessary to buy products that were fashionable and up to date. Owning such things helped satisfy the emerging cultural need for status distinctions, which had become more relevant in the relatively anonymous urban societies where fewer people knew about others' family backgrounds. Thus, people began to see consumption as an acceptable way to convey important social meanings. Finally, more people had disposable income and were willing to spend it to achieve social values.

These cultural changes, combined with the rapidly developing ability of industry to mass produce products of reasonable quality at "low" prices, created a dramatic increase in consumption in 18th-century England. Essentially, the same events occurred in France and North America during the 19th century, and the modern consumer society was born there, too.[1]

This brief summary of the beginnings of the modern consumption society points to the importance of culture in understanding consumer behaviour. To develop effective strategies, marketers need to identify important aspects of culture and understand how the cultural environment affects consumers. We begin this chapter by defining culture and examining how culture influences consumers' affect, cognitions, and behaviours. Then, we identify some important characteristics of Canadian culture and discuss the implications of cultural analysis for developing marketing strategies. Next we describe the cultural processes by which cultural meaning is transmitted through marketing strategies from the cultural environment to products and on to consumers, who acquire those cultural meanings for themselves. Finally, we discuss cross-cultural (international) differences and their implications for developing global marketing strategies.

WHAT IS CULTURE?

As the all-encompassing aspect of the macro social environment, culture has a strong and pervasive influence on consumers, although the term remains difficult for marketers to understand. Dozens of definitions have confused researchers about what "culture" is or how culture "works" to influence consumers.[2] We define **culture** broadly as *the meanings that are shared by (most) people in a social group.* In establishing a particular vision of the world, each society constructs its cultural view by creating and using meanings that reflect important distinctions in that society. For example, Consumer Perspective 15.1 describes some cultural meanings of the Christmas holiday that are unique to particular societies.

CONSUMER PERSPECTIVE

▶ **15.1**

Holiday buying around the world

A witch flies on a broomstick to drop Christmas gifts down Italian chimneys, a kindly old Saint Nicolas leaves gifts at the front doors of Scandinavian homes, a camel does the hauling in southern Syria, and the honourable porter's name is *Santa-san* in Japan. Although the exact method of delivery varies around the world, consumers fill the sacks with presents every holiday season.

Each year, eager shoppers record huge purchases during the Christmas holiday season. Most department stores record about one-third of their annual sales during this period. Toy vendors from London to Madrid to Vancouver expect to do about 50 percent of their yearly business in these three months.

Shopping for and giving presents at Christmastime has become a worldwide phenomenon. Even in Japan, where less than 1 percent of the population is Christian, Yuletide is widely celebrated with artfully packaged gifts and partying. West Germany's lively outdoor Christmas markets sell sausages, sweets, and holiday gifts. Shoppers in Rome's oval-shaped plaza Piazza Navona are bathed in light from stalls selling items like books, toys, records, candy, and video games while being entertained by street musicians and magicians. Even the energy shortages and sparsely stocked stores in Eastern Europe cannot extinguish Christmas cheer. Families in Warsaw, Bratislava, and Budapest surrender their bathtubs for a week to give freshwater carp, a holiday delicacy, a place to swim before they become dinner.

Holiday decorations, especially lights, are popular everywhere. For instance, Christmas trees decorate plazas around the globe (and are found in 85 percent of Canadian homes). In Scandinavia, candles glow from every window to brighten the darkness that arrives by midafternoon. The Stroget, Copenhagen's large pedestrian-only shopping district, is illuminated by thousands of coloured lights and stars. The Via Condotti, Rome's pedestrian-only shopping area, is decorated with hundreds of red poinsettias, called "Christmas stars" in Italian.

Marketers should consider several issues when analysing culture. First, cultural meaning can be analysed at different levels. At the macro level, we would look at the culture of an entire society or country (France or Kenya). Because culture refers to the meanings shared among a group of people of whatever size, marketers can also analyse the cultural meanings of subcultures (French Canadians, the elderly, or people who live in the Prairie provinces or Maritimes) or social classes (middle class versus working class). We discuss subcultures and social class in Chapter 16. Marketers also can analyse the shared cultural meanings of smaller groups such as a reference group (students who live on the same dorm floor, members of a sorority or a street gang, or a group of co-workers) or families (people in one's nuclear or extended family). We discuss reference groups and family influences in Chapter 17.

Second, the essence of culture as shared or common meaning is critical to understanding the concept. A meaning is cultural if many people in a social group share the same basic meaning or belief.[3] **Cultural meanings** are usually rather fluid and not rigidly defined in that not everyone in a social group has precisely the same meaning for any object or activity (an "old" person, an "environmentally safe" product, or a "good" bargain). Fortunately, meanings need only be "close enough" to be treated as shared or common.

Third, cultural meanings are created by people. Anthropologists often say cultural meanings are constructed or negotiated by people in a group through their social interactions. The construction of cultural meaning is most obvious at the level of smaller groups. (Consider the social meanings created by college students—what music

For many, the winter weather in the northern hemisphere heightens the holiday mood. But cold weather and lights in the early darkness are not prerequisites for Christmas spirit. South of the equator, the holiday falls in the middle of summer. So when enthusiastic shoppers in Australia and Rio get too hot, they just head for the beach to cool off.

There are differences, of course, among the consumers in various cultures, subcultures, and social classes. Marketers need to identify these factors and understand how they are related to purchasing and consumption behaviour. However, there are also similarities between cultures. One example is the generosity and good spirit of the Christmas season. Holiday spending and gift giving seem to be fairly universal in most societies with a strong consumption ethic. The details, of course, often differ. The weather (cold and snowy or hot, humid, and rainy), the most desirable gifts (fur coats in Northern Europe, ice-cream makers in Brazil), the particular details of the holiday rituals (who brings the gifts), and the religious symbolic meanings may vary considerably. Canadians have begun to change their views about Christmas. We tend to see the holiday less as a spiritual event than as an opportunity to spend time with our families. The core meaning of the holiday, captured by Charles Dickens in *A Christmas Carol*, seems fairly universal. "Christmas," Dickens wrote, "is the only time I know of, in the long calendar year, when men and women seem by one consent to open their shut-up hearts freely." And, we might note, they open their pocketbooks, too.

Source: Adapted with permission from Jaclyn Fierman, "Christmas Shopping around the World," *Fortune*, © 1987 Time Inc. All rights reserved; Nicolaas Van Rijn, "Canadians See Yule as Time for Family," *Toronto Star*, Dec. 24, 1993.

The cultural meanings of products such as clothing are created by advertising and the people who use the products.

or clothing look is "in" this semester?) At the level of society, cultural institutions such as governments, religious and educational organisations, and business firms also create cultural meanings.

A fourth issue is that cultural meanings are constantly in motion and can undergo rapid change. In the early days of the consumption society in England, for instance, the cultural changes in people's values, perceptions, and behaviours were so dramatic that one observer felt a kind of "madness" had taken over society. Later in this chapter, we examine the processes by which cultural meanings change and move about in the society, partly through marketing strategies.

Fifth, social groups differ in the amount of freedom their members have to adopt and use certain cultural meanings. North American and European societies afford people a great deal of freedom to select cultural meanings and use them to create a desired self-identity. In many other societies, such as China, India, or Saudi Arabia, people have less freedom to do so.

Marketers can understand cultural meaning from two useful perspectives. They can examine the *content* of a culture, or they can treat culture as a *process*.[4]

THE CONTENT OF CULTURE

The usual approach in marketing is to analyse culture in terms of its major features or attributes, which is to say its content. Although marketers typically focus on identifying the dominant values of a society, culture is more than values.[5] The **content of culture** includes the beliefs, attitudes, goals, and values that most people in a society hold, as well as the meanings of characteristic behaviours, rules, customs, and norms that most people follow. The content of culture also includes meanings of the significant aspects of the social and physical environment, including the major institutions in a society (governmental bodies, political parties, religions) and the typical physical objects (products, tools, buildings) used by people in a society.

Culture has a profound effect on how and where people shop for products, as shown in the open-air market in India and a Wal-Mart store in Canada.

The goal of cultural analysis is to understand the cultural meanings of concepts from the point of view of the people who create and use them.[6] For example, many Quebecers have similar affective responses to the raising of the Quebec flag (patriotic feelings). Canadians may respond to accidentally breaking something in a store (anxiety or guilt), or to a 50-percent-off sale (interest or enthusiasm). *Affective responses* vary across cultures. Many North Americans and northern Europeans become annoyed if kept waiting for 15 minutes in a checkout line, while people in other cultures might not have a negative reaction.

Behaviours can also have important cultural meanings. For instance, the meaning of shaking hands when greeting someone (welcome or friendliness) is shared by many peoples of the world, although in some cultures people bow or kiss instead. Protesters who raise the Quebec flag on Canada Day are communicating through their behaviour. Some consumption-related behaviours have a cultural meaning that is unique to particular societies. For instance, the bargaining behaviours that are common (and expected) among shoppers in the open market bazaars of northern Africa indicate a skilled and shrewd buyer. But in Canada, such bargaining behaviours are not appropriate for shopping in Zellers or Wal-Mart and would be considered naive or rude.

Aspects of the *social environment* can have rich cultural meanings. For instance, the cultural meanings of shopping for a new sweater at a self-service factory outlet store may be quite different from shopping in an upscale department store with attentive personal service from salespeople. Likewise, the physical or material environment—including the landscape, buildings, and the weather, as well as specific objects such as products—can have significant cultural meaning. For instance, objects such as wedding rings and new cars have cultural meaning for many consumers. All societies have certain objects that symbolize key cultural meanings. Consider the shared meanings that many Canadians associate with hockey, the Mounties, the House of Commons, Canadian healthcare, (pride, freedom, shared common safety and health).

Marketing strategies may also have shared meanings. Reactions to advertising, for instance, tend to be culturally specific.[7] In North America, many advertising appeals are straightforward and direct, but consumers in other societies consider such appeals blunt and even offensive. People in other countries consider many of our ads overly emotional and sentimental. Thus, a McDonald's ad featuring a young man with Down's syndrome

EXHIBIT 15.1a

Core cultural values in North America

Value	General Feature	Relevance to Consumer Behaviour
Achievement and success	Hard work is good; success flows from hard work	Acts as a justification for acquisition of goods ("You deserve it")
Activity	Keeping busy is healthy and natural	Stimulates interest in products that save time and enhance leisure-time activities
Efficiency and practicality	Admire things that solve problems (e.g., save time and effort)	Stimulates purchase of products that function well and save time
Progress	People can improve themselves; tomorrow should be better	Stimulates desire for new products that fulfill unsatisfied needs; acceptance of products that claim to be "new" or "improved"
Material comfort	"The good life"	Fosters acceptance of convenience and luxury products that make life more enjoyable
Individualism	Being one's self (e.g., self-reliance, self-interest, and self-esteem)	Stimulates acceptance of customised or unique products that help a person "express his or her own personality"
Freedom	Freedom of choice	Fosters interest in wide product lines and differentiated products
External conformity	Uniformity of observable behaviour; desire to be accepted	Stimulates interest in products that are used or owned by others in the same social group
Humanitarianism	Caring for others, particularly the underdog	Stimulates patronage of firms that compete with market leaders
Youthfulness	A state of mind that stresses being young at heart or appearing young	Stimulates acceptance of products that provide the illusion of maintaining or fostering youth
Fitness and health	Caring about one's body, including the desire to be physically fit and healthy	Stimulates acceptance of food products, activities, and equipment perceived to maintain or increase physical fitness.

Source: Leon G. Schiffman and Leslie Lazar Kanuk, *Consumer Behavior,* 4th ed., p. 424, © 1991. Reprinted by permission of Prentice Hall, Englewood Cliffs, NJ.

who found a job and acceptance at McDonald's was considered a tearjerker in North America but was booed and jeered at the International Advertising Film Festival in Cannes. The British tend to be embarrassed by a direct sell; their ads are noted for self-deprecating humour. In contrast, the French rarely use humour; they prefer stylish and rather indirect appeals, which Canadians may find surrealistic. For example, the best French ad in 1991 (also shown in North America) showed a lion and a tawny-haired woman crawling up opposite sides of a mountain; at the peak the woman outroars the lion for a bottle of Perrier. Most Japanese consumers prefer ads that emphasise affective mood and emotional tone over facts. Although some Japanese ads travel well to other cultures, many are not understood elsewhere.[8] As a final example, marketing strategies such as pricing or distribution have cultural content that can differ across societies. Many Canadian consumers have positive reactions to frequent sales promotions such as discounting, sales, and coupons, but consumers in other cultures may have more negative meanings and wonder whether something is wrong with the product.

Finally, *physical objects* such as products and brands have cultural meanings that marketers need to understand. For instance, an analysis of beverage products focused on the status and age meanings carried in various beverage products—milk, for example, is seen

Number of students in sample	Canada	United States	Australia	Israel
	125	169	279	71
Terminal Value				
Freedom				
(independence, free choice)	1	1	3	4
Happiness				
(contentedness)	2	2	7	3
Mature love				
(sexual and spiritual intimacy)	3	6	5	5
Self-respect				
(self-esteem)	4	4	6	11
True friendship				
(close companionship)	5	8	2	12
Inner harmony				
(freedom from inner conflict)	6	9	8	13
Family security				
(taking care of loved ones)	7	7	12	8
Wisdom				
(a mature understanding of life)	8	3	1	6
A sense of accomplishment				
(lasting contribution)	9	5	4	7
Equality				
(equal opportunity for all)	10	13	10	10
An exciting life				
(a stimulating, active life)	11	12	11	9
A world at peace				
(free of war and conflict)	12	10	9	1
A comfortable life				
(a prosperous life)	13	11	13	15
Pleasure				
(an enjoyable, leisurely life)	14	15	14	14
A world of beauty				
(beauty of nature and the arts)	15	18	15	17
Social recognition				
(respect, admiration)	16	14	16	16
National security				
(protection from attack)	17	17	17	2
Salvation				
(saved, eternal life)	18	16	18	18

EXHIBIT 15.1b

Eighteen terminal values among Canadian, American, Australian, and Israeli male university students in order of importance

Source: Adapted with the permission of The Free Press, a division of Macmillan, Inc. from *The Nature of Human Values* by Milton Rokeach (New York: Free Press, 1973), p. 89, Table 3.18. Copyright © 1973 by The Free Press.

as weak and appropriate for younger people, while wine is considered sophisticated and for mature adults.[9] Consumers look for certain cultural meanings in products and acquire them to create a desirable personal identity.

A typical marketing analysis of cultural content begins by identifying the core values of the particular social groups. **Core values** describe the *end goals* that people are striving to achieve in their lives. Knowing the core values held by people in a society can help marketers understand the basis for the customer/product relationship for those consumers. Many Canadians seem to value freedom and control of their lives and their environment. Their fascination with lawn care (control of nature), TV remote controls (control over entertainment), and time management systems (control over time) reflect this value. Perhaps this value will be held less closely as more people realise that some things (such as nature) cannot be rigidly managed or controlled. Exhibit 15.1a presents several core values that many Canadians and Americans share. Exhibit 15.1b ranks 18 terminal values among a sampling of Canadians, Americans, Australians, and Israelis.

The core values of Canadian culture

CONSUMER PERSPECTIVE

▶ **15.2**

Changing cultural meanings of products

No meaning lasts forever. Consider the decline of traditional "fast food." In the past, fast food was synonymous with burgers, shakes, and fries—all laden with fat and sodium. In fact, traditionally there were few choices for nutrition-conscious consumers. However, with increasing pressure from consumers, fast-food restaurants are finding that they must either adapt or risk being shunned by a growing segment of the market.

The McDonald's Corp. is one fast-food chain that recognises the need to improve the nutritional value of its menu. In 1991, McDonald's concocted a new burger, the McLean Deluxe, which is 9 percent fat by weight, compared to 20 to 30 percent for most hamburgers. It phased out ice cream, replacing it with frozen yogurt, and it replaced animal fat for french frying with vegetable oil. McDonald's is also test marketing more healthful foods, such as pasta and carrot and celery sticks.

Healthier eating habits have also meant big adjustments for many concepts. In one notable example, declining sales prompted Kentucky Fried Chicken to change its name to KFC, mostly so customers wouldn't be reminded of the "fried" word. The company recently introduced a healthy alternative to deep-fried chicken: chicken that is prepared rotisserie-style. The KFC trademark has also enabled the franchise to start selling other entrées besides chicken.

Not all the products introduced by fast-food chains to respond to the increasingly health-conscious nature of consumers are successful. However, these products demonstrate the need for franchises to adapt to lifestyle changes if they hope to remain successful.

Source: Deborah McKay-Stokes, "Trend-Spotting Key to Franchising," *Financial Post*, Feb. 18, 1994.

Changing values in North America

The constant changes in North American cultural values can affect the success of a company's marketing strategies. As people's values change, their means-end connections with existing products and brands also change, which can change the important consumer/product relationship. Consumer Perspective 15.2 describes several instances where a value change—healthier attitudes toward eating—played a role in the success or failure of certain restaurants.

Changes in values can create both problems and opportunities for marketers. For instance, after the consumption excesses of the 1980s, many consumers seemed to become less materialistic and more concerned about social issues such as protection of the environment. Certainly, the growth of environmentalism as a cultural value has affected the disposable diaper market dominated by Procter & Gamble and Kimberly-Clark, makers of Pampers and Huggies. By the late 1980s, an increasing number of consumers began to see disposable diapers as a significant contributor to the solid waste overflowing landfills. Essentially, disposable diapers had become a means to a negative end for some consumers. In response to these cultural changes, P&G and other companies claimed that reusable cloth diapers pose about the same environmental impact as disposables due to the water and energy required to clean and dry them. The major companies also worked to develop a more biodegradable diaper. Consumer Perspective 15.3 presents other examples of corporate responses to changing environmental values.

Changes in cultural values can create new marketing opportunities, too. Chicken, fish, and soybean products, for instance, have seen significant growth as Canadian consumers turned away from burgers to products seen as more healthful. Increasing health values

CONSUMER
PERSPECTIVE

15.3 ◀

Environmental
concern:
A growing
cultural value

Many companies are responding to consumers' growing environmental values. Trend watchers think the 1990s is the decade of environmentalism, which will become an important value for consumers all around the world. Some claim environmentalism is "absolutely the most important issue for business." Among the companies that are reacting:

▶ Procter & Gamble, along with many other marketers, is trying to cast it products in an environmentally friendly light by using recycled materials for packaging and reformulating some products to reduce pollution.

▶ Wal-Mart has asked all its suppliers for more recycled or recyclable products, which it then features prominently with in-store signs.

▶ Du Pont has stated a "zero pollution" goal. Among other initiatives, the company is getting out of a $750 million-per-year business in chlorofluorocarbons, which may damage the earth's ozone layer, and has spent nearly $200 million developing a safe alternative.

▶ McDonald's is working to cut the huge waste stream produced daily at 8,500 restaurants in the United States. For instance, it requires suppliers to use corrugated boxes containing at least 35 percent recyclable materials. McDonald's has tested reusable salad lids, nonplastic utensils, pump-style containers for condiments, and refillable coffee mugs.

▶ The Body Shop has a director of social inventions whose job includes finding ways to enhance the Canadian economy by producing environmentally sound jobs. The Body Shop's past business decisions include employing indigenous workers to pick brazil nuts for lotions and using recycled toilets from a demolished hotel in Toronto.

The growing environmental concern of consumers creates not just problems for companies, but also opportunities. Booming business is forecast for companies in recycling, pollution control technology, and pollution cleanup. Consider the opportunity to design environmentally friendly packaging for compact disks. CDs originally came in a plastic "jewel box" inside a long cardboard box. The long box was developed to discourage shoplifting and to fit into existing record racks in stores. Besides requiring near gorilla strength to open, the discarded cardboard created 23 million pounds of garbage in 1990.

Source: Stevens Wild, "Cultivating Viable Green Jobs," *Winnipeg Free Press*, June 25, 1994, p. A14; Frank Edward Allen, "McDonald's Launches Plan to Cut Waste," *The Wall Street Journal*, April 17, 1991, pp. B1, B4; Meg Cox, "Music Firms Try Out 'Green' CD Boxes," *The Wall Street Journal*, July 25, 1991, p. B1; and David Kirkpatrick, "Environmentalism: The New Crusade," *Fortune*, Feb. 12, 1990, pp. 44–55.

have led many restaurants to add "healthy or heart-conscious" items (with reduced levels of fat, sugar, and cholesterol) to their menus.

Changes in cultural values are usually accompanied by changes in behaviour. For instance, the values of convenience and time-saving led to increases in certain home shopping behaviours, including use of mail-order catalogues and TV shopping channels. Marketers often talk about behaviour in terms of lifestyles—ways people live their lives to achieve important end goals or values. Exhibit 15.2 lists several important lifestyle trends in North American society, along with examples of how each may affect marketing strategies. Marketers need to monitor these cultural changes and adjust their marketing strategies as necessary.

EXHIBIT 15.2

Lifestyle trends in North America

Lifestyle trend	Example
Control of time	North Americans increasingly value their time and seek greater control of its use.
Component lifestyles	Consumer behaviour is becoming more individualistic because of the wider array of available choices.
The culture of convenience	With the rising number of two-income households, consumers are spending more on services in order to have more free time for themselves.
Growth of home shopping	Consumers want more time for themselves and are frustrated by waiting in checkout lines.
Shopping habits of men and women to converge	Men continue to do more of the shopping, and working women take on many male shopping habits.
Escalation of home entertainment	The VCR is the force behind the boom in home entertainment, which will bring about increased purchases of takeout food and changes in the nature of home furnishings and appliances.
Dressing for success	There has been a widespread return to fashion and concern for one's appearance.
Spread of the diversified diet	North Americans are eating differently (e.g., lower beef consumption, greater fish consumption).
Self-imposed prohibition of alcohol	The trend has been toward lighter drinks (e.g., vodka, "lite" beer), as well as a decline in the overall consumption of alcohol.
The lightest drink of all—water	Bottled or sparkling water is considered chic; some people are concerned about the quality of their tap water.
The bifurcation of product markets	There is a growing distance between upscale and downscale markets, and companies caught in the middle may fare poorly.
Product and service quality—more important, if not everything	Products falling below acceptable quality standards will be treated mercilessly.

CULTURE AS A PROCESS

Understanding the content of culture is important for developing effective marketing strategies, but we can also think about *culture as a process*. Exhibit 15.3 presents a model of the cultural process in a highly developed consumer society.[10] The model shows that cultural meaning is present in three "locations": in the social and physical environment, in products and services, and in individual consumers. The **cultural process** describes *how this cultural meaning is moved about or transferred among these locations* by the actions of organisations (business, government, religion, education) and individuals in the society. Meaning is transferred in a consumption-oriented society in two ways. First, marketing strategies are designed to move cultural meanings from the cultural environment into products and services in an attempt to make them attractive to consumers. Second, consumers actively seek to acquire these cultural meanings in products to establish a desirable personal identity or self-concept.

Moving cultural meanings into products

Advertising has been the most closely studied method of transferring cultural meaning from the physical and social environment "into" products.[11] From a cultural process perspective, advertising can be seen as a funnel through which cultural meaning is poured into consumer goods.[12] Essentially, advertisers must decide what cultural meanings they want their products to have and create ads that communicate those cultural meanings, often using symbols (whether words or images) to stand for the desired cultural meanings.[13] For instance, to communicate cool, refreshing, summertime meanings for Nestlé's Nestea instant tea, ads showed people falling, fully clothed, into a cool swimming pool.

EXHIBIT 15.2

Continued

Lifestyle trend	Example
Heightened importance of visuals in advertising marketing	With the VCR revolution, the imperative for advertisers is to make the message seen, not heard.
Fragmentation of media markets	There will be new sources of programming as loyalty to network TV fades.
The return of the family	The family will be seen as something to join, as the baby-boom generation rears its children.
New employee benefits for two-income families	Employers will offer flexible work hours, job sharing, and day care services.
Growing appeal of work at home	Workers will want to work at home on their own computers.
Older Canadians— the next entrepreneurs	Older people want to work past the traditional retirement age and have the resources to invest in their own businesses.
The young Canadian—a new kind of conservative	Although 18- to 29-year-olds are socially liberal, they are economically and politically conservative.
Public relations— tough times ahead for business	Business does not receive the credit it deserves for the creation of new jobs, as people remain suspicious about how business operates.
The nation's mood— the new reality	The euphoric mood of the 1980s was divorced from economic realities. Canadians are economically more sober today.

Source: Adapted from "31 Major Trends Shaping the Future of American Business," *The Public Pulse* 2, no. 1 (New York: The Roper Organization, 1988).

To communicate relief from the misery of mid-February cold, Hall's mentholyptus lozenges ads show the warmth of penetrating heat waves. The long-running Ford Explorer ads seen regularly on "Hockey Night in Canada" showed various symbols of Canadian

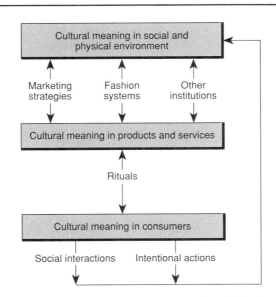

EXHIBIT 15.3

A model of the cultural process

Source: Adapted with permission from the University of Chicago Press from Grant McCracken, "Culture and Consumption: A Theoretical Account of the Structure and Movement of the Cultural Meaning of Consumer Goods," in *Journal of Consumer Research*, June 1986, pp. 71–84. © 1986 by the University of Chicago.

People often are unaware of the specific cultural origins of everyday objects in their environments, even though they may sense the fundamental meaning of these objects. Consider the Jolly Green Giant, the symbol of the Green Giant Company, canners of vegetables in the Le Sueur Valley of Minnesota. In print and TV ads, the Giant stands, hands on hips, towering over the valley and looking down on the hordes of happy, elfin workers harvesting the succulent produce below. He is green and is dressed entirely in green leaves. The Giant doesn't move or say much beyond the obligatory "Ho, Ho, Ho!" at the end of each ad.

What is the cultural meaning of the Jolly Green Giant? Is he merely a memorable brand symbol, or is he something more?

Figures clothed in leaves have deep cultural meanings that date back hundreds of years. James Frazer described many of these symbolic figures in his masterwork, *The Golden Bough*. In many early European cultures, people celebrated the return of spring by honoring the spirits of sacred trees or plants. By the 19th century, this ritual had become embodied in the form of people dressed in leaves or flowers. For instance, the Gypsies of Transylvania and Romania had "Green George," a boy "covered from top to toe in green leaves and blossoms." In Bavaria (southern Germany), the leaf person was "Quack"; in England, it was "Jack in the Green"; and in Switzerland, it was the "Whitsuntide Lout." Other popular names for the fertility symbol were the Leaf King, the Grass King, the May King, and the Queen of May.

Even as recently as 100 years ago, fertility figures representing the spirit of vegetation could be found in many parts of Eastern Europe, Germany, and England.

country and family values. Animals have distinctive symbolic meanings that marketers can associate with products (the moose in Moosehead beer, the polar bear in Sorel boots, the ram for Dodge "ram tough" trucks). The nude bodies shown in Calvin Klein's ads for Obsession cologne connote obvious meanings about the product. Consumer Perspective 15.4 describes another cultural symbol used in advertising.

Although advertising may be the most obvious marketing mechanism for moving meanings into products, other aspects of marketing strategy are involved as well. Consider pricing strategies. Discount stores like Zellers and Wal-Mart use low prices to establish the cultural meaning of their stores. For many consumers, high prices may have positive cultural meanings that can be linked to certain products (Mercedes-Benz, Rolex watches, Chivas Regal scotch, European designer clothing) to convey a deluxe, high-status image of high quality. As for product strategy, Japanese car companies intentionally design interior attributes (leather versus cloth seats, analogue versus digital gauges, wood versus plastic dash) as well as the location and feeling of the controls to transfer important cultural meanings into the car. Even distribution strategies can influence the transmission of meaning: the limited distribution of Burberry trenchcoats and similar products in better clothing stores enhances the products' image.

Other factors besides marketing strategies can influence the transfer of cultural meaning from the environment to products.[14] For instance, journalists who report the results of product tests of cars or stereo systems, or who review movies, are moving cultural meaning into these products. The fashion world, including designers, reporters, opinion leaders, and celebrities, transfers fashion-related meanings into clothing, cuisine, and home furnishings.[15] Consumer advocates such as Ralph Nader (who convinced people the Chevrolet Corvair was unsafe) and private organisations such as the Canadian Standards Association (which provides approval labels validating protective equipment) also transmit meanings to products through their pronouncements.

Although the details of the costume and the ritual varied from place to place, the overall concept and the representation of the central figure were consistent. A youthful person was dressed with leaves and other vegetation. Sometimes the person was symbolically dunked into a handy pond or stream. Thus were the spirits of fertility and water honoured, and the community was assured continued supplies of water and forage.

From a cultural perspective, the Jolly Green Giant can be seen as a 20th-century manifestation of these ancient European fertility symbols. Is this just a coincidence, or does the obvious symbolism of such a figure still convey compelling meanings to the sophisticated citizens of the modern world? Did the creative staff at Leo Burnett, Green Giant's ad agency, intentionally appropriate an ancient fertility symbol, or did the idea emerge from their collective unconscious? And how did the meanings of a giant get added into the equation? Whatever the answers, the Jolly Green Giant seems to represent deep, symbolic cultural meanings that may be partially responsible for the success of the product.

Modern advertising includes other examples of ancient cultural symbols: the Keebler elves, the genie-like Mr. Clean (called Mr. Proper in Germany/Austria), and the white knight of Ajax fame who rode in with lance at the ready and blasted the dirt out of the laundry.

Source: Reproduced by permission of the American Folklore Society from *Journal of American Folklore* 87:343, 1974, pp. 53–65. Not for sale or further reproduction.

Cultural meanings in products

Particular products, stores, and brands do express cultural or symbolic meanings.[16] For instance, Virginia Slims cigarettes are for women, Export A's are for men; Rollerblades and T-shirts are for young people, gardening tools and laxatives are for older people. Some products embody cultural meanings, such as the official NHL Players Association collection of high-quality reproductions of current and old-time hockey team jerseys, jackets, and caps.[17] Using such products makes their cultural meanings tangible and visible and communicates those meanings to others.

Cultural meanings of products are likely to vary across different societies or cultures. For instance, most societies have favourite foods, which represent important meanings in that culture but not in others. The Danes love eel, Mexicans love chilies, Irish love Guinness beer, French love cheese, Americans and Canadians love hamburgers and meat and potatoes. Not all people in a social group or society, however, perceive a product, brand, or activity to have the same cultural meaning. For example, some teenagers might begin to drink Labatt 50 beer to associate themselves with the positive lifestyle and cultural meanings they perceive to be associated with the act of drinking. Others will reject drinking to avoid taking on the negative meanings they perceive in the action.

While some of the cultural meanings in products are obvious to anyone who is familiar with that culture, other meanings are hidden. Nearly everyone would recognise the basic cultural meanings in different styles of clothing (jeans and a sweatshirt compared to a business suit), makes of car (Mercedes-Benz versus Ford versus Honda), types of stores (The Bay versus Zellers' versus Eaton's or Ogilvy's). But other, less obvious cultural meanings in products may not be fully recognised by consumers or marketers. This was the case in 1985 when Coca-Cola changed Coke's taste to make it slightly sweeter with less of a bite.[18] When it introduced new Coke, the company was surprised by an immediate flurry of protests from customers. Millions of people had consumed Coke from childhood and had strong cultural meanings for (and emotional ties to) the original product.

These consumers resented its removal from the marketplace and some of them even sued the company. In response, Coca-Cola quickly reintroduced the original product under the brand name Coca-Cola Classic.

Finally, many products have *personal meanings* in addition to cultural meaning. Personal meanings are moved into products by the actions of individual consumers. Although these meanings tend to be highly idiosyncratic and unique to each consumer, they are important as a source of personal relevance that can affect consumers' involvement with the product.

Moving meanings from products into consumers

The cultural process model in Exhibit 15.3 identifies rituals as ways of moving cultural meanings from the product to the consumer. A **ritual** is a *symbolic action that people engage in to create, affirm, evoke, or revise certain cultural meanings.*[19] For instance, the consumption ritual performed on Thanksgiving Day by most Canadian families, who come together to feast on a big turkey dinner, affirms the family's ability to provide abundantly for its needs. Not all rituals involve formal events such as a special dinner, a graduation, or a wedding. Many rituals are actually common actions in everyday life, although people may not recognise their behaviour as ritualistic. Here we discuss five specific consumption-related rituals involved in the movement of meaning from product to consumer: acquisition, possession, exchange, grooming, and divestment rituals.[20]

Some of the cultural meanings in products are transferred to consumers through specific *acquisition rituals* involved in purchasing and consuming the product. For instance, buying and eating an ice-cream cone is necessary to receive the cultural meanings the product conveys (fun, relaxation, a reward for hard work, a "pick-me-up"). Other acquisition behaviours have ritualistic characteristics that are important for meaning transfer. For example, collectors looking for scarce or unique products (antiques, stamps or coins, tools) may perform special *search rituals* when they go out on the hunt, including wearing special lucky clothes.

Another example of acquisition ritual is the *bargaining ritual* involved in negotiating the price of a car, a stereo system, or something at a garage sale, which can transfer important meanings to the buyer ("I got a good deal"). Consider how an avid antique collector describes the role of bidding rituals at an auction or flea market.

> There's no Alcoholics Anonymous for collectors. You just get bit by the bug and that's it. The beauty and craftsmanship of some of these things is amazing. They were made by people who cared. There's nothing like getting ahold of them for yourself. Especially if you get it for a song and you sing it yourself. It's not just *getting* a great deal, it's *knowing* that you've got a great deal that makes for the thrill. It's even better if you had to bid against someone for it.[21]

Possession rituals are another way consumers acquire the meanings in products. For instance, people moving into a new house or apartment have a housewarming party to show the place off and formally establish its meanings. Many consumers perform similar ritualistic displays of new purchases (a car, clothing, stereo system) to solicit the admiration of their friends and gain reassurance that they made a good purchase.

Other possession rituals involve moving personal meaning from the customer "into" the product. For instance, *product nurturing rituals* put personal meaning into the product (washing your car each Saturday; organising your CD collection; tuning your bicycle; tilling your garden).[22] At some point following the nurturing activity, such meanings can be moved back to the consumer, where they may be experienced and enjoyed as satisfaction or pride. Such possession rituals help create strong, involving relationships between products and consumers.

Personalising rituals serve a similar function. For instance, many people who buy a used car or a house they did not build perform ritualistic actions to remove meanings left

These products focus on a lifestyle trend toward drinking bottled water—the lightest drink of all.

over from the previous owner and transfer new meanings of their own into the product. The car owner might purchase special accessories to personalise it (new floor mats, a better radio, different wheels and/or tires, custom stripes). Repainting, wallpapering, and installing new carpeting are rituals that personalise a house.

Certain meanings can be transferred to consumers through *exchange rituals* such as giving gifts.[23] For instance, taking wine or flowers when you go to a dinner party is a ritual that transfers cultural meanings (thanks, courtesy, generosity). People often select gifts for anniversaries, birthdays, or special holidays that contain special cultural meanings to be transferred to the receiver. For instance, giving a nice watch, luggage, or a new car to a university graduate might be intended to convey cultural meanings of achievement, adult status or independence. Parents often give gifts to their children that are intended to transfer particular cultural meanings (a puppy represents responsibility; a bike represents freedom; a computer conveys the importance of learning and mastery).

Certain cultural meanings consumers acquire tend to fade over time. The central meanings embodied in personal care products such as shampoo, mouthwash, deodorants, and cosmetics, such as attractiveness, confidence, and influence over others, do not become a permanent part of the consumer. Consumers must continually renew these meanings by drawing them out of a product each time they use it. *Grooming rituals* describe people's particular ways of using personal care products that call up these cultural meanings and transfer them to the consumer. Some people engage in elaborate grooming rituals to obtain these important meanings (see Consumer Perspective 15.5).

Consumers perform *divestment rituals* to remove meaning from products. Certain products (clothing, a house, a car or motorcycle, a favourite piece of sports equipment) can embody considerable amounts of personal meaning. Products can acquire such personal meaning through long periods of use, or because they symbolise important meanings (a painting might be a family heirloom that has been handed down through the generations). Often consumers feel that some of these personal meanings must be removed before such products can be sold or discarded. Thus, people may wash or dry

CONSUMER PERSPECTIVE

▶ 15.5

Grooming rituals

A Canada-wide poll on grooming habits conducted by Angus Reid on behalf of S. C. Johnson and Son, manufacturers of Edge shaving gel, found that Canadian men spend just as much money and almost as much time primping and preening as do women. On average, Canadians spend 21.5 minutes in the bathroom getting ready in the morning, with women averaging 23.5 minutes and men 19. Both sexes spend $37 a month on such personal grooming items as shaving preps, body creams, hair sprays, hair gels, shampoos, and deodorants. Men over the age of 55 actually spend $5 more than their female counterparts.

The poll also found that only one man in 10 leaves the choice of grooming products to wives, girlfriends, or mothers. Blue-collar workers spend more on grooming products than professionals; single Canadians spend 28 percent more than married people. In Canada, it's the Quebecers who spend the most time grooming.

Another survey, conducted in 25 universities across North America, found that grooming plays a surprisingly important role on college campuses for both women and men, especially during job interviews.

Women perceive regular skin care products as the most important factor in grooming, while men consider a shaped body and wearing the right clothes as the most important. The primary reasons they give for spending a "great deal" or "fair" amount of time using grooming products are "Looking better makes me feel better" and "A good physical appearance is important if you want to succeed." Looking to the future, these respondents all expect that personal grooming will become even more important.

To discover consumers' deep, symbolic meanings for some products in the marketplace can be difficult. However, the knowledge may give marketers useful insights into consumers' reactions to their strategies.

Source: Laura Medcaff, "Genders Are Equal In Front of Mirror," *Marketing*, Feb. 8, 1993, p. 2; Marlene Habib, "Men Almost As Bad As Women For Time Spent Grooming," *Winnipeg Free Press*, Dec. 18, 1992, p. A8, "The 1986 Survey of College Grooming Habits," published by ASK Associates, Inc.

clean a favourite item of clothing that they plan to give away or donate to charity to remove some of the personal meanings in the product. Others might remove certain highly personal fixtures in a house (a special chandelier), attributes of a car (a special radio), or parts of a motorcycle (a custom seat) before selling it.

In certain cases, the personal meaning in a product is so great that the consumer cannot bear to part with the object. Thus, people hang onto old cars, clothes, or furniture that have sentimental personal meaning. One study found that some people had become so highly attached to their Levi's jeans that they kept them for 20 or 30 years.[24] These consumers associated many salient meanings with Levi's jeans, including the self-confidence they felt when wearing the product and the feeling that Levi's were appropriate in many social situations. Other consumers talked as if their Levi's were an old friend who had accompanied them on many adventures, and their jeans were valued for the memories they embodied. If divestment rituals are unable to remove these meanings, consumers may keep such objects practically forever, or at least until the personal meanings have faded and become less intense.

Cultural meanings in consumers

Consumers select products as one way to acquire cultural meanings to use in establishing their self-identities. Consider the sports fan who buys a team hat or jacket. Major League Baseball Properties, a licensing and marketing organisation, sells authentic jerseys from the Toronto Blue Jays (about $175) and the 1919 Chicago Black Sox ($245) to middle-age fans who want to identify with their favourite teams, present and past. Some people buy Ben & Jerry's Rain Forest Crunch ice cream (made from nuts grown in the Amazon rain forest) or Tide detergent packaged in recycled materials to express the environmental values these products embody. People buy such products to move important cultural meanings into themselves and to communicate these meanings to others.

Canadians have a lot of freedom to create different selves, through their choice of lifestyles and environments as well as products. Personality definition is especially intense during the teenage and young adult years. In trying different social roles and identities, young people often purchase products to gain meanings related to these roles. Thus, teenage rebellion against parental values often involves the purchase of products that symbolise the desired cultural meanings (often clothing). As most people mature, their self-concepts become more stable, and their interest in change lessens. Even so, consumers still use the cultural meanings in products to maintain and fine tune their current identities.

Although products transfer some useful meanings to consumers, goods cannot provide all the meanings that consumers need to construct a healthy self-concept. People obtain self-relevant meanings from many fundamental sources, including their work, family, religious experience, and various social activities. The meanings gained through these activities are likely to be more basic and more satisfying than those obtained through product consumption. In highly developed consumption societies, however, some people buy products in an attempt to define themselves through possessions. Some marketing strategies encourage this behaviour. These consumers may engage in excessive consumption as they desperately seek to acquire cultural meanings with which to construct a satisfactory identity. More often the result is debt and dissatisfaction.

Most people have favourite possessions that are imbued with significant self-relevant meanings, and they experience high levels of *involvement* with such objects.[25] For instance, older people tend to feel strong attachments to objects such as photographs and furniture that remind them of past events, while younger consumers tend to value objects that allow them to be active in self-relevant ways (sports or hobby equipment, work-related objects such as books or computers). Marketers who understand these consumer/product relationships can develop more effective marketing strategies.

Moving meanings to the cultural environment

The cultural process model in Exhibit 15.3 shows that the consumers' meanings can be transferred to the social and physical environment through their social behaviour. That is, in a society consisting of many individuals living and working together, culture (shared meaning) literally is created by those people. Much of the movement of meaning to the cultural environment is an automatic consequence of the daily social interactions among people. Sometimes, however, people intentionally try to create new cultural meanings in an attempt to change society. For instance, various interest groups in society (punks, greens or environmental activists, gay rights activists) try to influence others to adopt new cultural meanings.

Marketing implications

The cultural process is a continual movement of meanings between and among the physical and social environment, organisations, and individuals in the society. This focuses marketers' attention on the cultural meaning of their brands.[26] The shared cultural meanings of a brand are a large part of its economic value or its *brand equity,*[27] and managing the brand requires that marketers identify these shared brand meanings and monitor any changes. Means-end analysis is useful for this purpose. A marketer might try to maintain positive brand meanings or to create new favourable meanings by selecting appropriate meanings from the cultural environment and transferring them into products and brands by marketing strategies.

Consumption rituals or special occasions such as Thanksgiving help create or affirm important cultural meanings.

Although marketers usually think their strategies have little effect on culture, marketing strategies do influence the cultural environment in a number of ways. A conspicuous example is the proliferation of marketing information (stores, signs, billboards, ads), which changes cultural meaning of the physical environment. Less obvious is how the huge volume of marketing strategies in a consumption society affects the social environment and thereby the cultural meanings of modern life.[28]

Celebrity endorsers in ads

A popular advertising strategy in North America (and in Japan) for endowing products and brands with cultural meaning is to use celebrities to endorse a product.[29] Among the celebrities appearing in ads in the early 1990s were the actor Michael J. Fox (Pepsi), Cher and the ballet dancer Mikhail Baryshnikov (cologne), CEOs Lee Iacocca (Chrysler) and Victor Kiam (Remington razors), singers Whitney Houston and Michael Jackson, and basketball player Michael Jordan (Nike). Other examples include Celine Dionne and Anne Murray (The Bay), Wayne Gretzky (Thrifty Car Rentals), Eddie Shack (Days Inn motels), Pat Burns (Nutri-Slim), and Alan Thicke (Zellers).

From a cultural perspective, celebrities may be seen as cultural objects with specific cultural meanings. Consider, for instance, the meanings associated with Mark Tewkesbury, Isabelle Brasseur, and Lloyd Eisler, all talented athletes who are spokespeople for the beef industry in Canada.

In developing an effective celebrity endorsement strategy, marketers must be careful to select a celebrity who embodies appropriate meanings that are consistent with the overall marketing strategy (the intended meanings) for the product. For example, celebrities such as Bill Murray, Sylvester Stallone, or Suzanne Sommers convey relatively clear meanings that are based on the types of roles they usually play. Musicians such as Elton John and Sting (for Coke) or Ray Charles (for Pepsi) have distinctive cultural images related to their records, live performances, and video appearances, which enhance their appeal as celebrity spokespeople. Some celebrities, like Madonna, have shrewdly re-created their images (and their cultural meanings) over time as the appeal of one set of cultural meanings wanes. Interestingly, celebrities who tend to be typecast (something actors complain about) are more likely to evoke shared cultural meanings that can be associated with a product. Meryl Streep, for instance, might not be a desirable spokesperson because she has played a wide variety of roles and therefore does not convey a clear set of cultural meanings.

Sometimes the cultural meanings of a celebrity spokesperson are related to their credibility and expertise concerning the product. For instance, Cher and Elizabeth Taylor promote their own perfume brands. Jean Luc Brassard promotes Birk's jewellery (stopwatches) and Maurice Richard Grecian Formula hair products. In other cases, the person's cultural meanings are not logically linked to the product, but the marketer hopes the general meaning of the celebrity as a credible and trustworthy person will help transfer important meanings to the product. Apparently on this basis, Bill Cosby has been a spokesperson for Jell-O, E. F. Hutton, Kodak film, and Coke.

Marketers need to understand more about how celebrities transfer meanings to a product. What happens to the cultural meanings of celebrities who are disgraced (Ben Johnson is caught using steroids, Pete Rose is jailed for income tax evasion), or fall from public favour (an actor's performance is panned), or retire from public life (Larry Bird stops playing basketball, Ingmar Bergman stops making films), or return again to fame and favour in some way (Bob Dylan or Mickey Rooney)? How do marketers use such celebrities in transmitting cultural meanings? Do consumers gain the meanings embodied by a celebrity merely by purchasing the endorsed brand, or are ritualistic behaviours necessary? Although it is popular to criticise the North American and Japanese fascination with celebrities as juvenile, celebrities represent important cultural meanings that many consumers find personally relevant. By purchasing and using a product endorsed by a celebrity, consumers can assume some of those meanings and use them in constructing a satisfying identity.

Helping consumers obtain cultural meanings

If they understand the role of rituals in consumer behaviour, marketers can devise rituals that serve to transfer important cultural meanings from products to the customer. A real estate firm, for instance, might develop an elaborate purchase ritual, perhaps including an exchange of gifts, to symbolise the transfer of the house and its meanings to the buyer. Some upscale clothing stores go through elaborate shopping and buying rituals aimed at their affluent customers, including ushering the customer to a private room, serving coffee or wine, and presenting a selection of clothing. People dining in a fine restaurant participate in many rituals that transfer special meanings, including being seated by the maître d', talking to the wine steward, using different silverware and glasses, eating successive courses, and tipping.

Another example is the strategies Nissan uses to create rituals that help transmit meanings about the luxury car Infiniti to consumers.[30] Dealers will gently welcome customers Japanese-style, as "honoured guests" (not aggressively descend on the "mooches," as car salespeople sometimes describe naive customers). Tea or coffee is offered, served in fine Japanese china. Each Infiniti dealership has a special shoki-screened contemplation room where consumers can sit quietly with the car, "meditating" about their purchase and the consumer/product relationship. These rituals help reinforce the low-pressure, relaxed meanings Nissan wants to impart to the Infiniti experience.

CROSS-CULTURAL INFLUENCES

Foreign markets have become significant for many businesses. In the U.S. film industry, because domestic ticket sales were flat over the past decade (about 1 billion tickets per year), film companies have looked to foreign markets for growth. In 1990, major domestic film studios received about 35 percent of their total revenues from foreign markets (50 percent for smaller companies).[31] Film studios have come under pressure to develop films that will appeal to consumers both in North America and in foreign markets.

To develop strategies that are effective in multiple cultures, marketers must understand the differences in cultural meanings across societies. **Cross-cultural differences** in meanings create different cultural environments that influence consumers' behaviours, affects, and cognition. These cross-cultural differences must be considered in developing international marketing strategies.

Cross-cultural differences do not always coincide with national borders. This concept is obvious in Canada, with its two founding cultures of French and British. It is also obvious in many countries where the cultural differences between internal social factions can be as great as those between separate nations. Examples include the former Yugoslavia (which was made up of several distinct regions including Slovenia, Croatia, and Serbia), Belgium (with two language cultures—Flemish and French), Switzerland (with German, French, Italian, and Romansch-speaking regions). Understanding the multiple cultural influences in such regions requires an analysis of subcultures, discussed in Chapter 16.

Likewise, national borders do not always demarcate clear cross-cultural differences. For instance, many people living on either side of the long Canadian–U.S. border share similar cultural characteristics. Likewise, the people in southern Austria and northern Italy, or northern France and southern Belgium, share many cultural characteristics.

Cross-cultural differences

Marketers must consider cross-cultural differences when developing marketing strategies for foreign markets. We discuss some of these differences here.

Differences in consumption culture

The level of consumption orientation in different markets around the world is an important cross-cultural factor that must be considered in developing international marketing strategies. Canadian society, like the United States, Japan, and Western Europe, is a highly developed consumer culture. Even in relatively poor countries, significant segments of society may have a developing consumption culture. For instance, India, Mexico, and many South American countries have large middle classes able to consume at significant levels. The Pacific Rim countries have a rapidly growing middle class with substantial spending power. Consumer Perspective 15.6 provides more details on this vast market.

In much of the world, however, the majority of people are unable to participate fully in a consumption culture. For instance, the ordinary citizens of many Eastern European countries, the former Soviet Union, China, India, and most less developed countries do not have sufficient purchasing power to consume at high levels, nor are these societies able to produce goods in sufficient number and variety to meet the consumption needs of their people. A company's marketing strategies must be tailored to the level of consumption culture in the society.

Self-concept

People in different cultures may have strikingly different concepts of themselves and how they should relate to other people.[32] An example is the differences between the independent self-concept typical of North America and Western Europe and the social concept of self as highly interrelated with others that is more common in Japan, India, Africa, and South America. North Americans, with their strong individualistic orientation, tend to think of themselves in terms of personal traits and abilities that enable them to achieve their ideal goals of independence, freedom of choice, and personal achievement. The Japanese, by contrast, tend to value an individual who is sensitive to the needs of others, fitting harmoniously into the group and contributing positively to the well-being of its members. Such cross-cultural differences in self-concept are likely to affect how people in a cultural environment interpret and use products to achieve important ends in their lives.

Materialism

Materialistic values underlie the development of a mass consumption society, and people in different societies vary considerably in their level of materialism. Materialism has been defined as the "importance a consumer attaches to worldly possessions."[33] In fact, **materialism** is a multidimensional value including, for instance, *possessiveness, envy* (jealousy of someone's possessions), and *lack of generosity* (unwillingness to give or share possessions). Consumers with this value tend to acquire many possessions that they see as important for achieving happiness, self-esteem, or social recognition (all prominent values in Canadian culture). One study identifies four representations of materialism: possessions are symbols of success or achievement (also prominent Canadian values), a source of pleasure, a source of happiness, and representations of indulgence and luxury.[34]

The United States is usually considered the most materialistic culture in the world.[35] Canadians, on the other hand, have always viewed themselves as less materialistic than their neighbours to the south. With the rise of environmentalism in Canada, the theme of responsible consumerism has helped to reinforce this perception. The three Rs of reducing, re-using, and recycling have been promoted extensively, and marketers across Canada have had to respond accordingly. Clearly the theme of materialism, though still a strong factor in most of the developed world, is taking on a new face in the light of recent cultural changes.

Similar cross-cultural changes

It is becoming more common to find similar cultural changes occurring in many societies around the world at about the same time. For instance, the social roles for women in Canadian society have changed considerably over the past 20 years; as more women work outside the home, their values, goals, beliefs, and behaviours have changed.[36] Similar changes are now seen around the world. Modern women in North America and Europe, and increasingly in Japan and other countries, want more egalitarian marriages. They want their husbands to share in the housework and nurturing of children, and they want to establish a personal identity outside the family unit. These common cross-cultural changes have created similar marketing opportunities in many societies (particularly for convenience products and time-saving services). For instance, as the Japanese become more consumption oriented and price conscious, the number of malls and discount stores is increasing rapidly.[37]

In developed countries throughout the world, people want more leisure and more free time. Even the world champion workaholics in Japan, where up to 60 percent of workers spend Saturdays on the job, have begun to relax a bit.[38] Although the traditional Japanese values of hard work, dedication, and respect for the established order are still dominant, some Japanese, especially the young, are starting to see certain aspects of Western culture and lifestyle as preferable to their own.

A global culture?

Although some cross-cultural differences are distinctive, in other cases people from different cultures have rather similar values and consumer/product relationships. Some analysts, in fact, see the entire world as moving toward an "Americanised" culture, although

Significant cultural changes in Asia are opening up new marketing opportunities for companies. A number of factors are contributing these massive changes in culture.

People
About 1.7 billion people live in the Asian Pacific Rim region. It is estimated that by the turn of the century, Asia will have 259 million people, including 73 million households with annual incomes of $18,000. China will account for 150 million of these individuals, India for 75 million, and East Asia for the remainder. China and India together contain 40 percent of the world's population. Within China there are 40 cities with populations of more than one million (the United States has nine). This represents the largest potential consumer market in the next decade.

Income
There has been dramatic change in income in East Asia. Estimates are that per-capita incomes rose at an annual rate of 6.5 percent from 1983 to 1993. In China alone, incomes over that period grew 8.5 percent annually. The World Bank predicts that developing countries in Asia could have average gross domestic product (GDP) growth of 4.8 percent annually over the next 10 years (against 3.5 percent in the 1980s). Among them, China, Indonesia, India and South Korea are expected to double their share of global GDP to 20 percent by 2100. A recent survey found that 72 million people in the Pacific Rim (not including Japan) have average household incomes of U.S.$12,000 or more. The average individual pay had gone up 28 percent in the past two years. If this growth rate continues, annual salaries will reach U.S.$20,000 by 1999.

Cities
It was only a few years ago that Asia, excluding Japan, was mostly a low-cost, low-pay production site. With the impressive growth rates, China and India have embarked on far-reaching economic reforms. The same is true for smaller countries such as Vietnam and South Korea. This is all happening in conjunction with Taiwan's high-profile projects (U.S.$300 billion infrastructure programme), tariff reductions and the message that China's opening is for real. Asia has changed its image in the minds of the leading corporations and has the attention of the whole world as never before.

this observation is far from accepted. Consumer Perspective 15.7 discusses some examples of the exporting of Canadian and American popular culture. To the extent that cultural meanings are becoming similar across societies, marketers may be able to develop successful strategies that are indeed global in scope.

Developing international marketing strategies

Cross-cultural differences pose challenges for international marketers. Even translating a brand or model name into another language can cause problems. When Coca-Cola was introduced in China in the 1920s, the translated meaning of the brand name was "bite the wax tadpole"! Sales were not good, and the symbols were later changed to mean "happiness in the mouth." AMC's Matador model had problems in Puerto Rico because matador means "killer." Ford changed the name of the Comet to Caliente when it introduced this car in Mexico, then experienced low sales levels until it discovered that *caliente* is slang for streetwalker. Sunbeam Corp. introduced its mist-producing hair-curling iron in the German market under the name Mist-Stick, which translated meant "manure wand."[39]

North American companies are not the only ones that have difficulty translating brand names. The Chinese had to find better brand names for several products they hoped to

Women

It is also a great change that Asian men agree that women are at least as intelligent as men. The average income of women within the region has risen even faster than men's by 35 percent to U.S.$13,000. Almost everywhere in Asia, women are staying in school longer, marrying later, and entering the work force in greater numbers. They are having fewer children and having them later in life.

Families

As the number of children in each household decreases and the number of households increases, there has been a dramatic increase in the consumption of children's products. This is good news for companies that target children as their major customers, such as Disney. The Asia-Pacific region now accounts for about 25 percent of Disney's revenue from consumer products. Half of the 50 busiest McDonald's in the world are located in Hong Kong.

Communications

The incredible changes in technology enable consumers in Taiwan and Singapore to know what's happening in Canada or the rest of the world. Also, because of the intense competition in the telecommunications industry, the cost of communicating has decreased. People in Asia love to own whatever new gadget that their counterparts in the West enjoy. A large proportion of consumers in this Asian region are innovators who value ownership of high-tech equipment and firsthand news as symbols of status and superiority. These regions would be good test markets for many discontinuous innovations.

Singaporeans, the Hong Kong Chinese, and the Indonesians like to buy anything metal that goes beep. In fact, Jardine Fleming Securities, a Hong Kong firm, has estimated that between now and the year 2000, Asia (excluding Japan) will spend $1.15 trillion on power, transportation, telecommunications, water supplies, and sanitation.

Sources: *Far Eastern Economic Review*, "Special Reports on Asia Lifestyle," Dec. 30–Jan. 6, July 15, Aug. 11, Sept. 15, 1994; *Fortune*, May 30, 1994, pp. 74–90.

export, including "Double Happiness" bras, "Pansy" men's underwear, and "White Elephant" batteries.[40]

Clearly, cross-cultural differences in language and related meanings can affect the success of a marketing strategy. While differences in cultures can often be identified, marketers do not agree on how to treat them. There are at least three overall approaches. First, a firm can adapt its marketing strategy to the characteristics of each culture. Second, a firm can standardise its marketing strategy across several cultures. Arguments over which of these is the preferred approach have raged for more than 20 years. Third, a firm can use a marketing strategy to change the culture.

Adapt strategy to culture

The traditional approach to international marketing is to research each local culture to identify important differences from the domestic market. The goal is to understand differences in consumer needs, wants, preferences, attitudes, and values, as well as in shopping, purchasing, and consumption behaviours. Marketers then tailor a marketing strategy to fit the specific values and behaviours of the culture.

Celebrity endorsers are used to move cultural meaning into products.

The *adaptation* approach advocates modifying the product, the promotion mix, or any other aspect of marketing strategy to appeal to local cultures.[41] Black & Decker, for example, modifies its hand tools because electrical outlets and voltages vary in different parts of the world. Philip Morris had to alter its ads for Marlboro cigarettes in Britain, because the government believed British children were so impressed with American

Benetton uses a similar social awareness image strategy across the world.

**CONSUMER
PERSPECTIVE**

15.7 ◀

**Exporting
North American
popular culture**

Aspects of North American culture are found increasingly around the globe. Consider the worldwide presence of Coke and Pepsi, McDonald's and Pizza Hut, Mickey Mouse and Mickey Rourke, cowboys and jazz, Americana films and Disneyland. The spread of American culture has produced some incongruous scenes of Third World protesters burning the American flag or chanting anti-American slogans while dressed in Nikes and Levi's. Although some people consider American culture distasteful, others have adopted many of its forms. Even in anglophobic France, the uniform of young, upper-middle-class Parisian women in 1990 was pure Americana: Calvin Klein jeans, a white button-down oxford shirt, a navy blazer, Bass Weejuns penny loafers, and a Marlboro cigarette.

Clearly, consumers around the world are not attracted to American products solely for their intrinsic physical qualities. People don't buy blue jeans because of some universal aesthetic for denim, nor do Coke or Marlboros or Mickey Mouse have physical attributes that are so special. Rather, these prototypically American products are inbred with meanings that symbolise the United States.

What are these special American meanings? According to a Yale professor, "It's about a dream, a utopian fantasy. Certainly it is about freedom, the freedom of people to create themselves anew, redefining themselves through the products that they buy and use, the clothes they wear, the music they listen to." Blue jeans, perhaps more than any other product, symbolise America and the individualistic meanings it represents to many. Buying blue jeans is a way for consumers to share in the American dream of individualism, personal freedom, and other symbolic characteristics associated with America.

This international demand for North American culture has extended to Canadian culture as well. For example, Moosehead beer of Canada experienced great success when it introduced its namesake to the Swedish market. Since March 1993, when the first 4,200 cases left Canada, the Dartmouth, N.S., company's brand has rocketed to third place among 75 imported labels. In fact, what Moosehead executives expected to sell over an entire year sold out in only two months.

It is important to recognise that North American culture is popular partly because it is just that—a popular culture, not an elitist culture created by and for the aristocracy in a society. North American culture is for the masses. Moreover, it is a highly democratic culture, which everyone in the society helps to shape, not just the upper class. Finally, North American culture lends itself to export because it is itself a combination of diverse cultural elements brought together by millions of immigrants tumbled together to create something new and desirable.

Source: David Bartal, "Moosehead Defies Odds in Sweden," *Marketing*, Aug. 2/9, 1993, p. 15; Eric Felten, "Love It or Hate It, America Is King of Pop Culture," *Insight*, March 25, 1991, pp. 14–16.

cowboys they might be moved to take up smoking. Nestlé modifies the taste of its Nescafe coffee and the promotions for it in the adjoining countries of France and Switzerland to accommodate different preferences in each nation.[42]

Standardise strategy across cultures

The **global marketing** approach argues for marketing a product in essentially the same way everywhere in the world. Standardising strategy is not a new idea. Coca-Cola has used this basic approach for more than 40 years: "one sight, one sound, one sell." Eastman Kodak, Gillette, and Timex are among other companies that have marketed standard products in essentially the same way for several decades.

Many marketers are beginning to treat the standardised approach more seriously. One of its major advocates, Theodore Levitt, argues that increased world travel and worldwide telecommunications capabilities cause consumers the world over to think and shop in increasingly similar ways. Tastes, preferences, and motivations of people in different cultures are becoming more homogeneous, so a common brand name, packaging, and communication strategy can be used successfully for many products.[43] For example, given the international popularity of the "Dallas" TV show, actress Victoria Principal sold Jhirmack shampoo all over the world. Similarly, Victor Kiam sells his Remington shavers using the same pitch in 15 languages. Sales of Remington shavers went up 60 percent in Britain and 140 percent in Australia using this approach. Playtex markets its WoW bra in 12 countries using the same advertising appeal.

One advantage of the standardised approach is that it can be much less expensive.[44] Executives at Coca-Cola, for instance, estimate they save more than $8 million a year in the cost of thinking up new imagery. Texas Instruments runs the same ads throughout Europe rather than mounting individual ad campaigns for each country, and it estimates its savings at $30,000 per commercial. Playtex produced standardised ads for 12 countries for $250,000, while the average cost of producing a single Playtex ad for the United States was $100,000.[45]

For some products, a global or standardised marketing approach can work well, although many have severely criticised it.[46] Two issues cloud the debate between adapting versus standardising international marketing approaches. First is the nature of the product and how standardised the global approach is. For example, advocates of standardising recognise that Black & Decker had to modify its products to suit local electrical outlets and voltages; yet they would argue the basic meaning and use of such products is becoming similar across cultures. If so, the same type of promotion campaign should work in different cultures.

Second, and perhaps more important, is the question whether advocates of the standardising approach are identifying a long-term trend toward similarity across cultures or are suggesting that cultures are nearly identical today. If the former is true, this is a trend marketers should be aware of and adapt to when appropriate. Thus, in essence, both sides are arguing for marketers to adapt to cultural trends; there would seem to be little disagreement between the two positions at this level.

Change the culture

The first approach we discussed is to adapt marketing strategy to local cultures. The second approach assumes decreasing cross-cultural differences that, in some cases, can be ignored. Yet a third approach suggests marketing strategies can be developed to influence a culture directly to achieve organisational objectives. As the cultural process model in Exhibit 15.3 shows, marketing does not simply reflect changing cultural values and behaviours of consumers; marketing is an active part of the cultural process of creating and transferring cultural meaning.[47]

Marketing strategies can change cultural values and behaviours. Several years ago, Nestlé marketed vigorously to convince mothers in some Third World countries to change from breast-feeding to baby formula. The campaign attempted to convince mothers that breast-feeding was not as healthful for their children as the company's formula. The campaign did change their feeding practices. Unfortunately, lack of clean water and improper formula preparation led to an increase in infant mortality. Thus, the preference for and practice of breast-feeding had to be reinstilled in those countries, which was done successfully by Nestlé. This company changed cultural preferences and behaviours—and then changed them back—in a relatively short time.

Learning objective 1: *Define culture and cultural meaning.*
Culture is broadly defined as the meanings that are shared by most people in a social group. Those meanings that are similar or common among people in the group are called cultural meanings. Cultural meanings could refer to any component of the Wheel of Consumer Analysis: affect and cognition, behaviour, or any aspect of the environment, including marketing strategies. Cultural meanings are created by people in the social group and are in continual flux. Marketers can analyse the cultural meanings of very large groups such as an entire society, a subculture within a society, or quite small groups such as families or reference groups.

Learning objective 2: *Discuss aspects of the content of culture, including core values.*
The content of culture includes the beliefs, attitudes, goals, and values held by most people in a society as well as their emotions and feelings. Culture also refers to the shared meanings of characteristic behaviours, rules, customs, and norms that most people follow. The content of culture includes shared meanings of the significant aspects of the social and physical environment, including the major social institutions in a society (governmental bodies, political parties, religions) and the typical physical objects (products, tools, buildings) its people use. Core values describe the end goals people are striving to achieve in their lives and are among the most important aspects of culture. An understanding of the core values in a social group is essential for marketers in order to identify how those values are related to products through means-end chains.

Learning objective 3: *Describe the cultural process by which cultural meaning is moved from the environment into products and then into consumers.*
Cultural meaning is present in three locations—in the social and physical environment, in products and services, and in individual consumers. Cultural meaning is moved or transferred between locations through a cultural process effected by organisations (government, business, religion, education) and by individuals in the society. Two forces for meaning transfer in a consumption-oriented society are these: (1) Marketing strategies are designed to endow products and services with cultural meaning that makes them attractive to consumers. Advertising is the most obvious marketing strategy for transmitting meaning into products, but in fact all aspects of marketing strategy, including product design, pricing, and distribution, are involved. (2) Consumers actively seek the cultural meanings in products to use in establishing a desirable personal identity or self-concept. They engage in ritualistic behaviours to acquire the meanings in products.

Learning objective 4: *Give examples of how rituals move meaning from products into consumers and vice versa.*
Rituals are symbolic actions that people engage in to create, affirm, evoke, or revise certain cultural meanings. Some rituals involve formal ceremonies such as a wedding or a graduation, but rituals also are common behaviours in everyday life. Marketers are especially interested in the rituals consumers perform to transfer meanings from the product to themselves and vice versa. Acquisition rituals may be important in helping people acquire the cultural meanings of some products. For instance, shopping rituals may be important for consumers who are buying an important suit or special antiques. Bargaining rituals may be part of the acquisition process. Possession rituals such as showing off a new car help establish cultural meanings of ownership and pride. Divestment rituals are actions intended to remove meaning from a product before one disposes of it.

Learning objective 5: *Give some examples of important cross-cultural differences.*
Cross-cultural differences refer to differences in cultural meaning across societies, usually analysed in terms of national boundaries. Consumers in different societies or countries are likely to have different values, beliefs, emotional responses, and norms of

appropriate behaviour, as well as different social and physical environments. For instance, people in some societies may be more materialistic than in others. One important cross-cultural difference refers to people's self-concepts, or how they see themselves. Such cross-cultural differences can lead to distinctive consumer/product relationships. Cross-cultural differences in consumption behaviours, such as shopping, bargaining, or product use, can be important for marketing. Emotional reactions to marketing strategies (ads, displays, salespeople) may differ across cultures.

Learning objective 6: *Discuss three approaches to developing international marketing strategies.*

First, a company can adapt its marketing strategies to cultural factors found in various societies. This may require a company to develop special product configurations, advertising campaigns, and pricing and distribution strategies for each culture. A second possibility is to develop a standardised marketing strategy to be used in several cultures. A standardised strategy does not mean every tiny detail is identical in every culture, but the key aspects of the strategy are the same. A third approach to cross-cultural differences in international marketing is to attempt through marketing and general business strategies to change cultural values and behaviours in ways advantageous to the company. Most companies follow the first two approaches.

▶ **KEY TERMS AND CONCEPTS**

culture	core values	cross-cultural differences
cultural meanings	cultural process	materialism
content of culture	ritual	global marketing

▶ **REVIEW AND DISCUSSION QUESTIONS**

1. Define culture and describe three issues involved in cultural analysis.

2. Identify a major change in cultural values that seems to be occurring in your society (choose one not discussed in the book). Discuss its likely effects on consumers' affect, cognitions, and behaviours and on the social and physical environment.

3. Discuss two implications of your analysis in Question 2 for developing marketing strategies for a product of your choice.

4. Briefly describe one example of a price, product, and distribution strategy that moves cultural meaning into the product (do not use examples cited in the text).

5. Select a print ad and analyse it as a mechanism for moving cultural meaning into the product.

6. Choose a popular celebrity endorser and analyse the meanings that are being transmitted to the product the celebrity is endorsing.

7. Select a holiday in your culture other than Christmas. Discuss the cultural values reflected in this holiday celebration. What rituals does your family perform for this holiday, and how do these actions convey meaning?

8. Think about what you do when getting ready to go to a party or some other social event. Identify a grooming ritual you perform that involves some product (blow dryer, cologne, shampoo, cosmetics). What implications might this ritual have for marketing this product?

9. Describe a personal experience in which you performed a divestment ritual. What personal meanings did you remove through the ritual?

10. Discuss how the three main approaches to dealing with cross-cultural factors in international marketing could be applied to the marketing of a soft drink like Pepsi. Describe one problem with each approach. Which approach do you recommend?

CHAPTER 16

Subculture and Social Class Influences

LEARNING OBJECTIVES

After completing this chapter, you should be able to

▶ 1. Define subculture and discuss the analysis of subcultures.

▶ 2. Describe a geographic subculture and give several examples.

▶ 3. Describe age subcultures and give some examples.

▶ 4. Discuss the major ethnic subcultures in Canada.

▶ 5. Define consumer acculturation and describe its four stages.

▶ 6. Describe the major social classes in Canada and discuss how marketers can use social class distinctions.

THE BOOMERS MEET THE DOCKERS

For the first time since they began arriving after the second world war, the 86 million North Americans of the baby boom are being courted by large numbers of marketers, not for their seemingly endless youth, but for their encroaching middle age.

According to Statistics Canada's 1991 census, the number of working-age people as a proportion of the total population has reached an almost historic high. Unprecedented growth in the number of seniors is projected. In 1991, of the total population of about 27 million, 21 percent were under age 15, 48 percent were 15 to 44, 20 percent were 45 to 64, and 12 percent were 65 or older.

As the baby boomers born between 1945 and 1964 squint their way into their mid-40s, companies are striking gold with products that offer a bit of youth to these aging yuppies.

Retailers are ringing up profits with products like wide-seated jeans, frilly girdles, and expensive bifocals without telltale lines in the lenses. For example, in December 1991, the makers of Lee's jeans began a multimillion-dollar advertising campaign aimed at jeans wearers with youthful hearts but expanding behinds. Driving such innovations, analysts say, is a belief that the success of many products in the 1990s will depend on how well they adapt to the great transition in the population as these Canadians move into their middle years.

For years, jeans makers sold more than half of their products to consumers 14 to 24 years of age, and the companies' advertising was crowded with young, slim models. But now, more than 60 percent of jeans buyers are over 25, and Levi Strauss & Co. has sharply increased its market share with relaxed-fit jeans and its casual Dockers slacks, aimed at people in their 30s and 40s. The vice president of marketing for Lee announced that when the company targeted the "hip and trendier" younger market, it found it was alienating its prime customers, who are 25 to 40 years old. Lee decided not to lose them to khaki pants!

Maybelline has been aggressively targeting boomers heading into their forties. The company introduced new cosmetics colours with an ad campaign stressing that aging is natural and beautiful. Both the advertising and the products have been so well received by consumers that the North American Yardley business (10 percent of Maybelline's business) increased 75 percent during the second quarter of 1992.

People's values and goals tend to change as they age. Older boomers started to care about comfort, convenience, and financial security. They also had to start facing the reality of spreading waistlines and eyes that just can't read the fine print the way they used to. These aging boomers are not accepting the unfamiliar world of middle age easily. To the delight of marketers, in the years to come these boomers will significantly redefine the mature market with their desire for products to make them feel young. These are important considerations for marketers.[1]

Different age groups represent major subcultures in Canada (and elsewhere). The aging of the baby boomers is one example of how changing demographic characteristics of a subculture can be important to marketers. Subcultures and social class are two aspects of the macro social environment; culture is the third. The key distinction among the three is size. Culture usually is analysed at the level of a country or an entire society, whereas subcultures are subgroups or segments of a society. Social class is a special type of subculture defined in terms of social status. Subcultures and social classes are cultural groups in that their members share certain cultural meanings; both, however, are part of the larger society and therefore are influenced by the overall culture. Thus, we would not expect middle-class Germans and middle-class Canadians to have exactly the same meanings, behaviours, and lifestyles. Marketers use social class and subculture to segment markets, to help understand the shared cultural meanings of large groups of consumers, and to develop targeted marketing strategies.

In this chapter, we define subculture and discuss several subcultures found in Canada (and elsewhere in the world). We also discuss the social classes found in Canadian society. Throughout, we draw implications for marketing strategy.

SUBCULTURES

A **subculture** is a *distinctive group of people in a society who share cultural meanings.* These common cultural meanings may concern affective and cognitive responses (emotional reactions, beliefs, values, and goals), behaviours (customs, scripts and rituals, norms) and environmental factors (living conditions, geographic location, important objects). Although each subculture shares certain cultural meanings with the overall society and other subcultures, some of its meanings are unique and distinctive.

Major demographic changes relating to age and diversity make marketers' analyses of subculture more important than ever. As in most developed countries, the population in Canada is aging (in 2001, the median age will be 36; it was 32 in 1991).[2] Another change is that Canada is becoming more culturally diverse, largely through increased immigration of people from other cultures. About 31 percent of Canadians reported origins other than British or French in the 1991 census. This trend is expected to continue to grow well into the 21st century. These various subcultural groups, each with unique perspectives and cultural meanings, exert considerable influence on the overall culture. To understand this diversity, marketers try to identify and understand subcultures and develop marketing strategies to address their particular needs.

EXHIBIT 16.1

Types of subcultures

Demographic Characteristics	Examples of Subcultures
Age	Adolescent, young adult, middle-aged, elderly
Ethnic origin	British, French, Italian, German, Chinese, Greek
Gender	Female, male
Race	Black, Caucasian, Asian
Income level	Affluent, middle income, poor, destitute
Nationality	French, Malaysian, Australian, American
Religion	Jewish, Catholic, Protestant, Mormon, Muslim
Family type	Single parent, divorced/no kids, two parents/kids
Occupation	Mechanic, accountant, priest, professor, clerk
Geographic region	Atlantic Canada, Quebec, Prairies
Community	Rural, small town, suburban, city

Marketers generally use demographic characteristics to identify subcultures. Exhibit 16.1 lists several examples of subcultures and the demographic characteristics used to classify people into these cultural groups. Subcultures are not mutually exclusive—a person can simultaneously be an Egyptian middle-class female, with a moderate income, who resides in Alberta. Marketers often combine demographic distinctions to identify more precisely defined subcultures (such as affluent, Jewish, middle-aged consumers living in British Columbia).

Marketers can analyse subcultures at different levels. The analysis is often done in stages. First, a general subculture is identified according to some broad demographic characteristic (race: Asian Canadian; age: elderly French-speaking; income level: middle-income Italians). Then, depending on the marketing purpose, this broad group is segmented further into sub-subcultures using other demographic characteristics (income: affluent, middle-income, and poor Italian Canadians; physical health: elderly French Canadians who are healthy versus those who are ill; community environment: middle-income Italians living in large cities or small towns). If necessary, the segmentation process could continue, creating ever smaller and more narrowly defined subcultures.

Managers must determine the level of subculture analysis that is relevant for the marketing problem (how narrow should the subculture be?) and develop marketing strategies appropriate for consumers at that level. Consider Air Canada's strategy in developing the advertisement for direct flights to Germany. The company considered the large ratio of Germans (32 percent single origin) in Ontario relative to the total number of Germans in Canada. According to the 1991 census, 289,420 Germans reside in Ontario (out of the 911,560 Germans living in Canada). A domestic feeling surges when German eyes see "Guten Tag!," and the heart beats to "nonstop from Toronto to Berlin and Düsseldorf," making consumers feel closer to their families so far away. The authoritarian tone chosen for the ad also relates to the subculture itself.

The same approach used to understand culture can be used to analyse subcultures. Typically, marketers examine the *content* of a subculture by describing the cultural meanings (especially values and lifestyles) its members share. It is much less common for marketers to examine the *process* by which cultural meanings are moved from the physical and social environment of the subculture to products and services and on to the people in the subculture, but this could be done.

Because marketers seek to identify the *typical* characteristics, meanings, and behavioural tendencies shared by people in a subculture, its members sometimes are

Air Canada developed this advertisement to appeal to the subculture of Germans living in Ontario.

Guten Tag!

THE ONLY SCHEDULED NONSTOP FROM TORONTO TO BERLIN AND DÜSSELDORF
Air Canada and its Connector partners can get you from where you are in Ontario to where you want to be in Germany. Nonstop. Now this is how you say hello to the folks back home.

AIR CANADA
For all the world

characterized in a stereotyped way (Italians are loud, elderly people are weak and ill, yuppies are rich). This can lead to major mistakes when developing marketing strategies. In fact, most subcultures are made up of diverse members who do not respond in the same way to marketing strategies. For example, marketers have identified a subgroup of "young" elderly people, called Opals (old people with active lifestyles), who think and act younger than their years, have money to spend, and are healthy enough to do so. In fact, it is difficult to identify a "typical" person in a subculture. This should be clear in Consumer Perspective 16.1, which describes some characteristics of the "average" Canadian.

CONSUMER PERSPECTIVE

▶ 16.1

Do you fit the mold? Jane and John Doe

Jane Doe can be considered your average Canadian female. Jane is 34 years old, weighs 132 pounds, and is five foot three. Jane spends one-third of the family income on food and shelter, using her two to three credit cards.

After her usual eight hours of sleep, Jane begins her day with toast or cereal. Then she gets into her seven-year old white compact car, fastens her seat belt, and drives half an hour to work, usually exceeding the speed limit.

John Doe, her husband, wears glasses and believes he looks younger than his years. John is two years older than Jane; he stands five feet seven and weighs 170 pounds. John watches his fat and thinks he could be healthier if he exercised. John drinks one glass of alcohol a day, while Jane drinks only two or three a week. Neither smokes.

After a long day they come home to two kids. Jane does three hours of chores and John does one hour and 10 minutes. The Does own a seven-room house built after 1969 and still live in the same province as their birth (like 85 percent of Canadians). Together they earn $47,715. They own two TV sets, one FM radio, a VCR, and a washer/dryer. They normally watch over two hours of TV a night. From time to time, they read for half an hour, or make their usual four phone calls a night.

The Does believe the national economy is in trouble. However, they are very optimistic about their own finances. They try to help the growing pollution problem by buying recycled products, but they do not compost.

Nobody really fits the profile of Jane and John Doe, because we are all unique.

Source: Lawrence Nyveen, "Are You an Average Canadian?," *Readers Digest*, March 1994, p. 44.

Careful research and thoughtful analysis are necessary to clearly define and understand a subculture. Consider what happened with the group called yuppies (young urban professionals). Originally, this was a narrow subcultural group, but the term *yuppie* gradually became associated with any upscale, self-centered young person. With the intense media attention focused on this group in the 1980s, the term became virtually synonymous with the baby boomer generation. In fact, the best estimates are that yuppies represent a mere 5 percent of the baby boomer subculture.[3]

Age groups can be treated as subcultures because people of different ages often share distinctive values, meanings, and behaviours. Marketers must be cautious, however, about segmenting consumers on the basis of their actual ages. Many adults think of themselves as 10 to 15 years younger than they really are.[4] Their behaviour, affect, and cognitions are more related to their psychological age than their chronological age. (See Consumer Perspective 16.2 for an example.) Although many different **age subcultures** can be identified and analysed, we discuss four here: teens, baby boomers, the mature market, and the elderly.

Age subcultures

The Teen Market
The size of the teen market has been declining in Canada, but marketers' interest has been increasing due to the increased purchasing power of this group of Canadians. There were approximately 1.85 million 15- to 19-year-olds in Canada in 1991. Statistics Canada estimates that this figure will begin to rise again, to about 1.88 million in 1996 and 1.93 million in 2001.

Teenagers are important to marketers for more than their increased influence on many household purchases. Teens in Canada have substantial discretionary purchasing power. Research shows that teenage girls, for example, spend roughly $10 billion in any given year.[5] This money is typically spent on cosmetics, clothing, health care products, chewing

---

For most people, age is more a state of mind than a physical state. Consider this statement from an 89-year-old woman:

> I might be 89 years old. I feel good. I feel like I could fly the coop. I do. I feel younger, like I'm 45 or 50. I want to doll up, and I like to fuss. . . . I don't know I'm old. I feel like I'm going to live a long time.

At age 75, Toronto's Ella Neale belongs to a Gentle Fitness class. After a week of attending neighbourhood committee meetings, visiting day care centers, teaching crafts and line dancing, she said, "We all have a lot to share, even at my age, if we care enough to share it."

This suggests that marketers should analyse subjective or "cognitive age" (the age one thinks of oneself as being) rather than chronological or actual age.

A new subcultural age segment may be emerging—the "new-age elderly." Such people view themselves quite differently from the "traditional" elderly. They perceive themselves as younger and more self-confident, more in control of their lives, less materialistic and concerned with possessions, and more involved with new experiences, challenges, and adventures. They are a good market for concerts and plays, lectures and university courses, and vacation travel to exotic locations.

Sources: Leon G. Schiffman and Elaine Sherman, "Value Orientations of New-Age Elderly: The Coming of an Ageless Market," *Journal of Business Research* 22 (1991), pp. 187–94; Dibar Apartian, "The Challenge of Aging," *The Plain Truth*, August 1994, pp. 11–13.

CONSUMER PERSPECTIVE

16.2 ◄

The "new" elderly

gum, and magazines. Close to 42 percent of 15- to 19-year-olds are employed in sales, services, or clerical jobs. This group tends to know what they want and has the income to sustain their purchasing preferences. The number of employed teenagers is also projected to grow over the next 10 years.

While modern teenagers are still relatively materialistic in their purchasing, most have become much more concerned with social issues that affect them. Further, a recent study suggests that teens can be very brand loyal. They will buy, for example, Reebok sports shoes or Cover Girl make-up. They tend to enjoy snacking, eating fresh food, and microwaving their food. Brand loyalty in this segment is essential, as it cultivates buying patterns that will likely last a lifetime.

Baby Boomers

Baby boomers are individuals born between the years 1945 to 1964, a period when 8.1 million babies were born in Canada. Currently, baby boomers are in their 30s and 40s, and marketers believe this group will represent a very lucrative market for the next 45 years. In fact, baby boomers are expected to account for nearly half of all discretionary spending throughout the next decade.

Although the baby-boomer subculture is extremely diverse, some general traits have been identified. Baby boomers can be characterized as having a blend of traditional family values and a "me generation attitude." As a group, they strongly affect the values of other subcultures. Differences can even be drawn between boomers born in the earlier years compared to later. Research shows that the second half of baby boomers are more pragmatic, less idealistic, and more stressed out than the first half.[6] These boomers believe they are a unique group in society. In general, baby boomers demand more personal services and more attention from retail salespeople. It has been predicted that most boomers will value self-fulfillment less as they get older but will begin to value self-respect and excitement in life much more.

Baby boomers form a very lucrative market for many products. Single boomers demand vacations and convenience packaged goods, while married boomers spend lavishly on their homes and families.[7] This shift to family products will certainly lead to an expansion in the children's market. In fact, the growing popularity of Kids "R" Us can largely be attributed to this expansion. Many stores recognise the growing demand for children's products. For example, Sears unveiled a frequent shopper bonus program with a "wear out" guarantee for children's clothing. In 1991 Burger King introduced its BK Kids Club, which offers special meals targeted to children. Research also indicates that baby boomers are demanding healthful, environmentally sound, quality products. According to Statistics Canada, as baby boomers age many new services are expected to emerge, especially in the area of products designed for seniors.

The baby boomers represent a lucrative, challenging market. So it's not surprising that many firms are designing new products and redesigning and repositioning old products for this market. For example, Wheaties used to appeal to children as "the breakfast of champions." Now it's being promoted to adults with slogans like "what the big boys eat." Levi Strauss designed jeans to give a little more room in the seat to accommodate boomer bodies. Cadillac is also targeting this market (see Consumer Perspective 16.3). Even Clearasil, traditionally an anti-acne medication for teenagers, has developed Clearasil Adult Care to appeal to the growing number of adults with skin problems.

The mature market

The first baby boomers are hitting 50, and marketers and ad agencies have already addressed the changes in the mature market, which can be defined as consumers between 50 and 65. Marketers are taking advantage of the fact that in the 90s, three-quarters of

CONSUMER PERSPECTIVE

16.3 ◀

GM races for the baby boomers

Cadillac of General Motors Corp. broke baby boomers' resistance to North American automobiles with its advertising for the Eldorado and Seville models. Before that, the profile of a Cadillac owner was about 63 years old, with household income of $106,000. "Our unique design challenge is to bring the future to today so that we can fulfill consumer needs tomorrow," said Phil Guarascio of GM.

This success is due mainly to the fact that GM offers universal car designs with special features and appeals to specific target markets. It understands and tries to accommodate the needs of its target consumers. For example, GM used warranties and owner services programs on cars and trucks. It also offered loaners to the mature couple with money to spend but no time to spend at the mechanic.

Before GM launched the advertising campaign, it researched the attitudes of wealthy baby boomers age 45 and under. It then focused resources on advertising to this targeted market. In TV advertising, young, professional-looking people give voice to those attitudes with lines like "The luxury sedans of Europe and Japan seem to fit my lifestyle better." GM also resorted to direct marketing, offering 170,000 prospective buyers 8-minute videocassettes about each new car.

This aggressive advertising campaign was rewarding. Younger affluent consumers started to be drawn to Cadillac. According to a company survey, 45 percent of those who contacted the car dealers were under age 50 and had a household income of $75,000 or more. This was a new market opportunity for GM.

Perhaps the most direct result of the advertising effort was an unanticipated increase in sales. Initially, Cadillac predicted a sales increase of 32 percent in 1992; actual sales were up by 60 percent in some regions. This example shows the profitability of the baby-boomer market.

Sources: *Advertising Age*, Jan. 11, 1993, p. 29; Raymond Serafin, "Cadillac Ads Draw Affluent Baby Boomers," *Automotive News*, Dec. 9, 1991, p. 41.

the population growth is in the 50 to 65 range.[8] It is predicted that in the following 10 years, that age range will see 85 percent of the population growth. As baby boomers age, the mature market is expected to change, especially as graying boomers increase spending on education for their college-age children and look to retrain themselves for new careers.

According to Statistics Canada, the number of older people of working age (45–64) will increase to 9.4 million by the year 2036, compared to 5.4 million in 1991. This shift in the age distribution suggests a change in societal focus and economic policy. The needs and priorities of the dominant age group will likely shift the focus of public policy and change the nature of the goods and services provided by governments and industry alike. Marketers have already recognised that the men and women in this age group provide excellent marketing opportunities, especially in the areas of financial services, health promotion, nutritious products, luxury travel, adult education, and purchases of second homes. Many aging consumers will have ample disposable income as the financial burdens of raising a family are lifted. Recognising that extended families will be larger, Canadian Airlines International of Vancouver has launched a travel club to tap into this soaring seniors travel market. Its Global Horizons Club provides discounts on airfare, holiday packages, airport parking, hotels, and car rentals. Elderhostel pioneered "learning trips" excursion tours as well as cruise-line vacation packages, and Grandtravel targets the mature market with trips for grandparents and their grandchildren.

Marketers need to realise the unique characteristics of the mature market. This group currently holds 40 percent of all discretionary spending power; it purchases 43 percent of all new domestic cars and 48 percent of all luxury cars. Mature consumers also spend more on travel and eat out more than any other group. They own 75 percent of all the financial assets in North America and account for 40 percent of all consumer demand. (The group with the highest level of discretionary spending in Canada in 1991 was the age 55 to 64 group.) The book *Age Wave: The Challenges and Opportunities of an Aging America*[9] says nearly 1.8 million Canadian households are presently headed by "nearly retireds" and outlines ways society can change to meet the needs of this growing segment of the Canadian population.

The challenge facing marketers today is to develop strategies that appeal to older consumers without dwelling on the fact that they are aging. One company that has successfully targeted the mature market is the fast-food giant McDonald's. As early as 1987, McDonald's successfully boosted sales to seniors and became a forerunner in mature marketing. In 1992 McDonald's made famous "The Usual" commercial, where a mature gentleman orders "the usual" while being urged by his woman friend to "come on and live a little." The man decides to take this advice and orders large fries instead of his usual, provoking her to exclaim, "You're a wild man!"

The elderly market

Over the past 20 years, Canada has experienced great demographic changes, especially in the increased size and composition of the group reaching retirement age. This greying of Canada can be attributed to several factors, the most significant being increased longevity and a decline in fertility. It is estimated that by 2036 the elderly will represent 23.2 percent of the total Canadian population, with an especially pronounced growth among those over 75.

Women outnumber men, and this trend increases with age. According to the 1991 census, Canada's elderly population was 42 percent male and 58 percent female; this translates to a ratio of 723 men per 1,000 women (compared to a Canadian national average of 972 men per 1,000 women).

The elderly subculture is not a homogenous group. It can be divided according to age into three subgroups, which vary according to seniors' needs at each stage.

▷ ages 65–74: younger seniors.
▷ ages 75–84: intermediate seniors.
▷ age 85 and older: older seniors.

Of Canada's 3.2 million seniors, 60 percent are in the 65–74 range, 31 percent are in the 75–84 range, and 9 percent are 85 or older. The 1991 census predicts that by 2036 the number of younger seniors will more than double in size and the population aged 75–84 could represent more than 4 million seniors (3.4 times its 1991 size). The proportion of those age 85 and older is predicted to increase by a factor of 24 since 1951.

Many factors influence seniors' lifestyles, among them the following:

▷ education levels.
▷ marital status.
▷ living arrangements.
▷ income sources.

Education levels Statistics Canada data show that education levels of the Canadian population have been rising gradually. In 1991, only 20 percent of seniors 85 or older had post-secondary education, with 52 percent having only elementary education (grades 1–8) or no schooling at all. This is in contrast to seniors aged 75–84. 23 percent had post-secondary education and only 42 percent had an elementary education or no schooling.

The younger seniors (65–74) had the highest rate of post-secondary education at 29 percent and the lowest level of seniors with an elementary education or no schooling (35 percent).

Marital status In 1991, most of Canada's 3.2 million seniors were either married (57 percent) or widowed (33 percent). The proportion of single seniors was fairly stable until 1971, when it fell considerably. It is interesting to note that although the proportion of divorced seniors from 1931 to 1991 was small (approximately 3 percent), a trend toward divorce is evident.

Living arrangements In 1991, the majority of seniors occupied private households (2.2 million of Canada's 10 million private households). Many of the rest resided in collectives.

Income sources In 1990, nine-tenths of all seniors had incomes between $5,000 and $50,000 (average income of $19,500), with government retirement income making up 40 percent of total income (accounting on average for about $7,800 per person). The next most important source of income for all seniors was investment income accounting for 23 percent of total income (or $4,400), followed by employment (13 percent or $2,600).

Aging is an inevitable process that often presents physical, emotional, and financial hurdles. However, aging can generate opportunities, primarily in the area of increased leisure activities. According to Statistics Canada, seniors particularly enjoy going to the movies, travelling out of town, attending seniors' centres, club meetings, bingo and card games, and going to church. Many seniors also find a renewed interest in returning to school.[10]

Many products are marketed to consumers in the mature market.

Ethnic subcultures

Canada is a very culturally diverse society, mostly due to the large number of minority groups that have come to Canada from many other places. As of the 1991 census, most Canadians still considered themselves of British, French, Asian, German, or Italian heritage. These larger ethnic subcultures grew at unequal rates, mainly due to different immigration patterns and birth rates.

For instance, there was a large influx of Asians to Canada in the early 1990s. The Chinese, Japanese, and Korean populations, together with other ethnic groups from the Asian subculture, comprise roughly 4 percent of the total Canadian population. The single largest group, after those of British origin (28 percent), is French Canadians, who make up 23 percent. Germans account for 3.4 percent, Italians for almost 3 percent, and other groups, such as the Greek community, account for slightly more than 0.5 percent of Canadian society (see Exhibit 16.2). The ethnic diversity of Canada is expected to increase further into the next century.

Marketers must remember that ethnic subcultures are not distributed equally across Canada. Montreal, Edmonton, and Hamilton are among the most culturally diverse cities in Canada. The Prairies are not nearly as culturally diverse; the majority of their population is of either British or other European origin. The most prominent ethnic subcultures in Canada—French Canadians, Asians, Germans, Italians, and Greeks—are discussed in the following pages. Also considered are Native peoples, a subculture that deserves special attention.

French–Canadian market

The French–Canadian market requires special attention from Canadian marketers not only because it is very different from English markets (due to a unique culture and linguistic differences), but because it is quite substantial. It is in fact the second-largest market in Canada, with approximately 7 million consumers in 1996. Unfortunately, marketers often experience difficulty distributing and promoting specific products to French–Canadians, due largely to a basic lack of understanding of the group's distinctiveness.

Lefrancois and Chatel define the French–Canadian market as "including eight adjacent counties in Ontario" and "seven counties in New Brunswick," in addition to the province of Quebec. The authors claim this definition accounts for approximately 93 percent of all French Canadians.[11] There have been many ways to define and describe the French–Canadian marketplace, including comparative and structural approaches provided by well-known Quebec political historians such as Mallen, Henault, and Bouchard.[12] Other authors, such as Rosenblatt and Bergier,[13] have used other marketing research measures to attempt to define English and French groups—for example, linguistic criteria, such as language spoken at home, language of returned questionnaire, and mother tongue.

When the French–Canadian market is compared to the English–Canadian, some interesting findings are apparent. For example, English Canadians are more evenly distributed among the provinces; French Canadians are more concentrated, accounting for about 75 percent of the population of Quebec, and 34 percent of New Brunswick.

The French–Canadian culture can be identified as a mix of "the American way," the English system, and the French culture. In comparison to English Canadians, French Canadians tend to be more hedonistic. In a study conducted by the firm Le Groupe Leger Leger, enjoyment of life topped the list of 32 topics respondents rated by importance, while voting ranked second. Other findings indicate that Quebecers are very security conscious, put great importance on appearance and having a family, and desire to be au courant with the news. Quebecers also consider cultivating friends much more important than do Canadians as a whole. It is also interesting to note that Quebecers tend to look at advertising as a form of pop art and entertainment and are in general emotional buyers who respond to sensitive advertising.

EXHIBIT 16.2   Ethnic origins

Provinces	Total	British Only	French Only	British and French	British and/or French and Other	Other	Other Main Groups	Single Responses as % of Total Population
Newfoundland		88.3	1.7	3.9	3.6	2.5	Aboriginal	0.9
Percent	100.0						German	0.2
Number	563,940						Canadian	0.2
Prince Edward Island							Dutch	1.0
Percent	100.0	65.6	9.4	12.3	8.7	4.0	Canadian	0.6
Number	128,100						German	0.5
Nova Scotia							German	2.8
Percent	100.0	58.2	6.3	9.0	15.5	10.9	Black	1.2
Number	890,950						Canadian	1.1
New Brunswick							Canadian	1.3
Percent	100.0	44.0	33.5	9.2	8.3	4.9	German	0.6
Number	716,495						Aboriginal	0.6
Quebec							Italian	2.6
Percent	100.0	5.1	74.6	2.7	3.7	13.9	Jewish	1.1
Number	6,810,300						Aboriginal	1.0
							Greek	0.7
Ontario							Canadian	5.3
Percent	100.0	34.9	5.3	4.6	15.5	39.7	Italian	4.9
Number	9,977,055						German	2.9
							Chinese	2.7
Manitoba							German	8.7
Percent	100.0	24.8	5.0	2.9	19.8	47.4	Aboriginal	6.9
Number	1,079,390						Ukrainian	6.9
Saskatchewan							German	12.4
Percent	100.0	23.4	3.1	2.5	25.2	45.8	Aboriginal	6.8
Number	976,040						Ukrainian	5.7
Alberta							German	7.4
Percent	100.0	27.7	3.0	3.3	24.6	41.5	Ukrainian	4.1
Number	2,519,185						Canadian	3.7
British Columbia							Chinese	5.6
Percent	100.0	35.2	2.1	3.3	21.7	37.7	German	4.8
Number	3,247,505						East Indian	2.7
							Aboriginal	2.3
Yukon							Aboriginal	13.7
Percent	100.0	29.6	3.2	4.2	28.6	34.4	German	3.8
Number	27,655							
Northwest Territories							Aboriginal	51.2
Percent	100.0	14.7	2.4	2.5	16.1	64.3	Canadian	1.8
Number	56,430							
Canada							German	3.4
Percent	100.0	28.1	22.8	4.0	14.2	30.9	Canadian	2.8
Number	26,994,040						Italian	2.8
							Chinese	2.2

Source: Statistics Canada, 1991 Census of Canada.

A very significant finding and a source of worry for French Canadians is the fact that the gap between the median incomes of individual Anglophones and Francophones more than doubled to 10.3 percent in 1992 from 4.4 percent in 1977. Among families, the gap grew to 14.1 percent in 1992 from 9.9 percent in 1977. Francophones outside Quebec still tend to be in lower-paid primary industries, such as farming and mining, rather than in high-paid urban jobs. In 1992, the median income of French-speaking men in Quebec was

CONSUMER PERSPECTIVE

▶ **16.4**

French Canadians

In 1992, the firm Legendre Lubawin Goldfarb studied the perception that Quebecers are a homogeneous group. This belief turned out to be a falsehood. Quebecers can in fact be largely classified into three psychographic groups: joiner activists, day-to-day watchers, and old-fashioned puritans.

Joiner activists are liberals who like to keep up with new fashions, technology, and the like. Puritans are conformists who adhere to a traditional lifestyle, resist change, and often cling to familiar brands of products. Day-to-day watchers are satisfied with what life has to offer. Legendre discovered an unusually high number of activists in Quebec in relation to the rest of Canada, and attributed this discovery to Quebec's strong Roman Catholic heritage.

In 1995, Goldfarb Consultants undertook another study of Canadian society. It found the breakdown of Quebec shown in the table.

1995 Goldfarb Segments

Segment	Canada (% of population)	Quebec (% of population)
Old-fashioned puritans	16%	15%
Disinterested self-indulgents	17%	12%
Joiner activists	21%	26%
Aggressive achievers	10%	14%
Responsible survivors	12%	10%
Day-to-day watchers	24%	23%

It is interesting to note that by 1995, the percentage of puritans in Quebec had fallen slightly below the national average.

Source: "Portrait of the Quebec Consumer: Two Research Firms Look into the Hearts, Minds and Buying Habits of the Quebecois", *Marketing*, March 22, 1993, p. 14; Goldfarb Consultants.

12 percent higher than that of English-speaking men, but even so Francophone families in Quebec have not surpassed the median income of the English. A possible explanation for this phenomenon could be the fact that Francophone women living in Quebec make significantly less money than English women in the same province.[14]

Most studies of French–Canadian consumption behaviour use the comparative or structural approaches.[15] The comparative, or descriptive, approach usually involves a researcher administering identical questionnaires to French and English Canadians (in either French or English). The responses of the two groups are then compared to determine if there are any significant differences. In the structural approach, the researcher attempts to gain a more complete understanding of the behavioural patterns of the French–Canadian market.

Comparative approach Most studies involving the differences between French and English consumers are comparative in nature and as such as purely descriptive. Some proponents of this approach are Lefrancois and Chatel, who attribute the behavioural differences between the French and the English to differences in socioeconomic characteristics (differences in educational levels, income, employment, etc.) Lefrancois and Chatel believe that if these differences were eliminated, English and French Canadians would exhibit more similar purchasing behaviours.

Many studies in this vein have investigated the socioeconomic and purchasing pattern differences between English and French Canadians. The attempt to understand any underlying socioeconomic differences has always been based largely on the assumption that differences in socioeconomic status would likely lead to different purchasing patterns. If and when the underlying socioeconomic structure of the two societies was eliminated, so too would be any differences in consumption patterns. While the income gap has narrowed, most researchers still show that English and French Canadians do differ on consumption and purchasing behaviour. Many recent studies show that with respect to credit-card usage, store patronage, brand loyalty, durable and nondurable products and media viewing habits, there are substantive differences between the two groups.

Structural approach   Many researchers in Canada (mostly private, but some published) have developed their own theories about the consumption characteristics and behaviour traits of French Canadians. This structural approach is based on discovering common traits within the French–Canadian market. Three main published profiles of French–Canadian cultural traits have been developed by George Henault, Bruce Mallen, and Jacques Bouchard.

George Henault was one of the first authors to develop a French–Canadian cultural profile for marketing purposes. He identified eight cultural characteristics and two tendencies in which the French and English show significant differences. They are ethnic origin, religion, language spoken, intellectual attitude, family, leisure time, attitude toward the individual vis-a-vis the environment, business management, political tendencies, and consumption attitudes. Briefly, French Canadians have Latin origins and follow the Catholic religion. The family tends to be patriarchal in nature and plays a large role in everyday life. English Canadians have Anglo-Saxon origins and follow the Protestant religion. The English family is usually matriarchal in nature, and the family plays a large role in the professional class.

Bruce Mallen argues that three major traits affect French–Canadian consumption behaviour: the sensate, the conservative, and the nonprice cognitive traits. The sensate trait involves appeals to the senses: touch, taste, smell, sight, hearing and social hedonism. Research shows that French Canadians do not like foods or drinks that are bitter; in fact, they enjoy very sweet food, such as maple syrup. The conservative trait involves the French Canadian tendency for low-risk behaviour and strong family orientation. Perhaps this could explain the relatively high degree of brand loyalty among French Canadians. Finally, the nonprice cognitive trait is related to the other two traits in that if a product is liked (sensate trait), it will be purchased regularly (conservative trait) and its price will be less likely to have a negative impact on repurchase behaviour.

Jacques Bouchard identified six common historical and cultural roots of French Canadians: rural, minority, North American, Catholic, Latin, and French. In other words, the fact that French Canadians have a strong rural background not affected by industrialisation, that Francophones have generally been a small group in terms of the whole of North America, and that they have been affected by the American culture, as well as Catholicism, Latin traits, and the French heritage, all contribute to the consumption patterns of French Canadians (See Consumer Perspective 16.4 for the Goldfarb psychographic profiles of French Canadians).

Asian Canadians

Although they represented less than 3 percent of the population in 1991, Asian Canadians are the most rapidly growing ethnic group in Canada (and comprised more than 4 percent of the population by 1995). In fact, the population of people with Asian ancestry increased 34 percent to 961,225 between 1981 and 1991. Asians can be said to include individuals with Filipino, Indian, Vietnamese, Korean, Japanese or Chinese ancestry. Immigrants with Chinese origins (mostly from Hong Kong) represent the largest group of Asian immigrants. The Canadian Advertising Foundation predicts that by the end of 2001 the Chinese population will number 1.3 million.

The largest concentration of Asian Canadians is in Ontario (47 percent), followed by British Columbia (31 percent) and Alberta (12 percent). This group is highly urbanised, most of its members live in central metropolitan areas. Asian Canadians, in particular Chinese Canadians, are considered a lucrative niche for many marketers as they are well-educated, demand quality products, and generally earn higher household incomes than the average Canadian. According to one survey, individuals from Hong Kong earn household incomes of approximately $111,300, compared to the average Canadian household income of $51,300.[16] DJC Research found that Hong Kong immigrants had bought more than $9 billion worth of capital between 1987 and 1991.[17]

Many companies are trying to attract these affluent Chinese consumers. CIBC recently opened a storefront banking centre for Asians in Richmond Hill, Ontario, in an attempt to target mature and affluent Asians. The bank gives the utmost consideration to these customers' cultural preferences when handling transactions.[18]

Asian culture is extremely different from Western culture. Marketers must analyse the consumption behaviour of the Asian market carefully before marketing products to this group. A survey conducted by Burson-Marsteller found that recent Chinese immigrants deem quality more important than price in purchasing. It also discovered that word of mouth and advice from reference groups play large roles in Asian decision making.[19] A survey on Chinese consumers discovered that 94 percent of respondents favour Sunday shopping.[20] All of these factors need to be taken into consideration when a firm attempts to market to this group.

German Canadians

German Canadians represent 3.4 percent of the total Canadian population. Most live west of Ontario. They represent 12.4 percent of the population of Saskatchewan, 8.7 percent of Manitoba, and 7.4 percent of Alberta. Like other Northern European groups, German Canadians have rejected the idea of complete assimilation and have worked to maintain their ethnicity through rituals and celebrations. They are served by at least six German publications, the largest being the *Deutsche Presse,* and by several radio stations.

German Canadians can be said to be driven by four major values:[21]

▷ A strong sense of family: Group members gather support and strength in time of crisis from their families (including extended families).

▷ A strong work ethic: Germans have made great contributions in farming and industrial development in Canada. They are thorough, pay attention to detail, and exhibit pride in their work.

▷ Strong drive for education: Academic success is highly praised and parents are willing to sacrifice financially to provide their children with a good education.

▷ A strong sense of justice: Contributions to the family and society are noted and evaluated by other members of the community.

Italian Canadians

Italians first immigrated to Canada in 1861, but 80 percent arrived in the 1950s after the second world war. After many decades of assimilation into Canadian society, Italian Canadians have achieved a remarkable presence. In 1991, Italians made up 2.8 percent of the population in Canada, living mostly in Ontario and Quebec.

Italians tend to have a strong sense of family orientation. According to a survey conducted by the *Toronto Star* and Goldfarb Consultants, 55 percent of Italians consider it important to transfer their own language and culture to their children.[22] Almost 70 percent of all Italian Canadians have Italian as their mother tongue, and 32 percent still speak Italian mainly at home. As with many other subcultures, their primary relations are with people of their own background. Italians own and predominantly frequent their own stores, cinemas, and social events. There are more than 15 publications in Italian, with the largest being *Il Cittadino Canadese*.

Almost 90 percent of all Italians who live in Canada reside in the provinces of Quebec and Ontario, and 90 percent of these individuals live in the metropolitan areas. Further, 90 percent of all Italian Canadians in Toronto own their own homes, preferring a home with a garden to an apartment.

Italians are mostly Roman Catholic. They maintain the habit of going to church regularly. A study conducted by Canadian Cleric found that 98 percent of young Italians consider the role of the church as "attempting to solve conflicts between parents and youths." This reveals that young Italians attend church not only for religious but also for cultural reasons. On the other hand, older Italians go to church to protect their traditional values. This shows a change in the role of religion among Italian Canadians.

Greek Canadians

According to the 1991 census, approximately 151,150 Greeks live in Canada (about 0.5 percent of the total population). About 70,000 reside in Toronto, 55,000 in Montreal, 10,000 in Vancouver, and most of the rest in other urban centres such as Windsor, Winnipeg, Ottawa, Saskatoon, Edmonton, Calgary, Hamilton, and London, Ontario.

Marketers have identified five broad social groups.[23] The *old-timers* are immigrants, mainly of rural stock, who came to Canada before the second world war and had little or no formal education. The *Canadian-born* are generally well integrated within the general Canadian society, but nevertheless maintain strong connections with their cultural group. Members of this group tend to be successful professionals or entrepreneurs. The *immigrant elite* is a rather small group including highly educated immigrants of urban middle-class origin. Among them are professionals, scientists, artists and ship owners.

Immigrant entrepreneurs are those immigrants who have come to Canada from rural areas since the second world war and have relatively low levels of formal education and occupational training. This group is active in the restaurant business, the fur business, and fruit and grocery wholesale and retail firms. These small businesses are usually informal gathering places where men accustomed to the village cafenio (coffee house) meet to exchange views and information. The *skilled and unskilled workers* who came to Canada after the second world war probably constitute the majority of Greeks in Canada. They can be found in restaurant and hotel enterprises working as unskilled labour, and in maintenance, the garment industry, hospital staffs, and heavy industry.

To reach Greek consumers efficiently and effectively, marketers can use opinion leaders such as the Greek Orthodox church. For many Greeks, the church is the centre of their social as well as religious life. Another method would be to advertise in one of the numerous Greek–Canadian newspapers, which perform an important function in the Greek community. The largest is *Greek Canadian Action.* For marketers who want to target women as their customers, the Montreal Greek newspaper contains a women's section as well as a sports page. The weekly independent newspaper *Eleftheros Typos* (*The Hellenic Free Press*) has been published in the Greek language in Toronto since 1966.

Native Canadians

Over five hundred thousand people in Canada reported one or more Aboriginal origins in 1991. This was up from roughly three hundred and fifty thousand in 1986. A five-year increase of this magnitude cannot be explained by demographic factors. Clearly, many people who had not previously reported Aboriginal ancestry did so in 1991. This was most likely due to a heightened awareness of Aboriginal issues, resulting from the considerable attention given to these issues in the year prior to the 1991 census.[24]

The sharp increase in the number of people reporting Aboriginal origins resulted in a rise in the proportion of the population with this ancestry. In 1991, 2 percent of Canada's population reported Aboriginal origins in combination with other backgrounds, up from 1.4 percent in 1986. There was also a smaller increase for those reporting exclusively Aboriginal origins (to 1.7 percent from 1.5 percent).

While Aboriginals are distributed throughout most of the provinces, the Northwest Territories were the only province or territory where neither British nor French constituted the largest ethnic group. Over half of the population reported single Aboriginal origins in 1991: 32 percent Inuit, 15 percent North American Indian, and 4 percent Metis.

The Yukon also had a relatively large Aboriginal population. In 1991, 14 percent of the territory's population reported singly Aboriginal origins, the largest exclusive response group after the British.

Values often associated with Native Canadians include:[25]

▷ A time orientation that focuses on the present and stresses a cyclical rather than linear orientation.

▷ An emphasis on understanding and working in harmony with the forces of nature, rather than attempting to control or manipulate them.

▷ A strong orientation to the group or collectivity rather than the individual. This includes communal living and the sharing of many material possessions.

▷ A tenet of "being in becoming," which means in part that the constant evolution of individuals is central to natural human growth.

▷ The pervasive orientation that most humans are generally of good intention, and some have mixed intentions, but few if any are evil.

Unfortunately, little scientific market research has been conducted about Canadian Native peoples, so we do not truly understand much of their consumption patterns. However, there are at least two Native agencies in Canada, one in Winnipeg (CrossCom Group) and one in Brampton, Ontario, which work on advertising messages directed specifically to Native Canadians.[26] Given the growth and market potential of this subcultural group, more data will probably be published in years to come.

Gender as a subculture

Despite the modern tendency to downplay differences between men and women, there is ample evidence that men and women do differ in many respects other than physical characteristics. Women are typically more sympathetic and nurturing and less dominant than men. At times gender differences may be significant enough to consider the two sexes as distinctive subcultures with their own meanings and norms. Many psychologists believe that women value possessions that enhance their interpersonal relationships, while men favour possessions that they can dominate. In the husband–wife role differentiation, instrumental goal-oriented behaviour has been associated with the wife.

Women now occupy an increasingly important role in society, not only in terms of their interaction with their families, but also within the labour market. From 1975 to 1993, women accounted for three-quarters of all employment growth in Canada. By 1993, 51 percent of all women over age 14 worked outside the home, an increase from 41 percent in 1975. While women have succeeded in entering the work force, they still face significant obstacles. For example, studies show that women comprise the largest proportion of part-time workers. In 1993, at least one-third of female part-time workers desired full-time work but were unable to find it. Women also earn significantly less than men. In 1992, women in the paid work force working full-time all year round made 72 percent of the average earnings of their male counterparts. While this ratio is up from 68 percent in 1990, the fact that equal work does not seem to warrant equal pay is still disturbing.

Selected Characteristics	Low	Middle (Average Canadian)	High
Average family income	$11,704	$51,300	$164,400
Number of census families	972,860	906,130	528,340
Percentage of census families	13.2%	12.3%	7.2%
Average income of wife	< $ 6,000	$15,800	$ 59,700
Occupation Group (%)			
Managerial	3.4	16.8	42.3
Sales	9.2	8.4	9.4
Clerical	13.2	5.6	1.5
Farming, fishing, forestry	14.5	3.9	2.6
Services	21.0	7.9	1.7
Other	38.7	57.4	42.5
Highest Level of Education Completed (%)			
University degree	6.8	18.5	62.7
Secondary school	37.2	57.3	29.7
Less than secondary school	36.4	24.2	7.6

EXHIBIT 16.3

Characteristics of three income subcultures

Source: "The Nation" *Statistics Canada,* Cat. #93–331.

It is interesting to note that women have made considerable inroads into certain occupations. In 1993, 26 percent of all doctors, dentists, and health-diagnosing and treating professionals were women, up from 18 percent in 1982. Women have also sharply improved their share of managerial and administrative jobs. Unfortunately, women still remain considerably underrepresented among professionals employed in natural sciences, engineering, and mathematics.

In 1992, 61 percent of husband–wife families enjoyed the income of two earners, with wives' earnings contributing about 31 percent to the family's total income. While this statistic is encouraging, one must remember that women who work outside the home are still responsible for most work around the house. They typically spend approximately two hours more than men each day on domestic work, primarily child care and shopping.

This added burden of work in the labour force combined with family responsibilities creates unique marketing opportunities targeting women. Many studies show that these women desire convenience products, such as microwave ovens and the vast array of either fresh or frozen prepared foods.[27]

Income as a subculture

Marketers can consider level of income as a subculture, because people with similar incomes tend to have similar cultural meanings, values, behaviours, and lifestyles. Income can also be used to segment a subculture defined on some other characteristics (age, ethnic group, gender, etc.). There are many myths that can confuse the marketer. For instance, it has been said that low-income homes are usually minority households. But in Quebec, the majority of low-income households are French in origin. It was further believed that affluence increased with age. However, many Canadians get poorer as they age.[28]

Canadian society can be divided into three distinct income levels: high, middle, low. In 1991, low-income families earned, on average, $11,704; middle-income families averaged, $51,300; and high-income families averaged $164,400.

In 1991, the average Canadian family earned approximately $53,000 and fell into the middle-income category. Exhibit 16.3 illustrates the average family income, number of

EXHIBIT 16.4 **Nine Nations of North America**

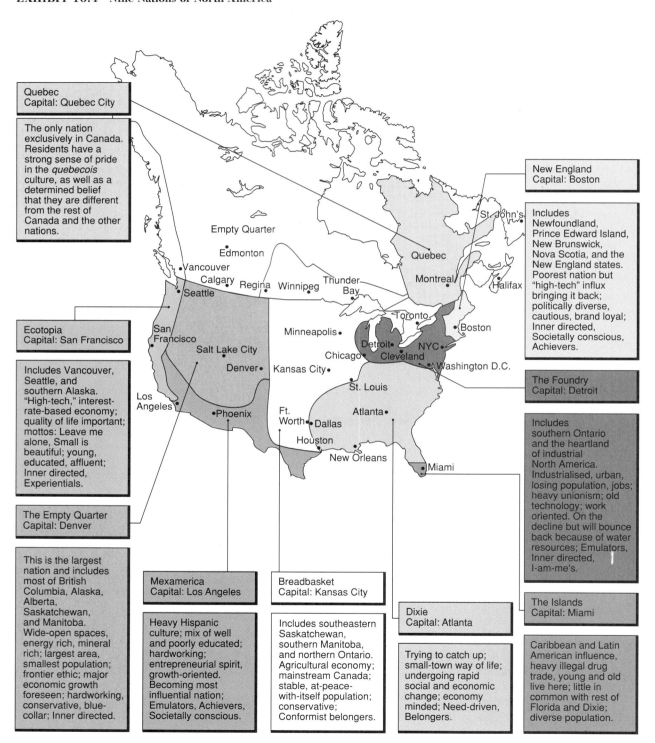

Quebec
Capital: Quebec City

The only nation exclusively in Canada. Residents have a strong sense of pride in the *quebecois* culture, as well as a determined belief that they are different from the rest of Canada and the other nations.

New England
Capital: Boston

Includes Newfoundland, Prince Edward Island, New Brunswick, Nova Scotia, and the New England states. Poorest nation but "high-tech" influx bringing it back; politically diverse, cautious, brand loyal; Inner directed, Societally conscious, Achievers.

Ecotopia
Capital: San Francisco

Includes Vancouver, Seattle, and southern Alaska. "High-tech," interest-rate-based economy; quality of life important; mottos: Leave me alone, Small is beautiful; young, educated, affluent; Inner directed, Experientials.

The Foundry
Capital: Detroit

Includes southern Ontario and the heartland of industrial North America. Industrialised, urban, losing population, jobs; heavy unionism; old technology; work oriented. On the decline but will bounce back because of water resources; Emulators, Inner directed, I-am-me's.

The Empty Quarter
Capital: Denver

This is the largest nation and includes most of British Columbia, Alaska, Alberta, Saskatchewan, and Manitoba. Wide-open spaces, energy rich, mineral rich; largest area, smallest population; frontier ethic; major economic growth foreseen; hardworking, conservative, blue-collar; Inner directed.

Mexamerica
Capital: Los Angeles

Heavy Hispanic culture; mix of well and poorly educated; hardworking; entrepreneurial spirit, growth-oriented. Becoming most influential nation; Emulators, Achievers, Societally conscious.

Breadbasket
Capital: Kansas City

Includes southeastern Saskatchewan, southern Manitoba, and northern Ontario. Agricultural economy; mainstream Canada; stable, at-peace-with-itself population; conservative; Conformist belongers.

Dixie
Capital: Atlanta

Trying to catch up; small-town way of life; undergoing rapid social and economic change; economy minded; Need-driven, Belongers.

The Islands
Capital: Miami

Caribbean and Latin American influence, heavy illegal drug trade, young and old live here; little in common with rest of Florida and Dixie; diverse population.

census families, average income of wife, major occupational groups, and educational characteristics of the three main income subcultures in Canada.

Canadians typically view the country as a mosaic of cultures and topography. Different parts of the country have very different physical environments (topography, climate, natural resources) and social environments (economics, population demographics, lifestyles). These factors create **geographic subcultures** of people with shared cultural meanings that can influence their buying behaviour.

Geographic subcultures

There are many ways to analyse **geographic subcultures.** Canada is typically subdivided into the 10 provinces and two territories, or the regions of the Maritimes, Quebec, Ontario, the Prairies and British Columbia.

An innovative way to study geographic subcultures is described by Joel Garreau in *The Nine Nations of North America*.[29] Garreau argues that regional similarities may often transcend traditional political boundaries (such as Canadian provinces or countries), as the values and lifestyles of individuals are often based on economic, social, cultural, political, topographical, and natural resource factors (see Exhibit 16.4).

Garreau has redrawn the map of North America into nine nations whose citizens have historically led unique lives. Six of these nations are at least partially in Canada: Quebec, New England, the Foundry, Ecotopia, the Empty Quarter, and the Breadbasket. Three nations—Dixie, Mexamerica, and the Islands—are indigenous to the United States and Latin America.

With the exception of Quebec, these geographic subcultures create boundaries that are very different from the usual political (state, provincial, national) boundaries. British Columbia is made up of Ecotopia and the Empty Quarter. Alberta is located within the Empty Quarter, as are Saskatchewan and Manitoba. Ontario is made up mostly of the Foundry, The Breadbasket and the Empty Quarter. Ottawa is located in the Foundry. Quebec is obviously located in Quebec, while the Maritime provinces are located in the New England nation. As Garreau notes, "Economically and philosophically, Calgary is far more kin to Fairbanks, Salt Lake City, or Denver than it is to Ottawa."

A process of acculturation begins when a person moves to a different culture to live and work or becomes a member of a different subculture. **Acculturation** refers to how people in one culture or subculture understand and adapt to the meanings of another subculture or culture. Consumer acculturation refers to how people acquire the ability and knowledge to be skilled consumers in a different cultural environment. It is important for marketers to understand the concept of acculturation because often an understanding of the different cultural meanings consumers hold is a determining factor in a firm's success.

THE ACCULTURATION PROCESS

Acculturation is common and necessary in the modern world. Many countries that experience an influx of immigrants face difficulties assimilating people from different cultural backgrounds to the host culture. Canada experienced difficulty with assimilation during the 1980s and 1990s as many Asians immigrated.

Acculturation is also a very important process for those who move to different regions within the same country. For example, the number of Canadians who will move to British Columbia is expected to increase. These Canadians may experience some problems in adapting to the culture of that province.

The level of cultural interpenetration—the amount and type of social interactions individuals have with people in the host subculture—determines the degree to which immigrants become accultured into a new culture. Social interactions can be direct or indirect.

Direct social interaction occurs through working, shopping, and living arrangements. Indirect social interaction can be seen through observation of the mass media. An individual who has more opportunities to interact with people from the host culture may penetrate into the host culture better than those who do not.

When individuals try to interact with a subculture, they may go through four **stages of acculturation.** In the first, or *honeymoon stage*, individuals are excited by confronting an entirely new culture. Acculturation is minimal at this stage since cultural interpenetrations are not deep enough. Then the *rejection stage* occurs. As their interpenetration increases, individuals realise that many of the established behaviours and meanings that were taken for granted in their old subculture are inadequate for acting appropriately in the new subculture. These individuals may reject the values of the new subculture. Usually, cultural conflict occurs in this stage.

The *tolerance stage* occurs when individual interpenetration deepens. People may understand more about the new culture and start to appreciate it. Then they reach the final stage, the *integration stage*. Here some adjustments to the new culture are often seen.

Understanding different acculturation stages is critical for Canadian marketers because different opportunities occur at different stages. It is commonly believed that language proficiency is important for successful assimilation into a new culture, especially in North America. Most Canadians will agree that immigrants to Canada who live and work in environments where only their native language is spoken are not likely to penetrate far into Canadian society and may only become partially acculturated. Immigrants with more education are more likely to speak English or French and will likely obtain better jobs, which, in turn, will allow for greater cultural penetration and more complete acculturation. This is strongly believed by the government of Quebec which requires all new immigrants to Quebec to send their children to schools in the French language sector to learn to speak French. In the Chinese communities in Canada, many recent immigrants from Hong Kong and Taiwan have been accused by their own members of not doing enough to learn the customs, traditions and languages of Canada. Acculturation and assimilation also cause much concern. Elderly Chinese immigrants have concerns that Canadian-born Chinese have failed to learn to speak Chinese well, and that their old customs and traditions will soon be forgotten.[30]

SOCIAL CLASS

An expert in social class research makes some useful observations about class:

> There are no two ways about it: social class is a difficult idea. Sociologists, in whose discipline the concept emerged, are not of one mind about its value and validity. Consumer researchers, to whose field its use has spread, display confusion about when and how to apply it. The American public is noticeably uncomfortable with the realities about life that it reflects. All who try to measure it have trouble. Studying it rigorously and imaginatively can be monstrously expensive. Yet, all these difficulties notwithstanding, the proposition still holds: social class is worth troubling over for the insights it offers on the marketplace behaviour of the nation's consumers.[31]

We agree with these observations concerning both the problems and the value of social class analysis. For our purposes in this text, **social class** refers to a status hierarchy by which groups and individuals are distinguished in terms of esteem and prestige. In Canada, the most often used measure of social class is the Pineo-Porter-McRoberts socioeconomic classification.

The 16 Pineo-Porter-McRoberts socioeconomic occupation groups are classified according to prestige and form four major social class divisions: the upper class, the middle class, the working class, and the lower class. The 16 occupation groups can help consumer researchers determine the most likely social class of individuals who participate in surveys. The complete list of occupational titles used by the census is much more extensive, but Exhibit 16.5 shows the major larger groups of Canadians. The percentage of the population that fits into each occupational group is shown in parentheses.

Social class is clearly not the same as income. The Economic Council of Canada says social class measures can tell you whether you are middle income, but you must ask yourself whether you are middle class or not. Occupation, though not a completely reliable predictor of class membership, is usually the best indicator available. Exhibit 16.5 describes these groups and identifies some marketing implications for each.

Identification with a social class is influenced most strongly by one's level of education and occupation (including income as a measure of work success). But social class is also affected by social skills, status aspirations, community participation, family history, cultural level, recreational habits, physical appearance, and social acceptance by a particular class. Thus, social class is a composite of many personal and social attributes rather than a single characteristic such as income or education. The social classes can be considered as large subcultures because their members share many cultural meanings and behaviours.

Social class is an important source of consumers' beliefs, values, and behaviours.[32] Most of the people an individual interacts with on a day-to-day basis are likely to be members of that person's social class. Family, peer groups, and friends at work, at school, and in the neighbourhood are all likely to be of the same social class. Association with these people teaches the individual appropriate values for the class as well as behaviour norms that are acceptable. This learning process can occur either through direct statement ("You don't have a chance any more unless you go to college") or by example (an individual sees friends going to college, graduating, and purchasing new cars).

Social class and values

Social classes are useful for understanding why consumers develop different beliefs, values, and behaviour patterns. For example, the upper class may well be socially secure and not find it necessary or desirable to purchase the most expensive brands to impress other people. Middle-class people, on the other hand, often engage in such conspicuous consumption. As Consumer Perspective 16.5 shows, even homeless people (perhaps the lowest social class in Canadian society) engage in consumption behaviour that reflects their values.

Although the members of each social class share distinct values and behaviour patterns to some degree, the four major groups can be differentiated even further. There are vast differences in family situations and income totals among subgroups. For instance, families in each social class can be classified further as relatively overprivileged, average, or underprivileged.[33] *Overprivileged* families in each social class are those with incomes usually 25 percent to 30 percent above the median for the class, who therefore have money left over to seek forms of a "better life" preferred by the class. At the same time, because these families continue to share values, behaviours, and associations with other members of the class, they typically do not "move" to a higher social class. The *average* families are those in the middle income range of the class who can afford the kind of house, car, apparel, food, furniture, and appliances expected by their peers. Finally, the *underprivileged* families have incomes at least 15 percent below the class midpoint, so they must scrimp and sacrifice to purchase the proper products for their class.

Social class and income

There has long been a debate about whether social class or income is the better variable for understanding consumer choice for market segmentation. Advocates of each position muster a number of arguments for the superiority of their favourite variable and point out a variety of methodological and conceptual problems with the other one.

EXHIBIT 16.5

Pineo/Porter/ McRoberts social class structure

Upper Class (11 percent of population)

This group consists of the upper-upper, lower-upper, and upper-middle class. They have common goals and are differentiated based on the prestige and status society ascribes to different occupations. Depending on income level and values, activities include attending symphony orchestras, the opera, the ballet; yachting, drama, summer camp for children, sailing, hiking; mountaineering, golfing, ice skating, and investing in art. Prestige schooling for their offspring is a priority.

Self-employed professionals (1.0%)
Employed professionals (7.3%)
High-level management (2.6%)

Middle Class (28 percent of population)

This consumer group is characterised by its preoccupation with "correct" behaviours, doing the "right thing" and appearing "respectable" to avoid losing status. The older generation of this group, many without university degrees, often try to aim their children toward achieving a higher education. They sense that upward social mobility or landing a good job depends very much on having more formal/higher education. This class includes the following occupations:

Semiprofessionals (4.8%)   Supervisors (3.1%)
Technicians (2.0%)   Foremen/women (4.1%)
Middle management (6.5%)   Skilled clerical, sales, service (7.2%)

Working Class (41 percent of population)

This is the largest social stratum in Canadian society. This class has a certain pride in its social position. It is composed of people in the skilled crafts and trades (e.g., police officers, tailors and dressmakers, auto mechanics, plumbers, firefighters, printers, carpenters). It also includes semiskilled manual occupations (e.g., meat packers, shoemakers, fishers, butchers, bakers, bus drivers) and the white collar semiskilled jobs (e.g., guides, farmers, restaurant servers, hairdressers, typists, cashiers, tellers). Working-class people usually have a lower education level than the higher classes, but most have completed elementary education. The class is characterised by its "limited horizons, the centrality of family and clan, the chauvinistic devotion to nation and neighbourhood," and its pursuit of ease of labour and leisure.
Skilled crafts and trades (14.0%)

Farmers (2.5%)
Semiskilled clerical, sales, service (12.0%)
Semiskilled manual (12.2%)

Lower Class (20 percent of population)

This class consists of around 20% of Canada's labour force. It is subdivided into "a lower group of people but not the lowest" and the "real lower-lower" class.
The lower class lives above the poverty line but below the living standard of the working class. Occupationally, it consists of unskilled service workers such as servants and maids, mail clerks, mail carriers and messengers, street vendors, taxi or truck drivers, nursing attendants, janitors, house cleaners, and the like. Members of this group are characterised by limited sociogeographic horizon and education.
Members of the lower-lower class are usually out of work and visibly poverty-stricken. They are homeless, live in multi-story tenements or row houses, or take shelter in private charitable institutions such as halfway houses or the Salvation Army. They are primarily people on welfare. "Bag ladies and bums" are visible lower-lower class examples.

Unskilled clerical, sales, service (3.7%)
Unskilled manual (14.9%)
Farm labourers (3.1%)

Sources: Richard P. Coleman, "The Continuing Significance of Social Class to Marketing," *Journal of Consumer Research* 10, December 1983; Peter C. Pineo, "Revisions of the Pineo-Porter-McRoberts Socioeconomic Classification of Occupations for the 1981 Census, "Qsep Research Report No. 125 (Hamilton, ON: Program for Quantitative Studies in Economics and Population, Faculty of Social Sciences, McMaster University), February 1985, p. 12, Table 1.

CONSUMER
PERSPECTIVE

16.5

The homeless:
Canada's lowest
social class

In the last decade, demographers have linked the term "growing underclass" to the increasing number of homeless men and women found in Canadian cities. The latest estimates say that 4.2 million people fall into the circle of poverty. The bottom of the social class hierarchy is often associated with having no home and no job. However, the homeless are still consumers despite their low status. They may not have money, but they still have a basic set of consumption behaviours. These activities include finding a warm place to sleep, looking for food, and having some meagre possessions that are safe.

Society often paints the homeless as alcoholic and unemployed. But a closer look reveals insights contrary to this stereotype. A 1992 survey revealed that only 16 percent of 468 homeless people surveyed actually reported drinking. Most homeless individuals do have jobs, jobs that nobody else wants. They make small change from recycling. A few creative homeless people have begun their own newspaper in an effort to save themselves from poverty. These people can't afford a decent apartment, and the subsidised housing lists are long. So they live in makeshift homes. A shopping cart is a good possession because you can move around the streets easily with all your other possessions. A warm blanket is almost a luxury to some in this cold, harsh climate.

The lowest needs defined by Maslow, such as food, shelter and safety, are the most important "products" to the homeless. By definition they do not have a home, but they do have makeshift homes. These range from park benches to cardboard boxes in the streets to abandoned buildings; many live under bridges or in hostels. Their criterion for choosing an area is warmth.

Food is the next need the homeless try to satisfy. If money is extremely hard to come by, then they visit food banks like 2 million other Canadians. Soup kitchens and some group homes distribute food to the homeless as well.

Clothing is important, especially during the cold winter months in Canada. Many layers of clothes are usually worn to ward off the cold and possible physical attack. Clothes are usually received from centres for the homeless.

The homeless need health care. They do not necessarily have different health problems, but they have different lives. Hostels are a place to sleep at night, but most do not offer sleeping accommodations during the day. The poor do not have disinfectants or dressings or even reliable access to water, so they are more prone to disease. They are often refused care. Smaller clinics and drop-in centres were designed to right these wrongs, but the problems still grow.

Sources: Sandro Contenta, "The Forgotten Homeless", *The Toronto Star,* Oct. 10, 1993, pp. H1–H8. Morris Wolfe, "Homeless Magazines Worth the Price," *The Globe and Mail,* Oct. 26, 1993, p. C5. Sherri Davis-Barron, "Feeding the Hungry," *The Vancouver Sun,* Oct. 16, 1991, p. A4. Jane Coutts, "Homeless Recount Health-Care Barriers," *The Globe and Mail,* May 12, 1992.

Recently, consumer researchers have recognised that each variable has its advantages and disadvantages, and whether to use social class, income, or a combination of the two depends on the product and the situation. Some tentative generalisations come from study of the issue:[34]

1. Social class is a better predictor than income of areas of consumer behaviour that do not involve high dollar expenditures but do reflect underlying differences in lifestyles or values (drinking imported wines). Social class is superior for understanding the purchase of highly visible, symbolic, and expensive objects such as living room furniture.

2. Income is generally superior for understanding purchases of major kitchen and laundry appliances and products that require substantial expenditure but are not status symbols within the class.

3. The combination of social class and income is generally superior for understanding purchases of product classes that are highly visible, serve as symbols of social class or status within class, and require either moderate or substantial expenditure (clothing, cars, TV sets).

Determining whether social class or income or a combination of these or other variables is the dominant factor in a given marketing analysis requires careful examination of the relationship between the product and the consumer.

▶ **SUMMARY**

Learning objective 1: *Define subculture and discuss the analysis of subcultures.*
Subcultures are distinctive groups of people in a society that share cultural meanings. These common meanings may concern affective and cognitive responses (emotional reactions, beliefs, values, and goals), behaviours (customs, scripts and rituals, behavioural norms), and environmental factors (living conditions, geographic location, important objects). Subcultures share certain cultural meanings with the overall society and/or other subcultures, but some of a subculture's meanings are unique and distinctive. Subcultures in a society can be analysed at different levels depending on the marketing purpose: broader groups (middle-age French) or more narrowly defined groups (middle-age French, low income, living in rural areas). Marketers normally analyse a subculture in terms of its content (shared values, lifestyles, or beliefs). Although the people in a subculture have certain cultural meanings in common, analysis of nearly any subculture also reveals great diversity. Marketers must attempt to identify subcultural groups large enough to be useful, without ignoring important differences among people in each group.

Learning objective 2: *Describe a geographic subculture and give several examples.*
In any country, groups of people living in different regions have the characteristics of subcultures. That is, consumers in geographic subcultures have different values, behaviour norms, beliefs, and lifestyles. These different cultural meanings lead to differences in consumption behaviour. In Canada, a province or a large city could be analysed as a geographic subculture. Other geographic subcultures can be identified that do not correspond exactly to governmental boundaries—the Maritimes, central Canada, the Prairies, and the West Coast regions are commonly considered geographic subcultures. The nine nations of North America divide the continent into geographic subcultures based on common cultural meanings.

Learning objective 3: *Describe age subcultures and give some examples.*
Age subcultures are based on the chronological (actual) ages of people. Teenagers (13 to 19), baby boomers (mid-30s to mid-40s), mature market (age 50 to 65) and elderly (over 65) are four age subcultures. Age subcultures within the elderly market include younger seniors (65–74), intermediate seniors (75–84), and older seniors (85 and over). People in these age categories can be considered subcultures because they share certain meanings (values, beliefs, lifestyles). But as with any other social group, the consumers in any age subculture are also highly diverse (not all elderly feel they are that age).

Learning objective 4: *Discuss the major ethnic subcultures in Canada.*
Canada has many ethnic subcultures. The major ones, according to Statistics Canada data, are French, Asian, German, and Italian heritage. Since the 1991 Canadian census, there has been a large influx of Asians to Canada. The Chinese, Japanese, and Korean

populations, together with other ethnic groups from the Asian subculture, now comprise roughly 4 percent of the total Canadian population. The single largest group after those of British origin (28 percent), are French Canadians, who make up 23 percent of all Canadians; the majority reside in Quebec or Ontario. Germans account for 3.4 percent of Canada's population, Italians for almost 3 percent. Many other ethnic subcultures in Canada, such as the Greek community, each account for less than 1 percent of Canadian society. A special ethnic subculture is Native (Aboriginal) Canadians, who now number just over one-half million. The ethnic diversity of Canada is expected to keep increasing into the next century.

Learning objective 5: *Define consumer acculturation and describe its four stages.*
Acculturation refers to how people in one culture or subculture come to understand and adapt to the meanings (values, beliefs, behaviours, rituals, lifestyles) of another culture or subculture. Consumer acculturation refers to how people acquire the ability and cultural knowledge to be skilled consumers in a different culture or subculture. Acculturation is highly relevant for immigrants to a new culture, people who move within a country and experience a new subculture, and marketers who manage international marketing strategies in many countries. The degree to which people become acculturated into a new culture or subculture depends on their level of cultural interpenetration—the amount and type of social interactions they have with people in the "host" culture. When people come into contact with a new culture or subculture, they may go through four stages of acculturation corresponding to four levels of cultural interpenetration. In the honeymoon stage, people (often tourists) are fascinated by the exotic foreign culture or subculture, but because their culture interpenetration is usually shallow and superficial, little acculturation occurs. If cultural interpenetration increases, people may enter a rejection stage, develop antagonistic attitudes toward the new subculture, and reject its key values and meanings. If cultural interpenetration continues and deepens, people may reach the tolerance stage, where they begin to appreciate the meanings of the subculture. Finally, in the integration stage, acculturation is adequate for a person to function satisfactorily in the new culture or subculture. Although acculturation may never become total, people view the new culture as a valid alternative way of life that they value for its good qualities.

Learning objective 6: *Describe the major social classes in Canada and discuss how marketers can use social class distinctions.*
Most of the schemes to subdivide Canadian society into social classes are similar to the four social classes described in the text—the upper, middle, working, and lower classes. Upper-class Canadians (about 11 percent) tend to have college educations and professional occupations. They value quality merchandise and self-expression. About 28 percent of Canadians are middle class. They look to the upper class for inspiration and have a more cosmopolitan outlook than working-class Canadians (about 41 percent), who have narrower world views and stronger family ties. Lower-class Canadians (about 20 percent of the population) are the least educated and have the lowest income levels. Because people in different social classes have rather different beliefs, values, and lifestyles, marketers can use social class as a basis for creating large market segments. As with any subculture, each social class shares certain cultural characteristics but can be diverse in some elements.

---

subculture	geographic subculture	social class	▶ **KEY TERMS**
age subculture	acculturation		**AND**
ethnic subculture	stages of acculturation		**CONCEPTS**

1. Define a subculture. Are college students a subculture? Explain why or why not.

2. Discuss how subcultures (and social class) can influence the way consumers learn cultural meanings (values, behaviours, lifestyles). Give a specific example.

3. What ethical factors should a marketer consider in developing marketing strategies targeted at particular subcultures or social classes? (What is your reaction to selling fortified wine to homeless people, cigarettes to Hispanics, or diet plans to overweight working-class people?)

4. Identify the age subcultures among members of your own family (or neighbourhood). How do these cultural differences affect their consumption behaviours for food, personal care products, and clothing?

5. Think of three subcultures not discussed in the text and describe them. Discuss one marketing implication for each one. (What product categories would be most relevant?)

6. Discuss the acculturation process by describing what might happen if you come into long-term contact with a different subculture (imagine you move to a different area of the country or city).

7. Discuss the concept of cultural interpenetration in terms of the acculturation of groups of immigrants in your country. What problems and opportunities do you see for marketing strategies?

8. Define the concept of social class and identify the major social class groups in your country. What are the major social class groups in the immediate community where you live? How do you recognise these social class groupings?

9. Select a product class (perhaps a food, beverage, clothing, car, or furniture product). How might each of the social classes you identified above respond to marketing strategies for these products?

CHAPTER 17

Reference Groups and Family Influences

LEARNING OBJECTIVES

After completing this chapter, you should be able to

► 1. Define reference groups and give several examples of types of reference groups.

► 2. Discuss three types of reference group influence on consumers.

► 3. Define household and family and explain the types of each.

► 4. Describe various roles in family decision making.

► 5. Describe the sources of conflict in family decision making and discuss how conflict can be handled.

► 6. Discuss consumer socialisation and give an implication for marketing.

► 7. Describe the family life cycle and discuss its implications.

Barney: Copyright © 1995 The Lyons Group. Reprinted with permission.

BARNEYMANIA AND THE BABY BOOMLET

Kids all over the country have gone Barney crazy. It seems this big purple dinosaur has taken over where the Teenage Mutant Ninja Turtles left off. Kids all across Canada are wearing Barney clothing, playing with Barney dolls, and watching Barney's popular videocassettes.

Spending on children, by both parents and children themselves, is going through the roof. Fueling this spending are the baby boomers who are having children later in life, creating a baby boomlet. Boomers in their 30s and 40s can afford to indulge their children because their earning power is greater than that of younger parents, and they already own many of the material things in life. Also, many affluent families have only one or two children, which leaves more money to spend on each child.

Many different markets are being affected by this new boom. Sales of traditional toys, such as Mattel's Barbie doll, are booming to the point that Mattel has introduced new lines just to keep up with demand. The videocassette market is also going through the roof. Many parents are buying their kids videos to have as collector items and also so they can watch them as many times as they wish. Disney is one beneficiary of this trend. *Aladdin* is the all-time best-selling video, surpassing another Disney film called *Beauty and the Beast.*

Another product for children is Hallmark's new line of greeting cards, "To Kids with Love." These cards are intended to convey affection and encouragement from busy working parents who sometimes do not see their children all day. Clearly children and their parents represent a very large and growing market.[1]

Evolutionary changes in the social environment of the family influence marketing strategies targeted at children or adults who buy for kids. In making these purchasing decisions, mothers and fathers influence each other's affective responses, cognitions, and behaviours. Parents are also influenced by other people in the social environment, including their relatives, friends, and peers (the latter is highly influential for both kids and adults). In this chapter, we discuss two types of environmental influences: reference groups and family.

Reference groups and family are aspects of a consumer's micro social environment. Social interaction with reference groups and family is often direct and face to face, meaning it can have immediate influence on consumers' cognitive, affective, and behavioural responses to marketing strategies.[2] Reference groups and family are involved in transferring or moving cultural meanings from the overall society, subculture, and social class to individual consumers. For all these reasons, reference groups and family have significant marketing implications.

REFERENCE GROUPS

Individuals may belong to many sorts of groups. A **group** consists of *two or more people who interact with each other to accomplish some goal*. Important groups include families, close personal friends, co-workers, formal organisations (Shriners, church youth group, professional association), leisure or hobby groups (a bowling team or gourmet diners), and neighbours. Any of these groups may become a reference group.

A **reference group** involves *one or more people someone uses as a basis for comparison or "point of reference" in forming affective and cognitive responses and performing behaviours*. Reference groups can be of any size (from one person to hundreds of people); they may be tangible (the actual people in your office), or intangible and symbolic (successful business executives or sports heroes you observe from afar). A person's reference group may be from the same or another social class, subculture, or even culture. Reference groups are cultural groups in that members share certain common meanings. For instance, groups of college students tend to develop specific meanings and behaviour norms about appropriate clothing, and groups of teenage boys share certain meanings about what types of athletic shoes are "in." Such reference groups can influence the affective and cognitive responses of consumers as well as their purchase and consumption behaviour.

Marketers try to determine the *content* of the shared meanings of various reference groups (the common values, beliefs, behavioural norms, lifestyles). Then they select certain reference groups to associate with or promote their products. Marketers seldom examine the *process* by which reference groups move cultural meaning into products and from products into consumers.

Reference groups can have both positive and negative effects on consumers. Social groups that have favourable cultural meanings may become *associative reference groups* that consumers want to emulate or associate with. Other social groups that embody undesirable meanings may serve as a negative point of reference that people want to avoid; they become *dissociative reference groups.*

Exhibit 17.1 lists several types of reference groups and their key distinguishing characteristics. Characteristics may be combined to describe quite specific groups. For example, your immediate co-workers constitute a formal, primary membership group. While these distinctions can be useful, most consumer research focuses on two primary, informal groups—peers and family. The issues that interest marketers about reference groups include:

EXHIBIT 17.1

Types of reference
groups

Type of Reference Group	Key Distinctions and Characteristics
Formal/informal	Formal reference groups have a clearly specified structure; informal groups do not.
Primary/secondary	Primary reference groups involve direct, face-to-face interaction; secondary groups do not.
Membership	People become formal members of membership reference groups.
Aspirational	People want to join or emulate aspirational reference groups.
Dissociative	People avoid or reject dissociative reference groups.

1. What types of influence do reference groups exert on consumers?

2. How does reference group influence vary across products and brands?

3. How can marketers use their understanding of reference groups to develop more effective marketing strategies?

Most people belong to several primary informal groups and a few formal, membership groups (church, PTA, chamber of commerce). Most people could also be associated with many secondary groups, both formal and informal. Why do people use some of these groups as reference groups and not others? And how do these reference groups influence

Type of reference group influence

Danskin uses these athletes with expertise as a credible reference group for product information.

consumers' affect, cognitions, and behaviours? Basically, people identify and affiliate with particular reference groups for three reasons: to gain useful knowledge, to obtain rewards or avoid punishment, and to acquire meanings for constructing, modifying, or maintaining their self-concept. These goals reflect three types of reference group influence: informational, utilitarian, and value-expressive.

Informational reference group influence occurs when a group transmits information to a consumer about other people or about aspects of the physical environment such as products, services, and stores. This information can be conveyed directly, either in words or by direct demonstration. For instance, a consumer thinking about buying running shoes or stereo equipment might ask friends who know about such products. A person learning to play tennis might ask friends to show how to serve or how to hit a backhand shot.

Consumers tend to be influenced by reference groups to the degree that they perceive the information is reliable and relevant to the problem at hand and the information source is trustworthy.[3] Reference sources can be a single person, as when Jean Luc Brassard extols the merits of Pert Plus shampoo. Because highly credible reference groups are more likely to have an informational influence on consumers, marketers may hire recognised experts to endorse a product and tell consumers why it is good (famous extreme skier Scott Schmidt is spokesperson and model for North Face, manufacturer of ski clothing).

Consumers can also obtain information indirectly through vicarious observation of a reference group. People who like fishing will pay attention to the brands of equipment famous bass fishers use in a fishing tournament or on TV fishing shows. This is common behaviour; many golfers, skiers, mountain climbers, and other sports enthusiasts engage in similar vicarious observation of the brands used by their reference group. This is why Nike hired basketball star Michael Jordan (obviously an expert) to wear its Air Jordan basketball shoes.

Reference groups can transmit information to consumers in three ways. Sometimes consumers intentionally seek information to reduce the perceived risk of making a decision or to learn how to perform certain behaviours. Thus, most beginning skydivers listen very carefully to their new reference group of experienced skydiving instructors as they explain how to pack a parachute or how to land correctly. Consumers buying a new computer may seek out a reference group of more experienced users who can help them learn how to use the product. In other cases, the reference group may accidentally transmit information; perhaps someone will overhear reference group members talking about a product or happen to observe them using a particular brand. A third way information may be transmitted to the consumer is for reference group members to initiate the process. This can occur when enthusiastic reference group members talk up an activity and encourage people to try it. For example, in-line skaters might try to persuade others to take up the sport. A marketing strategy consistent with informational reference group influence is to encourage current customers to create new customers (bring along a friend for dinner and get your meal for half-price).

Utilitarian reference group influence on consumers' behaviours and affective and cognitive responses can occur when the reference group is in charge of rewards and punishments that matter to the consumers. Basically, people will comply with the desires of a reference group if (*a*) they believe the group can control rewards and punishments, (*b*) the behaviour is visible or known to the group, and (*c*) they are motivated to gain rewards or avoid punishment.

For example, in some work environments (a formal, membership reference group), people are expected to wear business attire. Other work groups may encourage casual dress (jeans and T-shirts in some Silicon Valley companies). The rewards and punishments for compliance with the appropriate form of dress may be tangible (people get raises or bonuses, or they get fired), or more psychological and social (approving looks, or disparaging remarks behind your back). Peer groups routinely administer such psychosocial rewards and punishments for adherence to or violation of the reference group code. We can all cite examples of how our own peer reference group influences (even controls) our dressing behaviour and attitude. Marketing strategies that use utilitarian reference group appeals include portrayal of social sanctions in TV commercials (people recoiling from someone's offensive body odour or bad breath or the evidence of dandruff).

Value-expressive reference group influence can affect people's self-concepts. As cultural units, reference groups create and embody cultural meanings (beliefs, values, goals, behavioural norms, lifestyles). As you learned in Chapter 15, people constantly look for desirable cultural meanings to use in constructing, enhancing, or maintaining their self-concepts. When they identify and affiliate with particular reference groups that express these desired meanings, consumers can draw out some of these meanings and use them in their own self-construction.

Consider a group of people who buy Harley-Davidson motorcycles and associated gear—they are largely middle and upper-class professional people, including doctors, dentists, lawyers, and professors. These RUBs (rich urban bikers) or weekend warriors, as the hard-core Harley owners (the tattooed and bearded renegades) refer to them, look to the traditional Harley owners as an aspirational reference group (although very few RUBs will ever become hard-core bikers).[4] The hard-core Harley bikers express several desirable meanings and values for the RUBs, which they can gain through association and through purchase of Harley-Davidson products, including feelings of freedom from work and family, independence, and belonging to a special, unique group. Some RUBs even may inspire a bit of the fascination that the hard-core Harley bikers relish from nonbikers or owners of other brands. Value expressive reference group meanings can

Hard-core Harley bikers like these are a reference group for some Harley owners.

EXHIBIT 17.2

**Effects of public–
private and luxury–
necessity dimensions
on reference group
influence for product
and brand choice**

	Necessity	Luxury

Public	**Public necessities**
	
	Reference group influence
	    Product: Weak
	    Brand: Strong
	
	Examples: Wristwatch, car, man's suit
		Public luxuries
		
		Reference group influence
		    Product: Strong
		    Brand: Strong
		
		Examples: Golf clubs, skis, sailboat

Private	**Private necessities**
	
	Reference group influence
	    Product: Weak
	    Brand: Weak
	
	Examples: Mattress, floor lamp, refrigerator
		Private luxuries
		
		Reference group influence
		    Product: Strong
		    Brand: Weak
		
		Examples: TV game, trash compactor, icemaker

Source: Adapted with permission of the University of Chicago Press from "Reference Group Influences on Product and Brand Purchase Decisions," by Bearden and Etzel, in *Journal of Consumer Research*, September 1982, p. 185. © 1982 by the University of Chicago.

influence affect, cognitions, and behaviour, in this case including purchases of biker clothing and accessories. Harley-Davidson markets a variety of products to satisfy these desires, including black leather jackets, "colours" (clothing with insignias and biker logos), many biking accessories, and even a Harley-Davidson brand of beer.

In summary, reference groups can influence consumers' affect, cognitions, and behaviours in several ways. In fact, all three types of reference group influence can occur through a single reference group. As a reference group for the weekend biker, the hard-core Harley-Davidson bikers can be a source of information (magazine articles and observation), reward or punishment (returning a wave or ignoring the RUBs on the road), and cultural meanings (the values of individualism and independence).

**Reference group
influence on
product and brand
purchase**

It is unlikely that reference groups influence all product and brand purchases to the same degree. Research suggests that reference group influence on consumers' purchase decisions varies on at least two dimensions.[5] The first dimension concerns the degree to which the product or brand is a necessity or a luxury. A *necessity* is owned by virtually everyone (a flashlight, a clock, a bed), while a *luxury* is owned only by consumers in particular groups (a sailboat, a camcorder, a tuxedo). The second dimension is the degree to which the object in question is conspicuous or visible to other people.[6] A *public good* is one that other people are aware an individual owns and uses, one for which they can identify the brand with little or no difficulty (a car). A *private good* is used at home or in private, so other people (outside the immediate family) are unaware of its possession or use (a hair dryer).

Combining these two dimensions produces the matrix shown in Exhibit 17.2. It suggests that reference group influence will vary depending on whether the products and brands are public necessities, private necessities, public luxuries, or private luxuries. Consider wristwatches, which are public necessities. Because everyone can see whether a person is wearing a wristwatch, the *brand* may be susceptible to reference group influence. Because this product class is owned and used by most people, however, there is likely to be little reference group influence on whether one should purchase a watch.

We have seen that reference groups exert an important influence on consumers.[7] Members of primary informal groups affect not only consumer knowledge, attitudes, and values, but also the purchase of specific products and brands—and even the choice of stores in which purchases are made. In some cases, an analysis of primary informal group influences can be used to develop marketing strategies. For example, in industrial marketing, a careful analysis of the group influence dynamics among the various people who have a role in a purchase decision may be useful for determining appropriate marketing approaches.[8] Similarly, peer group influence is a major asset to firms that sell to groups of consumers (perhaps at "parties" in the home), like Tupperware. Individuals tend to conform to the norms of the group by purchasing some items. Occasionally, marketers may try to stimulate reference group influence—a health club might offer you two months' membership free if you get a friend to sign up for a year.

Salespeople may attempt to create a reference group influence by describing how a customer is similar to previous purchasers of the product: "There was a couple in here last week very much like you. They bought the JVC speakers." Or they may describe themselves as a reference group: "Oh, your children go to East High School? My kids go there, too. We bought them a new notebook computer to help them with their school projects."

Finally, soliciting experts to aid in the direct sale of products can be a successful strategy for some firms. For example, a consumer's dentist is likely to be a highly influential reference individual, particularly for products related to dental care. Thus, it could be effective for a manufacturer of, say, the Water Pik to offer gifts to dentists for encouraging patients to use the product. The company could keep track of a dentist's referrals by asking consumers to list their dentist on the warranty card for the product. Of course, experts can also have a negative impact on sales of a new product if they convey negative information.[9]

For most mass-marketed products, a detailed analysis of the interactions of specific primary informal groups (groups of close friends or co-workers) is impractical. Instead marketers tend to portray both primary informal and aspirational groups in advertising:

> Reference group concepts have been used by advertisers in their efforts to persuade consumers to purchase products and brands. Portraying products being consumed in socially pleasant situations, the use of prominent attractive people endorsing products, and the use of obvious group members as spokespersons in advertising are all evidence that marketers and advertisers make substantial use of potential reference group influence on consumer behaviour in the development of their communications. . . . Reference groups expose people to behaviour and lifestyles, influence self-concept development, contribute to the formation of values and attitudes, and generate pressure for conformity to group norms.[10]

There are many examples of the use of reference group concepts in advertising. Pepsi has featured popular stars such as Ray Charles and Michael Jackson and popular athletes such as Joe Montana and Dan Marino, with whom many young people identify. Bauer, Cooper, Nike, and other sports equipment companies for many years spent a large portion of their promotion budget on giveaways to successful athletes, as well as hiring these athletes to wear and recommend their brands. The popular series of Miller Lite ads featuring well-known retired athletes likely appealed to baby boomers who followed their careers and considered some of them heroes. Consumer Perspective 17.1 describes the aspirational reference group appeals used by American Express.

Marketing implications

CONSUMER
PERSPECTIVE

▶ 17.1

Reference group
advertising

Sometimes the reference group is a single person—a referent other. Thus, movie stars like Meryl Streep or Mickey Rourke (highly popular in France) or musicians like Madonna or Garth Brooks can serve as a reference group for some people.

American Express has based its advertising on single-person, reference group appeals since the early 1970s, beginning with the classic campaign, "Do You Know Me?" Each ad featured a person who was famous for his or her achievements but whose face was not familiar to the public. In 1987, American Express modified the ad strategy and produced the highly praised "Portraits" campaign, with photos of famous people who held American Express credit cards. Featured were the likes of Mikhail Baryshnikov, Luciano Pavarotti, and Ella Fitzgerald, implying that slapping down the Amex card put one in the league of such talent. The reference group strategy seems to have worked for American Express, as earnings grew at a 20 percent rate between 1970 and 1990.

Visa had used a different promotion approach since the middle 1980s, developing ads intended to convince consumers that Visa is a more practical card because it is accepted in more places than American Express. This ad campaign finally paid off in the 1990s when prestige and high status no longer seemed so important. In fact, value was what cardholders wanted. As a result, American Express lost 400,000 cardholders in Canada, leaving current membership at only 1.1 million. Many more cardholders were lost in the United States.

Due to this decreased market share, American Express has rethought its image. Amex's latest media blitz reinforces the card's connection to fiscal prudence, while encouraging spending. To do this, it redefined prestige—this time as financial responsibility. To promote this new image, Amex recruited comedian Jerry Seinfeld, star of the sitcom of the same name on NBC. Jerry can be seen making a series of puns to a goldfish "drowning in debt." He then urges a man shopping in a busy Christmas season to "stick with American Express—no interest and no revolving debt."

Although there is debate over the appropriateness of using Jerry Seinfeld as a spokesperson, no one can deny the change in consumer demand for value in credit cards. Amex is hoping that by renewing its image and connecting with consumers, it will prevent its market share from declining further.

Source: Marina Strauss, "Amex Leaves Attitude at Home," *Globe and Mail*, March 14, 1994, p. B1; Stuart Elliot, "Seinfeld's Jabs Give Amex a 1–2 Punch," *Globe and Mail*, Dec. 3, 1992, p. B4; "Amex's New Pitch to Status Seekers: Prudent Spending," *Financial Times of Canada*, p. 21; "American Express Pulls Trigger with New Ads," *Marketing News*, March 4, 1991, p. 6; Derrick Niederman, "Image Can Be a Fickle Thing," *Investment Vision*, October/November 1991, p. 30.

FAMILY

In most consumer behaviour research, marketers take the individual consumer as the unit of analysis. The usual goal is to describe and understand how individuals make purchase decisions so that marketing strategies can be developed to influence this process most effectively. The area of family research is an exception: it views the family as the unit of analysis.[11]

Actually, marketers are interested in both families and households. The distinction between a family and a household is important.[12] A housing unit is defined as having its own entrance (inside or outside) and basic living facilities. The people living in the housing unit constitute a **household.** Except for homeless people, most Canadians live in households. These households are highly diverse, involving many different living arrangements such as houses, townhouses, apartments and condos, college dorm rooms, fraternity houses, and nursing homes. The *householder* is the person or people who rent or own the household. Households can be categorised into types on the basis of the relationship of the residents to the householder. Marketers are mainly concerned with two types of house-holds, families and nonfamilies.

Nonfamily households include unrelated people living together, such as college roommates or unmarried couples of opposite sexes or the same sex. In 1991, fewer than 3 in 10 Canadian households (2.6 out of 10 million households) were nonfamilies. A **family** by contrast has at least two people—a husband and a wife, with or without unmarried children, or a single parent with unmarried children living in the same dwelling. Common-law partners are also considered as families by Statistics Canada. About 75 percent of Canadian households are families. The difference between nuclear and extended families is an important distinction. The *nuclear family* includes one or more parents and one or more children living together in a household. The *extended family* is a nuclear family plus other relatives, usually grandparents, living in one household.

Marketers are highly interested in **family decision making**—how family members interact and influence each other when making purchase choices for the household.[13] Research shows that different people in the family may take on different social roles and perform different behaviours during decision making and consumption.[14] For example, the person who purchases Kraft peanut butter for lunchtime sandwiches (the father) may not be the same person who makes the sandwiches (the mother) or who eats them (the children).

Family decision making

Decision roles and influence

To understand family decision making fully, marketers need to identify which family members take on what roles. Decision-making roles encompass the following:

▷ *Influencers* provide information to other family members about a product or service (a child tells parents about a new brand of breakfast cereal).

▷ *Gatekeepers* control the flow of information into the family (a mother does not tell her children about a new toy she saw at the store).

▷ *Deciders* have the power to determine whether to obtain a product or service (a husband decides to buy a new snack chip at the grocery store).

▷ *Buyers* actually purchase the product or service (a teenager buys milk for the family at the convenience store).

▷ *Users* consume or use the product or service (the kids eat canned spaghetti that the parents bought).

▷ *Disposers* discard a product or discontinue use of a service (a father throws out a partially eaten pizza; a mother cancels a magazine subscription).

These definitions show how different family members may be involved in particular aspects of the purchase decision and use of the product or service that is bought. From the perspective of the Wheel of Consumer Analysis, each family member and his or her roles and behaviours are part of the social environment for the other family members. Understanding family decision making is a difficult research challenge that requires marketers to study the social interactions and patterns of influence among family members. These interactions and influences vary for different purchases depending on which family members are involved and how much is at stake.

Some products are purchased for use by the entire family (orange juice), while others are purchased for use by one person in the family (deodorant). Developing successful marketing strategies for selling products to families requires attention to questions such as these:

1. Is the product to be used by one person or several family members?
2. Is the product to be purchased with funds from a single person or family funds?

3. Is the product expensive enough that the purchase requires the family to make trade-offs in buying other items it needs?

4. Do family members disagree about the value of the product? How do they reduce the conflict?

5. If the product is to be used by several people in the family, what product modifications are necessary to accommodate each user?

6. Which family members will influence the product purchase decision? What media and information are used by each influencer?

7. Do different family members prefer different product forms, brands, models, or stores?

Consider the purchase of a car by a family. Answers to these questions will influence the marketing strategies used by car manufacturers and dealers. The appropriate marketing strategies for selling cars will vary if the car is to be used as a second family car for commuting to work, or by a teenager to drive to school, versus if it is the only car in the family.

Because of these variations, relatively few generalisations can be offered about family decision making. Essentially, marketers can expect to find substantial differences in the people involved at each stage of the decision-making process, their roles, and their influences on the decision outcome.[15] This means researchers must analyse the dynamics of family decision making for each marketing problem they face, including identifying which family members are involved, what roles they play, and who has the major influence. These analyses are useful in developing effective marketing strategies targeted at the appropriate family member.

Most research on family decision making has focused on husband/wife roles and influence, while children (and other members of extended families) have not received much attention.[16] Yet we know the children's market is large and important. Both younger kids and teenagers can have major influences on the family's budget allocation decisions and purchase choices. The birth of a child, for example, is a major event for a family, which creates demand for a wide variety of products most couples never needed to consider purchasing previously. Consumer Perspective 17.2 describes some of these purchases.

Conflict in family decision making

When more than one person in a family is involved in making a purchase decision, some degree of conflict is likely.[17] **Decision conflict** arises when family members disagree about some aspect of the purchase decision. The means–end chain model provides a useful framework for understanding decision conflict. Family members may disagree about the desired end goals of a purchase. Consider the choice of where to spend a family vacation. The husband might want to go somewhere for lazy relaxation, the wife wants good shopping and night life, and the kids want adventure and entertainment. Differences in end goals or values can create major conflict because very different choice alternatives are likely to be related to these incompatible ends. Serious negotiations may be required to resolve the conflict.

In other cases, family members agree on the desired end goal yet disagree about the best means to achieve it. For instance, everyone might want to go out to eat or see a movie, but the kids think a fast-food restaurant or an action film is the best choice, while the parents prefer a full-service restaurant or a dramatic film. Again, some means of resolving the conflict is necessary. Often, an alternative (a new means to the end) is chosen as a compromise (everyone goes out for pizza or to see a comedy film). Finally, if either the end or the means is not agreed on, family members are also likely to disagree about the choice criteria for evaluating alternatives (in the case of a new car, these could include the appropriate price range, the necessary options, the best colour).

CONSUMER
PERSPECTIVE

17.2

The cost of
raising a family

The number of births in Canada rose in 1990 to 405,486, as compared to 370,709 in 1980. Both these levels are lower than those of the previous high birthrate periods when the baby boomers were born during the late 1940s, 50s, and early 1960s. By 1993 the number of births in Canada had declined once again to approximately 387,796.

However, the costs of raising a family have increased dramatically in recent years. In 1992, the total average household expenditure was up 29 percent over 1986, based on a survey of 9,500 households. The overall costs of running a household have increased, and the costs of raising a family have gone up even faster. The major expenditures are shelter, food, clothing, recreation, and widespread child care. These costs rose by a whopping 51 percent from 1986 to 1992. One research study in the United States estimated that in the first year of life an infant's parents spend $500 on infant formula, $570 on disposable diapers, $850 on high chairs and baby food, $350 on clothes, $1,000 on cribs and baby furniture, and another $225 on bedding and bath products.

These first-year expenditures are only a sample of what is yet to come. It is clear that the cost of raising a family is climbing and will continue to rise into the next century. It is also clear that families and children represent very large markets and marketing opportunities.

Source: Blayne Cutler, "Rock-A-Buy Baby," *American Demographics*, January 1990, pp. 35–39. Reprinted with permission © *American Demographics*, January 1990. Statistics Canada, *Canadian Social Trends*, Summer 1993.

When family members disagree about such factors in a purchase situation, conflict may be severe.[18] If so, family members can do several things. Some consumers procrastinate, ignoring the problem and hoping the situation will improve by itself. Others may try to get their way by attempting to influence other family members. Exhibit 17.3 describes several influence strategies that have been identified in family research.[19] Depending on the product at issue, the family members involved in the decision, the social class and subculture of the family, and the environment, a family member might use any of these strategies to influence other members of the family.

Although serious conflicts can occur in family decision making, many family purchases probably do not involve major conflicts. For one thing, many family purchases are recurring, in that many products and brands are bought repeatedly over a long period. So, even though conflict may have been present at one time, it usually has been resolved. To minimise friction, families may develop choice plans to avoid potential conflict. For instance, a family with two children might allow one to choose the breakfast cereal or ice cream flavour one week and the other to choose the next week.

Another reason decision conflict among family members concerning purchase and consumption decisions is not often serious is that many purchases in a household are made by individuals to meet their own personal needs or those of other family members. To the degree that such purchases are reasonably consistent with family values and do not place an undue burden on family resources, there is likely to be little conflict. For instance, we would expect that purchases of books, personal care items, and many food products do not involve much family conflict.

It is through socialisation processes that families transmit the cultural meanings of society, subculture, and social class to their children, thereby influencing their children's affect, cognitions, and behaviours. **Consumer socialisation** refers to the way children

Consumer socialisation

EXHIBIT 17.3

Six common types of family influence strategies

Expert
Influence is reflected by a spouse providing specific information concerning the various alternatives. For example, one spouse can try to convince the other that she/he is more knowledgeable concerning the products under consideration by presenting detailed information about various aspects of these products.
Legitimate
Influence deals with one spouse's attempts to draw upon the other's feelings of shared values concerning their role expectations. Therefore, the spouse's influence is based on the shared belief that she/he should make the decision because she/he is the wife/husband. For example, the husband can argue that since he is the "man of the house," he should make a particular decision.
Bargaining
Involves attempts by one spouse to turn the joint decision into an autonomous one in return for some favor granted to the other spouse. For example, in return for autonomy in a particular decision, one spouse may agree to give the other autonomy in another decision when she/he had previously refused to do so. "If you do this, I'll do that" may be the most common type of bargaining attempt.
Reward/referent
Influence is based on a combination of the reward and referent power/influence strategies. Reward influence is based on an individual's ability to reward another by doing something that the other would enjoy. Referent influence is the influence based on the identification or feeling of oneness (or desire for such an identity) of one person with another. Referent influence in marriage stems from the desire of spouses to be like their concepts of the "ideal" husband or wife.
Emotional
Influence attempts involve displaying some emotion-laden reaction. For example, one spouse may get angry at the other. These attempts are often nonverbal techniques. For example, one person may cry or pout, while another may try the "silent treatment."
Impression management
Encompasses premeditated persuasive attempts to enhance one's influence differential in a dyadic relationship. For example, one spouse may claim that the other's preferred brand was "out of stock" when, in fact, it wasn't. The objective is to convince the spouse to attribute the influence attempt to external pressures beyond the influencer's control.

Source: Reprinted by permission of the University of Chicago Press from "Persuasion in Family Decision Making," by Rosann L. Spiro, in *Journal of Consumer Research,* March 1983, p. 394. © 1983 by the University of Chicago.

acquire knowledge about products and services and various consumption-related skills (how to buy carefully, how to apply for a loan).[20] Younger children acquire much of their consumer knowledge from their parents, but adolescents learn from their peers as well. Both younger and older children absorb consumer knowledge and skills from social institutions such as the media (TV, magazines, movies) and advertising.[21]

Socialisation can occur indirectly through observation and modelling or directly through intentional instruction. Indirect socialisation occurs when parents take their children on shopping trips or discuss products and brands. In other cases, parents intentionally talk to their children about consumer skills such as how to look for products, find the

Many companies have recognised segments of the family life cycle such as divorced or widowed middle-age people.

JAN: Here I am. 40 and dating again.
ANNCR: How Colgate Tartar Control gave Jan her smile back.
JAN: I took a really good look at myself. And my smile didn't look clean.

My dentist removed the tartar and said Colgate Tartar Control helps keep it off.
ANNCR: Colgate fights the tartar that traps bacteria and stains . . . For cleaner teeth.

RANDY: I LOVE TO SEE YOU SMILE.
ANNCR: Colgate Tartar Control.
Because your smile was meant to last a lifetime.

best price, bargain with salespeople, return unsatisfactory products for a refund, and dispose of products (recycling, holding a garage sale).[22]

The consumer knowledge formed in childhood can influence people in later years. Some adults still use the same brands their parents bought when they were children. A number of long-lived brands may be purchased and used throughout an adult's life (Campbell's soup, Crest or Colgate toothpaste, Heinz ketchup, and Tide laundry detergent are examples). Thus, developing early brand awareness and loyalty is an important marketing strategy for many companies. BCTel Mobility for instance, sponsors events such as the World Cup freestyle skiing championships in Whistler, British Columbia. Even though teenagers are not often purchasers of cellular phones, they can have a significant influence on their parents' choices. Chevrolet has advertised on Much Music to attract today's teens and tomorrow's new car buyers.[23]

Socialisation is not restricted to the influence of parents on young children. Children can socialise their parents, especially where new products are concerned (teens may introduce their parents to new music styles).[24] In some instances, adult children can influence the consumption behaviour of their parents, as in decisions on retirement housing.[25] Finally, consumer socialisation occurs throughout life as people continue to learn new consumer skills and acquire product knowledge. Consider the socialisation that occurs when people marry or move in together. Each person learns from the other as they adjust to different preferences and consumption behaviours.

Changes in Canadian families

Many cultural and social changes in recent years have influenced the structure of Canadian families (and families elsewhere, too). We briefly discuss four of these changes that are interrelated: women's employment, marriage and divorce, family planning and child-rearing practices, and household composition.

Women's employment

At one time in Canadian society (say, 40 years ago), the typical role of women was as homemakers. Today, over two-thirds of all women are in the labour force.[26] Working women are not distributed equally across all age groups, however. Over two-thirds of women in their 20s, 30s and 40s are employed outside the home, but fewer women older than that have outside jobs. Of the women who do work, 45 percent are employed full-time the year around, compared to 65 percent of men who work full-time all year. More than half of young women with preschool children are working, up from 30 percent in 1970.

The disposable income of married-couple households increases dramatically when both spouses work outside the home. The average household income for dual-earner couples with children was $60,246 in 1992, compared to $43,511 for one-earner households.[27]

Marriage and divorce

Canadian society has undergone major changes in people's attitudes and behaviours concerning marriage and divorce.[28] Young people are delaying marriage (in 1991, the median age of first marriage was 25 for women and 27 for men, a near record). Increasing numbers of Canadians may never marry (in 1987, the marriage rate in Canada (per 1,000) was 6.9. This rate has declined steadily, and was estimated at about 5.5 in 1993).

In the 1990s, marriage is likely to become even more of an optional lifestyle. Increasing numbers of single women are remaining unmarried and raising children alone. Divorced and widowed people are waiting longer to remarry, and increasing numbers of them will never remarry. And more Canadians are living together outside marriage. Although some people claim cohabiting is a way to cut the chance of divorce (because people learn more about a future spouse before marriage), divorce rates actually are higher for couples who cohabit before marriage (53 percent of first marriages that begin with cohabitation end in divorce, compared to 28 percent of those where the partners did not live together before marriage).

The net result is that more Canadians spend less of their lives married. This change has profound implications for many consumer businesses that may have assumed their market consists of traditional families. Still, most Canadians eventually do marry (or remarry), and many of them have children. Current estimates are that 90 percent of Canadian women will marry at some time in their lives. The point is that marketers must consider a greater variety of family types than they once did.

Family planning and child-rearing practices

As more baby boomers start families, the number of births increased to near record levels (nearly 406,000 in 1990).[29] The number of births is up because there are more potential parents among the baby boomers, not because families are having more children. In fact, the number of children per family has decreased steadily since the mid-1960s. Women currently bear an average of fewer than two children, down from nearly three in 1965. Despite the trend toward smaller families, there are still some large families in Canada. In 1991, over 400,000 families had three or more children (representing 12 percent of families with kids, down from 14 percent in 1986).[30] These relatively larger families constitute significant markets for certain products such as breakfast cereal, milk, toothpaste, and toilet paper. At the same time, the fact that many women marry later and have children later than their mothers did changes how they raise their kids and relate to them. Finally, women live many years after their children leave home. All of these changes together mean people spend less of their lives in child-oriented households, which has a strong influence on their consumption behaviour.

Household composition

Canadian family and nonfamily households have undergone major demographic changes during the past few decades that have important implications for marketers. Exhibit 17.4 summarises some of these changes. First, the number of people in households grew to 26.7 million by 1991. The number of people in family households grew in numbers but actually shrank as a percentage of people in households (from 88.3 percent in 1980 to 84.4 in 1991). In 1991 there were 22.6 million people in households compared to 21.9 million in 1985.

The number of people in families composed of husbands, wives, common-law partners, or lone parents increased in number but again decreased as a percentage of the total number of people in households. In 1991 there were 13.3 million people in this category, representing 49.7 percent of all people in households (compared to 12.6 million and 50.9 percent in 1986). Common-law partners refers to two people of the opposite sex who are not legally married to each other but live together as husband and wife in the same dwelling.

The number of never-married sons and daughters in families decreased in both number and percentage of total people in households. In 1991 this category represented 31.9 percent of the total, or 8.5 million people (compared to 1986, when it was 34.6 percent and 8.6 million people). Never-married sons and daughters refers to blood, step, or adopted children who have never married (regardless of age) and are living in the same dwelling as their parent(s).

People living in nonfamily households totalled 655,000, a very small percentage (2/10 of 1 percent) of the total. This was a decrease from 1986, when the total number of people living in nonfamily households was 683,000. Nonfamily people refers to household members who do not belong to a census family. They may be related to the household reference person (a cousin or brother-in-law) or unrelated (a lodger or roommate).

	1991		1986	
	Households	**Percent Distribution**	**Households**	**Percent Distribution**
People in households	26,731,000	100.00	24,773,000	100.00
People in family households	22,558,000	84.40	21,878,000	88.30
Husbands, wives, common-law partners, or lone parents	13,287,000	49.70	12,616,000	50.90
Never-married sons and daughters	8,514,000	31.90	8,578,000	34.60
People in nonfamily households	655,000	0.02	683,000	0.03
People not in families	4,173,000	15.60	2,894,000	11.70

EXHIBIT 17.4

Changes in Canadian family and nonfamily households

CONSUMER PERSPECTIVE

▶ 17.3

Singles

The 1991 Canadian census reports that there are 672,495 people over the age of 25 who have never been married. This is up from the total number of never-marrieds from 1986. Two factors account for this trend: (1) many individuals are making conscious decisions either not to marry or to delay marriage; and (2) a large number of marriages end in divorce.

These singles, plus college students and other young adults living with their parents, constitute a huge market with significant annual income (estimated at $60 billion). It will certainly come as no surprise that singles are disproportionate consumers of convenience products, fast-food and regular restaurant meals, and travel.

As with any social segment, there is a great diversity among singles, including carefree 21-year-olds, middle-age divorced people, and elderly widows. Some marketers have treated all singles as an "extramarital aberration," which is undoubtedly foolhardy. To be successful, marketers must deal with the diversity of this group.

Consider the 1991 ad campaign "Friends and Family" from Sprint Canada. Singles use the telephone to keep in touch with their families and friends. In Sprint's promotion, if consumers got their friends and families to join, each party received a 20 percent discount on all calls made to each other. The promotion was very successful. Bell Canada, recognising that many families have members in both Quebec and Ontario, developed a similar promotion entitled "Between Friends," which offered substantial discounts on long-distance rates between these two provinces.

Source: Blayne Cutler, "Single and Settled," *American Demographics*, May 1991, p. 10.

The number of people not in families increased substantially. In 1986 these people numbered 2.9 million, or 11.7 percent of the total people in households; in 1991 the numbers had grown to 4.2 million or 15.6 percent.

The number of single people living alone has been increasing. This can be attributed to two factors. First, more and more people are marrying at a later age or never at all. Second, many people who do marry end up single again due to divorce. This social trend creates major opportunities for marketers, some of which are described in Consumer Perspective 17.3.

Family life cycle

Analysis of the many demographic changes in family composition and structure can be complicated. To apply an organising framework, marketers can use the concept of the family life cycle to identify key family segments and develop effective marketing strategies for those households.

Some 40 years ago, most Canadians followed the same life path and went through about the same stages of life. People got married, had children, stayed married, raised their children and sent them on their way, grew old, retired, and eventually died. This sequence of family types delineated by major life events (marriage, birth of children, aging, departure of children, retirement, death) is called the *traditional family life cycle*.[31]

Recent cultural changes in Canadian society such as delayed marriages, childless marriages, working women, and increased divorce rates have rendered the traditional family life cycle somewhat inadequate. Exhibit 17.5 presents a **modern family life cycle** that includes the traditional family life cycle and adds several other family types to describe the more diverse family structures of the 1990s.[32] The modern family life cycle can account for most types of families in Canadian society, including childless couples, divorced people, and single parents with children.

EXHIBIT 17.5   A modern family life cycle

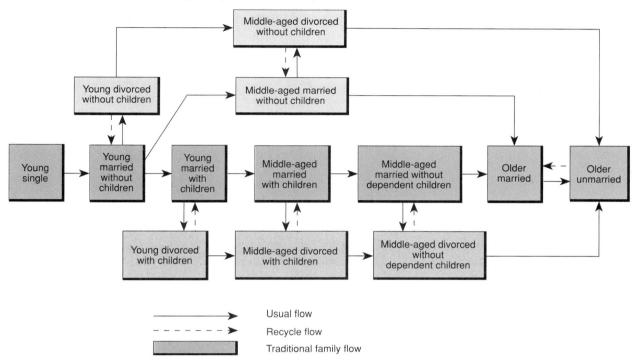

Source: Reprinted by permission of the University of Chicago Press from "A Modernized Family Life Cycle," by Murphy and Staples, in *Journal of Consumer Research,* June 1979, pp. 12–31. © 1979 by the University of Chicago.

▷ *Single-parent families* are usually headed by a woman. In fewer than half of these families does the adult work full-time. On the average they spend about $2,500 more than the income received, and almost 80 percent of their total expenditures are for current consumption. The percentages spent on food and clothing are the highest of all households. About 35 percent of single parents are homeowners, which may explain in part the high debt level. From these numbers it is evident that these families are living through a difficult stage in their finances.

▷ *Young singles* are people in one-person households under the age of 45. They have the largest percentage of total expenditures on tobacco, alcoholic beverages, recreation, reading, and education. They also spend more than other unattached individuals on clothing, security, insurance, and transportation, and less for food, shelter, and personal and health care. Very few (19.1 percent) are homeowners. This pattern of consumption reflects the needs and lifestyles of young single or divorced individuals: appearance, entertainment, smoking and drinking.

▷ *Older singles* are people in one-person households over the age of 45. They see a gradual drop in income as they grow older. Between 30 and 37 percent own their own homes. As they grow older, they spend an increasing amount of money on shelter and personal health care and a decreasing amount on clothing, recreation, reading, and education.

▷ *Married couples with children* includes three important subcategories. First are the couples with one or more children under the age of 4. They are in the home formation stage and spend a high proportion of their expenditures on furnishings and equipment. About 65 percent of these families own their own homes. The second subcategory is couples with children between the ages of 5 and 15. About 77 percent of these are homeowners, and a higher percentage of wives work full time now that the kids are older. In the third category, the children are all over 16 years of age. The percentage of wives working increases but the percentage of homeowners decreases. This category has the highest expenditures on transportation, tobacco, and alcoholic beverages and the lowest on food and personal and health care.

Television producers seem to cover many of these stages in the family life cycle in creating situation comedies (see Consumer Perspective 17.4).

Two cautions are worth mentioning about the modern family life cycle in Exhibit 17.5. First, this scheme does not include nonfamily households, which currently represent nearly 24 percent of all Canadian households. This diverse category includes people who remain single and never marry, cohabiting couples, and shared households that include various combinations of unrelated residents. Although these diverse households may be difficult to categorise and target with marketing strategies, the fact that they number 2.4 million households (over 4 million people or 16% of Canadian society) makes them attractive markets for many products.

Second, the family life cycle framework does not capture every possible change in family status that can occur. For instance, a new life cycle stage may be developing called the "boomerang age."[33] This refers to the increasing number of young adults (mostly in their 20s) who left home for work or college but are now returning to live with their parents. Although there were more of these people in 1991 than at any time since the Depression, living with parents past high school and even college is not so unusual. This boomerang segment of the family life cycle may offer some marketing opportunities.

Marketing implications

Marketers can use the family life cycle to segment the market, analyse market potential, identify target markets, and develop more effective marketing strategies. The family segments identified by the family life cycle include diverse types of people. Each family type

Young singles (9 percent of all households) are an important market segment for many products.

is made up of people from every social class and every age, racial, ethnic, and regional subculture in the country.

Marital status

Consider the young single or bachelor stage of the family life cycle. In 1991, nearly 23 percent of all households in Canada consisted of a single adult, up from 21 percent in 1986. Much of this growth is attributable to the "new" bachelors created by divorce. The number of divorced individuals in Canada in 1991 was approximately 14 percent of all families.

The various types of bachelors constitute rather different markets. For instance, 18- to 24-year-old men in the swinging years (99 percent have never married, but most will someday) are a prime market for tape decks, sixpacks, and hot cars. But 35- to 45-year-old unmarried men (many of whom are divorced) are more interested in toys for their kids, living room furniture, and toiletbowl cleaners. Many divorced men are really only temporary bachelors, because many will remarry within an average of three years. Finally, widowers, with an average age of 61, behave more like married men their age than other bachelors. In sum, developing marketing strategies for this diverse bachelor segment is a real challenge for marketers.

Size of market

Another point to recognise is that some stages in the family life cycle are more important markets than others. For instance, households headed by people age 45 to 64 have the highest average income and total expenditures.[34] This segment of middle-aged households will become even more important through the 1990s as it grows by 20 percent when all the baby boomers enter this life cycle stage. Most of these boomers will have children and will spend heavily on them.

Effect of time pressure

The family life cycle can help marketers understand how important cultural trends affect family structures and consumption behaviour. For example, consider the "time-starved" consumers in Canada. Time is more precious to many people as the pace of family and work life becomes more hectic and more families have two wage earners (two-thirds of married couples with children are dual-income households) or are headed by a single parent. Millions of people are stressed about time, believe they don't have enough time, and try to conserve time. They are prime candidates for convenience products of all types that can save time, which then can be used for more enjoyable or profitable purposes.

For many of these people, shopping is a painful chore that interferes with their leisure. Many Canadians believe shopping is drudgery. According to one survey in the United States, these perceptions are strongest among married-couple families with children, especially if both parents are working. Eleven million of these people do not enjoy shopping, and half believe it adds to their stress level. The interest in shopping is gone for many (though not all) Americans.

These attitudes are reflected in various consumption-related behaviours. For instance, in 1988, the average consumer in the United States spent 90 minutes on a shopping trip to the mall; in 1990, shopping time was down to 68 minutes. Some consumers develop shopping strategies to save time. For instance, some people shop for clothes only two or three times a year. Some shoppers follow established paths through the store to avoid duplicating effort. One executive buys a car at a dealer located near the airport, so he can have the car serviced during business trips. In an extreme case, one consumer shops for groceries only on Tuesday from 4:45 to 5:50 P.M. As she rushes through the store virtually on automatic pilot, a new marketing strategy is unlikely to catch her attention.

Although relatively few marketers have done much to reduce shopping time and stress, there are many ways to appeal to the time-stressed shopper. These need not be highly sophisticated strategies—one department store changed to a central-aisle layout to make it easier for customers to find their way. Following are several marketing strategies to help reduce consumers' shopping time and stress.

> ▷ *Provide useful information.* Marketers who provide useful information to help consumers make the right choices save their customers time and reduce shopping stress. For instance, Blockbuster Video has a computerised database to help customers find films made by a certain director or starring a particular actor. Computer technology could help consumers make the right choices of colour, size, and styles for clothing, cars, and home furnishings. Coordinating displays of related products, such as showing entire ensembles, can serve the same purpose.

> ▷ *Assist in purchase planning.* People often try to cope with time stress by carefully planning their shopping excursions. Marketers who help consumers form purchase plans will help them reduce stress. High-quality sales assistance in the clothing store or appliance showroom can help a time-stressed customer develop a decision plan. Marketers might suggest alternatives when a product is unavailable. Blockbuster tries to give customers movie alternatives if their first choice is unavailable.

> ▷ *Develop out-of-store selling.* Although shopping may once have been a pleasant and enjoyable experience, today many consumers would rather relax at home. This trend creates problems for retailers but also creates new opportunities for

selling in the home or at the workplace. Avon, for example, now sells its products to groups of co-workers at the work site.

▷ *Automate transaction processes.* Companies that can automate and thereby speed up transaction processes appeal to time-stressed consumers. At one supermarket, customers can use a computer to enter their deli orders so they don't have to wait in line to be served; they pick up the deli orders as they leave the store. A&P and Shop Rite are experimenting with automated checkout systems to reduce waiting time in the checkout line. At certain Subway restaurants in Toronto, you can fax in your lunch order and it will be ready when you arrive. Car rental companies like Hertz and Avis offer an automated check-in service at major airports. Hand-held computers speed the check-in process so customers receive an invoice on the spot as they leave the car in the parking lot. Customers can speed to the airport with no waiting.

▷ *Improve delivery.* Nothing upsets a time-stressed consumer more than having to wait at home all day for a service person to come to fix the washing machine. For years, GE has made precise appointments for its service calls. Sears now offers repair services six days a week and in the evening. Service courts are being developed where consumers can obtain a variety of services (dry cleaning, shoe repair, small appliance repairs, mailing) in one stop.

▶ SUMMARY

Learning objective 1: *Define reference groups and give several examples of types of reference groups.*
A reference group consists of one or more people whom someone uses as a basis for comparison or a point of reference in forming and evaluating his or her affective responses, cognitions, and behaviours. Reference groups can be of any size (from one person to hundreds of people) and may be tangible (actual people) or intangible and symbolic (successful business executives or sports heroes). A person's reference groups may be from the same or a different social class, subculture, and culture. Reference groups may be formal or informal (professional associations versus friends), primary or secondary (direct versus no direct social interaction), aspirational or dissociative (want to join or emulate versus want to avoid).

Learning objective 2: *Discuss three types of reference group influence on consumers.*
People identify and associate with reference groups for three basic reasons: to gain useful knowledge, to gain reward or avoid punishment, and to acquire desirable cultural meanings. These goals correspond to three types of influences reference groups can have on consumers' affective responses, cognitions, and behaviours. Informational reference group influence occurs when a group transmits relevant information to consumers about themselves, other people, or aspects of the physical environment such as products, services, and stores. Utilitarian reference group influence can occur when the reference group controls rewards and punishments that are relevant to the consumers. Finally, value-expressive reference group influence can affect people's self-concept. Reference groups are cultural units that embody cultural meanings (beliefs, values, goals, behavioural norms, lifestyles). People constantly look for desirable cultural meanings to construct, enhance, or maintain their self-concepts. By identifying and affiliating with particular reference groups that express these desired meanings, consumers can draw out some of these meanings and use them in their own self-construction.

Learning objective 3: *Define household and family and explain the types of each.*
A household consists of people living in a housing unit—a dwelling with its own entrance (inside or outside) and basic living facilities. Canadian households are diverse, involving

many different living arrangements such as houses, townhouses, apartments and condos, college dorm rooms, fraternity houses, and nursing homes. The person who rents or owns the household is the householder. Types of households are defined in terms of the relationship of household residents to the householder. Marketers are concerned with two main types of households, families and nonfamilies. A family consists of at least two people—the householder and someone related to him or her by blood, marriage, common law or adoption. A nuclear family includes one or more parents and one or more children living together in a household. An extended family is a nuclear family plus other relatives, such as grandparents, living in one household. In contrast, nonfamily households include unrelated people living together, such as college roommates or unmarried couples.

Learning objective 4: *Describe various roles in family decision making.*

In family decision making, different people in the family may take on different social roles during the purchase choice process. In these roles, people have varying types and amounts of influence on the final choice outcome. For example, the husband may purchase peanut butter at the store (playing the buyer role). A son or daughter may provide information about choice alternatives (the influencer role). The mother may control which information is considered in the decision process (the gatekeeper role), and she may choose what brand to buy (the decider role). The child might eat a peanut butter sandwich for lunch (the user role) and throw it away half-eaten (the disposer role). To understand family decision making, marketers should identify which family members take on which roles and determine how they influence the course of the decision-making process.

Learning objective 5: *Describe the sources of conflict in family decision making and discuss how conflict can be handled.*

Decision conflict arises when family members disagree about some aspect of the purchase decision. Family members may disagree about the desired end goals of a purchase. Dissimilar end goals can create major conflict, because very different choice alternatives are likely to be related to incompatible ends. In other cases, family members may agree on the desired end goal, yet disagree about the best means to achieve it. When either the end or the means is not agreed on, family members are also likely to disagree about the choice criteria for evaluating alternatives. Sometimes, family members attempt to handle conflict by trying to influence others to change their minds. Their influence may be based on expertise, legitimate role status, or control of rewards. Some family members try to bargain with others to reduce conflict or resort to emotional reactions (anger, tears).

Learning objective 6: *Discuss consumer socialisation and give an implication for marketing.*

Families transmit the cultural meanings of society, subculture, and social class to their children through socialisation processes. Consumer socialisation describes how children acquire knowledge about products and services and learn various consumption-related skills (how to buy carefully, how to get a loan). Socialisation can occur indirectly through observation and modelling or directly through intentional instruction. Indirect socialisation occurs when parents take their children on shopping trips or talk about products, brands, and stores. Some socialisation occurs when parents intentionally try to teach their children consumer skills such as how to look for products, find the best price, bargain with salespeople, return products for a refund, and dispose of products (recycling, holding a garage sale). The consumer knowledge formed in childhood can influence people all their lives. Some adults still use the same brands their parents purchased when they were children.

Learning objective 7: *Describe the family life cycle and discuss its implications.*

The typical stages in family life are defined by major life events (marriage, birth of children, aging, departure of children, retirement, death). This sequence is called the traditional family life cycle. Marketers use the family life cycle as a basis for segmenting consumers into broad large segments.

Recent cultural changes in Canadian society such as delayed marriages, childless marriages, working women, and increased divorce rates have created new stages not included in the traditional family life cycle. The modern family life cycle includes the stages of the traditional family life cycle, while adding several other family types to describe the more diverse family structures of the 1990s. The modern family life cycle can account for most types of families in Canadian society, including childless couples, divorced people, and single parents with children.

group	value-expressive reference group influence	decision conflict	▶ **KEY TERMS AND CONCEPTS**
reference group		consumer socialisation	
informational reference group influence	household	modern family life cycle	
	nonfamily households		
utilitarian reference group influence	family		
	family decision making		

▶ **REVIEW AND DISCUSSION QUESTIONS**

1. Identify two reference groups that influence your consumption behaviour. Describe each according to the types listed in the text and tell what categories of purchases each influences.

2. From a marketing manager's viewpoint, what are some advantages and problems associated with each type of reference group influence?

3. Describe how public visibility and the distinction between luxury and necessity goods affect reference group influence on choice at the product and brand levels.

4. What is the family life cycle? Discuss how marketers can use it to develop effective marketing strategies.

5. Identify three family purchases where you have played a role in the decision process. What role did you play? Discuss the interpersonal interactions involved in the decisions.

6. Suggest two ways that marketing strategies could influence the decision process in your family or household. How are these different from strategies that might be used to influence individual decisions?

7. Offer examples of conflict in family household decision making that you have experienced or observed. What types of marketing strategies could help to reduce such conflict?

8. Discuss the differences between households and families. Describe how each is important to marketers.

9. How are family influence strategies similar to or different from other reference group influences? Are there marketing implications related to these patterns?

10. Work with another student to identify two different household or family compositions. Assume that each unit has the same level of income. Discuss how the decision processes and conflicts in each household might vary for products such as a car, a vacation, and a stereo system.

18

Environmental Influences on Marketing Practices

LEARNING OBJECTIVES

After completing this chapter, you should be able to

▶ 1. Explain why society needs controls for marketers.

▶ 2. List the basic rights of Canadian consumers.

▶ 3. Explain four constraints society uses for controlling marketing activities.

FAST FOOD STUFFED WITH R&D

Since 1985, Yves Potvin, a former gourmet chef, has been developing a new product category—healthy fast food. Besides wieners, his company, Yves Veggie Cuisine of Vancouver, British Columbia, makes its own brand-name burger patties (three varieties) and deli slices for sandwiches. All use vegetable protein from soybeans, wheat, onions, mushrooms, and carrots.

Potvin's segment of the food market is so new he claims to have little direct competition. Some companies make vegetable patties, but "nobody else has a full line of products or mass-market packaging," he maintains. In the United States, which generates 40 percent of his more than $7 million in annual sales, competitors are five years behind, he says.

Potvin's key ingredient is research and development in products and processes: "Because we're pioneers in this field, it's important to always make improvements." With the support of a full-time food technologist, he hopes to develop two new products a year. Among the current projects: vegetable-based breakfast sausages, paté, and pepperoni.

Yves Veggies' fast growth—including five successive years of profitability—is capturing attention. In 1995 it won the federal government's Canada Awards for Business Excellence in two categories, for small business and entrepreneurship. Among the factors cited were its commitment to R&D and its alertness to changing consumer tastes.[1]

EXHIBIT 18.1

Some problem areas
in marketing

Product Issues	Promotion Issues
Unsafe products	Deceptive advertising
Poor-quality products	Advertising to children
Poor service/repair/maintenance after sale	Bait-and-switch advertising
Deceptive packaging and labelling practices	Anxiety-inducing advertising
Environmental impact of packaging and products	Deceptive personal selling tactics
Pricing Issues	**Distribution Issues**
Deceptive pricing	Sale of counterfeit products and brands
Fraudulent or misleading credit practices	Pyramid selling
Warranty refund problems	Deceptive in-store selling influences

In this text, we have discussed the relationships among consumer affect and cognition, behaviour, and the environment. One of our major premises is that marketing is an important and powerful force in society. Properly designed and executed marketing strategies can often change consumer affect, cognitions, and behaviours in ways that help organisations achieve their objectives.

So far in this section of the text, we have discussed a number of environmental influences on consumers, including the impact of culture, subculture, social class, reference groups, and family. In this last chapter, however, the focus changes. While we are still concerned with environmental influences, we look now at their impact not on consumers but on organisations and their marketing strategies. Given that marketing is a powerful force and that marketers can misuse this power, it is important for society to have checks to restrain marketing strategies.

Three points are worth making in our discussion of rights and powers. First, we believe marketing and the free enterprise system offer the best and most effective system of exchange that has ever been developed. This does not mean the system could not be improved. For example, there is still a large group of poor, uneducated, needy people in our society who have little chance of improving their lot.

Second, while marketing may come in for the brunt of society's criticism of business, marketing managers are no more or less guilty of shortcomings than other business executives. Corporate responsibility to society is shared by all business executives, regardless of their functional field. Nor are marketing executives any more or any less ethical than most other groups in society. Similarly, while business, particularly big business, is commonly singled out for criticism, there is no question that other fields—including medicine, engineering, and law—also contribute their share of societal problems. And consumers could also be criticised for the billions of dollars of merchandise that is shoplifted annually, as well as for other crimes against businesses and society.

Third, while some critics target marketing practices in general, many abuses are traceable to a relatively small percentage of firms and practices. Exhibit 18.1 lists some of the most often cited areas of concern, divided into product, promotion, pricing, and distribution issues. Many of these practices are regulated by law.

THE RIGHTS OF MARKETERS AND CONSUMERS

Both marketers and consumers are granted certain rights by society, and both have a degree of power. Overall, many people believe marketers have considerably more power than consumers. One researcher frames the rights granted to marketers (sellers) as follows:

1. Sellers have the right to introduce any product in any size, style, colour, or whatever, so long as the product meets minimum health and safety requirements.
2. Sellers have the right to price the product as they please, so long as they avoid discrimination that is harmful to competition.
3. Sellers have the right to promote the product using any resources, media, or message, in any amount, so long as no deception or fraud is involved.
4. Sellers have the right to introduce any buying schemes they wish, so long as they are not discriminatory.
5. Sellers have the right to alter the product offering at any time.
6. Sellers have the right to distribute the product in any reasonable manner.
7. Sellers have the right to limit the product guarantee or post-sale services.[2]

While this list is not exhaustive, it illustrates the considerable latitude marketers have.

Since the establishment in 1968 of Consumer and Corporate Affairs (now Industry Canada), many rights advocated by consumerists have been enshrined in legislation. In Canada, consumers have eight basic rights:

1. *The right to be informed.* The right to have as much good information as possible to help the consumer to make informed decisions, and to be protected against fraudulent, deceitful, or misleading advertising.
2. *The right to safety.* The right to have safe products and services that will not cause harm or be hazardous under normal use.
3. *The right to choose.* The right to choose freely without undue pressure and to have a broad selection.
4. *The right to redress.* The right to have some action in response to a complaint of a violation.
5. *The right to be heard.* The right to have a voice, which includes assurance that their interests will be fully and fairly considered in the formulation of government policy.
6. *The right to fair value.* The right to have a product or service turn out to be what the seller promised.
7. *The right to a fair price.* The right to a price that is set fairly in the marketplace.
8. *The right to an improved quality of life.*

Consumers have the right to choose which products they prefer.

While these rights may appear to provide consumers considerable protection, note one important weakness: most of these rights depend on the assumption that consumers are both able and willing to be highly involved in purchase and consumption. In fact, however, many consumers are neither. Young children, many elderly people, and the less educated poor often do not have the cognitive abilities to process information well enough to be protected. Furthermore, even those consumers who do have the capacity often are not willing to invest the time, money, cognitive energy, and effort it would take to ensure their rights.

The right to choose is also predicated on the assumption that consumers are rational, autonomous, and knowledgeable decision makers. While we believe most consumers are capable of being so, evidence suggests that they often do not behave this way.[3] The right to choose also ignores the power of marketing to influence attitudes, intentions, and behaviours. Consumers' needs, wants, and satisfaction can be shaped through the conditioning and modelling processes that marketers use, for instance. Thus, the assumption of consumer autonomy is not easily supported.

Finally, no matter how much effort consumers exert to ensure they are choosing a good product, they cannot process information that is not available. For example, consumers cannot be aware of product safety risks that are hidden from them.

Overall, then, if there were no other forces operating in society, marketers might well have more rights and power than consumers do. This is not to say that consumers cannot exert countercontrol on marketers, or that consumers do not vary in the degree to which they are influenced by marketers. However, as our society and system of government and exchange have evolved, a number of constraints or societal influences on marketing activities have also developed. As shown in Exhibit 18.2, these include legal, political, competitive, and ethical influences.

Legal influences

Legal influences include federal, provincial, and municipal legislation and the agencies and processes by which these laws are upheld. Some laws are designed to control practices in specific industries (such as food); others are aimed at controlling functional areas (such as product safety).

EXHIBIT 18.2

Major sources of consumer protection

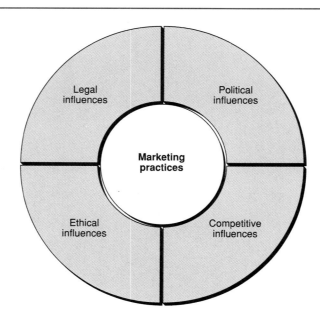

A variety of government agencies are involved in enforcing these laws and investigating questionable business practices. In addition to provincial and local agencies, this includes a number of federal agencies, such as those listed in Exhibit 18.3.

One marketing practice of major interest to Industry Canada is deceptive advertising—advertising that misleads consumers. One approach to dealing with this problem is **corrective advertising,** which requires firms that have misled consumers to rectify the deception in future ads.[4] The following examples illustrate legal influences on advertising.

▷ *Procter & Gamble.* Recent Pampers diaper ads designed to capitalise on changing environmental trends and associated consumer values promoted the diapers as being compostable. Several environmental groups raised complaints and urged revision of the ads. Though Procter & Gamble quickly complied by changing the wording used in the ads, complaints continued due to artwork illustrating disposable diapers in a compost heap changing into a growing tree. Diapers, of course, are not easily composted.

▷ *Du Pont & Co.* Recent Du Pont ads on Canadian television depict a woman who looks about 30 and is encouraged to seek regular professional breast examinations as opposed to conducting self-exams, which are often adequate for her age group. Several critics and groups, including many breast cancer specialists and agency representatives, took offense to this ad, as it is generally agreed that regular mammograms are a necessity only in the 40 to 50 age range. As the ads were presented in a fashion similar to public service announcements,

---

Industry Canada (formerly Consumer and Corporate Affairs Canada) has wide responsibility for administering numerous consumer protection laws and provides support for new programs aimed at furthering Canadians' interests. Industry Canada administers numerous areas of legislation (see below). There are six major aspects to its mandate: (1) to establish and administer rules and guidelines for business conduct; (2) to ensure that information is accurate so consumers can make informed decisions; (3) to maintain and encourage competition among businesses; (4) to establish, administer, and enforce standards for trade in commodities and services; (5) to provide protection from product-related hazards; and (6) to encourage the disclosure and diffusion of technological information. (See Exhibit 18.3b.)

The Food and Drug Act is administered by the Health Protection Branch of **Health Canada** (formerly Health and Welfare Canada). Its prime responsibility is to regulate the sale of food, drugs, cosmetics, and medical devices. The Food and Drug Act deals with quality standards, packaging, labelling, and advertising, as well as the manufacturing practices and selling policies of food and drug manufacturers.

The **Canadian Radio and Television Commission (CRTC)** regulates the broadcast industry in terms of cable offerings, Canadian content, and standards as well as advertising.

Legislation administered by Industry Canada includes the following:

Bankruptcy Act	Hazardous Products Act
Boards of Trade Act	Industrial Design Act
Canada Business Corporation	National Trademark and True Labelling Act
Canada Cooperative Associations Act	Patent Act
Canada Corporations Act	Pension Fund Societies Act
Competition Act	Precious Metals Marking Act
Companies' Creditors Agreement Act	Public Servants Invention Act
Consumer Packaging and Labelling Act	Tax Rebate Discounting Act
Copyright Act	Textile Labelling Act
Dept. Consumer and Corporate Affairs Act	Timber Marking Act
Electricity and Gas Inspection Act	Trademarks Act
Government Corporations Operation Act	Weights and Measures Act

Legislation below is administered jointly with other departments:

Bills of Exchange (with Finance)	Food and Drug Act (with Health)
Canada Agricultural Products Standards Act (with Agriculture)	Maple Products Industry Act (with Agriculture)
Canada Dairy Products (with Agriculture)	Shipping Conference Exemption Act (with Transport)
Fish Inspection Act (with Fisheries and Oceans)	Winding Up Act (with Finance)

EXHIBIT 18.3a

The role of government

EXHIBIT 18-3b

Industry Canada on Internet

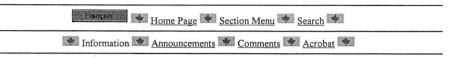

Welcome to Industry Canada

Français   Home Page   Section Menu   Search

Information   Announcements   Comments   Acrobat

More About Industry Canada

Industry Canada is the federal government's key department in charge of national economic issues. It was created to promote jobs and growth in Canada in a world characterized by global integration and the growth of knowledge-based economies. The department's main function is to provide policy advice, industry sector information and business services. The role of Industry Canada is to create a marketplace that is efficient, competitive, supportive, fair, and driven by informed consumers as well as a marketplace that will encourage Canadian businesses to take advantage of opportunities at home and abroad, and apply scientific and technological advances.

Industry Canada joins within a single organization:

Industry, Science and Technology Canada's responsibilities for international competitiveness, economic development and excellence in science
the **Department of Communication's** telecommunications policy and programs
Consumer and Corporate Affairs Canada's market, business framework and consumer policy activities, and
Investment Canada's responsibilities for investment research, policy and review.

Under the direction of the Minister of Industry, <u>John Manley</u>, and supported by the Secretary of State (Science, Research and Development), <u>Jon Gerrard</u>, the responsibilities of the Minister of Industry extends to the areas of industry and technology in Canada; trade and commerce; science; consumer affairs; corporations and corporate securities; competition and restraint of trade, including mergers and monopolies; bankruptcy and insolvency; patents, copyrights, trademarks, industrial designs and integrated circuit topographies; standards of identity, packaging and performance in relation to consumer products and services, except in relation to the safety of consumer goods; legal metrology; telecommunications, except in relation to (i) the planning and coordination of telecommunications services for departments, boards and agencies of the Government of Canada and (ii) broadcasting, other than in relation to spectrum management and the technical aspects of broadcasting; the development and utilization generally of communication undertakings, facilities, systems and services for Canada; investment; small businesses; and tourism.

Last update: September 11, 1995 (jp)
http://info.ic.gc.ca/ic-data/general/more-e.html

---

ethics standards in many provinces came into question. Du Pont, which makes the film used in mammographies, may have compromised its position.

▷ *Oriental Rug Center Ltd.* In a number of retail industries, ads for sales based on bankruptcies or liquidations catch many a hopeful consumer's eyes. But the actual distress related to the sale is not always present. Oriental Rug Center Ltd., a leading Canadian retailer in the lucrative Persian and Oriental rug trade, was recently accused on six charges of misleading advertising. In a market valued at $60 million per year, Canada's biggest and most successful rug dealer faced potential fines amounting to $150,000 due to sales based on phony store "bankruptcies." Huge discounts on highly inflated prices have also come into question. While rug retailing has been singled out here, several other cases in the home furnishing market are being investigated.

Legal influences and the power of government agencies to regulate business and marketing practices grew dramatically in the 1970s, but the 1980s witnessed a decrease in many areas of regulation. In fact, NAFTA and the deregulation of business were the major

The biggest problem facing toy marketers in Quebec is that it's against the law to advertise anything directly to children under the age of 13. Animation is out and the times of day when children's ads can be shown on television are also restricted.

Nobody knows this better than Irwin Toys of Toronto, which spent hundreds of thousands of dollars fighting the law. Passed in 1980 in Quebec, the law (Sections 248 and 249 of the Quebec Consumer Protection Act) was overturned by the Quebec Court of Appeals a few years ago. But it was upheld by the Supreme Court of Canada in 1989. In 1991, Vickers and Benson was fined $10,500 for some Toys "R" Us commercials, while J. Walter Thompson was fined $3,500 for a Mattel campaign.

The restrictions on advertising have had some negative fallout. First, no Quebec agency handles a major toy account, because most toy advertising is done on television, which is now heavily regulated. Second, original French-language children's programs are virtually nonexistent in Quebec. "What you get instead is a translation of American programs, which are violent," said Niquette Delage, director general of the Conseil des Normes de la Publicite.

There are exceptions. Radio Quebec has at least three very popular children's programs on the air. They are "Passe Partout" (for ages 3 to 6), "Robin et Stella" (for ages 6 to 9) and "Le Club de 100 Watts (for ages 9 to 12). These shows and other like them are largely financed from Radio Quebec's own operating budget, sponsorships, and product-licensing agreements.

Outside Quebec, advertising aimed at children is self-regulated by the Canadian Advertising Foundation. All broadcast advertising geared to children must be cleared by the foundation before being aired.

Source: Brian Dunn, "Quebec Law Restricts Ads Aimed at Children," *The Globe and Mail*, Dec. 14, 1992, p. C9. Marina Strauss, "Quebec Charges Five Firms over Ad Campaigns," *The Globe and Mail*, July 3, 1990, p. B6.

thrust in that period, and government agencies considerably reduced their involvement in controlling business practices. The 1990's have witnessed a resurgence of legal influences at the federal level aimed at consumer and environmental protection. Consumer Perspective 18.1 shows how the government of Quebec handles ads aimed at children.

By **political influences** we mean the pressure various consumer groups can exert to control marketing practices. These groups use many methods to influence marketing practice, such as lobbying with various government agencies to enact legislation or working directly with consumers in redress assistance and education. Exhibit 18.4 lists a few of the many organisations established to serve consumer interests.

Bloom and Greyser argue that consumerism has reached the mature stage of its life cycle and that its impact has been fragmented.[5] Yet they believe consumerism will continue to have some impact on business, and they offer three strategies for business to address it. First, businesses can try to accelerate the decline of consumerism by *reducing demand* for it. They could do this by improving product quality, expanding services, lowering prices, and moderating advertising claims.

Second, businesses can *compete* with consumer groups by establishing active consumer affairs departments that offer redress assistance and consumer education. Alternatively, a business could fund and coordinate activities designed to "sell" deregulation and other pro-business causes. Third, businesses can *cooperate* with consumer groups by providing financial and other support.

Political influences

EXHIBIT 18.4

Some political groups and consumerism

International groups
  Greenpeace

Broad-based national groups
  Consumers Association of Canada
  Canadian Wildlife Federation
  Canadian Environmental Defense Fund
  Canadian Health Organisation of Canada

Smaller multi-issue organisations
  Association of Consumer Consultants
  Citizens for a Safe Environment
  C. D. Howe Institute

Special-interest groups
  Jane Goodall Institute
  Canadian Council on Smoking and Health
  Canadian Cancer Society

Local groups
  Smokers' Freedom Society
  Citizens against Metro Garbage
  Heritage Montreal

Overall, most of these strategies would likely further reduce the impact and importance of political influences. Essentially, to the degree that following these strategies leads business firms to become more socially responsible, consumers should benefit.

Competitive influences

Competitive influences refer to actions of competing firms intended to affect other companies and consumers. These actions can be taken in many ways. For example, one firm might sue another firm or point out what it alleges as fraudulent activities to consumers. Johnson & Johnson frequently took competitors to court to protect its Tylenol brand of pain reliever from being shown in competitive ads. Burger King publicly accused McDonald's of overstating the weight of its hamburgers.

Perhaps the most important consumer protection generated by competition is that it reduces the impact of information from any single firm. In other words, in a marketing environment where there are many active competitors, no single firm can dominate the information flow to consumers. In this sense, conflicting competitive claims, images, information, and offers may insulate consumers from undue influence by a single firm or brand. Conversely, competition may also lead to information overload.

Consumers may also benefit from the development and marketing of better products and services brought about by competitive pressure. Current merger trends and the concentration of various industries may lessen these competitive constraints and societal advantages, however.

Ethical influences

Perhaps the most important constraints on marketing practices are **ethical influences,** which involve self-regulation by marketers. Many firms have consumer affairs offices that seek to make sure the consumers are treated fairly. A number of companies have developed a positive image through consumer-oriented marketing practices such as offering toll-free lines for information and complaints, promoting unit pricing, and supporting social causes. Codes of ethics govern practices in many professions. The American Marketing Association has several Canadian chapters for example, in Montreal and Toronto. Its code is shown in Consumer Perspective 18.2.

It is difficult to discuss ethical constraints because there is no single standard by which actions can be judged. Gene Laczniak summarises five ethical standards proposed by various researchers:

1. **The Golden Rule:** Act in the way you would like others to act toward you.

2. **The utilitarian principle:** Act in the way that results in the greatest good for the greatest number.

Members of the American Marketing Association (AMA) are committed to ethical professional conduct. They have joined together in subscribing to this Code of Ethics embracing the following topics:

Responsibilities of the Marketer
Marketers must accept responsibility for the consequence of their activities and make every effort to ensure that their decisions, recommendations, and actions function to identify, serve, and satisfy all relevant publics: customers, organizations, and society. Marketers' professional conduct must be guided by:

1. The basic rule of professional ethics: not knowingly to do harm;
2. The adherence to all applicable laws and regulations;
3. The accurate representation of their education, training, and experience; and
4. The active support, practice, and promotion of this Code of Ethics.

Honesty and fairness
Marketers shall uphold and advance the integrity, honour, and dignity of the marketing profession by:

1. Being honest in serving consumers, clients, employees, suppliers, distributors, and the public;
2. Not knowingly participating in conflict of interest without prior notice to all parties involved; and
3. Establishing equitable fee schedules including the payment or receipt of usual, customary, and/or legal compensation or marketing exchanges.

(continued)

CONSUMER PERSPECTIVE

18.2

Code of Ethics of the American Marketing Association

3. **Kant's categorical imperative:** Act in such a way that the action taken under the circumstances could be a universal law or rule of behaviour.
4. **The professional ethic:** Act in a way that would be viewed as proper by a disinterested panel of professional colleagues.
5. **The TV test:** Ask: "Would I feel comfortable explaining to a national TV audience why I took this action?"[6]

Following any one of these standards could result in many different interpretations of what is ethical. If you doubt this, consider how you might apply them to the scenarios below.

▷ **Scenario 1**
The Thrifty Supermarket Chain has 12 stores in the city of Knowlton, Alberta. The company's policy is to maintain the same prices for all items at all stores. The distribution manager nevertheless sends the poorest cuts of meat and the lowest-quality produce to the store located in the low-income section of town. He justifies this action by the fact that this store has the highest overhead because of factors such as employee turnover, pilferage, and vandalism. *Is the*

CONSUMER
PERSPECTIVE

▶ 18.2

Concluded

Rights and Duties of Parties in the Marketing Exchange Process
Participants in the marketing exchange process should be able to expect that:

1. Products and services offered are safe and fit for their intended uses;
2. Communications about offered products and services are not deceptive;
3. All parties intend to discharge their obligations, financial and otherwise, in good faith; and
4. Appropriate internal methods exist for equitable adjustment and/or redress of grievances concerning purchases.

It is understood that the above would include, *but are not limited to,* the following responsibilities of the marketer:

In the area of product development and management,

▶ disclosure of all substantial risks associated with product or service usage;

▶ identification of any product component substitution that might materially change the product or impact on the buyer's purchase decision;

▶ identification of extra-cost added features.

In the area of promotions,

▶ avoidance of false and misleading advertising;

▶ rejection of high-pressure manipulation or misleading sales tactics;

▶ avoidance of sales promotions that use deception or manipulation.

In the area of distribution,

▶ not manipulating the availability of a product for purpose of exploitation;

▶ not using coercion in the marketing channel;

▶ not exerting undue influence over the reseller's choice to handle the product.

distribution manager's economic rationale sufficient justification for his allocation method?

▷ **Scenario 2**
The independent Chevy Dealers of Valley, British Columbia, have undertaken an advertising campaign headlined by the slogan: "Is your family's life worth 45 MPG?" The ads say that while Chevy subcompacts are not as fuel efficient as foreign imports and cost more to maintain, they are safer, according to government-sponsored crash tests. The ads imply that responsible parents purchasing a car should trade off fuel efficiency for safety. *Is it ethical for the dealers' association to use this sort of appeal to offset an economic disadvantage?*

▷ **Scenario 3**
Some studies have linked the presence of the artificial sweetener subsugural to incidence of cancer in laboratory rats. While the validity of these findings has been debated by medical experts, the Health Protection Branch has ordered

In the area of pricing,

▶ not engaging in price fixing;

▶ not practicing predatory pricing;

▶ disclosing the full price associated with any purchase.

In the area of marketing research,

▶ prohibiting selling or fund raising under the guise of conducting research;

▶ maintaining research integrity by avoiding misrepresentation and omission of pertinent research data;

▶ treating outside clients and suppliers fairly.

Organizational Relationships

Marketers should be aware of how their behaviour may influence or impact on the behaviour of others in organizational relationships. They should not demand, encourage, or apply coercion to obtain unethical behaviour in their relationships with others, such as employees, suppliers, or customers. They should:

1. Apply confidentiality and anonymity in professional relationships with regard to privileged information;

2. Meet their obligations and responsibilities in contracts and mutual agreements in a timely manner;

3. Avoid taking the work of others, in whole or in part, and representing this work as their own or directly benefiting from it without compensation or consent of the originator or owner;

4. Avoid manipulation to take advantage of situations to maximize personal welfare in a way that unfairly deprives or damages the organization or others.

Any AMA member found to be in violation of any provision of this Code of Ethics may have his or her Association membership suspended or revoked.

Source: The American Marketing Association, Chicago.

products containing the ingredient banned from sale in Canada. The Jones Company sends all of its sugar-free J.C. Cola (which contains subsugural) to European supermarkets because the sweetener has not be banned there. *Is it acceptable for the Jones Company to send a potentially unsafe product to another market without waiting for further evidence?*

▷ **Scenario 4**

The Acme Company sells industrial supplies through its own sales force, which calls on company purchasing agents. Acme has found that providing the purchasing agent with small gifts helps cement a cordial relationship and creates goodwill. Acme follows the policy that the bigger the order, the bigger the gift to the purchasing agent. The gifts range from a pair of tickets to a sports event to outboard motors and snowmobiles. Acme does not give gifts to personnel at companies that it knows have an explicit policy prohibiting their acceptance. *Assuming no laws are violated, is Acme's policy of providing gifts to purchasing agents ethically acceptable?*

▷ **Scenario 5**

The Buy Canadian Electronics Company has been selling its highly rated System X color TV sets (21, 19, and 12 inches) for $700, $500, and $300, respectively. These prices have been relatively uncompetitive in the market. After some study, Buy Canadian substitutes several cheaper components (which engineering says may slightly reduce the quality of performance) and passes on the savings to consumers in the form of a $100 price reduction on each model. Buy Canadian institutes a price-oriented promotional campaign, which neglects to mention that the second-generation System X sets are different from the first. *Is the company's competitive strategy ethical?*

▷ **Scenario 6**

The Smith & Smith Advertising Agency has been struggling financially. Smith is approached by the representative of a small South American country that is on good terms with the Department of External Affairs. He wants S&S to create a multimillion-dollar advertising and public relations campaign that will bolster the image of the country and increase the likelihood that it will receive foreign aid assistance and attract investment capital. Smith knows the country is controlled by a dictatorship that has been accused of numerous human rights violations. *Is it ethical for the Smith & Smith Agency to undertake the proposed campaign?*[7]

What constitutes ethical marketing behaviour is a matter of social judgment. Even in areas like product safety, it's not always clear. While at first blush it might be argued that all products should be either completely safe or not allowed on the market, deeper inspection reveals questions such as "How safe?" and "For whom?" Bicycles, for example, often head the list of the most hazardous products, yet few consumers or marketers would argue that bicycles should not be sold. Much of the problem in determining product safety concerns whether harm attributable to a product results from an inherent lack of product safety or unsafe use by the consumer.

CONCLUSIONS ABOUT CONSUMER BEHAVIOUR AND MARKETING PRACTICE

This text presents a comprehensive overview of consumer behaviour and demonstrates its importance for marketing and for the success of organisations in general. The first section discussed how successful organisations design and market products and services that consumers want and are willing to purchase. A framework for understanding consumer behaviour, called the Wheel of Consumer Analysis, was introduced. This wheel consists of three major elements: affect and cognition, behaviour, and environment. The next three sections of the book offer detailed discussions of these three elements and illustrate how analysis of each aids in successful marketing. A consistent theme of the book is that carefully researching and understanding all three parts of the wheel enhances the success of marketing strategies.

Another theme of the book is that marketing is a powerful force that has a strong influence on society and consumers' lives. Marketers' ability to research consumers and understand their affect and cognitions, behaviours, and environments could lead to an organisation having too much power in society. For this reason, legal, political, competitive, and ethical influences control the power of marketing organisations. This final chapter of the book discussed these influences in hopes that future marketers will carefully consider their social responsibilities and develop strategies that are good for society and consumers as well as for the organisations for which they work.

▶ **SUMMARY**

Learning objective 1: *Explain why society needs controls for marketers.*

Marketing is a powerful force in society, and power is subject to abuse if marketers misuse it to influence consumer affect, cognitions, and behaviours. Marketers have considerable freedom in designing and executing product strategies, but to keep marketers from becoming unduly influential, society exerts some checks.

Learning objective 2: *Learn the basic rights of Canadian consumers.*

Consumers have eight basic rights: (1) the right to be informed (to have as much information as possible to make informed decisions, and to be protected against fraudulent, deceitful, or misleading advertising; (2) the right to have safe products and services that will not cause harm or be hazardous under normal use; (3) the right to choose freely without undue pressure and to have a broad selection; (4) the right to redress (to have some action in response to a complaint of a violation; (5) the right to be heard (to have a voice, which includes assurance that their interests will be fully and fairly considered in the formulation of government policy; (6) the right to fair value (to have products or services turn out to be what the seller promised); (7) the right to a price that is set fairly in the marketplace; and (8) the right to an improved quality of life.

Learning objective 3: *Explain four constraints society uses for controlling marketing activities.*

First, there are legal constraints or influences. These include federal, state, and local legislation and the agencies that uphold these laws. Second, there are political influences, which include the pressure various consumer groups can exert to control marketing practices. Third, there are competitive influences, which means actions of competing firms intended to affect companies and consumers. Fourth, there are ethical influences, which take the form of various codes and sanctions by which professions regulate their own activities.

---

legal influences	political influences	ethical influences	▶ **KEY TERMS AND CONCEPTS**
corrective advertising	competitive influences		

▶ **REVIEW AND DISCUSSION QUESTIONS**

1. Compare the rights of marketers and the rights of consumers. Which group do you think has more power?

2. Which of the buyer and seller rights become a problem if we assume consumers are not highly involved in most purchases?

3. Define the four major components of consumer protection. In which of them can the consumer participate?

4. Evaluate the actions in each of the six ethical scenarios in the chapter.

5. Which of the ethical standards proposed in the text do you think would be most useful to you as a marketing manager? Why?

6. In a bait-and-switch ad, the retailer advertises a low price on an item but either doesn't stock the item or pressures consumers into buying a more expensive item when they come into the store. Evaluate the ethics of this practice.

7. Select three newspaper ads that you consider misleading. Tell what elements of the communication are deceptive and what groups of consumers might be harmed.

8. Discuss with other members of the class the ethics of tobacco or liquor marketing. Could you develop a code of personal ethics to guide you as a promotion manager in these industries?

9. Prepare lists of obligations to complement the lists of rights for marketers and consumers.

CASES IN CONSUMER BEHAVIOUR

CASES

► 1. Toyota

► 2. Wal-Mart Canada

► 3. Ralph Lauren

► 4. Nike

► 5. Black & Decker

► 6. Coca-Cola

► 7. Buying a Lancer

► 8. A Business Trip

► 9. The Intel Pentium

► 10. Price Costco

► 11. Elegant Traditions

► 12. Bauer In-Line Skates

► 13. The Train Trip

► 14. Movie Theatres

► 15. Selling in Foreign Markets

► 16. Hyatt and Marriott: Building Retirement Housing

► 17. Breastfeeding in Canada in the 1990s

► 18. The Tylenol Crisis

► 19. Advice for a New Friend

► 20. Purchasing a Treadmill

► CASE V.1

Toyota

If any one word describes the Toyota company, it is *kaizen,* which means "continuous improvement." While some companies strive for dramatic breakthrough, Toyota keeps doing lots of little things better and better. Consider the subcompact Tercel, the smallest Toyota sold in Canada. While this model contributes only modestly to its profits, Toyota made the 1991 Tercel faster, roomier, and quieter than its predecessor—with less weight, equally good mileage, and, remarkably, the same price for the basic four-door sedan. It's cheaper than GM's new Saturn and as much as $1,600 less than other competing models.

One consultant calls Toyota's strategy "rapid inch-up": Take enough tiny steps, and pretty soon you outdistance the competition. By introducing six all-new vehicles within 14 months, Toyota grabbed a crushing 43 percent share of car sales in Japan. In the 1990 model year, it sold more than 1 million cars and trucks in North America and was poised to move up from its number 4 position in the Canadian market; Toyota is now the number 3 automaker in the world market. The company, which enjoys the highest operating margins in the world auto industry, is so rich that it makes more money on financial investments than it does on operations. With Toyota's cash reserve it could buy both Ford and Chrysler with nearly $5 billion to spare.

Toyota simply is tops in quality, production, and efficiency. From its factories pour a wide range of cars, built with unequalled precision. Toyota turns out luxury sedans with Mercedes-like quality using *one-sixth* the labour Mercedes does. The company originated just-in-time (JIT) production and remains its leading practitioner. It has close relationships with its suppliers and rigourous engineering specifications for the products it purchases.

Toyota pioneered quality circles, which involve workers discussing ways to improve their tasks and avoid what it calls the three Ds: the dangerous, dirty, and demanding aspects of factory work. The company invested $770 million to improve worker housing, add dining halls, and build new recreational facilities. On the assembly line, quality is defined not as zero defects but, as another Toyota slogan has it, as "building the very best and giving customers what they want." Because workers serve as customers for the process just before theirs, they become quality-control inspectors. If a piece isn't installed properly when it reaches them, they won't accept it.

Toyota's engineering system allows it to take a new car design from concept to showroom in less than four years, compared to more than five years for North American companies and seven years for Mercedes-Benz. This cuts costs, allows quicker correction of mistakes, and keeps Toyota more in tune with market trends. Gains from speed feed on themselves. Toyota accomplishes its advanced engineering and design more quickly because, as one manager puts it, "We are closer to the customer and thus have a shorter concept time." New products are the province of a chief engineer who has complete responsibility and authority for the product from design and manufacturing through marketing and has direct contacts with both dealers and consumers. New-model bosses in North American companies seldom have such control and almost never have direct contact with dealers or consumers.

In Toyota's manufacturing system, parts and cars don't get built until dealers request them. In placing orders, dealers essentially reserve a portion of factory capacity. The system is so effective that rather than wait several months for a new car, the customer can get a built-to-order car in a week to 10 days.

"We have learned that universal mass production is not enough," says the head of the Toyota's Tokyo Design Center. "In the 21st century, you personalise things more to make them more reflective of individual needs." The winners in carmaking will be those who target narrow customer niches most successfully with specific models.

Discussion Questions

1. In what ways is Toyota's new-product development system designed to serve customers?
2. In what ways is Toyota's manufacturing system designed to serve customers?
3. How does Toyota personalise its cars and trucks to meet individual consumer needs?
4. How do you think the Toyota Tercel stacks up against the competition in its price range?

Source: Reprinted with permission from "Why Toyota Keeps Getting Better and Better and Better," by Alex Taylor III, *Fortune,* © 1990 Time Inc. All rights reserved.

▶ **CASE V.2**

Wal-Mart Canada

For many years, North Americans bought more goods from Sears, Roebuck & Co. than from any other retailer. But in 1991, Wal-Mart became the number one retailer and Sears slipped to third behind Kmart. That year, during one of the worst recessions in recent years, Wal-Mart sales rose 26 percent to more than $32 billion. Wal-Mart's phenomenal growth has continued, and by the end of 1994, sales had reached more than $83 billion, with more than $2.8 billion in profits. In 1986 there were 859 Wal-Mart stores worldwide. By 1994, this number had risen to over 2,560 stores, 122 of them in Canada.

Wal-Mart began in Canada in 1994 by acquiring 122 Woolco stores for about $300 million. To spruce up the stores, Wal-Mart invested over $275 million, adding conveyor-belt checkouts, new lighting and bright new floors and walls.

Wal-Mart's arrival in Canada was greeted with a blizzard of warnings that this giant would ruin the Canadian domestic retail market and turn the main streets of rural towns into commercial graveyards. Wal-Mart responded by plastering its stores with "Buy Canadian" signs and by trumpeting its contracts and supply agreements with Canadian businesses.

Wal-Mart sells a variety of standard consumer goods ranging from laundry detergent to sporting goods. One factor contributing to the company's success is consumer willingness to travel past nearby stores to a Wal-Mart. Rhona Lynn, for instance, drove 25 minutes from her Mount Royal home to shop at a Wal-Mart for a portable radio for her son. "I thought I could get the best price," she said, remembering a previous purchase she had made at Wal-Mart.

A trip down the aisles of any Wal-Mart offers some clues to its marketing strategy. Other than a monthly full-colour advertising circular distributed in local newspapers, in-store signs are virtually all the advertising Wal-Mart does. Brightly coloured signs hang from the ceiling and steer shoppers toward tables offering tantalizing bargains on shoes, garden supplies, diapers, and toothpaste. Signs under a hair-care display boast everyday low prices of $1.19 for a 16-ounce bottle of shampoo. A nearby discount health and beauty aids store will sell the same bottle for $1.79. A popular outdoor barbecue grill sells for $149.99; a leading competitor in a nearby mall sells it for $179.99. If consumers bring in an ad for a product sold by a competitor at a lower price, Wal-Mart lowers its price to match. Department managers and other price-checkers routinely shop other stores to compare price and log the prices that beat theirs into their store computer.

Wal-Mart's expansion strategy has always been to build stores in trading areas that could support only one large discount store. In this way it avoided competition with other discounters such as Kmart and Zellers. As Wal-Mart has grown and become more profitable, it has expanded into larger trading areas. However, Wal-Mart still avoids shopping malls, preferring to locate on the edges of cities where property is less expensive.

Wal-Mart is an expert at holding down overhead costs. Sophisticated warehouse and information systems enable it to keep operating costs down to an enviable 16 percent, the lowest in the industry. Wal-Mart sends checkout-line information on sales of some Procter & Gamble products, such as diapers, directly to P&G at the same time it records the sales in its own computer records. This electronic data interface (EDI) technology provides P&G with immediate information on sales so it can adjust production and delivery schedules to allow efficient replenishment of Wal-Mart's stock. Wal-Mart sells such huge volumes of merchandise that it can demand the best prices and service from manufacturers such as P&G. The efficiencies that a Wal-Mart can generate often get paid back to consumers. One year after the introduction of Wal-Mart to Canada, the average cost of a consumer basket of goods in Canada had fallen roughly 8 percent.

The company has numerous employee programs to promote sales and friendly service. For example, each in-store sales associate selects one piece of merchandise to sponsor for a year. The sales associate builds a display for it and keeps it clean and stocked. In a store with more than 200 employees, this means someone is watching 200 of the store's products extra carefully. Individual rewards for sponsoring a product are not monetary; workers simply seek recognition for their efforts from fellow employees and bosses (all of whom are on a first-name basis). The best of the merchandising ideas make their way to headquarters, allowing small but good concepts to be adopted nationwide.

Wal-Mart stores in Canada move an average of $297 worth of merchandise per square foot, more than twice as much as its average Canadian competitor. Here's how Wal-Mart Canada explains its success:

▷ **Give them what they want.** The average Wal-Mart carries about 75,000 items, compared with 56,000 items at Zellers. Daily inventory replenishment ensures that Wal-Mart shoppers can always find the newest hot items.

▷ **Excellent Pricing—low mark-ups.** Wal-Mart has the best prices anywhere for light bulbs, paper towels, motor oil, and other widely purchased items, thereby leading people to assume that all Wal-Mart merchandise is a bargain.

▷ **The irresistible impulse.** Sam Walton pioneered the "action alley," a row of bins and racks packed with peanuts, batteries, razors, and other impulse items. It is the home stretch on the way to the checkout counter.

▷ **Many happy returns.** Wal-Mart takes back almost any item with no questions asked. If the price of the returned item is not indicated, it will refund the full purchase retail price.

▷ **Cart tricks.** Wal-mart's greeters don't just say hello, they offer every shopper a cart. Smart move. Retail surveys show that people buy more when they have shopping carts to fill.

▷ **Keep them moving.** If more than three people are lined up at a checkout counter, Wal-Mart promises to open another one. Clerks verify credit cards via Wal-Mart's own satellite in 3 to 5 seconds.

Canadian retailers have responded to the Wal-Mart challenge. Zellers spent more than $150 million improving their 290 outlets, Canadian Tire spent over $100 million on expansion and renovations, and retailers such as Eaton's and The Bay promote equal quality and service offered by uniquely Canadian companies.

The introduction of Wal-Mart to Canada shook up the retail scene. As a result, Canadian consumers will likely be provided with an increased number of product offerings at even lower prices.

Discussion Questions

1. Based on the case information and your personal experiences, list at least five things you know about Wal-Mart. The list gives some idea of your cognitions about this retail chain

2. Based on the case information and your personal experiences, list at least five things you like or dislike about Wal-Mart. This list gives some of your affect for this retail chain.

3. Based on your personal shopping experiences at Wal-Mart (or another discount store if you haven't shopped there), list at least five behaviours you have performed in a shopping trip. This list gives you some idea of the behaviours involved in shopping at a discount store.

4. Based on the case information and your personal experiences, list at least five things Wal-Mart has done in the environment to influence consumers to shop there. This list gives you some idea of how the environment influences cognition, affect, and behaviour.

5. Write a brief description of a purchase you made at a Wal-Mart. Did the purchase involve cognition, affect, behaviour and environmental components?

Source: Kevin Kelly and Amy Dunkin, "Wal-Mart Gets Lost in the Vegetable Aisle," *Business Week,* May 28, 1990, p. 48; Marianne Taylor, "Wal-Mart Prices Its Way to Top of Retail Mountain," *Wisconsin State Journal,* May 5, 1991, pp. 1c, 2c; Canadian data provided by Wal-Mart Canada, 1995.

▶ **CASE V.3**

Ralph Lauren

Ralph Lauren is one of the most successful designers in the world. He has a unique approach. While other designers create product lines, he first designs lifestyles and then develops a wide range of products to reflect those themes. Lauren creates romantic worlds where handsome families ride to hounds, play lawn tennis with wooden racquets, or dress for dinner on safari. They wear crested blazers and trousers of crisp linen while watching polo matches in Palm Beach. They sip cognac by the fireplace of a chalet, nestled in a Navajo blanket. Phyllis Posnick, executive fashion editor of *Vogue,* says, "He takes an American fantasy of a lifestyle and he creates a Ralph Lauren world—and he does it better than anyone else."

The world where Ralph Lauren grew up was quite different. Born Ralph Lifshitz in a Bronx neighborhood, he was clothes conscious at an early age. He wore canvas jackets and button-down shirts to school (in contrast to the typical student, who looked like Fonzie in jeans and black leather jackets). At 22, Lauren went to work for a Boston necktie manufacturer, travelling to meet his customers dressed in tweeds and driving a Morgan sports car. His first designs were 4-inch-wide ties to replace the narrow 2½-inch ties then in fashion. Lauren selected the name Polo for his line of ties, because the word connoted to him a lifestyle mood of athletic grace and discreet elegance and an image of men who wore well-tailored, classic clothes with style. Printed on vibrant Italian silk, his creations were priced at $15 (double the typical price). He sold $500,000 worth in 1967, his first year.

The next year, Lauren began producing an entire menswear line, including wide-collar shirts and wide-lapel suits. He used only the finest fabrics to create the Lauren "look"—distinctive and innovative, but classic and refined at the same time. His suits combined the Ivy League natural-shoulder look with the fitted shape and expensive fabrics of the best European custom-tailored clothing. His shirts were all-cotton and richly patterned.

Over the years, Ralph Lauren created several product lines targeted at new consumer segments. In 1971, he introduced a line of women's clothing with the image of understated elegance and femininity. Later, he created the Chaps line of men's clothing for executives who wanted a traditional American look at a less expensive price. He introduced the Polo University Club line of sportswear for college students and young businessmen who were beginning to form their professional wardrobe. In 1983, he created a collection of home furnishings, including bedding, towels, rugs, and wall coverings. The collection expanded in 1986 to include furniture. All the Lauren furnishings were designed to reflect a lifestyle look and were marketed using ads showing entire coordinated rooms. For instance, the "Bride" was a romantic collection in rich cream fabrics, while "Estate" combined the elegance and beauty of white linen with mahogany carved furniture, woven wicker, and bent rattan. In addition, Lauren produces two fragrances—Polo for men and Lauren for women—and he markets a collection of handmade shoes, boots, and moccasins.

By the late 1980s, Ralph Lauren was an international presence in the fashion world. His Polo clothing is distributed in Italy, Japan, Canada, Hong Kong, Singapore, Taiwan, Malaysia, Korea, Panama, Mexico, Germany, Austria, Belgium, Brazil, Uruguay, the Netherlands, Luxembourg, Scandinavia, Switzerland, Spain, England, and France. He has free-standing stores and boutiques in department stores all over the world, but his showcase store is in New York City. In 1987, Lauren converted the Rhinelander mansion on Madison Avenue into the ultimate showcase for the Lauren lifestyle image. He remodelled the five-story limestone structure at a cost of $14 million and fitted it with hand-carved mahogany woodwork, oriental rugs, and fine antique furniture. The clothing displays share spaces with saddles, trophies, top hats, and billiard cues, making the place feel more like a London club than a retail store. (Ralph Lauren was not the first to use such a retailing strategy. In 1863, department store magnate A. T. Stewart chose an oriental motif for the interior of a store he built at Broadway and 10th Street in New York City. The store had "luxurious hassocks . . . soft Persian rugs . . . and fairy-like frostings of lace draperies.")

Lauren begins the design process by imagining a lifestyle that he develops like a play, including describing the characters/actors, how and where they live, and the types of clothing they wear. Based on these rich images, his designers create the costumes (clothing products) and the stage sets (retail displays) for the latest dream world. "I want only to make the things I love," Lauren has said repeatedly. "A lot of people have good taste. I have dreams." To make his dreams a reality, he puts great effort into the ads and retail displays. Nothing is left to chance. From the furniture to the props to the models who portray the characters, everything is carefully chosen to create a very specific look. Each ad and retail display creates a mood and evokes a lifestyle. Every ad invites the reader to share the fantasy and enter the dream world of Ralph Lauren.

Ralph Lauren is a master of mood. His home-furnishing arrangements are opulent and luxurious. A bed might have eight pillows, all with ruffles and contrasting fabrics. The idea is that a customer will want to buy the entire package to acquire the Ralph Lauren look. In the stores, he surrounds his products with loads of charming and inventive "treasures," many of them for sale. Rather than displaying only a blazer or a skirt, he also presents a whole pile of goodies, such as antique tobacco horns and framed pictures of families, that complete the picture and establish the lifestyle mood.

Ralph Lauren creates moods, dreams, and fantasies, and he offers consumers the opportunity to share his dreams and perhaps acquire new identities by purchasing his carefully orchestrated products. No other designer has created a product range so wide, a retailing network so extensive, and a marketing image so well defined.

By the early 1990s, the Ralph Lauren fashion empire had retail sales approaching $1.5 billion, up over 400 percent since 1981.

Source: Adapted from "A Dream World Labeled Lauren," *Marketing Insights,* June 1989, pp. 91–95; and Valerie Free, "100 Years Ago: Through a Distant Mirror," *Marketing Insights,* Spring 1990, pp. 20–21.

Discussion Questions

1. What types of affective responses to the Ralph Lauren ads and retail displays might be created by consumers' affective systems? How might the cognitive system interpret these responses?

2. What types of cognitions (knowledge) do Ralph Lauren customers have about Ralph Lauren and Lauren products? What types of schemas might consumers have for the Polo brand?

3. How could consumers' knowledge about Lauren and Polo be activated? How might the affective system react to these cognitive responses? How might this knowledge influence consumers' decision making and contribute to Ralph Lauren's success?

4. How might consumers' affective and cognitive responses influence their decision making and contribute to Ralph Lauren's success?

5. How are consumers' scripts relevant for the marketing of Ralph Lauren products?

▶ **CASE V.4**

Nike

By mid-1985 the signs were becoming clear: after years of mystique and spectacular growth, jogging was puffing into middle age. In 1984, for instance, unit sales of running shoes decreased 17 percent, and dollar sales were off by 15 percent. Nike, the market leader in 1983 with a 31 percent market share, sold about $270 million worth of running shoes. By 1984, Nike's share of the running shoe market was down 26 percent. The decline continued so that by 1987 Nike had only an 18.6 percent share of the market for athletic shoes, a market it had dominated just a few years earlier. What happened?

Nike had become successful as a manufacturer of technically sophisticated shoes for the serious runner, but the market for running shoes had peaked. According to the director of the National Sporting Goods Association, "We've probably reached pretty close to the maximum participation in running." The running shoe market was saturated, as nearly everyone who wanted to run had tried it.

Part of the reason is demographic. During the late 1970s and early 1980s, the large baby-boomer group represented the primary market for running gear, ages 25 to 40. But in the mid- to late-1980s, fewer people were entering this age group, thus decreasing overall demand. As the leading age of this group pushed toward 40, lacing up the old shoes for another 5-mile run began to seem less fun than it had at age 24.

The running shoe market had also become highly segmented by the mid-1980s—a sure sign of a mature market. Marketers had to pay even closer attention to consumers' needs, goals, and values and produce product variations for smaller groups of consumers. And, finally, the industry had begun to engage in sporadic price cutting as companies fought to maintain their market share.

Another reason for the drop-off in running concerns consumers' ideas about health. Running develops the legs and cardiovascular system but little else. Many runners had begun to notice that the rest of their bodies needed conditioning too. Athletically oriented people became increasingly interested in total fitness.

All these changes meant that fewer people were taking up running and that the millions of joggers who were still on the run were doing fewer laps. This translated into fewer replacement shoes sold by Nike, Converse, New Balance, Brooks, and all the others. As the biggest manufacturer in the business, Nike had the most to lose.

From one perspective, makers of running shoes had enjoyed a long run, especially in the sports equipment market, which is often dominated by short-lived fads. Consider tennis, for example. Sales of tennis racquets peaked in 1976 when an estimated 8.6 million racquets were sold. Despite technological innovations and space-age materials such as Kevlar, boron, and graphite, the industry sold only 3.2 million racquets in 1984. Instead, the big boom in 1984 and 1985 was in aerobics gear and home gym equipment.

Some commentators believe Nike didn't react quickly enough to these fundamental changes in the consumer markets. One company that did capitalise on these changes was Reebok International. Its sales shot up from $84 million in 1984 to $307 million the next year, with profits increasing sixfold to $39 million. According to Reebok president Paul Fireman, "We go out to consumers and find out what they want. Other companies don't seem to do that."

It seems that what many consumers wanted in the mid-1980s was fashion. Perhaps this would have been evident by simple observation of consumers' product use behaviours. It is estimated that between 70 and 80 percent of the shoes designed for basketball and aerobic exercise are actually used for street wear. These products must have been satisfying some fashion needs or ends.

So when Reebok introduced its first soft-leather Freestyle aerobic shoes in 1983, the brilliant colours and soft leather made them an overnight sensation. Reebok actually expanded the overall market for athletic shoes by attracting women customers from more traditional shoe manufacturers such as Bass. People began to think of this product class as something more than "just sneakers." Reebok's spectacular popularity continued, and by 1986 it eclipsed Nike as number one.

During 1987 and 1988, Nike worked feverishly (and with some success) to recapture the lead in this expanding and profitable market. In 1987, Nike introduced its Air shoes, headed by the successful basketball shoe Air Jordan, named after Chicago Bulls basketball star Michael Jordan, who wore and promoted the product. Nike spent heavily on TV and print advertising to introduce this innovative product. But perhaps the best strategy was to produce its top-of-the-line models with a transparent "cut-out" in the sole so the consumer could actually see how the air cushioned the impact. In 1988, Nike spent some $34 million on advertising, the highest level yet for the company that once eschewed mass advertising as unnecessary and somewhat demeaning. Of course Reebok, the once-small competitor, wasn't sitting still; it increased its own advertising spending, with a substantial amount channelled to TV.

In response to these changes in consumers, Nike expanded its product line beyond running shoes in the mid-1980s. The company began to produce shoes for the aerobic market and other specialty sports activities, including a line of walking shoes to appeal to a submarket that had emerged rapidly in the mid-1980s (perhaps as aging baby boomers found running too stressful on their joints).

Finally, in 1988 and throughout the 1990's, Nike continues to introduce fashion-oriented shoes to compete head-on with archrival Reebok. The new shoes are targeted at women, the primary buyers of such shoes, and was called IE. They do not carry the Nike name. Prices are between $65 and $100, somewhat below the price for the average

Nike shoe. "With the IE, Nike is attempting to penetrate the very market (the fashion market) where it has been weakest historically," said one industry analyst. The independent brand name seemed a good strategy, as it would not give its core customers (serious and would-be athletes) mixed signals about the meaning of the Nike brand.

Discussion questions

1. Apparently there are two market segments of consumers for many product forms of athletic shoes: those who use them for the designated athletic activity and those who use them primarily for casual wear and seldom engage in the athletic activity.

   a. Discuss the differences between these two segments in means-end chains and especially end goals, needs, and values for running, basketball, aerobics, or tennis shoes.

   b. Draw means-end chains to illustrate your ideas about how these two segments differ.

   c. What types of special difficulties does a marketer face in promoting its product to two segments of consumers who use the product in very different ways?

2. Many manufacturers of athletic shoes promote so-called technological advances such as the "air sole" or the "energy wave." How do consumers make sense of such attributes? Which types of attributes are likely to have a major impact on their purchasing behaviour?

3. As the market for athletic shoes has become more segmented, marketers have produced shoes for very specialised purposes. Why? Discuss the special types of means-end chains held by people who buy athletic shoes for particular purposes (walking, tennis, aerobics). Analyse the source of consumers' involvement in these products—personal or situational. How can these analyses help marketers understand the consumer/product relationship and develop more effective marketing strategies?

4. Analyse the changes that have occurred over time in consumers' product/self relationships for running shoes (or some other type of athletic shoe). Consider changes in consumers' affective responses and their product knowledge, as well as their overt behaviours and general environmental factors. How could Nike have kept better track of these changes so that its marketing strategies would have been more effective in the mid-1980s?

Sources: Adapted from Marcy Magiera, "Nike Plans Rebound with Fashion Shoe," *Advertising Age,* Jan. 25, 1988, p. 1; Patrick McGeehan, "Wave Action: Converse Goes Toe-to-Toe with Nike High-Performance," *Advertising Age,* Feb. 22, 1988, p. 76; Richard Phalon, "Out of Breath," *Forbes,* Oct. 22, 1984, pp. 38–40; and Lois Therrien and Amy Borrus, "Reeboks: How Far Can a Fad Run?" *Business Week,* Feb. 24, 1986, pp. 89–90.

▶ **CASE V.5**

Black & Decker

At the end of 1985, Black & Decker was about halfway through the biggest brand-name swap in marketing history. The company, once best known for its power tools, bought General Electric's small-appliance business in 1984 for $300 million. Black & Decker had until mid-1987 to bring all of GE's 150 or so appliance products under its own logo.

By renaming the GE appliances, B&D did for its competitors something they could not possibly have accomplished by themselves; it eliminated the best-known brand name in the small-appliance business. But these other companies—including Sunbeam, Rival, Hamilton Beach, and Norelco—did not show much gratitude. Sensing confusion in the market and weakness in their competitor, they increased their advertising budgets and introduced new products in an attempt to intercept GE customers before they got to Black & Decker. In return, Black & Decker unleashed a new product blitz of its own and began a $100 million advertising and promotion campaign, the largest ever in the small-appliance industry.

For years, GE had been the best-loved name in the appliance game. It still was in 1985. In one survey, consumers were asked to name small-appliance makers: GE came up a remarkable 92 percent of the time. Sunbeam was a distant second at 41 percent, and Black & Decker was mentioned only 12 percent of the time. In fact, another 1985 survey showed that most consumers didn't know GE had left the game.

Kenneth Homa, vice president for marketing, directed the complex Black & Decker strategy to make GE's name its own. The company broke the changeover process for each product into about 140 steps to be completed over 14 months. According to Black & Decker, the process went so smoothly that the timetable was completed by the end of 1986.

Black & Decker decided to launch each product as if it were new. For some products, it made alterations ranging from simple changes in colour to major redesigns. For instance, GE's under-the-cabinet Spacemaker products—including a coffee maker, a toaster oven, and a can opener—were remodelled into sleeker units. Black & Decker also doubled the warranty period for every GE product to two years.

One big question for Black & Decker was whether to use its own brand name alongside GE's in the initial promotion and advertising. When research revealed that consumers associate similar reliability and durability qualities with Black & Decker as with GE, Black & Decker tried to keep consumer confusion to a minimum by making a clean switch—the Black & Decker name for GE. For instance, the popular Spacemaker line was remarketed without a reference to GE. TV commercials emphasised the Spacemaker brand name and ended with the tag line "Now by Black & Decker."

Competitors, of course, did not stand still while the brand-name switch occurred. In particular, Sunbeam wanted consumers to forget both GE and Black & Decker. It increased its 1985 advertising budget to $42 million, four times what had been planned, to take advantage of the potential for confusion.

Irons are an important part (about 25 percent) of Black & Decker's small-appliance business. Thus, the company delayed conversion until it had experience with other lines. Research showed that 40 percent of customers go into a store intending to buy a particular brand of iron (usually GE). Therefore, Black & Decker modified its "clean switch" strategy and included GE's name next to its own in print ads for irons and in promotional materials in the stores. On TV, however, it was more difficult to explain the switch, so Black & Decker promoted the irons under its own name in television commercials.

The short-run concerns with the name change were not the only problems Black & Decker faced. Most appliance sales are to people replacing worn-out items, rather than to first-time buyers. Therefore, in any given year, only about 10 percent of the small-appliance market turns over. This means most consumers who now own GE products won't buy new ones until after the GE name is long gone from the small-appliance scene. What will they think when they go into the store and find no GE products?

Discussion questions

1. Describe some typical situations where consumers would be (a) accidentally and (b) intentionally exposed to information about Black & Decker's new line of appliances. What implications would the type of exposure have for Black & Decker's approach to making the name switch from GE?

2. Discuss how consumers' prior knowledge about Black & Decker and GE corporate images could have affected their comprehension of the small appliances now marketed by Black & Decker.

   a. What types of inferences might consumers have drawn when they first became aware that Black & Decker was now selling small appliances?

   b. How would these inferences change over time as consumers became familiar with Black & Decker's appliances?

3. In what ways might consumers become confused by marketing information from Black & Decker? What could Black & Decker do about this?

4. Analyse the pros and cons of Black & Decker's decision not to mention the GE name in its brand changeover. How do you feel about the decision to feature the GE name only on electric irons?

5. What types of strategies could Sunbeam (or some other competitor) have used to try to derail Black & Decker's strategy? How could Black & Decker have countered each of these attacks?

Source: Excerpted from Bill Saporito, "Ganging Up on Black & Decker," *Fortune,* Dec. 23, 1985, pp. 63–72.

The past 15 years or so have seen tumultuous changes in the soft-drink industry. After years of slow growth and little product innovation in the 1970s, the 1980s were full of activity. No company exemplifies these changes more than the Coca-Cola Company.

> ▶ **CASE V.6**
>
> **Coca-Cola**

For most of its 100-year history, Coca-Cola has dominated the soft-drink business, largely through sheer size rather than savvy marketing. But Coke's complacency vanished in 1977 when PepsiCo's brand, Pepsi, threatened to become the market leader and take over Coke's role as the top brand in food-store sales. Coke responded with a number of marketing strategies, including some that would have been unthinkable a few years earlier. In the process, the company learned something about North American consumers' brand attitudes toward Coke.

In July 1982, Coca-Cola management did the unthinkable: It introduced a diet cola and called it Diet Coke. This was the first time in history that the company had allowed the world's best-known trademark to be put on a product other than the flagship Coca-Cola brand. Despite the perceived risks, Diet Coke was extremely successful. By 1984, it had become the third best-selling soft drink in North America, displacing 7UP. Then, in quick succession, Coca-Cola introduced decaffeinated versions of Coke, Diet Coke, and Tab.

But these decisions were soon overshadowed by another controversial marketing strategy. In the spring of 1985, chair Robert Goizueta announced the introduction of a new Coca-Cola with an improved taste. The 99-year-old secret formula for the original Coke with a secret ingredient (called Merchandise 7X, it was developed by John Styth Pemberton, an Atlanta pharmacist, in a 30-gallon brass kettle in his backyard) was to be locked in a bank vault in Atlanta, never to be used again. The new formula, with ingredient 7X-100, was to replace the old Coca-Cola. Goizueta called the new product "the most significant soft-drink development in the company's history."

Consumers got their first taste of the new Coke in late April 1985. In July, less than three months later, the company reversed its decision. A rather chagrined management announced that the old Coke was coming back under the brand name label

Coca-Cola Classic. What happened to Coca-Cola was a classic lesson in consumers' brand attitudes. Some critics thought Coca-Cola had made a giant marketing mistake, and some cynics thought the company had planned the whole thing for publicity value. According to Donald Keough, the president of Coca-Cola, "The truth is that we are not that dumb and we are not that smart."

The positive attitudes and beliefs that keep customers buying the same brand over and over again are called *brand loyalty.* Brand loyalty is an elusive concept. It begins with customers' positive attitudes and preferences for a brand based on "objective" beliefs about product attributes—the drink is sweeter or more carbonated. The brand name guarantees the customer will receive the same expected attributes and benefits from each product use. But once a product has been around for a while, it can accumulate a variety of emotionally laden meanings and beliefs. Some brands may become linked to consumers' lifestyles and self-images. For example, many consumers associated Coke with fond memories of days gone by.

Apparently these strong affective beliefs about Coke were activated when Coca-Cola announced the old "friend" was gone forever. Consumers inundated Coca-Cola's head office with protests. A group of brand loyalists threatened to sue the company. And when June sales didn't pick up as expected, the independent bottlers demanded to have the old Coca-Cola back.

Interestingly, the decision to retire the old Coke formula was not a casual one. It had been very carefully researched, and managers thought they had covered every angle. For instance, Coca-Cola spent over $4 million on many different taste tests of the new flavor, involving over 200,000 consumers in some 25 cities. These tests revealed more people liked the new, sweeter flavor than the old (about 55 percent to 45 percent). But apparently this research didn't measure everything. "All the time and money and skill poured into consumer research on the new Coca-Cola could not measure or reveal the deep and abiding emotional attachment to original Coca-Cola," Keough said later.

It is true that understanding consumers' brand loyalties and product attitudes can be difficult. According to John O'Toole, chair of the advertising agency Foote, Cone & Belding, "You can't get at people's private motivations. In any kind of interview or questionnaire, they want to seem sensible and prudent. They aren't going to tell you how they feel."

A variety of different types of beliefs, not all of them about product attributes, may be salient influences on attitudes. Consumers' attitudes toward the new and old Cokes included more than just their taste and mouth feel—the factors that were measured in the extensive taste tests. As a company spokesperson said, "We had taken away more than the product Coca-Cola. We had taken away a little part of them and their past. They said, 'You have no right to do that. Bring it back.' " So Coca-Cola did.

Then what happened? When the old Coke returned in the summer of 1985, consumers found six models of Coke on the supermarket shelf: (new) Coke, Coca-Cola Classic, caffeine-free Coke, Diet Coke, caffeine-free Diet Coke, and Cherry Coke. In 1980, there had been only one brand, Coca-Cola. Some marketing experts thought the company would have a tough time keeping a clear identity for the different brands in consumers' minds. But Robert Goizueta considered the lineup to be a "megabrand" and a marketing plus.

One advantage of the brand-name proliferation involves the environment of the supermarket shelf. Having six brands gives a company a lot more shelf facings, a great advantage in this market. In addition, it may be possible for consumers to have positive attitudes and be loyal to more than one brand in a product class. The phenomenon, known as *brand-cluster loyalty* or *multibrand loyalty,* may be more common than we realise.

Discussion questions

1. Discuss the concept of brand loyalty in terms of consumers' attitudes (both A_o and A_{act}) and purchase intentions. Do you think it is possible for consumers to be loyal to more than one brand of soft drink?

2. How do you think attitudes (and underlying belief structures) differ between the intensely loyal and the less-involved consumers?

3. Is it possible for positive attitudes from one brand to be transferred to a different but related brand, perhaps with the same name? What aspects of attitude theory would help marketers develop strategies to do this?

4. According to Morgan Hunter of Marketing Corp. of America, a Connecticut marketing firm, "It is important not to confuse a stated preference with what consumers actually do when they're in the store. They may not actually buy the brand they say they prefer." Do you agree? Justify your position in terms of the theoretical relationships among consumers' attitudes, purchase intentions, and actual behaviours.

Sources: Anne B. Fisher, "Coke's Brand-Loyalty Lesson," *Fortune,* Aug. 5, 1985, pp. 44–46; Carrie Gottlieb, "Products of the Year," *Fortune,* Dec. 9, 1985, pp. 106–12; and Thomas Moore, "He Put the Kick Back into Coke," *Fortune,* Oct. 26, 1987, pp. 46–56.

▶ **CASE V.7**

Buying a Lancer

Shortly after Doug Hanson started his new job at The Family Health Club in the spring of 1990, he realized that his 1980 Toyota Celica, which he bought from the original owner in 1982, was no longer a sporty new car. Each day when Doug drove to work, his need for a new car became more and more apparent. Every morning he said a quick prayer before turning the key in the ignition. When he actually made it into the parking lot at work, he let out a sigh of relief. He was thankful that his Celica, which had almost 330,000 kilometers on it, had survived another 20-kilometer journey.

Doug, who was born and raised in Pembroke, Ontario, had recently obtained his BA degree from the University of Ottawa. He selected this college because it offered good academics and was close to home. Upon graduation, Doug decided to move to Vancouver, which offered milder weather and an affordable graduate education. Doug planned to go to Simon Fraser University for his MBA.

Doug's trek to the West Coast was an adventure. The Celica broke down once while passing through Saskatchewan and had a tough time making it through the Rockies. When Doug finally arrived in Vancouver, he knew he had pushed the Celica to its limit. He realised that before long he would have to retire the 10-year-old car. In the spring of 1991, Doug began to work part-time on his MBA. This meant driving more miles each week to the SFU campus.

In fall 1992, Doug was promoted to manager of his department, and his salary increased significantly. He was now in a position to seriously consider replacing his car. Coincidentally, his landlady, Edna Johnson, was getting ready to trade in her 1986 Buick LeSabre. A friend at her bridge club had just purchased a 1993 Toyota Camry. Mrs. Johnson was so impressed with the maneuverability and handling of the Camry that she decided to buy one of her own.

Mrs. Johnson's Buick was in mint condition. She always kept the car in the garage, so it never saw dust, let alone a scratch. The Buick had been driven only 48,000 kilometers, and all parts appeared to be in perfect shape. The Toyota dealership offered her $3,000 for the Buick as a trade-in. Her car was in such good condition that she felt she would be giving it away at this price. However, she did not want the hassle of trying to sell it on the open market. As she saw Doug tinkering with his car once again, the thought crossed her mind to offer it to him. She told Doug that he could have the car for the same price the dealer had offered her. In addition, because Doug was such a reliable tenant, she would allow him to pay it off over six months.

Clearly this was a golden opportunity for Doug to solve his transportation problems. He knew the Buick was in excellent shape, and he could get at least $500 for his car. On top of that, she was willing to take payments! Doug told her that he would think it over. He had two days to make his decision before Mrs. Johnson picked up her new Toyota. Doug knew it was a great deal, yet he felt he would not be entirely happy with the Buick. Every day when he pulled into the parking lot at work, he admired the sports cars driven by his co-workers and clientele. Also, his girlfriend had recently bought a 1992 Acura Integra. Doug had hoped to purchase a car similar to hers.

The next morning while paging through the Vancouver *Sun,* Doug noticed an ad offering a "lease special" for 1993 Acura Integras. The lease price was only $250 a month. Doug's first impression was how affordable driving a brand-new Acura could be. He called the number in the ad. He knew that his girlfriend had put down $7,000 and was paying $200 a month on a $10,000 loan. Doug could not afford a $7,000 down payment, but $250 a month was no problem.

Leasing a car is certainly different from owning one. After the lease term, you have to give the car back. In addition, the dealership usually limits the mileage that can be driven each year. Doug considered these factors but felt that if he could drive an Acura for $250 a month without having to come up with a down payment, he would be satisfied. He planned to visit the dealership the following weekend.

When he arrived home from work one day, he saw his neighbour Jay Smith polishing his 1969 Corvette. The Corvette was one of three high-performance vehicles that Jay, a race enthusiast, owned. Jay would often help Doug when he was having trouble with the Celica. Doug asked Jay's opinion about purchasing Mrs. Johnson's car.

"Buick does make a decent car, but I've never been too impressed by their styling or performance," Jay responded. "I classify them as family cars. What you need is a sports car. There are a lot of new models out this year. For someone your age, shopping for a sports car should be like taking a kid to a candy store!"

"I only wish I could afford something sporty," returned Doug.

"What do you mean? in my latest issue of *Car and Driver,* I saw a handful of new sporty models for under $18,000. You just got a nice raise, and I'm sure you could afford the payments! Why don't you wait here and I'll go get the magazine for you."

"Maybe Jay is right," Doug thought as Jay ran inside. "Perhaps I need something sporty . . . ."

With all the ideas about cars floating around in his head, Doug decided to get more information. He called his uncle Barry, who lived back in Ontario. Barry was a mechanic. He had helped Doug fix his car a few times and even helped him put in a new clutch before he left for B.C. Doug respected his opinion.

Barry suggested that he look into the Chevy Cavalier. "Yeah, if I were in your shoes, I might consider the Cavalier. It has a good four cylinders and antilock brakes all around. It even has a decent stereo."

"Sounds interesting. Do you know what they're going for?" asked Doug.

"I think they're somewhere in the $12,000 range. And I read that they come standard with a four-year/80,000-kilometer warranty."

Doug's uncle also reminded him that he should buy Canadian. "Speaking of Canadian cars," said Doug, "Let me tell you about the deal my landlady offered me on her 1986 Buick . . . ."

"Gee, that sounds like a great deal," said Barry. "I wish I lived in Vancouver. I'd snap that one up in a second."

Doug woke up early Saturday morning, excited to begin his search for a car. He planned to spend the entire day test driving new cars. His first stop was the Acura dealership. He soon learned that since he had never had a previous car loan, he was not qualified for the lease program. This was not mentioned in the newspaper ad or during his telephone conversation with the dealer. The salesman tried to encourage Doug to buy an Acura, but they started at the high end of his price range. It became apparent to Doug that the ad was just a come-on. Annoyed with the misleading sales tactics, he decided to look elsewhere.

His next stop was the Toyota dealership where he had always taken his Celica for servicing. Doug had a great deal of confidence in Toyota; after all, his Celica had served him well for 10 years.

As he was browsing through the lot, he was approached by a salesman. He soon discovered the only Toyota besides the Celica that suited him, was the MR2. Doug did not want to buy another Celica because he was not impressed with the new body design. The MR2 was Toyota's four-cylinder sports model. He had seen one on the freeway and admired its sleek design. A major drawback was the fact that the MR2 was a small two-seater. Furthermore, it started at over $20,000.

His next stop was the Dodge dealer. He had seen the new Lancer model pictured in *Car and Driver* and was impressed with its looks. It came in three versions. The base model had a four-cylinder engine with very little horsepower. The mid-range version also had four cylinders, but its multivalve engine design gave it 50 percent more horsepower. The top-of-the-line car had the most powerful engine due to its turbo design. The base model started at around $14,000, the mid-range $17,000, and the highest-priced Lancer close to $20,000. Despite the different engines, all three models had the same body design.

Doug test drove the base model first. It drove smoothly, but it had very little pickup. The middle version was priced at the upper limits of his range, but he decided to test drive it anyway. He was extremely pleased with the overall performance of this car. The turbo model was priced beyond his range—not to mention the fact that the insurance would be almost double that of the other two models.

Doug really liked the mid-range Lancer and decided to negotiate a deal. The asking price for the car he was interested in was $18,300. It had all of the extras Doug wanted, and it was the only one on the lot that came in the color he wanted. He haggled the sales manager down to $17,300. The dealership gave Doug $1,000 for his Celica. He even qualified for the special first-time buyer interest rate for his car loan. Doug went with his gut feeling and decided to buy the car.

After signing the papers, a nearly numb Doug was given the keys to his first brand-new car. He was about to drive his car off the lot when the salesman ran after him. "What's the matter?!" asked Doug. The salesman replied, "Just give me a minute. You look so good next to that car, I want to take a picture." The salesman pulled out his camera and snapped the picture. Doug was flabbergasted, but managed to crack a big smile anyway.

As he pulled his new car into the driveway, Doug was greeted by Mrs. Johnson and Jay. They both admired his Lancer. Doug proudly took them for a spin and told them all about the great deal he got.

In the following weeks, Doug continued to enjoy his new car. He especially liked knowing that it would get him to work on time without fail. One day his mail contained a large envelope from the dealership. He opened it and found a calendar with a picture of him standing beside his new car. There were also coupons inside for discounts on an oil change, a tune-up, and other services. Doug reminisced about the day he had purchased his car and congratulated himself on making the right choice.

Discussion Questions

1. List the stages of the decision process Doug Hanson went through.
2. Describe Doug's search for relevant information.
3. What were Doug's main choice criteria and purchase end goals?
4. What type of problem solving was Doug's decision?

© 1993. Faculty of Administration, University of Ottawa. This case was written by Barbara Schneider and Doug Henkel under the supervision of David S. Litvack.

▶ **CASE V.8**

A business trip

The 7:30 A.M. Air Canada Rapid Air flight from Toronto to Montreal was delayed 45 minutes because of a heavy overnight snowstorm in Montreal. Finally, we boarded the Lockheed L-1011 and the cabin crew distributed copies of this morning's *Globe and Mail* to the passengers. I turned to the Report on Business section.

The feature story on the front page of the section was about the outlook for next year in the Canadian food-processing industry. As a marketing consultant with several food industry clients, I started reading this article. Out of the blue, the person sitting on my left mumbled something.

I said, "I'm sorry, but I didn't hear what you said."

He looked up at me with some embarrassment and said "Excuse me, I was so engrossed in this" (and he pointed to the same article that I was reading) "that I talked aloud to myself. I said that this writer really understands the plight of our industry. This article zeros in on the problems of my industry and on some decisions I must make before the end of March. By the way, I'm Herb Sherrington, president of Sherrington Food Products Ltd."

Just as I introduced myself, the plane started down the runway. As if by some unspoken agreement we were both silent during take-off, but once we were airborne Herb turned to me. "Food processing today is nothing like it was 25 years ago when I started to work for my father."

"In the early 1960s all of our products were sold under our own brand names (referred to as national brands or producer brands). They were good products that we took pride in and we constantly strove to make them even better."

"Today, not only do we compete with the brand names of other manufacturers, we face serious competition from brands owned by retailers and wholesalers (private label or dealer brands). Since 1978, we've had another type of competition: the no name products. They have about 5 percent of the market. Private label accounts for more than 35 percent of the market, and its share of the market continues to increase year after year."

"Oh, you thought private label would hold a bigger share of the market? It would, but manufacturers have been offering more frequent and richer deals to consumers and retailers. In fact, 10 years ago we sold two-thirds of our national brand production at full price. Today, to protect our volume, we sell more than two-thirds on deal. Back in the 1960s most of our branded products were sold at full price and only occasionally, in order to attract new customers, did we run a price-off special."

"We used to spend money promoting our brand names. People tried our products, liked them, and became loyal to them. Some people are still loyal to specific products, but they are a relatively small segment of the market. Many people today shop on price and will switch brands in order to save a few cents. And private-label products usually sell for less than the national brands."

"You ask what has caused these changes? We'll probably never know all the reasons, but part of the answer lies in environmental factors. First, there are the economic facts. During the high rates of inflation in the late 1970s and the double-digit unemployment levels for most of the last decade, consumers were forced to be price conscious. They tried the lower-priced private label products and found that the differences in quality, if any, were hardly noticeable."

"Second, today the population is better educated than in the past, and better educated people are less influenced by brand names. They tend to have more confidence in their ability to evaluate products and make their own buying decisions."

"Third, the nature of the grocery business has changed. More and more of the volume has passed into fewer hands. Only eight major chains control more than half of the retail grocery business. Competition is intense. Supermarkets will go to great lengths to encourage people to shop at their stores and to earn a few extra profit points on an item."

"The chains not only have their own private labels for high-volume prepared foods, they will private label anything that they sell in volume. They have their own brands of aluminium foil and garbage bags and their own versions of well-known brands such as Mr. Clean and Wisk."

"Private-label products costs less for the final consumer and usually generate above-average margins for the retailer. This is not the result of magic but of good business. Retailers negotiate better prices because of advance volume purchasing (contracts are signed before the growing season starts) and because they accept the responsibility of promoting their own brands."

"We spend a lot of money promoting our national label brands to the consumer and to wholesalers and retailers. The actual amount depends on many factors, including our corporation's sales objectives, the selected marketing mix, and general competitive and economic conditions. As a rule of thumb, we spend between 10 and 15 percent of our revenue for our own brands on promotion. The expenses are included when we cost our own brands but not when we cost private-label products."

"While we spend millions of dollars promoting our brand names, retailers spend little on their private labels. They occasionally advertise all their products under one brand name—or they do nothing. People who shop at supermarkets tend to have confidence in the store or else they would not shop there. There seems to be an unspoken communication: You trust us. You like us. These are our own brands; you can trust them because we stand behind them."

"My father, who was an astute businessman, read the trends correctly and 18 years ago we started to produce private-label brands for a major chain. Now we pack for two major chains and a large food wholesaler. It is clean, profitable business for us. We can order produce and schedule production in advance. We do not have to stock or promote the products—the retailer does that. The big negative is that if the retailer decides to change suppliers, for whatever reason, we lose that business completely. Consumers will never know that a different firm is now producing the product. Because we offer good products, we deliver on time, and our prices are very competitive, we have not yet lost any private-label customers. In fact, private label now generates 35 percent of our dollar volume and 41 percent of our unit volume. However, one can never tell what will happen with chain-store buyers."

"We have another group of customers—institutional wholesalers who handle large containers (4-litre size or larger), which they sell to restaurants, hotels, hospitals, prisons, and other large-scale meal providers. In this market there is no brand loyalty; as long as your quality is acceptable, price becomes the key purchasing variable. About 15 percent of our dollar sales are generated from this segment. Although we would prefer higher margins, the business is profitable."

"The balance of our volume comes from the promotion and sale of our own well-known brands. This business is profitable."

"I must try and resolve these issues before the end of March, when we contract with our farmers for the amount of produce we'll need from the next harvest. My problems are the same as those faced by all the producers of national-label products. There are no easy solutions, but we are looking at a number of alternatives:

1. Do nothing and allow our national brands to slowly die off.
2. Introduce new, potentially high-volume national-brand products to replace the volume lost to private-label brands.
3. Introduce new, potentially low-volume brands aimed at smaller market segments.
4. Spend more money advertising our brands to develop greater brand preference and brand loyalty.
5. Spend more money on trade promotions and high-pressure selling techniques to get the chains to promote our well-known national brands more actively.
6. Place more emphasis on doing private-label work for major retailers and wholesalers."

"As a marketing consultant, what course of action would you advise? Are any of my options sound, or are there other possibilities that I should consider? It may be good to have an outsider look at our marketing problems."

At that point the plane made a perfect landing at Montreal's Dorval airport. Herb and I exchanged cards and agreed to meet at his Toronto office in a few days for me to give him my recommendations.

▶ CASE V.9

The Intel Pentium

Michael Bureau ran a small accounting and bookkeeping service from his home in Mont St. Bruno, just outside Montreal, Quebec. He was also an MSc student in business administration at Concordia University, the statistician for the local minor hockey association, and the father of four: two boys already in high school, a girl who would be joining her brothers next year, and a third boy just entering primary school.

He was disturbed, irritated, and confused by the mail he had just opened from the manufacturer of his recently purchased $3,500 personal computer.

The Business

Michael, a Chartered Accountant, offered a completely computerised bookkeeping service—including general ledger, complete with payroll and all federal and provincial tax reports—to small manufacturing and retail businesses near his home, as well as to a number of high-income business executives. He ran the business from a small office that used to be the den on the first floor of his home. The business was small but efficient. Michael had adopted all the new communications technologies, including a fax machine, modem, high-speed laser printer, and high-quality photocopy machine. Most of his customers transferred their financial transactions electronically via either modem or fax. Many were exploring e-mail as well.

Requirements for the New PC

Michael had come to the conclusion some time ago that his old 286 machine could not process the volume of transactions that his growing practice demanded. He had decided to return to school to pursue an MSc to increase his competence in strategic planning and marketing in order to expand his consulting work in these areas. Having access to faster, more up-to-date technology through the computer facilities at the university increased his frustration with the machine he was using in his business. Furthermore, through his studies he quickly became aware of the tremendous potential of the Internet and began to explore these new opportunities as well as the intriguing possibilities for sophisticated analysis of research data that he was being exposed to in his coursework.

Michael also faced increasing pressure from his children to have access to high-resolution graphic games and CD-ROM multimedia. And the hockey association demanded stats that Michael accumulated using spreadsheet software.

Michael thought of himself as relatively computer literate. It was evident that his new PC, if it was to satisfy his needs for the next five or six years, would have to include the latest technology. He wanted Internet access as well as faster response and capability to use the new sophisticated multitasking software he was constantly hearing about. He had heard and read so much about Intel's new Pentium™ chip through TV ads and innumerable articles in personal computing magazines that he was convinced his new system should be based on the Pentium cpu. He was sufficiently comfortable with his knowledge of PCs, however, that he did not feel the need to purchase a name brand. As long as the Intel technology was included and the operating specifications met his requirements, he was quite willing to accept some risk in buying a "clone" that would cost substantially less.

The Intel Pentium

Not since the dawn of the computer age had there been such a large ad campaign (TV, radio, magazines) for one specific microprocessor. Many people who don't know even what a microprocessor is know the Intel Inside sticker and the name Pentium.

"Intel Inside" was a highly visible multimedia campaign using animated TV ads on such wide-reaching events as the Super Bowl. Through cooperative advertising, it appeared in virtually every computer specialty magazine accompanying advertisements for products incorporating the Intel chip and proudly announcing the association with the "Intel Inside" logo. The latest step forward, the Intel Pentium, boasted architecture that permitted response speeds in excess of 66 MHz.

The letter Michael had just received detailed a potential flaw in the Pentium chip that caused incorrect calculations under certain very specific circumstances. Although the letter stipulated that the likelihood of an error occurring was slim, it had been widely reported and its importance had been distorted in press reports as well as discussions on the Net. Michael, in spite of his experience and relative computer literacy, was overwhelmed by the plethora of bewildering acronyms associated with this problem. He was more than a little uncertain how to proceed. Since this was a situation in which he had invested considerable resources and ego, he was very uncomfortable with the conflicting reports coming from a number of sources. He was especially concerned with the posturing of Intel and IBM downplaying the potential for errors resulting from this defect.

On the one hand, he felt Intel had taken a rather haughty attitude toward the problem. After all, had it not conducted an extensive campaign to directly influence consumers to purchase products incorporating its chips? Michael remembered from his introductory marketing course that this was called a "pull" strategy designed to create primary demand for products using Intel processors. A response to this problem based solely on its technical analysis, although perhaps acceptable among experts in an industrial market, left all but the most sophisticated consumers unsure of what to do. Surely Intel had an obligation to be more forthright as a result of having taken this tack in its ad campaign!

On the other hand, IBM seemed to be having problems of its own. Suggestions were coming from a number of sources that Big Blue was attempting to profit from this situation through exaggerating the consequences and overpublicising the problem. (Its press release was sent to both the print media and a number of electronic bulletin boards.) This profit motive was at least a plausible explanation of the discrepancy between IBM's analysis and Intel's and tended to discredit IBM's position in Michael's mind.

In early January of 1995, Michael was very concerned about the consequences of a computational error given the nature of his business. More and more of the work he was taking on involved divisions much like those described by IBM, as did the spreadsheets for the hockey association and his coursework at university. The local distributor of the clone he had purchased was prepared to make the necessary changes to Michael's machine, although it was the dealer's opinion that Michael need not worry given the probabilities involved. Unfortunately, Michael would have to return the computer to the dealer and be without it for three to five days while the warranty was confirmed and the repair completed. The dealer also thought that a software-based fix was likely to be available within a few months.

Furthermore, it was common knowledge that Canadian distributors were relatively small and lacked the resources and market clout to be very effective in demanding service from suppliers that dwarfed them in size. From experience Michael thought the repair period would probably extend beyond the five days the dealer optimistically quoted.

Michael also wondered if this problem might corrupt his increased investment in high-resolution graphics for his children. He had heard that some of the algorithms used in such programs could also produce the flawed calculation. He knew that he was naive in this area of computing and felt very vulnerable. Could this flaw somehow damage his programs and other computing equipment?

Discussion Questions

1. How do you think Michael will go about resolving this dilemma?
2. Who is he likely to ask for information to help him reach a decision?
3. How might knowledge of consumer behaviour have helped Intel avoid this fiasco?

Source: This case was written by Tom Robertson of Bishops University, copyright 1995.

▶ **CASE V.10**

Price Costco

Jeffrey Michael's recent expedition to the new Club Price store in Montreal was no ordinary trip to a grocery store. "You go crazy," said Jeffrey, sounding a little shell-shocked. Overwhelmed by the vast selection, tables of samples, and discounts as high as 30 percent, he spent $76 on groceries—$36 more than he'd planned. Jeffrey fell prey to what a Price Costco executive calls "the wow factor," a shopping frenzy brought on by low prices and clever marketing. That's the reaction Price Costco's super warehouse stores strive for—and often get.

Price Costco (Price Club in Quebec) has been a leader in shaking up the food industry in Canada and forcing many conventional supermarkets to reduce prices, increase services, or—in some cases—go out of business. With Price Costco and other super warehouse stores springing up across the country, shopping habits are changing, too. Some shoppers drive 50 miles or more to a Price Costco store instead of going to their neighbourhood supermarket. Their payoff is that they find almost everything they need under one roof, and most of it is cheaper than at competing supermarkets. The low prices, smart marketing, and sheer size encourage shoppers to spend far more than they do in the average supermarket.

The difference between Price Costco and most supermarkets is obvious the minute a shopper walks through the doors. The shopper must present a valid membership card, which costs about $25. The ceiling joists and girders are exposed, giving the subliminal feeling of spaciousness. It suggests massive buying, which translates in a shopper's mind into tremendous savings.

The wide shopping carts, which are supposed to promote expansive buying, fit easily through the store's wide aisles, which channel shoppers toward high-profit impulse foods. The whole store exudes a seductive, horn-of-plenty feeling. At the beginning of each aisle you will find the best-selling items (known as "end-caps"), as well as items on promotion. The objective is to draw customers down the aisle toward lower-selling items that they may not have thought of buying. Customers typically buy in volume and spend on average $100 a trip, four times the supermarket average. The average Price Costco store has sales of $100,000 million per year or $2 million a week, quadruple the volume of conventional stores.

Price Costco has a simple approach to retailing: low prices, made possible by rigidly controlled costs and high-volume sales; exceptionally high quality products; and immense variety. It's all packaged in clean stores that are twice as big as most warehouse outlets and four times as big as most supermarkets. A Price Costco store stocks as many as 25,000 items, double the selection of conventional stores, mixing staples with luxury, ethnic, and hard-to-find foods. However, stores typically don't stock more than 2 or 3 brands (often only 1) of a particular product class. Mostly market leaders are sold in Price Costco.

In addition to all the food items, shoppers can buy games, office products, clothing, sporting goods, eyeglasses, home cleaning products, car accessories, and many electronic goods and home appliances.

Overall, Price Costco's gross margin—the difference between what it pays for its goods and what it sells them for—is 8 percent, seven to eight points less than most conventional stores. And because Price Costco relies mostly on word-of-mouth advertising, its ad budgets are 25 percent lower than those of other chains.

Discussion questions

1. List several marketing tactics Price Costco employs in its stores to increase the probability of purchase.
2. What accounts for Price Costco's success in generating such large sales per customer and per store?
3. Given Price Costco's lower prices, quality merchandise, excellent location, and superior assortment, what reasons can you offer for why many consumers in its trading areas refuse to shop there?

Source: Adapted from Steve Weiner and Betsy Morris, "Bigger, Shrewder, and Cheaper Cub Leads Food Stores into the Future," *The Wall Street Journal*, August 26, 1985, p. 17; also see Michael Garry, "Cub Embraces Non-Foods," *Progressive Grocer*, December 1991, pp. 45–48.

The Prince of Wales Hotel, the Shaw Festival, and Inniskillin Winery, and Fort George of Niagara-on-the Lake, Ontario, formed a partnership to offer a package to attract tourists to their facilities. The partnership was designed to gain customers for each of the participating organisations and create a spin-off effect for the whole community. (For each dollar spent by tourists, the multiplier effect produces $7 of economic benefit. For example, a person employed as a guide at Fort George spends some earnings at the supermarket, the supermarket employs people who spend some of their earning to get their hair cut, and this process repeats itself many times, producing the enhanced benefit to the area.)

The partners, four of Niagara-on-the-Lake's most popular tourist attractions, offer very different products, adding to the total enjoyment of visitors:

▷ *Prince of Wales Hotel,* a stately 131-year-old Victorian hotel completely expanded and refurbished, has been visited on several occasions by the British Royal Family. An award-winning gourmet chef and a superb wine cellar enhance visitors' enjoyment.

▷ *The Shaw Festival* is the second largest theatre company in North America and the only one in the world that specialises in plays written during George Bernard Shaw's lifetime (1856–1950).

▷ *Inniskillin Winery* produces award-winning wines from select grapes grown in the Niagara Penninsula.

▷ *Fort George* is a British fort that played a key role in the struggle for the Niagara frontier during the War of 1812. The fort has been restored to its state on the eve of the war.

The Elegant Traditions package included dinner, breakfast for two, and one night's accommodation at the Prince of Wales Hotel; two tickets to the Shaw Festival; a self-guided tour of Inneskillin Winery, a bottle of wine and a wine tote bag; and a tour of Fort George. Purchasers of the package could select their food from the hotel's regular menus and choose from any of Shaw's nine productions. Purchasers could also extend their stays and/or add more plays.

Since the target market selected for the program was relatively affluent travellers living in the three border states of New York, Ohio and Michigan, the package was priced in U.S. dollars: $265 per couple for the weekday package (Sunday to Thursday) and $310 for Friday and Saturday registrations. The weekend price was based on full list price. The weekday package offered a 15 percent savings, but more importantly, it gave prospective buyers an idea of what to do in the area and how much it would cost.

Promotion of the package included 80,000 four-colour elegant traditional brochures distributed by mail using lists provided by the partners. The brochure was supported by newspaper advertising in a number of local and regional publications as well as in two prestigious national magazines, *Travel & Leisure* and *Gourmet*. A total of 39 ads (mainly 1″ × 2″ in size) were placed for a total cost of $26,750. The two national magazines contained request forms for flyers. The Shaw Festival filled thousands of requests. The Prince of Wales Hotel handled all the bookings. Its toll-free telephone number was displayed prominently in all advertising. One reservation clerk was responsible for the Elegant Traditions package. She proved most effective at turning general accommodation inquiries into package sales. In fact, 127 packages were sold as the result of her personal selling effort.

Both the Prince of Wales and the Shaw Festival kept track of package purchases. The reservations clerk at the hotel asked buyers where they lived and how they had heard about the package (Table 1). From its computerised database, the Shaw also provided data on the points of origin of the package clientele (Table 2).

How did you hear about the Elegant Traditions packages?	
Television	1
Radio	2
Newspaper/magazine	14
Flyer from Shaw Festival	85
Brochure from the Prince of Wales Hotel	49
Word of mouth	30
Reservation clerk	127
No response/Other	93
Total	401

TABLE 1

Where our guests are from	
Michigan	85
New York	74
Ohio	58
Ontario	164
Pennsylvania	6
Other	20
Total	401

TABLE 2

The Results

The four partners agreed that the Elegant Traditions package was very successfully launched. With a total marketing budget of just under $46,000 (Table 3), sales of 401 packages for $137,000 were achieved. (The $137,000 included taxes and hotel gratuities but excluded additional hotel, theatre, and winery purchases, which were not tracked.) Three-quarters of the packages sold were for midweek use. From the partners' point of view this helped to increase business in the slower periods of the week. Although there is no hard evidence, it is likely that midweek visits are part of longer travel programs. Spending longer vacation periods in Canada brings in more foreign exchange (from foreign visitors) and discourages Canadians from spending money out of the country. Activities like this partnership can help reduce Canada's travel deficit.

Although a marketing expenditure of 34 cents for each revenue dollar seems somewhat high, the partners viewed this as a reasonable start-up investment and anticipate better returns in future years. The partnership could not afford to advertise frequently and the ads were very small. But there appears to be a direct link between sales achieved and the amount of local/regional advertising. Approximately the same amount ($5,000) was spent on New York State and Michigan and similar levels were noted. A smaller investment of $3,200 in Ohio produced lower sales, while in Pennsylvania, less than $750 was spent and only six packages were sold (Table 2).

The strong response from readers of the two national magazines requesting flyers is encouraging. We also know that 85 people who received flyers actually purchased the package. It may be inferred that 25 percent of all sales could be directly attributed to the

TABLE 3

Actual promotion expenditure, year one

Newspapers		$16,471
Michigan	$ 4,932	
New York	$ 7,574	
Ohio	$ 3,227	
Pennsylvania	$ 738	
Magazines		**$10,294**
Travel and Leisure	$ 6,990	
Gourmet	$ 3,304	
Other Expenses		**$19,209**
Flyers	$12,010	
Envelopes	$ 3,737	
Postage	$ 1,047	
Bulk distribution	$ 715	
Miscellaneous	$ 1,700	
	Total	**$45,974**

two magazine ads. If this is true, then $26,750 was spent to generate gross revenues of $34,350.

Personal selling proved far more effective than any of the partners anticipated. The package is easy to describe and attractively priced, so a general request for hotel accommodations can be turned into a package sale with just a little effort from an enthusiastic reservations clerk.

Questions

1. How would you evaluate the first year's promotion of the program? Was it as successful as the partners thought or not? Support your opinion.

2. Develop a plan that would allow for accurate evaluation of next year's promotion program.

▶ **CASE V.12**

Bauer In-Line Skates

The birth of the sport of in-line skating has been credited to Rollerblade Inc. of Minneapolis, Minnesota. The company founder, Scott Olson, was a hockey player with the Winnipeg Jets' farm teams in 1980 when he envisioned a roller skate with the action of an ice skate that hockey players and skiers could use to train during the off-season. At first, the plan was to use modern materials to construct a model based on an 18th-century design, but Olson discovered a similar in-line skate already on the market and purchased the patent from the Chicago Roller Skate Company. Olson and his brother, Brennan Olson, perfected the design using a plastic moulded ski-type boot atop a blade of polyurethane wheels. Their first sales were to Olson's teammates and a few sporting goods stores. Thus began the sport of blading.

When in-line roller skates appeared in the United States, Canstar Sports Inc. of Canada, the world's biggest maker of hockey equipment, saw their potential as a natural offshoot to its Bauer ice-hockey skate. In-line skates added a whole new dimension to the grassroots sport of road hockey. By adapting its stitch boot to in-line skates, Bauer revolutionised an industry that had known only moulded boots. The market finally caught on in 1991 and since then has increased exponentially. from 1989 until 1995, 3 million pairs of in-line skates were sold in Canada. In 1994 alone, 850,000 pairs were sold. Estimates for 1995 are pegged at 1.2 million.

In-line skating appeals to a wide cross-section of consumers for simple casual recreation, transportation, general fitness, a low-impact workout, cross-training, speed skating, stunt and ramp skating, and roller hockey. In-line skates generally cost twice as much as conventional roller skates, ranging from $100 to $380 for adult models, $60 to $130 for kids' models, and up to $600 for racing skates. They are purchased for two reasons. First, they are faster and therefore more exciting to use than conventional skates. Second, they use more muscles, providing skaters with a better aerobic workout. It is more difficult to learn how to use in-line skates, however, because they require better balance. And at faster speeds, falls may cause more, and more severe, injuries.

Although Rollerblade Inc. controls 70 percent of the North American market, in January 1995 the Canadian market was dominated by Canstar Sports Inc. with a 40 percent market share. Rollerblade Inc. and CCM Ultra Wheels held the number two and three positions respectively. In addition to developing skates for different uses, the companies continue to improve the technology of the boot and the braking system. Over 30 percent of in-line users are under the age of 14 (which guarantees sales of in-line products for at least the decade and probably longer). Not only will the young skaters grow out of their present boot but there is also the potential among all consumers for upgrades as their skill levels improve.

The fierce industry competition is not limited to product features. It includes other marketing mix elements as well. The industry prefers grassroots marketing activities and specialty programs over mainstream advertising. The objective has been to turn the fad into a sport with staying power. Employees go out to the streets and teach people how to skate in demonstrations and tournaments. All three manufacturers sponsor races, roller-hockey leagues, tournaments, and stunt competitions. Although limited in Canada, some companies have adopted spokespeople to promote their product. For example, Ultra Wheels signed Wayne Gretzky, the Los Angeles Kings hockey star, and his wife, Janet Jones Gretzky, to promote its skates. Competitors also moved into new retail markets, including discount and department stores. The top three retail outlets in 1993 were Canadian Tire, General Sporting Goods Stores, and Woolco/Wal-Mart.

A recognized leader within the NHL, the Bauer brand is poised to prosper. The sale of Canstar Sports to Nike in March 1995 further solidified its position as a world market leader. Bauer should benefit from Nike's brand-oriented marketing expertise, its solid capitalisation, and its worldwide distribution network. With sales of in-line skates growing, Bauer is feeling the pressure on capacity, as are the U.S. competitors—which may leave room for additional competitors to move in.

Discussion Questions

1. What role do you think modelling could have played in the diffusion of this innovation?

2. How could you use live, covert, and verbal modelling to teach a friend how to use Bauer in-line skates?

3. What factors make Wayne and Janet Jones Gretzky good models for Bauer's competitor?

4. If you were designing a commercial for Bauer in-line skates to be used for an in-store videotape demonstration, how would you design the commercial to take advantage of your knowledge of modelling?

This case was written by Cynthia Joy, © 1995.

Source: Based on "The 1993 Canadian In-line Skate Market," *Sports Business,* Feb. 1995, p. 121; "Rollin' Rollin' Rollin' In-line Skating for Fun, Fitness and Family," *Toronto Sun,* June 25, 1995, p. 50; "Skating Boom Has Gone Wild," *The Spectator* (Hamilton), June 19, 1995, p. D19; "Nike Plans Purchase of Montreal Hockey Giant," *The Ottawa Citizen,* Dec. 15, 1994, p. G1; "The Evolution of Roller Skating," *Globe & Mail* Metro Edition, July 19, 1994, p. C5–C7; "In-line Industry Streaking towards the Year 2000," *Sports Business,* Sept. 1995, pp. 6–8; "High Rollers; Canstar Keeps Growing as Hockey's Popularity Increases," *Daily News* (Halifax), June 6, 1994, p. 13.

▶ CASE V.13

The Train Trip

On July 21, 1993, Marianne and Robert relived their annoyance as they composed a letter to the French National Railway concerning a recent bad experience with the train system. It had been the only blight on a two-week family holiday in Europe in May/June 1993.

Planning the Family Holiday

Marianne Ricci, 41, and Robert Dupuis, 48, were a professional couple with one son, Michael, age 10. They lived in a small town in northeastern Nova Scotia. They usually took their family vacation at the same spot on the Gaspe Coast of Quebec. The summer of 1993 would be special, however. Marianne had a special leave from work, Robert was flexible in his job as an independent consultant, and Michael was now old enough to go with the flow of a big trip.

The family initially contemplated going across Canada. But Marianne had not been to Europe since 1978 and had always wanted to visit France with Robert because he spoke French fluently. At this point Michael would also appreciate a different cultural setting. Robert was less keen on going to Europe; he saw it as an expensive holiday with the risk of not accommodating the whole family in a truly holiday way. One debating point was that a trip to Europe would cost about $1,400 more than going across Canada, accounted for by being able to stay with friends or family in various parts of Canada. Michael became increasingly enthusiastic as Mom described her trips to Europe and what he might take with him and what he might see and do. After many discussions from November 1992 to February 1993, they decided on the trip to Europe. As usual, they would work within a predetermined budget.

The family narrowed down their range to France and Italy. Since Marianne had taken two holidays in Europe in the late 1970s, she felt that Robert and Michael should have first choice for places to visit. They decided to visit Paris, Venice, Florence (with a side trip to Pisa) and Milan, spending about four days in each of the first three cities. They worked out in detail what they would like to see and do.

Marianne investigated travel arrangements with the airlines. The travelling was complicated because they lived two and a half hours from the airport (in Halifax) and would have to fly to Montreal or Toronto, where virtually all international flights originate for travellers in Atlantic Canada. The return trip would involve staying overnight at the airport hotel in Halifax. They bought their tickets from Canadian Airlines, which could fly them into Paris on May 26 and out of Milan on June 9 for a reasonable price. The rest of the travel would be by train, since they were not interested in driving in Europe. The routes seemed direct and Marianne's experience on the European trains was very positive; she said they were comfortable, ran on time, and had frequent departures and various routes.

Robert was particularly concerned about accommodations and how they might get from one place to another at reasonable times and for reasonable prices. To enjoy the experience everyone would need adequate rest. Thus, Robert spent a lot of time gathering information on where to stay and how to get around. He spoke to friends and family members, collected brochures from tour companies, talked to travel agents, and spent over $100 during April phoning hotels in Europe. Marianne assisted with gathering this information, but Robert took primary responsibility for it. He wanted as few surprises as possible. They spent nearly $150 on travel guides.

A month before the trip, Robert called the French Embassy for the train schedule leaving Paris for Italy. The embassy forwarded his call to a Canadian agency that looked after train passes for Canadians travelling abroad. He determined that the best route would be a stay in Paris, followed by a 12-hour daytime train trip via Lausanne, Switzerland (with a bonus stopover of two hours), through Milan to Florence. After a few days in Florence, they could go up to Venice and then have a day in Milan before flying home. Robert carefully noted the times of arrivals and departures and took this information with him to Europe. Hotel reservations for each city were made and confirmed with deposits.

The Trip

The holiday went very well except for the train trip between Paris and Florence on May 31. On the previous day, Robert went to the international travel desk at Gare de Lyon (a major train station in Paris) and presented the schedule he had brought with him. The agent informed him that they had just been computerised and that Robert's schedule was incorrect. The agent had problems getting the tickets from the computerised setup, but finally printed them out after numerous attempts and consultation with various manuals. Robert paid 1,754 French francs for the tickets and three reserved seats (optional, unless you want your seats guaranteed). Although the agent seemed to know what he was doing, Robert still had doubts about the schedule.

The train arrived in Lausanne on time, giving the family an opportunity to have lunch and walk around Lausanne. Upon returning to the train station in plenty of time to catch their next train, however, they discovered that they had tickets and reservations for a train departure which did not exist! (In fact, the agent told Robert that the schedule obtained in Canada was correct and the agent in Paris had been working off the old schedule.) An unsettling chain of events unfolded.

EXHIBIT 1

**Letter to the French
National Railway**

> 12 Pinevale Drive
> Smalltown, Nova Scotia
> Canada B0Z 4X2
> July 21, 1993
>
> French National Railway (SNCF)
> Department Apres-Vente
> 10 Place Budapest
> Paris, France
>
> Dear sir or madam:
>
> On Saturday, May 29, 1993, my wife, my young son, and I made reservations and bought tickets at Gare de Lyon (in Paris) to go from Paris to Florence (Italy) on Monday, May 31. Our trip required that we change trains in Lausanne and Milan.
>
> While waiting for our train in Lausanne, we became alarmed when Train #323 leaving at 12:55 did not appear on the Departure Notice Board. We immediately spoke to a ticket agent and were informed that our train no longer existed, that a new schedule had recently come into effect, and that the train we should have been on had departed Lausanne for Milan at 11:13. The ticket agent told us to take the next train (#327) at 13:32 to arrive in Milan at 17:45. This was a second-class train and reservations were not required. The agent doubted that we would be able to catch Train #541, for which we had reservations, which was leaving Milan for Florence at 17:50. We were told to take Train #511, leaving Milan at 19:40 to arrive in Florence at 22:08, if we missed Train #541.
>
> Unfortunately, Train #327 was late, arriving in Milan at 17:50. Although we tried, it was impossible for us to catch Train #541 for Florence.
>
> The ticket agent we spoke to in Milan stamped our reservation card (Milan to Florence) as not having been used. However, the agent also informed us that Train #511 from Milan to Florence at 19:40 would cost us an additional 170,500 lire. Naturally, we protested, but were forced to pay the additional fee to get to our destination.
>
> The ticket agent at Gare de Lyon made a mistake when he issued our tickets and reservations. This mistake resulted in lost time, a great deal of frustration, and additional costs to us of 170,500 lire. We hold the SNCF responsible and hereby request a refund of our additional costs.
>
> You will find enclosed with this letter photocopies of our tickets, reservations, payment receipt, directions we were given in Lausanne, and our ticket from Milan to Florence with the costs indicated. Should you require the originals, I will be happy to forward them.
>
> I look forward to hearing from you.
>
> Sincerely,
>
> _____
>
> Robert S. Dupuis

They were able to use their tickets to get another train to Milan, but they did not make their original connection to Florence because the Lausanne train arrived five minutes late. In Milan, after spending nearly 90 minutes speaking to personnel at three different desks, Robert finally learned (through a half-French, half-Italian exchange) that the choice was to take a train that would arrive in Florence at 12:30 in the morning or buy tickets for the next train out of Milan, which was first-class only but would get them there at 10:00 P.M. They chose to take the first-class train and called the pensione (hotel) in Florence to say they would be late. The tickets cost 170,500 lire plus an additional 33,360 lire for the high exchange rate at the train station. The clerk would not refund the tickets bought in Paris because he insisted that there was no error in the system. However, he did stamp the tickets to indicate that they were not used.

The first-class service offered no consolation. The car was filled with fashionably dressed Europeans, many working on laptop computers and doing business. Neither the other passengers nor the two attendants seemed pleased at the presence of the family dressed very casually, carrying backpacks and duffel bags, and asking for extra water to quench their thirst. They were hot, tired, and annoyed. As they approached Florence, they realized that the train stopped only at the other end of the city from their pensione—which they had chosen because it was a short walk from the train station where they were supposed to arrive.

They managed to find a taxi quite easily, however, and the fare they paid the skillful driver was worth it in comic relief. The three passengers found themselves in a very small automobile travelling at what seemed incredible speed through very narrow streets in a strange city late at night. They were laughing by the time they reached their pensione, where they were greeted as expected guests. After a good night's sleep, they were determined to put the train ordeal behind them and enjoy the rest of the trip.

The Trip Revisited

When the family returned home, they were reminded of the train incident each time they described their trip to friends and families. The extra expense showed up in accounting for the budget for the trip. Both Marianne and Robert became increasingly annoyed over time. Although Robert was doubtful that anything would be achieved from such a long distance, Marianne convinced him that they should at least try to appeal for some compensation by writing a letter to the French National Railway. They composed a registered letter (shown in Exhibit 1) in English, since it would be too complicated to try to explain the situation in French.

Source: © 1995, Rosemary Polegato, Mount Allison University.

The price of admission to movie theatres sometimes buys an experience sensible people would pay to avoid. The dingy carpet in the lobby could be a relic from the silent screen era. The $1.25 bucket of popcorn (that's the small size!) holds 10 cents worth of corn tossed with a strange liquid, perhaps derived from petroleum. Beneath the worn-out seats, sticky coats of spilled soda pop varnish the floor. The screen is tiny, the sound tinny, and the audience rude. Oh, and one more thing—the picture isn't worth seeing.

Many theatre owners bought into the business at low prices after 1984, when antitrust rulings forced the major Hollywood studios, which had previously owned the leading theatre chains, to give up their movie houses. The new owners got a great deal. They owned the only show in town (sometimes literally), and the studios promoted the movies. As the easy profits rolled in, many exhibitors lost contact with their customers. They milked the business and let their theatres deteriorate.

But the success of video rentals and cable TV converted many moviegoers into stay-at-homers. By 1985, theatres were no longer the only show in town. Attendance dropped 12 percent over 1984 figures. The $5 billion-a-year North American movie theatre industry was fighting for survival.

This put the theatre owners in a bind. To regain their customers, they had to pour money into refurnishing, rebuilding, and restoring the glamour of moviegoing.

To survive, exhibitors developed some temporarily successful strategies. One was to focus on lobby concession stands as a source of revenues. To keep some of their customers, theatres had kept ticket prices fairly low. The average price in 1985 was about $3.50

► CASE V.14

Movie theatres

to $4, prices that lagged behind inflation. Once inside, though, moviegoers were a captive market for the popcorn, soda, and candy sold at stupendous markups of up to 500 percent or more. A well-run concession stand generates at least $1 of sales and as much as 75 cents of profit per ticket buyer.

What brands of candy were in the typical concession stand? Usually, it was a strange mix of oversized boxes that included very few of the best-selling brands. Theatres tended to stock candy brands like Milk Duds, Sno Caps, and Glosette Raisins, hardly big sellers elsewhere. Do moviegoers have different tastes from the rest of the population? Of course not. The movie-house operators preferred these brands because they were more profitable. With limited space available, the operators stocked the brands with the highest profit margins. Critics claim that by sticking to the most profitable brands, theatre owners are missing an opportunity to increase overall candy sales by stocking more popular brands. As it stands now, only about one-third of moviegoers buy anything from the concession stand.

The profits from concession sales can be considerable. For instance, a tub of popcorn that cost 30 cents sells for about $2—a markup of 567 percent. A soft drink (often a Coke) that cost the theater 10 cents sells for $2.00, a two-thousand percent markup. Candy produces a much smaller profit, with markups of "only" about 180 percent. On average, about 40 percent of annual concession sales came from popcorn, another 40 percent from soft drinks, and only about 20 percent from everything else.

The other strategy was the multiscreen theater. During the 1970s, exhibitors began chopping up their grand old theatres into smaller ones that many moviegoers have come to hate. Individual exhibitors did well, though (as long as they owned the only theatre in town). A theatre with four screens is four times as likely to book a hit picture: the exhibitor then shows the hit in the largest room and lesser movies in the smaller theatres.

But at a macro level, more seats were the last thing the industry needed. In 1985, the total number of tickets sold annually remained constant at about 1 billion, a number that hadn't varied much for 25 years. When the growing population is considered, this translates into a 24 percent per-capita decline in moviegoing. As a writer for *Variety* said, "Film-going used to be part of the social fabric. Now it is an impulse purchase." During the 1980s, the population began to age and the prime moviegoing segment of the under-30-year-olds to decline. When the damage done by VCRs and cable TV is added . . . well, you get the picture.

To survive the 1990s, exhibitors have learned how to woo moviegoers. There is admittedly something special about seeing a terrific film in a great theatre with an appreciative audience. And by using technologies such as widescreen 70-millimeter projection and wraparound Dolby sound, theatres can create a sense of spectacle that no TV set can match. Owners have made their theatres clean and comfortable again, maybe even palatial. In fact, many exhibitors have remodeled their old elegant theatres and restored them to their former grandeur. New construction is being upgraded. One successful exhibitor coddled customers in specially designed $130 seats, costing twice the national average.

Another exhibitor said, "We have to upgrade the quality of the moviegoing experience." His newest theatres have granite-floored lobbies, mural walls, spacious auditoriums, and first-rate sound and projection. The higher construction costs paid off in more customers at higher than average ticket prices.

As the drama of change pervades the movie exhibition industry, the major beneficiaries may even be the long-suffering moviegoers. When consumers enter the theatre of the future, they may not encounter a marvel of technology, but at least they won't stick to the floor.

Discussion questions

1. The VCR is an environmental change that has affected moviegoing behaviour. Compare and contrast the consumption situations of watching a movie in a theatre and seeing the same movie at home on your VCR. Discuss the interactions between and among environment, behaviour, and cognitive and affective responses. What long-term effects do you think the in-home VCR environments will have on moviegoing? What can movie theatres do to address the situation?

2. What macro environmental factors might affect moviegoing behaviours (both decreases and increases)? Consider their impacts on different market segments. What marketing implications does your analysis have for theatre owners or movie companies?

3. Analyse the information, purchasing, and consumption environments of different movie theatres that you know. What recommendations do you have for changing these environments to increase sales?

4. Analyse the effects of the consumption situation at movie theaters on consumers' purchase of snacks at the concession stand. What could theatre owners do to change the purchasing and consumption environment to encourage higher levels of snack consumption and greater sales at concession stands?

Source: Alex Ben Block, "Those Peculiar Candies that Star at the Movies," *Forbes,* May 19, 1986, pp. 174–76; and Stratford P. Sherman, "Back to the Future," *Fortune,* Jan. 20, 1986, pp. 909–14.

The Japanese market is the second richest in the world, after the United States. But it is notoriously difficult for foreign companies to succeed in marketing their products in Japan. Yet, in the late 1980s and early 1990s, North American companies have better opportunities than ever before to sell in Japan. The Japanese government has relaxed some trade barriers, and the powerful yen and relatively weak dollar have given North American firms the best price-cutting opportunity in decades. Recent cultural changes in Japan should increase marketing opportunities. After decades of austerity, Japanese are spending more on consumer goods. Some Japanese, especially young people, have a fondness for American culture.

But succeeding in Japan won't be easy. The Japanese market may just be the toughest on earth. The language is difficult, values and meanings are different, and customs and manners can be baffling to westerners. In addition, attitudes toward foreign products can be frosty. For example, a 1990 survey of Japanese consumers found that 71 percent considered Japanese products superior to North American. Only 8 percent of Japanese would even consider buying a North American car (3 percent would think of buying an American TV). Success requires an extraordinary commitment to quality, a willingness to adjust to cultural differences, a long-range perspective, and patience (lots of patience)—all qualities of the typical Japanese company. Foreign businesses intending to enter the Japanese market might analyse some earlier marketing mistakes to avoid repeating them. There are plenty of examples to choose from. Consider, for instance, some of the problems that Procter & Gamble had with doing business in Japan.

In 1973, Procter & Gamble charged into Osaka with the marketing strategies that had played so well at home. The results were disastrous. By some accounts, the huge company lost about a quarter of a billion dollars over the next decade or so. The gambit started off fairly well. By the late 1970s, P&G's Cheer brand of laundry detergent was the leading brand in Japan with a 10 percent market share, Camay bath soap had 3.5 percent

► **CASE V.15**

Selling in foreign markets

of a very competitive market, and Pampers, with little competition, had 90 percent of the disposable-diaper market. But P&G lost ground in all of these markets. Why it happened and what the company did to regain the lost ground provide useful lessons in the importance of understanding cultural factors and their relation to consumer behaviour.

In general, the Japanese seem to have learned such lessons better than most North American companies. When the Japanese enter a foreign market, they study it carefully. They do not assume that what goes in Japan also goes in Canada, for example. P&G apparently lacked this humility and cross-cultural perspective. As one bitter ex-P&G employee summed up the problem, "They [the company] didn't listen to anybody." Cheer detergent prospered at first because of heavy price discounting. But this strategy partially backfired because it devalued the company's reputation in the eyes of many Japanese consumers. According to one expert, "Unlike Europe and the U.S., once you discount in Japan it is hard to raise prices later." The price-cutting strategy also overlooked several other cultural factors. Because many Japanese do not have a car, they shop in small neighbourhood stores where close to 30 percent of detergents are sold. Owners of these small stores do not like to carry discounted products because they make less money on them.

The advertising also missed the mark. In the late 1970s, Japanese viewers voted Cheer ads the least liked on TV. They were repelled by a typical North American hard-sell approach that stressed product benefits and user testimonials. Bad advertising also hurt Camay soap. In one commercial, a man meeting a woman for the first time compared her skin to that of a fine porcelain doll. Although the ad had worked well in the Philippines, South America, and Europe, the Japanese were insulted. Japanese ad executives had warned P&G that women would find the commercial offensive—"For a Japanese man to say something like that to a Japanese woman means he's either unsophisticated or rude"—but their warnings went unheeded.

The worst story was in the disposable-diaper market. P&G had literally created the market in 1978 and invested heavily in educating Japanese consumers about the advantages of disposable diapers. By the time a small Japanese manufacturer entered the market in 1981, P&G controlled over 90 percent of a $100 million business. By 1985, it had only about 5 percent. The company had underestimated both the capabilities of the Japanese competitor and the favourable response of Japanese consumers to a higher-quality product.

Unfortunately, there was more to come. P&G stuck too long to its policy of advertising the brand, not the company. In Japan, consumers like to know the company, and they tend to form a personal relationship with it. Most Japanese ads end with a flash of the company's name. But P&G didn't add this to its ads until 1986.

But all was not lost. P&G learned from its very expensive mistakes and is in Japan to stay. Its Ultra Pampers product made inroads into the Japanese market and the advertising is now more in tune with Japanese cultural sensibilities. P&G is gaining back some of its lost market share.

P&G's mistakes should not be taken to imply that Japanese companies are always perfect marketers. They have made some embarrassing blunders of their own in trying to market Japanese products in foreign cultures. But often the Japanese are so determined that they succeed anyway. Their remarkable desire to please the customer is a big factor in their success, according to one P&G executive.

Consider the experience of Shiseido, a giant cosmetics company, in introducing its line of cosmetics into the United States in the mid-1960s. Only after getting its products into more than 800 stores, including Bloomingdale's and Saks, did the company realize how different American women's tastes in cosmetics were from those of their Japanese counterparts. Application of Shiseido's makeup required a lengthy series of steps. Apparently

Japanese women didn't mind, but American women balked. The cosmetics flopped, and the company pulled out of more than 600 stores. But Shiseido didn't quit. Instead, it designed a new line of products to meet the needs of American women, beautifully packaged, easy to use, and graced with subtle scents. To promote these products, the company relied less on advertising, as is the typical approach, and more on the extraordinary personal service it gives its customers in Japan. According to an executive of Estée Lauder, a competitor, "The service level in Japan is the highest in the world. It starts with the fact that the store manager and his executives come down to the entrance of the store every morning for 15 or 20 minutes to greet the customers." In North America, Shiseido trains its saleswomen to treat the customer lavishly, including offering free facial massages at demonstration counters. By the early 1990's, Shiseido's sales were growing at about 25 percent a year, and its products were available in over 1,000 stores across North America.

Discussion questions

1. Sometimes even rather subtle cultural factors can make a significant difference in the success of a marketing strategy. Describe several examples of these cultural factors from the case. How can a company learn about these cultural factors? What things should the company consider in deciding whether to adapt its marketing strategies to reflect them?

2. Using the model of the cultural process in Exhibit 15.3, discuss the transmission of cultural meaning involved in Shiseido's marketing of cosmetics in North America.

3. Discuss the stands taken by advocates of global and local marketing strategies in the context of this case. Do you think P&G can sell its household and personal care products around the world using the same marketing strategies? Defend your answer, and then discuss your position on the debate about global marketing strategies.

4. In 1988, Kao, the $4-billion-a-year Japanese manufacturer of detergents, diapers, and toothpaste, entered the North American market. Kao is a direct competitor of P&G in Japan. Many of its products were under the Jergens name, a company Kao bought in 1988. Identify some of the more important cultural and subcultural factors that Kao should have considered in introducing its shampoo into the Canadian market. What implications do these cultural aspects of the social environment have for devising effective marketing strategies?

Source: Joel Dreyfuss, "How to Beat the Japanese at Home," *Fortune,* Aug. 31, 1987, pp. 80–83; Brian Dumaine, "Japan's Next Push in U.S. Markets," *Fortune,* Sept. 26, 1988, pp. 135–40; Frederick Katayama, "Japan's Prodigal Young Are Dippy about Imports," *Fortune,* May 11, 1987, p. 118; Jeffrey A. Trachtenberg, "They Didn't Listen to Anybody," *Forbes,* Dec. 15, 1986, pp. 168–69; and Carla Rapoport, "How the Japanese Are Changing," *Fortune,* Sept. 24, 1990, pp. 15–22.

As the number of older people increases, businesses are beginning to pay more attention to the diversity in this subcultural group. Many companies are rushing to identify the needs of the elderly and to develop products to meet those needs. Both Marriott Corp. and Hyatt Hotels, for example, developed retirement community "products" for the elderly market. Retirement communities combine retirement housing, various services, and nursing care. They offer personal living quarters in apartments of varying sizes, a wide range of activities and entertainment, housekeeping services, food service options (a dining

► **CASE V.16**

Hyatt and Marriott: building retirement housing

room for some meals, along with one's own kitchen), along with varying levels of on-site health care, including full nursing home services for some people.

The market for retirement communities is immense, but it is a fallacy to assume everyone over 65 is a potential customer for a retirement community. Actually, the prime customers are in their late 70s or early 80s. Also, it is untrue that many elderly are feeble and ripe for the nursing home. Contrary to popular belief, not all elderly live alone; many are married. It should be obvious that the "mature market" is quite diverse; only the over-85 subgroup is somewhat homogeneous. The implication is that marketers must analyse the elderly subculture very carefully.

Elderly people differ considerably in how they want to live in retirement. Some prefer a single-family home, while others want apartments or condominiums. Some want community, social interaction, and recreational amenities, while others prefer solitude and independence.

Both Hyatt and Marriott conducted detailed research using focus groups and telephone and written surveys to understand these needs. One research study identifies three sub-subcultures in the elderly subcultures—the "go-go's" (65 to 75, who travel and play golf), and "slow-go's" (75 to 85, still active, but slowing down), and the "no-go's" (85 and older, somewhat active but staying closer to home). The prime target customer for retirement communities is the slow-go group. The go-go's will be potential customers in another 10 years, while the no-go's are potential customers for the more intensive levels of nursing care.

In earlier days, marketing of retirement community products was rather simplistic—some fancy four-colour brochures and corporate print ads placed in magazines and newspapers. Early research generally was confined to simple demographic analyses of age, income, and competition. Many marketers did not investigate the elderly market further to understand how its members perceive their own needs. There is a big affective and cognitive problem in marketing retirement communities, for example. Typically, a consumer's first response is "I'm not ready yet." Most elderly people want to stay in their own homes and remain independent until it becomes impossible. Getting consumers to buy into a retirement community requires that they think about the unthinkable (their own mortality and failing health)—not easy for most people. In fact, many elderly, especially those in the affluent subgroup, perceive themselves as younger and more fit than they actually are.

Marriott opened its first two high-rise retirement developments (350 to 400 apartments) in 1988. One retirement community offers a pool, maid service, and a health club, in addition to 24-hour meals, emergency call buttons in each bathroom and bedroom, a floor with skilled nursing care, and another floor for those who don't require nursing care but need other types of daily help (in bathing themselves, for example).

One industry consultant has suggested that direct mail is the most effective approach for marketing retirement communities. Every month, a company might send something to potential customers: a postcard invitation to an event, a letter describing some service, a newsletter describing people in the retirement community, even recipes. Marriott successfully used a direct-mail promotion to generate early interest in its unbuilt retirement community. Brochures and information were mailed to affluent elderly residents of the area. For a $1,000 deposit, people could reserve a $100,000 to $260,000 apartment in the luxury complex. The mailing generated a phenomenal 4 percent response rate (2 or 3 percent is considered good). Over the next several years, Marriott spent more than $1 billion to construct some 150 retirement communities. Marriott also intends to continue to build additional developments that offer only two living options, assisted living and nursing care.

Hyatt developed its retirement community, Classic Residences by Hyatt, in 1990. Classic Residences are upscale apartment complexes that offer a set of services similar to Marriott's. Hyatt's initial research also showed that elderly people have a strong initial negative reaction to retirement communities. Even people living in metropolitan areas who are exposed to a great deal of marketing information about these products think of "retirement communities" as a euphemism for the dreaded nursing home. Thus, Hyatt's marketing promotions tend to emphasise "maintain an active lifestyle" rather than "be taken care of forever."

Hyatt also found that many elderly people believe retirement communities are extremely expensive or that they have to sign away their life savings to get in. So Hyatt salespeople explicitly compared the costs of living in one's own home to living in the retirement community. Most people did not factor in how much they were spending to live in their own house, and this discovery had some influence on their conviction that "I'm not ready yet." Marriott, finding the same thing, is experimenting with different pricing strategies, including charging a lower initial payment with higher monthly rent or fees, so their prospects don't have to use so much of their accumulated savings.

Finally, both Hyatt and Marriott have developed other marketing strategies. Their sales presentations include seminars about retirement planning, health issues, and motivational topics. Open houses often include entertainment to draw in customers. If necessary, incentives are offered to encourage prospects to take that final step, including free rent for a few months, paid moving expenses, free interior decorating advice, or expense-paid vacations.

In sum, developing successful retirement community products and marketing strategies is largely a matter of listening to the prospects and understanding their needs and interests. Many elderly consumers know what they want, and they respond to the same types of marketing strategies used to sell other services.

Discussion questions

1. Discuss the submarkets (sub-subcultures) within the elderly subculture that are relevant in the case of retirement communities. Discuss how social class can be combined with age subcultures to define the market segments for retirement communities more precisely. What marketing strategies would be necessary to target these different segments of the elderly market?

2. Identify the key target segments for Marriott's new health care-oriented retirement communities (they offer only some level of health care). For the most attractive segment, identify and analyse the most important behaviours, affective responses, and cognitions in shopping for, purchasing, and living in such a retirement community.

3. Discuss the marketing strategies that Marriott could use to market its new health care-oriented retirement units to the key market segments. What different promotional strategies are likely to appeal to these subcultural groups?

4. The customer/product relationship may be a useful way to think about marketing retirement communities. What aspects of this relationship should Marriott and Hyatt consider, and why? Contrast the marketing strategies Marriott and Hyatt could use to develop the customer/product relationship before the purchase with the strategies they might institute after the sale to enhance and maintain this relationship.

Source: Sally Chapralis, "Retirement Community Marketers End Their Retirement," *Marketing News,* July 8, 1991, p. 2; Jame Gollub and Harold Javitz, "Six Ways to Age," *American Demographics,* June 1989, pp. 28–37; and Janet Novack, "Tea, Sympathy, and Direct Mail," *Forbes,* Sept. 18, 1989, pp. 210–11.

**Breastfeeding
in Canada
in the 1990s**

Marie André McCord, chair of the National Capital Region Health Department's strategic planning committee, is reviewing a report she recently received on current Canadian attitudes and practices about breastfeeding. She must decide if there is a need for a breastfeeding campaign in the National Capital Region and what should be the strategic thrust of this campaign (which messages should be communicated and to which target audiences). Social marketing campaigns such as the one contemplated on breastfeeding usually promote the acceptance of positive social behaviour that improves the quality of individual lives and benefits society as a whole.

Ottawa-Hull, Canada's fourth-largest CMA, is a mixture of many languages and cultures. According to the last census, 53 percent of the population reported English as their mother tongue while 33 percent spoke French as their initial language. The remaining 14 percent of the population reported a wide variety of languages, each of which represents 1.5 percent or less of the population.

Here is the report Ms. McCord reviewed:

Mother Nature and some mothers are in conflict over the purpose and use of female human breasts. Mother Nature intended breasts primarily as a source of nourishment for babies and as a secondary sexual characteristic. In some cultures, the population and nature are in agreement. However, in Canada, the human breast is not always used according to the best interest of either the mother or the child, in that:

1. Some mothers of newborns who are able to breastfeed decide not to do so at all. This pattern is especially evident in mothers who are less educated and poor and among Quebec francophone mothers. When the French and English populations are adjusted for education and income, language is no longer a meaningful factor.

   It has been especially difficult to encourage women of low socioeconomic status (maternal family income, occupation and education levels) to initiate and continue breastfeeding. The profile of a mother who initiates breastfeeding at birth is an older mother who is married, has more formal education, earns higher income, does not smoke, and has a supportive social network.

   There is a strong correlation between low self-esteem of the expectant mother and a decision not to breastfeed. Low self-esteem includes the lack of confidence to produce the amount of milk needed and to provide the on-demand attention breastfeeding requires.

2. Many mothers who start breastfeeding discontinue the practice significantly earlier than the minimum of six months recommended by the Canadian Paediatrics Society Nutrition Committee.

Although the decision-making process followed by prospective mothers is not fully documented, it appears that the decision may be made before conception, during pregnancy, or immediately after delivery. There is evidence that women tend to follow through with their initial decisions concerning breastfeeding and duration. Prenatal instructors report that expectant mothers have already made their breastfeeding decisions before they start prenatal classes (about the fourth month of pregnancy). The instructors report that their attempts to convert expectant mothers who have decided to bottle feed are seldom successful.

There appear to be at least four major influences on the mother's decision to breastfeed:

▷ the baby's maternal grandmother.
▷ the baby's father.
▷ the mother's peers.
▷ medical professionals including physicians, nurses, and public health workers.

TABLE 1
Benefits of Breastfeeding

For the infant
Perfect nutritional balance for children
Ease of absorption of nutrients
Healthier infants

▷ lower incidence of gastrointestinal, respiratory, and middle ear illnesses
    ▷ better protection against infectious diseases and infections
    ▷ protection against Hodgkin's Disease

May reduce the risk of SIDS (sudden infant death syndrome)
Higher IQ at age 7.5 years than nonbreastfed babies (even after adjustment for mother's education and social class)
Better bonding and self-esteem
For the mother
Reduced risk of developing some cancers, especially breast and ovarian cancer
Facilitates weight loss and return to prepregnancy weight
Reduced chance of developing osteoporosis
No cost
No need to prepare formulas and bottles

Once implemented, a decision not to breastfeed or to discontinue the practice is not reversible. However, a decision to breastfeed may be easily changed.

Insight to the issues may be gained from looking at the position and arguments of each of the opposed groups. First, let's look at a mother's reasons for initiating and continuing to breastfeed for at least six months. Medical research has conclusively identified benefits for the child and for the mother. Most mothers will do almost anything for the benefit of their babies. And nursing mothers benefit from reduced risk of certain types of cancer, faster return to prepregnancy weight and improved uterine condition. (A more complete list of benefits to babies and mothers is found in Table 1.)

Breastfeeding is advocated by all health professionals, many levels of government, and at least two major nonprofit organisations (La Leche League Canada [Ligue La Leche in Quebec] and the Infant Feeding Action Coalition [Infact]). Health Canada plays a major role through its own education programs, for the most part providing factual data to interested parties and funding, to some extent, programs initiated by others. It has also developed a social marketing program to promote breastfeeding.

Provincial health departments have their own breastfeeding initiatives, which are implemented on a provincewide basis by the provincial government and/or by local and regional health units. For example, since the fall of 1993, Quebec has paid $50 per month to nursing mothers who are receiving welfare. This payment, intended to provide nursing mothers with the funds to purchase supplementary vitamins and minerals to ensure the health of the mother and child, is viewed as a cost saving to the provincial treasury. Breastfed babies are healthier than bottle-fed babies and require less costly medical care at the province's expense.

In Ontario and other provinces, regional and local health units run breastfeeding programs for pregnant women. Some programs are offered at no cost to participants; others have modest fees. Many hospitals across the country, as part of prenatal courses, also advocate nursing babies and provide some training.

La Leche League Canada and the Infant Feeding Action Coalition both encourage mothers to breastfeed. However, they approach the issue differently. La Leche provides information and support, often on a one-to-one basis; Infact is more concerned with fostering the cause with the population, leading to changes in how society in general views breastfeeding.

Although these organisations work to educate the population and foster positive attitudes towards breastfeeding, the medical community has the primary responsibility of working with pregnant women on a one-to-one basis to encourage a positive decision. Physicians may see the benefits of breastfeeding, but because of time pressures (and their own billings), some physicians are reluctant to make more than passing mention of the topic to their patients. In some communities, nurses, some with special training, have established fee-for-service practices to prepare prospective mothers to breastfeed and to provide support for the practice.

Based on the facts and the support of governments, nonprofit organisations, and the health community, it might be expected that all mothers would nurse for at least the minimum recommended time. However, this is far from the case. Several forces operate in opposition.

First, the excellent marketing skills of the producers and distributors of commercial infant formula affect prospective mothers. For many years, these firms have used substantial promotion budgets to extol the benefits of prepared formula to prospective mothers and to the parents of newborns. Physicians are provided with abundant supplies of samples to be given to mothers. In many cases, the manufacturers have obtained the names, addresses, and phone numbers of prospective and/or new mothers and approached them directly at the time when the final decision to breastfeed or not is being made.

There is evidence that the manufacturers' practice of distributing gift packs of formula to breastfeeding mothers results in mothers feeding for shorter periods to time. This trend is especially noted in less educated mothers, first-time mothers, and those who become ill. The cost of bottle feeding is high ($1,500 to $3,000 per year versus almost no cost to breastfeeding). In some circles, it was once viewed as a sign of love to lavish money on formula. Breastfeeding was viewed as something that only people who could not afford formula did. It was believed that the more affluent, knowledgeable people fed scientifically balanced commercial formulas.

Social and cultural pressures also discourage breastfeeding. A segment of the population views breastfeeding as a bodily function that should not be seen or discussed in public. Some people link the process to sex. For example, Jim Duff, a talk-show host on Montreal radio station CJAD, invited a guest expert to talk about breastfeeding. He received several phone calls saying that radio was not the place to talk about sexual matters and telling him to get this "dirty stuff" off the air!

Recently a woman breastfeeding her baby in public in Westmont Square (an upscale Montreal shopping centre) was asked to leave by a security guard. Although she left, the incident was reported to the media and was featured in the news, alerting many people to the issue of breastfeeding in public. As a result of the extensive coverage, the management of the shopping centre issued an apology.

The Canadian (and American) obsession with women's breasts as sex objects has caused some people to lose sight of their primary function. For example, a surprisingly large number of women have undergone expensive, painful breast enlargement that jeopardises their health. Hooters, a slang expression for the female breast, became the name for a fast-growing U.S. restaurant chain that features women servers wearing skimpy clothing. The obsession with breasts is misleading in that the breasts exposed in

TABLE 2

Reasons for Stopping Breastfeeding

Insufficient milk

Inconvenience/fatigue

Technique

Nipple engorgement

Illness (mother's or infant's)

Planned to stop early

Infant weight loss

Inadequate diet of mother

Back to work

Other

ads, movies, and other public settings tend to be those of women who have never been pregnant.

The success of encouraging new mothers to breastfeed is largely intuitive and based on a number of regional studies. Although a Canadian benchmark study was conducted in 1982, there has not been a recent national study. Experts believe that the percentage of women who breastfeed has risen over the years, but it is still significantly below the total number of mothers who are capable of feeding (it is estimated that fewer than 5 percent of mothers have medical reasons for not breastfeeding). Recent estimates place Canadian breastfeeding initiation rates at about 80 percent (compared to 70 percent in 1982 and 38 percent in 1963). This means that a large percentage of currently pregnant women were themselves bottle-fed rather than breastfed. It is possible that how these women were fed may influence their decision on how to feed their own children. However, the percentage of the mothers breastfeeding at six months has remained constant at 30 percent. The average duration is estimated at three months.

Work still remains to increase the participation rate, especially in Quebec and the Maritimes and with Aboriginal and poor, less educated women.

It is desirable to extend the length of time that babies are nursed. Clearly, mothers who start but then discontinue quickly begin with a positive attitude towards nature's choice of feeding babies. Many reasons are cited for ceasing to breastfeed (see Table 2). The most common reasons include:

▷ lack of facilities or locations to feed in public (some people do not accept the sight of a baby feeding in front of them).

▷ the need for the mother to be present for all feedings. The task cannot be shared with another person, even in the middle of the night when the mother is exhausted.

▷ the mother's returning to work.

▷ lack of support from the father, family members, and health care providers.

Solutions exist for each of these problems. To achieve acceptance, we must educate the public to the natural, necessary act of feeding a baby, and train mothers on techniques for feeding in public areas, and reassure them that breastfeeding is acceptable at any time and place. We must also educate mothers on techniques for managing the availability and storage of their milk.

TABLE 3

Number of Births

	1992	Rate per 1,000
Newfoundland	7,510	13.0
Prince Edward Island	1,890	14.5
Nova Scotia	11,990	13.2
New Brunswick	9,570	13.1
Quebec	97,520	14.1
Ontario	152,190	15.0
Manitoba	17,420	15.9
Saskatchewan	15,430	15.6
Alberta	42,580	16.6
British Columbia	46,040	13.9
Yukon	570	20.2
North West Territories	1,580	28.0
CANADA	404,290	14.7

Source: Statistics Canada

Studies in which mothers were contacted by health professionals every two or three weeks to answer questions and to reinforce the activity show significantly higher rates of continuance to at least the minimum recommended time. Similar results are achieved when the mother's partner, peers, and other family members support the process. In addition to convincing mothers to breastfeed for at least the recommended time, we must encourage their immediate family and friends to support their decision for at least six months.

Although it is beneficial to make health professionals aware of the positive impact they can have on breastfeeding, the economic realities are that there are limited resources available to support the program formally. Major support has to be obtained from nonprofessional sources, who must be made aware of the role that they could play.

The target market for breastfeeding promotion is relatively small and spread across Canada. Approximately 15 babies are born in any year for every 1,000 Canadians. If the statistics are recalculated to include only women in the main child-bearing ages of 20 to 34 years, the rate increases dramatically. Table 3 provides a breakdown of births by province.

Table 4 estimates the number of various types of health professionals in each province who may be active in some way in the decision to breastfeed and the length of time mothers continue.

Discussion Questions

1. List and evaluate at least seven areas in which marketing may help to change attitudes and behaviour towards breastfeeding.

2. Decide which opportunity you would like to address, justify your choice, and then develop a marketing strategy for your province, keeping in mind the limited resources available.

	Community Health Nurses	GPs and Family Medicine	Paediatrics	Obstetrics and Gynaecology
Canada	**10,880**	**27,929**	**1,891**	**1,583**
Newfoundland	329	590	34	21
Prince Edward Island	80	105	4	10
Nova Scotia	433	981	60	48
New Brunswick	474	600	23	49
Quebec	1,691	7,019	486	421
Ontario	5,133	10,402	752	650
Manitoba	784	1,073	116	59
Saskatchewan	379	948	41	37
Alberta	695	2,415	171	124
British Columbia	827	3,722	202	161
Yukon and North West Territories	55	74	2	2

TABLE 4

Selected Health Professionals by Province

▶ **CASE V.18**

The Tylenol crisis

Pain relievers are a lucrative, $1.2-billion-a-year industry. Until recently, there were no chemical or medicinal differences among brands of nonaspirin pain relievers, so aggressive marketing was the key to gain market share—$130 million was spent on advertising for pain relievers in one recent year. Johnson & Johnson, producer of Tylenol analgesic, developed very successful marketing strategies and obtained the largest share of the pain reliever market, 37 percent, in a matter of a few years.

In 1959, Johnson & Johnson acquired McNeil Laboratories, which had introduced the Tylenol brand in 1955 in the form of an elixir for children without the irritating side effects of aspirin. Traditionally, Tylenol was sold "ethically" through physicians and pharmacists and not directly to end-use consumers. It was sold only as a prescription drug until 1960 and then as a nonprescription drug advertised only to doctors and pharmacists, who in turn recommended it to patients.

In 1975 Bristol-Myers introduced its own nonaspirin pain reliever, Datril, successfully marketing it directly to end users. Datril's success spurred Johnson & Johnson to expand its marketing effort to end users. The company cut prices, formed a sales force, and spent $8 million on advertising representing Tylenol as an alternative to aspirin. Tylenol's solid reputation among pharmacists and physicians gave it a definite competitive advantage with end-use consumers because they perceived it as a safe product endorsed by health professionals. In fact, two of every three Tylenol customers started using the product because it was recommended by their doctors.

In 1976, Extra-Strength Tylenol was introduced, the first product to contain 500 milligrams of painkiller per tablet. Market research then indicated that many consumers believed Tylenol was too gentle to be effective. Extra-Strength Tylenol was advertised as the "most potent pain reliever available without a prescription." Tylenol's market share rose from 4 percent to 25 percent in 1979, due largely to the extra-strength version of the brand. In 1982, Tylenol had a 37 percent market share, as shown in Exhibit 1.

Competitors frantically tried to defend their brands against Tylenol. Excedrin, Anacin, and Bayer each introduced extra-strength versions with little success. Datril turned out to be a noncontender in the fight for market share because of a failure to build a favourable reputation among physicians and pharmacists. Tylenol seemed unbeatable. The product

EXHIBIT 1

Market shares: pain reliever industry

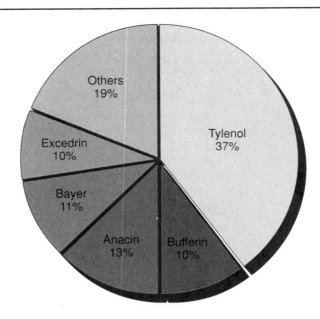

became the largest-selling health and beauty aid, outstripping the 18-year dominance of Procter & Gamble's Crest toothpaste.

Tylenol employed very aggressive competitive tactics to dominate the industry. Litigation became a significant competitive strategy, as Johnson & Johnson took several competitors to court with claims of infringement on Tylenol's trademark and name. Tylenol found that the use of litigation kept competitors from active competition for up to two years. After that time, the competition emerged in a weakened market position and seldom recovered. This strategy was especially effective against Anacin. Tylenol sued Anacin four times, once for trademark infringement and three times for false advertising, winning each time. One marketing expert went so far as to credit Johnson & Johnson with inventing the fifth "P" of marketing—plaintiff.

Then, in the early fall of 1982, a tragedy threatened the company's strong position. Eight Chicago-area consumers of Extra-Strength Tylenol took capsules that had been tampered with and laced with cyanide. The coupling of the Tylenol name with their deaths caused Tylenol's market share to drop from 37 percent to 7 percent overnight.

Research indicated many consumers came away with misconceptions about the poisoning incidents. Many consumers did not learn that (1) the company was absolved of all responsibility by the investigating authorities, (2) Tylenol's production process conformed to all safety standards, (3) only Tylenol capsules were involved, not tablets, and (4) the tragic deaths were confined to that single incident.

Tylenol's competitors benefited greatly from the tragedy. Anacin won about 25 percent of Tylenol's lost business, mainly by aggressively advertising Anacin-3, and Bufferin and Bayer each took 20 percent of Tylenol's business. Most experts predicted the Tylenol brand would never recover. The situation was described as a consumer goods marketer's darkest nightmare.

Very soon after the crisis, Johnson & Johnson made a strategic decision to attempt to save the Tylenol brand that had been so successful and profitable. The company had built up a reservoir of consumer trust and loyalty that management felt could play a key role in the brand's recovery. The company had always tried to live up to the credo set for it in the

1940s by its leader, General Robert Wood Johnson: "We believe our first responsibility is to the doctors, nurses, and patients, to mothers and all others who use our products and services. In meeting their needs, everything we do must be of high quality." Company management interpreted the crisis as a monumental challenge to live up to this credo against overwhelming odds.

Discussion questions

1. What tactics should Johnson & Johnson have used to rebuild consumer trust in Tylenol?

2. What lessons are there for marketers of drug products in Tylenol's response to the crisis, which resulted in the recovery of 90 percent of the lost market share in less than one year?

3. Should Johnson & Johnson have abandoned Tylenol and marketed a new brand?

Source: This case was prepared by Margaret L. Friedman, Assistant Professor, School of Business, University of Wisconsin–Whitewater. Used by permission. Based on "Tylenol, the Painkiller, Gives Rivals Headache in Stores and in Court," *The Wall Street Journal,* Sept. 2, 1982; "A Death Blow for Tylenol?" *Business Week,* Oct. 18, 1982, p. 151; "The Fight to Save Tylenol," *Fortune,* Nov. 29, 1982, pp. 44–49; "Rivals Go After Tylenol's Market, but Gains May Be Only Temporary," *The Wall Street Journal,* Dec. 2, 1982, pp. 25ff; and taken from J. Paul Peter and James M. Donnelly, *Marketing Management: Knowledge and Skills* (Homewood, Ill.: Richard D. Irwin, 1989), pp. 573–76.

▶ **CASE VI.19**

Advice for a new friend

My wife and I were spending our first evening at the Club Med village on the island of Eleuthera in the Bahamas. When we entered the dining room the hostess, as is the custom at Club Med, seated us at a table with six strangers who introduced themselves, followed by the usual Club Med questions: "Where are you from? Have you been to Club Med before (and if yes, which ones)? What do you do for a living?"

At this first evening's dinner, my wife and I were fortunate to meet another couple, Jackie and Peter Throtmorton, who live in Montreal. The four of us hit it off and we started to spend a lot of time together.

Later in the week Peter and I were sitting on the beach having a drink while we watched the sun sink behind the Carribean sea. Peter looked at me, took a deep breath, and began to speak.

"I know that we are both on vacation, but something's bothering me. I hope you will indulge a new friend and allow me to talk business with you, and perhaps take advantage of your marketing expertise to solve my problem."

"In all modesty I am an excellent dentist. I graduated near the top of my class. I lecture at McGill's Faculty of Dentistry one morning per week. Other dentists consult me about the latest dental techniques. However, it bothers me that less competent dentists who have been in practice for less time than I, have bigger, more lucrative practices. Perhaps, since you are a marketing consultant, you could advise me on how to improve my practice."

"One problem is that the marketing of dentistry is very different and more limited than the marketing of most goods and services. Dentistry, like professions such as medicine, law, architecture, pharmacy and engineering, is regulated by a professional association that has been granted certain legal rights by the provincial government. In Quebec, the Order of Dentists has the authority to regulate the practice of dentistry, including the authority to reprimand, fine, or suspend the license to practice of dentists who do not adhere to the order's regulations."

"Perhaps I should start by telling you about my office. I have a staff of three competent, hard-working women (a receptionist, a hygienist, and a dental assistant) who have been with me for many years. My offices are located in a downtown medical/dental building. I have been in the same offices since I started to practice dentistry 11 years ago. When I set up my offices, I spent most of my money on installing the finest dental equipment. The waiting room is a simple, functional room. I didn't have extra money to spend on it. Besides, I think if your office is too lavish, your patients sit there and think, 'The dentist has got to get the cost of the office back. I'm paying for this beautiful office in high fees.' "

"By the way, that's not true. Every year the Order of Dentists publishes a suggested fee schedule for each dental procedure. Most dentists follow the suggested fees, although some do charge less. The suggested fee schedule is also used by insurance companies to set the rates they will pay on behalf of their clients. Between 30 and 40 percent of patients have some form of dental insurance. However, in most cases the insured patient still pays part of the bill."

"Regardless of the facts or of the insurance coverage, the cost of dentistry is an important concern of patients. A recent survey that asked people what they disliked most about going to the dentist ranked the cost second (after the noise of the drill and before the pain of the needle)."

"One of the things I am considering to improve my practice is to move to a shopping center when the lease on my present offices expires next spring. Opening dental offices in shopping centers is the hottest thing in dentistry today. Patients really like the convenience. They can combine their trips to the dentist with shopping and other errands. (The dental offices are open the same long hours as the other stores in the centers, which usually requires two dentists.)"

"In 1980 an Ontario firm called Trident started opening dental clinics in shopping centers. Eight years later the company has more than 90 franchised locations and is listed on the Toronto stock exchange. In Montreal, another firm has recently started to do the same thing."

"These shopping center locations produce a lot of business for a dentist. A good downtown practice has about 1,500 patients who come in regularly for a checkup, a cleaning, and any other treatment that may be needed. A good suburban practice may have 2,000 regular patients plus another 1,000 who come in when they have a problem. A shopping center location, once developed, could serve 4,000 or 5,000 patients."

"At present, I have 1,120 regular patients in my practice. It is not only a question of building my practice to the desired level, but of keeping it there. Every year I lose between 5 and 10 percent of my patients because of things that cannot be controlled. Some move away, some die, and some leave because they are dissatisfied for various reasons. It is not realistic to expect to keep all your patients happy. For that matter, when a new patient comes to see you, it does not mean that he or she will stay with you. In my practice, about 40 percent of the people who come in for a first examination stay and become regular patients."

"The process of selecting a dentist is rather difficult for people. Patients can't see what is going on in their mouth. Even if they could, they wouldn't be qualified to judge the quality of the work. I really don't know how most people pick a dentist."

"Last year I hired a third-year marketing student from McGill to do a little marketing research for me. He called a sample of my current patients as well as a sample of those who had left my practice. He summarized the respondents' comments for me (see Table 1). But I am not sure how to interpret them and what use, if any, they may have in making my practice grow."

"Why don't I advertise for more patients? Occasionally I do run ads in the professional classified section of the *Gazette*. However, advertising is strictly regulated by the Quebec

TABLE 1

Responses to Dentist's Questionnaire

A. Why do you go to Dr. Throtmorton?

"He is close to where I work."
"Some of my friends go to him and they are satisfied."
"His office is close to my children's school. It's easy to get there with the kids."
"I heard from somebody that he is a really good dentist."
"His office is close to my house. I make my appointments so that I see him on the way to or from work."
"He hardly ever hurts me—he must be good."
"If he teaches dentistry at McGill, he must be a good dentist."
"The subway takes me right to his building."
"My G.P. once looked in a patient's mouth and saw an especially well-looked-after set of teeth. He asked the name of the patient's dentist and he and his family started to go to Dr. Throtmorton. If Dr. Throtmorton is good enough for my doctor, he is good enough for me."
"I don't know. I don't know who would be a better dentist."

B. Reasons why patients stopped going to Dr. Throtmorton (excluding those who moved away from Montreal or who died).

"I sat in his chair for an hour at a time and he hardly said anything to me. I got bored."
"His fees are too high. My other dentist charges less for a checkup and a cleaning."
"I can't put my finger on it exactly, but I got the feeling from sitting in his waiting room that he is not successful. Who wants to go to a second-rate dentist?"
"I don't like his personality."
"His breath smells."
"Every time I went to him he talked about the same things—skiing and the high cost of living."
"Often when my mouth was open and full of dental apparatus, he would accept a phone call from a friend and talk about some social thing."
"I just didn't feel comfortable in his office."
"I can't afford his prices. I don't have any dental insurance."
"I am nervous enough when I go to the dentist. His waiting room seems to depress me. Can't he afford to redo his office in a bright, cheerful decor?"
"I changed jobs and found a dentist close to my new office."

Order of Dentists. I am permitted to advertise in a purely professional manner (calling card advertising: my name, address, phone number, specialty, and educational degrees). I am prohibited from advertising anything else, such as the prices I charge, or the fact that I offer my patients nitrous oxide (laughing gas), or that my chairs are now equipped with stereo headphones. The promotion regulations are comprehensive. They even cover when I am permitted to include my photograph in an ad and the size and wording of the sign outside my office."

"There is a little leeway in getting my name in front of the public. The Order of Dentists does allow dentists to appear on radio or TV shows or to write a newspaper column about dentistry in general. However, the dentist may not use the occasion to promote his or her own practice. That is, in the introduction I could state my name, profession, and specialty (if any), but I could not mention my address or phone number or suggest that callers or writers contact me for diagnosis or treatment."

"Because of the very limited number of shows and columns that media offer about dentistry, the competition is very strong for these few openings. In addition, some dentists solicit invitations to talk to groups and clubs about general interest dental topics. However, it takes a certain type of personality to appear on shows or to speak to large groups of people. I don't think I would feel comfortable doing it."

"Occasionally I get new patients because people see my sign outside my office or they find my name in the Yellow Pages. This type of patient comes to my office because it is conveniently located. It does not have anything to do with my expertise."

"Because of the severe promotional limitation, most dentists build their practices through word-of-mouth advertising by friends, relatives, and satisfied patients. When somebody refers a patient to me, I call to thank him or her. I hope this will encourage them to tell more people about my practice. I don't know what else I can do to encourage people to refer patients to me."

"I apologize for talking business while we are on vacation, but I am very concerned about the possibility of moving my office. Moving is very expensive because a dental office requires special plumbing and electrical installations. Beyond the cost, I don't know if the move will expand my practice to the size it should be, based on my expertise and years of practice."

"What do you think? What should I do?"

▶ **CASE V.20**

Purchasing a treadmill

Saturday, September 2

Dear Diary: Today Myra and I decided to buy our daughter Stephanie a gift. She just moved to Long Island, New York, to start medical school and she misses her daily exercise on the treadmill we have at home. I remembered receiving a Warehouse Store catalogue that featured a 2 horsepower treadmill (with speeds up to 10 miles per hour) on sale for $349.50 U.S. plus 7 percent tax. After converting to Canadian funds, the treadmill will cost us $517.

We called the 800 number from the catalogue and found out that the treadmill could be delivered within a 21-mile radius of a store for a cost of $38.50. Fortunately, a store within the stipulated distance of Stephanie's home had the treadmill in stock.

Then the problem started.

The representative took all the information, including my credit card number. Then she told us that Stephanie would have to go to the store and pay the $38.50 for delivery. This was not what we wanted; Stephanie did not know her way around Long Island, and she didn't have the time to go to the store. We explained this, but the rep said she did not have the authority to change the rules for us. We asked to speak to the supervisor and started the whole process over again. She too said, "I'm sorry I can't do anything about the store rules, even if you are willing to pay C.O.D. or send us a cheque by mail. But if you don't mind holding I will call the store and speak to the manager and find out if she can do something for you." After a minute or two Suzanne Jefferson, the supervisor, returned with a ray of hope. "The store manager does not have the authority to help you. However, she said if you call Jack French after 9.00 A.M. local 3450 at this same toll-free number (1 (800) 555-1212) on Tuesday (Monday is Labour Day) she is sure that he will be able to do something for you. In the meantime, I will process the order as a pickup so that you will still get the sale price (which ends tomorrow)."

Tuesday, September 5

Dear Diary: Today I spent a lot of time on the phone. First I called the 800 number to speak to Jack French. The woman who answered asked for my name, phone number, and zip code and then asked how she could help me. I insisted on speaking to Jack French. He said he would arrange for the cost of delivery to be added to my credit card bill. The trucking company would call Stephanie to arrange for delivery at a suitable time (apparently the Warehouse Store contracts out its deliveries).

I left my office for a meeting with a client. When I returned there were two messages on my voice mail from the store's order verification department. The first said that because the banks were closed for Labour Day, credit verification could not be made and the pre-paid pickup order would not be ready before Wednesday. (No problem, we wanted delivery on Friday or Saturday.) The second message was that the order information was incomplete. They needed my full address, zip code, phone number, and the name of my bank. (For some reason the address they had for was Johnson City, Tennessee.) I was to call another 800 number, 1 (800) 555-6286.

Unfortunately, this second toll-free number was not valid from Canada, so I called Jack French's number and was asked for my name, phone number, and zip code. The clerk now entered the order number that had been left on my voice mail. He said this could not be my order because it was for somebody in Johnson City, Tennessee. Nor he did know how to access the other 800 number, which was not familiar to him.

After returning from another client meeting, I found the third message from the store's order verification department (apparently the same nameless person). This time she said that since I hadn't returned her call, she was cancelling the order. If I wanted to reorder, I should provide all the needed information, including a daytime phone number where I could be reached.

Wednesday, September 6

Dear Diary: Since I knew that this would be an especially busy day for me, first thing in the morning I called Jack French. Again I was asked for my name, phone number, and zip code, followed by "How can I help you?" My answer was short and direct: "I want to talk to Jack French or the president of the Warehouse Store and I don't care which one you put on the line." (When I asked for the name and fax number of the president the clerk told me his name but said that she could not give me his fax number.)

Shortly after that I was connected to Jack French. He assured me that he would reinstate the order at the sale price. After he entered the order number into his computer, he was able to piece together the problem. The computer could not match my zip code and phone number with the delivery address. This flagged the order to the attention of the fraud and order verification department. The person entering the order had problems entering Canadian data with a U.S. delivery address, and Johnson, Tennessee was where the Warehouse Store's mail order centre was located. Jack apologized for cancelling the order and told me that of the store's 15 toll-free numbers, only one worked from Canada. Unfortunately, the person in order verification did not know this.

I told him that I had spent about four hours on the phone trying to order the machine and at my hourly rate I had already put in more time than the treadmill is worth. Since I knew that many reputable firms offer compensation when customers are inconvenienced, I asked what the store would do for me. Without hesitation, Jack offered to pay for the delivery of the treadmill, a saving of $38.50. He promised to have the store call Stephanie to arrange for delivery on Friday. Let's hope the problem has been resolved.

Thursday, September 7

Dear Diary: We spoke to Stephanie at 11:00 tonight. She still has not heard from the store and she was wondering if she should wait at home tomorrow morning for the delivery.

Friday, September 8

Dear Diary: Today started like many other days this week. I called the Warehouse Store, gave my name, phone number, and zip code, and had to insist on speaking to Jack French.

I started by telling him how difficult it was to get through to him and how frustrating was the routine of name, phone number, zip code and how can I help you. He said he knew because he had called in acting as a customer. The 800 number was for mail order and answered 24 hours a day. Because customer service was short staffed and worked shorter hours, mail order answered its calls. The store recently recognised the importance of improving its customer service, because any competitor can match prices. The opportunity for differentiation and customer loyalty is through superior customer service. Unfortunately, all the needed changes are not yet in place, but he assured me they are working on it.

He was surprised that Stephanie had not heard from the store. He promised to call the store and get back to me shortly. About two hours later he called back.

The store had found that there was only one treadmill in stock, the box was broken, and the treadmill might be damaged. They did not want to take the chance and send it to Stephanie. However, they had a discontinued version that was being cleared out and I could save $75 if I accepted this model. The older model was smaller and slower than the one that we wanted, so we decided to wait for the new shipment of treadmills, which is supposed to arrive in about 10 days.

Jack French, then offered to reduce our price by $25 so that we would pay $325 including delivery. I accepted and I told him that I would call him in about a week.

Thursday, September 21
Dear Diary: Stephanie told us that she is feeling very lethargic. After full days at school followed by long hours of studying, she really needs her treadmill. I called 1 (800) 555-1212 and went through the whole ritual of name, phone number, and zip code. Two hours later, Jack French called back to say the treadmill is still in transit and he will call me when it comes in.

Monday, October 2
Dear Diary: Stephanie is getting very impatient. So instead of waiting for Jack French to call me, I will call him tomorrow morning in the hope that Stephanie will have her treadmill this Friday afternoon.

Post Script
Stephanie finally received the treadmill in early November, a full two months after the process began.

Discussion Questions

1. Is the buying behaviour of the diary writer typical or not? How might other people act when the order taker said she did not have the authority to change the rules for the customer?

2. Evaluate the customer service of each of the people/positions that the diary writer came into contact with. What should the Warehouse Store do to make it easier for customers to do business with the firm?

▼ Notes

Chapter 1

1. The popular business press frequently features articles on the importance of organisations staying close to consumers. For examples, see Terence P. Pare, "Banks Discover the Consumer," *Fortune,* February 12, 1990, pp. 96–104; Stephen Phillips et al., "King Customer," *Business Week,* pp. 88–94; Patricia Sellers, "What Customers Really Want," *Fortune,* June 4, 1990, pp. 58–68; Frank Rose, "Now Quality Means Service Too," *Fortune,* April 22, 1991, pp. 97–108.

2. Peter D. Bennett, *Dictionary of Marketing Terms* (Chicago: American Marketing Association, 1988), p. 40.

Chapter 2

1. See Albert Bandura, "The Self System in Reciprocal Determinism," *American Psychologist,* April 1978, p. 346; also see Albert Bandura, *Social Foundations of Thought and Action: A Social Cognitive Theory* (Englewood Cliffs, N.J.: Prentice Hall, 1986).

2. See Keith H. Hammond, "The 'Blacktop' Is Paving Reebok's Road to Recovery," *Business Week,* August 12, 1991, p. 27.

Chapter 3

1. Geoffrey Smith, "Does Gillette Know How to Treat a Lady?" *Business Week,* August 27, 1990, pp. 64–6.

2. This discussion of VALS 2 is abstracted from Martha Farnsworth Riche, "Psychographics for the 1990s," *American Demographics,* July 1989, pp. 24–26ff. Besides the famous VALS 2 and Goldfarb Consultants segmentation schemes, many Canadians have attempted to segment the market in a variety of innovative ways. See Bruce Cameron, "Varying Shades of Green: Segmenting Canadian Consumers on Environmental Attitudes and Behaviour," *Marketing,* vol. 14, Administrative Sciences Association of Canada, 1993, p. 290; Thomas P. Novak and Bruce MacEvoy, "On Comparing Alternative Segmentation Schemes: The List of Values (LOV) and Values and Lifestyles (VALS)," *Journal of Consumer Research* 17, 1, June 1990, pp. 105–109; Anne T. Hale, "A Method for Monitoring Temporal Changes in Market Segmentations," *Marketing,* vol. 14, 1993, pp. 96–105; Lanita Carter, "A Market Segmentation Model for Food Consumption Behaviour," *Marketing,* vol. 11, 1990, pp. 74–83; Christian Dussart and Jean-Pierre Bayard, "Segmentation . . . To Be or Not to Be? That Is Not the Right Question!," *Marketing,* vol. 11, 1990, pp. 118–127; Eugene Kaciak amd Jerome N. Sheahan, "Marketing Segmentation: An Alternative Principal Components Approach," *Marketing,* vol. 9, 1988, pp. 139–148; Patrick G. Buckley, "A Psychographic Profile of Students Involved in Adult Education," *Marketing,* vol. 9, 1988, pp. 149–158.

3. Lisa Kassenaar, "Card Holders Scramble for Points Payoff," *Financial Post,* September 10, 1994, p. S23. For other interesting approaches to market segmentation, see Anne T. Hale, "A Method for Monitoring Temporal Changes in Market Segmentations," *Marketing,* vol. 14, pp. 96–105; Lanita S. Carter, "A Market Segmentation Model for Food Consumption Behaviour," *Marketing,* vol. 11, 1990, pp. 74–83.

4. Peter R. Dickson, "Person-Situation: Segmentation's Missing Link," *Journal of Marketing,* Fall 1982, p. 57.

5. Shirley Young, Leland Ott, and Barbara Feigin, "Some Practical Considerations in Market Segmentation," *Journal of Marketing Research,* August 1978, p. 405.

6. David Greising, "Whap! Ace. Point. You Call This Tennis?" *Business Week,* September 9, 1991, p. 71.

7. Alex Taylor III, "How Buick Is Bouncing Back," *Fortune,* May 6, 1991, pp. 83–88.

Chapter 4

1. Bob Macklin, "Dole Doles Out New Juices," *Marketing*, November 1993.

2. C. E. Izard, "Emotion-Cognition Relationships and Human Development," in *Emotions, Cognition, and Behavior,* ed. C. E. Izard, J. Kagan, and R. B. Zajonc (New York: Cambridge University Press, 1984), pp. 17–37; Rom Harre, David Clarke, and Nicola De Carlo, *Motives and Mechanisms: An Introduction to the Psychology of Action* (London: Methuen, 1985), ch. 2, pp. 20–39; Martin L. Hoffman, "Affect, Cognition, and Motivation," in *Handbook of Motivation and Cognition,* ed. R. M. Sorrentino and E. T. Higgins (New York: Guilford Press, 1986), pp. 244–80; and Robert Plutchik, *Emotion: A Psychoevolutionary Synthesis* (New York: Harper & Row, 1980).

3. Rik G. M. Pieters and W. Fred Van Raaij, "Functions and Management of Affect: Applications to Economic Behavior," *Journal of Economic Psychology* 9 (1988), pp. 251–82.

4. Werner Kroeber-Riel, "Activation Research: Psychobiological Approaches in Consumer Research," *Journal of Consumer Research,* March 1979, pp. 240–50.

5. Meryl Paula Gardner, "Mood States and Consumer Behavior: A Critical Review," *Journal of Consumer Research,* December 1985, pp. 281–300.

6. See Harre et al., *Motives and Mechanisms: An Introduction to the Psychology of Action;* Robert B. Zajonc and Hazel Markus, "Affective and Cognitive Factors in Preferences," *Journal of Consumer Research* 9 (1982), pp. 123–31; Hoffman, "Affect, Cognition, and Motivation," pp. 244–80; Robert B. Zajonc, "On the Primacy of Affect," *American Psychologist* 39 (1984), pp. 117–23; and Richard S. Lazarus, "On the Primacy of Cognition," *American Psychologist* 39 (1984), pp. 124–29.

7. Michael K. Hui and John E. G. Bateson, "Perceived Control and the Effects of Crowding and Consumer Choice on the Service Experience," *Journal of Consumer Research,* September 1991, pp. 174–84; and Michael Hui and Lianxi Zhou, "The Effects of Waiting Time Information on Consumers' Reactions to Delays in Services," *Marketing,* vol. 14, 1993, pp. 123–130.

8. For example, see the exchange between Yehoshua Tsal, "On the Relationship between Cognitive and Affective Processes: A Critique of Zajonc and Markus," *Journal of Consumer Research* 12 (1985), pp. 358–64; Zajonc and Markus, "Affective and Cognitive Factors in Preferences"; and Robert B. Zajonc and Hazel Markus, "Must All Affect Be Mediated by Cognition?" *Journal of Consumer Research* 12 (1985), pp. 363–64.

9. Lazarus, "On the Primacy of Cognition," pp. 124–29; Pieters and Van Raaij, "Functions and Management of Affect: Applications to Economic Behavior," pp. 251–82; and Richard S. Lazarus, "Cognition and Motivation in Emotion," *American Psychologist,* April 1991, pp. 352–67; and Louis Fabien, "L'habilite cognitive et les strategies d'acquisition de l'information du consommateur," *Marketing,* vol. 9, 1988, pp. 78–87. For a discussion of children's cog-

nitive processing, see Caroline Espiard and Corinne Berneman, "La comprehension des messages publicitaires et le developpement cognitif des enfants," *Marketing,* vol. 14, 1993, pp. 67–76.

10. S. S. Tomkins, "Affect Theory," in *Emotion in the Human Face,* ed. P. Ekman (Cambridge, England: Cambridge University Press, 1983); Robert B. Zajonc, "On the Primacy of Affect," *American Psychologist* 39 (1984), pp. 117–23; and Richard S. Lazarus, "On the Primacy of Cognition," *American Psychologist* 39 (1984), pp. 124–29; and Laurette Dube-Rioux, "Affective Categorization: A New Perspective on Customer Satisfaction," *Marketing,* vol. 10, 1989, pp. 118–129.

11. For example, see Julie A. Edell and Marian Chapman Burke, "The Power of Feelings in Understanding Advertising Effects," *Journal of Consumer Research,* December 1987, pp. 421–33; William J. Havlena, and Morris B. Holbrook, "The Varieties of Consumption Experience: Comparing Two Typologies of Emotion in Consumer Behavior," *Journal of Consumer Research,* December 1986, pp. 394–404; Morris B. Holbrook and Rajeev Batra, "Assessing the Role of Emotions as Mediators of Consumer Responses to Advertising," *Journal of Consumer Research,* December 1987, pp. 404–20; and Rajeev Batra and Douglas M. Stayman, "The Role of Mood in Advertising Effectiveness," *Journal of Consumer Research,* September 1990, pp. 203–14.

12. For example, see Hoffman, "Affect, Cognition, and Motivation," pp. 244–80.

13. Dawn Dobni and George M. Zinkhan, "In Search of Brand Image: A Foundation Analysis," in *Advances in Consumer Research,* vol. 17, eds. M. Goldberg, G. Gorn, and R. Pollay (Provo, Utah: Association for Consumer Research, 1990), pp. 110–19; and Ernest Dichter, "What's in an Image?" *Journal of Consumer Marketing,* Winter 1985, pp. 75–81.

14. John R. Rossiter, Larry Percy, and Robert J. Donovan, "A Better Advertising Planning Grid," *Journal of Advertising Research,* October–November 1991, pp. 11–21; and Brian Ratchford, "New Insights about the FCB Grid," *Journal of Advertising Research,* August–September 1987, pp. 24–38.

15. Mark Maremont, "They're All Screaming for Haagen-Dazs," *Business Week,* October 14, 1991, p. 121.

16. Kathleen Deveny, "As Lauder's Scent Battles Calvin Klein's, Cosmetics Whiz Finds Herself on the Spot," *The Wall Street Journal,* June 27, 1991, pp. B1, B6.

17. One complex information processing model of consumer decision making is by John Howard and Jagdish Sheth, *The Theory of Buyer Behavior* (New York: John Wiley & Sons, 1969). Another is James R. Bettman, *An Information Processing Model of Consumer Choice* (Reading Mass.: Addison-Wesley, 1979).

18. Alan M. Collins and Elizabeth F. Loftus, "A Spreading Activation Theory of Semantic Memory," *Psychological Review* 82 (1975), pp. 407–28.

19. John R. Anderson, "A Spreading Activation Theory of Memory," *Journal of Verbal Learning and Verbal Behavior*

22 (1983), pp. 261–75; and Collins and Loftus, "A Spreading Activation Theory of Semantic Memory," pp. 407–28.

20. John A. Bargh, "Automatic and Conscious Processing of Social Information," in *Handbook of Social Cognition,* vol. 3, ed. R. S. Wyer and T. K. Srull (Hillsdale, N.J.: Lawrence Erlbaum, 1984), pp. 1–43; and Richard M. Shiffrin and Susan T. Dumais, "The Development of Automatism," in *Cognitive Skills and Their Development,* ed. John R. Anderson (Hillsdale, N.J.: Lawrence Erlbaum, 1981), pp. 111–40.

21. Jeffrey F. Durgee and Robert W. Stuart, "Advertising Symbols and Brand Names that Best Represent Key Product Meanings," *Journal of Advertising,* Summer 1987, pp. 15–24.

22. Wayne A. Wickelgren, "Human Learning and Memory," in *Annual Review of Psychology,* ed. M. R. Rosenzweig and L. W. Porter (Palo Alto, Calif.: Annual Reviews, 1981), pp. 21–52.

23. John R. Anderson, *The Architecture of Cognition* (Cambridge, Mass.: Harvard University Press, 1983); and Terence R. Smith, Andrew A. Mitchell, and Robert Meyer, "A Computational Process Model of Evaluation Based on the Cognitive Structuring of Episodic Knowledge," in *Advances in Consumer Research,* vol. 9, ed. Andrew A. Mitchell (Ann Arbor, Mich.: Association for Consumer Research, 1982), pp. 136–43.

24. Endel Tulving, "Episodic and Semantic Memory," in *Organization of Memory,* ed. Endel Tulving (New York: Academic Press, 1972), pp. 382–404.

25. Merrie Brucks and Andrew Mitchell, "Knowledge Structures, Production Systems, and Decision Strategies," in *Advances in Consumer Research,* vol. 8, ed. Kent B. Monroe (Ann Arbor, Mich.: Association for Consumer Research, 1982).

26. Donald A. Norman, *The Psychology of Everyday Things* (New York: Basic Books, 1988).

27. Bruce Nussbaum and Robert Neff, "I Can't Work This Thing!" *Business Week,* April 29, 1991, pp. 58–66.

28. Although many types of memory structures have been proposed, most can be reduced to the more general associative network model. See James R. Bettman, "Memory Factors in Consumer Choice: A Review," *Journal of Marketing,* Spring 1979, pp. 37–53; Andrew A. Mitchell, "Models of Memory: Implications for Measuring Knowledge Structures," in *Advances in Consumer Research,* vol. 9, ed. Andrew A. Mitchell (Ann Arbor, Mich.: Association for Consumer Research, 1982), pp. 45–51; and Edward Smith, "Theories of Semantic Memory," in *Handbook of Learning and Cognitive Processes,* vol. 6, ed. W. K. Estes (Hillsdale, N.J.: Lawrence Erlbaum, 1978), pp. 1–56.

29. Joseph W. Alba and Lynn Hasher, "Is Memory Schematic?" *Psychological Bulletin,* March 1983, pp. 203–31; and Donald E. Rumelhart and Anthony Ortony, "The Representation of Knowledge in Memory," in *Schooling and the Acquisition of Knowledge,* eds. R. C. Anderson, R. J. Spiro, and W. E. Montague (Hillsdale, N.J.: Lawrence Erlbaum, 1977), pp. 99–136.

30. Thomas W. Leigh and Arno J. Rethans, "Experiences with Script Elicitation within Consumer Decision-Making Contexts," in *Advances in Consumer Research,* vol. 10, ed. R. P. Baggozzi and A. M. Tybout (Ann Arbor, Mich.: Association for Consumer Research, 1983), pp. 667–72; and Roger C. Schank and Robert P. Abelson, *Scripts, Plans, Goals, and Understanding: An Inquiry into Human Knowledge Structures* (Hillsdale, N.J.: Lawrence Erlbaum, 1977).

Chapter 5

1. Gary Lamphler, "Chrysler in the Minivan Driver's Seat," *Financial Times,* August 19, 1985, p. 1; "Auto Sales Still Falling: Minivan Movement One of the Few Bright Spots in the Market," *Financial Post,* March 4/6, 1995, p. 3; and Data Sources: R. L. Polk Audit, Blackburn Polk Registration Services.

2. Eleanor Rosch, Carolyn B. Mervis, Wayne D. Gray, David M. Johnson, and Penny Boyes-Braem, "Basic Objects in Natural Categories," *Cognitive Psychology,* July 1976, pp. 382–439; Mita Sujan, "Consumer Knowledge: Effects on Evaluation Strategies Mediating Consumer Judgments," *Journal of Consumer Research,* June 1985, pp. 31–46; Joel Cohen and Kunal Basu, "Alternative Models of Categorization: Toward a Contingent Processing Framework," *Journal of Consumer Research,* March 1987, pp. 455–72; Carolyn B. Mervis, "Category Structure and the Development of Categorization," in *Theoretical Issues in Reading Comprehension,* ed. Rand Spiro et al. (Hillsdale, N.J.: Lawrence Erlbaum, 1980), pp. 279–307.

3. For examples, see Joseph W. Alba and Amitava Chattopadhyay, "The Effects of Context and Part-Category Cues on the Recall of Competing Brands," *Journal of Marketing Research,* August 1985, pp. 340–49; Mita Sujan and Christine Dekleva, "Product Categorization and Inference Making: Some Implications for Comparative Advertising," *Journal of Consumer Research,* September 1987, pp. 141–54; Mita Sujan and James R. Bettman, "The Effects of Brand Positioning Strategies on Consumers' Brand and Category Perceptions: Some Insights from Schema Research," *Journal of Marketing Research,* November 1989, pp. 454–67.

4. Michael D. Johnson, "The Differential Processing of Product Category and Noncomparable Choice Alternatives," *Journal of Consumer Research,* December 1989, pp. 300–09; Jerry A. Rosenblatt and Michel J. Bergier, "A Critical Review of Past and Current Methodologies Used for Classifying English and French Canadians," in *Marketing,* vol. 3, 1982; and Jerry A. Rosenblatt and Michel J. Bergier, "Cross-Cultural Differences: Back to the Drawing Board," in *Marketing in the 1980s,* Proceedings of the Southern Marketing Association, New Orleans, 1982.

5. Zachary Schiller and Mark N. Varmmos, "Liquid Tide Looks like Solid Gold," *Business Week,* December 24, 1984, p. 32.

6. For example, Elizabeth C. Hirschman, "Attributes of Attributes and Layers of Meaning," in *Advances in Consumer Research,* vol. 7, ed. Jerry C. Olson (Ann Arbor, Mich.: Association for Consumer Research, 1980), pp. 7–12; and Lyle V. Geistfeld, George B. Sproles, and Susan B.

Badenhop, "The Concept and Measurement of a Hierarchy of Product Characteristics," in *Advances in Consumer Research,* vol. 4, ed. H. Keith Hunt (Ann Arbor, Mich.: Association for Consumer Research, 1977), pp. 302–7; Eugene Kaciak and Joan Mount, "A Comparison of Two Approaches to Measuring Attribute Importance," *Marketing,* vol. 11, 1990, pp. 167–177. An alternative way to measure attribute importance is shown by John P. Liefeld, Marjorie Wall, Greta Hofstra, and Louise Heslop, "Explicit vs. Conjoint Measurement of Attribute Importance: Convergent Validity," *Marketing,* vol. 9, 1988, pp. 38–47; Robert M. MacGregor, "Symbolic Slavery: Symbolic Consumption and Representational Images in the Exchange Processes," *Marketing,* vol. 10, 1989, pp. 216–224.

7. Theodore Levitt, "Marketing Myopia," *Harvard Business Review,* July–August 1960, pp. 45–56.

8. Paul E. Green, Yoram Wind, and Arun K. Jain, "Benefit Bundle Analysis," *Journal of Advertising Research,* April 1972, pp. 32–36; and Russell I. Haley, "Benefit Segmentation: A Decision-Oriented Research Tool," *Journal of Marketing,* July 1972, pp. 30–35.

9. For instance, Jonathan Gutman and Donald E. Vinson, "Values Structures and Consumer Behavior," in *Advances in Consumer Research,* vol. 6, ed. William L. Wilkie (Ann Arbor, Mich.: Association for Consumer Research, 1979), pp. 335–39; Janice G. Hanna, "A Typology of Consumer Needs," in *Research in Marketing,* vol. 3, ed. Jagdish N. Sheth (Greenwich, Conn.: JAI Press, 1980), pp. 83–104; and Lynn Kahle, "The Values of Americans: Implications for Consumer Adaptation," in *Personal Values & Consumer Psychology,* ed. Robert E. Pitts, Jr., and Arch G. Woodside (Lexington, Mass.: Lexington Books, 1984), pp. 77–86.

10. Anthony G. Greenwald and Anthony R. Pratkanis, "The Self," in *The Handbook of Social Cognition,* eds. Robert S. Wyer and Thomas K. Srull (Hillsdale, N.J.: Lawrence Erlbaum, 1984), pp. 129–78; Hazel Markus and Paula Nunus, "Possible Selves," *American Psychologist,* September 1986, pp. 954–69; John F. Kihlstrom and Nancy Cantor, "Mental Representations of the Self," in *Advances in Experimental Social Psychology,* 1984, pp. 1–47; Hazel Markus, "Self-Schemata and Processing Information about the Self," *Journal of Personality and Social Psychology,* 1977, pp. 63–78; and Hazel Markus and Keith Sentis, "The Self in Social Information Processing," in *Psychological Perspectives on the Self,* ed. J. Suis (Hillsdale, N.J.: Lawrence Erlbaum, 1982), pp. 41–70.

11. The basic idea of means-end chains can be traced back at least to Edward C. Tolman, *Purposive Behavior in Animals and Men* (New York: Century, 1932). Among the first to suggest its use in marketing was John A. Howard, *Consumer Behavior Application and Theory* (New York: McGraw-Hill, 1977). Jon Gutman and Tom Reynolds have been active proponents of means-end chain models. For example, see Jonathan Gutman and Thomas J. Reynolds, "An Investigation of the Levels of Cognitive Abstraction Utilized by Consumers in Product Differentiation," in *Attitude Research under the Sun,* ed. John Eighmey (Chicago: American Marketing Association, 1979), pp. 125–50; and Jonathan Gutman, "A Means-End Chain Model Based on Consumer Categorization Processes," *Journal of Marketing,* Spring 1982, pp. 60–72.

12. Shirley Young and Barbara Feigen, "Using the Benefit Chair for Improved Strategy Formulation," *Journal of Marketing,* July 1975, pp. 72–74; James H. Myers and Alan D. Schocker, "The Nature of Product-Related Attributes," in *Research in Marketing,* ed. J. N. Sheth (Greenwich, Conn.: JAI Press, 1981), pp. 211–36; Joel B. Cohen, "The Structure of Product Attributes: Defining Attribute Dimensions for Planning and Evaluation," in *Analytic Approaches to Product and Marketing Planning,* ed. A. D. Shocker (Cambridge, Mass.: Marketing Science Institute, 1979), pp. 54–86; Jonathan Gutman, "A Means-End Chain Model Based on Consumer Categorization Processes," *Journal of Marketing,* Spring 1982, pp. 60–72; and Jerry C. Olson, "The Theoretical Foundations of Means-End Chains," *Verbeforschung & Praxis* 5, 1990, pp. 174–78.

13. Jerry C. Olson and Thomas J. Reynolds, "Understanding Consumers' Cognitive Structures: Implications for Marketing Strategy," in *Advertising and Consumer Psychology,* vol. 1, ed. Larry Percy and Arch Woodside (Lexington Mass.: Lexington Books, 1983), pp. 77–90.

14. For a good example, see Sunil Mehrotra and John Palmer, "Relating Product Features to Perceptions of Quality: Appliances," in *Perceived Quality,* ed. Jacob Jacoby and Jerry Olson (Lexington, Mass.: Lexington Books, 1985), pp. 81–96.

15. Thomas J. Reynolds and Jonathan Gutman, "Laddering Theory, Method, Analysis, and Interpretation," *Journal of Advertising Research,* February–March 1988, pp. 11–31; Jonathan Gutman, "Exploring the Nature of Linkages between Consequences and Values," *Journal of Business Research,* 1991, pp. 143–48.

16. For a good example, see Jonathan Gutman and Scott D. Alden, 'Adolescents' Cognitive Structures of Retail Stores and Fashion Consumption: A Means-End Chain Analysis of Quality," in *Perceived Quality,* ed. Jacob Jacoby and Jerry Olson (Lexington, Mass.: Lexington Books, 1985), pp. 99–114.

17. One of the first and most influential writers about involvement was Herbert E. Krugman. See his "The Impact of Television Advertising: Learning without Involvement," *Public Opinion Quarterly,* 1965, pp. 349–56; and "The Measurement of Advertising Involvement," *Public Opinion Quarterly,* 1967, pp. 583–96.

18. For instance, see John H. Antil, "Conceptualization and Operationalization of Involvement," in *Advances in Consumer Research,* vol. 11, ed. Thomas C. Kinnear (Ann Arbor, Mich.: Association for Consumer Research, 1984), pp. 203–09; Andrew A. Mitchell, "Involvement: A Potentially Important Mediator of Consumer Behavior," in *Advances in Consumer Research,* vol. 6, ed. William Wilkie (Ann Arbor, Mich.: Association for Consumer Research, 1979), pp. 191–96; Robert N. Stone, "The Marketing Characteristics of Involvement," in *Advances in Consumer Research,* vol. 11, ed. Thomas C. Kinnear (Ann Arbor, Mich.: Association for Consumer Research, 1984), pp. 210–15; Peter N. Bloch, "An Exploration into the Scaling of Consumers' Involvement with a Product Class," in *Advances*

in Consumer Research, vol. 8, ed. Kent B. Monroe (Ann Arbor, Mich.: Association for Consumer Research, 1981), pp. 61–65; and Judith Lynne Zaichkowsky, "Measuring the Involvement Construct," *Journal of Consumer Research,* December 1985, pp. 341–52; Jerry A. Rosenblatt, "Interactive Effects in Information Processing: A Conceptual Framework of the Relationship of Consumer Involvement and Brand Categorization," in *Developments in Marketing Science,* Proceedings of the Academy of Marketing Science, May 1988; Jacques Csipak, Jean-Charles Chebat and Jerry A. Rosenblatt, "The Interactive Effects of Involvement and Information Processing Strategies: An Examination of the Transportation Service Sector," *Marketing,* vol. 15, 1994.

19. This section draws on Richard L. Celsi and Jerry C. Olson, "The Role of Involvement in Attention and Comprehension Processes," *Journal of Consumer Research,* September 1988, pp. 210–24; also see Andrew A. Mitchell, "The Dimensions of Advertising Involvement," in *Advances in Consumer Research,* vol. 8, ed. Kent B. Monroe (Ann Arbor, Mich.: Association for Consumer Research, 1981), pp. 25–30; and William L. Moore and Donald R. Lehmann, "Individual Differences in Search Behavior for a Nondurable," *Journal of Consumer Research,* December 1980, pp. 296–307.

20. Beth A. Walker and Jerry C. Olson, "Means-End Chains: Connecting Products with Self," *Journal of Business Research,* 1991, pp. 111–18.

21. Joel B. Cohen, "Involvement and You: 100 Great Ideas," in *Advances in Consumer Research,* vol. 9, ed. Andrew A. Mitchell (Ann Arbor, Mich.: Association for Consumer Research, 1982), pp. 324–27; Harold H. Kassarjian, "Low Involvement—A Second Look," in *Advances in Consumer Research,* vol. 8, ed. Kent B. Monroe (Ann Arbor, Mich.: Association for Consumer Research, 1981), pp. 31–34.

22. Celsi and Olson, "The Role of Involvement in Attention and Comprehension Processes," pp. 210–24. A similar perspective is provided by Peter H. Bloch and Marsha L. Richins, "A Theoretical Model of the Study of Product Importance Perceptions," *Journal of Marketing,* Summer 1983, pp. 69–81. Some researchers treat these two factors as two forms of involvement—enduring and situational involvement, respectively. For instance, see Michael J. Houston and Michael L. Rothschild, "Conceptual and Methodological Perspectives on Involvement," in *1978 Educators Proceedings,* ed. S. C. Jain (Chicago: American Marketing Association, 1978), pp. 184–87. We believe it is clearer to treat these factors as sources of involvement.

23. For a similar proposal, see Peter H. Bloch, "Involvement beyond the Purchase Process: Conceptual Issues and Empirical Investigation," in *Advances in Consumer Research,* vol. 9, ed. Andrew A. Mitchell (Ann Arbor, Mich.: Association for Consumer Research, 1982), pp. 413–17.

24. John Harris, "I Don't Want Good, I Want Fast," *Forbes,* October 1, 1990, p. 186.

25. Russell W. Belk, "Worldly Possessions: Issues and Criticisms," in *Advances in Consumer Research,* vol. 10, ed. Richard P. Baggozzi and Alice M. Tybout (Ann Arbor, Mich.: Association for Consumer Research, 1983),

pp. 514–19; and Terence A. Shimp and Thomas J. Madden, "Consumer-Object Relations: A Conceptual Framework Based Analogously on Sternberg's Triangular Theory of Love," in *Advances in Consumer Research,* vol. 15, ed. Michael J. Houston (Ann Arbor, Mich.: Association for Consumer Research, 1988), pp. 163–68; and Karen Finlay, "The Role of Corporate Indentification on the Perception of Brand Extensions: Integrations of Memory and Persuasion Approaches," *Marketing,* vol. 13, Administrative Sciences Association of Canada, 1992, pp. 78–87.

26. For a similar idea in an advertising context, see Thomas J. Reynolds and Jonathan Gutman, "Advertising Is Image Management," *Journal of Advertising Research,* February–March 1984, pp. 27–37.

27. Bill Brubaker, "Athletic Shoes: Beyond Big Business," *Washington Post,* March 10, 1991, pp. A1, A18.

28. For a detailed description of the perceived personal relevance (involvement) of some consumer researchers, see Donald R. Lehmann, "Pumping Iron III: An Examination of Compulsive Lifting," in *Advances in Consumer Research,* vol. 14, ed. Melanie Wallendorf and Paul Anderson (Ann Arbor, Mich.: Association for Consumer Research, 1987), pp. 129–31; and Debra Scammon, "Breeding, Training, and Riding: The Serious Side of Horsing Around," in *Advances in Consumer Research,* vol. 14, ed. Melanie Wallendorf and Paul Anderson (Ann Arbor, Mich.: Association for Consumer Research, 1987), pp. 125–28.

29. Sunil Mehrotra and John Palmer, "Relating Product Features to Perceptions of Quality: Appliances," in *Perceived Quality,* ed. Jacob Jacoby and Jerry C. Olson (Lexington, Mass.: Lexington Books, 1985), pp. 81–96.

30. Grant McCracken, "Advertising: Meaning or Information," in *Advances in Consumer Research,* vol. 14, ed. Melanie Wallendorf and Paul Anderson (Ann Arbor, Mich.: Association for Consumer Research, 1987), pp. 121–24.

31. Joshua Levine, "I Gave at the Supermarket," *Forbes,* December 25, 1989, pp. 138–40; and Jaclyn Fierman, "The Big Muddle in Green Marketing," *Fortune,* June 3, 1991, pp. 91–101.

Chapter 6

1. Patty Summerfield, "Nielson: Partners in Decisions," *Strategy,* October 5, 1992, p. 23; Howard Schlossberg, "Case of Missing TV Viewers," *Marketing News,* September 17, 1990, pp. 1, 7; Lynn G. Coleman, "People Meter Rerun," *Marketing News,* September 2, 1991, pp. 1, 44.

2. Sharon E. Beatty and Scott M. Smith, "External Search Effort: An Investigation across Several Product Categories," *Journal of Consumer Research,* June 1987, pp. 83–95; Peter H. Bloch, Daniel Sherrell, and Nancy M. Ridgway, "Consumer Search: An Extended Framework," *Journal of Consumer Research,* June 1986, pp. 119–26; Joseph W. Newman, "Consumer External Search: Amount and Determinants," in *Consumer and Industrial Buying Behavior,* ed. A. G. Woodside, J. N. Sheth, and P. D.

Bennett (New York: Elsevier-North Holland, 1977), pp. 79–94; and Richard R. Olshavsky and Donald H. Granbois, "Consumer Decision Making—Fact or Fiction," *Journal of Consumer Research*, June 1979, pp. 63–70.

3. "Advertising vs. Promotion—Game Over?" *Marketing*, February 7, 1994, p. 23.

4. Peter H. Bloch and Marsha L. Ritchins, "Shopping without Purchase: An Investigation of Consumer Browsing Behavior," in *Advances in Consumer Research*, vol. 10, ed. R. P. Baggozi and A. M. Tybout (Ann Arbor, Mich.: Association for Consumer Research, 1983), pp. 389–93.

5. Joanne Lipman, "CNN Ads Get Extra Mileage during the War," *The Wall Street Journal*, February 27, 1991, pp. B1, B4.

6. Avery Abernethy and Hubert Rotfield, "Zipping through TV Ads Is Old Tradition—But Viewers Are Getting Better at It," *Marketing News*, January 7, 1991, pp. 6, 14.

7. Dennis Kneale, "Zapping of TV Ads Appears Pervasive," *The Wall Street Journal*, April 25, 1988, p. 21.

8. Christine Dugas, "Ad Space Now Has a Whole New Meaning," *Business Week*, July 29, 1985, p. 52.

9. David W. Schumann, Jennifer Gayson, Johanna Ault, Kerri Hargrove, Lois Hollingsworth, Russell Ruelle, and Sharon Seguin, "The Effectiveness of Shopping Cart Signage: Perceptual Measures Tell a Different Story," *Journal of Advertising Research*, February–March 1991, pp. 17–22.

10. Suzanne Alexander, "Saturating Cities with Stores Can Pay," *The Wall Street Journal*, September 11, 1990, p. B1.

11. Joanne Lipman, "Brand-Name Products Are Popping Up in TV Shows," *The Wall Street Journal*, February 19, 1991, pp. B1, B3.

12. Roy Lachman, Janet L. Lachman, and Earl C. Butterfield, *Cognitive Psychology and Information Processing: An Introduction* (Hillsdale, N.J.: Lawrence Erlbaum, 1979).

13. Daniel Kahneman, *Attention and Effort* (Englewood Cliffs, N.J.: Prentice Hall, 1973); Anthony A. Greenwald and Clark Leavitt, "Audience Involvement in Advertising: Four Levels," *Journal of Consumer Research*, June 1984, pp. 581–92; and Chris Janiszewski, "The Influence of Nonattended Material on the Processing of Advertising Claims," *Journal of Marketing Research*, August 1990, pp. 263–78.

14. Schumann et al., "The Effectiveness of Shopping Cart Signage."

15. David M. Sanbonmatsu and Frank R. Kardes, "The Effects of Physiological Arousal on Information Processing and Persuasion," *Journal of Consumer Research*, December 1988, pp. 379–85; Meryl Paula Gardner, "Mood States and Consumer Behavior," *Journal of Consumer Research*, December 1985, pp. 281–300; and Noel Murray, Harish Sujan, Edward R. Hirt, and Mita Sujan, "The Effects of Mood on Categorization: A Cognitive Flexibility Hypothesis," *Journal of Personality and Social Psychology*, September 1990, pp. 411–25.

16. Marvin E. Goldberg and Gerald J. Gorn, "Happy and Sad TV Programs: How They Affect Reactions to Commercials," *Journal of Consumer Research*, December 1987, pp. 387–403.

17. See Richard L. Celsi and Jerry C. Olson, "The Role of Involvement in Attention and Comprehension Processes," *Journal of Consumer Research*, September 1988, pp. 210–24.

18. Sana Siwolop, "You Can't (Hum) Ignore (Hum) That Ad," *Business Week*, September 21, 1987, p. 56.

19. Both examples are taken from "Intuition: Microstudies, Humanized Research Can Identify Emotions that Motivate Consumers," *Marketing News*, March 19, 1982, p. 11.

20. Ann L. McGill and Punam Anand, "The Effect of Vivid Attributes on the Evaluation of Alternatives: The Role of Differential Attention and Cognitive Elaboration," *Journal of Consumer Research*, September 1989, pp. 188–96.

21. Cathryn Donohoe, "Whittle Zeroes In on His Target," *Insight*, August 14, 1989, pp. 50–52.

22. Fergus I. M. Craik and Robert S. Lockhart, "Levels of Processing: A Framework for Memory Research," *Journal of Verbal Learning and Verbal Behavior*, 1972, pp. 671–89; and Jerry C. Olson, "Encoding Processes: Levels of Processing and Existing Knowledge Structures," in *Advances in Consumer Research*, vol. 7, ed. J. C. Olson (Ann Arbor, Mich.: Association for Consumer Research, 1980), pp. 154–59.

23. John R. Anderson and Lynne M. Reder, "An Elaboration Processing Explanation of Depth of Processing," in *Levels of Processing in Human Memory*, ed. Larry S. Cermak and Fergus I. M. Craik (Hillsdale, N.J.: Lawrence Erlbaum, 1979), pp. 385–404; and Richard E. Petty and John T. Cacioppo, "The Elaboration Likelihood Model of Persuasion," in *Advances in Experimental Social Psychology*, vol. 19, ed. Leonard Berkowitz (New York: Academic Press, 1986), pp. 123–205.

24. Alain d'Astous and Marc Dubuc, "Retrieval Processes in Consumer Evaluative Judgment Making: The Role of Elaborative Processing," in *Advances in Consumer Research*, vol. 13, ed. Richard J. Lutz (Provo, Utah: Association for Consumer Research, 1986), pp. 132–37; Jerry C. Olson, "Encoding Processes: Levels of Processing and Existing Knowledge Structures," in *Advances in Consumer Research*, vol. 7, ed. J. C. Olson (Ann Arbor, Mich.: Association for Consumer Research, 1980), pp. 154–59; and Douglas M. Stayman and Rajeev Batra, "Encoding and Retrieval of Ad Affect in Memory," *Journal of Consumer Research*, May 1991, pp. 232–39.

25. Kevin Lane Keller, "Memory Factors in Advertising: The Effect of Advertising Retrieval Cues on Brand Evaluations," *Journal of Consumer Research*, December 1987, pp. 316–33; and Joan Myers-Levy, "Priming Effects on Product Judgments: A Hemispheric Interpretation," *Journal of Consumer Research*, June 1989, pp. 76–86.

26. Gary T. Ford and Ruth Ann Smith, "Inferential Beliefs in Consumer Evaluations: An Assessment of Alternative Processing Strategies," *Journal of Consumer Research*, December 1987, pp. 363–71; Richard J. Harris, "Inferences in Information Processing," in *The Psychology of Learning and Motivation*, vol. 15, ed. Gordon A. Bower (New York: Academic Press, 1981), pp. 81–128; and Mita Sujan and Christine Dekleva, "Product Categorization and

Inference Making: Some Implications for Comparative Advertising," *Journal of Consumer Research,* December 1986, pp. 372–78.

27. Amna Kirmani, "The Effect of Perceived Advertising Costs on Brand Perceptions," *Journal of Consumer Research,* September 1990, pp. 160–71; and Amna Kirmani and Peter Wright, "Money Talks: Perceived Advertising Expense and Expected Product Quality," *Journal of Consumer Research,* December 1989, pp. 344–53.

28. See Joseph W. Alba and J. Wesley Hutchinson, "Dimensions of Consumer Expertise," *Journal of Consumer Research,* March 1987, pp. 411–54; and Jerry C. Olson, "Inferential Belief Formation in the Cue Utilization Process," in *Advances in Consumer Research,* vol. 5, ed. H. Keith Hunt (Ann Arbor, Mich.: Association for Consumer Research, 1978), pp. 706–13.

29. Carl Obermiller, "When Do Consumers Infer Quality from Price?" in *Advances in Consumer Research,* vol. 15, ed. Michael J. Houston (Provo, Utah: Association for Consumer Research, 1988), pp. 304–10; Jerry C. Olson, "Price as an Informational Cue: Effects on Product Evaluations," in *Consumer and Industrial Buying Behavior,* ed. Arch G. Woodside, Jagdish N. Sheth, and Peter D. Bennett (New York: North Holland, 1977), pp. 267–86; and Valarie A. Zeithaml, "Consumer Perceptions of Price, Quality, and Value," *Journal of Marketing,* July 1988, pp. 2–22.

30. Frank R. Kardes, "Spontaneous Inference Processes in Advertising: The Effects of Conclusion Omission and Involvement on Persuasion," *Journal of Consumer Research,* September 1988, pp. 225–33; Richard D. Johnson and Irwin P. Levin, "More than Meets the Eye: The Effect of Missing Information on Purchase Evaluations," *Journal of Consumer Research,* June 1985, pp. 169–77; Carolyn J. Simmons and John G. Lynch, Jr., "Inference Effects with Inference Making? Effects of Missing Information on Discounting and Use of Presented Information," *Journal of Consumer Research,* March 1991, pp. 477–91.

31. For examples of inferring means-end chains, see Zeithaml, "Consumer Perceptions of Price, Quality, and Value," pp. 2–22; and Sunil Mehrotra and John Palmer, "Relating Product Features to Perceptions of Quality: Appliances," in *Perceived Quality,* ed. Jacob Jacoby and Jerry C. Olson (Lexington, Mass.: Lexington Books, 1985), pp. 81–96.

32. Durairaj Maheswaran and Brian Sternthal, "The Effects of Knowledge, Motivation, and Type of Message on Ad Processing and Product Judgments," *Journal of Consumer Research,* June 1990, pp. 66–73.

33. James R. Bettman and Mita Sujan, "Effects of Framing on Evaluation of Comparable and Noncomparable Alternatives by Expert and Novice Consumers," *Journal of Consumer Research,* September 1987, pp. 141–54; Joseph W. Alba and J. Wesley Hutchinson, "Dimensions of Consumer Expertise," *Journal of Consumer Research,* March 1987, pp. 411–54; Eric J. Johnson and J. Edward Russo, "Product Familiarity and Learning New Information," *Journal of Consumer Research,* June 1984, pp. 542–50; Larry J. Marks and Jerry C. Olson, "Toward a Cognitive Structure

Conceptualization of Product Familiarity," in *Advances in Consumer Research,* vol. 8, ed. Kent B. Monroe (Ann Arbor, Mich.: Association for Consumer Research, 1981), pp. 145–50; and Mita Sujan, "Consumer Knowledge: Effects on Evaluation Processes Mediating Consumer Judgments," *Journal of Consumer Research,* June 1985, pp. 31–46.

34. Michael O'Neal, "Attack of the Bug Killers," *Business Week,* May 16, 1988, p. 81.

35. Richard E. Petty, John T. Cacioppo, and David Schumann, "Central and Peripheral Routes to Advertising Effectiveness: The Moderating Role of Involvement," *Journal of Consumer Research,* September 1983, pp. 135–44.

36. Peter L. Wright and Barton Weitz, "Time Horizon Effects on Product Evaluation Strategies," *Journal of Marketing Research,* November 1977, pp. 429–43.

37. Christine Moorman, "The Effects of Stimulus and Consumer Characteristics on the Utilization of Nutrition Information," *Journal of Consumer Research,* December 1990, pp. 362–74.

38. Deborah J. MacInnis and Linda L. Price, "The Role of Imagery in Information Processing: Review and Extensions," *Journal of Consumer Research,* March 1987, pp. 473–91; and Elizabeth C. Hirschman, "Point of View: Sacred, Secular, and Mediating Consumption Imagery in Television Commercials," *Journal of Advertising Research,* December–January 1991, pp. 38–43.

39. Ronald Alsop, "Marketing: The Slogan's Familiar, but What's the Brand?" *The Wall Street Journal,* January 8, 1988, p. B1.

40. Jacob Jacoby and Wayne D. Hoyer, "Viewer Miscomprehension of Televised Communication: Selected Findings," *Journal of Marketing,* Fall 1982, pp. 12–26; and Jacob Jacoby and Wayne D. Hoyer, "The Comprehension/Miscomprehension of Print Communication: Selected Findings," *Journal of Consumer Research,* March 1989, pp. 434–43.

41. Some researchers feel these estimates are too high, because there are problems in measuring miscomprehension. See Gary T. Ford and Richard Yalch, "Viewer Miscomprehension of Televised Communication—A Comment," *Journal of Marketing,* Fall 1982, pp. 27–31; and Richard W. Mizerski, "Viewer Miscomprehension Findings Are Measurement Bound," Journal of Marketing, Fall 1982, pp. 32–34.

42. Industry Canada regulates misleading advertising in Canada and publishes the *Misleading Advertising Bulletin.* In the United States, misleading advertising is monitored by the FTC. The following articles have been published on misleading advertising. Gary T. Ford and John E. Calfee, "Recent Developments in FTC Policy on Deceptions," *Journal of Marketing,* July 1986, pp. 82–103; and Ivan L. Preston and Jef I. Richards, "The Relationship of Miscomprehension to Deceptiveness in FTC Cases," in *Advances in Consumer Research,* vol. 13, ed. Richard J. Lutz (Provo, Utah: Association for Consumer Research, 1986), pp. 138–42.

43. Chris Janiszewski, "The Influence of Print Advertisement Organization on Affect toward a Brand Name," *Journal of Consumer Research,* June 1990, pp. 53–65; James M.

Munch and Jack L. Swasy, "Rhetorical Questions, Summarization Frequency, and Argument Strength Effects on Recall," *Journal of Consumer Research,* June 1988, pp. 69–76; and Thomas J. Olney, Morris B. Holbrook, and Rajeev Batra, "Consumer Responses to Advertising: The Effects of Ad Content, Emotions, and Attitude toward the Ad on Viewing Time," *Journal of Consumer Research,* March 1991, pp. 440–53.

44. Jacob Jacoby, Robert W. Chestnut, and William Silberman, "Consumer Use and Comprehension of Nutrition Information," *Journal of Consumer Research,* September 1977, pp. 119–28; and Joyce A. Vermeersch and Helene Swenerton, "Interpretations of Nutrition Claims in Food Advertisements by Low-Income Consumers," *Journal of Nutrition Education,* January–March 1980, pp. 19–25; and Moorman, "The Effects of Stimulus."

Chapter 7

1. "Winning Over Canadian Wine Drinkers: Vintners are Marketing Aggressively to Alter the Image of Homegrown Wines," *Marketing,* November 11, 1991, p. 6; and "Ontario Wineries Trying to Shake Old Plonk Image," *Financial Post,* March 5, 1991, p. 37.

2. Martin Fishbein and Icek Ajzen, *Belief, Attitude, Intention, and Behavior: An Introduction to Theory and Research* (Reading, Mass.: Addison-Wesley, 1975); and Martin Fishbein, "Attitude, Attitude Change, and Behavior: A Theoretical Overview," in *Attitude Research Bridges the Atlantic,* ed. Philip Levine (Chicago: American Marketing Association, 1975), pp. 3–16.

3. Many authors have defined attitudes in this way, including Russell H. Fazio, "How Do Attitudes Guide Behavior?" in *Handbook of Motivation and Cognition: Foundations of Social Behavior,* ed. R. M. Sorrentino and E. T. Higgins (New York: Guilford Press, 1986), pp. 204–43.

4. For an excellent overview, see Elnora W. Stuart, Terence A. Shimp, and Randall W. Engle, "Classical Conditioning of Consumer Attitudes: Four Experiments in an Advertising Context," *Journal of Consumer Research,* December 1987, pp. 334–49; also see Chris T. Allen and Thomas J. Madden, "A Closer Look at Classical Conditioning," *Journal of Consumer Research,* December 1985, pp. 301–15; Terence A. Shimp, Elnora W. Stuart, and Randall W. Engle, "A Program of Classical Conditioning Experiments Testing Variations in the Conditioned Stimulus and Context," *Journal of Consumer Research,* June 1991, pp. 1–12.

5. Chike Okechuka and Stuart Brockbank, "Predicting Message Acceptance from Concurrent Cognitive Thoughts," *Marketing,* vol. 14, 1993, pp. 228–239; Alain d'Astous and Marc Dubuc, "Retrieval Processes in Consumer Evaluative Judgment Making: The Role of Elaborative Processing," in *Advances in Consumer Research,* vol. 13, ed. Richard J. Lutz (Provo, Utah: Association for Consumer Research, 1986), pp. 132–37; Paul W. Miniard, Thomas J. Page, April Atwood, and Randall L. Ross, "Representing Attitude Structure: Issues and Evidence," in *Advances in Consumer Research,* vol. 13, ed. Richard

J. Lutz (Provo, Utah: Association for Consumer Research, 1986), pp. 72–76; Russell H. Fazio, Martha C. Powell, and Carol J. Williams, "The Role of Attitude Accessibility in the Attitude-to-Behavior Process," *Journal of Consumer Research,* December 1989, pp. 280–88; and Ida E. Berger and Andrew A. Mitchell, "The Effect of Advertising on Attitude Accessibility, Attitude Confidence, and the Attitude-Behavior Relationship," *Journal of Consumer Research,* December 1989, pp. 269–79.

6. Kenneth E. Miller and James L. Ginter, "An Investigation of Situational Variation in Brand Choice Behavior and Attitude," *Journal of Marketing Research,* February 1979, pp. 111–23.

7. This section draws on Peter H. Farquhar, "Managing Brand Equity," *Marketing Research,* September 1989, pp. 24–33.

8. Norman C. Berry, "Revitalizing Brands," *Journal of Consumer Marketing,* Summer 1988, pp. 15–20.

9. David M. Boush and Barbara Loken, "A Process-Tracing Study of Brand Extension Evaluation," *Journal of Marketing Research,* February 1991, pp. 16–28; and C. Whan Park, Sandra Milberg, and Robert Lawson, "Evaluation of Brand Extensions: The Role of Product Feature Similarity and Brand Concept Consistency," *Journal of Consumer Research,* September 1991, pp. 185–93.

10. Fishbein and Ajzen, *Belief, Attitude, Intention, and Behavior;* Andrew A. Mitchell and Jerry C. Olson, "Are Product Attributes the Only Mediators of Advertising Effects on Brand Attitude?" *Journal of Marketing Research,* August 1981, pp. 318–32; and P. Peter Yannopoulos, "Salient Factors in Shopping Centre Choice," *Marketing,* vol. 12, 1991, pp. 294–302.

11. Susan B. Hester and Mary Yuen, "The Influence of Country of Origin on Consumer Attitudes and Buying Behavior in the United States and Canada," in *Advances in Consumer Research,* vol. 14, ed. Melanie Wallendorf and Paul Anderson (Provo, Utah: Association for Consumer Research, 1987), pp. 538–42; Sung-Tai Hong and Robert S. Wyer, "Determinants of Product Evaluation: Effects of the Time Interval between Knowledge of a Product's Country of Origin and Information about Its Specific Attributes," *Journal of Consumer Research,* December 1990, pp. 277–88; Tony Schellinck, "Determinants of Country of Origin Cue Usage," *Marketing,* vol. 10, 1989, pp. 268–275; Sadrudin A. Ahmed and Alain d'Astous, "L'influence du pays d'origine sur l'evaluation de produits suscitant differents niveaux d'implication: Une approche multi-attributs," *Canadian Journal of Administrative Sciences* vol. 10(1), 1993, pp. 48–59; Marjorie Wall, John Liefeld, and Louise A. Heslop, "Impact of Country of Origin Cues and Patriotic Appeals on Consumer Judgments: Covariance Analysis," *Marketing,* vol. 10, 1989, pp. 306–315; and Jerry A. Rosenblatt, "Perceptions of Fine Wood Furniture Imported from Mexico: An Analysis of Ottawa Residents' Perceptions," Concordia University Working Paper Series, #92-03-16, 1992.

12. See William L. Wilkie and Edgar A. Pessemier, "Issues in Marketing's Use of Multiattribute Attitude Models," *Journal of Marketing Research,* November 1973, pp. 428–41.

Relatively little work has investigated the integration process itself—see Joel B. Cohen, Paul W. Miniard, and Peter R. Dickson, "Information Integration: An Information Processing Perspective," in *Advances in Consumer Research,* vol. 11, ed. Thomas C. Kinnear (Ann Arbor, Mich.: Association for Consumer Research, 1980), pp. 161–70. Another influential model, particularly in the early days of marketing research on attitudes, was developed by Milton J. Rosenberg, "Cognitive Structure and Attitudinal Affect," *Journal of Abnormal and Social Psychology,* November 1956, pp. 367–72. Although different terminology is used, the structure of Rosenberg's model is quite similar to Fishbein's.

13. Fishbein and Ajzen, *Belief, Attitude, Intention, and Behavior.*

14. Ibid.

15. See Philip A. Dover and Jerry C. Olson, "Dynamic Changes in an Expectancy-Value Attitude Model as a Function of Multiple Exposures to Product Information," in *Contemporary Marketing Thought,* ed. B. A. Greenberg and D. N. Dellenger (Chicago: American Marketing Association, 1977), pp. 455–59; Robert E. Smith and William R. Swinyard, "Information Response Models: An Integrated Approach," *Journal of Marketing,* Winter 1982, pp. 81–93; and Russell H. Fazio and Mark P. Zanna, "Attitudinal Qualities Relating to the Strength of the Attitude-Behavior Relationship," *Journal of Experimental Social Psychology,* 14 (1987), pp. 398–408.

16. Richard J. Lutz and James R. Bettman, "Multiattribute Models in Marketing: A Bicentennial Review," in *Consumer and Industrial Buying Behavior,* ed. A. G. Woodside, J. N. Sheth, and P. D. Bennett (New York: Elsevier-North Holland Publishing, 1977), pp. 137–50.

17. Monci Jo Williams, "Why Is Airline Food So Terrible?" *Fortune,* December 19, 1988, pp. 169–72. Other studies dealing with airline choice include Line Ricard, Jean Perrien, Serge Merineau, and Etienne Bastin, "Le processus de choix d'un mode de transport," *Marketing,* vol. 10, 1990, pp. 296–308; Jacques Csipak, Jean-Charles Chebat, and Jerry A. Rosenblatt, "The Interactive Effects of Involvement and Information Processing Strategies: An Examination of the Transportation Service Sector," *Marketing,* vol. 15, 1994.

18. Christopher Power, Walecia Konrad, Alice Z. Cuneo, and James B. Treece, "Value Marketing: Quality, Service, and Fair Pricing Are the Keys to Selling in the 90s," *Business Week,* November 11, 1991, pp. 132–40.

19. John B. Palmer and Russ H. Crupnick, "New Dimensions Added to Conjoint Analysis," *Marketing News,* January 3, 1986, p. 62.

20. Richard J. Lutz, "Changing Brand Attitudes through Modification of Cognitive Structure," *Journal of Consumer Research,* March 1975, pp. 49–59; Andrew A. Mitchell, "The Effect of Verbal and Visual Components of Advertisements on Brand Attitudes and Attitude toward the Advertisement," *Journal of Consumer Research,* June 1986, pp. 12–24; and Jerry A. Rosenblatt, Michel Laroche, and John A. Howard, "Some Determinants of Attitude Change Following Product Usage," in *Marketing,* vol. 2, 1981.

21. Keith H. Hammonds, " 'Has-Beens' Have Been Very Good to Hasbro," *Business Week,* August 5, 1991, pp. 76–77.

22. Frank Rose, "If It Feels Good, It Must Be Bad," *Fortune,* October 21, 1991, pp. 91–108.

23. Martin Fishbein, "An Overview of the Attitude Construct," in *A Look Back, A Look Ahead,* ed. G. B. Hafer (Chicago: American Marketing Association, 1980), p. 3.

24. See Icek Ajzen and Martin Fishbein, "Attitude–Behavior Relations: A Theoretical Analysis and Review of Empirical Research," *Psychological Bulletin,* September 1977, pp. 888–918; and Alan W. Wicker, "Attitudes versus Action: The Relationship of Verbal and Overt Behavioral Responses to Attitude Objects," *Journal of Social Issues* 25 (1969), pp. 41–78.

25. See Fishbein, "An Overview of the Attitude Construct," pp. 1–19; and Fishbein and Ajzen, *Belief, Attitude, Intentions, and Behavior.*

26. Icek Ajzen and Martin Fishbein, *Understanding Attitudes and Predicting Social Behavior* (Englewood Cliffs, N.J.: Prentice Hall, 1980); and Fishbein and Ajzen, *Belief, Attitude, Intention, and Behavior.* Note that choosing behaviour with positive consequences is consistent with our means-end chain conceptualisation of consumers' product knowledge.

27. For a detailed exposition, see Terence A. Shimp and Alican Kavas, "The Theory of Reasoned Action Applied to Coupon Usage," *Journal of Consumer Research,* December 1984, pp. 795–809.

28. Ajzen and Fishbein, "Attitude–Behavior Relations: A Theoretical Analysis and Review of Empirical Research," pp. 888–918.

29. Richard P. Baggozzi and Paul R. Warshaw, "Trying to Consume," *Journal of Consumer Research,* September 1990, pp. 127–40.

30. Barbara Loken, "Effects of Uniquely Purchase Information on Attitudes toward Objects and Attitudes toward Behaviors," in *Advances in Consumer Research,* vol. 10, ed. R. P. Baggozzi and A. M. Tybout (Ann Arbor, Mich.: Association for Consumer Research, 1983), pp. 88–93; and G. Douglas Olsen, "The Infuence of Method of Deal Expression on Deal Perception and Behavioural Intentions," *Marketing,* vol. 14, 1993, pp. 240–246.

31. Some researchers have argued that the strong distinction between A_{act} and SN may not be justified. See articles by Paul W. Miniard and Joel B. Cohen, "Isolating Attitudinal and Normative Influences in Behavioral Intentions Models," *Journal of Marketing Research,* February 1979, pp. 102–10; and Paul W. Miniard and Joel B. Cohen, "An Examination of the Fishbein-Ajzen Behavioral Intentions Model's Concepts and Measures," *Journal of Experimental Social Psychology* 17 (1981), pp. 309–39. Alternatively, the underlying salient beliefs for both A_{act} and SN could be considered as one set of activated beliefs that are combined to form a single, global A_{act}. One version of such a model is proposed by Paul W. Miniard and Joel B. Cohen, "Modeling Personal and Normative Influences on Behavior," *Journal of Consumer Research,* September 1983, pp. 169–80. For simplicity, however, we follow the separate approach advocated by the theory of reasoned action.

32. Pat McIntyre, Mark A. Barnett, Richard Harris, James Shanteau, John Skowronski, and Michael Klassen, "Psychological Factors Influencing Decisions to Donate Organs," in *Advances in Consumer Research*, vol. 14, ed. Melanie Wallendorf and Paul Anderson (Provo, Utah: Association for Consumer Research, 1987), pp. 331–34; William O. Bearden and Randall L. Rose, "Attention to Social Comparison Information: An Individual Difference Factor Affecting Consumer Conformity," *Journal of Consumer Research*, March 1990, pp. 461–71.

33. Cited in Kenneth A. Longman, "Promises, Promises," in *Attitude Research on the Rocks*, ed. L. Adler and L. Crespi (Chicago: American Marketing Association, 1968), pp. 28–37. For further studies on car purchases in Canada, see Marjorie Wall, Greta Hofstra, and Louise Heslop, "Imported versus Domestic Car Owners: Demographic Characteristics and Attitudes," *Marketing*, vol. 11, 1990, pp. 391–400. The following study measured intentions of Canadians to shop in U.S. retail outlets: Edward Bruning, Larry Lockshin, and Gary Lantz, "A Conjoint Analysis of Factors Affecting Intentions of Canadian Consumers to Shop in U. S. Retail Centres," *Marketing*, vol. 14, pp. 12–21.

34. Ibid., "Promises, Promises".

35. For an interesting discussion of this issue, see Gordon R. Foxall, "Consumers' Intentions and Behavior: A Note on Research and a Challenge to Researchers," *Journal of the Market Research Society* 26 (1985), pp. 231–41.

Chapter 8

1. Adapted from Barbara Hayes-Roth, "Opportunism in Consumer Behavior," in *Advances in Consumer Research*, vol. 9, ed. A. A. Mitchell (Ann Arbor, Mich.: Association for Consumer Research, 1982), pp. 132–35.

2. Flemming Hansen, "Psychological Theories of Consumer Choice," *Journal of Consumer Research*, December 1976, pp. 117–42.

3. Richard W. Olshavsky and Donald H. Granbois, "Consumer Decision Making—Fact or Fiction?" *Journal of Consumer Research*, September 1979, pp. 93–100.

4. A similar notion is presented by Girish N. Punj and David W. Stewart, "An Interaction Framework of Consumer Decision Making," *Journal of Consumer Research*, September 1983, pp. 181–96.

5. Daniel Kahneman and Amos Tyersky, "Choices, Values, and Frames," *American Psychologist* 39 (1984), pp. 341–50; Christopher P. Puto, "The Framing of Buying Decisions," *Journal of Consumer Research*, December 1987, pp. 301–15; William J. Qualls and Christopher P. Puto, "Organizational Climate and Decision Framing: An Integrated Approach to Analyzing Industrial Buying Decisions," *Journal of Marketing Research*, May 1989, pp. 179–92; James R. Bettman and Mita Sujan, "Effects of Framing on Evaluation of Comparable and Noncomparable Alternatives by Experts and Novice Consumers," *Journal of Consumer Research*, September 1987,

pp. 141–54; Joshua L. Wiener, James W. Gentry, and Ronald K. Miller, "The Framing of the Insurance Purchase Decision," in *Advances in Consumer Research*, vol. 13, ed. Richard J. Lutz (Provo, Utah: Association for Consumer Research, 1986), pp. 257–62; and Peter Wright and Peter D. Rip, "Product Class Advertising Effects on First-Time Buyers' Decision Strategies," *Journal of Consumer Research*, September 1980, pp. 176–88.

6. Lawrence A. Crosby and James R. Taylor, "Effects of Consumer Information and Education in Cognition and Choice," *Journal of Consumer Research*, June 1981, pp. 43–56; John G. Lynch and Thomas K. Srull, "Memory and Attentional Factors in Consumer Choice: Concepts and Research Methods," *Journal of Consumer Research*, June 1982, pp. 18–37; Gabriel Biehal and Dipankar Chakravarti, "Consumers' Use of Memory and External Information in Choice: Macro and Micro Perspectives," *Journal of Consumer Research*, March 1986, pp. 382–405; Gabriel Biehal and Dipankar Chakravarti, "Information Accessibility as a Moderator of Consumer Choice," *Journal of Consumer Research*, June 1983, pp. 1–14; and Valerie S. Folkes, "The Availability Heuristic and Perceived Risk," *Journal of Consumer Research*, June 1988, pp. 13–23.

7. Peter H. Bloch, Daniel L. Sherrell, and Nancy M. Ridgway, "Consumer Search: An Extended Framework," *Journal of Consumer Research*, June 1986, pp. 119–26; and Louise Heslop, John P. Liefeld, Majorie Wall, and Nicholas Papadopoulos, "An Experimental Study of the Effects of Intrinsic and Extrinsic Cues and Consumer Characteristics on Product Evaluations and Choice," *Marketing*, vol. 14, 1993, pp. 113–122.

8. David B. Klenosky and Arno J. Rethans, "The Formation of Consumer Choice Sets: A Longitudinal Investigation at the Product Class Level," in *Advances in Consumer Research*, vol. 15, ed. Michael J. Houston (Provo, Utah: Association for Consumer Research, 1988), pp. 13–18; John R. Hauser and Birger Wernerfelt, "An Evaluation Cost Model of Consideration Sets," *Journal of Consumer Research*, March 1990, pp. 393–408; and John H. Roberts and James M. Lattin, "Development and Testing of a Model of Consideration Set Composition," *Journal of Marketing Research*, November 1991, pp. 429–40. For alternative views on how consumers categorise brands, see Jerry A. Rosenblatt, "How Consumers Categorize Brands: Basic Framework and Managerial Implications," *Proceedings of the Southern Marketing Association*, November 1986; Jerry A. Rosenblatt, "Interactive Effects in Information Processing: A Conceptual Framework of the Relationship of Consumer Involvement and Brand Categorization," in *Developments in Marketing Science*, Proceedings of the Academy of Marketing Science, May 1988; Michel Larouche, Jerry A. Rosenblatt, and Jacques E. Brisoux, "Consumer Brand Categorization: Basic Framework and Managerial Implication," *Marketing Intelligence and Planning*, vol. 4, no. 4, pp. 60–74, 1986; Michel Laroche, Jerry A. Rosenblatt, Alan Hochstein, and Robert Ransom, "The Economic Impact of Price–Quality Evaluations on Brand Categorization: The Examination of the Micro-Computer Market," September 1989, pp. 1–11.

9. John Howard and Jagdish N. Sheth, *The Theory of Buyer Behavior* (New York: John Wiley & Sons, 1969); and Prak-

ash Nedungadi, "Recall and Consumer Consideration Sets: Influencing Choice without Altering Brand Evaluations," *Journal of Consumer Research,* December 1990, pp. 263–76. For alternative conceptualisation of the evoked set, see Jerry A. Rosenblatt, "The Consumer Brand Categorization Process: The Relationship of Involvement and the Evoked Set Phenomenon," *Marketing,* vol. 5, 1984.

10. Sharon E. Beatty and Scott M. Smith, "External Search Effort: An Investigation across Several Product Categories," *Journal of Consumer Research,* June 1987, pp. 83–95.

11. Wayne D. Hoyer and Steven P. Brown, "Effects of Brand Awareness on Choice for a Common, Repeat-Purchase Product," *Journal of Consumer Research,* September 1990, pp. 141–48.

12. William Baker, J. Wesley Hutchinson, Danny Moore, and Prakash Nedungadi, "Brand Familiarity and Advertising: Effects on the Evoked Set and Brand Preference," in *Advances in Consumer Research,* vol. 13, ed. Richard J. Lutz (Provo, Utah: Association for Consumer Research, 1986), pp. 637–42.

13. Kristian E. Moller and Pirjo Karppinen, "Role of Motives and Attributes in Consumer Motion Picture Choice," *Journal of Economic Psychology* 4 (1983), pp. 239–62; and Michel Laroche, Jerry A. Rosenblatt, and Terrill Manning, "Services Used and Factors Considered Important in Selecting a Bank: An Investigation Across Diverse Demographic Segments," *International Journal of Bank Marketing,* vol. 4, no. 1 (1986), pp. 35–55.

14. Joel E. Urbany, Peter R. Dickson, and William L. Wilkie, "Buyer Uncertainty and Information Search," *Journal of Consumer Research,* September 1989, pp. 208–15.

15. Klaus G. Grunert, "Cognitive Determinants of Attribute Information Usage," *Journal of Economic Psychology* 7 (1986), pp. 95–124; and C. Whan Park and Daniel C. Smith, "Product-Level Choice: A Top-Down or Bottom-Up Process?" *Journal of Consumer Research,* December 1989, pp. 289–99.

16. John U. Farley, Jerrold Katz, and Donald R. Lehmann, "Impact of Different Comparison Sets on Evaluation of a New Subcompact Car Brand," *Journal of Consumer Research,* September 1978, pp. 138–42; Srinivasan Ratneshwar, Allan D. Shocker, and David W. Stewart, "Toward Understanding the Attraction Effect: The Implications of Product Stimulus Meaningfulness and Familiarity," *Journal of Consumer Research,* March 1987, pp. 520–33; Merrie Brucks and Paul H. Shurr, "The Effects of Bargainable Attributes and Attribute Range Knowledge on Consumer Choice Processes," *Journal of Consumer Research,* March 1990, pp. 409–19; Kim P. Corfman, "Comparability and Comparison Levels Used in Choices among Consumer Products," *Journal of Marketing Research,* August 1991, pp. 368–74; Noreen M. Klein and Manjit S. Yadav, "Context Effects on Effort and Accuracy in Choice: An Enquiry into Adaptive Decision Making," *Journal of Consumer Research,* March 1989, pp. 411–21; and Rashi Glazer, Barbara E. Kahn, and William L. Moore, "The Influence of External Constraints on Brand Choice: The Lone Alterna-

tive Effect," *Journal of Consumer Research,* June 1991, pp. 119–27.

17. Mark I. Alpert, "Unresolved Issues in Identification of Determinant Attributes," in *Advances in Consumer Research,* vol. 7, ed. Jerry C. Olson (Ann Arbor, Mich.: Association for Consumer Research, 1980), pp. 83–88.

18. Valerie S. Folkes, "The Availability Heuristic and Perceived Risk," *Journal of Consumer Research,* June 1988, pp. 13–23; and John W. Vann, "A Conditional Probability View of the Role of Product Warranties in Reducing Perceived Financial Risk," in *Advances in Consumer Research,* vol. 14, ed. Melanie Wallendorf and Paul Anderson (Provo, Utah: Association for Consumer Research, 1987), pp. 421–25.

19. Narasimhan Srinivasan and Brian T. Ratchford, "An Empirical Test of a Model of External Search for Automobiles," *Journal of Consumer Research,* September 1991, pp. 233–42; and Keith B. Murray, "A Test of Services Marketing Theory: Consumer Information Acquisition Activities," *Journal of Marketing,* January 1991, pp. 10–25.

20. Robert S. Billings and Lisa L. Scherer, "The Effects of Response Mode and Importance on Decision-Making Strategies: Judgment versus Choice," *Organizational Behavior and Human Decision Processes* 41 (1988), pp. 1–19; and Peter Wright, "Consumer Choice Strategies: Simplifying versus Optimizing," *Journal of Marketing Research,* February 1975, pp. 60–67; and Jerry A. Rosenblatt, Michel Laroche, Alan Hochstein, Ronald McTavish, and Maureen Sheahan, "Commercial Banking in Canada: A Study of the Selection Criteria and Service Expectations of Corporate Treasurers," *International Journal of Bank Marketing,* vol. 6, no. 4 (1988), pp. 19–30; and Jerry A. Rosenblatt and Michel Laroche, "Brand Categorization Strategies in an Extensive Problem Solving Situation: A Study of University Choice," in *Advances in Consumer Research,* vol. XI, Association for Consumer Research, 1984.

21. James R. Bettman and C. Whan Park, "Effects of Prior Knowledge and Experience and Phase of the Choice Process on Consumer Decision Processes: A Protocol Analysis," *Journal of Consumer Research,* December 1980, pp. 234–48; Joel B. Cohen, Paul W. Miniard, and Peter Dickson, "Information Integration: An Information Processing Perspective," in *Advances in Consumer Research,* vol. 7, ed. Jerry C. Olson (Ann Arbor, Mich.: Association for Consumer Research, 1980), pp. 161–70; Wayne D. Hoyer, "An Examination of Consumer Decision Making for a Common Repeat Purchase Product," *Journal of Consumer Research,* December 1984, pp. 822–29; and David J. Curry, Michael B. Menasco, and James W. Van Ark, "Multiattribute Dyadic Choice: Models and Tests," *Journal of Marketing Research,* August 1991, pp. 259–67.

22. James R. Bettman, *An Information Processing Theory of Consumer Choice* (Reading, Mass.: Addison-Wesley, 1979); Denis A. Lussier and Richard W. Olshavsky, "Task Complexity and Contingent Processing in Brand Choice," *Journal of Consumer Research,* September 1979, pp. 154–65; and Merrie Brucks and Andrew A. Mitchell, "Knowledge Structures, Production Systems and Decision Strategies," in *Advances in Consumer Research,* vol. 8,

ed. Kent B. Monroe (Ann Arbor, Mich.: Association for Consumer Research, 1981).

23. Bettman and Park, "Effects of Prior Knowledge," pp. 234–48; and Hoyer, "An Examination of Consumer Decision Making for a Common Repeat Purchase Product," pp. 822–29.

24. James R. Bettman, "Presidential Address: Processes of Adaptivity in Decision Making," in *Advances in Consumer Research,* vol. 15, ed. Michael J. Houston (Provo, Utah: Association for Consumer Research, 1988), pp. 1–4; Surjit Chabra and Richard W. Olshavsky, "Some Evidence for Additional Types of Choice Strategies," in *Advances in Consumer Research,* vol. 13, ed. Richard J. Lutz (Provo, Utah: Association for Consumer Research, 1986), pp. 12–16; Wayne D. Hoyer, "Variations in Choice Strategies across Decision Contexts: An Examination of Contingent Factors," in *Advances in Consumer Research,* vol. 13, ed. Richard J. Lutz (Provo, Utah: Association for Consumer Research, 1986), pp. 32–36; James R. Bettman and Michel A. Zins, "Constructive Processes in Consumer Choice," *Journal of Consumer Research,* September 1977, pp. 75–85; Bettman and Park, "Effects of Prior Knowledge," 234–48; Hoyer, "Examination of Consumer Decision Making," pp. 822–29; John Payne, "Task Complexity and Contingent Processing in Decision Making," *Organizational Behavior and Human Performance* 16 (1976), pp. 366–87; and David Grether and Louis Wilde, "An Analysis of Conjunctive Choice: Theory and Experiments," *Journal of Consumer Research,* March 1984, pp. 373–85.

25. C. Whan Park and Richard J. Lutz, "Decision Plans and Consumer Choice Dynamics," *Journal of Marketing Research,* February 1982, pp. 108–15.

26. David K. Tse, Franco M. Nicosia, and Peter C. Wilton, "Consumer Satisfaction as a Process," *Psychology & Marketing,* Fall 1990, pp. 177–93.

27. Reviews of the literature on consumer satisfaction include Stephen A. Latour and Nancy C. Peat, "Conceptual and Methodological Issues in Consumer Satisfaction Research," in *Advances in Consumer Research,* vol. 6, ed. W. L. Wilkie (Ann Arbor, Mich.: Association for Consumer Research, 1979), pp. 431–37; and Denise T. Smart, "Consumer Satisfaction Research: A Review," in *Consumer Behavior: Classical and Contemporary Dimensions,* ed. J. U. McNeal and Stephen W. McDaniel (Boston: Little Brown, 1982), pp. 286–306.

28. See Marsha L. Richins, "Negative Word-of-Mouth by Dissatisfied Consumers: A Pilot Study," *Journal of Marketing,* Winter 1983, pp. 69–78; and Jagdip Singh, "Consumer Complaint Intentions and Behavior: Definitional and Taxonomical Issues," *Journal of Marketing,* January 1988, pp. 93–107.

29. See Richard L. Oliver, "A Cognitive Model of the Antecedents and Consequences of Satisfaction Decisions," *Journal of Marketing Research,* November 1980, pp. 460–69; Richard L. Oliver and Wayne S. DeSarbo, "Response Determination in Satisfaction Judgments," *Journal of Consumer Research,* March 1988, pp. 495–507; and Priscilla A. LaBarbara and David Mazursky, "A Longitudinal As-

sessment of Consumer Satisfaction/Dissatisfaction: The Dynamic Aspect of the Cognitive Process," *Journal of Marketing Research,* November 1983, pp. 393–404.

30. There are many sources on cognitive dissonance, stemming from the original work by Leon Festinger, *A Theory of Cognitive Dissonance,* (Stanford, Calif.: Stanford University Press, 1957).

31. This terminology comes from John Howard, *Consumer Behavior: Applications of Theory* (New York: McGraw-Hill, 1979). Studies that have attempted to combine brand categorisation theory with different problem-solving strategies include Nancy J. Church, Michel Laroche, and Jerry A. Rosenblatt, "Consumer Brand Categorization for Durables with Limited Problem Solving: An Empirical Test and Proposed Extension of the Brisoux-Laroche Model," *Journal of Economic Psychology* 6 (1985), pp. 231–253; Jerry A. Rosenblatt and Michel Laroche, "Brand Categorization Strategies in RRB Situations: Some Empirical Results," in *Advances in Consumer Research,* vol. X, 1983.

32. Robert J. Meyer, "The Learning of Multiattribute Judgment Policies," *Journal of Consumer Research,* September 1987, pp. 155–73; and Lawrence W. Barsalou and J. Wesley Hutchinson, "Schema-Based Planning of Events in Consumer Contexts," in *Advances in Consumer Research,* vol. 14, ed. Melanie Wallendorf and Paul Anderson (Provo, Utah: Association for Consumer Research, 1987), pp. 114–18; and Jacques A. Nantel and Renee Robillard, "The Effect of Experience and Expertise on the Complexity of the Decision-Making Process," *Marketing,* vol. 9, 1988, pp. 88–97.

33. Kevin Lane Keller and Richard Staelin, "Effects of Quality and Quantity of Information on Decision Effectiveness," *Journal of Consumer Research,* September 1987, pp. 200–13.

34. Dennis W. Rook, "The Buying Impulse," *Journal of Consumer Research,* September 1987, pp. 189–99.

35. Interrupts are discussed by Bettman, *An Information Processing Theory of Consumer Choice;* also see Robert M. Schlinder, Michael Berbaum, and Donna R. Weinzimer, "How an Attention Getting Device Can Affect Choice among Similar Alternatives," in *Advances in Consumer Research,* vol. 14, ed. Melanie Wallendorf and Paul Anderson (Provo, Utah: Association for Consumer Research, 1987), pp. 505–09; and Tony Schellinck, "Exploring Issues Relevant to the Development of a Theory of Cue Usage," *Marketing,* vol. 10, 1989, pp. 276–285.

Chapter 9

1. James Pollock, "CFL Chief Is TAMA's Marketer of the Year," *Marketing,* October 24, 1994, p. 8; and David Israelson, "Stranger but True: Head of the Trouble-Plagued CFL Is Named Marketer of the Year," *Toronto Star,* October 14, 1994, p. F1.

2. C. Whan Park, Bernard J. Jaworski, and Deborah J. MacInnis, "Strategic Brand Concept Image Management," *Journal of Marketing,* October 1986, pp. 135–45; and

Thomas J. Reynolds and Jonathan Gutman, "Advertising Is Image Management," *Journal of Advertising Research,* February–March 1984, pp. 27–37.

3. Kevin Higgins, "Billboards Put Nike Back in the Running," *Marketing News,* June 7, 1985, p. 7.

4. "Advertising versus Promotion—Game Over?" *Marketing,* February 7, 1994, p. 23.

5. "McDonald's Olympic Promotion Gets the Gold."

6. Mary Ann Falzone, "Survey Highlights Lower Costs, Higher Productivity of Telemarketing," *Telemarketing Insider's Report* (Special Report, 1985), pp. 1–2.

7. Stewart W. Cross, "Can You Turn a 1985 Salesperson into a TSR?" *Telemarketing Insider's Report,* April 1985, p. 2.

8. Michael Wahl, "Eye POPping Persuasion," *Marketing Insights,* 1989, pp. 130–34.

9. W. E. Philips, "Continuous Sales (Price) Promotion Destroys Brands: Yes," *Marketing News,* January 16, 1989, pp. 4, 8; Bill Robinson, "Continuous Sales (Price) Promotion Destroys Brands: No," *Marketing News,* January 16, 1989, pp. 4, 8; Chris Sutherland, "Promoting Sales Out of a Slump," *Marketing Insights,* Winter 1990, pp. 41–43; and Wahl, "Eye POPping Persuasion."

10. Deborah J. MacInnis and Bernard J. Jaworski, "Information Processing from Advertisements: Toward an Integrative Framework," *Journal of Marketing,* October 1989, pp. 1–24.

11. Alan J. Bush and Gregory W. Boller, "Rethinking the Role of Television Advertising During Health Crises: A Rhetorical Analysis of the Federal AIDS Campaigns," *Journal of Advertising* 20, no. 1 (1991), pp. 28–37.

12. Brian Sternthal, Ruby Dholakia, and Clark Leavitt, "The Persuasive Effect of Source Credibility: Tests of Cognitive Response," *Journal of Consumer Research,* March 1978, pp. 252–60.

13. Lynn R. Kahle and Pamela M. Homer, "Physical Attractiveness of the Celebrity Endorser: A Social Adaptation Perspective," *Journal of Consumer Research,* March 1985, pp. 954–61; and John C. Mowen and Stephen W. Brown, "On Explaining and Predicting the Effectiveness of Celebrity Endorsers," in *Advances in Consumer Research,* vol. 8, ed. Kent B. Monroe (Ann Arbor, Mich.: Association for Consumer Research, 1981), pp. 437–41.

14. David A. Aaker, Douglas M. Stayman, and Michael R. Hagerty, "Warmth in Advertising: Measurement, Impact, and Sequence Effects," *Journal of Consumer Research,* March 1986, pp. 365–81; Calvin P. Duncan, James E. Nelson, and Nancy T. Frontczak, "The Effect of Humor on Advertising Comprehension," in *Advances in Consumer Research,* vol. 11, ed. Thomas C. Kinnear (Ann Arbor, Mich.: Association for Consumer Research, 1984), pp. 432–37; Mary C. Gilly, "Sex Roles in Advertising: A Comparison of Television Advertisements in Australia, Mexico, and the United States," *Journal of Marketing,* April 1988, pp. 75–85; Michael A. Kamins and Henry Assael, "Two-Sided versus One-Sided Appeals: A Cognitive Perspective on Argumentation, Source Derogation, and the Effect of Disconfirming Trial on Belief Change," *Journal of Marketing Research,* February 1987, pp. 29–39; Leo Bo-

gart and Charles Lehman, "The Case of the 30-Second Commercial," *Journal of Advertising Research,* February–March 1983, pp. 11–20; Morris B. Holbrook and Rajeev Batra, "Assessing the Role of Emotions as Mediators of Consumer Responses to Advertising," *Journal of Consumer Research,* December 1987, pp. 404–20; and George M. Zinkhan and Claude R. Martin, Jr., "Message Characteristics and Audience Characteristics: Predictors of Advertising Response," in *Advances in Consumer Research,* vol. 10, ed. Richard P. Baggozzi and Alice M. Tybout (Ann Arbor, Mich.: Association for Consumer Research, 1983), pp. 27–31.

15. Terry L. Childers, Michael J. Houston, and Susan E. Heckler, "Measurement of Individual Differences in Visual versus Verbal Information Processing," *Journal of Consumer Research,* September 1985, pp. 125–34; Julie A. Edell and Richard Staelin, "The Information Processing of Pictures in Print Advertisements," *Journal of Consumer Research,* June 1983, pp. 45–61; Andrew A. Mitchell, "The Effect of Verbal and Visual Components of Advertisements on Brand Attitudes and Attitude toward the Advertisement," *Journal of Consumer Research,* June 1986, pp. 12–24; and Deborah J. MacInnis and Linda L. Price, "The Role of Imagery in Information Processing: Review and Extensions," *Journal of Consumer Research,* March 1987, pp. 473–91.

16. John Deighton, Daniel Romer, and Josh McQueen, "Using Drama to Persuade," *Journal of Consumer Research,* December 1989, pp. 335–43.

17. Gregory W. Boller and Jerry C. Olson, "Experiencing Ad Meanings: Crucial Aspects of Narrative/Drama Processing," in *Advances in Consumer Research,* vol. 18, ed. R. Holman and M. Solomon (Provo, Utah: Association for Consumer Research, 1991), pp. 172–75.

18. Scott S. Liu and Patricia A. Stout, "Effects of Message Modality and Appeal on Advertising Acceptance," *Psychology and Marketing* 3 (1987), pp. 167–87.

19. See Peter H. Webb and Michael L. Ray, "Effects of TV Clutter," *Journal of Advertising Research,* June 1979, pp. 7–12; and Joanne Lipman, "Ads on TV: Out of Sight, Out of Mind," *The Wall Street Journal,* May 14, 1991, pp. B1, B8.

20. Scott Hume, "Coupon Use Jumps 10% as Distribution Soars," *Advertising Age,* October 5, 1992, pp. 3, 44.

21. Kapil Bawa and Robert W. Shoemaker, "The Effects of a Direct Mail Coupon on Brand Choice Behavior," *Journal of Marketing Research,* November 1987, pp. 370–76; P. S. Raju and Manoj Hastak, "Consumer Response to Deals: A Discussion of Theoretical Perspective," in *Advances in Consumer Research,* vol. 7, ed. Jerry C. Olson (Ann Arbor, Mich.: Association for Consumer Research, 1980), pp. 296–301; and Robert Blattberg, Thomas Biesing, Peter Peacock, and Subrata Sen, "Identifying the Deal Prone Segment," *Journal of Marketing Research,* August 1978, pp. 369–97.

22. For a review of various measures of advertising effectiveness, see David W. Stewart, Connie Pechmann, Srinivasan Ratneshwar, John Stroud, and Beverly Bryant, "Advertising Evaluation: A Review of Measures," in

Marketing Communications—Theory and Research, ed. Michael J. Houston and Richard J. Lutz (Chicago: American Marketing Association, 1985), pp. 3–6. For a discussion of copy testing, see Benjamin Lipstein and James P. Neelankavil, "Television Advertising Copy Research: A Critical Review of the State of the Art," *Journal of Advertising Research,* April–May 1984, pp. 19–25; Joseph T. Plummer, "The Role of Copy Research in Multinational Advertising," *Journal of Advertising Research,* October–November 1986, pp. 11–15; and Harold M. Spielman, "Copy Research: Facts and Fictions," *European Research,* November 1987, pp. 226–31.

23. Lawrence D. Gibson, "Not Recall," *Journal of Advertising Research,* February–March 1983, pp. 39–46; Herbert E. Krugman, "Low Recall and High Recognition of Advertising," *Journal of Advertising Research,* February–March 1986, pp. 79–86; and Jan Stapel, "Viva Recall: Viva Persuasion," *European Research,* November 1987, pp. 222–25.

24. Jeffrey A. Trachtenberg, "Viewer Fatigue?" *Forbes,* December 26, 1988, pp. 120, 122.

25. Marvin E. Goldberg and Jon Hartwick, "The Effects of Advertiser Reputation and Extremity of Advertising Claim on Advertising Effectiveness," *Journal of Consumer Research,* September 1990, pp. 172–79; Jerry C. Olson, Daniel R. Toy, and Philip A. Dover, "Do Cognitive Responses Mediate the Effects of Advertising Content on Cognitive Structure?" *Journal of Consumer Research,* December 1982, pp. 245–62; Arno J. Rethans, John L. Swasy, and Lawrence J. Marks, "Effects of Television Commercial Repetition, Receiver Knowledge, and Commercial Length: A Test of the Two-Factor Model," *Journal of Marketing Research,* February 1986, pp. 50–61; and Daniel R. Toy, "Monitoring Communication Effects: A Cognitive Structure Cognitive Response Approach," *Journal of Consumer Research,* June 1982, pp. 66–76.

26. Jon Gutman and Thomas J. Reynolds, "Coordinating Assessment to Strategy Development: An Advertising Assessment Paradigm Based on the MECCAS Approach," in *Advertising and Consumer Psychology,* vol. 3, ed. Jerry Olson and Keith Sentis (New York: Praeger, 1987).

27. This section is adapted from John R. Rossiter and Larry Percy, *Advertising and Promotion Management* (New York: McGraw-Hill, 1987), pp. 129–64.

28. William T. Moran, "Brand Presence and the Perceptual Frame," *Journal of Advertising Research,* October–November 1990, pp. 9–16; and H. Rao Unnava and Robert E. Burnkrant, "Effects of Repeating Varied Ad Executions on Brand Name Memory," *Journal of Marketing Research,* November 1991, pp. 406–16.

29. Kevin Lane Keller, "Memory and Evaluation Effects in Competitive Advertising Environments," *Journal of Consumer Research,* March 1991, pp. 463–76.

30. Punam Anand and Brian Sternthal, "Ease of Message Processing as a Moderator of Repetition Effects in Advertising," *Journal of Marketing Research,* August 1990, pp. 345–53.

31. Banwari Mittal, "The Relative Roles of Brand Beliefs and Attitude toward the Ad as Mediators of Brand Attitude: A Second Look," *Journal of Marketing Research,* May 1990, pp. 209–19.

32. Cornelia Pechmann and David W. Stewart, "The Effects of Comparative Advertising on Attention, Memory, and Purchase Intentions," *Journal of Consumer Research,* September 1990, pp. 180–91.

33. Wahl, "Eye POPping Persuasion."

34. Aradhna Krishna, "Effect of Dealing Patterns on Consumer Perceptions of Deal Frequency and Willingness to Pay," *Journal of Marketing Research,* November 1991, pp. 441–51.

35. Richard E. Petty, John T. Cacioppo, and David Schumann, "Central and Peripheral Routes to Advertising Effectiveness: The Moderating Role of Involvement," *Journal of Consumer Research,* September 1983, pp. 135–46.

36. Richard L Celsi and Jerry C. Olson, "The Role of Involvement in Attention and Comprehension Processes," *Journal of Consumer Research,* September 1988, pp. 201–24; Deborah J. MacInnis and C. Whan Park, "The Differential Role of Characteristics of Music on High- and Low-Involvement Consumers' Processing of Ads," *Journal of Consumer Research,* September 1991, pp. 161–73; David W. Schumann, Richard E. Petty, and D. Scott Clemons, "Predicting the Effectiveness of Different Strategies of Advertising Variation: A Test of the Repetition-Variation Hypotheses," *Journal of Consumer Research,* September 1990, pp. 192–202; H. Rao Unnava and Robert E. Burnkrant, "An Imagery-Processing View of the Role of Pictures in Print Advertisements," *Journal of Marketing Research,* May 1991, pp. 226–31.

37. Manoj Hastak and Jerry C. Olson, "Assessing the Role of Brand-Related Cognitive Responses as Mediators of Communication Effects on Cognitive Structure," *Journal of Consumer Research,* March 1989, pp. 444–56; and John L. Swasy and James M. Munch, "Examining the Target of Receiver Elaborations: Rhetorical Question Effects on Source Processing and Persuasion," *Journal of Consumer Research,* March 11, 1985, pp. 877–86.

38. Andrew A. Mitchell and Jerry C. Olson, "Are Product Attribute Beliefs the Only Mediator of Advertising Effects on Brand Attitude?" *Journal of Marketing Research,* August 1981, pp. 318–32; Meryl Paula Gardner, "Does Attitude toward the Ad Affect Brand Attitude under a Brand Evaluation Set?" *Journal of Marketing Research,* May 1985, pp. 192–98; Thomas J. Olney, Morris B. Holbrook, and Rajeev Batra, "Consumer Responses to Advertising: The Effects of Ad Content, Emotions, and Attitude toward the Ad on Viewing Time," *Journal of Consumer Research,* March 1991, pp. 440–53; Scott B. MacKenzie, Richard J. Lutz, and George E. Belch, "The Role of Attitude toward the Ad as a Mediator of Advertising Effectiveness: A Test of Competing Explanations," *Journal of Marketing Research,* May 1986, pp. 130–43; Andrew A. Mitchell, "The Effect of Verbal and Visual Components of Advertisements on Brand Attitudes and Attitude toward the Advertisement," *Journal of Consumer Research,* June 1986, pp. 12–24; Pamela M. Homer, "The Mediating Role of Attitude toward the Ad: Some Additional Evidence," *Journal of Marketing Research,* February 1990, pp. 78–86; and Douglas M. Stay-

man and Rajeev Batra, "Encoding and Retrieval of Ad Affect in Memory," *Journal of Consumer Research,* May 1991, pp. 232–39.

39. Celsi and Olson, "The Role of Involvement," pp. 210–24; Hastak and Olson, "Assessing the Role of Brand-Related Cognitive Responses," pp. 444–56; and Deborah J. MacInnis, Christine Moorman, and Bernard J. Jaworski, "Enhancing and Measuring Consumers' Motivation, Opportunity, and Ability to Process Brand Information from Ads," *Journal of Marketing,* October 1991, pp. 32–53.

40. George E. Belch, "An Examination of Comparative and Noncomparative Television Commercials: The Effects of Claim Variation and Repetition on Cognitive Response and Message Acceptance," *Journal of Marketing Research,* August 1981, pp. 333–49; and Cornelia Droge and Rene Y. Darmon, "Associative Positioning Strategies through Comparative Advertising: Attribute versus Overall Similarity Approaches," *Journal of Marketing Research,* November 1987, pp. 377–88; Cornelia Pechmann and S. Ratneshwar, "The Use of Comparative Advertising for Brand Positioning: Association versus Differentiation," *Journal of Consumer Research,* September 1991, pp. 145–60; and Cornelia Droge, "Shaping the Route to Attitude Change: Central versus Peripheral Processing Through Comparative versus Noncomparative Advertising," *Journal of Marketing Research,* May 1989, pp. 193–204.

41. Jon Gutman, "Analyzing Consumer Orientations toward Beverages through Means-End Chain Analysis," *Psychology and Marketing* 3/4 (1984), pp. 23–43; and Joan Mount and Eugene Kaciak, "Transforming the Laddering Technique into a Research Tool for Everyday Use," *Marketing,* vol. 14, 1993, pp. 205–217.

42. See David Berger, "Theory into Practice: The FCB Grid," *European Research,* January 1986, pp. 35–46; Richard Vaughn, "How Advertising Works: A Planning Model," *Journal of Advertising Research,* October 1980, pp. 27–33; Richard Vaughn, "How Advertising Works: A Planning Model Revisited," *Journal of Advertising Research,* February–March 1986, pp. 57–66; and Chung K. Kim and Kenneth R. Lord, "A New FCB Grid and Its Strategic Implications for Advertising," *Marketing,* vol. 12, 1991, pp. 51–60.

43. Roberto Friedman and V. Parker Lessig, "A Framework of Psychological Meaning of Products," in *Advances in Consumer Research,* vol. 13, ed. Richard J. Lutz (Provo, Utah: Association for Consumer Research, 1986), pp. 338–42.

44. Julie A. Edell, "Nonverbal Effects in Ads: A Review and Synthesis," in *Nonverbal Communication in Advertising,* ed. David Stewart and Sidney Hecker (Lexington, Mass.: Lexington Books, 1988); Werner Kroeber-Riel, "Emotional Product Differentiation by Classical Conditioning," in *Advances in Consumer Research,* vol. 11, ed. Thomas C. Kinnear (Ann Arbor, Mich.: Association for Consumer Research, 1984), pp. 538–43; and Marian Chapman Burke and Julie A. Edell, "The Impact of Feelings on Ad-Based Affect and Cognition," *Journal of Marketing Research,* February 1989, pp. 69–83.

45. Belch, "An Examination of Comparative and Noncomparative Television Commercials," pp. 333–49; and William L. Wilkie and Paul W. Farris, "Comparison Advertising Problems and Potential," *Journal of Marketing,* October 1975, pp. 7–15; and Auleen Carson and Marshall Rice, "The Incidence of Comparative Advertising: A Content Analysis of Canadian and American Magazines," *Marketing,* vol. 11, 1990, pp. 65–73; Normand Turgeon, "Comparative Advertising: Some Positive Findings," *Marketing,* vol. 11, 1990, pp. 359–368.

46. Thomas J. Peters and Robert H. Waterman, Jr., *In Search of Excellence: Lessons from America's Best-Run Companies* (New York: Warner Books, 1982), p. 158.

47. Celsi and Olson, "The Role of Involvement," pp. 210–24; and C. Whan Park and S. Mark Young, "Consumer Response to Television Commercials: The Impact of Involvement and Background Music on Brand Attitude Formation," *Journal of Marketing Research,* February 1986, pp. 11–24.

48. Marian C. Burke and Julie A. Edell, "Ad Reactions over Time: Capturing Changes in the Real World," *Journal of Consumer Research,* June 1986, pp. 114–18.

49. Thomas J. Reynolds and John P. Rochon, "Means-End Based Advertising Research: Copy Testing Is Not Strategy Assessment," *Journal of Business Research* 22 (1991), pp. 131–42.

50. Material for this section is derived from Jerry C. Olson and Thomas J. Reynolds, "Understanding Consumers' Cognitive Structures: Implications for Advertising Strategies," in *Advertising and Consumer Psychology,* ed. Larry Percy and Arch Woodside (Lexington, Mass.: Lexington Books, 1983), pp. 77–90.

51. Thomas J. Reynolds and Alyce Byrd Craddock, "The Application of the MECCAS Model to the Development and Assessment of Advertising Strategy: A Case Study," *Journal of Advertising Research,* April–May 1988, pp. 43–54.

52. Thomas J. Reynolds and Charles Gengler, "A Strategic Framework for Assessing Advertising: The Animatic vs. Finished Issue," *Journal of Advertising Research,* June–July 1991, pp. 61–71.

Chapter 10

1. Robert C. Blattberg and Scott A. Neslin, *Sales Promotion: Concepts, Methods, and Strategies* (Englewood Cliffs, N.J.: Prentice Hall, 1990), p. 3.

2. J. Paul Peter and James H. Donnelly, Jr., *A Preface to Marketing Management,* 5th ed. (Homewood, Ill.: Richard D. Irwin, 1990), p. 151.

3. "Study: Some Promotions Change Consumer Behavior," *Marketing News,* October 15, 1990, p. 12.

4. For further discussion and examples of research, see Alan E. Kazdin, *Behavior Modification in Applied Settings,* 4th ed. (Pacific Grove, Calif.: Brooks/Cole Publishing, 1989); Lee Smith, "Getting Junkies to Clean Up," *Fortune,* May 6, 1991, pp. 103–8; and A. D. Wayne Taylor and Katherine Henderson, "AIDS and Ontario's Public Education

Campaign: A Social Marketing Calamity," *Canadian Journal of Administrative Sciences*, vol. 9 (1), 1992, pp. 58–65. Also, see recent issues of the *Journal of Applied Behavior Analysis*. For example, the Spring 1991 issue has a series of articles on improving safe driving.

Chapter 11

1. *Montreal Gazette*, March 26, 1994, p. A6.

2. Much of the material in this chapter is based on Walter R. Nord and J. Paul Peter, "A Behavior Modification Perspective on Marketing," *Journal of Marketing*, Spring 1980, pp. 36–47; and J. Paul Peter and Walter R. Nord, "A Clarification and Extension of Operant Conditioning Principles in Marketing," *Journal of Marketing*, Summer 1982, pp. 102–7.

3. Gerald J. Gorn, "The Effects of Music in Advertising on Choice Behavior: A Classical Conditioning Approach," *Journal of Marketing*, Winter 1982, pp. 94–101.

4. Werner Kroeber-Riel, "Emotional Product Differentiation by Classical Conditioning," in *Advances in Consumer Research*, vol. 11, ed. Thomas C. Kinnear (Provo, Utah: Association for Consumer Research, 1984), pp. 538–43.

5. Richard A. Feinberg, "Classical Conditioning of Credit Cards: Credit Cards May Facilitate Spending," in *Proceedings of the American Psychological Association, Division of Consumer Psychology*, ed. Michael B. Mazis (Washington, D.C.: American Psychological Association, 1982), pp. 28–30; also see Richard A. Feinberg, "Credit Cards as Spending Facilitating Stimuli: A Conditioning Interpretation," *Journal of Consumer Research*, December 1986, pp. 348–56.

6. B. C. Deslauriers and P. B. Everett, "The Effects of Intermittent and Continuous Token Reinforcement on Bus Ridership," *Journal of Applied Psychology*, August 1977, pp. 369–75.

7. J. Ronald Carey, Stephen H. Clicque, Barbara A. Leighton, and Frank Milton, "A Test of Positive Reinforcement of Customers," *Journal of Marketing*, October 1976, pp. 98–100.

8. A. J. McSweeney, "Effects of Response Cost on the Behavior of a Million Persons: Charging for Directory Assistance in Cincinnati," *Journal of Applied Behavioral Analysis*, Spring 1978, pp. 47–51.

Chapter 12

1. Albert Bandura, *Principles of Behavior Modification* (New York: Holt, Rinehart & Winston, 1979), p. 167.

2. See Joseph R. Cautela, "The Present Status of Covert Modeling," *Journal of Behavior Therapy and Experimental Psychiatry*, December 1976, pp. 323–26.

3. Cautela, "Present Status," pp. 323–26.

4. Viola Catt and Peter L. Benson, "Effect of Verbal Modeling on Contributions to Charity," *Journal of Applied Psychology*, February 1977, pp. 81–85.

5. See Charles C. Manz and Henry P. Sims, "Vicarious

Learning: The Influence of Modeling on Organizational Behavior," *Academy of Management Review*, January 1981, pp. 105–13. For discussions of model characteristics in advertising, see Michael J. Baker and Gilbert A. Churchill, Jr., "The Impact of Physically Attractive Models on Advertising Evaluations," *Journal of Marketing Research*, November 1977, pp. 538–55; "Models' Clothing Speaks to Ad Market: Study," *Marketing News*, November 22, 1985, p. 16; and Lynn R. Kahle and Pamela M. Homer, "Physical Attractiveness of the Celebrity Endorser: A Social Adaptation Perspective," *Journal of Consumer Research*, March 1985, pp. 954–61.

6. Manz and Sims, "Vicarious Learning," p. 107.

7. Albert Bandura, *Social Learning Theory* (Englewood Cliffs, N.J.: Prentice Hall, 1977), p. 89.

8. Mary Dee Dickerson and James W. Gentry, "Characteristics of Adopters and Nonadopters of Home Computers," *Journal of Consumer Research*, September 1983, pp. 225–35. Also see William E. Warren, C. L. Abercrombie, and Robert L. Berl, "Characteristics of Adopters and Nonadopters of Alternative Residential Long-Distance Telephone Services," in *Advances in Consumer Research*, vol. 15, ed. Michael J. Houston (Provo, Utah: Association for Consumer Research, 1987), pp. 292–98; Peter Sianchuk and Laurel de Yturralde, "Adoption and Use/Continuance of Technologically Advanced Consumer Products: Research Implications for the Study of Technophobia," *Marketing*, vol. 12, 1991, pp. 243–252; and Roger A. More, "Generating Profit from New Technology: Adoption as a Major Management Problem," *Canadian Journal of Administrative Sciences*, vol. 6, no. 1 (1989), pp. 29–35.

Chapter 13

1. James B. Treece and Mark Landler, "Beep, Beep! There Goes Ford's Explorer," *Business Week*, January 28, 1991, pp. 60–61. Canadian data provided by Ford Canada product information manager, April 14, 1995.

2. Sharon E. Beatty and Scott M. Smith, "External Search Effort: An Investigation across Several Product Categories," *Journal of Consumer Research*, June 1987, p. 84.

3. For a complete discussion of these issues, see Howard Beales, Michael B. Mazis, Steven Salop, and Richard Staelin, "Consumer Search and Public Policy," *Journal of Consumer Research*, June 1981, pp. 11–22.

4. "American Express Plays Its Trump Card," *Business Week*, October 24, 1983, p. 62; also see "Credit Cards: The U.S. Is Taking Its Time Getting 'Smart,'" *Business Week*, February 9, 1987, pp. 88–89.

5. Susan Caminiti, "What the Scanner Knows about You," *Fortune*, December 3, 1990, pp. 51–52; also see Jeffrey Rothfeder et al., "How Software Is Making Food Sales a Piece of Cake," *Business Week*, July 2, 1990, pp. 54–55; Dom Del Prete, "Advances in Scanner Research Yield Better Data Quicker," *Marketing News*, January 7, 1991, p. 54; and Howard Schlossberg, "IRI Expands Sales Tracking to Drugstores, Mass Merchandisers," *Marketing News*, May 27, 1991, pp. 1, 10.

Chapter 14

1. Doug Naime, "High-Tech Bingo Palace Lures Gamblers," *Winnipeg Free Press,* June 19, 1993, p. A14.

2. Adapted from Jack Block and Jeanne H. Block, "Studying Situational Dimensions: A Grand Perspective and Some Limited Empiricism," in *Toward a Psychology of Situations: An Interactional Perspective,* ed. David Magnusson (Hillsdale, N.J.: Lawrence Erlbaum, 1981), pp. 85–102. Also see Annette Ribordy and David Gillingham, "Are There Specific Environmental Requirements for the Development of New Products?,"*Canadian Journal of Administrative Sciences,* vol. 9, no. 3 (1992), pp. 203–212.

3. For example, see Robert J. Graham, "The Role of Perception of Time in Consumer Research," *Journal of Consumer Research,* March 1981, pp. 335–42; Laurence P. Feldman and Jacob Hornik, "The Use of Time: An Integrated Conceptual Model," *Journal of Consumer Research,* March 1981, pp. 408–19; Jacob Hornik, "Situational Effects on the Consumption of Time," *Journal of Marketing,* Fall 1982, pp. 44–55; and Jacob Hornik, "Subjective versus Objective Time Measures: A Note on the Perception of Time in Consumer Behavior," *Journal of Consumer Research,* June 1984, pp. 615–18.

4. See Debra A. Michal's, "Pitching Products by the Barometer," *Business Week,* July 8, 1985, p. 45; Ronald Alsop, "Companies Look to Weather to Find Best Climate for Ads," *The Wall Street Journal,* January 19, 1985, p. 27; and Fred Ward, "Weather, Behavior Correlated in New Market Test," *Marketing News,* June 7, 1985, p. 9.

5. See Mark Harris, "Evaluate Lighting Systems as a Marketing Device, Not Overhead," *Marketing News,* October 26, 1984, p. 1.

6. Joseph A. Bellizzi, Ayn E. Crowley, and Ronald W. Hasty, The Effects of Color in Store Design," *Journal of Retailing,* Spring 1983, pp. 21–45. Also see J. Edward Russo, Richard Staelin, Catherine A. Nolan, Gary J. Russell, and Barbara L. Metcalf, "Nutrition Information in the Supermarket," *Journal of Consumer Research,* June 1986, pp. 48–70.

7. Carl P. Zeithaml and Valarie A. Zeithaml, "Environmental Management: Revising the Marketing Perspective," *Journal of Marketing,* Spring 1984, pp. 46–53.

8. The figures and part of the discussion of store layout are based on J. Barry Mason, Morris L. Mayer, and Hazel F. Ezell, *Retailing,* 3rd ed. (Plano, Texas: Business Publications, Inc., 1988), pp. 244–77.

9. Gary F. McKinnon, J. Patrick Kelly, and E. Doyle Robinson, "Sales Effects of Point-of-Purchase In-Store Signing," *Journal of Retailing,* Summer 1981, pp. 49–63.

10. See Rockney G. Walters and Scott B. MacKenzie, "A Structural Equations Analysis of the Impact of Price Promotions on Store Performance," *Journal of Marketing Research,* February 1988, pp. 51–63; and V. Kumar and Robert P. Leone, "Measuring the Effect of Retail Store Promotions on Brand and Store Substitution," *Journal of Marketing Research,* May 1988, pp. 178–85.

11. J. B. Wilkinson, J. Barry Mason, and Christie H. Paksoy, "Assessing the Impact of Short-Term Supermarket Strategy Variables," *Journal of Marketing Research,* February 1982, pp. 72–86.

12. Ronald E. Milliman, "Using Background Music to Affect the Behavior of Supermarket Shoppers," *Journal of Marketing,* Summer 1982, pp. 86–91.

13. Ibid., p. 91. For additional support for these ideas, see Ronald E. Milliman, "The Influence of Background Music on the Behavior of Restaurant Patrons," *Journal of Consumer Research,* September 1986, pp. 286–89.

14. See James H. Leigh and Claude R. Martin, "A Review of Situational Influence Paradigms and Research," in *Review of Marketing* (1981), ed. Ben M. Enis and Kenneth J. Reering (Chicago: American Marketing Association, 1981), pp. 57–74; Pradeep Kakkar and Richard J. Lutz, "Situational Influences on Consumer Behavior," in *Perspectives in Consumer Behavior,* 3rd ed., ed. Harold H. Kassarjian and Thomas S. Robertson (Glenview, Ill.: Scott, Foresman, 1981), pp. 204–15; and Joseph A. Cote, Jr., "Situational Variables in Consumer Research: A Review," Working Paper, Washington State University, 1985.

15. See Russell W. Belk, "The Objective Situation as a Determinant of Consumer Behavior," in *Advances in Consumer Research,* vol. 2, ed. Mary J. Schlinger (Chicago: Association for Consumer Research, 1975), pp. 427–38; and Richard J. Lutz and Pradeep K. Kakkar, "The Psychological Situation as a Determinant of Consumer Behavior, in *Advances in Consumer Research,* vol. 2, ed. Mary J. Schlinger (Chicago: Association for Consumer Research, 1975), pp. 439–54.

16. Geraldine Fennell, "Consumers' Perceptions of the Product Use Situation," *Journal of Marketing,* April 1978, pp. 38–47; Russell W. Belk, "Situational Variables and Consumer Behavior," *Journal of Consumer Research,* December 1976, pp. 156–64; Kenneth E. Miller and James L. Ginter, "An Investigation of Situational Variation in Brand Choice Behavior and Attitude," *Journal of Marketing Research,* February 1979, pp. 111–23.

17. Kenneth E. Miller and James L. Ginter, "An Investigation of Situational Variation in Brand Choice Behavior and Attitude," *Journal of Marketing Research,* February 1979, pp. 111–23.

18. J. Edward Russo, Richard Staelin, Catherine A. Nolan, Gary J. Russell, and Barbara L. Metcalf, "Nutrition Information in the Supermarket," *Journal of Consumer Research,* June 1986, pp. 48–70.

19. Dennis L. McNeill and William L. Wilkie, "Public Policy and Consumer Information: Impact on the New Energy Labels," *Journal of Consumer Research,* June 1979, pp. 1–11.

20. These examples come from Skip Wollenberg, "P-O-P Campaigns Increase as Profile of Shoppers Change," *Marketing News,* April 11, 1988, p. 25.

21. Joe Agnew, "P-O-P Displays Are Becoming a Matter of Convenience," *Marketing News,* October 9, 1987, pp. 14, 16.

22. J. Davis Illingworth, "The Personal Plus," *Marketing Insights,* Winter 1991, pp. 31–33, 45.

23. Illingworth, "The Personal Plus."

24. "Hallmark Now Marketing by Color," *Marketing News,* June 6, 1988, p. 18.

25. Meryl P. Gardner and George J. Siomkos, "Toward Methodology for Assessing Effects of In-Store Atmospherics," in *Advances in Consumer Research,* vol. 13, ed. Richard J. Lutz (Provo, Utah: Association for Consumer Research, 1986), pp. 27–31; and Robert J. Donovan and John R. Rossiter, "Store Atmosphere: An Environmental Psychology Approach, *Journal of Retailing,* Spring 1982, pp. 34–37.

26. Diane Schneidman, "Visual Aura, Kinetics Help Stabilize Store Image," *Marketing News,* October 23, 1987, p. 4.

27. Michael Solomon, "The Missing Link: Surrogate Consumers in the Marketing Chain," *Journal of Marketing,* October 1986, pp. 208–18.

28. Russell W. Belk, John Sherry, and Melanie Wallendorf, "A Naturalistic Inquiry into Buyer and Seller Behavior at a Swap Meet," *Journal of Consumer Research,* March 1988, pp. 449–70.

Chapter 15

1. Adapted from Grant McCracken, *Culture and Consumption: New Approaches to the Symbolic Character of Consumer Goods and Activities* (Bloomington, Ind.: Indiana University Press, 1988), Ch. 1; and Janeen A. Costa, "Toward an Understanding of Social and World Systemic Processes in the Spread of Consumer Culture: An Anthropological Case Study," in *Advances in Consumer Research,* 17, ed. (Provo, Utah: Association for Consumer Research, 1991), pp. 826–32.

2. Over 160 definitions of culture are reported in Frederick D. Sturdivant, "Subculture Theory: Poverty, Minorities, and Marketing," in *Consumer Behavior: Theoretical Sources,* ed. Scott Ward and Thomas S. Robertson (Englewood Cliffs, N.J.: Prentice Hall, 1973), pp. 469–520.

3. McCracken, *Culture and Consumption.*

4. John F. Sherry, "The Cultural Perspective in Consumer Research," in *Advances in Consumer Research,* vol. 13, ed. Richard J. Lutz (Provo, Utah: Association for Consumer Research, 1986), pp. 573–75.

5. Ann Swidler, "Culture in Action: Symbols and Strategies," *American Sociological Review,* April 1986, pp. 273–86. Most consumer behaviour textbooks focus on the content of culture, describing the values and lifestyles of consumers in different cultures. For example, see Leon G. Shiffman and Leslie Lazar Kanuk, *Consumer Behavior,* 4th ed. (Englewood Cliffs, N.J.: Prentice Hall, 1991); and William L. Wilkie, *Consumer Behavior,* 2nd ed. (New York: John Wiley & Sons, 1990).

6. Craig J. Thompson, William B. Locander, and Howard R. Pollio, "Putting Consumer Experience Back into Consumer Research: The Philosophy and Method of Existential Phenomenology," *Journal of Consumer Research,* September 1989, pp. 133–47; and Craig J. Thompson, William B. Locander, Howard R. Pollio, "The Lived Meaning of Free Choice: An Existential-Phenomenological Description of Everyday Consumer Experiences of Contemporary Married Women," *Journal of Consumer Research,* December 1990, pp. 346–61.

7. Margot Hornblower, "Advertising Spoken Here," *Time,* July 15, 1991, pp. 71–72.

8. David Kilburn, "Japan's Sun Rises," *Advertising Age,* August 3, 1987, p. 42.

9. Sidney J. Levy, "Interpreting Consumer Mythology: A Structural Approach to Consumer Behavior," *Journal of Marketing,* Summer 1981, pp. 49–61.

10. This model is an adaptation and extension of the cultural process described by Grant McCracken, in *Culture and Consumption,* focusing on how cultural meanings are first transferred to products and then passed on to individuals.

11. Grant McCracken, "Culture and Consumption: A Theoretical Account of the Structure and Movement of the Cultural Meaning of Consumer Goods," *Journal of Consumer Research,* June 1986, pp. 71–84.

12. McCracken, *Culture and Consumption,* p. 79.

13. Jeffrey F. Durgee and Robert W. Stuart, "Advertising Symbols and Brand Names that Best Represent Key Product Meanings," *Journal of Advertising,* Summer 1987, pp. 15–24.

14. Elizabeth C. Hirschman, "The Creation of Product Symbolism," in *Advances in Consumer Research,* vol. 13, ed. R. J. Lutz (Provo, Utah: Association for Consumer Research, 1986), pp. 327–31.

15. For a brief discussion of the meaning transfer aspects of the fashion system, see McCracken, "Culture and Consumption."

16. Mihaly Csikszentmihalyi and Eugene Rochberg-Halton, *The Meaning of Things: Domestic Symbols and the Self* (Cambridge: Cambridge University Press, 1981); Sidney J. Levy, "Interpreting Consumer Mythology: A Structural Approach to Consumer Behavior," *Journal of Marketing,* 1981, pp. 49–61. Michael Solomon, "The Role of Products as Social Stimuli: A Symbolic Interactionism Perspective," *Journal of Consumer Research,* December 1983, pp. 319–29.

17. Seth Lubove, "Going, Going, Sold!" *Forbes,* October 14, 1991, pp. 180–81.

18. Anne B. Fisher, "Coke's Brand-Loyalty Lesson," *Fortune,* August 5, 1985, pp. 44–46.

19. McCracken, *Culture and Consumption;* and Dennis W. Rook, "The Ritual Dimension of Consumer Behavior," *Journal of Consumer Research,* December 1985, pp. 251–64.

20. The last four rituals are described in McCracken, "Culture and Consumption," pp. 71–84.

21. John F. Sherry, Jr., "A Sociocultural Analysis of a Midwestern American Flea Market," *Journal of Consumer Research,* June, pp. 13–30.

22. Peter H. Bloch, "Product Enthusiasm: Many Questions, A Few Answers," in *Advances in Consumer Research,* vol. 13, ed. R. J. Lutz (Provo, Utah: Association for Consumer Research, 1986), pp. 61–65.

23. Russell W. Belk, "Gift-Giving Behavior," in *Research in Marketing,* vol. 2, ed. Jagdish Sheth (Greenwich, Conn.: JAI Press, 1979), pp. 95–126.

24. Michael R. Solomon, "Deep-Seated Materialism: The Case of Levi's 501 Jeans," in *Advances in Consumer Research,* vol. 13, ed. R. J. Lutz (Provo, Utah: Association for Consumer Research, 1986), pp. 619–22.

25. Edmund Sherman and Evelyn S. Newman, "The Meaning of Cherished Personal Possessions for the Elderly," *Journal of Aging and Human Development* 8, no. 2 (1977–78), pp. 181–92; and Terence A. Shimp and Thomas J. Madden, "Consumer-Object Relations: A Conceptual Framework Based Analogously on Sternberg's Triangular Theory of Love," in *Advances in Consumer Research,* vol. 15, ed. M. Houston (Provo, Utah: Association for Consumer Research, 1988), pp. 163–68.

26. Thomas Reynolds and Jonathan Gutman, "Advertising Is Image Management," *Journal of Advertising Research,* 1984, 24(1), pp. 27–36; for a similar viewpoint, see C. Whan Park, Bernard J. Jaworski, and Deborah J. MacInnis, "Strategic Brand Concept-Image Management," *Journal of Marketing,* October 1986, pp. 135–45.

27. Peter H. Farquhar, "Managing Brand Equity," *Marketing Research,* September 1989, pp. 24–33.

28. Russell W. Belk, "ACR Presidential Address: Happy Thought," in *Advances in Consumer Research,* vol. 14, ed. M. Wallendorf and P. Anderson (Provo, Utah: Association for Consumer Research, 1986), pp. 1–4.

29. This section is adapted from Grant McCracken, "Who Is the Celebrity Endorser? Cultural Foundations of the Endorsement Process," *Journal of Consumer Research,* December 1989, pp. 310–21. See also Chike Okechuku, Ignatius va Kooten, and Pauline Tsang, "The Effectiveness of Celebrity Endorsement in Print Advertising," *Marketing,* vol. 12, 1991, pp. 212–223.

30. Joshua Levine, "The Sound of No Dealers Selling," *Forbes,* February 19, 1990, pp. 122–24.

31. Some foreign markets are not growing because of competition from television and home videos (box-office receipts in Finland were down about 15 percent in 1990, for example). See Kathleen A. Hughes, "You Don't Need Subtitles to Know Foreign Film Folk Have the Blues," *The Wall Street Journal,* March 5, 1991, p. B1.

32. Hazel Rose Markus and Shinobu Kitayama, "Culture and Self: Implications for Cognition, Emotion, and Motivation," *Psychological Review* 98, no. 2 (1991), pp. 224–53.

33. Russell W. Belk, "Materialism: Trait Aspects of Living in the Material World," *Journal of Consumer Research,* December 1985, pp. 265–79.

34. Marsha L. Richins and Scott Dawson, "Measuring Material Values: A Preliminary Report of Scale Development," in *Advances in Consumer Research,* 17, eds. M. Goldberg, G. Gorn, and R. Pollay (Provo, Utah: Association for Consumer Research, 1990), pp. 169–75.

35. Scott Dawson and Gary Bamossy, "Isolating the Effect of Non-Economic Factors on the Development of a Consumer Culture: A Comparison of Materialism in the Netherlands and the United States," in *Advances in Consumer Research,* vol. 17, eds. (Provo, Utah: Association for Consumer Research, 1990), pp. 182–85.

36. Thompson et al., "The Lived Meaning of Free Choice."

37. Carla Rapoport, "How the Japanese Are Changing," *Fortune,* September 24, 1990, pp. 15–22.

38. Laurel Anderson and Marsha Wadkins, "Japan—A Culture of Consumption?" in *Advances in Consumer Research,* vol. 18, eds. R. Holman and M. Solomon (Provo, Utah: Association for Consumer Research, 1991), pp. 129–34; and Yumiko Ono, "Japan Becomes Land of the Rising Mall," *The Wall Street Journal,* February 11, 1991, pp. B1, B6.

39. For further discussion of these and many other examples, see David A. Ricks, *Big Business Blunders: Mistakes in Multinational Marketing* (Homewood, Ill.: Dow Jones-Irwin, 1983).

40. Lynne Reaves, "China's Domestic Ad Scene: A Paradox," *Advertising Age,* September 16, 1985, p. 76.

41. "Global Advertisers Should Pay Heed to Contextual Variations," *Marketing News,* February 13, 1987, p. 18; and A. Tansu Barker and Nizamettin Aydin, "Globalization versus Adaptation: A Marketing Perspective," *Marketing,* vol. 11, 1990, pp. 25–34.

42. See Anne B. Fisher, "The Ad Biz Gloms onto 'Global,'" *Fortune,* November 12, 1984, pp. 77–80. The examples in this section are taken from this article. Also see Bill Saporito, "Black & Decker's Gamble on 'Globalization,'" *Fortune,* May 14, 1984, pp. 40–48.

43. For example, see "Levitt: Global Companies to Replace Dying Multinationals," *Marketing News,* March 15, 1985, p. 15; Theodore Levitt, *The Marketing Imagination* (New York: The Free Press, 1983), Ch. 2; and Theodore Levitt, "The Globalization of Markets," *Harvard Business Review,* May–June 1983, pp. 92–102.

44. Subrata N. Chakravarty, "The Croissant Comes to Harvard Square," *Forbes,* July 14, 1986, p. 69.

45. Christine Dugas and Marilyn A. Harris, "Playtex Kicks Off a One-Ad-Fits-All Campaign," *Business Week,* December 16, 1985, pp. 48–49.

46. Julie Skur Hill and Joseph M. Winski, "Good-bye Global Ads: Global Village Is Fantasy Land for Big Marketers," *Advertising Age,* November 16, 1987, pp. 22–36; Joanne Lipman, "Marketers Turn Sour on Global Sales Pitch Harvard Guru Makes," *The Wall Street Journal,* May 12, 1988, pp. 1, 10; and N. Papadopoulos, L. A. Heslop, and J. J. Marshall, "Domestic and International Marketing of Canadian Cultural Products: Some Questions and Directions for Research," *Marketing,* vol. 11, 1990, pp. 266–275.

47. McCracken, "Culture and Consumption," pp. 71–84.

Chapter 16

1. Bob Papoe, "Maybelline Revamps Line to Lure Mature Women," *Toronto Star,* November 2, 1991, p. C3; *Canadian Social Trends,* Statistics Canada, Cat #11-008E, Summer 1993; *Chronicle Herald,* December 3, 1991, p. B1; *Fortune,* December 14, 1992, p. 15; and Susan

Garland, "Those Aging Baby Boomers," *Business Week,* May 20, 1991, pp. 106–12.

2. Alecia Swasy, "Changing Times," *The Wall Street Journal,* March 22, 1991, p. B6.

3. Diane Crispell, "Guppies, Minks, and Ticks," *American Demographics,* June 1990, pp. 50–51.

4. Associated Press, "Survey: Age Is Not Good Indicator of Consumer Need," *Marketing News,* November 21, 1988, p. 6. Also see Thomas E. Muller, "The Implications of Change in the Value Orientations of Canada's Aging Population," *Marketing,* vol. 10, 1989, pp. 245–246; and Thomas A. Muller, Lynn R. Kahle, and Emmanuel J. Cheron, "Value Trends and Demand Forecasts for Canada's Aging Baby Boomers," *Canadian Journal of Administrative Sciences,* vol. 9, no. 4 (1992), pp. 294–304.

5. Alexander Bruce, "Canadian Teen Mag Will Fill a Void," *Marketing,* April 5, 1993, p. 24; J. Marney, "Youthful Shoppers Can Be Savvy and Skeptical," *Marketing,* May 31, 1993, p. 26; J. Marney, "Youth Culture Is Key to a Huge Market," *Marketing,* August 5, 1991, p. 16; J. Marney, "New Perspectives on the Teen Market," *Marketing,* June 16, 1986, p. 9; J. Marney, "Teenagers: Power in Numbers," *Marketing,* February 19, 1990, p. 17; and J. Marney, "Brand Loyalty: A Marketer's Teen Dream," *Marketing,* December 9, 1991, p. 14. For a discussion of advertising to the youth market, see Anne M. Lavack, "Using Brand Image to Compete for the Youth Market: The Case of Export 'A' and Player's," *Marketing,* vol. 14, 1993, pp. 142–151.

6. Thomas Muller, Lynn Kahle, and Emmanuel Cheron, "Value Trends and Demand Forecasts for Canada's Aging Baby Boomers," *Canadian Journal of Administrative Sciences,* vol. 9, no. 4 (1992), pp. 294–304.

7. Faith Popcorn, *The Popcorn Report,* (New York: Doubleday, 1991).

8. *Canadian Social Trends,* Statistics Canada, Cat #11-008E, Summer 1993.

9. Ken Dychtwald and Joe Flower, *Age Wave: The Challenges and Opportunities of an Aging America,* (New York: Bantam, 1990).

10. Much of the above discussion comes from the following sources: "Ethnic Diversity in the 90s," *Canadian Social Trends,* Statistics Canada, Cat #11-008E, Autumn 1993, pp. 1, 20; B. Singh Bolaria, "Social Issues and Contradictions in Canadian Society," p. 198; *Elderly in Canada,* Statistics Canada, Cat #91-533E, pp. 12, 14; *Profile of Canada's Seniors,* Statistics Canada, Cat #96-312E, pp. 11, 14, 21, 32, 39, 43; and *General Social Survey Analysis Series: Health and Social Support 1985,* Statistics Canada, Cat #11-612E, p. 204.

11. P. C. Lefrancois and G. Chatel, "The French-Canadian Consumer," *Canadian Marketer,* vol. 2, no. 2 (Spring 1967), pp. 4–7.

12. George Henault, "Les Consequences du Biculturalisme sur la Consommation," *Commerce,* vol. 73, no. 9 (September 1971), pp. 90–91; K. S. Palda, "A Comparison of Consumers' Expenditures in Quebec and Ontario," *Canadian Journal of Economics and Political Science,* vol. 33 (February 1967), p. 26; D. R. Thomas, "Cultural and Consumption Behaviours in English and French Canada," in *Marketing in the 1970s and Beyond,* ed. B. Stidsen (Montreal: Administrative Sciences Association of Canada, 1975), pp. 255–61; B. Mallen, *French Canadian Consumer Behaviour* (Montreal: Advertising and Sales Executive Club of Montreal, October 1977), p. 8; "Buying Habits of Quebec Consumers: Points to Ponder," *Marketing,* May 27, 1985, pp. 13–27; J. Bouchard, "The French Evolution," *Marketing,* September 26, 1983, p. 60; and J. Bouchard, *Differences* (Montreal: Editions Heritage, 1980).

13. Michel Bergier and Jerry A. Rosenblatt, "A Critical Review of Past and Current Methodologies For Classifying English and French Canadians," in *Marketing,* vol. 3, 1982, pp. 11–20.

14. "Ethnic Diversity in the 90s," *Canadian Social Trends,* Statistics Canada, Cat #11-008E, Autumn 1993; "Portrait of the Quebec Consumer: Two Research Firms Look into the Hearts, Minds and Buying Habits of the Quebecois," *Marketing,* March 22, 1993, p. 14; Alanna Mitchell, "Hopes for Bilingualism Unrealised: Statistics Show Gap in French-English Incomes Has Grown," *Globe and Mail,* March 23, 1994, pp. A1, A7; and Alanna Mitchell, "Francophones Alarmed by Income Gap: Data Refute Myth that French Speakers Get Too Much Funding," *Globe and Mail,* March 24, 1994, p. D6.

15. For an excellent review of this subject see G. Kindra, M. Laroche and T. Muller, *Consumer Behaviour: The Canadian Perspective*, Scarborough: Nelson Canada, 1994, pp. 342–351.

16. "Asia Lifestyles Special Report," *Far East Economic Review,* July 14, 1994, p. 35.

17. David Chilton, "Study to Track Chinese Buyers," *Strategy,* March 8, 1993, p. 7.

18. Phil Johnson, "CIBC Opens 'Asian' Branch," *Strategy,* August 10, 1992, p. 2.

19. "New Chinese Buy Quality, Survey Finds," *Toronto Star,* June 2, 1992, p. D1.

20. Ibid.

21. H. Winaker-Steiner and N. A. Wetzel, "German Families," in *Ethnicity and Family Therapy,* ed. M. McGoldrick, J. K. Pierce, and J. Giordano (New York: The Guilford Press, 1982), pp. 247–68.

22. Franca Damiani Carella, "The Powerful Role of Church," *Toronto Star,* June 4, 1992, p. F8; and Lois Sweet, "Tale of Italian Community One of Metro's Success Stories," *Toronto Star,* July 19, 1992, pp. A1, A6–A7.

23. *The Canadian Family Tree,* Department of Secretary of State, Supply and Services Canada, 1979, pp. 96–98.

24. "Ethnic Diversity in the 90s," *Canadian Social Trends,* Statistics Canada, Cat #11-008E, Autumn 1993, pp. 19–22.

25. C. Attneave, "American Indians and Alaska Native Families: Immigrants in Their Own Homeland," in *Ethnicity and Family Therapy,* ed. M. McGoldrick, J. K. Pierce, and J. Giordano (New York: The Guilford Press, 1982).

26. G. Sinclair, Jr. "Advertisers Poised to Tap into Native Demographics," *Winnipeg Free Press,* October 1, 1991, p. 3.

27. Much of the discussion in this section comes from the following sources: *Women in the Labour Force,* Statistics Canada, Cat #75-001E, Winter 1994 Perspectives; Joan Myers-Levy and Durairaj Maheswaran, "Exploring Differ-

ences in Males' and Females' Processing Strategies," *Journal of Consumer Research,* June 1991, pp. 63–70; and Floyd Rudmin, "German and Canadian Data on Motivations for Ownership: Was Pythagoras Right?," in *Advances in Consumer Research,* vol. 17, eds. M. Goldberg, G. Gorn, and R. Pollay (Provo, Utah: Association for Consumer Research), 1990, pp. 176–81.

28. *Poverty Profile 1992,* Statistics Canada, Spring 1994; Alanna Mitchell, "Hopes for Bilingualism Unrealised: Statistics Show Gap in French-English Incomes Has Grown," *Globe and Mail,* March 23, 1994, pp. A1, A7; and "Plus riches hors Quebec," *Globe and Mail,* March 26, 1994, p. D6.

29. Joel Garreau, *The Nine Nations of North America* (New York: Avon Books, 1981). For a critical perspective, see Lynn R. Kahle, "The Nine Nations of North America and the Value Basis of Geographic Segmentation," *Journal of Marketing,* April 1986, pp. 37–47; and Thomas E. Muller, "The Two Nations of Canada versus the Nine Nations of North America: A Cross-Cultural Analysis of Consumers' Personal Values," *Journal of International Consumer Marketing,* vol. 1, no. 4, pp. 57–79.

30. Much of the above discussion on acculturation comes from the following sources: Robert Matas, "A Banana Split in Vancouver," *Globe and Mail,* February 25, 1994, p. A17; Ronald J. Farber, Thomas C. O'Guinn, and John A. McCarty, "Ethnicity, Acculturation, and the Importance of Product Attributes," *Psychology & Marketing,* Summer 1987, pp. 121–34; and Lisa N. Penaloza, "Immigrant Consumer Acculturation," in *Advances in Consumer Research,* 16 (Provo, Utah: Association for Consumer Research), 1989, pp. 110–18.

31. Richard P. Coleman, "The Continuing Significance of Social Class to Marketing," *Journal of Consumer Research,* December 1983, pp. 265–80. Much of the discussion in this part of the chapter is based on Coleman's view of social class as described in this article.

32. Ibid.

33. James E. Fisher, "Social Class and Consumer Behavior: The Relevance of Class and Status," in *Advances in Consumer Research,* vol. 14, ed. Melanie Wallendorf and Paul Anderson (Provo, Utah: Association for Consumer Research, 1987), pp. 492–96.

34. Adapted from Charles M. Schaninger, "Social Class versus Income Revisited: An Empirical Investigation," *Journal of Marketing Research,* May 1981, pp. 192–208.

Chapter 17

1. Information supplied by the Lyons Group, Mattel, the Walt Disney Company, and Hallmark Canada.

2. Lakshman Krishnamurthi, "The Salience of Relevant Others and Its Effects on Individual and Joint Preferences: An Experimental Investigation," *Journal of Consumer Research,* June 1983, pp. 62–72.

3. C. Whan Park and V. Parker Lessig, "Students and Housewives: Differences in Susceptibility to Reference Group Influences," *Journal of Consumer Research,* September 1977, pp. 102–10; and William O. Bearden, Richard G. Netemeyer, and Jesse E. Teel, "Measurement of Consumer Susceptibility to Interpersonal Influence," *Journal of Consumer Research,* March 1989, pp. 473–81.

4. John W. Schouten and James H. Alexander, "Hog Heaven: The Structure, Ethos, and Market Impact of a Consumption Culture," a paper presented at the Annual Conference of the Association for Consumer Research, Chicago, October 1991.

5. William O. Bearden and Michael J. Etzel, "Reference Group Influences on Product and Brand Purchase Decision," *Journal of Consumer Research,* September 1982, pp. 183–94. The discussion in this section relies heavily on this excellent work.

6. David Brinberg and Linda Plimpton, "Self-Monitoring and Product Conspicuousness in Reference Group Influence," in *Advances in Consumer Research,* vol. 13, ed. Richard J. Lutz (Provo, Utah: Association for Consumer Research, 1986), pp. 297–300.

7. For further discussion and an alternative approach to studying reference group influences, see Peter H. Reingen, Brian L. Foster, Jacqueline Johnson Brown, and Stephen B. Seidman, "Brand Congruence in Interpersonal Relations: A Social Network Analysis," *Journal of Consumer Research,* December 1984, pp. 771–83.

8. Julia M. Bristor, "Coalitions in Organizational Purchasing: An Application of Network Analysis," in *Advances in Consumer Research,* vol. 15, ed. Michael J. Houston (Provo, Utah: Association for Consumer Research, 1988), pp. 563–68; Jacqueline Johnson Brown and Peter H. Reingen, "Social Ties and Word-of-Mouth Referral Behavior," *Journal of Consumer Research,* December 1987, pp. 350–62; and Peter H. Reingen, "A Word-of-Mouth Network," in *Advances in Consumer Research,* vol. 14, ed. Melanie Wallendorf and Paul Anderson (Provo, Utah: Association for Consumer Research, 1987), pp. 213–17.

9. Dorothy Leonard-Barton, "Experts as Negative Opinion Leaders in the Diffusion of a Technological Innovation," *Journal of Consumer Research,* March 1985, pp. 914–26.

10. Bearden and Etzel, "Reference Group Influences," p. 184.

11. Joel Rudd, "The Household as a Consuming Unit," in *Advances in Consumer Research,* vol. 14, ed. Melanie Wallendorf and Paul Anderson (Provo, Utah: Association for Consumer Research, 1987), pp. 451–52.

12. This section is adapted from Diane Crispell, "How to Avoid Big Mistakes," *American Demographics,* March 1991, pp. 48–50.

13. Sunil Gupta, Michael R. Hagerty, and John G. Myers, "New Directions in Family Decision Making Research," in *Advances in Consumer Research,* vol. 10, ed. Richard P. Baggozzi and Alice M. Tybout (Ann Arbor, Mich.: Association for Consumer Research, 1983), pp. 445–50; and Jagdish N. Sheth, "A Theory of Family Buying Decisions," in *Modes of Buyer Behavior, Conceptual, Quantitative, and Empirical,* ed. J. N. Sheth (New York: Harper and Row, 1974), pp. 17–33.

14. Dennis L. Rosen and Donald H. Granbois, "Determinants of Role Structure in Family Financial Management,"

Journal of Consumer Research, September 1983, pp. 253–85; Irene Raj Foster and Richard W. Olshavsky, "An Exploratory Study of Family Decision Making Using a New Taxonomy of Family Role Structure," in *Advances in Consumer Research,* vol. 16, ed. T. K. Srull (Provo, Utah: Association for Consumer Research, 1989), pp. 665–70; and Jerry A. Rosenblatt, "A Study of the Contents of Husbands' and Wives' Evoked Sets," Proceedings of the XVIII European Academy of Marketing Annual Conference, 1989.

15. Benny Rigaux-Bricmont, "La prise de decision risquee dans le couple," *Marketing,* vol. 11, 1990, pp. 322–327; H. L. Davis and B. P. Riguax, "Perceptions of Marital Roles in Decision Processes," *Journal of Consumer Research,* June 1974, pp. 51–62; Pierre Filiatrault and J. Brent Ritchie, "Joint Purchasing Decisions: A Comparison of Influence Structure in Family and Couple Decision-Making Units," *Journal of Consumer Research,* September 1980, pp. 131–40; C. Kim and H. Lee, "Sex Role Attitudes of Spouses and Task Sharing Behaviour," *Advances in Consumer Research,* Association for Consumer Research, 1989, pp. 671–79; William J. Quails, "Household Decision Behavior: The Impact of Husbands' and Wives' Sex Role Orientation," *Journal of Consumer Research,* September 1987, pp. 264–79; Rosen and Granbois, "Determinants of Role Structure in Family Financial Management," Charles M. Schaninger, W. Christian Buss, and Rajiv Grover, "The Effect of Sex Roles on Family Economic Handling and Decision Influence," in *Advances in Consumer Research,* vol. 9, ed. Andrew A. Mitchell (Ann Arbor, Mich.: Association for Consumer Research, 1982), pp. 43–47; Daniel Seymour and Greg Lessne, "Spousal Conflict Arousal: Scale Development," *Journal of Consumer Research,* December 1984, pp. 810–21; Harry L. Davis, "Decision Making within the Household," *Journal of Consumer Research,* March 1976, pp. 241–60; and George P. Moschis and Linda G. Mitchell, "Television Advertising and Interpersonal Influences on Teenagers' Participation in Family Consumer Decisions," in *Advances in Consumer Research,* vol. 13, ed. Richard J. Lutz (Provo, Utah: Association for Consumer Research, 1986), pp. 181–86.

16. George E. Belch, Michael A. Belch, and Gayle Ceresino, "Parental and Teenage Child Influences in Family Decision Making," *Journal of Business Research* 13 (1985), pp. 163–76; and Ellen R. Foxman, Patriya S. Tansuhaj, and Karin M. Ekstrom, "Family Members' Perceptions of Adolescents' Influence in Family Decision Making," *Journal of Consumer Research,* March 1989, pp. 482–91.

17. Alvin Burns and Donald Granbois, "Factors Moderating the Resolution of Preference Conflict in Family Automobile Purchasing," *Journal of Marketing Research,* February 1977, pp. 68–77; Alvin C. Burns and Jo Anne Hopper, "An Analysis of the Presence, Stability, and Antecedents of Husband and Wife Purchase Decision Making Influence Assessment and Disagreement," in *Advances in Consumer Research,* vol. 13, ed. Richard J. Lutz (Provo, Utah: Association for Consumer Research, 1986), pp. 175–80; Margaret C. Nelson, "The Resolution of Conflict in Joint Purchase Decisions by Husbands and Wives: A Review and Empirical Test," in *Advances in Consumer Research,*

vol. 15, ed. Michael J. Houston (Provo, Utah: Association for Consumer Research, 1988), pp. 436–41; and William J. Quails, "Toward Understanding the Dynamics of Household Decision Conflict Behavior," in *Advances in Consumer Research,* vol. 15, ed. Michael J. Houston (Provo, Utah: Association for Consumer Research, 1988), pp. 442–48.

18. Kim P. Corfman and Donald R. Lehmann, "Models of Cooperative Group Decision-Making and Relative Influence: An Experimental Investigation of Family Purchase Decisions," *Journal of Consumer Research,* June 1987, pp. 1–13; Burns and Granbois, "Factors Moderating the Resolution of Preference Conflict," pp. 68–77; and Pierre Filiatrauit and J. R. Brent Ritchie, "Joint Purchasing Decisions: A Comparison of Influence Structure in Family and Couple Decision-Making Units," *Journal of Consumer Research,* September 1980, pp. 131–40; and Dennis L. Rosen and Richard W. Olshavsky, "The Dual Role of Informational Social Influence: Implications for Marketing Management," *Journal of Business Research* 15 (1987), pp. 123–44.

19. Rosann L. Spiro, "Persuasion in Family Decision Making," *Journal of Consumer Research,* March 1983, pp. 393–402.

20. Scott Ward, Donna M. Klees, and Daniel B. Wackman, "Consumer Socialization Research: Content Analysis of Post-1980 Studies, and Some Implications for Future Work," in *Advances in Consumer Research,* vol. 17, ed. M. E. Goldberg and G. Gorn (Provo, Utah: Association for Consumer Research, 1990), pp. 798–803; and George P. Moschis, "The Role of Family Communication in Consumer Socialization of Children and Adolescents," *Journal of Consumer Research,* March 1985, pp. 898–913.

21. Gilbert A. Churchill, Jr., and George P. Moschis, "Television and Interpersonal Influences on Adolescent Consumer Learning," *Journal of Consumer Research,* June 1979, pp. 23–35.

22. Sanford Grossbart, Les Carlson, and Ann Walsh, "Consumer Socialization Motives for Shopping with Children," *AMA Summer Educators' Proceedings* (Chicago: American Marketing Association, 1988); Bonnie B. Reece, Sevgin Eroglu, and Nora J. Rifon, "Parents Teaching Children to Shop: How, What, and Who?" *AMA Summer Educators' Proceedings* (Chicago: American Marketing Association, 1988), pp. 274–278; and Les Carlson and Sanford Grossbart, "Parental Style and Consumer Socialization of Children," *Journal of Consumer Research,* June 1988, pp. 77–94.

23. Ellen Graham, "Children's Hour: As Kids Gain Power of Purse, Marketing Takes Aim at Them," *The Wall Street Journal,* January 10, 1988, pp. 1, 24.

24. Karin M. Ekstrom, Patriya S. Tansuhaj, and Ellen Foxman, "Children's Influence in Family Decisions and Consumer Socialization: A Reciprocal View," in *Advances in Consumer Research,* vol. 14, ed. Melanie Wallendorf and Paul Anderson (Provo, Utah: Association for Consumer Research, 1987), pp. 283–87; Elizabeth S. Moore-Shay and Richard J. Lutz, "Intergenerational Influences in the Formation of Consumer Attitudes and Beliefs about the Marketplace: Mothers and Daughters," in *Advances in*

Consumer Research, vol. 15, ed. Michael J. Houston (Provo, Utah: Association for Consumer Research, 1988), pp. 461–67; and Scott Ward, Thomas S. Robertson, Donna M. Klees, and Hubert Gatignon, "Children's Purchase Requests and Parental Yielding: A Cross-National Study," in *Advances in Consumer Research,* vol. 13, ed. Richard J. Lutz (Provo, Utah: Association for Consumer Research, 1986), pp. 629–32.

25. Susan E. Heckler, Terry L. Childers, and Ramesh Arunachalam, "Intergenerational Influences in Adult Buying Behaviors: An Examination of Moderating Factors," in *Advances in Consumer Research,* 16, ed. T. Srull (Provo, Utah: Association for Consumer Research, 1990), pp. 276–84; Patricia Sorce, Lynette Loomis, and Philip R. Tyler, "Intergenerational Influence on Consumer Decision Making," in *Advances in Consumer Research,* vol. 16, ed. T. Srull (Provo, Utah: Association for Consumer Research, 1990), pp. 271–75; and George P. Moschis, "Methodological Issues in Studying Intergenerational Influences on Consumer Behavior," in *Advances in Consumer Research,* vol. 15, ed. Michael J. Houston (Provo, Utah: Association for Consumer Research, 1988), pp. 569–73.

26. For a review of these issues, see Michael D. Reilly, "Working Wives and Convenience Consumption," *Journal of Consumer Research,* March 1982, pp. 407–18. Also see Charles M. Schaninger and Chris T. Allen, "Wife's Occupational Status as a Consumer Behavior Construct," *Journal of Consumer Research,* September 1981, pp. 189–96; and Charles B. Weinberg and Russell S. Winer, "Working Wives and Major Family Expenditures: Replication and Extension," *Journal of Consumer Research,* September 1983, pp. 259–63.

27. Gordon Green and Edward Welniak, "The Nine Household Markets," *American Demographics,* October 1991, pp. 36–40.

28. This section draws from Martha Farnsworth Riche, "The Postmarital Society," *American Demographics,* November 1988, pp. 22–26, 60.

29. *Population Dynamics in Canada,* Statistics Canada, Cat #96-305E; and Martha Farnsworth Riche, "The Future of the Family," *American Demographics,* March 1991, pp. 44–46.

30. *Population Dynamics in Canada,* Statistics Canada, Cat #96-305E; and Diane Crispell, "Three's a Crowd," *American Demographics,* January 1989, pp. 34–38.

31. For a review, see Patrick E. Murphy and William A. Staples, "A Modernized Family Life Cycle," *Journal of Consumer Research,* June 1979, pp. 12–22.

32. Ibid. For other approaches and discussion, see Frederick W. Derrick and Alane K. Lehfeld, "The Family Life Cycle: An Alternative Approach," *Journal of Consumer Research,* September 1980, pp. 214–17; Mary C. Gilly and Ben M. Enis, "Recycling the Family Life Cycle: A Proposal for Redefinition," in *Advances in Consumer Research,* vol. 8, ed. Andrew Mitchell (Ann Arbor, Mich.: Association for Consumer Research, 1982), pp. 271–76; Janet Wagner and Sherman Hanna, "The Effectiveness of Family Life Cycle Variables in Consumer Expenditure Research," *Journal of Consumer Research,* December 1983, pp. 281–91.

33. Martha Farnsworth Riche, "The Boomerang Age," *American Demographics,* May 1990, pp. 25–27, 30, 52.

34. Margaret Ambry, "The Age of Spending," *American Demographics,* November 1990, pp. 16–23, 52.

35. This section is adapted from Eugene H. Fram, "The Time-Compressed Shopper," *Marketing Insights,* Summer 1991, pp. 34–39; and Eugene H. Fram and Joel Axelrod, "The Distressed Shopper," *American Demographics,* October 1990, pp. 44–45.

Chapter 18

1. Patricia Lush, "Fast Food Stuffed with R&D," *Globe and Mail,* December 8, 1992, p. B18.

2. Philip Kotler, "What Consumerism Means for Marketers," *Harvard Business Review,* May–June 1972, pp. 48–57. Also see Joseph V. Anderson, "Power Marketing: Its Past, Present, and Future," *Journal of Consumer Marketing,* Summer 1987, pp. 5–13.

3. For example, see Richard W. Olshavsky and Donald H. Granbois, "Consumer Decision Making: Fact or Fiction?" *Journal of Consumer Research,* September 1979, pp. 93–100; and T. K. Clarke, Susan Stewart, and F. G. Crane, "The Dark Side of Marketing: A Psychological Perspective," *Marketing,* vol. 12, 1991, pp. 61–67.

4. Robert G. Wyckham, "Industry and Government Advertising Regulation: An Analysis of Relative Efficiency and Effectiveness," *Canadian Journal of Administrative Sciences,* vol. 4, no. 1 (1987), pp. 31–51; S. Burke, *1991 Advertising Standards Council Complaints Summary,* (Toronto: Canadian Advertising Foundation, 1992). For an excellent, comprehensive discussion of corrective advertising, see William L. Wilkie, Dennis L. McNeill, and Michael B. Mazis, "Marketing's 'Scarlet Letter': The Theory and Practice of Corrective Advertising," *Journal of Marketing,* Spring 1984, pp. 11–31.

5. Paul N. Bloom and Stephen A. Greyser, "The Maturing of Consumerism," *Harvard Business Review,* November–December 1981, pp. 130–39.

6. Gene R. Laczniak, "Framework for Analyzing Marketing Ethics," *Journal of Macromarketing,* Spring 1983, pp. 7–18.

7. Ibid.

Glossary of Consumer Behaviour Terms

abstract attributes Intangible, subjective characteristics of the product, such as the quality of a blanket or the stylishness of a car.

accessibility The probability that a meaning concept will be (or can be) activated from memory. Highly related to top-of-mind awareness and salience.

accidental exposure Occurs when consumers come into contact with marketing information in the environment that they haven't deliberately sought out. Compare with *intentional exposure*.

acculturation The process by which people in one culture or subculture learn to understand and adapt to the meanings, values, lifestyles, and behaviours of another culture or subculture.

activation The essentially automatic process by which knowledge, meanings, and beliefs are retrieved from memory and made available for use by cognitive processes.

adopter categories A classification of consumers based on the time of initial purchase of a new product. Typically, five groups are considered: innovators, early adopters, early majority, late majority, and laggards.

adoption curve A visual representation of the cumulative percentage of people who adopt a new product across time.

adoption process An ambiguous term sometimes used to refer to a model of stages in the purchase process ranging from awareness to knowledge, evaluation, trial, and adoption. In other cases, it is used as a synonym for the diffusion process.

advertising Any paid, nonpersonal presentation of information about a product, brand, company, or store.

affect A basic mode of psychological response that involves a general positive/negative feeling and varying levels of activation or arousal of the physiological system that consumers experience in their bodies. Compare with *cognition*. See also *affective responses*.

affective and cognitive segmentation Identifying groups of consumers based on similarities in their knowledge, meanings, beliefs, and affective responses.

affective responses Consumers can experience four types of affective responses—emotions, specific feelings, moods, and evaluations—that vary in level of intensity and arousal.

age subcultures Groups of people defined in terms of age categories (teens, elderly) with distinctive behaviours, values, beliefs, and lifestyles.

AIO An acronym standing for activities, interest, and opinions. AIO measures are the primary method for investigating consumer lifestyles and forming psychographic segments.

aspirational group A reference group an individual consumer wants to join or be similar to.

associative network of knowledge An organised structure of knowledge, meanings, and beliefs about some concept such as a brand. Each meaning concept is linked to other concepts to form a network of associations.

attention The process by which consumers select information in the environment to interpret. Also the point at which consumers become conscious or aware of certain stimuli.

attitude A person's overall evaluation of a concept. An attitude is an affective response at a low level of intensity and arousal. General feelings of favourability or liking.

attitude models See *multiattribute attitude models*.

attitude toward objects (A_o) Consumers' overall evaluation (like/dislike) of an object such as a product or store. May be formed in two different ways: a cognitive process that involves relatively controlled and conscious integration of information about the object, and a largely automatic and unconscious response of the affective system linked to an object through classical conditioning.

attitude toward the ad (A_{ad}) Consumers' affective evaluations of the advertisement, not the product or brand being promoted.

attitude toward the behaviour or action (A_{act}) The consumer's overall evaluation of a specific behaviour.

automatic processing Cognitive processes tend to become more automatic—to require less conscious control and less cognitive capacity—as they become more practiced and familiar.

baseline The frequency of the problem behaviour before an intervention strategy.

behaviour Overt acts or actions that can be directly observed.

behaviour approach   An approach to studying consumer behaviour that focuses on the relationship between overt behaviour and the environment.

behaviour change strategy   A strategy developed to change the frequency or quality of a problem behaviour.

behaviour effort   The effort consumers expend when making a purchase.

behavioural intention (*BI*)   A plan to perform an action: "I intend to go shopping this afternoon." Intentions are produced when consumers consider and integrate their beliefs about the behavioural consequences of the action and social normative beliefs to evaluate alternative behaviours and select among them.

behavioural segmentation   Grouping consumers on the basis of similarities in their overt behaviour.

behaviours   Specific overt actions of consumers.

belief evaluation (*e₍ᵢ₎*)   The degree of liking or favourability a consumer feels for an attribute or consequence associated with a product.

belief strength (*b₍ᵢ₎*)   The perceived strength of association between an object and its relevant attributes or consequences.

beliefs   The perceived association between two concepts. May be stored in memory as a proposition. Beliefs about products often concern their attributes or functional consequences. For example, after trying a new brand of toothpaste, a consumer may form a belief that it has a minty taste. Beliefs are synonymous with knowledge and meaning in that each term refers to consumers' interpretations of important concepts.

benefit segmentation   The process of grouping consumers on the basis of the benefits they seek from the product. For example, the toothpaste market may include one segment seeking cosmetic benefits such as white teeth and another seeking health benefits such as decay prevention.

benefits   Desirable consequences or outcomes that consumers seek when purchasing and using products and services.

brand choice   The selection of one brand to purchase from a consideration set of alternative brands.

brand equity   The value of a brand. From the consumer's perspective, brand equity is reflected by the brand attitude based on beliefs about positive product attributes and favourable consequences of brand use.

brand indifference   A purchasing pattern characterised by a low degree of brand loyalty.

brand loyalty   The degree to which a consumer consistently purchases the same brand within a product class.

brand switching   A purchasing pattern characterised by a change from one brand to another.

central route to persuasion   One of two types of cognitive processes by which persuasion occurs. In the central route, consumers focus on the product messages in the ad, interpret them, form beliefs about product attributes and consequences, and integrate these meanings to form brand attitudes and purchase intentions. See *peripheral route to persuasion*.

choice   Evaluating alternative actions or behaviours and forming a behavioural intention or plan to engage in the selected behaviour. The outcome of the integration processes involved in consumer decision making. See also *behavioural intention*.

choice alternatives   The different product classes, product forms, brands, or models considered for purchase.

choice criteria   The specific product attributes or consequences consumers use to evaluate and choose from a set of alternatives.

choice decision   Requires that consumers integrate their product knowledge about choice criteria to evaluate the choice alternatives in the consideration set and choose one.

classical conditioning   A process through which a previously neutral stimulus, by being paired with an unconditioned stimulus, comes to elicit a response very similar to the response originally elicited by the unconditioned stimulus.

cognition   The mental processes of interpretation and integration, and the thoughts and meanings they produce.

cognitive activity   The mental thought and effort involved in interpreting and integrating information, as in a purchase decision. Often considered as a cost.

cognitive approach   An approach to studying consumer behaviour based on current research on topics such as information processing and cognitive science.

cognitive dissonance   A psychologically uncomfortable condition brought about by an imbalance in thoughts, beliefs, attitudes, or behaviour. For example, behaving in a way that is inconsistent with one's beliefs creates cognitive dissonance and a motivation to reduce the inconsistency.

cognitive processes   The mental activities (both conscious and unconscious) by which external information in the environment is transformed into meanings and combined to form evaluations of objects and choices about behaviour.

cognitive response   The thoughts one has in response to a persuasive message, such as support arguments or acceptance thoughts, counterarguments, and curiosity thoughts.

communication   A type of behaviour that marketers attempt to increase, involving two basic audiences: consumers who can provide the company with marketing information and consumers who can tell other potential consumers about the product and encourage them to buy it.

communication model   A simple representation of the communication process that focuses on characteristics of the source, message, medium, and receiver.

communication process   The broad goal of marketing communications is to communicate or convey a set of meanings to consumers. See *communication model*.

compatibility   The degree to which a product is consistent with consumers' current cognitions and behaviours.

compensatory integration processes   In decision making, the combination of all the salient beliefs about the consequences of the choice alternatives to form an overall evaluation or attitude (A_{act}) toward each behavioural alternative. A consumer will select the alternative with the highest overall evaluation on a set of criteria. Criteria evaluations are done separately and combined such that positive evaluations can offset (or compensate for) negative evaluations. Also called the compensatory rule and compensatory model. See also *noncompensatory integration processes*.

competitive influences Actions of competing firms intended to affect each other and consumers.

comprehension The cognitive processes involved in interpreting, understanding, and making sense of concepts, events, objects, and persons in the environment and behaviour.

concrete attributes Tangible, physical characteristics of a product such as the type of fibre in a blanket or the front-seat legroom in a car.

confirmation In consumer satisfaction theory, confirmation refers to a situation in which a product performs exactly as it was expected to (i.e., prepurchase expectations are confirmed).

consideration set A set of alternatives the consumer evaluates in making a decision. Compare with *evoked set.*

consumer acculturation The process by which a person acquires the ability and cultural knowledge to be a skilled consumer in a different culture or subculture.

consumer behaviour (1) The dynamic interaction of cognition, behaviour, and environmental events by which human beings conduct the exchange aspects of their lives; (2) a field of study concerned with (1) above; (3) a college course concerned with (1) above; and (4) the overt actions of consumers.

consumer behaviour management model Based on ideas in applied behaviour analysis, this model is concerned with developing and maintaining consumer behaviour.

consumer decision making The cognitive processes by which consumers interpret product information and integrate that knowledge to make choices among alternatives.

consumer information processing The cognitive processes by which consumers interpret and integrate information from the environment.

consumer/product relationship The relationship between target consumers and the product or brand of interest. How consumers perceive the product as relating to their goals and values. Important to consider in developing all phases of a marketing strategy. See also *means-end chain.*

consumer satisfaction The degree to which a consumer's prepurchase expectations are fulfilled or surpassed by a product.

consumer socialisation How children or adults acquire knowledge about products and services and various consumption-related skills.

consumption Use of a product.

consumption situation The social and physical aspects of the environments where consumers actually use and consume the products and services they have bought.

content of culture All the beliefs, attitudes, goals, and values shared by most people in a society, as well as the typical behaviours, rules, customs, and norms that most people follow, plus characteristic aspects of the physical and social environment.

continuous reinforcement schedule A schedule of reinforcement that provides a reward after every occurrence of the desired behaviour.

core values The abstract, broad, general end goals that people are trying to achieve in their lives.

corrective advertising Ads that are mandated by Industry Canada to correct the false beliefs created by previous misleading or deceptive advertising.

covert modelling In this type of modelling, no actual behaviours or consequences are demonstrated; instead, subjects are told to imagine observing a model behaving in various situations and receiving particular consequences.

cross-cultural differences How the content of culture (meanings, values, norms) differs between different cultures.

cross-cultural research Studies in which marketers seek to identify the differences and similarities in the cultural meaning systems of consumers living in different societies.

cultural interpenetration The amount and type of social interaction between newcomers to a culture (immigrants) and people in the host culture. Influences the degree of acculturation the newcomers can attain. See also *acculturation.*

cultural meanings The shared or similar knowledge, meanings, and beliefs by which people in a social system represent significant aspects of their environments.

cultural process The process by which cultural meaning is moved or transferred among three locations in a society—the social and physical environment, products and services, and individual consumers.

culture The complex of learned meanings, values, and behavioural patterns shared by a society.

deal proneness A consumer's general inclination to use promotional deals such as buying on sale or using coupons.

decision A choice between two or more alternative actions or behaviours. See also *choice* and *behavioural intention.*

decision conflict Arises when family members disagree about various aspects of the purchase decision, such as goals and appropriate choice criteria.

decision making See *consumer decision making.*

decision plan The sequence of behavioural intentions produced when consumers engage in problem solving during the decision-making process. See also *behavioural intention.*

demographic segmentation Dividing a market by demographic characteristics such as age, income, family size, gender.

diffusion The process by which new ideas and products become accepted by a society. See also *adopter categories.*

disconfirmation In consumer satisfaction theory, disconfirmation refers to a situation in which a product performs differently from expected. See also *negative disconfirmation* and *positive disconfirmation.*

discriminant consequences Only those consequences that differ across a set of alternatives that may be used as choice criteria.

discriminative stimulus A stimulus that by its mere presence or absence changes the probability of a behaviour. For example, a "50 percent off" sign in a store window could be a discriminative stimulus.

disposition situation The physical and social aspects of the environments in which consumers dispose of products, as well as consumers' goals, values, beliefs, feelings, and behaviours while in those environments.

dissatisfaction Occurs when prepurchase expectations are negatively confirmed (when the product performs less well than expected).

dissociative reference group A reference group with undesirable meanings that an individual does not want to join or be similar to.

early adopters   The second group of adopters of a new product.

early majority   The third group of adopters of a new product.

elaboration   The extensiveness of comprehension processes; the degree of elaboration determines the amount of knowledge or the number of meanings produced during comprehension as well as the richness of the interconnections among those meanings.

Elaboration Likelihood Model (ELM)   Identifies two cognitive processes by which promotion communications can persuade consumers: central and peripheral routes.

end goal   The most abstract or most basic consequence, need, or value a consumer wants to achieve or satisfy in a given problem-solving situation.

enduring involvement   The personal sources of relevance or involvement of a product or activity. Compare with *situational sources of involvement*.

environment   The complex set of physical and social stimuli in consumers' external world.

environmental prominence   The marketing strategy of making certain stimuli obvious or prominent in the environment to attract consumers' attention.

episodic knowledge   Cognitive representations of specific events in a person's life. Compare with *semantic knowledge*.

ethical influences   Basic values concerning right and wrong that constrain marketing practices.

ethnic subcultures   Large social groups based on consumers' ethnic background. In Canada, the largest ethnic subcultures include French Canadians, Asians, Germans, Italians, and Greeks.

evaluation   An overall judgment of favourable/unfavourable, pro/con, or like/dislike. An attitude toward an object such as a brand, an ad, or a behavioural act.

evoked set   The set of choice alternatives activated directly from memory.

expertise   Occurs when consumers are quite familiar with a product category and specific brands, possessing substantial amounts of general and procedural knowledge organised in schemas and scripts.

exposure   Occurs when consumers come into contact with information in the environment, sometimes through their own intentional behaviours and sometimes by accident.

extensive problem solving   A choice involving substantial cognitive and behavioural effort, as compared to limited decision making and routine choice behaviour.

extinction   The process of arranging the environment so that a particular response results in neutral consequences, thus diminishing the frequency of the behaviour response over time.

family   A group of at least two people in a household formed on the basis of marriage, cohabitation, blood relationships, or adoption. Families often serve as a basis for various types of consumer analysis.

family decision making   The processes, interactions, and roles of family members involved in making decisions as a group.

family life cycle   A sociological concept that describes changes in families across time. Emphasis is placed on the effects of marriage, births, aging, and deaths on families and the changes in income and consumption through various family stages.

fixed ratio schedule   A type of reinforcement schedule where every second, third, tenth, etc., response is reinforced.

focal attention   A controlled, conscious level of attention that focuses cognitive processes on relevant or prominent stimuli in the environment.

Foote, Cone & Belding (FCB) Grid   A two-by-two grid developed by the Foote, Cone & Belding advertising agency for analysing consumers and products. The FCB Grid categorises products based on consumers' level of involvement (high or low) and on whether consumers' dominant response to the product is cognitive or affective (thinking or feeling).

four stages of acculturation   Four levels of acculturation a newcomer to a culture could achieve, depending on the level of cultural interpenetration: honeymoon, rejection, tolerance, and integration stages.

free-flow layout   A store layout that permits consumers to move freely rather than being constrained to movement up and down specific aisles.

functional consequences   The immediate tangible outcomes of product use that consumers can experience directly. For instance, a toothpaste may get your teeth white.

funds access   The behaviours by which consumers obtain money for their purchases. Primary marketing issues include the methods consumers use to pay for particular purchases and the marketing strategies used to increase the probability that consumers can access their funds for purchase.

general knowledge   The meanings that consumers construct to represent important informational stimuli they encounter in the environment. Sometimes called declarative knowledge. Compare with *procedural knowledge*.

geographic segmentation   Dividing a market by geographic characteristics, such as regions in a country or areas of a city.

geographic subculture   Large social groups defined in geographic terms. For instance, people living in different parts of a country may exhibit differences in cultural meanings.

global marketing   An approach that argues for marketing a product in essentially the same way everywhere in the world.

goal hierarchy   The end goal and the subgoals that are involved in achieving it.

Goldfarb Psychographic Profile   A psychographic segmentation profile of Canadian consumers, developed by Goldfarb Consultants.

grid layout   A store layout where all counters and fixtures are at right angles to each other, with merchandise counters acting as barriers and guides to traffic flow.

group   Two or more people who interact with each other to accomplish some goal. Examples include families, co-workers, bowling teams, and church members.

heuristics   Propositions connecting an event with an action. Heuristics simplify problem solving. For example, "buy the cheapest brand" could be a choice heuristic that would simplify purchase choice.

hierarchy of effects model An early model that depicted consumer response to advertising as a series of stages including awareness, knowledge, liking, preference, conviction, and purchase.

hierarchy of needs See *Maslow's need hierarchy.*

high involvement See *involvement.*

household The people living in a housing unit (a dwelling with its own entrance and basic facilities).

ideal self-concept The ideas, attitudes, and meanings people have about themselves concerning what they would be like if they were perfect or ideal. Compare with *self-concept.*

impulse purchase A purchase choice typically made quickly, in the store, with little decision-making effort.

inferences Meanings or beliefs that consumers construct to represent the relationships between concepts that are based not only on explicit information in the environment but also on consumers' prior knowledge.

information acquisition situation Includes physical and social aspects of environments where consumers acquire information relevant to a problem-solving goal, such as a store choice or a decision to buy a particular brand.

information contact A common early stage in the purchase sequence that occurs when consumers come into contact with information about the product or brand. This often occurs in promotions, where such contact can be intentional (consumers search newspapers for coupons) or accidental (a consumer just happens to come into contact with a promotion while engaging in some other behaviour). See also *exposure.*

information processing See *consumer information processing.*

information-processing model Used to divide complex cognitive processes into a series of simpler subprocesses that are more easily measured and understood.

information search Consumers' deliberate search for relevant information in the external environment.

informational reference group influence Information from a group that is accepted if the consumer believes it will help achieve a goal.

innovativeness A personality trait to account for the degree to which a consumer accepts and purchases new products and services.

innovators The first group of consumers to adopt a new product.

instrumental conditioning See *operant conditioning.*

instrumental values One of two major types of values proposed by Milton Rokeach. Instrumental values represent preferred modes of conduct or preferred patterns of behaviour. See also *terminal values.*

integration process The process by which consumers combine knowledge to make two types of judgments. *Attitude formation* concerns how different types of knowledge are combined to form overall evaluations of products or brands. *Decision making* concerns how knowledge is combined to make choices about what behaviours to perform.

intentional exposure Occurs when consumers are exposed to marketing information due to their own intentional, goal-directed behaviour. Compare with *accidental exposure.*

interpretation processes The processes by which consumers make sense of or determine the meaning of important aspects of the physical and social environment as well as their own behaviours and internal affective states.

interrupts Stimuli that interrupt or stop the problem-solving process, such as unexpected information encountered in the environment.

involvement The degree of personal relevance a product, brand, object, or behaviour has for a consumer. Experienced as feelings of interest and importance. *A high-involvement* product is one a consumer believes has important personal consequences or will help achieve important personal goals. A *low-involvement* product is one that is not strongly linked to important consequences or goals. Determined by personal and situational sources of involvement.

knowledge Meanings and beliefs about products, brands, and other aspects of the environment that are stored in memory. See *meanings* and *beliefs.*

laggards The last group to adopt a new product.

late majority The next-to-last group to adopt a new product.

legal influences National, provincial, and municipal legislation and the government agencies and processes by which these laws are upheld.

level of competition A key aspect of the promotion environment for a product category; as competition heats up, marketers' use of promotions usually increases.

level of comprehension Refers to the different types of meanings that consumers construct during interpretation processes. Shallow meanings concern physical attributes and functional consequences; deeper meanings concern psychosocial consequences and values.

levels of abstraction Consumers have product knowledge at different levels of abstraction, from concrete attributes to more abstract functional consequences to very abstract value outcomes.

lifestyle The manner in which people conduct their lives, including their activities, interests, and opinions.

limited capacity The notion that the amount of knowledge that can be activated and thought about at one time is quite small.

limited problem solving A choice process involving a moderate degree of cognitive and behavioural effort. See also *extensive problem solving.*

macro social environment The broad, pervasive aspects of the social environment that affect the entire society or at least large portions of it, including culture, subculture, and social class.

market segmentation The process of dividing a market into groups of similar consumers and selecting the most appropriate group(s) for the firm to serve.

marketing concept A business philosophy stating that organisations should satisfy consumer needs and wants to make profits.

marketing mix The various elements of marketing strategy, including product, price, promotion, and channels of distribution. The goal of marketing management is to develop an effective mix of these elements so they all work together to serve the target market.

marketing strategy A plan designed to influence exchanges to achieve organisational objectives usually focused on consumers' behaviours; includes product, price, promotion, and channels of distribution; a part of the environment consisting of a variety of physical and social stimuli.

Maslow's need hierarchy A popular theory of human needs developed by Abraham Maslow. The theory suggests humans satisfy their needs in a sequential order starting with physiological needs (food, water, sex), and ranging through safety needs (protection from harm), belongingness and love needs (companionship), esteem needs (prestige, respect of others), and, finally, self-actualisation needs (self-fulfillment).

materialism A multidimensional value held by many consumers in developed countries. Materialism includes possessiveness, envy of other people's possessions, and nongenerosity.

meanings People's personal interpretations of stimuli in the environment. See *knowledge* and *beliefs*.

means-end chain A simple knowledge structure that links product attributes to functional and social consequences and perhaps to high-level consumer values. Means-end chains organise consumers' product knowledge in terms of its self-relevance.

MECCAS model Attempts to simplify the difficult task of developing effective advertising strategies by identifying five key factors; stands for means-end chain conceptualisation of advertising strategy.

micro social environment Important aspects of consumers' immediate social environment, especially reference groups and family.

modelling See *vicarious learning*.

modern family life cycle The various life stages for modern Canadian families, including the stages of the traditional family life cycle, plus other stages found in modern culture such as divorced, never married, and single parents.

multiattribute attitude models Models designed to predict consumers' attitudes toward objects (such as brands) or behaviours (such as buying a brand) based on their beliefs about and evaluations of associated attributes or expected consequences.

multiple-baseline design Commonly used in applied behaviour analysis, these designs demonstrate the effect of an intervention across several different behaviours, individuals, or situations at different times.

negative disconfirmation In consumer satisfaction theory, negative disconfirmation refers to a situation in which a product performs worse than expected.

negative reinforcement Occurs when an adverse stimulus is removed to increase the frequency of a given behaviour. See also *reinforcement*.

noncompensatory integration processes Choice strategies in which the positive and negative consequences of the choice alternatives do not balance or compensate for each other. Compare with *compensatory integration processes*. When alternatives are evaluated using noncompensatory rules, their positive and negative consequences do not compensate for each other. Types of noncompensatory integration processes include conjunctive, disjunctive, and lexicographic. The *conjunctive rule* suggests consumers establish a minimum acceptable level for each choice criterion and accept an alternative only if it equals or exceeds the minimum cutoff level for every criterion. The *disjunctive rule* suggests consumers establish acceptable standards for each criterion and accept an alternative if it exceeds the standard on at least one criterion. The *lexicographic rule* suggests consumers rank choice criteria from most to least important and choose the best alternative on the most important criterion.

nonfamily households Unrelated people living together in the same household—about 25 percent of Canadian households.

observability The degree to which products or their effects can be perceived or observed by other consumers.

operant conditioning The process of altering the probability of a behaviour by changing the consequences of the behaviour.

opportunity to process The extent to which consumers have the chance to attend to and comprehend marketing information; can be affected by factors such as time pressure, consumers' affective states, and distractions.

overt modelling The most common form of vicarious learning, this requires that consumers actually observe the model performing the behaviour.

penetration price policy A pricing strategy that includes a plan to raise prices sequentially after introducing a new product at a relatively low price.

perceived environment Those parts of the environment that are attended to and interpreted by a particular consumer on a particular occasion.

perceived risk The expected negative consequences of performing an action such as purchasing a product.

peripheral route to persuasion One of two types of cognitive processes by which persuasion occurs. In the peripheral route, the consumer focuses not on the product message in an ad but on "peripheral" stimuli such as an attractive, well-known celebrity or popular music. Consumers' feelings about these other stimuli may indirectly influence beliefs and attitude about the product by first influencing their attitude toward the ad. Compare with *central route to persuasion*.

personal selling Direct personal interactions between a salesperson and a potential buyer.

personal sources of involvement A consumer's personal level of self-relevance for a product. Represented in memory by the means-end chains of product/self relationships that consumers have learned through experience. Compare with *situational sources of involvement*.

personality The general, relatively consistent pattern of responses to the environment exhibited by an individual.

persuasion The cognitive and affective processes by which consumers' beliefs and attitudes are changed by promotion communications.

physical environment The collection of nonhuman, physical, tangible elements that comprises the field in which consumer behaviour occurs. Compare with *social environment*.

place utility Occurs when goods and services are made available where the consumer wants to purchase them.

political influences The pressure various consumer groups exert to control marketing practices.

positioning See *product positioning*.

positive disconfirmation In consumer satisfaction theory, positive disconfirmation refers to a situation in which a product performs better than expected.

positive reinforcement Occurs when rewards are given to increase the frequency with which a given behaviour is likely to occur. See also *reinforcement*.

prepurchase expectations Beliefs about anticipated performance of a product.

problem recognition Occurs when a consumer notices that the current state of affairs is not the ideal or desired state. Involves activation of a goal and a certain level of involvement.

problem solving A general approach to understanding consumer decision making. Focuses on consumers' perception of the decision as a problem. Important aspects of the problem representation include end goals, subgoals, and relevant knowledge. Consumers construct a decision plan by integrating knowledge within the constraints of the problem representation.

procedural knowledge Consumers' knowledge or beliefs about how to perform behaviours. See also *script*.

product contact Occurs when a consumer comes into physical contact with a product.

product positioning Designing and executing a marketing strategy to form a particular mental representation of a product or brand in consumers' minds. Typically, the goal is to position the product in some favourable way relative to competitive offerings.

product symbolism The various abstract meanings of a product to a consumer and what the consumer experiences in purchasing and using it.

promotion clutter The growing number of competitive promotion strategies in the environment.

promotion communications See *promotion strategies*.

promotion strategies Used by marketers to help achieve their promotion objectives, these include advertising, sales promotions, personal selling, and publicity.

promotions Information that marketers develop to communicate meanings about their products and persuade consumers to buy them.

psychographic segmentation Dividing markets into segments on the basis of consumer lifestyles, attitudes, and interests.

psychosocial consequences This term refers to two types of outcomes or consequences of product use: Psychological consequences (I feel good about myself) and social consequences (Other people are making fun of me).

publicity Any unpaid form of communication about the marketer's company, products, or brand.

pull strategies Ways to encourage the consumer to purchase the manufacturer's brand, such as cents-off coupons.

punishment A term used to describe the process of a response being followed by a noxious or aversive event, which decreases the frequency of the response.

purchase intentions A decision plan or intention to buy a particular product or brand. See also *behavioural intention*.

purchase transactions Behaviours involving the exchange of funds for products and services.

purchasing situation Includes the physical and social stimuli that are present in the environment where the consumer actually makes the purchase.

push strategies Ways to influence the selling efforts of retailers, such as trade discounts.

rate of usage The rate at which a consumer uses or consumes a product.

reference group People who serve as a point of reference and who influence an individual's affect, cognitions, and behaviours.

reinforcement A consequence occurring after a behaviour that increases the probability of future behaviour of the same type.

reinforcement schedule The rate at which rewards or reinforcements are offered in attempts to operantly condition behaviour. See *reinforcement*.

relative advantage The degree to which an item has a sustainable, competitive differential advantage over other product classes, product forms, and brands.

relevant knowledge Appropriate or useful knowledge that is activated from memory in the context of a decision or interpretation situation.

respondent conditioning See *classical conditioning*.

response hierarchy The total list of behaviours a consumer could perform at any given time, arranged from most probable to least probable.

reversal design In this approach, the problem behaviour of a subject or group of subjects is first assessed to determine baseline performance. After a stable rate of behaviour is determined, the intervention is introduced until behaviour changes. The intervention is then withdrawn and then reintroduced to determine if it is influencing the behaviour.

rituals Actions or behaviours performed by consumers to create, affirm, evoke, revise, or obtain desired symbolic cultural meanings.

routinised choice behaviour A purchase involving little cognitive and behavioural effort and perhaps no decision. Purchase could be merely carrying out an existing decision plan. Compare with *limited* and *extensive problem solving*.

sales promotions Direct inducements to the consumer to make a purchase, such as coupons or cents-off deals.

salient beliefs The set of beliefs activated in a particular situation; may be represented as an associative network of linked meanings.

satisfaction/dissatisfaction Useful concept for understanding consumer behaviour; refers to the consumer's affective and cognitive reactions to the chosen product after purchase.

scanner cable method A method of monitoring a number of stages in a purchase sequence. One such system, BehaviorScan, is designed to predict which products will be successful and which ads will work best to sell them.

schema An associative network of interrelated meanings that represents a person's general knowledge about some concept. Compare with *script*.

script A sequence of productions or knowledge about the appropriate actions associated with particular events. Consumers often form scripts to organise their knowledge about behaviours to perform in familiar situations. Compare with *schema*.

segmentation See *market segmentation*.

segmentation strategy The general approach marketers use to approach markets—for example, mass marketing or marketing to one or more segments.

selective exposure A process by which people selectively come into contact with information in their environment. For instance, consumers may avoid marketing information by leaving the room while commercials are on TV or not opening junk mail.

self-concept The ideas, meanings, attitudes, and knowledge people have about themselves.

self-regulation A form of ethical influence employed by marketers; many professions have codes of ethics and many firms have their own consumer affairs offices that seek to make sure consumers are treated fairly.

semantic knowledge The general meanings and beliefs people have acquired about their world. Compare with *episodic knowledge*.

shaping A process of reinforcing successive approximations of a desired behaviour, or of other required behaviours, to increase the probability of the desired response.

shopping situation The physical and spatial characteristics of the environments where consumers shop for products and services.

simplicity The degree to which a product is easy for a consumer to understand and use.

situation The ongoing stream of interactions among goal-directed behaviours, affective and cognitive responses, and environmental factors that occur over a defined period of time. Situations have a purpose and a beginning, middle, and end.

situational sources of involvement Temporary interest or concern with a product or a behaviour brought about by the situational context. Aspects of the immediate physical and social environment that activate important consequences and values and link them to product attributes, thus making products and brands seem self-relevant. For example, consumers may become situationally involved with buying a water heater if their old one breaks. Compare with *personal sources of involvement*.

social class A status hierarchy by which groups and individuals are categorised on the basis of esteem and prestige. For example, one classification divides Canadian society into upper class (11 percent of the population), middle class (20 percent of the population), working class (41 percent of the population), and lower class (20 percent of the population).

social environment Includes all human activities in social interactions, direct or indirect.

social marketing Programs and strategies designed to change behaviour in ways that are deemed good for consumers and for society.

social stratification See *social class*.

socialisation The processes by which an individual learns the values and appropriate behaviour patterns of a group, insti-

tution, or culture. Socialisation is strongly influenced by family, reference groups, and social class.

sociocultural segmentation Dividing a market by social and cultural characteristics (ethnicity, country of origin, social class).

speed Refers to how fast the consumer experiences the benefits of the product.

spreading activation Through this usually unconscious process, interrelated parts of a knowledge structure may be activated during interpretation and integration processes (or even daydreaming).

stages of acculturation Four stages of acculturation are the honeymoon stage, rejection stage, tolerance stage, and integration stage.

store atmosphere Affective and cognitive states that consumers experience in a store environment but may not be fully conscious of while shopping.

store contact An important set of behaviours for most consumer-goods purchases, this includes locating, travelling to, and entering the outlet.

store image The set of meanings consumers associate with a particular store.

store layout The basic floor plan and display of merchandise within a store. At a basic level, this influences such factors as how long consumers stay in the store, how many products they come into visual contact with, and what routes they travel within the store. Two basic types are *grid* and *free-flow layouts*.

store location Where a store is situated in a specific geographic area; influences the ease of store contact.

store loyalty The degree to which a consumer consistently patronises the same store when shopping for particular types of products.

store patronage The degree to which a consumer shops at a particular store relative to competitive outlets.

subcultures Segments within a culture that share a set of distinguishing meanings, values, and patterns of behaviour that differ in certain respects from those of the overall culture.

subjective or social norms (*SN*) Consumers' perceptions of what other people want them to do; influence behavioural intentions.

subliminal perception A psychological view that suggests attitudes and behaviours can be changed by stimuli that are not consciously perceived.

symbolic meaning The set of psychological and social meanings products have for consumers. More abstract meanings than physical attributes and functional consequences.

target behaviour The earliest behaviour in a purchase sequence not being performed, or not being performed appropriately or frequently enough to lead to the next behaviour. Also known as *problem behaviour*.

target market Group of consumers selected as potential customers for a product or service; the consumers targeted to receive marketing strategies.

terminal values One of two major types of values proposed by Milton Rokeach. Terminal values represent preferred end states of being or abstract, global goals that consumers are trying to achieve in their lives. Compare with *instrumental values*.

theory of reasoned action Assumes consumers consciously consider the consequences of alternative behaviours and choose the one that leads to the most desirable outcomes. The theory states behaviour is strongly influenced by behavioural intentions, which in turn are determined by attitudes toward performing the behaviour and social normative beliefs about the behaviour.

trade promotion Marketing tactics, such as advertising or display allowances, designed to get channel members to provide special support for products or services.

traditional family life cycle The typical stages of life followed by most Canadian families some 30 to 40 years ago. Each stage is distinguished by a major life event: marriage, birth of children, aging, retirement, and death.

transactions The exchanges of funds, time, cognitive activity, and behaviour effort for products and services. In a micro sense, the primary objective of marketing, where consumers' funds are exchanged for products and services.

trialability The degree to which a product can be tried on a limited basis or divided into small quantities for an inexpensive trial.

usage situation segmentation Grouping consumers on the basis of product usage situations (buying ice cream for an after-dinner dessert versus an afternoon snack).

utilitarian reference group influence Compliance of an individual with perceived expectations of others to obtain rewards or avoid punishments.

VALS An acronym for Values and Life-Styles. VALS and VALS 2 are well-known psychographic segmentation schemes marketed by SRI International.

value-expressive reference group influence An individual's use of groups to enhance or support his or her self-concept.

values The cognitive representations of important, abstract life goals that consumers are trying to achieve. See also *terminal* and *instrumental values*.

variable ratio schedule Occurs when a reinforcer follows a desired consequence on an average of one-half, one-third, one-fourth, etc., of the time the behaviour occurs, but not necessarily every second or third time, etc.

verbal modelling Modelling in which behaviours are not demonstrated and people are not asked to imagine a model performing the behaviour; instead, people are told how others similar to them behaved in a particular situation.

vicarious learning Changes in an individual's behaviour brought about through observation of the actions of others and the consequences of those actions.

Wheel of Consumer Analysis A simple model of the key factors in understanding consumer behaviour and guiding marketing strategy. Consists of four parts: affect and cognition, behaviour, environment, and marketing strategy.

word-of-mouth (WOM) communication Occurs when consumers share information with friends about products and/or promotions (good deals on particular products, a valuable coupon in the newspaper, or a sale at a retail store).

▼ Credits and Acknowledgments

Chapter 1

p. 3, Melissa Dehncke/Archive Photos;
p. 6, Courtesy Beta Research Corporation;
p. 7, Courtesy Blockbuster Entertainment;
p. 11, Courtesy General Motors of Canada Ltd.

Chapter 2

p. 15, Courtesy Banque Nationale du Canada; **p. 21**, Courtesy LePage's Ltd.; **p. 25** (left) Michael Putland/Retina Ltd. and (right) Mark Allan/Globe Photos, Inc.; **p. 27** (both), Courtesy Harry Rosen Menswear

Chapter 3

p. 31, Melanie Carr/Zephyr Pictures;
p. 34, Courtesy Rolex Watch USA, Inc.;
p. 43, Courtesy of Oscar Mayer Foods Corporation. Oscar Mayer, Lunchables, the Oscar Mayer rhomboid and Nothing But The Best are registered trademarks of Oscar Mayer Foods Corporation, Madison, Wisconsin; **p. 48**, Courtesy Shimano American Corporation.

Chapter 4

p. 53, Peter Correz/Tony Stone Images;
p. 57, Courtesy Guerlain, Inc.; **p. 63**, © 1992 Norelco Consumer Products Company; **p. 65**, Reprinted with special permission of King Features Syndicate.

Chapter 5

p. 73, Courtesy Chrysler Canada Ltd.;
p. 75, Courtesy of Dairy Farmers of Ontario;
p. 88, Courtesy McCann-Erickson Worldwide;
p. 91, Courtesy Reebok International Ltd.

Chapter 6

p. 99, Courtesy Nielsen Media Research;
p. 108, Reprinted with permission of Anderson Consulting; **p.115**, Courtesy Molson Brewery.

Chapter 7

p. 121, Courtesy Wine Council of Ontario;
p. 123, Christopher Pillitz-Network/Matrix;
p. 127, Courtesy Bristol-Myers Squibb Company.

Chapter 8

p. 145, Melanie Carr/Zephyr Pictures;
p. 149, © Sterling Winthrop Inc. Reprinted with permission of Sterling Winthrop Inc.;
p.155, Courtesy Audio Centre; **p. 162**, Courtesy Duracell, Inc.

Chapter 9

p. 169, photo by John E. Sokolowski;
p. 171, Mike Clemmer/Picture Group;
p. 175, Courtesy American Suzuki Motor Corporation; **p. 185**, Courtesy Jean Patou.

Chapter 10

p. 195, TM Registered Trademark of General Motors Corporation, TD licensed user of the Trademark. Courtesy General Motors of Canada Ltd. and the Toronto Dominion Bank;
p. 198, Courtesy General Motors of Canada Ltd.; **p. 204**, Courtesy Zellers; **p. 205**, © 1995 Seth Resnick; **p. 206**, Courtesy Participaction.

Chapter 11

p. 211, Courtesy Societe des Loteries de Quebec; **p. 214**, Courtesy Wrangler; agency: The Martin Agency; **p. 216**, Courtesy Moosehead; **p. 218**, Martha Bates/Stock Boston; **p. 220**, Courtesy mmmuffins Canada Corporation; **p. 221**, Courtesy Pepsi-Cola Canada Ltd.; **p. 224**, Courtesy Vickers & Benson Direct.

Chapter 12

p. 229, Courtesy Sega Inc.; **p. 237**, Courtesy Russell Corporation; **p. 239**, Courtesy 3M.

Chapter 13

p. 245, Courtesy Ford Motor Co.; **p. 250**, (left), T. Collicot/Zephyr pictures, (top), Michael Krasowitz/FPG, and (bottom), Michael Keller/FPG; **p. 251**, Courtesy Leon's Furniture Ltd.; **p. 255**, Joe Jacobson/Nawrocki Stock Photo;
p. 256, Courtesy Avia.

Chapter 14

p. 267, Courtesy Manitoba Lottery;
p. 270, Brian Lovell/Nawrocki Stock Photo;
p. 271, Courtesy Pfizer, Inc. photo: David Langley; **p. 272**, Reprinted with permission of the Thomas J. Lipton Company; **p. 277**, Courtesy Albertson's; **p. 287**, Courtesy West Edmonton Mall.

Chapter 15

p. 293, The Bettman Archive; **p. 296**, Courtesy Levi Strauss & Co.; **p. 297** (left), John Elk/Stock Boston and (right) Courtesy Wal-Mart Stores, Inc.; **p. 307**, Michael J. Hruby; **p. 310**, Mug Shots/The Stock Market; **p. 316** (top), Courtesy Labatt Breweries of Canada; agency: Axmith McIntyre Wicht Ltd. and (bottom) Courtesy Benetton Services Corporation.

Chapter 16

p. 323, Courtesy Levi Strauss & Co.;
p. 326, Courtesy Air Canada; **p. 331**, Reprinted courtesy of the Wm. Wrigley Jr. Company.

Chapter 17

p. 351, Copyright © 1995 The Lyons Group. Reprinted With Permission. The name and character Barney R are trademarks of the Lyons Group; **p. 353,** Reprinted with permission of Danskin, Inc.; Team Danskin as of 1994; **p. 355,** Michael Brohm/Nawrocki Stock Photo; **p. 363,** Courtesy Colgate-Palmolive Company; **p. 369,** Courtesy Midas International Corporation.

Chapter 18

p. 375, Courtesy Yves Veggie Cuisine; **p. 377,** Bob Daemmrich/Stock Boston.

Name Index

A

A. C. Nielsen Company, 99-100, 179, 257
A. L. Van Houte, 47, 102, 103
Aaker, David A., 449 n
A & B Sound Ltd., 4
A & P grocery chain, 218, 285, 371
A & W Food Services of Canada, 90
Aapri facial cleaner, 31
Abelson, Robert P., 439 n
Abercrombie, C. L., 452 n
Abernathy, Avery, 442 n
ActMedia, 104, 274
Acura, 111
Acura Integra, 402
Adler, L., 446 n
Agnew, Joe, 453 n
Ahmed, Sadrudin A., 444 n
Air Canada, 137, 138, 187, 248
Air Canada Aeroplan, 137
Air Canada Rapid Air flight, 404
Air Jordan shoes, 354, 396
Air Miles, 248
Ajax, 305
Ajzen, Icek, 444 n, 445 n
Aladdin (film), 351
Alba, Joseph W., 439 n, 443 n
Alcan, 173
Alden, Scott D., 440 n
Alexander, James H., 457 n
Alexander, Suzanne, 442 n
Allemang, Peter, 172
Allen, Chris T., 444 n, 459 n
Allen, Frank Edward, 301
Allstate Insurance, 231
Alpert, Mark I., 447 n
Alsop, Ronald, 443 n
Ambry, Margaret, 459 n
AMC Matador, 314
American Airlines, 248
American Express, 251, 253, 254, 358, 452 n
Amstel Brewery of Canada Ltd., 132
Anacin, 429-430

Anacin-3, 430
Anand, Punam, 442 n, 450 n
Anderson, John R., 58, 438 n, 439 n, 442 n
Anderson, Joseph V., 459 n
Anderson, Laurel, 455 n
Anderson, Paul, 441 n, 444 n, 446 n, 447 n,
    448 n, 455 n, 457 n, 458 n
Anderson, R. C., 439 n
Andre LaLonde Sports, 248
Andres Wines, 121
Animal House (film), 36
Antil, John H., 440 n
Apartian, Dibar, 327
Apple Computers, 239
Araldite, 106
Arbitron, 99
Arm & Hammer, 231
Arunachalam, Ramesh, 459 n
Assael, Henry, 174, 449 n
Association of Canadian Advertisers,
    200, 201
Attneave, C., 456 n
Atwood, April, 444 n
Audio Centre of Montreal, 154, 155
Ault, Johanna, 442 n
Avia International Ltd., 107
Avis, 114, 371
Avon, 171, 371
Axelrod, Joel, 459 n
Aydin, Nizamettin, 455 n

B

Babe, 111
Badenhop, Susan B., 439 n-440 n
Baggozzi, Richard P., 151, 439 n, 441 n,
    442 n, 445 n, 449 n, 457 n
Bain de Soleil, 133
Baker, Michael J., 452 n
Baker, Stuart, 216
Baker, William, 447 n

Bandura, Albert, 437 n, 452 n
Bank of Montreal, 248
Bank of Montreal MasterCard, 187
Barbie doll, 351
Barclay cigarettes, 261
Bargh, John A., 439 n
Barker, A. Tansu, 455 n
Barmossy, Gary, 455 n
Barnett, Mark A., 446
Barney, 351
Barsalou, Lawrence W., 448 n
Baryshnikov, Mikhail, 310, 358
Baskin-Robbins, 61, 74, 78
Bass, 396
Bass Weejuns, 317
Bastin, Etienne, 445 n
Basu, Kunai, 439 n
Bateson, John E. G., 438 n
Batra, Rajeev, 438 n, 442 n, 444 n, 449 n,
    450 n, 451 n
Bauer in-line skates, 155
    case, 412-413
Bauer sporting goods, 202, 357
Bawa, Kapil, 449 n
Bay, The, 62, 124, 132, 146, 156, 251, 285,
    305, 310, 392
Bayard, Jean-Pierre, 437 n
Bayer, 429-430
BCTel Mobility, 363
Beales, Howard, 452 n
Bearden, William O., 356, 446 n, 457 n
Beatty, Sharon E., 441 n, 447 n, 452 n
Beauty and the Beast (film), 351
Beef Industry Council, 132-133
Belch, George E., 450 n, 451 n, 458 n
Belch, Michael A., 458 n
Belk, Russell W., 441 n, 453 n, 454 n, 455 n
Bell Canada, 187, 213, 366
Bellizzi, Joseph A., 453 n
Bell Mobility Cellular, 113
Ben & Jerry's Rain Forest Crunch, 309
Benihana restaurants, 287

Bennett, Peter D., 186, 437 n, 441 n-442 n, 443 n, 445 n
Benson, Peter L., 452 n
Berbaum, Michael, 448 n
Berger, David, 184, 451
Berger, Ida E., 444 n
Bergier, Michel J., 332, 439 n, 456 n
Bergman, Ingmar, 311
Berkowitz, Leonard, 442 n
Berl, Robert L., 452 n
Berneman, Corinne, 438 n
Berry, Norman C., 444 n
Best, Roger, Jr., 249
Best Foods, 202
Beta Research, 6
Bettman, James R., 439 n, 443 n, 445 n, 446 n, 447 n, 448 n
Bic pen, 62, 75
Biehal, Gabriel, 446 n
Biesing, Thomas, 449 n
Big Mac, 70
Billings, Robert S., 447 n
Birk's jewellery, 311
BK Kids Club, 328
Black, John B., 68
Black and Decker, 163, 316, 318
    case, 397-398
Blacktop shoes, 23
Blackwell, Paxton, 179
Blattberg, Robert C., 449 n, 451 n
Bloch, Peter H., 87, 151, 440 n, 441 n, 442 n, 446 n, 454 n
Block, Alex Ben, 419
Block, Jack, 453 n
Block, Jeanne H., 453 n
Blockbuster Video, 7, 370
Bloom, Paul N., 381, 459 n
Bloomingdale's, 420
BMW, 63, 74, 75, 114, 124, 245
BMX bikes, 74
Bochove, Danielle, 204
Body of Evidence (film) 25
Body Shop, 81, 123, 301
Bogart, Leo, 449 n
Bolaria, Singh, 456 n
Boller, Gregory W., 449 n, 449 n
Borts, Morris, 428, 434, 436
Bouchard, Jacques, 332, 335, 456 n
Boush, David M., 444 n
Bower, Gordon A., 68, 442 n
Boyd, Robert S., 38
Boyes-Braem, Penny, 439 n
Brassard, Jean Luc, 311
Brasseur, Isabelle, 310
Brent, Paul, 204
Brick, 251
Bride fabrics, 394
Bride magazine, 60
Bridgestone tires, 132
Brim coffee, 45
Brinberg, David, 457 n
Brisoux, Jacques E., 446 n
Bristol-Myers Squibb, 127, 429
Bristor, Julia M., 457 n
Brockbank, Stuart, 444 n
Brooks, Garth, 358
Brooks shoes, 396
Brown, Jacqueline Johnson, 457 n

Brown, Stephen W., 449 n
Brown, Steven P., 447 n
Brown & Williamson, 261
Brubaker, Bill, 441 n
Bruce, Alexander, 456 n
Brucks, Merrie, 439 n, 447 n
Bruning, Edward, 446 n
Bryant, Beverly, 449 n
Buck stores, 124
Buckley, Patrick G., 437 n
Bud Light, 107
Budreau, Craig, 270
Budreau, Mary Ellen, 270
Budweiser, 114
Bufferin, 430
Buick, 46, 171, 401-403, 437 n
Bulkeley, William M., 107
Burberry, 304
Burger King, 90, 187, 328, 382
Burke, Marian Chapman, 438 n, 451 n
Burke, S., 459 n
Burnkrant, Robert E., 450 n
Burns, Alvin C., 458 n
Burns, Pat, 310
Bush, Alan J., 449 n
Bush, George, 113
Business Depot, 124
Buss, W. Christian, 458 n
Butterfield, Earl C., 442 n

C

Cachet, 111
Cacioppo, John T., 442 n, 443 n, 450 n
Cadillac, 103, 171, 195, 240, 329
Calcutta 200 reel, 48, 49
Calfee, John E., 443 n
Calgary Flames, 90
Calvin Klein, 60, 304
Calvin Klein cosmetics, 438 n
Calvin Klein jeans, 317
Camay soap, 278, 419-420
Cameron, Bruce, 437 n
Caminiti, Susan, 452 n
Campbell's soup, 126, 363
Campbell Soup Company, 8, 53, 273
Campus Network, 36
Campus Plus "Canadian Campus Survey", 36
Camry, 401
Canada Awards for Business Excellence, 375
Canada Dry, 147
Canada Post, 127
Canadian Action, 337
Canadian Airlines, 138, 187, 329
Canadian Dietetic Association, 112
Canadian Gold Card, 253
Canadian Heart Association, 133
Canadian Imperial Bank of Commerce, 137
Canadian Milk and Poultry Marketing Boards, 152
Canadian Olympic Team, 202
Canadian Tire, 35, 203, 252, 413
Canadian Wildlife Federation, 202
Canon, 93
Canstar Sports Inc., 202, 413
Cantor, Nancy, 440 n

Car and Driver, 402, 403
Caravan, 73
Carella, Franca Damiani, 456 n
Carey, J. Ronald, 452 n
Carleton Cards Ltd., 202
Carlson, Les, 458 n
Carson, Auleen, 451 n
Carson, Patrick, 81
Carter, Lanita S., 437 n
Carter Products, 269
Catt, Viola, 452 n
Cautela, Joseph R., 452 n
CBC, 196
CBC Newsworld, 85, 101
CCM Ultra Wheels, 413
Celica, 401-403
Celsi, Richard L., 87, 441 n, 442 n, 450 n, 451 n
Centraide, 202
Ceresino, Gayle, 458 n
Cerissa, 111
Cermak, Larry S., 442 n
Chabra, Surjit, 448 n
Chakravarti, Dipankar, 446 n
Chakravarty, Subrata N., 455 n
Chanel, 111
Chaps men's clothing, 394
Charles, Ray, 310, 357
Charlie, 111
Chatel, G., 332, 334, 456 n
Chattopadhyay, Amitava, 439 n
Chebat, Jean-Charles, 441 n, 445 n
Cheer, 202, 419-420
Cheney, Margaret, 112
Cher, 310, 311
Cheron, Emmanuel J., 456 n
Cherry Coke, 400
Chestnut, Robert W., 444 n
Chevrolet, 46, 136, 195, 363
Chevrolet Cavalier, 402
Chevrolet Corvair, 304
Chevrolet dealers, 384
Chicago Roller Skate Company, 413
Childers, Terry L., 449 n, 459 n
Chilton, David, 456 n
Chivas Regal, 304
Choice Hotels, 35
Chretien, Jean, 214
Chrysler Corporation, 74, 76, 310
Chrysler minivan, 73, 93, 439 n
Church, Nancy J., 448 n
Churchill, Gilbert A., Jr., 452 n, 458 n
Ciara, 111
CIBC/Aerogold Visa card, 137
CIBC/Aeroplan Visa card, 253
Cie, 111
Citizen watches, 127
Clairol, 230
Clarion Cosmetics, 282
Clarke, David, 438 n
Clarke, T. K., 459 n
Classic Residences, 423
Classy Formal Wear, 126
Clearasil Adult Care, 328
Clemons, D. Scott, 450 n
Clicque, Stephen H., 452 n
Clinique Canada, 285
Club Biz, 124, 131

Club Med, 431
Club Price store, 408
Club Regent, 267
Club Z, 204, 262
CNN, 101, 442 n
Coca-Cola Classic, 126, 306, 400
Coca-Cola Company, 8, 74, 76, 85, 86,
    107, 108, 126, 181, 187, 212, 213,
    305-306, 314, 317-318
    case, 399-400
Cohen, Joel B., 439 n, 440 n, 441 n, 445 n,
    447 n
Coke, 89, 103, 114, 152, 164, 202, 305-306,
    310, 317
Coleman, Lynn G., 441 n
Coleman, Richard P., 344, 457 n
Colgate toothpaste, 8, 55, 91, 152, 156, 363
Collins, Alan M., 438 n
Compaq Computers, 103
Compusearch Market and Social
    Research, 100
Condom Shack, 269
Coney, Kenneth A., 249
Consumer Reports, 101, 153, 156
Contac cold remedy, 137
Converse shoes, 396
Cooper, Simon, 5
Cooper hockey equipment, 20, 21
Cooper sports equipment, 357
Corelle dinnerware, 42
Corfman, Kim P., 447 n, 458 n
Corning Glass Works, 77
Corvette, 402
Cosby, Bill, 64, 311
Costa, Janeen A., 454 n
Costco, 131
Cote, Joseph A., Jr., 453 n
Cotric, Bill, 36
Country Crock, 126
Coutts, Jane, 345
Cover Girl, 328
Cox, Meg, 301
Cracklin' Oat Bran, 8
Craddock, Alyce Byrd, 451 n
Craik, Fergus I. M., 442 n
Crane, F. G., 459 n
Crespi, L., 446 n
Crest toothpaste, 128, 152, 261, 275,
    363, 430
Crispell, Diane, 456 n, 457 n, 459 n
Crosby, Lawrence A., 446 n
Cross, Stewart W., 449 n
CrossCom Group, 338
Crowley, Ayn C., 453 n
Crupnick, Russ H., 445 n
Csikszentmihalyi, Mihaly, 454 n
Csipak, Jacques, 441 n, 445 n
Cuneo, Alicd Z., 445 n
Curry, David J., 447 n

D

D. H. Howden and Company Ltd., 163
Dairy Council of Canada, 232
Dairy Queen, 284
Daiwa, 48
Darmon, Rene Y., 451 n

D'Astous, Alain, 44 n, 442 n
Datril, 429
Davis, Harry L., 458 n, 458 n
Davis-Barron, Sherri, 345
Dawson, Scott, 455 n
Days Inn motels, 310
De Carlo, Nicola, 438 n
Deep Magic skin cream, 31
Deighton, John, 449 n
Dekleva, Christine, 439 n, 442 n
Dellenger, D. N., 445 n
Del Monte, 8
Delta Hotels and Resorts, 5
Derrick, Frederick W., 459 n
DeSarbo, Wayne S., 448 n
Deslauriers, B. C., 452 n
Deutsch, Nancy, 270
Deutsche Presse, 336
Deveny, Kathleen, 438 n
Dholakia, Ruby, 449 n
Diaperene baby washcloths, 202
Dichter, Ernest, 438 n
Dickens, Charles, 295
Dickerson, Mary Dee, 452 n
Dickson, Peter R., 437 n, 445 n, 447 n
Dick Tracy (film), 25
DieHard battery, 176
Diet Coke, 107, 126, 399
Diet Pepsi, 76, 129-130
Diet 7Up, 76
Dionne, Celine, 310
Dippity-Do hair treatment, 31
Discount car rental, 132
Disney Company; see Walt Disney Company
Disneyland, 286, 317
DJC Research, 336
Dobni, Dawn, 438 n
Dockers slacks, 323-324
Dodge Lancer, 403
Dodge trucks, 304
Doeden, Daniel, 111
Dofasco Inc., 81
Dole Food Products, 53, 56, 438 n
Dollar Bill, 124
Domino's Pizza, 252
Donnelly, James H., Jr., 431, 451 n
Donohoe, Cathryn, 442 n
Donovan, Robert J., 438 n, 454 n
Doulton China, 42
Dover, Philip A., 445 n, 450 n
Dow Chemical, 170
Dreyfuss, Joel, 421
Driscoll, Lisa, 253
Droge, Cornelia, 451 n
Dryden, Ken, 90
Dry Idea, 114
Dube-Rioux, Laurette, 438 n
Dubow, Joel S., 213
Dubuc, Marc, 442 n, 444 n
Dufferin Street Mall, 284
Dugas, Christine, 442 n, 455 n
Dumaine, Brian, 421
Dumais, Susan T., 439 n
Du Maurier cigarettes, 152
Duncan, Calvin P., 449 n
Duncan Hines cake mix, 200
Dunkin, Amy, 393
Dunn, Brian, 381

Du Pont, 301, 379
Duracell, 197
Durgee, Jeffrey F., 439 n, 454 n
Dussart, Christian, 437 n
Dychtwald, Ken, 456 n
Dylan, Bob, 311

E

E. F. Hutton, 311
Eastern Airlines, 113
Eastman Kodak; see Kodak
Easton hockey sticks, 236
Easy Line, 66
Easy-Off oven cleaner, 111
Eaton's, 62, 124, 146, 151, 156, 305, 392
Eaton Centre, 151
Economic Council of Canada, 343
Edell, Julie A., 438 n, 449 n, 451 n
Edge shaving gel, 308
Edmonton Oilers, 54, 90
Eighmey, John, 440 n
Eisler, Lloyd, 310
Ekman, P., 438 n
Ekstrom, Karin M., 458 n
Elderhostel, 329
Elegant Traditions, 410-411
Elle magazine, 106
Elliot, Stuart, 358
Embassy Suites, 35
Enis, Ben M., 453 n, 459 n
Epoch Condom, 269
Eroglu, Sevgin, 458 n
Espiard, Caroline, 438 n
Esso, 93, 132, 262
Esso Medals of Achievement, 93
Estate, 394
Estes, W. K., 439 n
Estée Lauder, 60, 438 n
Eternity cologne, 60
Etzel, Michael J., 356, 457 n
Evans, Mark, 124
Everett, P. B., 452 n
Evert, Chris, 34
Excedrin, 429
Extra Strength Tylenol, 429-431
Ezell, Hazel F., 277, 453 n

F

Fabien, Louis, 438 n
Falzone, Mary Ann, 449 n
Farber, Ronald J., 457 n
Farley, John U., 447 n
Farquhar, Peter H., 444 n, 455 n
Farris, Paul W., 451 n
Fazio, Russell H., 444 n, 445 n
Federal Express, 79
Feigin, Barbara, 437 n, 440 n
Feinberg, Richard A., 452 n
Feldman, Laurence P., 453 n
Fennell, Geraldine, 150, 453 n
Festin de Gouverneur, 287
Festinger, Leon, 448 n
Fierman, Jaclyn, 295, 441 n
Filiatrault, Pierre, 458 n

Filman, Hugh, 269
Financial Post, 81
Finlay, Karen, 441 n
Fireman, Paul, 396
Firestone tires, 132
Fishbein, Martin, 444 n, 445 n
Fisher, Anne B., 86, 401, 454 n, 455 n
Fisher, James E., 457 n
Fitzgerald, Ella, 358
Flower, Joe, 456 n
Folger's coffee, 75, 200, 282
Folkes, Valerie S., 446 n, 447 n
Foote, Cone and Belding, 400
Ford, Gary T., 442 n, 443 n
Ford Caliente, 314
Ford Canada, 73, 245
Ford Crown Victoria, 198
Ford dealerships, 196
Ford Escort, 195, 275
Ford Explorer, 245, 303
Ford Grand Marquis, 198
Ford Merkur, 111
Ford Motor Company, 36, 75, 124, 136, 224,
    248, 305
Ford Motor Company of Canada, 199
Foster, Brian L., 457 n
Foster, Irene Raj, 458 n
Foster's beer, 75
Fox, Michael J., 310
Foxall, Gordon R., 446 n
Foxman, Ellen R., 458 n
Fram, Eugene H., 459 n
Franklin, Gary, 4
Frazer, James, 304
Free, Valerie, 395
Freedman, Adele, 151
Freestlye aerobic shoes, 396
French National Railway, 414, 416-417
Friedman, Margaret L., 431
Friedman, Roberto, 451 n
Frito Lay, 258
Frontczak, Nancy T., 449 n
Future Shop, 152, 203

G

G. I. Joe doll, 132
Gallop, Richard, 169
Gap, The, 37, 156
Gap jeans, 62
Gap sportswear, 78
Garcia, Jerry, 3
Gardner, Meryl Paula, 438 n, 442 n, 450 n,
    453 n
Garland, Susan, 455 n-456 n
Garreau, Joel, 340-341, 457 n
Gatignon, Hubert, 459 n
Gatorade, 202
Gayson, Jennifer, 442 n
Geistfeld, Lyle V., 439 n
General Electric, 114, 126, 371, 397-398
General Foods, 258
General Foods of Canada, 137
General Mills, 258
General Motors, 34, 73, 198, 240, 329, 390

General Motors of Canada, 42, 195, 201
General Sporting Goods Stores, 413
Gengler, Charles, 451 n
Gentle Fitness, 327
Gentry, James W., 446 n, 452 n
Gerrard, Jon, 380
Gherson, Giles, 124
Gibson, Lawrence D., 450 n
Gillette, 8, 31, 82, 317, 437 n
Gillette Atra, 202
Gillette Canada, 202
Gillingham, David, 453 n
Gilly, Mary C., 449 n, 459 n
Ginter, James L., 444 n, 453 n
Giordano, J., 456 n
Girard, Daniel, 124
Girard, Joe, 187
Glazer, Rashi, 447 n
Global Horizons Club, 329
Globe and Mail, 404
GMC Truck, 195
Godiva, 110
Goizueta, Robert, 399, 400
Gold's Gym, 257
Goldberg, Marvin E., 438 n, 442 n, 450 n,
    455 n, 457 n, 458 n
Golden Almond, 110
Goldfarb Consultants, 39, 334, 336
GO magazine, 108
Gorn, Gerald J., 214-215, 438 n, 442 n,
    452 n, 455 n, 457 n, 458 n
Gottlieb, 401
Gourmet Cup, 47
Gourmet magazine, 410
Graham, Ellen, 458 n
Graham, Robert J., 453 n
Granbois, Donald H., 442 n, 446 n, 457 n,
    458 n, 459 n
Grand and Toy, 124
Grandtravel, 329
Grateful Dead, 3
Gray, Wayne D., 439 n
Grecian Formula, 235, 311
Green, Carolyn, 204
Green, Gordon, 459 n
Green, Paul E., 440 n
Greenberg, B. A., 445 n
Green Giant Company, 304
Greenwald, Anthony A., 440 n, 442 n
Greising, David, 437 n
Gremlins (film), 170
Grether, David, 448 n
Gretzky, Janet Jones, 413
Gretzky, Wayne, 310, 413
Grey Cup, 212
Greyser, Stephen A., 459 n
Grocery Industry Foundation Together, 202
Grossbart, Sanford, 458 n
Grover, Rajiv, 458 n
Grunert, Klaus G., 447 n
Guarascio, Phil, 329
Gucci handbags, 35
Guerlain, 57
Guess? jeans, 146, 240
Gupta, Sunil, 457 n
Gutman, Jonathan, 440 n, 441 n, 449 n,
    450 n, 451 n, 455 n

H

Haagen-Dazs, 60, 438 n
Haberstroh, Jack, 176
Hafer, G. B., 135, 445 n
Haggerty, Michael R., 449 n, 457 n
Hale, Anne T., 437 n
Haley, Russell I., 440 n
Haliechuk, Rick, 204
Hallmark, 136, 213, 284, 351, 454 n
Hallmark Canada, 457 n
Hamilton Beach, 397
Hammond, Keith H., 437 n, 445 n
Hampton Inns, 35
Hanna, Janice G., 440 n
Hanna, Sherman, 459 n
Hansen, Flemming, 446 n
Hargrove, Kerri, 442 n
Harley-Davidson, 355-356
Harre, Rom, 438 n
Harris, John, 441 n
Harris, Marilyn A., 455 n
Harris, Richard J., 442 n, 446 n
Harrod and Merlin, 216
Harry Rosen menswear, 23, 26-27, 126, 171
Hartmann luggage, 35
Hartwick, Jon, 450 n
Harvey's restaurants, 77-78, 89, 90, 252, 275
Hasbro, Inc., 132, 445 n
Hasher, Lynn, 439 n
Hastak, Manoj, 449 n, 450 n
Hasty, Ronald W., 453 n
Hauser, John R., 446 n
Havlena, William J., 438 n
Hawaiian Tropic, 133
Hawkins, Del I., 249
Hayes-Roth, Barbara, 446 n
Head and Shoulders, 111, 224, 231
Head's Discovery, 44
Heart and Stroke Foundation, 169
Hecker, Sidney, 451 n
Heckler, Susan E., 449 n, 459 n
Hefty bags, 231
Heinz ketchup, 247, 363
Heinzl, John, 163, 204, 262
Hellenic Free Press, 337
Help Wanted Cafe, 286
Helsop, Louise A., 455 n
Henault, George, 332, 335, 456 n
Henderson, Katherine, 451 n
Hershey Foods, 201, 202
Hertz Rent-A-Car, 202, 371
Heslop, Louise A., , 440 n, 444 n, 446 n
Hester, Susan B., 444 n
Higgins, E. T., 438 n, 444 n
Higgins, Kevin, 449 n
Hill, Julie Skur, 455 n
Hirschman, Elizabeth C., 439 n, 443 n, 454 n
Hirt, Edward R., 442 n
Hitachi, 126
Hitchcock, Bob, 4
Hochstein, Alan, 446 n, 447 n
Hockey Hall of Fame, 172
Hoffman, Martin L., 438 n
Hofstra, Greta, 440 n, 446 n
Holbrook, Morris B., 438 n, 444 n, 449 n,
    450 n
Holiday Inn, 35, 124

Hollingsworth, Lois, 442 n
Holman, R., 455 n
Holt Renfrew and Company, 32, 115
Holub, Bruce, 112
Homa, Kenneth, 398
Home Depot, 102
Homer, Pamela M., 449 n, 450 n, 452 n
Honda, 34, 111, 305
Honda Civic, 58
Hong, Sung-Tai, 444 n
Hooter's Restaurants, 287
Hopper, Jo Anne, 458 n
Hornblower, Margot, 454 n
Hornik, Jacob, 453 n
Hostess potato chips, 124
Hostess snack chips, 162
Houston, Michael J., 441 n, 443 n, 446 n,
        448 n, 449 n, 450 n, 452 n, 455 n, 457 n,
        458 n, 459 n
Houston, Whitney, 310
Howard, John A., 438 n, 440 n, 445 n, 446 n,
        448 n
Howe, Karen, 113
Hoyer, Wayne D., 161, 443 n, 447 n, 447 n,
        448 n
Huggies, 300
Hughes, Kathleen A., 455 n
Hugo Boss, 27
Hui, Michael K., 438 n
Hume, Scott, 449 n
Hunt, H. Keith, 440 n, 443 n
Hutchinson, J. Wesley, 443 n, 447 n, 448 n
Hyatt Hotels, case, 421-423
Hyundai, 114

I

Iacocca, Lee, 310
IBM, 102, 162, 407-408
IE shoes, 396
IGA stores, 93
Il Cittadino Canadese, 337
Illingworth, J. Davis, 453 n, 454 n
Imari stoneware, 146, 149
Infant Feeding Action Coalition, 425-426
Infiniti, 124, 311
Information Resources, Inc., 179, 257-258
Inniskillen Winery, 410
Intel Pentium, case, 406-408
Internet, 286
in View magazine, 108
Irwin Toys, 381
Israelson, David, 448 n
Ivory Soap, 8
Izard, C. E., 438 n

J

J. Walter Thompson, 381
Jackson, Michael, 102, 310, 357
Jacoby, Jacob, 440 n, 441 n, 443 n, 444 n
Jaguar, 65
Jain, Arun K., 440 n
Jain, S. C., 441 n
Janiszewski, Chris, 442 n, 443 n
Jaworski, Bernard J., 448 n, 449 n, 451 n,
        455 n

Jeep Cherokee, 245
Jeep YJ Renegades, 221
Jell-O, 64, 311
Jockey, 37
John, Elton, 310
John Forsyth Company Ltd., 126
John Labatt Ltd., 115; *see also* Labatt
Johnson's Baby Shampoo, 224
Johnson, Ben, 311
Johnson, David M., 439 n
Johnson, Eric J., 443 n
Johnson, Michael, D., 439 n
Johnson, Phil, 456 n
Johnson, Richard D., 443 n
Johnson, Robert Wood, 431
Johnson & Johnson, 93, 382
    case, 429-431
Jolly Green Giant, 70, 304-305
Jordan, Michael, 170, 310, 396
Journey's End, 35
Jujyfruits, 418
JVC speakers, 357

K

Kaciak, Eugene, 437 n, 440 n, 451 n
Kagan, J., 438 n
Kahle, Lynn R., 440 n, 449 n, 452 n, 456 n,
        457 n
Kahn, Barbara E., 447 n
Kahneman, Daniel, 442 n, 446 n
Kakkar, Pradeep, 453 n
Kamins, Michael A., 449 n
Kanuk, Leslie Lazar, 298, 454 n
Kardes, Frank R., 442 n, 443 n
Karppinen, Pirjo, 447 n
Kassarjian, Harold H., 441 n, 453 n
Kassenar, Lisa, 253, 437 n
Katayama, Frederick, 421
Katz, Jerome, 447 n
Kavas, Alican, 445 n
Kazdin, Alan E., 451 n
Keane, Bil, 65
Keebler elves, 305
Keller, Kevin Lane, 442 n, 448 n, 450 n
Kellogg's, 133, 202
Kellogg's All-Bran, 110
Kellogg's Mini Buns, 201
Kellogg's Raisin Squares, 20
Kelly, J. Patrick, 278, 453 n
Kelly, Kevin, 393
Kentucky Fried Chicken, 200, 284, 300
Keough, Donald, 400
Kessler, Felix, 179
Key, Wilson, 176
Kiam, Victor, 310
Kids "R" Us, 328
Kihlstrom, John F., 440 n
Kilburn, David, 454 n
Killoran, Cameron, 36
Kim, Chung K., 451 n, 458 n
Kimberly-Clark, 300
Kinnear, Thomas C., 440 n, 445 n, 449 n,
        451 n, 452 n
Kirkpatrick, David, 301
Kirmani, Amna, 443 n
Kitayama, Shinobu, 455 n

Klassen, Michael, 446 n
Klees, Donna M., 458 n, 459 n
Klein, Noreen M., 447 n
Klenosky, David B., 446 n
KLM Canada, 138
Kmart, 65, 115, 124, 173, 254, 391-392
Kneale, Dennis, 442 n
Knorr soups, 45
Kodak, 8, 311, 317
Konika, 93
Konrad, Walecia, 445 n
Kotler, Philip, 459 n
Kraft, 133, 359
Krishna, Aradhna, 450 n
Krishnamurthi, Lakshman, 457 n
Kris Kross, 195
Kroeber-Riel, Werner, 438 n, 451 n, 452 n
Krugman, Herbert E., 440 n, 450 n
Kumar, V., 453 n
Kuntz, Mary, 137
Kuryllowicz, Kara, 279

L

LaBarbara, Priscilla A., 448 n
Labatt, 22, 75, 124, 132, 173, 316
Labatt beer, 162
Labatt Blue beer, 152
Labatt Genuine Draft, 115
La Cage Aux Sports, 100, 287
Lachman, Janet L., 442 n
Lachman, Roy, 442 n
Laczniak, Gene R., 382, 459 n
Lakeport beer, 152
La Leche League Canada, 425-426
Lamphler, Gary, 439 n
Landler, Mark, 452 n
Landor Associates, 53
Lantz, Gary, 446 n
Laroche, Michel, 445 n, 446 n, 447 n, 448 n
Lasker, David, 285
Latour, Stephen A., 448 n
Lattin, James M., 446 n
Laura Secord, 110
Lauren, Ralph, 113-114, 182
    case, 393-395
Lauren, Sara, 15
Lavack, Anne M., 456 n
Lazarus, Richard S., 438 n
Leavitt, Clark, 442 n, 449 n
Lee, H., 458 n
Lefrancois, P. C., 332, 334, 456 n
Legendre Lubawin Goldfarb, 334
Le Groupe Leger Leger, 332
Lehfeld, Alane K., 459 n
Lehman, Charles, 449 n
Lehmann, Donald R., 441 n, 447 n, 458 n
Leigh, James H., 453 n
Leigh, Thomas W., 439 n
Leighton, Barbara A., 452 n
Lenox china, 145
Lenscrafters, 202
Leo Burnett, 305
Leon's, 251
Leonard-Barton, Dorothy, 457 n
Leone, Robert P., 453 n

LePage's Child's Play School Glue, 21
Lessig, V. Parker, 451 n, 457 n
Lessne, Greg, 458 n
Levi's, 146, 240, 296, 308, 317, 323, 455 n
Levi's Dockers, 323-324
Levin, Irwin P., 443 n
Levine, Art, 235
Levine, Joshua, 441 n, 455 n
Levine, Philip, 444 n
Levi Strauss and Company, 323-324, 328
Levitt, Theodore, 440 n, 455 n
Levy, Sidney J., 59, 454 n
Lewis, Carl, 170
Lexus, 124, 275, 282, 283
Liefeld, John P., 440 n, 444 n
Linen Chest, 203
Lipman, Joanne, 179, 442 n, 449 n, 455 n
Lipstein, Benjamin, 450 n
Lipton instant tea, 45
Lipton's Noodles and Sauce, 103
Liquid-Plumr, 111
Liquid Tide, 76, 107, 126, 172, 439 n
Liu, Scott S., 449 n
Loblaw International Merchants Inc., 18, 20,
    81, 161, 236
Locander, William B., 454 n
Lockhart, Robert S., 442 n
Lockheed L-1011, 404
Lockshin, Larry, 446 n
Loftus, Elizabeth F., 438 n
Loken, Barbara, 444 n, 445 n
London Life insurance, 150
Longman, Kenneth A., 126, 446 n
Loomis, Lynette, 459 n
Lord, Kenneth R., 451 n
Lotto-Quebec, 211
Loyalty Management Group Canada, Inc.,
    187, 248
Lubove, Seth, 454 n
Lunchables, 43
Lush, Patricia, 459 n
Lussier, Denis A., 447 n
Lutz, Richard J., 442 n, 443 n, 444 n,
    445 n, 446 n, 448 n, 450 n, 451 n, 453 n,
    454 n, 454 n, 457 n, 458 n, 459 n
Lynch, John G., Jr., 443 n, 446 n
Lynn, Rhona, 391
Lyons Group, 457 n

M

Mac's convenience stores, 252
MacEvoy, Bruce, 437 n
MacGregor, Robert M., 440 n
MacGregor, Roy, 90
MacInnis, Deborah J., 443 n, 448 n, 449 n,
    450 n, 451 n, 455 n
Macintosh computers, 103
Mack, Toni, 77
MacKenzie, Scott B., 450 n, 453 n
Macklin, Bob, 53, 438 n
Macklin, Bruce, 18, 24
Madden, Thomas J., 441 n, 444 n, 455 n
Madonna, 23-25
Magiera, Marcy, 397
Magnusson, David, 453 n
Mahatma rice, 278

Maheswaran, Durairaj, 443 n, 456 n
Mallen, Bruce, 332, 335, 456 n
Maloff, Bretta, 112
Manitoba Lottery Foundation, 267
Manning, Terrill, 447 n
Manz, Charles C., 234, 452 n
Maremont, Mark, 438 n
Marino, Dan, 357
Marketing magazine, 169
Marks, Lawrence J., 443 n, 450 n
Mark's Work Warehouse, 41, 152
Markus, Hazel Rose, 438 n, 440 n, 455 n
Marlboro cigarettes, 316, 317
Marney, Jo, 275, 456 n
Marriott Corporation, 202
    case, 421-423
Mars chocolate bar, 246
Marshall, J. J., 455 n
Martin, Claude R., Jr., 449 n, 453 n
Mary Kay Cosmetics, 171
Mason, J. Barry, 277, 453 n
MasterCard, 36, 248, 251
Mastercraft powerboat, 246
Matas, Robert, 457 n
Matheson, Scot, 269
Matinee, 173
Mattel, Inc., 351, 381, 457 n
Maurice Richard Grecian Formula, 311
Maxwell House, 75, 282
Maybelline, 314, 455 n
Mayer, Morris L., 277, 453 n
Mazda, 85, 93
Mazis, Michael B., 452 n, 459 n
Mazursky, David, 448 n
McCarty, John A., 457 n
McCord, Marie André, 424
McCorry, Jean, 267
McCracken, Grant, 441 n, 454 n, 455 n
McDaniel, Stephen W., 448 n
McDonald's, 89, 103, 108, 122-123, 125, 181,
    187, 254-255, 284, 297-298, 300, 301,
    315, 330, 382, 449 n
McDonald's Canada, 202
McGill, Ann L., 442 n
McGoldrick, M., 456 n
McIntyre, Pat, 446 n
McKay-Stokes, Deborah, 300
McKinnon, Gary F., 278, 453 n
McNeal, J. U., 448 n
McNeill, Dennis L., 453 n, 459 n
McNeil Laboratories, 429
McQueen, Josh, 449 n
McSweeney, A. J., 452 n
McTavish, Ronald, 447 n
Mehrotra, Sunil, 440 n, 441 n, 443 n
Menasco, Michael B., 447 n
Mennen Speed Stick, 202
Mercedes-Benz, 35, 103, 114, 124, 126, 245,
    304, 305, 390
Merineau, Serge, 445 n
Mervis, Carolyn B., 439 n
Metcalf, Barbara L., 453 n
Metro supermarkets, 93, 161
Meyer, Robert J., 439 n, 448 n
Michal, Debra A., 453 n
Michelin, 132
Mickey Mouse watches, 127
Milberg, Sandra, 444 n

Milk Duds, 418
Miller, Kenneth E., 444 n, 453 n
Miller, Ronald K., 446 n
Miller Geniune Draft, 115
Miller Lite, 22, 75, 357
Milliman, Ronald E., 453 n
Milton, Frank, 452 n
Miniard, Paul W., 444 n, 445 n, 447 n
Mintz, Jan, 428, 436
Mist-Stick, 314
Mitchell, Alanna, 456 n, 457 n
Mitchell, Andrew A., 439 n, 440 n, 441 n,
    444 n, 445 n, 446 n, 447 n, 449 n, 450 n,
    458 n, 459 n
Mitchell, Linda G., 458 n
Mittal, Banwari, 450 n
Mizerski, Richard W., 443 n
MMMuffins, 220
Mohawk Oil, 81
Moishe's restaurant, 287
Moller, Kristian E., 447 n
Molson's Export, 152
Molson Breweries of Canada, 22, 115,
    157, 158
Molson Dry, 75
Monarch margerine, 126
Monet watch line, 127
Monroe, Kent B., 439 n, 441 n, 443 n, 448 n,
    449 n
Montague, W. E., 439 n
Montana, Joe, 357
Montreal Canadiens, 90
Montreal Jazz Festival, 12, 173
Moore, Danny, 447 n
Moore, Thomas, 401
Moore, Timothy E., 176
Moore, William L., 441 n, 447 n
Moore-Shay, Elizabeth S., 458 n
Moorman, Christine, 443 n, 444 n, 451 n
Moosehead beer, 216, 304, 317
Moran, William T., 126, 450 n
More, Roger A., 452 n
Morgenson, Gretchen, 126
Moschis, George P., 48 n, 459 n
Motomaster, 45
Mount, Joan, 440 n, 451 n
Mountain Dew, 221
Mowen, John C., 449 n
Moyer Vico Corporation, 4
Mr. Clean, 305, 405
Mr. Proper, 305
Much Music, 363
Muller, Thomas E., 456 n, 457 n
Mulroney, Brian, 113
Munch, James M., 443 n-444 n, 450 n
Munson, J. Michael, 80
Murphy, Patrick E., 367, 459 n
Murray, Keith B., 447 n
Murray, Noel, 442 n
Myers, James H., 440 n
Myers, John G., 457 n
Myers-Levy, Joan, 442 n, 456 n

N

Nabisco, 8
Naime, Doug, 453 n
Nakanishi, Masao, 80

Nantel, Jacques A., 448 n
National Bank of Canada, 15
National Cancer Institute, 110
National Capital Regional Health
    Department, 424
National Football League, 195
National Hockey League, 236
National Sporting Goods Association, 395
Nautilus Plus, 257
Nedungadi, Prakash, 446 n-447 n
Neelankavil, James P., 450 n
Neff, Robert, 439 n
Nelson, James E., 449 n
Nelson, Margaret C., 458 n
Nescafe coffee, 103
Neslin, Scott A., 451 n
Nestea, 160, 303
Nestlé, 317, 318
Netemeyer, Richard G., 457 n
Network People Meter Service, 99-100
Nevica, 107
New Balance shoes, 396
Newcomb, Peter, 25
Newman, Evelyn S., 455 n
Newman, Joseph W., 441 n
Nexxus shampoo, 78
NHL Players Asociation, 305
Nicosia, Franco M., 448 n
Niederman, Derrick, 358
Nielsen, Leslie, 70
Nielsen Broadcast Index, 99-100
Nielsen Marketing Research, 161
Nike, 90-91, 95, 107, 217, 310, 354, 357,
    413, 449 n
    case, 395-397
Nike basketball shoes, 70
Nike running shoes, 67, 76, 109
Nikon, 93
Nilson Report, 137
Nintendo Entertainment System, 229
Nintendo of Canada Ltd., 229
Nissan, 75, 311
Nolan, Catherine A., 453 N
Nord, Walter R., 232, 452 n
Norelco, 397
Norman, Donald A., 439 n
North America Life Insurance Company, 33
North Face, 354
Novak, Thomas P., 437 n
Nunus, Paula, 440 n
Nussbaum, Bruce, 439 n
NutraSweet, 126
Nutri-Slim, 310
Nyquil, 232
Nyveen, Lawrence, 326

O

Obermiller, Carl, 443 n
Obsession cologne, 60, 304
Ogilvy's department store, 106
O'Guinn, Thomas C., 457 n
Okechuku, Chike, 455 n
Okhai, Adam, 4
Oldsmobile, 46, 195
Oliver, Richard L., 448 n
Olney, Thomas J., 444 n, 450 n

Olsen, G. Douglas, 445 n
Olshavsky, Richard W., 442 n, 446 n, 447 n,
    448 n, 458 n, 459 n
Olson, Brennan, 413
Olson, Jerry C., 87, 188, 439 n, 440 n, 441 n,
    442 n, 443 n, 444 n, 445 n, 447 n, 449 n,
    450 n, 451 n
Olson, Scott, 412-413
Olympic Cap, 202
Olympus, 93
O'Neal, Michael, 443 n
O'Neal, Shaquille, 162, 183
Oreo Double Stufs, 12
Oreos, 12, 19
Oriental Rug Center, Ltd., 380
Ortho Pharmaceuticals, 269
Ortony, Anthony, 439 n
OshKosh B'Gosh, 47
O'Toole, John, 400
Ott, Leland, 437 n
Ottawa-Hull, 424
Outdoors magazine, 106

P

Paas Products, 172
Page, Thomas J., 444 n
Paksoy, Christine H., 278, 453 n
Palda, K. S., 456 n
Palmer, John B., 440 n, 441 n, 443 n, 445 n
Pampers, 202, 224, 300, 420
Panasonic, 164
Papadopoulos, Nicholas, 446 n, 455 n
Papoe, Bob, 455 n
Parcher, Robert, 178
Pare, Terence P., 437 n
Park, C. Whan, 444 n, 447 n, 448 n, 450 n,
    451 n, 455 n, 457 n
ParkLane Ventures Ltd., 5
Pavlov, Ivan P., 212, 213
Payless, 132
Payne, John, 448 n
PC World, 171
Peacock, Peter, 449 n
Pearson International Airport, 151
Peat, Nancy C., 448 n
Pechmann, Cornelia, 449 n, 450 n, 451 n
Pemberton, John Styth, 399
Penaloza, Lisa N., 457 n
Pennzoil, 45
Pepsi, 19, 25, 86, 102, 103, 107, 152, 164,
    187, 202, 217, 310, 317
PepsiCo, 221, 399
Pepys, Samuel, 47
Percy, Larry, 188, 438 n, 440 n, 450 n, 451 n
Pereira, Joseph, 107
Perreault, W. D., 80
Perrien, Jean, 445 n
Perrier water, 79, 298
Pert Plus, 354
Pessemier, Edgar A., 444 n
Peter, J. Paul, 150, 232, 431, 451 n, 452 n
Peters, Thomas J., 451 n
Petro-Canada, 217
Petty, Richard E., 442 n, 443 n, 450 n
Phalon, Richard, 397
Philip Morris, 8, 316

Philips, W. E., 449 n
Philips Electronics, 66
Phillips, Stephen, 437 n
Pierce, J. K., 456 n
Pieters, Rik G. M., 438 n
Piggly Wiggly pie shells, 278
Pilot pens, 75
Pineo, Peter C., 344
Pitts, Robert E., Jr., 440 n
Pizza Hut, 133-134, 217, 221, 284, 317
Playboy, 53
Players' Challenge tennis tournament, 124
Player's cigarettes, 173
Plimpton, Linda, 457 n
Plummer, Joseph T., 450 n
Plutchik, Robert, 438 n
Pollay, R., 438 n, 455 n, 457 n
Pollio, Howard R., 454 n
Pollock, James, 448 n
Polo brand, 26, 182, 317, 393-394
Polo shops, 113-114
Polo University Club, 394
Pontiac, 46, 195
Pontiac Grand AM, 11, 289
Popcorn, Faith, 456 n
Porky's (film), 36
Porsche, 134
Porter, Lyman W., 439 n
Posnick, Phyllis, 393
Potvin, Yves, 375
Powell, Johanna, 81
Powell, Martha C., 444 n
Power, Christopher, 445 n
Pratkanis, Anthony R., 440 n
Prentice, Michael, 187
President's Choice brands, 126, 236
Preston, Ivan L., 443 n
Prete, Dom Del, 452 n
Previa, 177
Price, Linda L., 443 n, 449 n
Price Club, 163
Price Costco, 124, 163
    case, 408-409
Prince's Vortex, 44
Prince of Wales Hotel, 410
Pringle's potato chips, 162
Procter & Gamble, 76, 172, 200, 202,
    223-224, 258, 261, 300-301, 379,
    392, 430
    case, 419-421
Pro Hardware, 163
Provigo supermarkets, 93, 248
Publisher's Clearinghouse, 213
Pudding Pops, 111
Punj, Girish N., 446 n
Purolator Courier Ltd., 127
Puto, Christopher P., 446 n
Pyrex, 77

Q

Quails, William J., 446 n, 458 n
Quaker Oats, 202
Quaker Oat Squares, 103
Quaker State, 45
Quebec Nordiques, 90
Quebec Order of Dentists, 432-433

R

Radford, John, 199
Radio Quebec, 381
Raid, 112
Raju, P. S., 449 n
Ralph Lauren shirts, 217; *see also* Lauren, Ralph
Ransom, Robert, 446 n
Rapoport, Carla, 455 n
Ratchford, Brian T., 438 n, 447 n
Ratneshwar, Srinivasan, 447 n, 449 n, 451 n
Ray, Michael L., 449 n
RCA, 75, 239-240
Reaves, Lynne, 455 n
Reder, Lynne M., 442 n
Reebok, 23, 107, 162, 183, 328, 396
Reebok basketball shoes, 70
Reece, Bonnie B., 458 n
Reering, Kenneth J., 453 n
Reese's Crunchy, 201
Reilly, Michael D., 459 n
Reingen, Peter H., 457 n
Relax Hotels, 35
Remington Razors, 310, 318
Reno-Depot, 102
Rethans, Arno J., 439 n, 446 n, 450 n
Reynolds, Thomas J., 188, 440 n, 441 n, 449 n, 450 n, 451 n, 455 n
Ribordy, Annette, 453 n
Ricard, Line, 445 n
Ricci, Marianne, 414
Rice, Marhsall, 451 n
Richard, Maurice, 235
Richards, Jef I., 443 n
Riche, Martha Farnsworth, 40, 368, 437 n, 459 n
Richins, Marsha L., 87, 151, 441 n, 442 n, 448 n, 455 n
Ricks, David A., 455 n
Riddell, Ken, 221, 262
Rider Travel, 4
Ridgway, Nancy M., 441 n, 446 n
Rifon, Nora J., 458 n
Rigaux-Bricmont, Benny, 458 n
Ringer, David, 121
Rip, Peter D., 446 n
Ritchie, J. Brent, 458 n
Ritz crackers, 171, 180
Rival, 397
Roberts, Gilles des, 248
Roberts, John H., 446 n
Robertson, Laird, 21
Robertson, Thomas S., 453 n, 454 n, 459 n
Robillard, Renee, 448 n
Robinson, Bill, 449 n
Robinson, E. Doyle, 278, 453 n
Rochberg-Halton, Eugene, 454 n
Rochon, John P., 451 n
Rokeach, Milton J., 80, 299
Rolex, 34, 304
Rollerblade Inc., 412-413
Romain, Ken, 199
Romer, Daniel, 449 n
Ro-Na Hardware, 248
Rook, Dennis W., 448 n
Rooney, Mickey, 311
Roots sweatshirts, 129

Rosch, Eleanor, 439 n
Rose, Frank, 437 n, 445 n
Rose, Randall L., 446 n
Rosen, Dennis L., 457 n, 458 n
Rosenberg, Milton J., 445 n
Rosenblatt, Jerry A., 332, 439 n, 441 n, 444 n, 445 n, 446 n, 447 n, 448 n, 456 n, 458 n
Rosenzweig, M. R., 439 n
Ross, Randall L., 444 n
Rossiter, John R., 438 n, 450 n, 454 n
Rotfield, Hubert, 442 n
Rothfeder, Jeffrey, 452 n
Rothschild, Michael L., 441 n
Rourke, Mickey, 317, 358
Roy, Patrick, 214
Royal Bank of Canada, 253
Royal Trust MasterCard, 137
Rudd, Joel, 457 n
Rudmin, Floyd, 457 n
Ruelle, Russell, 442 n
Ruffles potato chips, 189
Rumelhart, Donald E., 439 n
Russell, Gary J., 453 n
Russo, J. Edward, 443 n, 453 n

S

S. C. Johnson Company, 112, 308
Saab, 114
Saatchi & Saatchi, 177
Safeway, 161
Saks, 420
Sanbonmatsu, David M., 442 n
Santini, Gary, 5
Saporito, Bill, 455 n
Saran Wrap, 187
Saturn automobile, 34, 390
Scammon, Debra, 441 n
Schaninger, Charles M., 457 n, 458 n, 459 n
Schank, Roger C., 439 n
Schellinck, Tony, 444 n, 448 n
Scherer, Lisa L., 447 n
Schiffman, Leon G., 298, 327, 454 n
Schifrin, Matthew, 25
Schiller, Zachary, 8, 12, 439 n
Schlinger, Mary J., 453 n
Schlossberg, Howard, 441 n, 452 n
Schneidman, Diane, 454 n
Schocker, Alan D., 440 n
Schouten, John W., 457 n
Schumann, David W., 442 n, 443 n, 450 n
Scoffield, Heather, 284
Scope, 181
Scot Foto, 257
Scoundrel cologne, 111
Sealtest ice cream, 133
Sears, 47, 65, 124, 146, 151, 173, 187, 371, 391
Second Cup, The, 47, 102, 286
Sega Genesis, 229
Seguin, Sharon, 442 n
Seidman, Stephen B., 457 n
Seiko watches, 127
Seinfeld, Jerry, 358
Sellers, Patricia, 240, 437 n
Sen, Subrata, 449 n

Sensor blades/razor, 31, 82
Sentis, Keith, 440 n, 450 n
Serafin, Raymond, 329
ServiceMaster Canada Ltd., 4
7Up, 8, 129, 130, 154, 221
Sexuality shop, 269
Seymour, Daniel, 458 n
Shanteau, James, 446 n
Sharpe, Thom, 113
Shaw Festival, 410
Sheahan, Jerome N., 437 n
Sheahan, Maureen, 447 n
Shell Canada Ltd., 81, 248
Shelter Aid, 93
Sherman, Edmund, 455 n
Sherman, Elaine, 327
Sherman, Stratford P., 419
Sherrell, Daniel L., 441 n, 446 n
Sherrington, Herb, 404
Sherrington Food Products, 404
Sherry, John F., Jr., 454 n
Sheth, Jagdish N., 186, 438 n, 440 n, 441 n, 443 n, 445 n, 446 n, 457 n
Shields, 269
Shiffrin, Richard M., 439 n
Shimano, 48-49
Shimp, Terence A., 441 n, 444 n, 445 n, 455 n
Shiseido cosmetics company, 420-421
Shocker, Allan D., 447 n
Shoemaker, Robert W., 449 n
Shurr, Paul H., 447 n
Sianchuk, Peter, 452 n
Silberman, William, 444 n
Silkience, 31
Simmons, Carolyn J., 443 n
Sims, Henry P., 234, 452 n
Sinclair, G., 456 n
Singh, Jagdip, 448 n
Sinutab, 195-196
Siomkos, George J., 454 n
Siwolop, Sana, 442 n
Skippy peanut butter, 202
Skowronski, John, 446 n
Smart, Denise T., 448 n
Smith, Daniel C., 447 n
Smith, Edward, 439 n
Smith, Geoffrey, 437 n
Smith, Larry, 169
Smith, Lee, 451 n
Smith, Robert E., 445 n
Smith, Ruth Ann, 442 n
Smith, Scott M., 441 n, 447 n, 452 n
Smith, Terence R., 439 n
Smith, Vivian, 161
Snicker's candy, 66, 146
Sno Caps, 418
Solomon, Michael R., 59, 449 n, 454 n, 455 n
Sony Corporation, 4, 12, 75, 164
Sony stereo system, 78
Sony Walkman, 101
Sorce, Patricia, 459 n
Sorel boots, 304
Sorrentino, R. M., 444 n
Sotheby's, 285
Spacemaker, 398
Spellbound cologne, 60
Spielman, Harold M., 450 n
Spiro, Rand J., 439 n

Spiro, Rosann L., 362, 458 n
Sprint Canada, 366
Sproles, George B., 439 n
SRI International, 38
Srinivasan, Narasimhan, 447 n
Srull, Thomas K., 439 n, 440 n, 446 n, 458 n, 459 n
Staelin, Richard, 448 n, 449 n, 452 n, 453 n
Stanley Cup, 212
Stapel, Jan, 450 n
Staples, William A., 367, 459 n
Star, 336
Starbucks, 47
StarKist, 45
Starter sports clothes, 103
Static Guard, 187
Stayman, Douglas M., 438 n, 442 n, 449 n, 450 n-451 n
Steinhart, Jim, 163
Sternthal, Brian, 443 n, 449 n, 450 n
Stevenson, Mark, 158
Stewart, A. T., 394
Stewart, David W., 446 n, 447 n, 449 n, 450 n, 451 n
Stewart, Susan, 459 n
Stidsen, B., 456 n
Stone, Robert N., 440 n
Stout, Patricia A., 449 n
Strauss, Marina, 132, 179, 358, 381
Streep, Meryl, 358
Stroud, John, 449 n
Stuart, Elnora W., 444 n
Stuart, Robert W., 439 n, 454 n
Sturdivant, Frederick D., 454 n
Subway restaurants, 371
Suis, J., 440 n
Sujan, Harish, 442 n
Sujan, Mita, 439 n, 442 n, 443 n, 446 n
Summerfield, Patty, 441 n
Sunbeam Corporation, 314, 397-298
Sun Chips snacks, 152, 258
Sunoco, 132
Sure deodorant, 105
Sutherland, Chris, 449 n
Swasy, Alecia, 456 n
Swasy, John L., 444 n, 450 n
Swatch watches, 127
Sweet, Lois, 456 n
Swenerton, Helene, 444 n
Swidler, Ann, 454 n
Swinyard, William R., 445 n

T

Taco Bell, 131, 284
Tansuhaj, Patriya S., 458 n
Tarpey, Lawrence X., Sr., 150
Taster's Choice, 86, 88
Taylor, A. D. Wayne, 451 n
Taylor, Alex, III, 437 n
Taylor, James R., 446 n
Taylor, Marianne, 393
TD-GM Visa card, 42, 137
Technics, 164
Teel, Jesse E., 457 n
Teenage Mutant Ninja Turtles, 4, 351
Telecom Canada, 195-196

Teleglobe Canada, 195
Television Spending Index, 100
Texas Instruments, 318
Therrien, Lois, 8, 397
Thicke, Alan, 173-174
Thomas, D. R., 456 n
Thompson, Craig J., 454 n, 455 n
Thrifty Car Rentals, 310
Thrifty Supermarket Chain, 383
Tide, 202
Tilden car rental, 132
Timex, 127, 246, 317
Timex Canada, 127
Tim Horton's, 131, 181, 219
Timothy's, 47, 102
Tolman, Edward C., 440 n
Tomkins, S. S., 438 n
Toni home permanent, 31
Tonka toys, 132
Toronto Blue Jays, 308
Toronto Dominion Bank, 42, 137, 195, 196, 254
Toronto Maple Leafs, 90
Touch of Sweden, 105
Toy, Daniel R., 450 n
Toyota, 5, 12, 282, 401-403
    case, 390
Trachtenberg, Jeffrey A., 111, 450 n
Trans-Optique, 274
Travel and Leisure magazine, 410
Treece, James B., 445 n, 452 n
Trident, 432
Trojans, 269
Tropicana orange juice, 218
Tsai, Yehoshua, 438 n
Tsang, Pauline, 455 n
Tse, David K., 448 n
Tulving, Endel, 439 n
Tupperware, 257, 357
Turbo, 132
Turgeon, Normand, 451 n
Turner, Terrence J., 68
Tybout, Alice M., 151, 439 n, 441 n, 442 n, 445 n, 449 n, 457 n
Tyersky, Amos, 446 n
Tylenol, case, 429-431
Tyler, Philip R., 459 n

U

Ultra Pampers, 420
Ultra Tide, 84, 126
Ultra Wheels, 413
Unnava, H. Rao, 450 n
Upper Deck, 214
Ups and Downs, 284
Urbany, Joel E., 447 n

V

Van Ark, James W., 447 n
Vancouver Canucks, 90
Vancouver Sun, 402
Van Heusen, 126
Vanity Fair, 60
Vann, John W., 447 n

Van Raaij, W. Fred, 438 n
Van Rijn, Nicolaas, 295
Variety, 418
Varmmos, Mark N., 439 n
Vaseline Intensive Care lotion, 105
Vaughn, Richard, 451 n
Vermeersch, Joyce A., 444 n
VIA Rail, 275
Vickers & Benson Advertising Ltd., 132, 381
VideoCart, Inc., 103
Vinson, Donald E., 80, 440 n
Virginia Slims, 305
Visa card, 137, 146, 251, 358
Visine, 271
Vogue, 60
Votre cologne, 111
Voyageur cars, 73

W

W. W. Electronics, 273
Wackman, Daniel B., 458 n
Wadkins, Marsha, 455 n
Wagner, Carlton, 57
Wagner, Janet, 459 n
Wahl, Michael, 449 n
Walker, Beth A., 441 n
Wall, Marjorie, 440 n, 444 n, 446 n
Wallendorf, Melanie, 441 n, 444 n, 446 n, 447 n, 448 n, 454 n, 455 n, 457 n, 458 n
Wal-Mart, 65, 104, 131, 147, 156, 173, 203, 217, 275, 289, 301, 304
Wal-Mart Canada, case, 391-393
Walsh, Ann, 458 n
Walt Disney Company, 127, 457 n
Walters, Paul, 204
Walters, Rockney G., 453 n
Walton, Sam, 392
Ward, Fred, 453 n
Ward, Scott, 454 n, 458 n, 459 n
Warehouse Store, 434
Warner-Lambert, 196
Warren, William E., 452 n
Warshaw, Paul R., 445 n
Waterman, Robert H., Jr., 451 n
Water Pik, 357
Webb, Peter H., 449 n
Weder, Adele, 204
Wedgwood stoneware, 145-146
Weinberg, Charles B., 459 n
Weinzimer, Donna R., 448 n
Weitz, Barton A., 443 n
Welniak, Edward, 459 n
Wendy's, 90, 125
Wernerfelt, Birger, 446 n
West Edmonton Mall, 283, 286, 287
Westmont Square, Montreal, 426
Wetzel, N. A., 456 n
White House apple juice, 278
White Rain shampoo, 31
Wickelgren, Wayne A., 439 n
Wicker, Alan W., 445 n
Wiener, Joshua L., 446 n
Wild, Stevens, 301
Wilde, Louis, 448 n
Wilkie, William L., 440 n, 444 n, 447 n, 448 n, 451 n, 453 n, 459 n

Wilkinson, J. B., 453 n
Williams, Carol J., 444 n
Williams, Monci Jo, 445 n
Wilson's Hammer, 44
Wilson, Rick, 36
Wilton, Peter C., 448 n
Winaker-Steiner, H., 456 n
Wind, Yoram, 186, 440 n
Winer, Russell S., 459 n
Winnipeg Jets, 412
Winski, Joseph M., 455 n
Wisk, 405
Wolfe, Morris, 345
Wollenberg, Skip, 453 n
Wonderland, 286
Woodley, Don, 169
Woodside, Arch G., 186, 188, 440 n, 441 n,
    443 n, 445 n, 451 n
Woolco stores, 391

Woolco/Wal-Mart, 413
World Wildlife Fund, 81
World Wildlife Fund of Canada, 9
Wrangler jeans, 62, 214
Wright, Peter L., 443 n, 446 n, 447 n
Wrigley's, chewing gum, 8
Wyckham, Robert G., 459 n
Wyer, Robert S., 439 n, 440 n, 444 n

Y

Yadav, Manjit S., 447 n
Yalch, Richard, 443 n
Yannopoulos, P. Peter, 444 n
Yardley, 324
Young, S. Mark, 451 n
Young, Shirley, 437 n, 440 n
Yturralde, Laurel de, 452 n

Yuen, Mary, 444 n
Yves Veggies, 375

Z

Zaichkowsky, Judith Lynne, 441 n
Zajonc, Robert B., 438 n
Zanna, Mark P., 445 n
Zeithaml, Carl P., 453 n
Zeithaml, Valerie A., 443 n, 453 n
Zellers, 104, 115, 124, 147, 173, 204, 217,
    262, 297, 304, 305, 310, 392
Zhou, Lianxi, 438 n
Zinkhan, George M., 438 n, 449 n
Zins, Michael A., 448 n
Ziploc, 170

Subject Index

A

Aboriginal, 337-338
Abstract attributes, 76
Accidental exposure, 101
Acculturation process, 341-342
Achievers, 40
Acquisition rituals, 306
Action-oriented consumers, 39
Action-oriented groups, 9
Activation of knowledge, 63
Activities, 87
Activity, interest, and opinion questions, 38
Actualizers, 40
Adaptation approach to marketing, 315-316
Adoption, 246
Adoption curve, 236-237
Advertising
   celebrity endorsers, 310-311, 413
   to children, 381
   corrective, 379-380
   definition, 170
   failures, 420-421
   MECCAS strategy model, 188-189
   media, 176-177
   message, 174-176
   reference group appeals, 358
   subliminal, 176
Advertising Film Festival, 298
Affect, 8; *see also* Cognition
   and attention, 104-105
   definition, 16-17
   marketing implications, 58-60
   as psychological response, 54-55
   relationship to cognition, 56-58
   relation to cognition, 20
Affective and cognitive segmentation, 41
Affective responses, 54-55, 297, 393-395
Affective system, 55
Age subcultures, 327-331
Age Wave, 330
Aggressive achievers, 41
AIDS, 269

AIO questions; *see* Activity, interest, and
   opinion questions
Alternatives, 153
American Marketing Association, 7
   Code of Ethics, 383-385
American Marketing Association Awards, 169
Applied behaviour analysis, 196
Asian mass markets, 314-315
Asian Canadians, 335-336
Association of Canadian Advertisers, 201,
   201
Associative network of knowledge, 67
Associative reference groups, 352
Attention, 61
   definition, 104
   factors influencing, 104-105
   marketing implications, 106-108
Attitude, 122-128, 198
Attitude-change strategies, 132-133
Attitudes toward behaviours, 133-138
Attitudes toward objects, 128-132
Attitude tracking studies, 127
Automated transaction process, 371
Automatic affective responses, 56-57
Automatic cognitive processing, 64
Automatic processing, 108-109
Automobile industry, 390, 401-404
Average families, 343
Awareness, 104

B

Baby Boomers, 323-324, 328, 329
Bargaining rituals, 306
Basic research group, 9
Behaviour, 8, 17; *see also* Consumer
   behaviour
   attitudes toward, 133-138
   cultural meanings, 297
   definition, 17, 135-136
   and lighting, 273-274
   promotion to influence, 182, 195-196

Behaviour—Cont.
   reactions to colour, 274
   and time, 273
   and weather, 273
Behavioural intention, 136, 137
Behavioural marketing strategy, 199
   to influence consumer behaviour, 200-206
   social marketing, 205-206
Behavioural responses
   desired, 232
   developing, 230-231
   and effectiveness of modelling, 233-235
   undesired, 231-232
Behavioural segmentation, 42
Behaviour approach, 196-200
   misconceptions about, 206-208
Behaviour change measurement, 261
Behaviour change strategy, 261
Behaviour maintenance, 261-262
Behaviour modification, 207
Beliefs, 61
Belief strength, 129-130
Believers, 40
Benefits, 77, 78
Benefit segmentation, 41, 78
Bikers, 355-356
Blue-light specials, 254
Boomerang age, 368
Brand attitudes, 61-62, 124-127, 181, 400
   measuring, 133-138
   vulnerability analysis, 186-187
Brand awareness, 180-181
Brand-cluster loyalty, 400
Brand equity, 126-127, 309
Brand indifference, 224
Brand loyalists, 91
Brand loyalty, 220, 223-224, 400
Brand-loyalty switches, 223-224
Brand name recognition, 53
Brand names
   confusion of, 115
   of new products, 111

Brand names—Cont.
  strategies, 314-315
Brand purchase decision, 181-182
Brands, 74
  consumer relationship to, 91-93
  cultural meanings in, 304-305
  private-label, 405
  reference group influence, 356
Brand switchers, 93
Breast feeding, 424-429
British Columbia, 121
Browsing, 151
Bundles of attributes, 76-77
Bureau of Broadcast Measurement, 100
Buyers, 359

C

Canada
  age subcultures, 327-331
  ethnic origins by province, 333
  ethnic subcultures, 332-341
  families in, 364-366
  government role in marketing, 378-381
  social class, 342-346
Canada Automobile Protection Plan, 9
Canada Pension Plan, 15
Canada Standards Association, 304
Canadian culture, 299
Canadian Radio and Television Commission, 379
Canadian Registered Retirement Savings Plan, 15
Canadians Against Drunk Driving, 23
Celebrity endorsers, 310-311, 413
Central route to persuasion, 182
Channels of distribution, 46-47
Channel surfing, 102
Child-rearing, 364-365
Children
  consumer socialisation, 361-363
  regulation of advertising to, 381
  spending by, 351
Choice, 147
Choice alternatives, 151-152
Choice criteria, 153-154
Choice decision, 154-156
Choice heuristics, 156
Cholesterol, 112
Classical conditioning, 212-217, 223-225
Clean switch strategy, 398
Clothing designers, 393-395
Clutter, 107-108
Code of Ethics, 383-385
Coffee shops, 47
Cognition, 8, 15, 16, 393-395
  consumer decision making, 61-65
  definition, 17, 54
  marketing implications, 58-60
  nature of knowledge, 65-69
  as psychological response, 55-56
  relation to affect, 20, 56-58
Cognitive approach to behaviour, 196-200
Cognitive dissonance, 158-159
Cognitive system, 55-56
  aspects of, 61-64
  and attention, 104
  attitudes, 122-124

Cognitive variables, 246
College market, 36
Colour, 56-57, 274
Communication, 260, 282-283; see also Promotion
  from consumer to marketer, 256-257
  in East Asia, 315
  media, 176-177
  process, 173-180
  receivers of, 177-179
Companies; see Firms
Compatibility, 238
Compensatory integration process, 154-155
Competitive influences, 382
Comprehension, 61
  definition, 108
  factors influencing, 111-114
  inferences during, 110-111
  marketing implications, 114-116
  variations in, 108-110
Compusearch Market and Social Research, 100
Concrete attributes, 76
Consequences, 77
Consideration set, 151-152
Consumer and Corporate Affairs, 377
Consumer behaviour
  affect and cognition, 54-60
  basic questions about, 18, 19-20
  characteristics, 8-9
  definition, 7
  groups interested in, 9-10
  and intention, 138-139
  marketers' analysis, 257-262
  means of influencing, 200-206
  model of, 246-257
  and operant conditioning, 218-219
  predicting, 138-139
  and symbolic meanings, 59
  undesired behaviour, 106
Consumer behaviour research theory, 6-7
Consumer confidence, 429-431
Consumer decisions, 146-148
  browsing, 151
  cognitive process, 61-65
  levels of problem solving, 159-163
  model of, 61-62
  problem-solving process, 148-158
Consumerism, 293
Consumer/product relationship, 33-35, 90-93
  in advertising strategies, 189
  FCB Grid, 184-186
  vulnerability analysis, 186-187
Consumer promotions, 200; see also Promotion
Consumer research; see also Marketing research
  on classical conditioning, 214-217
  on operant conditioning, 221-223
Consumers
  attention to information, 104-108
  attitudes, 122-127
  attitudes toward objects, 128-132
  behaviour versus cognitive views, 196-200
  brand attitudes, 122-127
  communication from, 256-257
  comprehension of information, 108-116
  consumption behaviour, 255-256

Consumers—Cont.
  cultural meanings, 306-308
  exposure to information, 101-103
  exposure to television, 99-100
  families and households, 358-371
  firms outreach to, 4-5
  funds access, 250-252
  individual, 23-24
  information contact, 247-250
  interpretation of information, 116
  levels of analysis of, 22-24
  levels of product knowledge, 74-75
  lifestyle types, 39-41
  mailing lists of, 7
  means-end chain of knowledge, 81-85
  measuring attitudes, 133-138
  obtaining cultural meanings, 311
  product contact, 253-254
  product involvement, 85-89
  product knowledge, 76-80
  purchase decision reasons, 89-90
  purchase transactions, 254-255
  receivers of communication, 177-179
  store contact, 252-253
  time pressure, 370-371
  wheel of consumer analysis, 16-22
Consumers' Association of Canada, 9
Consumer situations, 281-288
Consumer socialisation, 361-363
Consumers' rights, 377-378
Consumption, 255-256, 260
Consumption culture, 312
Consumption situations, 286-287
Content of culture, 296-302
Contingencies, 260-261
Continuous improvement, 390
Continuous schedule, 219
Core values, 80, 80, 299
  North American, 300-301
Corrective advertising, 379-380
Counterarguments, 182
Coupons, 177
Covert modelling, 233
Credit card points payoff, 253
Cross-cultural changes, 313
Cross cultural differences, 312-314
Cross-cultural influence, 312-318
Cues, 110
Cultural analysis, 297
Cultural environment, 308
Cultural meanings, 295-296
  and consumers, 306-308
  environmental issues, 301
  in foreign marketing/promotion, 419-421
  helping consumers obtain, 311
  of products, 300, 302-306
Cultural process, 302-311
Cultural revolution, 293
Cultural values, strategies to change, 318
Culture; see also Subcultures
  Canadian, 299
  characteristics of, 294-296
  content of, 296-302
  global, 313-314
  marketing implications, 309-311
  North American values, 300-301
  rituals of, 306-308
  terminal values, 299

D

Database marketing programs, 33
Daydreaming, 63
Day-to-day watchers, 39
Deciders, 359
Decision; *see* Consumer decisions
Decision conflict, 360-361
Decision-making roles, 359-360
Decision plan, 156
Deep comprehension, 109
Defective products, 257
Delivery service, 371
Demographic changes, 324
    Canadian families, 364-366
Demographic segmentation, 36-37
Dentistry, 431-434
Designated market areas, 99
Disconfirmation of consumer expectations,
    157-158
Discriminant consequences, 153
Discriminative stimuli, 217-218
Disinterested self-indulgents, 39
Displays, 278
Disposers, 359
Disposition situations, 287
Dissatisfaction level, 156-158
Dissociative reference groups, 352
Distribution decisions, 46-47
Divestment rituals, 307-308
Divided brand loyalty, 224
Divorce, 364
Drama ads, 175-176
Driving force of advertising, 189
Dynamic behaviour, 8

E

Early adopters, 236-237
Early majority, 237
East Asia, 314-315
Economic Council of Canada, 343
Elaboration, 109-110
Elaboration Likelihood Model, 182-183
Elderly market, 327, 330-331
Electronic data interchange, 163
Emotions, 54
    and classical conditioning, 212-213
End-caps, 409
End goods, 149-150
Environment, 15-16, 87
    basic questions about, 19
    in context of situations, 279-288
    cultural value, 301
    definition, 17-18, 268
    marketing implications, 274-279
    physical, 272-274
    social, 269-272
Environmental events, 9
Environmental influences, 131-132
Episodic knowledge, 66
Ethical influences, 382-386
Ethnic subcultures, 332-341
Evaluation, 55, 122
    of alternatives, 153
    and salient beliefs, 130-131
Evoked set, 152

F

Facilitating exchange, 254
Factory work, 390
Family, 358-371
    consumer socialisation, 361-363
    cost of raising, 361
    in East Asia, 315
Family decision making, 359-361
Family life cycle, 366-371
Family planning, 364-365
Fast food, 300, 375
FCB Grid; *see* Foote, Cone and Belding Grid
Fear appeals, 250
Feelings, 54
Feel products, 185
Final transaction, 285-286
Financial risks, 78
Firms
    Canadian, 81
    consumer behaviour research, 6-7
    consumer focus, 4-6
    improved marketing research, 5-6
    mailing lists, 7
Fixed ratio schedule, 219
Foote, Cone and Belding Grid, 184-186
Foreign marketing, 410-421
Four-wheel drive vehicles, 245
Free-flow store layout, 277
French Canadian market, 332-335
Frequent-buyer scheme, 248
Front-end displays, 279
Fulfilleds, 40
Functional consequences, 77-78
Functional risk, 78
Funds access, 250-252, 260, 285-286

G

Gambling technology, 267
Gatekeepers, 359
Gender subculture, 338-339
General knowledge, 65-66
Geographic segmentation, 35
Geographic subcultures, 341
German Canadians, 336
Global culture, 313-314
Global marketing, 317-318
Golden Bough (Frazer), 304
Goldfarb Psychographic Profiles, 39-41
Greek Canadians, 337
Grid store layout, 275-276
Grooming rituals, 307, 308
Group, 352

H

Health Canada, 9
Health professionals, 429
Heuristics, 154-156
Higher involvement, 184-185
Hockey, 90
Holiday shopping, 294
Homeless, 345
Honeymoon stage of acculturation, 342
Hotel business, 421-423
Household
    compensation, 365-366
    definition, 358-359

I

Ice hockey, 90
Image advertising, 114, 175
Immigrant elite, 337
Immigrant entrepreneurs, 337
Incentives, 137
Income
    and social class, 343-346
    subcultures, 339-341
Individual brand loyalty, 223
Industrial Revolution, 293
Industry Canada, 9, 115, 377
    responsibilities, 379-380
Inferences, 110-111
Influencers, 359
Infomercials, 236
Information
    attention to, 104-108
    comprehension of, 108-116
    environmental prominence, 106
    exposure of, 101-103
    interpretation of, 116
    promotion message, 174-176
    relevant, 150-152
    sources, 249
    useful, 370
Information acquisition, 282-283
Informational ads, 175
Informational reference group influence, 354
Information contact, 247-250, 260, 282
Information search, 150-152, 249, 401-404
Information seekers, 92
In-line skating, 412-413
Innovation diffusion, 236-240
Innovators, 236-237
In-store displays, 278
In-store environment, 19
Instrumental values, 79-80
Integration, 61-62
    in decision making, 147
    process, 122
Integration stage of acculturation, 342
Intensity of attention, 104
Intention and behaviour, 138-139
Intentional exposure, 101
Intention to buy, 62
Interactions, 8-9
International marketing strategies, 314-317
Interpretation, 61, 116
Interviews, 84-85

Involvement, 309
    and attention, 105-106
    and comprehension, 112-113
    definition, 85-86
    factors influencing, 87-89
    focus of, 86-87
    higher and lower, 184-185
    personal sources, 87, 91-93
    situational sources, 88-89, 93
Italian Canadians, 336-337

J-K

Joiner-activists, 39-41
Just-in-time production, 390
Just-in-time retailing, 392
Kaizen (continuous improvement), 390
Knowledge, 61
    means-end chain, 81-82
    structure of, 67-68
    types of, 65-67
Knowledge in memory, 111-112

L

Laddering interview, 84-85
Laggards, 237
Late majority, 237
Learned responses, 55
Lecture ads, 175
Legal influences, 378-381
Legislation, 379
Level of comprehension, 109
Leverage point, 189
Liberal Party of Canada, 214
Lifestyle segmentation, 37-41
Lifestyle trends, 302-303
Lighting, 273-274
Limited capacity of cognition, 64
Limited problem solving, 159-160, 161
Live modelling, 230
Lotteries, 211
Lower class, 344
Lower involvement, 184-185
Luxury, 356

M

Macro-environment, 268, 269
Macro social environment, 269-270
Magazine subscriptions, 251
Mailing lists, 7
Makers, 40
Manipulation, 207
Manufacturing system, 390
Marital status, 369
Marketable segment, 43
Marketers' rights, 376-377
Marketing
    behaviourist view, 199
    and classical conditioning, 213-214,
        223-225
    competitive influences, 382
    consumer issues, 10
    and culture, 309-311

Marketing—Cont.
    ethical influences, 382-386
    legal influences, 378-381
    political influences, 381-382
    problem areas, 376
    product knowledge implications, 89-93
Marketing concept, 4
Marketing managers
    analysis of consumer model, 257-262
    analysis of situations, 280-281
    attitude-change strategies, 132-133
    use of wheel of consumer analysis, 20-22
Marketing mix
    definition, 43-44
    distribution decisions, 46-47
    price decisions, 44-45
    product decisions, 44
    product positioning, 48-49
    promotion decisions, 46
Marketing research
    on consumer/product relationship, 184-187
    improved quality of, 5-6
Marketing strategies, 10-11
    aimed at price, 154-155
    cultural meanings, 297-298
    diagnosing, 131
    directed at women, 31
    in foreign markets, 419-421
    international, 314-318
    types of, 19
Market segmentation, 395-397, 421-423
    consumer/product relationships, 33-35
    definition, 32-33
    determining bases of, 35-43
    by family life cycle, 368-371
    strategy selection criteria, 42-43
Market segments, 23
Marriage, 364
Married couples with children, 367-368
Mass market, 35
    Asian, 314-315
Materialism, 313
Mature market, 328-330
Meaningful segment, 43
Meanings, 61
Means-end chain, 81-85
Measurable segment, 43
MECCAS model, 188-189
Media, 176-177
Memorability, 110
Memory, 65-69, 111-112
Message, 173, 174-176
Micro-environment, 268-269
Microprocessors, 406-408
Micro social environment, 270
Middle brands, 124
Middle class, 344
Minivans, 73
Miscomprehension, 114-115
Misleading Advertising Bulletin, 115
Mobile shopping environments, 284
Modelling
    apes versus humans, 235
    covert and verbal, 233
    and diffusion of innovation, 236-240
    factors influencing effectiveness, 233-235
    through infomercials, 236

Modelling—Cont.
    marketing implications, 236-240
    overt, 230-232
Models, 74
Modern family life cycle, 366-368
Moods, 54-55
    and attention, 104-105
Mothers Against Drunk Driving, 23
Motivation to comprehend, 112-113
Movie theatres, 417-418
Multiattribute attitude model
    definition, 129-131
    marketing implications, 131-132
Multibrand loyalty, 400
Music, 278-279

N

Native Canadians, 337-338
Necessity, 356
Needs, 198-199
Negative reinforcement, 218
Network People Meter Service, 99
New products; *see also* Products
    brand names, 111
    characteristics, 238-240
    development of, 390
    diffusion process, 236-240
Nine Nations of North America (Garreau),
    340, 341
Noncompensatory integration process, 155
Nonfamily households, 359
North America
    lifestyle trends, 302
    popular culture, 317
    value changes, 300-301
North American Free Trade Agreement, 124,
    380-381
Novel stimuli, 106
Novice consumers, 112
Nuclear family, 357

O

Observability, 238
Older singles, 367
Old-fashioned puritans, 39
Operant conditioning, 217-223
Opportunity to comprehend, 113-114
Other people, 86-87
Out-of-store selling, 370-371
Overprivileged families, 343
Overt modelling, 230-232

P

Pain relievers, 429-431
Perceived environment, 268
Perceived risk, 78-79
Peripheral route to persuasion, 182-183
Personal computers, 406-408
Personal interviews, 84
Personalizing rituals, 306-307
Personal meaning, 306
Personal selling, 170-171
Personal sources of involvement, 87

Persuasion
    definition, 182
    Elaboration Likelihood Model, 182-183
Physical environment, 272-274
Physical objects, 86
    cultural meanings, 298-299
Physical risk, 78
Pineo-Porter-McRoberts socioeconomic
    classification, 342-342, 344
Political influences, 381-382
Pollution, 301
Popular culture, 317
Positive reinforcement, 218
Possession rituals, 306
Postpurchase use and re-evaluation, 156-159
Power tools, 397-398
Prestige market, 35
Price competition, 390
Price decisions, 44-45
Price increases, 45
Price strategies, 154-155
Principle-oriented consumers, 39
Private good, 356
Private-label brands, 405
Problem behaviour, 259-260
Problem recognition, 148, 149-150
Problem solving
    changes with experience, 160
    choice criteria, 153-154
    choice decision, 154-156
    evaluation of alternatives, 153
    levels of, 159-163
    marketing implications, 152-153
    postpurchase use and re-evaluation,
        156-159
    problem recognition, 149-150
    process, 148-158
    purchase decision, 156
    search for relevant information, 150-152
    stages, 148-149
Procedural knowledge, 66-67
Product class, 75
Product contact, 253-254, 260, 284
Product form, 74
Product involvement, 85-89
    personal sources, 91-93
Production (mental)
    memory as, 66
    schemas, 68
    scripts, 68-69
Product knowledge
    of consumers, 76-80
    and involvement, 62
    levels of, 74-75
    marketing implications, 89-93
    means-end chain, 81-85
Product nurturing rituals, 306
Product positioning, 48-49
Products; see also New products
    benefits and risks, 77-79
    bundles of attributes, 76-77
    bundles of benefits, 77-79
    changing cultural meanings, 300
    in consumer decision making, 61-65
    continuous improvement, 390
    cultural meanings, 302-306
    defective, 257
    environmentally friendly, 81

Products—Cont.
    in marketing mix, 44
    middle brands, 124
    personal meaning, 306
    seasonal factors, 274-275
    stimulating need for, 180
    symbolic meanings, 59
    as value satisfiers, 79-80
Product symbolism, 240
Promotion, 410-412
    for behaviour change, 195-196
    communication process, 173-180
    and consumer action, 179-180
    effects of, 180-182, 180-182
    in foreign markets, 419-421
    incentives, 137
    in marketing mix, 46
    message, 173, 174-176
    message source, 173-174
    persuasion process, 182-183
    types of communication, 170-173
Promotion mix, 172-173
Prompts, 255
Psychographic segmentation, 37-41
Psychological consequences, 78
Psychosocial consequences, 78
Psychosocial risk, 78
Public good, 356
Publicity, 171-172
Pull strategy, 408
Punishment, 219
Purchase, 246
Purchase consequences, 89
Purchase/consumption process, 33-35
Purchase decision, 156, 401-404
    key reasons for, 89-90
Purchase location, 203
Purchase planning, 370
Purchase probability, 201-202
Purchase quantity, 202-203
Purchase sequence, 246-257
Purchase timing, 203
Purchase transaction, 254-255, 260
Purchasing situation, 285-286

Q-R

Quality circles, 390
Quebec Consumer Protection Act, 381
Radio advertising, 113
Rapid inch-up strategy, 390
Recall ability, 178
Reference group advertising, 358
Reference groups
    definition, 352-353
    marketing implications, 357
    product and brand influence, 356
    types of influence, 353-356
Reinforcement schedule, 219-220
Rejection stage of acculturation, 342
Relative advantage, 239-240
Remembering, 114
Responsible survivors, 39
Retailing, 391-393, 434-436
Retirement communities, 421-423
Revenue Canada, 33
Risks, of products, 78-79

Rituals, 306-308
Romance, 60
Routine brand buyers, 91
Routinized choice behaviour, 160, 161,
    162-163
Running shoes, 395-397

S

Sales promotions
    definition, 170
    effectiveness, 203-205
    to influence behaviour, 200-205
Salient beliefs, 128-129
    changes in, 132-133
    and evaluations, 130-131
Satisfaction level, 156-158
Satisfying/maintenance end goal, 150
Scanner cable method, 257
Schemas, 68
Scripts, 68
Search for relevant information, 150-152
Search heuristics, 156
Seasonal factors, 274-275
Selection and attention, 104
Selective demand, 253
Selective exposure, 101-102
Self-concept, 312-313
Semantic knowledge, 66
Shallow comprehension, 109
Shaping, 220-221
Shelf space, 278
Shopping situation, 283-285
Signs, 277-278
Simplicity, 239
Single-parent families, 367
Single persons, 366
Situational sources of involvement, 88-89
Situations, 279-288
Small appliances, 397-398
Social causes, 93
Social class, 342-346
Social consequences, 78
Social environment, 269-272
    cultural meanings, 297
Socialisation, 361-363
Social marketing, 205-206
Society, 22
Sociocultural segmentation, 37-41
Socioeconomic classification, 342-346
Soft-drink industry, 399-400
Source of message, 173-174
Space-age materials, 396
Specific feelings, 54
Speed of benefits, 239
Spreading activation, 64
Stages of acculturation, 342
Standardized approach to marketing,
    317-318
Statistics Canada, 33, 329, 359
Status-oriented consumers, 39
Stimuli, 55
    in classical conditioning, 212-216
    in operant conditioning, 217-218
Store contact, 252-253, 260, 283
Store environment, 285
Store layout, 275-277

Store loyalty, 224-225, 262
Strivers, 40
Strugglers, 40
Subcultures
    age groups, 327-331, 421-423
    baby boomers, 323-324, 328, 329
    definition and characteristics, 324-327
    ethnic, 332-341
    gender, 338-339
    geographic, 341
    by income, 339-341
    types of, 325
Subjective norm component of behaviour,
    136-137
Subliminal advertising, 176
Support arguments, 182
Supreme Court of Canada, 381
Sustainable, competitive differential
    advantage, 239
Symbolic meanings, 59
Symbolic modelling, 230

T

Target behaviour, 259-260
Target market, 421-423
    college students, 36
    definition, 32
Teen market, 327-328
Telemarketing, 171
Television
    channel surfing, 102
    commercials, 213
    family life cycle on, 368
    viewing and ratings, 99-100

Television Spending Index, 100
Terminal values, 79-80, 299
Theory of reasoned action, 135-136
Think product, 185
Time, 273
Time pressure, 370-371
Tolerance stage of acculturation, 342
Top-of-mind awareness, 152
Tourism, 410-412, 414-417
Toy marketers, 381
Tracking studies, 127
Trade promotions, 200
Traditional family life cycle, 366
Train travel, 414-417
Trialability, 238

U

Underclass, 345
Underprivileged families, 343
Upper class, 344
Usage situation strategy, 42
Users, 359
Utilitarian reference group influence, 354-355

V

VALS/VALS2 profiles, 38-41
Value-expressive reference group influence,
    355-356
Value-laden products, 5
Values, 79-80
    and social class, 343
Variable rate schedule, 219-220

VCRs, 417-418
Verbal modelling, 233
Vicarious learning
    definition, 230
    modelling effectiveness, 233-235
    overt modelling, 230-232
    verbal modelling, 233
VideoCart, 103
Video games, 229
Videotape commercials, 177
Vivid images, 106
Vulnerability analysis, 186-187

W-Y

Warehouse stores, 408-409
Weather, 273
Wheel of consumer analysis
    applying, 20-22
    components, 16-20
    environmental factors, 268-269
    and individual consumers, 23-24
    and industry, 22-23
    and market segments, 23
    and society, 22
Window-shopping environment, 270
Wine producers, 121
Women
    in East Asia, 315
    marketing strategy directed at, 31
    role in society, 338-339
    in work force, 364
Working class, 344
World Health Organization, 269
Young singles, 367, 369